Moshe Bar-Asher

Studies in Classical Hebrew

Studia Judaica

Forschungen zur Wissenschaft des Judentums

Begründet von
Ernst Ludwig Ehrlich

Herausgegeben von
Günter Stemberger, Charlotte Fonrobert
und Alexander Samely

Band 71

Moshe Bar-Asher

Studies in Classical Hebrew

Edited by Aaron Koller

DE GRUYTER

ISBN 978-3-11-048593-6
e-ISBN 978-3-11-030039-0
ISSN 0585-5306

Library of Congress Cataloging-in-Publication Data
A CIP catalog record for this book has been applied for at the Library of Congress

Bibliographic information published by the Deutsche Nationalbibliothek
The Deutsche Nationalbibliothek lists this publication in the Deutsche Nationalbibliografie; detailed bibliographic data are available in the Internet at http://dnb.dnb.de.

Typesetting: Meta Systems Publishing & Printservices GmbH, Wustermark
Printing and Binding: Hubert & Co. GmbH & Co. KG, Göttingen
♾ Printed on acid-free paper
Printed in Germany

www.degruyter.com

Preface

In this volume I have collected twenty-five of my published studies that deal with three divisions of the classical Hebrew language: Biblical Hebrew, the Hebrew of the Dead Sea Scrolls, and Mishnaic Hebrew. What is included here is but a sampling of the studies I have published in these fields. The growing interest in the last generation or two, in Europe and in the United States, in Israeli research into the Hebrew language, which is generally published in modern Hebrew, is sufficient reason for the publication of these studies in the language which has been for some time the international language of scholarship.

Some of the chapters in this book have been previously published in English, and many were translated specifically for the current volume. By the nature of scholarship, most of the chapters have been updated to some degree, both with regard to the data and with regard to the scholarly literature published in the interim.

De Gruyter's has long been a major force in the publication of research in Jewish Studies, including in the study of the Hebrew language. I wish to express my gratitude to the directors of the press, and especially to Dr. Albrecht Döhnert, Editorial Director for Religious Studies, for their decision to include this book in their Studia Judaica series and for their attentiveness to its production and quality. The staff of the press worked hard to produce a volume with the same high quality of production to which one is accustomed from De Gruyter's books.

This book could not have been published without the dedicated and educated work of my friend, Dr. Aaron Koller. He translated most of the articles into English, saw to the production of a unified bibliography, and oversaw the preparation of the indexes for the book. He also read a number of drafts of the entire book, and edited it carefully. Dr. Koller is a scholar with his own impressive accomplishments in the fields of Hebrew and Aramaic, and I could not have found someone more appropriate to do the editorial work needed for this volume. His devotion to the project is evident on every page of the book, and for this I offer him my deep gratitude.

MBA

Contents

Preface — v

Introduction — 1
A — **1**
B — **1**
C — **4**

A Biblical Hebrew — 7

1 **The *Qal* Passive Participle of Geminate Verbs in Biblical Hebrew — 9**
1.1 Introduction — **9**
1.2 נִדָּה and נִדָּה — **9**
1.2.1 נִדָּה ‘menstrual impurity’ / נִדָּה ‘sprinkling’ — **9**
1.2.2 נִדָּה (abstract noun) / נִדָּה (designating a female) — **11**
1.3 Qal Passive Participle of Geminate Verbs — **16**
1.4 Conclusion — **20**

2 **יְדִידְיָה – וה' אֲהֵבוֹ: The morphology and meaning of the word ידיד — 23**
2.1 Background Notes — **23**
2.2 On the Meaning of the Word — **24**
2.3 On the Morphology of the Word — **39**
2.4 Concluding Remarks — **45**

3 **The Bible Interpreting Itself — 47**
3.1 Introduction — **47**
3.2 Words that Explain and Words that are Explained — **48**
3.2.1 Parallelism and Parallel Verses — **48**
3.2.2 The Explicit Suggestion of the Explanation — **52**
3.2.3 The Use of an Explanatory Word or Expression — **54**
3.2.4 Explanatory Words in Similar Structures — **56**
3.3 Conclusion — **59**

4 **Gesenius’ Thesaurus and Mishnaic Hebrew Studies — 63**
4.1 Introductory Remarks — **63**
4.2 Data in need of correction — **65**
4.3 Augmentation of incomplete data — **68**

4.4 Early signs of MH scholarship — 70
4.5 Summary remarks — 74

5 איש יהודי היה בשושן הבירה: When did יהודי Come to Denote 'Jew'? — 75

6 Biblical Language in Mishnaic Texts — 81
6.1 Introductory comments — 81
6.2 Relationship of the Mishna to Biblical Hebrew — 82
6.3 Substantive changes due to biblical influence — 86
6.3.1 בין האולם ולמזבח — 86
6.3.2 הזורע והחורש והקוצר — 89
6.4 Concluding comment — 93

7 וְצִוִּתִךָ אַל יִכְבַּד לִבֶּךָ: Regarding One Sentence from the Letter to Pelatyahu — 95

8 The verse שְׁמַע יִשְׂרָאֵל ('Hear, O Israel') in Greek transcription on an ancient amulet — 103
8.1 The text — 104
8.2 Linguistic comments — 104
8.3 Summary — 108

B Qumran Hebrew — 109

9 A Few Remarks on Mishnaic Hebrew and Aramaic in Qumran Hebrew — 111
9.1 Mishnaic Hebrew and Qumran Hebrew — 111
9.1.1 Example 1 — 111
9.1.2 Example 2 — 113
9.2 Aramaic at Qumran — 114
9.2.1 Example 1 — 115
9.2.2 Example 2 — 116
9.3 Summary — 118

10 On Several Linguistic Features of Qumran Hebrew — 119
10.1 ריקמה — 119
10.2 מאחד — 127
10.3 עם החביב — 129
10.4 התקיים — 131

10.4.1 קם = התקיים — 131
10.4.2 התקומם = התקיים — 135
10.5 Concluding remarks — 137

11 Qumran Hebrew Between Biblical and Mishnaic Hebrews: A Morphological Study — 139
11.1 Introductory Comments — 139
11.2 Third-person Pronominal Suffixes on Plural Nouns with the Ending ־וֹת — 140
11.2.1 Biblical Hebrew — 140
11.2.1.1 Distribution patterns in some biblical books — 142
11.2.2.1 Analysis of one late biblical text — 142
11.2.2 Mishnaic Hebrew — 143
11.3 A note on the Samaritan Pentateuch — 145
11.4 QH and Ben Sira — 146
11.5 Summary of the findings within Hebrew — 149
11.6 Concluding comments — 150

12 Mistaken Repetitions or Double Readings? — 153
12.1 The Data and the Interpretations Current in the Scholarly Literature — 153
12.2 A Proposal for a New Explanation of the Phenomenon — 156
12.3 Conclusion — 164

13 Two Issues in Qumran Hebrew: Synchronic and Diachronic Perspectives — 165
13.1 Introductory Comments — 165
13.2 מָבוֹא/מָבוֹי (מָבוֹאִי) — 167
13.3 עָשָׂה and הֶעֱשָׂה (הֶעֱשִׂיא) — 174
13.4 Concluding Comments — 179

14 Grammatical and Lexicographic Notes on a Qumran Fragment (4Q374 ii) — 181
14.1 Introductory Remarks — 181
14.2 ארץ חמדות כל הארצות — 181
14.3 מחיגה — 187
14.4 Conclusion — 195

15 כיון הצלמים / כיניי הצלמים — 197
15.1 Introductory Remarks — 197

15.2 A biblical expression in the Damascus Covenant and its pesher — **198**
15.3 Concluding Statements — **205**

16 The Patterns *Pe'ila* and *Pi"ul* in Qumran Hebrew — 207
16.1 Introductory Comments — **207**
16.2 Specifics and Generalities in the relationship of Qumran Hebrew to Mishnaic Hebrew — **210**
16.3 The Pattern *Pe'ila* — **211**
16.4 The Pattern *Pi"ul* — **217**
16.5 Concluding Remarks — **223**

C. Mishnaic Hebrew and Aramaic — 227

17 Mishnaic Hebrew: An Introductory Survey — 229
17.1 Mishnaic Hebrew and Rabbinic literature — **229**
17.2 The Origin of Mishnaic Hebrew — **231**
17.3 Biblical Hebrew and Mishnaic Hebrew — **232**
17.3.1 Common and Contrasting Features — **232**
17.3.2 Diachronic Differences — **233**
17.3.3 Dialectal differences — **234**
17.3.4 Difference of Tradition — **236**
17.3.5 Literary Influence of Biblical Hebrew upon Mishnaic Hebrew — **237**
17.4 Unity and Diversity in Mishnaic Hebrew — **239**
17.4.1 The assumption of uniformity re-examined — **239**
17.4.2 Contrasts between the language of the Tannaim and the language of the Amoraim — **240**
17.4.3 Mishnaic Hebrew and its different dialects — **241**
17.4.4 Linguistic differences within the Mishnah — **243**
17.4.5 Editions and manuscripts — **244**
17.4.6 Linguistic types in the manuscripts of the Mishnah — **246**
17.4.7 Special traditions — **247**
17.4.8 Written and Oral Traditions — **248**
17.5 Mishnaic Hebrew and Other Languages — **249**
17.5.1 The situation of multi-lingualism — **249**
17.5.2 Mishnaic Hebrew and Aramaic — **250**
17.5.3 Borrowings from Greek and Latin — **253**
17.6 Mishnaic Hebrew from indirect sources — **254**
17.6.1 Direct and indirect sources — **254**

17.6.2 Documents from the Judean Desert — **256**
17.6.3 The Samaritan tradition — **257**
17.6.4 Greek and Latin Transcriptions — **259**
17.6.5 The language of Liturgy and the Piyyut — **260**
17.7 Conclusion — **260**

18 The Study of Mishnaic Hebrew Grammar Based on Written Sources: Achievements, Problems, and Tasks — 263
18.1 Introductory Remarks — **263**
18.2 Research and Achievements — **264**
18.2.1 Description of Mishnaic Hebrew Studies — **264**
18.2.2 Some Central Questions in the Study of Mishnaic Hebrew — **264**
18.2.3 Results of Mishnaic Hebrew Research — **272**
18.2.4 Unity of Mishnaic Hebrew — **275**
18.3 Problems and Tasks — **280**
18.3.1 Investigations of Reliable Manuscripts and other Manuscripts — **280**
18.3.1 Strata versus Traditions — **282**
18.3.3 Reliable Traditions and Scribal Corrections — **284**
18.3.4 Expanding the Fields of Research — **285**
18.3.4.1 Investigation of the Different Periods of Mishnaic Hebrew — **285**
18.3.4.2 Investigation of Traditions and Other Manuscripts — **286**
18.3.4.3 Investigation of Traditions and Examination of General Grammatical Topics — **287**
18.3.4.5 Proportions between Research Fields — **288**
18.3.5 Preparing a New Grammar of Mishnaic Hebrew — **289**
18.4 Concluding Remarks — **290**

19 The Different Traditions of Mishnaic Hebrew — 293
19.1 Introduction — **293**
19.2 The Division of Mishnaic Hebrew into Different Traditions — **294**
19.3 The Western tradition vis-à-vis the Eastern tradition within the Palestinian branch — **296**
19.4 The Palestinian branch vis-à-vis the Babylonian branch — **298**
19.5 Comments on the Proposed Divisions — **300**
19.6 The Western and Eastern traditions of the Palestinian branch — **304**
19.6.1 Gemination of *rēš* — **304**
19.6.2 The relative *šīn* with *šəwa* — **306**

19.6.3 The realization of the short vowel [u] — **306**
19.6.4 The Final Vowel in the *Qatt* and Related Noun Patterns — **309**
19.6.5 The Definite Article with *segol* before *'aleph* with *qameṣ* — **309**
19.6.6 Noun Pattern *po'lān/pa'lān* — **310**
19.6.6.1 צְפֹרֶן/צִפֹּרן — **312**
19.6.6.2 The plural אֲחָיוֹת/אַחְיוֹת — **311**
19.7 The Nature of the Differences between the Western and Eastern Traditions — **312**
19.8 The Historical Background of the Different Traditions of the Western Branch — **313**
19.9 The Palestinian Branch and the Babylonian Branch — **317**
19.10 Background of the Linguistic Differences between the Two Branches — **318**
19.11 Conclusion — **325**

20 The System of *binyanim* in Mishnaic Hebrew (A Morphological Study) — 329
20.1 The *binyanim* in general — **329**
20.2 Comments on the common *binyanim* — **330**
20.3 Comments on the uncommon *binyanim* — **332**
20.3.1 *Pu'al* — **332**
20.3.2 *Nuf'al* — **335**
20.3.3 *Nippə'al* — **339**
20.3.4 *Pē'ēl (pā"ēl), po'al (məfo"āl), niṯpā"al* — **341**
20.3.5 *Pē'ēl* — **342**
20.3.6 *Pō'al* — **344**
20.3.7 *Niṯpā'al* — **344**
20.4 Comments on these three binyanim — **345**
20.4.1 *Po'ēl, Niṯpo'ēl* — **348**
20.4.2 *Po'ēl* — **349**
20.4.3 *Niṯpō'al* — **349**
20.4.4 *Niṯṯap̄'al* — **352**
20.5 Other *binyanim?* — **354**
20.6 Conclusion — **354**

21 The Formation of the *Nif'al* III-*yod* Participle in Mishnaic Hebrew — 359
21.1 The Readings Traditions in the Bible — **359**
21.2 The Mishnaic Hebrew Traditions that have been Studied — **360**
21.3 Other Traditions of Mishnaic Hebrew — **361**

21.4 MS Antonin — **362**
21.5 MS Parma B — **362**
21.6 MS Kaufmann, MS Paris, and the Livorno Edition — **364**
21.7 Summary — **368**
21.8 Appendix — **372**

22 Comments on the Morphology of Nouns in Mishnaic Hebrew: Nouns Attested and Unattested in Biblical Hebrew — 375
22.1 Introduction — **375**
22.2 Nouns Attested in BH — **376**
22.3 Nouns Not in BH — **380**
22.4 Summary — **381**

23 Mishnaic Hebrew and Biblical Hebrew — 383
23.1 Introductory Remarks — **383**
23.2 Rabbinic Hebrew vis-à-vis Biblical Hebrew in Nominal Morphology — **386**
23.2.1 Nouns borrowed from the Bible — **387**
23.2.2 Nouns Common to the Languages of the Bible and the Mishnah — **390**
23.3 Conclusion — **392**

24 On the Language of the Beit ʻAmar Papyrus — 395
24.1 Preliminary Notes — **395**
24.2 On the General Nature of the Language in the Document — **396**
24.3 Orthography — **397**
24.4 Orthography and phonology — **399**
24.5 Minor items in Configuration and Syntax — **404**
24.6 Concluding note — **405**

25 From Oral Transmission to Written Transmission (Concerning the meaning of some orthographic forms in the manuscripts of the Mishnah and of Rabbinic Literature) — 407
25.1 Introductory Comments — **407**
25.2 Unusual orthographic forms and their meanings — **408**
25.2.1 רובע עצמות/רוב עצמות – a quarter-*qab* of bones — **408**
25.2.2 בָּאָת/בָּאָה – has arisen — **408**
25.2.3 עֵינָב/עֵינָיו — **409**
25.2.4 היות/להיות — **411**

25.3 Additions — 413
25.3.1 לָהּ > לַ, as in וקוצה לה חלה > וקוצה לחלה — 413
25.3.2 לֹא > לֹ — 415
25.3.3 The spelling of short words — 416
25.4 Summary — 416

Bibliography — 419

Indexes — 437

Introduction

A

Classical Hebrew is the language that was written in the eras when Hebrew was a spoken language. This is the language in which the Bible, the Dead Sea Scrolls, Ben Sira, and Tannaitic literature were all composed. By the nature of languages, this is not a single homogenous dialect, but a complex of dialects stretching over at least 1300 years, approximately from 1100 BCE until 200 CE, when Hebrew ceased to be a spoken language. Clearly over a period as lengthy as this one no language can remain entirely unified, and with the passage of time and generations, not to mention the vicissitudes and ruptures of history, numerous changes, small and large, are evident within Classical Hebrew.

Within the Bible itself, which alone spans nearly a millennium, are evident numerous strata within the history of Hebrew, and the literary products of the post-biblical era differ even more starkly from the biblical texts. These differences are evident both in the consonantal orthographies of the texts and in the reading traditions which have come down to us (Tiberian, Babylonian, Samaritan, and what can be inferred from Greek and Latin transcriptions).

Furthermore, there is no doubt that the various corpora of classical Hebrew texts were differentiated by dialects. For example, it is evidence that the language of the First Temple biblical books, known as Standard Biblical Hebrew (SBH), and the language of the Tannaim, known as Mishnaic Hebrew (MH), do not merely reflect different stages in the history of the language, but in fact represent distinct dialects. Scholars generally assume, justifiably, that SBH reflects the dialect from the area of Jerusalem, but this may not be the case with regard to MH. This reflects, apparently, a dialect from some other region of the country, which descended from a sister-dialect of SBH.

Despite this, it is important not to ignore the textual connections that exist between the later corpora of Classical Hebrew and the biblical texts and language. Or, to put it differently: Ben Sira, the sectarian texts from Qumran, and Tannaitic literature are all shaded with the colors of the Bible, in language and style. Each of them has words and phrases borrowed from the Bible, which do not reflect their own contemporary language but hark back to earlier eras.

B

The volume presented here is only a selection of the studies I have written about Classical Hebrew. The twenty-five chapters in the book include lexical and grammatical studies about three literary corpora: the Bible, the Dead Sea Scrolls, and Tannaitic literature. Because of the intimate contact between Qumran Hebrew and Mishnaic Hebrew, on the one hand, and Aramaic on the other, studies of Aramaic are also included.

These studies present synchronic analyses of linguistic issues, without disregarding the diachronic data and explanations relevant to each issue. In some of the chapters, one can see the changes that occurred over time with regard to certain words, forms, or other linguistic phenomena.

A. The first eight chapters, which are devoted to Biblical Hebrew, include broad studies and detailed investigations. Chapters 1–4 and 6 cast a wide net within each of the issues studied. Chapters 5 and 7–8, on the other hand, are devoted to narrowly defined studies of only the particular details needed by the topics addressed therein.

Here are some examples. Chapter 1 deals with the internal passive form of the participle in the Qal of geminate verbs. Here the data discussed include forms from within the Bible itself, as well as evidence from the ancient translations (the Septuagint, Onqelos on the Pentateuch and Jonathan on the Prophets, as well as the Peshiṭta and the Vulgate). In this study a previously-unrecognized ancient Hebrew grammatical form is uncovered. The study also draws on data from Mishnaic Hebrew and interpretations ascribed to lexemes in the Bible by ancient translators and commentators.

In Chapter 2, two separate discussions are presented: semantic and grammatical studies of the same word, the noun ידיד. The two studies in this chapter are again based on varied types of data, each of which can reveal a different aspect of the meaning or morphology of this noun. Here, too, the testimony of the ancients – translators and interpreters – turns out to be decisive. This chapter also presents a method for semantic and grammatical investigation of words from ancient Hebrew, where the relevant data are fragmentary and partial. There are also here insights into the various reading traditions extant in Jewish communities throughout the centuries, when Hebrew was only a liturgical and literary language.

An example of one of the shorter chapters is Chapter 5, which traces the semantic changes that befell the word *yəhudi* (יְהוּדִי) in the transition between the eras of the First Temple and the Second Temple. Here language intersects with other realms of inquiry, as the semantic change appears to be the result of extra-linguistic changes that occurred within Jewish history with the Babylonian exile, as is reflected within the Bible itself, and within the Rabbis' references to the meanings of this word.

B. Eight chapters – Chapter 9 through 16 – then deal with the Hebrew of the Dead Sea Scrolls. Here, too, there are broad synthetic studies and narrow investigations into particular grammatical phenomena. As is known, many important studies have already been written by the greatest of Hebraists since the discovery of the texts from Qumran more than sixty years ago. These studies have dealt broadly with both the grammar and the lexicon of the texts, as well as the relationship between the language of these texts and SBH, Aramaic, and MH. Not a few studies also dealt with the unique features of this language, again both in the realm of the lexicon and the realm of grammar. Still, there are more than a few general topics, and many details, in need of further study, both in terms of collecting and presenting all the relevant data, and in terms of accurately explaining it all. In the past decade I have devoted a series of studies, including the eight presented here, to furthering this field of research.

For example, I present different aspects of Qumran research in Chapters 11 and 13. Chapter 11 follows a grammatical phenomenon from the earliest layer of biblical literature through the texts of the Tannaim, and shows the changes that can occur – and did occur – in the spoken language over the generations. At the same time, however, it also shows the tendency of the literary texts to present a static and unchanging literary language, as the literary dialect found in Ben Sira and the Dead Sea Scrolls tends strongly to stick to archaic patterns from centuries earlier. Chapter 13 shows that words and grammatical features in the Hebrew of the Dead Sea Scrolls reveal various realities. One phenomenon in QH may be comparable to what is known from SBH, while another is more closely comparable to the colloquial dialect of the day, reflected later on in MH. Chapter 12, too, is a comprehensive study of a linguistic feature which peeks out from the medieval copy of the Damascus Covenant: there we find two versions of the same words, one in its ancient formulation and the other, alongside, in its later variation.

C. In the nine chapters 17–25, devoted primarily to Mishnaic Hebrew but also partially to Aramaic, I give a sampling of my primary field of research over the past 40 years and more: Mishnaic Hebrew. My first publication in this field was in 1971, and since then I have been intensively occupied with it. The studies presented here include some introductory presentations and overviews (Chapters 17–19), and some broad synthetic studies such as the new description of the system of *binyanim* of MH presented in Chapter 20. There are also other studies of great interest, such as the investigation into the question of the transition of Tannaitic literature from oral transmission to written texts (Chapter 25).

Like the studies of my teachers, my colleagues, and my students, the scholars of the "Jerusalem school", these studies establish the status of MH as a spoken language. In our generation there is hardly any scholar worthy of the name who still holds the position that MH was not a spoken language. It should be admitted, however, that there are still voices heard insisting – entirely mistakenly – that MH was an artificial scholastic language; this ignores the modern study of the dialect, which began to crystallize around the studies of M. Z. Segal and H. Yalon in the early parts of the twentieth century and continued in the following generations.

D. Epigraphic materials. In each of the three sections of the book, I have included studies of epigraphic texts which did not come from Qumran: chapters 7, 8, 24. These include the amulet from the third century CE found in Austria (Chapter 8) in which there is a transcription of the verse "Shema" (Deut. 6:4) into Greek letters. Another example is the document from Beit 'Amar (Chapter 24) which reveals important information about the contact between Hebrew and Aramaic, as well as about the presence of Greek in the language of Hebrew and Aramaic speakers (and writers) in the generation of Shimon Bar Koseba.

There is no epigraphic Hebrew (or Aramaic) text found that does not add to our knowledge of the history of the Hebrew language, whether with regard to a detail or to a more general issue. The text from Beit 'Amar, for example, provides firm evidence for the linguistic variation, or the dialectal diversity, in the pronunciation of the relative particle -ש in the generation of Bar Koseba and in MH. To my mind, it is clear that alongside the pronunciation with an [e] vowel, *še-*, there was also a pronunciation with an [a] vowel, as *ša-*. There is no doubt that the epigraphic data is of singular important for the study of Classical Hebrew, being texts untouched by copyists and editors, and arriving on our desks in their pristine forms. The study of this material often shows that the transmission of Jewish literature – Bible and rabbinic literature – in reliable manuscripts is remarkably accurate.

C

As I mentioned, theses 25 chapters are only a selection of my studies devoted to Classical Hebrew. This selection brings between two covers a sampling of the studies dealing with a cross-section of topics on the various strata of Classical Hebrew and its literary corpora. I have drawn encouragement in the past generation from the increasingly common phenomenon of scholars and students around the world studying not only the Hebrew of the Bible, but also of the literary texts from later centuries.

It is of course clear that one who wishes to follow modern scholarship on the Hebrew language in all the various eras and ages, and in all its literary crystallizations, ought to read the many important studies being published, in various forums, in modern Hebrew. Despite this, it is important to realize that there are many contexts in universities in different countries in which the Hebrew of Qumran and of rabbinic literature is studied. A handful of books and numerous articles published in European languages in recent years serve this community of research, scholarship, and learning. With this volume I add the voice that emerges from these collected essays to this effort.

A Biblical Hebrew

1 The *Qal* Passive Participle of Geminate Verbs in Biblical Hebrew

1.1 Introduction

§ 1 I would like to suggest the possible existence of a previously unidentified grammatical form in Biblical Hebrew. All grammatical conclusions are based on an exact understanding of the words in any given corpus, and I will therefore begin by investigating the meaning (or meanings) of one Hebrew word. To be more precise, I will begin with an investigation into the meanings that have been attributed to the word throughout the history of Hebrew, and which are attributed to it today. The topic is the word נִדָּה, which has been discussed extensively in recent years.

§ 2 I believe that an examination of נִדָּה and the identification of other forms from the root נד"ד and other geminates might reveal a grammatical category among geminate verbs, well attested for strong verbs, which has so far eluded recognition. Such an inquiry can potentially aid in the elucidation of other forms. Two meanings are usually assigned to נִדָּה: "menstrual impurity" and "sprinkling."

1.2 נִדָּה and נִדָּה

1.2.1 נִדָּה 'menstrual impurity' / נִדָּה 'sprinkling'

§ 3 In addition to the entries found in biblical dictionaries and commentaries, mention should be made of two short but important studies devoted to נִדָּה that were written in the past few years. The first is "Word Studies III" by Ze'ev Ben-Ḥayyim,[1] and the second is "The Etymology of נִדָּה (Menstrual Impurity)" by Moshe Greenberg, which was published in the Festschrift for Jonas Greenfield.[2]

In his article, Ben-Ḥayyim discusses five Hebrew and Aramaic lexical entries; the shortest of the discussions concerns נדה.[3] He begins by saying that

> "the noun נדה is derived in dictionaries from the root נד"ד either with the meaning of 'impurity,' 'female impurity' or in the expression מֵי נִדָּה 'waters of sprinkling' and these

1 Ben-Ḥayyim 1980–1981.

2 Greenberg 1995.

3 Ben-Ḥayyim 1980–1981:199–200.

waters were intended in biblical times to purify an impurity. Since the noun apparently means one thing and its opposite, one usually resolves the contradiction by assuming that the 'waters of sprinkling' were called such because they served to purify the impure."

As is his wont, Ben-Ḥayyim begins with the greatest of the medieval linguists (Ibn Janah and Radaq) and concludes with the modern scholars (the dictionary of Koehler-Baumgartner). He examines the midrashic and contextual interpretations of the words as they appear in the Babylonian Talmud in *Avoda Zara* 75b and the Targumim (Onqelos and the Peshitta). His conclusion is that two homonyms exist within Hebrew: (1) נִדָּה from the root נד"ד and (2) נִדָּה from the root נד"י.[4] In more detail: (1) means menstrual impurity, from the root נד"ד, and is inflected like other nouns from geminate roots such as דִּבָּה, גִּנָּה, סִבָּה, and כַּלָּה;[5] and (2) "sprinkling,"[6] from the root נד"י (cognate to נז"י),[7] which is inflected like nouns from final weak roots such as פִּנָּה, אַוָּה, הַוָּה, and עַוָּה.[8]

§ 4 Greenberg in his study examines in depth the etymology of נִדָּה meaning "menstrual impurity." He thoroughly reviews the dictionaries[9] and modern commentators,[10] and he describes in some detail the usages of the root נד"ד in the *targumim* and the *Peshitta*. He makes a good argument for deriving the noun נִדָּה from נד"ד and rejects the view that it should be derived from נד"י, which had been suggested by J. Milgrom and B. Levine.[11] The basis for this

4 Ben-Ḥayyim 1980–1981:200.

5 Ben-Ḥayyim 1980–1981:99 relates the noun pattern קִטָּה (*qitta[h]*) to the pattern קַטָּה (*qatta[h]*).

6 In addition to the expression מֵי נִדָּה / מֵי הַנִּדָּה (Num 19:9, 13, 20, 21;31:23), some of the early translations also understood the expression לחטאת ולְנִדָּה (Zech 13:11) meaning towards 'sprinkling.' This is apparent from Targum Jonathan כמה דמידכן במי אדיותא ובקטם תורתא דחטתא ('as those who purify themselves in the waters of sprinkling and by the ashes of the cow of sin') and from the Peshitta לרססא ולדכיתא ('for sprinkling and for purification'). Clearly the two *targumim* hint at a reverse order of the two nouns, as if it were written לנדה ולחטאת.

7 Ben-Ḥayyim 1980–1981:199 comments on additional pairs of Hebrew roots such as נזר/נדר, נצר/נטר "regardless of whether the doublets have arisen within Hebrew or as a result of loans from Aramaic." See also Rabin 1970:290–297.

8 Ben-Ḥayyim 1980–1981:200. Here, too, he believes there is a connection between the noun pattern קִטָּה (*qiṭṭa[h]*) and קַטָּה (*qaṭṭa[h]*).

9 He is interested primarily in modern European dictionaries beginning with the dictionary of Gesenius-Buhl (17th edition from 1915) and ending with *HALOT* (1967–1996). He also examines concordances to the Old Testament, Mishna, *Targum Onqelos*, and the *Peshitta*.

10 The commentaries of Milgrom (1991) and Levine (1989 and 1993).

11 Even though Milgrom suggests a derivation from נד"י, he recognized the fact that נִדָּה is inflected like קִטָּה from a geminate root. Moreover, he points out the alternation between geminate and final weak verbs (such as שג"ג and שג"ה). Levine takes נִדָּה as a *Nif'al* passive participle from the root נד"י (< נִנְדָּה).

suggestion was the verbal forms הַמְנַדִּים (Amos 6:3) and מְנַדֵּיכֶם (Isa 66:5), as well as comparative evidence. Greenberg, however, cites additional material from the *targumim*, *Peshitta*, and Ben-Sira that substantiates his conclusion that נִדָּה is derived from נד"ד meaning physical or spiritual removal (loathing). He believes that הַמְנַדִּים (Amos 6:3) and מְנַדֵּיכֶם (Isa 66:5) are denominative verbs from נִדָּה.

§ 5 Thus Ben-Ḥayyim and Greenberg conclude (like the medievals) that נִדָּה marking female impurity is derived from נד"ד and not from נד"י. I would like to argue, however, that one should distinguish between (1) נִדָּה, an abstract noun referring to menstrual impurity and (2) נְדָּה, a designation for an impure woman, which functions as both a noun and adjective. Greenberg points out this distinction in his article.[12] He did not, however, go one step further and come to what I think is the logical conclusion, namely, that these are two separate grammatical forms.

§ 6 I should stress that the general, scholarly consensus holds that נִדָּה is only an abstract noun. This is the impression one gets from looking at three biblical dictionaries that are widely used today: BDB, *HALOT* (Koehler-Baumgartner), and that of Ben-Yehuda. BDB defines נִדָּה as "impurity (as abhorrent, shunned)" and suggests two secondary meanings: (1) impurity; (2) figuratively an impure thing. This dictionary cites all twenty-nine occurrences of the word in the Hebrew Bible, including the expression מֵי נִדָּה.[13] The form נִידָה (Lam 1:8) is also included in this entry.[14] *HALOT* suggests two meanings: (1) bleeding, menstruation of a woman, and the expression מֵי נִדָּה is included under this meaning;[15] (2) separation, abomination, defilement.[16] Ben Yehuda lists three meanings: (1) female menstruation; (2) anything despised (e.g., ואיש כי יקח את אשת אחיו, נדה היא Lev 20:21); (3) water of impurity.[17]

1.2.2 נִדָּה (abstract noun) / נְדָּה (designating a female)

§ 7 Yet it is clear that נִדָּה is not an abstract noun designating menstrual impurity in every passage in which it occurs in the Old Testament. We also

12 See Greenberg 1995:75–76 (and § 8 below).

13 See § 3 above and n. 6. Zech 13:1 is not included in this dictionary under the category of מֵי נִדָּה.

14 נִידָה is cited as a separate entry, but at the end of the entry is it noted (= נִדָּה).

15 See n. 13 above. Zech 13:1 is cited under the second definition.

16 This dictionary lists נִידָה as a separate entry under נו"ד. Only at the end of the entry is it noted that it might be a reflex of נִדָּה.

17 Ben Yehuda 1960: 7.3533–3534 also does not include Zech 13:1 under this definition. See above nn. 6, 13, and 15.

find passages in which הָאִשָּׁה נִדָּה appears to be an adjective/noun designating a woman during her menstrual period, as is the case in Mishnaic Hebrew.[18] See, e.g., ואל אשה נִדָּה לא יקרב (Ezek 18:6) in which אִשָּׁה נִדָּה is a collocation composed of a noun and its modifying adjective and not an abstract noun. In this collocation נִדָּה designates an impure woman similar to the common mishnaic usage. It is true that the noun נִדָּה functions as an abstract noun with the meaning "female impurity" in many of its occurrences in Mishnaic Hebrew (according to Ben Yehuda: "the status of the woman during her period"),[19] such as ... יוצאת אשה בחוטי צמר... ובטוטפת ובסונבוטין ...בכבול ובפאה נכרית במוך שבאזנה ובמוך שבסנדלה ובמוך שהתקינה לְנִדָּתָה (m. Sabb. 6:5). Nonetheless, נִדָּה meaning an "impure woman" is also quite common, e.g., נִידָּה שבדקה עצמה יום שביעי שחרית (m. Nid. 10:2), בנות כותים נידות מעריסתן (m. Nid. 4:1), הנידות והיולדות טובלות כדרכן ביום הכיפורים (t. Kip. 4[5]:5).

§ 8 Greenberg already pointed out the unique use of נִדָּה in the phrase אשה נִדָּה (Ezek 18:6), which he interprets as two nouns in apposition.[20] On this interpretation, נִדָּה in this expression means "an impure [woman]," and not "female impurity," and that therefore the mishnaic usage can be found already in the Bible.[21] However, Greenberg argues that all meanings developed within one form, which originally possessed an abstract meaning (נידה = "menstrual impurity"), which developed secondarily into a concrete usage (נידה = "an impure thing," "an impure woman"). I would like to suggest, on the contrary, that we should consider the possibility of two separate grammatical forms. Before offering my interpretation, I shall review what the ancient versions had to say.

§ 9 The ancient biblical versions translate the noun נִדָּה with two different grammatical forms. Let us begin with Targum Onqelos. Of thirteen occurrences of נִדָּה[22] in the Pentateuch (all in the book of Leviticus), Onqelos trans-

18 For some reason Ben Yehuda 1960:7.3533–3534 also includes in his definition (נִדַּת האשה = מעמד האשה בזמן וסתה בזיבת דמה החדשי) the passages from Mishnaic Hebrew in which נידה deals with a woman, e.g., נידה שבדקה עצמה יום שביעי שחרית (m. Niddah 10:2).

19 Ben Yehuda 1960:7.3533–3534.

20 "In אשה נדה of Ezekiel, the word נדה, in apposition to the word אשה, denotes an embodiment of menstrual impurity, a woman, a menstruant = a menstruous woman on the pattern of אשה זונה 'a harlot woman'" (Greenberg 1995:75). I do not understand the necessity of taking the collocations אשה נדה and אשה זונה as constructions consisting of nucleus and apposition as against noun and modifying adjective. These constructions are identical to אשה גדולה (2 Kgs 4:8), אשה זרה (Prov 2:16), אשה יפה (Prov 11:22), אשה עזובה (Isa 54:6), etc.

21 It should be stressed that Greenberg 1995:76 also recognizes the fact that what is attested in Mishnaic Hebrew (נִדָּה as a title for a woman which also has the plural form נִדּוֹת), already can be found in the Hebrew Bible in the phrase לְנִדָּה היתה (Lam 1:17).

22 This number does not include the six occurrences of מֵי נִדָּה / מֵי הַנִּדָּה, which as already noted (§ 3), do not belong here.

lates נִדָּה twelve times as a verbal noun, which also functions as an abstract noun: רִיחוּק. Thus, the expression נִדַּת דותה (Lev 12:2) is translated ריחוק סאובתה (also in Lev 12:5; 15:19,20,24,25[3×], 26[2×],33; 18:19). In one passage, however, Onqelos uses a Pa‘‘el passive participle from the root רח"ק: ואיש אשר יקח את אשת אחיו, נִדָּה היא (Lev 20:21) is translated וגבר דיסב ית איתת אחוהי, מְרַחֲקָא[23] היא (not רחוק but מְרַחֲקָא 'far away,' or 'removed')! In this passage Onqelos translates נדה as in the expression אשה נדה (Ezek 18:6),[24] which we mentioned above,[25] and corresponds to the second meaning of נדה in Mishnaic Hebrew. I should add that מרחקא also can be found in Targum Lamentations (1:17): היתה ירושלם לנִדָּה ביניהם is translated הות ירושלים דמיא לאיתתא מרחקא[26] ביניהון.[27]

§ 10 In the Peshitta, too, there is evidence of a distinction between the abstract noun and the designation of a woman during her impurity. The abstract noun may be translated by one of several nouns: כפסא (*kefsā*), טמאותא (*ṭam'ūṯā*), נדתא (*neddəṯā*), or עולא (*'awlā*). Here are some examples: the word בְּנִדָּתָהּ is translated by איך כפסה in Lev 12:5 and in all its other occurrences in Leviticus, with the exception of the verse ואיש כי יקח את אשת אחיו, נדה היא (Lev 20:21) where one finds עולא (= עָוֶל 'iniquity'). לְנִדָּה in Lam 1:17 and לְנִידָה Lam 1:8 are both rendered נדתא. The expression בנדת עמי הארצות (Ezra 9:11) is translated בטמאותא דעממֿא ודמדינֿתא ('because of the impurity of nations and cities'). The expression והוציאו את הנדה (2 Chr 29:5) is translated ואפרֿקו עבדֿיכון בֿישא. Note that the noun נִדָּה is translated in this

23 We should add that the data from the Palestinian Targumim as reflected in Targum Neofiti and in Targum Pseudo-Jonathan match what we find in Targum Onqelos. All the occurrences which Targum Onqelos renders ריחוק are translated in Targum Neofiti by רחוק/ריחוק, נדה, ריחוק נדה, נדת סאבתא, (נדתה). The passage in which נידה is translated by Onqelos as מרחקא is rendered also in Neofiti as מרחקה (with *heh* as a final *mater lectionis*). In Pseudo-Jonathan the data are identical to those of Onqelos. ריחוק translates נדה wherever Onqelos does (the third occurrence in Lev 15:25, however, is omitted), and the same is true for מרחקא.

24 Yet it should be noted that one always find in Targum Jonathan to Ezekiel an abstract noun, e.g., לְנִדָּה (Ezek 7:19, 20) is translated by לבוסרן ('in scorn'). The expression אִשָּׁה נִדָּה (Ezek 18:6) is translated אִתָּא טומאה. (It is almost certain that the version אתא מסאבא found in the First [1515–1517] and Second [1524–1525] Rabbinic Bible as evidenced by Sperber's edition is not the original version). טְמֵאַת הנדה (Ezek 22:10) is translated אתא טְמאה, but the expression בטֻמאת הנדה (Ezek 36:17) is translated כסואבת איתא טְמאה ('according to the female impurity she was made impure'); in this passage the translator included the noun איתא and also used a construction made up of nucleus and apposition.

25 See § 8.

26 See n. 29 below.

27 Greenberg 1995:74 notes that the participle מְרַחֲקָא also translates the nouns תּוֹעֵבָה (e.g., Deut 7:26; Isa 1:13) and פִּגּוּל (Lev 7:18; 17:7) in the targumim. Even though מְרַחֲקָא translates nouns, its status as a passive participle is not changed, even if it functions as a noun.

verse by an abstract noun and a modifying adjective עבדִּיכוֹן בִּישָׁא ('your evil deeds'). וְאֶל אִשָּׁה נִדָּה (Ezek 18:6) is translated וּלְאִתְּתָא בְּכַפְסָה; in this passage the translator added a *beth* before the noun and a 3 f.s. pronominal suffix (בכפסה) in order to avoid the syntactic construction of noun and modifying adjective.

§ 11   In the Peshitta, נִדָּה is also translated by concrete nouns, i.e., words referring to a menstruating woman. For example, וְטֻמְאַת הַנִּדָּה (Ezek 22:10) is translated וטנפותא דכפסניתא ('the pollution of the menstruating woman'), and the expression כְּטֻמְאַת הַנִּדָּה (Ezek 36:17) is rendered ואיך טמאותא דכפסניתא ('and like the impurity of the menstruating woman'). It is important to add that *kefsanita* also translates the participial הַדָּוָה[28] (Lev 15:13). The word נִדָּה is sometimes translated as a passive participle of *Afʿel* of the verb אסלי: מסליא (*maslayā* "removed," "rejected," "condemned," "violated"); this is the case in Ezek 7:19–20. נִדָּה can be translated, too, by a participle טמאא (= *ṭamā* < *ṭam'ā*) 'impure.' I would like to emphasize that in one verse the word נדה is attested twice: הָאָרֶץ אֲשֶׁר אַתֶּם בָּאִים לְרִשְׁתָּהּ אֶרֶץ נִדָּה הִיא, בְּנִדַּת עַמֵּי הָאֲרָצוֹת (Ezra 9:11). The Syriac translator interprets the first occurrence of נדה as an adjective and translates it as a participle, whereas the second occurrence is taken as an abstract noun designating impurity and thus he translates ארעא דעאלין אנתון לה למארתה טמאא הי בטמאותא דעממא ודמדינתא ('the land you are entering to inherit it, is impure because of the impurity of the nations and cities').

§ 12   Several centuries before Targum Onqelos and the Peshitta, one finds that the Septuagint already distinguishes in translation between forms of נִדָּה. In passages where the word is understood as an abstract noun, it is translated by the appropriate Greek word, and where it is perceived as designating a woman, it is translated by a participle. Representative examples are כִּימֵי נִדַּת דְּוֹתָהּ (Lev 12:2), which is translated κατὰ τὰς ἡμέρας τοῦ χωρισμοῦ τῆς ἀφέδρου αὐτῆς; χωρισμός means 'separation,' 'removal'; נִדָּתָהּ (Lev (15:24) is translated ἡ ἀκαθαρσία αὐτῆς ('her impurity') and is commonly translated by ἄφεδρος ('the impurity of the menstruant'), e.g., בְּנִדָּתָהּ (Lev 15:19,20) is translated ἐν τῇ ἀφέδρῳ αὐτῆς. In contrast, the expression כְּטֻמְאַת הַנִּדָּה (Ezek 36:17) is translated κατὰ τὴν ἀκαθαρσίαν τῆς ἀποκαθημένης ('like the impurity of [the woman] who moves herself to the side' or 'who sits herself down on the side'). Ἀποκαθημένη is a feminine medial participle of the verb ἀποκάθημαι ('to sit oneself down on the side'). This is identical to what occurs in translating the

---

28 In Biblical Hebrew דָּוָה is a participle designating a menstruating woman (אין דוה אלא נדה Sifra Qed. 11:1).

collocation טֻמְאַת הַנִּדָּה (Ezek 22:10), and this is what we find in the translation of לְנִדָּה (Lam 1:17)[29]: εἰς ἀποκαθημένην.

§ 13 The Vulgate also distinguishes between נִדָּה as an abstract noun and נִדָּה as designating a woman, e.g., it translates נִדַּת in the collocation נִדַּת דותה (Lev 12:2) *separationis* ('separation'). On the other hand, in the verse ואל אשה נדה לא יקרב (Ezek 18:6) the Vulgate translates a medio-passive participle *menstruatam* ('a woman during her monthly period'). We also find in the Vulgate that נִדָּה in the collocations טֻמְאַת הנדה (Ezek 22:10), כטומאת הנדה (Ezek 36:17) translated by the genitive *menstruate*. A similar translation is also found in the verse היתה ירושלים לְנִדָּה ביניהם (Lam 1:17): *facta est Ierusalem quasi polluta*

---

29 In the Tiberian vocalization to Lam 1:8,17 נִידָה and נִדָּה are clearly distinguished: חטא צוה ה' ליעקב סביביו צריו, היתה ירושלם לְנִדָּה ביניהם (1:18), חטאה ירושלם על כן לנִידָה היתה (1:17). In v. 8 נִידָה is from נו"ד and in v. 17 נִדָּה is from נד"ד. The Tiberian vocalization is confirmed by the ancient translations and from the midrash, which give a historical dimension to both forms. The Septuagint translates לְנִידָה as εἰς σάλον; σάλος means "shaking." נִידָה is similar to קִימָה from the root קו"ם and to שִׁיבָה from the root שו"ב. נִדָּה, on the other hand, is translated by ἀποκαθημένην "to the one who sits down by the side," "to the one who moves away." This is what we find in Targum Lamentations 1:8 לְנִידָה היתה, which is translated by בטלטול הוות, and the clause היתה ירושלים לְנִדָּה ביניהם (Lam 1:17) is translated הוות ירושלים דמיא לאתתא מרחקא ביניהון. One should probably read מְרַחֲקָא along with Targum Onqelos. There is some similarity to Midrash Lamentations: על כן לנידה היתה – לטלטול היתה (Parasha 1, sect. 36), היתה ירושלים לנדה ביניהם – לריחנק היתה (Parasha 1 § 60). The midrash too distinguishes between two versions, but in v. 17 it uses the verbal noun ריחוק as does Onqelos in all the passages where נִדָּה is interpreted as an abstract noun.

Note also that later generations preserved the distinction in translating the words (since they considered them separate words). Sa'adia Ga'on translated לנידה היתה (Lam 1:8) as צארת נאידה (became a wanderer; see R. Y. Qafih to the verse), היתה ירושלים לְנִדָּה (Lam 1:17) וצארת ירושלים מבערה (נדה is translated 'distanced'!). Sa'adia translates with participles in the two verses. In Rashi's commentary one hears echoes of the midrash and the targum: לנידה (v. 8); לשון 'נע ונד' – לגולה. לְנִדָּה (v. 17) – לריחוק לבוז. In explaining נִידָה, Rashi takes it as a participle in explaining נִדָּה he interprets it as a verbal noun (as in the midrash). Ibn Ezra also explains נִידָה in v. 8 from the root נו"ד, though he believes the intent is one of mocking as in מנוד ראש and it is from the same verbal class as the expression נע ונד. Several modern commentators maintain this distinction. For example, Perles (1902–1903) correctly states that נידה (vs. 8) "in targum and in midrash the word is to be interpreted from נו"ד (shaking) and this is more correct." On the other hand, he follows Ibn Ezra in seeing this as mocking. Perles did not notice that the distinction between נידה and נִדָּה exists already in the Septuagint. He does cite some scholars who believe that נידה is a reflex (an erroneous one?) of נִדָּה (see Perles ad loc.). This is apparent in the concordances of Mandelkern and Even-Shoshan, both of whom list נידה in the entry of נִדָּה. The modern dictionaries also relate נידה to נִדָּה (see nn. 14 and 16 above). Perles also did not notice that the blurring of the distinction between נידה and נדה can be observed in the *Peshitta*, where in both verses one finds נדתא (see § 10 above). The evidence from the Tiberian Masorah, supported by the Septuagint, Midrash Lamentations, and the Jewish Aramaic Targum Lamentations outweighs the evidence from the Peshitta.

menstruis intereos (= 'Jerusalem was as if polluted by the menstrual period among them'); *polluta* is a feminine passive participle of *polluo*.

§ 14 In sum, it is impossible to ignore the accumulated evidence from the ancient translations, which distinguish between נִדָּה, an abstract noun, and נִדָּה, a designation for a woman. Sometimes נדה marking a woman is translated as a passive: מְרַחֲקָא in *Targum Onqelos* (and in other Jewish *targumim* including *Targum Lamentations*), *masləya* in the *Peshitta*, and *polluta* in the Vulgate, and other times it is translated differently, such as *kefsaniṯa* (adjective) and *ṭama* (*pə'el* participle) in Syriac, or ἀποκαθημένη (medial participle) in Greek. All point to the same thing: they choose a translation that designates a menstruating woman. These data line up with the collocation אשה נִדָּה (Ezek 18:6) as I have interpreted it and with the common usage of Mishnaic Hebrew, such as נדה שבדקה (*Nid* 10:1).

1.3 Qal Passive Participle of Geminate Verbs

§ 15 We have already noted that Greenberg[30] considers נִדָּה as designation for a woman to be concretization of an originally abstract noun: נִדָּה ("impurity") > נִדָּה ("an impure thing," "an impure woman").[31] However, it appears to me that another solution is possible: perhaps the word נִדָּה includes two homonyms that have merged into one noun. The first is an abstract noun in the *qiṭṭa(h)* pattern, similar to בִּזָּה and סִבָּה. The second, the noun designating a menstruating woman, is a passive participle in the *qiṭṭ* (> *qeṭ*) pattern, whose feminine is *qiṭṭa(h)*. I propose the existence of the pattern *qeṭ*[32] (< *qiṭṭ*) / *qiṭṭa(h)* in geminate verbs, cognate with passive participles of the pattern *qāṭīl* in the strong verb, such as קָרִיא and שְׂנִיאָה in biblical Hebrew and שְׁלִיחַ in Mishnaic Hebrew, and to the pattern *qil* in medial weak verbs, such as שִׂים (Num 24:21) and שִׂימָה (*ketiv* 2 Sam 13:32).[33]

§ 16 If this is indeed the case, then נִדָּה is the feminine passive participle of נֵד. Perhaps the masculine form is attested in the verse נֵד קציר ביום נחלה (Isa 17:11), i.e., "the harvest is shaken (or removed) on the day of (benefitting from) the inherited land." It is of course true that this is a difficult verse, as

30 Greenberg 1995:75–76.

31 Metonymy as revealed in an abstract noun becoming a concrete noun is a well-known phenomenon, e.g., אנכי ולא אהיה מפי הגבורה נאמרו, הגבורה is the גיבור himself. In קובי היה האהבה הגדולה שלה, אהבה is a designation for the lover himself.

32 The length of the vowel in this form is discussed below in § 24.

33 These are cognate with *qetil* and שִׂים in Aramaic.

A. B. Ehrlich notes in his commentary to Isaiah.[34] I must confess that the ancient translations offer no support for the proposed interpretation of this verse, since most of them have attempted to bypass the *peshat*. Targum Jonathan, for example, translates the entire verse (ביום נטעך תשגשגי ובבקר זרעך תפריחי, נד קציר ביום נחלה וכאב אנוש) midrashically: באתר דאתקדשתון למהוי עם, תמן קלקילתון עובדיכון, ואף כד עלתון לארע בית שכינתי, תמן הוה חזי לכון למפלח, שבקתון פולחני ופלחתון לטעוותא, ארחיקתון יום תיובא עד די מְטָא יום תברכון, בכין הוה כיבכון למפחת נפש. The translator has diverged significantly from the *peshat*, to the extent that it is difficult to see any connection between the Hebrew word נֵד and Targumic מְטָא, which ostensibly translates it. The Peshitta translates the expression נֵד קציר as איך נירא דקטפא, reading reads נִר (= נִיר "ploughed field") instead of נֵד. The Septuagint translates εἰς ἀμητόν = עַד קציר.[35] We have here a difficult phrase in a difficult verse.

§ 17 In order to understand נֵד one must look at the broader context. V. 11 (see above § 16) should be interpreted in the light of vv. 9 and 10: (9) ביום ההוא יהיו ערי מעוזו כעזובת החרש והאמיר אשר עזבו מפני בני ישראל והיתה שממה. (10) כי שכחת אלהי ישעך וצור מָעֻזֵּךְ לא זכרת על כן תטעי נטעי נעמנים וזמורת זר תזרענו., which are a continuation of vv. 4–8. V. 9 mentions the punishment, v. 10 talks of the sin, and v. 11 returns to the punishment, allow me to elaborate: v. 9 indicates the destruction and desolation of the strong cities of Jacob (mentioned in v. 4), v. 10 mentions the reason (the sin) ...כי שכחת אלהי ישעך. The strong punishment is to be presented through an amazingly unconventional idea (v. 11): הזורעים ברינה, בדמעה יקצורו. In the words of the verse: "On the day of planting you will blossom, and in the morning of sowing, you will bloom, but on the day in which you expect produce from the inheritance, the harvest will be removed and in its place will come incurable pain."[36]

§ 18 Presumably, the intent of נֵד קציר is "the harvest is shaken" ("removed" or "distanced."[37]).[38] There may already be in the Vulgate a basis

---

34 "This passage cannot be explained the way it is written." See Ehrlich 1899–1901:3.38.

35 Ehrlich 1899–1901:3.38.

36 See Ehrlich for a similar interpretation, however, it is possible to explain נד קציר ביום נחלה וכאב אנוש as 'the harvest will be removed on the day that the great blow and incurable pain come to you.' See Radak on this verse and following him many of the modern commentators.

37 Cf. מְרַחֲקָא in the translation of נִדָּה in Targum Onqelos, in other Pentateuchal targumim, and in the Targum to Lamentations (see § 9 and n. 23 above).

38 In the style of this passage one can see representative features of poetry: 1: absence of the definite article on the noun (קציר, כאב and not הקציר, הכאב); 2) complete grammatical parallelism between the two hemistiches – passive participle (which functions as the predicate), noun (which function as the subject). This parallelism appears in the chiasm: נֵד קציר (נֵד pss. ptc.) / וכאב אָנוּשׁ (אָנוּשׁ pss. ptc.), i.e., the harvest is removed (and consequently) the

for this interpretation. One finds *ablata est messis* ("the harvest is removed"). There is no reason to believe that the Vulgate reads[39] נָד קציר (or נַד). Frequently, the Vulgate translates a Hebrew passive participle with a Latin passive participle. For example, the *Qal* passive participial forms are translated from time to time with the *participium perfectum indicative passive* (and other forms), e.g., כאשר צוה משה עבד ה' את בני ישראל כַּכָּתוּב בספר תורת משה (Josh 8:31): *sicut praeceperat Moses famulus Domini filiis Israel et scriptum est in volumine legis Mosi.* כָּתוּב is translated by *scriptum est.* ויתר דברי אבים יכל אשר עשה הלוא הם כְּתוּבִים על ספר דברי הימים למלכי יהודה (1 Kgs 15:7) is translated by *reliqua autem sermonum Abiam et omnia quae fecit nonne haec scripta sunt in libro verborum dierum regum luda.* Here הם כתובים is translated by *scripta sunt.* Thus it is possible that the passive participle נֵד underlies the translation *ablata est* ("removed," distanced").[40]

§ 19 If I am right, then we have the complete inflection of the passive participle of נד"ד in *Qal*: נֵד, נְדָּה, [נְדִים], נְדוֹת. Only the m.pl. form is reconstructed. נֵד and נְדָּה are attested in Biblical Hebrew and נְדוֹת and נְדָּה are attested in Mishnaic Hebrew. In the only occurrence of נֵד, the root נד"ד has a general meaning of "shaken,""removed." The feminine form נִדָּה at first was limited to a woman who was "removed,""put aside during her impurity," and later it came to designate a thing that was spiritually removed (loathed).[41]

§ 20 It is possible that there is a similar participial pair among geminate verbs. Shorn fleece is called in Biblical Hebrew גֵּז or גִּזָּה: וראשית גֵּז צאנך תתן לי (Deut 18:4), ומִגֵּז כבשי יתחמם (Job 31:20), אם טל יהיה על הַגִּזָּה (Judg 6:37 and six more occurrences in vv. 37–39). גֵּז can also designate cut grass: ירד כמטר על גֵּז (Ps 72:6), והנה לקש אחרי גִּזֵּי המלך (Amos 7:1). One could simply say that גֵּז and גִּזָּה are nouns, however, one could also suppose interpret them as passive participial forms. My conjecture is supported by the Targumim. Even though גֵּז and גִּזָּה are translated by -גִּיזַּת, גִּזְּתָא (Deut 18:4 in Targum Onqelos

pain is severe". 3) The occurrence of the predicate (נֵד) before the subject in the first hemistich does not deviate from the poetic norm.

39 This emendation can be found in BH.

40 Occasionally one finds that the passive participle is translated by forms of the passive perfect. Here is one example from Targum Onqelos (ed. Sperber): ואת הכסף המושב (Gen 32:12) is translated וית כספא דְאִתְּתַב ("and the money that was returned").

41 Greenberg 1995:76 was correct in saying that נִדָּה has an element of physical removal (geographical distancing or separation) and a moral side (removal with loathing). It is interesting that the relationship between נד"ד and הרחיק relating to נִדָּה, which is apparent from the Pentateuchal targumim, Targum Lamentations, and Midrash Lamentations (see above § 9) nn. 23 and 29, is echoed also in the language of R. Simeon du Mans, the author of אתה הנחלת תורה לעמך וכאב את בן אותם יִסַּרְתָּ; line 16 of the *piyyut* begins with the words עריות להפריש נִדָּה לְהַרְחִיק.

and also Targum Jonathan in all of the occurrences in Judges 6), Targum Jonathan, on the other hand, translates Amos 7:1 as בתר דְּאִתְגְּזֵיזַת שיחתא דמלכא ("after the corn of the king was cut"). The translator used a passive perfect form in translating גִּזֵּי.[42] Moreover, the Targum to Psalms interprets ירד כמטר על גֵּז (Ps 72:6) as יחות היך מטרא דרעוא על עסבא דגזיז מן גובאי ("descended like rain of desire on the grass cut by locusts"). The passive participle (גְּזִיז) is used to translate the Hebrew גֵּז, and so, there is a basis for interpreting גֵּז and גִּזָּה as forms of the *Qal* passive participle. Of course, if originally these were forms of the passive participle, they have since becomes substantivized. Thus, we might possess the full inflection of the *Qal* passive participle of גז"ז: גֵּז, גִּזָּה, גִּזִּים[43], [גִּזּוֹת]. It is by chance that the form of the feminine plural גִּזּוֹת is unattested in Biblical Hebrew.

§ 21 It is clear that if these are forms of the passive participle, one should expect parallel forms of the active participle. Many geminate verbs, however, are intransitive, and as such, one expects a participle indicating a stative situation like עַז or קַל. Yet, there are verbs that express action such as גָּזַז or a dynamic situation such as נָדַד. In these verbs one would expect to find an active participle functioning alongside a passive participle. This is the case in both verbs we have discussed, גָּזַז and נָדַד. If my hypothesis is correct, we have active and passive participle for both verbs.

In a transitive verb like גָּזַז, the opposition between the active participle and the passive participle expresses active (shearing others) versus passive (others shearing it). In an intransitive verb such as נָדַד, the opposition between the two participial forms would express dynamic (moves on his own) as against passive or stative (others moving him).

Active participle	Passive participle (conjectured)
§ 1 גֹּזֵז (1 Sam 25:4)	גֵּז
גֹּזְזִים (1 Sam 25:7)	גִּזֵּי
	גִּזָּה
§ 2 נוֹדֵד (Isa 16:2)	נֵד
נֹדְדִים (Hos 9:17)	נִדָּה
נוֹדֶדֶת (Prov 27:8)	נְדוֹת (Mishnaic Hebrew)

42 See n. 40 above.

43 Preserved only in the construct גִּזֵּי המלך. If this is a participial form, there is no need to argue that גִּזֵּי is the construct of גִּזּוֹת as is the case with absolute אִילָנוֹת and קְבָרוֹת, and the construct אִילָנֵי and קִבְרֵי. See Sharvit 1990:337.

1.4 Conclusion

§ 22 I conclude with a few comments.

First, my suggestion is that that נִדָּה "impurity" reflects two homonyms. The first is an abstract noun from נד"ד in the *qiṭṭa(h)* pattern like בִּזָּה (from בז"ז), זִמָּה (זמ"ם), and סִבָּה (סב"ב), and the second is a passive participle of the pattern קֵט (< *qiṭṭ*) with a feminine form קִטָּה (*qiṭṭa[h]*). However, at some point the second form was absorbed by the first. This need not surprise us, since the distinction between homonyms frequently becomes blurred and one form ultimately prevails. This may have been what happened with נִדָּה from נד"ד ("female impurity") and נִדָּה from נד"י ("sprinkling") as shown by Ben-Ḥayyim[44] as well as with נָבָל ("low," "mean," "evil" from נב"ל) and נָבָל ("fool" *Nif'al* of בל"ל).[45] The elimination of a distinction is liable to occur not only in words from different roots, but also in different forms of one root, as I have pointed out recently in the case of מַעֲשֶׂה, מַעֲשִׂים (*Hif'il* participial forms of הֶעֱשָׂה), which merged with the noun מַעֲשֶׂה and its plural מַעֲשִׂים.[46] There is no reason to doubt that this is also what took place with נִדָּה, the *Qal* passive participle of נד"ד, which merged with נִדָּה, an abstract noun from נד"ד of the nominal pattern קִטָּה.

§ 23 Second, נֵד, גֵּז and גִּזָּה have not been recognized until now as forms of the passive participle. נֵד may be analyzed (from נד"ד[47]) like מֵת, the perfect or the participle of מו"ת. גֵּז can easily be parsed as a noun from גז"ז in the nominal pattern קֵט (< *qiṭṭ*) like חֵץ. גִּזָּה may be understood like בִּזָּה (from בז"ז) and גִּנָּה (גנ"ן). Even if גִּזָּה originally marked the action of the shearer, it was capable of shifting and marking the result of the action, i.e., the shorn wool, as is the case with the verbal noun מְצִיאָה (action of the finder, e.g., הטמאות כשעת מציאתן m. Teharot 3:5), which developed into a concrete noun meaning "the thing found" (רָאָה את המציאה m. B. Mesi'a 1:4). However, if I am correct, the interpretation I propose here for the pairs נֵד- נִדָּה and גֵּז-גִּזָּה presents one grammatical framework, which uncovers a previously unknown grammatical form.

§ 24 Third, it is important to clarify one grammatical detail. I proposed that *qiṭṭ* > *qeṭ* parallels *qaṭīl* in the strong verb, and *qīl* in medial weak verbs.

---

44 See § 3 above.

45 See Ben-Ḥayyim 1980–1981:197, concerning changes of homonyms. (Ben-Ḥayyim notes on p. 198 that the *Historical Dictionary of the Hebrew Language* should distinguish three roots for נב"ל).

46 See Chapter Thirteen, n. 66 in the present volume.

47 It has been explained as a corruption of נֵד [see e.g., the Even Shoshan concordance, though he includes it with the entry נֵד – wall], as well as a corruption of נֵד from נד"ד [see *HALOT*].

In both forms there is a long vowel /ī/. If so, then we would expect to find /ī/ also in geminate verbs. We can assume that this was the original situation, namely, the passive participle was *qīṭṭ* (with a long vowel), but the long vowel in the closed syllable was shortened. *Qīṭṭ* became *qiṭṭ*, just as *qāmti* > *qamti* and *'āsāt* > *'āsat*.[48] In essence, there is nothing to prevent us from reconstructing a geminate passive participle of the form *qīṭṭ* > *qiṭṭ* > *qeṭ*.

§ 25 Fourth, it should be noted that the pattern *qaṭil* as *Qal* passive participle (*qīl* in medial weak verbs: *qeṭ* in geminates) is not the principal pattern for the *Qal* passive participle. Rather, one finds *qaṭul* (שָׁמוּר, כָּתוּב, etc.) and in medial weak verbs one finds the corresponding pattern *qul*, e.g., סוּג (Prov 14:14), לוּטָה (1 Sam 21:10), סוּגָה (Cant 7:3), and שׂוּמָה (*qere* 2 Sam 13:32). We should have expected in geminate verbs the pattern *quṭṭ* > *qoṭ*/קֹט,[49] i.e., from נד"ד one would expect *nod* נֹד and from גֹּז from גז"ז. Presumably, there were forms like these in verbs that could take a passive participle (in other words, in verbs expressing action or a dynamic situation). Indeed, there is such as form in Biblical Hebrew: שן רֹעָה ורגל מועדת (Prov. 25:19).[50] רֹעָה developed from *ru"a(h)* with compensatory lengthening. This is a variant of רעועה. But the forms m. *qoṭ*, f. *quṭṭa(h)* were rejected or blocked because of their morphological identicalness with the patterns *quṭṭ* > *qoṭ*/קֹט fem. *Quṭṭa(h)*/ קֻטָּה designating abstract nouns such as עֹז, קֹל,[51] חֹק[52] and the fem. חֻקָּה, סֻכָּה. Ulti-

48 The evidence for the shift from *'āsāt* > *'āsat* is farily certain. See Bar-Asher 1999a:185–252 (§§ 16,40,60–63).

49 Here also we should mention *qūṭṭ* which became *quṭṭ* according to the process described above in § 24.

50 After completing this study, I came across Halper 1910:42–57, 99–126, 201–8. He deals at length with *qeṭ* and *qoṭ* as passive participles of geminate verbs. Among other things, he indicates that גִּזָּה is something גָּזוּז, an alternate form of גְּזִיזָה (p. 53), צִנִּים is a variant of צְנִינִים (ibid.), עַד in some contexts is a variant of עָדוּד (p. 56), רֹעָה in the expression שן רֹעָה (Prov. 25:19) is a variant of רְעוּעָה (ibid.), בֹּר in the phrase והזכותי בבר כפי (Job 9:30) is a variant of בָּרוּר, as well as many additional examples. This article reflects an approach based on phonological and morphological considerations (with comparison to Arabic and Aramaic) that greatly exaggerates in interpreting many nouns belonging to the patterns *qeṭ/qiṭṭa(h)* and *qoṭ/quṭṭ1a(h)* as *Qal* passive participles. I, on the other hand, have limited my discussion and based my arguments on the understanding of the early versions. Nonetheless, Halper's article should be read.

51 קֹל meaning "lightness" is attested in the Hebrew Bible in Jer 3:9: והיה מקֹל זנותה ותחנף את הארץ. Targum Jonathan translates והוה מדקלילה בעיניהא טעותה (Bar-Asher 1980:56 n. 269). קֹל is usually found in Mishnaic Hebrew (primarily in the collocation קול וחומר) as demonstrated by Kutscher 1972a:32–33.

52 A thorough investigation of the nouns חֹק and חֻקָּה is called for. Are all the occurrences of these words abstract nouns in the pattern *quṭṭ* > *qoṭ*/קֹט, *quṭṭa(h)*/קֻטָּה or do some of the occurrences reflect a passive participle of חַק and חָקַק, and as such חֹק reflects [something] חָקוּק? As is known, there are forms of the passive participle that have become substantivized,

mately, Biblical Hebrew chose to inflect the passive participle of geminate verbs according to the pattern of strong verbs, as in שָׁדוּד and צָרוּר, and בְּלוּלָה and שְׁדוּדָה.

§ 26 Fifth, and finally, it should be added that in one Aramaic dialect there is a passive participle of geminate verbs with *i* that reflects the pattern *qᵉṭil*. Specifically, the form *qil* in Babylonian Aramaic in the passive participle of geminate verbs, which are identical to the passive participle of medial weak verbs[53] such as גִ׳יס (from גס״ס), כיף (כפ״ף), עיל (על״ל), קיל (קל״ל), and the feminine דיקא (דק״ק), זילא (זל״ל), etc. These have been collected by J. N. Epstein,[54] Y. Kara,[55] and S. Morag[56] for Babylonian Talmudic Aramaic, and by M. Morgenstern for the Babylonian Gaonic Aramaic.[57] Note that *qil* is not the only form in Babylonian Aramaic. It is attested alongside *qəṭiṭ*, which is patterned after the strong verb, e.g., רעיע (Babylonian Talmudic Aramaic), בריר (Gaonic responsa).[58]

e.g., כָּתוּב in Mishnaic Hebrew which functions as a noun, and a substitute for the words פסוק and מקרא – (דיבר הכתוב). פסוק itself is a substantivized passive participle. At this point, however, it is merely a hypothesis.

53 The similarity of geminate verbs to medial weak verbs is a well-known feature of Eastern Aramaic.

54 See Epstein 1960:83.

55 Kara and Morag 1983:274–275.

56 Morag 1988:237–238.

57 Morgenstern 2002:285–286. He indicates that the pattern קיל attested in Babylonian Aramaic only in the root קל״ל.

58 See nn. 54–57.

2 וה' אֲהֵבוֹ – יְדִידְיָה: The morphology and meaning of the word ידיד

2.1 Background Notes

§ 1 Amos Hakham is a man of the Bible and teacher to the masses. The books of the Bible for on he wrote commentaries in the *Daat Miqra* series are known to be the finest in the series. His commentaries are filled with linguistic discussions, both lexical and grammatical, elucidated clearly and precisely. In his honor, and in honor of his contribution to the study of Bible and its commentaries in our generation, I would like to discuss a word which Hakham also worked to explain: ידיד. Despite the previous scholarship on this word, Hakham also "learned and left more to study," for others to come and add to the solution of this problem in his wake.

This word is primarily found in Biblical Hebrew, but it is also attested infrequently in Rabbinic literature; there it is almost always in connection to the Bible.[1] It is also found often in *piyyut*, because of the close connection of that genre to biblical Hebrew.[2] It has also had, as is well known, a resurgence in the contemporary Hebrew, as a noun in the same semantic field as the nouns חָבֵר and רֵעַ. It is even common today in the onomasticon, mainly as a surname.[3]

§ 2 This study deals with the morphology and meaning of the word ידיד in Biblical Hebrew and in a number of its appearances in Rabbinic literature.[4] To be more specific, this study has two goals. First, I intend to clarify whether the original form of the word in the absolute was יָדִיד, in the פָּעִיל pattern, or

---

1 The 'Arukh, s. v. ידיד, cites two Rabbinic texts from in which the word is found: (a) The blessing at the circumcision (t. Berakhot 6:3, y. Berakhot 9 [14a], b. Shabbat 137b); (b) b. Menahot 53a–b (see below § 14). It is also attested in other rabbinic texts, e.g., Mekhilta de-R. Ishmael, Beshalah, § 5 (ed. Horowitz-Rabin, p. 106, where alternative readings are given): באו' שע' [= באותה שעה] אמר לו המק' למשה: משה, ידידי משוקע במים והים סוגר, ושונא רודף, ואתה עומד ומרבה בתפילה "At that moment God said to Moses: 'Moses, my beloved (ידידי) is sunk in the water, and the sea is closing in, the enemy is hot in pursuit, and you are standing and praying at length?!'" (The text is cited here according to the reading in the Ma'agarim; there one can see that is a parallel in the Mekhilta de-R. Shim'on bar Yohai). One can also add the appearance of the word in the blessing following the morning Shema ("אמת ויציב"; see the citations in Ma'agarim and see below § 13). Like many Biblical words, this one is also widespread in *piyyut* and medieval poetry. It is also found often in the poetry of later periods from all regions of the world (see some of the examples suggested below in §§ 22–23).

2 Many attestations in early *piyyut* are found in Ma'agarim, s. v. ידיד.

3 See below, end of § 21.

4 E.g., see the examples suggested in footnote 1 above.

יָדִיד, in the פְּעִיל pattern. Second, I will try to establish the precise meaning of the word, or, more particularly, to clarify the meaning ascribed to it by the ancients.[5]

In the discussion here, the order of topics will be reversed. First I will deal with the meaning of the word, and only afterwards will I discuss its morphology. As mentioned, I will try to focus especially on the meaning that the ancients ascribed to the word, although I will not, of course, ignore the views of modern scholars. I will investigate its traditional readings, and consider the forms that dictionaries and grammars have given it.[6]

2.2 On the Meaning of the Word

§ 3 I begin with the Jewish translations to Aramaic. The sole appearance of ידיד in the Torah – לבנימין אמר יְדִיד ה' ישכן לבטח עליו (Deut. 33:12) – is translated in Targum Onqelos with the passive participle רְחִים: רְחִימָא דה' ישרי לרוחצן עלוהי. The same is true in the Palestinian Targum Neofiti: רחימה דיי ישרי לרחצן עלוי. רחימה / רְחִימָא is the determined form of the Aramaic Qal passive participle, רְחִים (= "beloved"). Something similar is found in Targum Pseudo-Jonathan, except that here a synonym is substituted for רְחִים: חביביה דה' ישרי לרוצחן עלוי. חביביה means the חביב "beloved" of God.[7] The form חֲבִיב is on the קְטִיל pattern, used for adjectives which interchange with the Qal passive participle (פְּעִיל).[8] A similar translation is found in Targum Jonathan to Jeremiah 12:15 מא לעמא דהוה חֲבִיב קדמי: מה לִידִידִי בביתי.[9] Targum Psalms follows in the footsteps of Onqelos in three of the four appearances of the noun in the book. In a verse that appears in two psalms – למען יחלצון ידידיך (60:7, 108:7) – we find in one instance the translation מן בגלל זכותיה דיצחק

5 Establishing the meaning attributed to a word by the early interpreters is not only worthwhile as a stage in clarifying the original meaning of the word, but is also a notable achievement in its own right.

6 I will not deal with the etymology of the word or its cognates in Semitic languages; these are presented comprehensively in modern scholarly dictionaries; see BDB and HALOT s. v. ידיד. Numerous and interesting data are presented there, and I have no intention to add anything to these.

7 There is no targum to this verse in Deuteronomy (33:12) among the Fragments of the Palestinian Targum published in Klein 1980.

8 This interchange is often found in geminate roots, though not exclusively (and see below § 5 and the bibliographic reference in n. 22).

9 Targum Jonathan to Isaiah 5:1, whose first half renders according to the midrash, will be discussed below in § 4.

יתפציין[10] רחימיך (60:7), and the second a slight variation, מן בגלל דישתזבון רחימייך[11] (108:7). The form רחימיך (רחימייך[12]) means "your beloved" (pl.). Similarly, in the verse מה יְדִידֹת[13] משכנותיך ה' צבאות (Ps 84:2), we find מא רחימין הנון[14] משכניך, that is to say, "How beloved are your dwelling places." However the fourth appearance, כן יתן לידידו שנא (Ps 127:2), the Targum reads, וכיון יתן ה' לרחמיה[15] דמכא. In the printed editions, the word is vocalized לְרָחֲמֵיהּ; this is the form רָחֵם (the Qal active participle) with a pronominal suffix "his lover" (אוהבו). If the version לרחימיה is not in fact attested in a reliable manuscript, we will be forced to conclude that Targum Psalms translates ידיד at least once with an active participle rather than a passive form.

§ 4 Isaiah 5:1 was translated somewhat midrashically in our targumim. The Hebrew text reads, אשירה נא לִידִידִי שירת דודי לכרמו כרם היה לִידִידִי בקרן בן שמן. Targum Jonathan translates, אמר נבייא אשבחיה כען לישראל דמתיל בכרמא דאברהם רָחֲמִי תושבחת רָחֲמִי לכרמיה עַמִּי חַבִּיבִי ישראל יהבית להון אחסנא בטור רם בארע שמינא. The first appearance of לידידי was translated "to Israel, who is compared to the vineyard of the one who loves me, Abraham."[16] In the second appearance of the word לידידי, it is translated "my nation, my beloved, Israel." It seems to me that in the first appearance, after the translator said that Israel is comparable to Abraham, who is known as "the ydyd God" (see b. Menahot 53b),[17] he is influenced by another text that dis-

---

10 This is the text of MS Paris 110 (and also in the printed texts), as Dr. Barak Dan kindly informed me. All the citations from this MS mentioned here are courtesy of Dr. Dan, and I am indebted to him for this. Incidentally, one might note that we should have expected the form יתפצון here. The forms יפעיין, יתפעיין, etc., are found elsewhere in MS Paris 110, but this detail and other matters of the grammar in this manuscript and other manuscripts of Targum Tehillim still require clarification.

11 This is the text of MS Paris 110.

12 It is clear that one *yod* before the final *kaf* is extra.

13 One might note that ידדֹת in this verse is the plural form of ידיד. We would have expected, of course, the plural form יְדִידִים, to agree with the masculine noun משכנות, which is the subject of the sentence (*מה ידידים משכנותיך), but the plural form of ידיד was formed as ידידות by attraction to משכנותיך. On the other hand, the form יְדִידוֹת in the expression שיר ידידת (Ps 45:1), widely interpreted as "a love song" (thus most of the modern dictionaries mentioned below in § 16) is not necessarily a plural form, and it can be explained as a feminine singular noun ending in -וֹת, like הוֹלֵלֹת/הוֹלֵלוֹת (Ecc. 1:17, 2:12) and חָכְמוֹת בנתה ביתה (Prov. 9:1).

14 I have cited the text as found in MS Paris 110 of Targum Tehillim, which preserves the correct word order (רחימין הנון): the pronoun הנון follows the predicate, rather than preceding it as in the corrupt text found in the printed editions.

15 Again, this is the text of MS Paris 110.

16 From the entire context it is possible to see that the noun דודי is also translated רחמי "my lover."

17 See below § 15.

cusses Abraham, in fact, the very text in which the expression "the one who loves me, Abraham" appears (Isa 41:8), which the Targumist quotes in Aramaic translation.[18] However in the second appearance the Targum employed חֲבִיב "beloved," which is, as mentioned, the equivalent of רְחִים, the most common translation of ידיד in most biblical verses.

§ 5 The Peshitta consistently translates ידיד with the word חֲבִיב: יְדִיד ה' (Deut. 33:12) – חֲבִיבָה דמריא; לִידִידִי (...) אשירה נא לִידִידִי (Is. 5:1) – לַחֲבִיבִי (...)[19]; מה ידידות[20] משכנותיך (Ps. 84:2) – מא חביבין משכניך. Likewise, twice the word ידידיך (ibid. 60:7, 108:7) is translated, חֲבִיבַיךְ, and the Peshitta translated similarly, לידידו (Ps. 127:2) – לַחֲבִיבָוהי. In this verse, it understood the noun as a mass noun, and therefore translated it in plural form. Again, we find an example in Jeremiah (11:15), with a slight grammatical variation: מה לידידי – למנא חֲבִיבְתִי (= why my beloved?).[21] In Syriac, חֲבִיב serves as an alternative for the passive participle of the Qal – חֲבִיב[22] – like all the pairs קְטִיל/קַטִיל, which often interchange with each other.

§ 6 The understanding of the word ידיד as "beloved" is already reflected in LXX,[23] many years before our Aramaic translations, and before the Peshitta. The LXX employs two alternate translations with the same meaning – medial perfect form, or adjective. יְדִיד ה' (Deut. 33:12) is translated ἠγαπημένος ὑπὸ κυρίου (= "beloved by the Lord"). We find something similar in the LXX to

---

18 The phenomenon of intertextuality within Targum Jonathan (and in and other targumim) is widespread and well-recognized. For example, for the word ספונים in the verse העת לכם אתם לשבת בבתיכם ספונים והבית הזה חרב (Haggai 1:4) Tg Jonathan writes דמטללין בכיורי ארזיא. The translator connected Haggai's ספונים to the expression וְסָפוּן בארז (Jer. 22:14), which is translated by him, ומטלל (נ"א: ומטליל) בכיורי ארזיא, since both here and there speak of the building of a house. Nevertheless, the Targum to the Book of Haggai differs from the expression וְסִפֻּן/וְסָפוּן בארז (1 Kings 7:3,7); this is translated in Targum Jonathan וחפי נסרין דארזא. Indeed, both books (Kings and Haggai) speak of the building of the Temple (the intertextuality in Targum Jonathan to Prophets is considered – like other topics – in the doctoral work of M. Kahana, "Language and Interpretation in Targum Jonathan to the Prophets, from Nahum to Malachi" (Hebrew University, Jerusalem, 2009).

19 The Peshitta also translates דּוֹדִי in this verse with an identical form; the expression שירת דודי is translated there תשבוחתא דחֲבִיבִי.

20 In the Masoretic formulation this word is written without a *waw*, as cited above in § 3; henceforth I quote it with the *waw* and without vocalization.

21 It is possible that the next part of the verse, which has a verb attached to a 3fs pronoun, which is in apposition to ידידי, the subject of the sentence – עֲשׂוֹתָהּ המזמתה – is the same that led to the replacement of the masculine form with the feminine.

22 See: Payne Smith (Margoliouth) 1967:122, 123.

23 For help with clarifying the data in the LXX and Vulgate, I was advised by my friend, Professor Cyril Aslanov. He has my gratitude for this.

Isaiah 5:1, where לִידִידִי is translated twice τῷ ἠγαπημένῳ "to my beloved." The word is also translated in this way in the expression מָה לִידִידִי in Jeremiah 11:15: τί ἡ ἠγαπημένη "What, my beloved."[24] The LXX to Psalms uses another form with a meaning identical the participial form just mentioned: it translates ידיד with the adjective ἀγαπητός ("beloved"), as in: לידידו (Ps. 127:2) – τοῖς ἀγαπητοῖς αὐτοῦ = "to his beloveds" (it is translated as if the text read לידידיו[25]); ידידיך (60:7, 108:7) – οἱ ἀγαπητοί σου; מה ידידות משכנותיך (84:2) – ὡς ἀγαπητὰ τὰ σκηνώματά σου.[26]

§ 7 In contrast with most of the translations mentioned previously, the Vulgate is inconsistent in its translations. Certainly it commonly translates ידיד with a word that means "beloved," but also attested as translations are words that mean "lover," and nouns with the senses of "friend" or "colleague." The following are the most important data: לידידי (...) לידידי (Isaiah *ibid.*) – *dilecto meo ... dilecto meo* "to my beloved ... to my beloved"; לידידי (Jeremiah *ibid.*) – dilectus meus "my beloved"; the expression מה ידידות משכנותיך (Psalm 84:2): quam dilecta tabernacula tua[27] "how beloved are your tabernacles"; ידידיך (Psalm 108:7): dilecti tui "your beloved." In the parallel verse, however, the Vulgate translated differently: ידידיך (Psalm 60:7): *amici tui* "your friends." It nevertheless should be noted that the LXX reading in the two psalms mentioned above (60:7, 108:7) were translated by the Vulgate with *dilecti tui* "your beloved," but in two other verses the Vulgate translated ידיד with an active form: ידיד ה' (Deuteronomy *ibid.*) – *amantissimus Domini* "who greatly loves the Lord"; לידידו (Psalm 127:2) – *diligentibus se* "those who love him," although the Vulgate translated the LXX's reading in Psalm 127 with *dilectis suis* "his beloved ones." Finally, the expression שיר ידידת (Psalm 45:1) is translated *canticum amantissimi*[28] "song of the best lover."

24 It should be noted that the LXX is already using the feminine (see above footnote 21).

25 Regarding this detail, too, the LXX serves as a precedent for the Peshitta (see below § 5 and nn. 21, 24). Was the Peshitta influenced by the LXX?

26 This expression in the LXX is translated in Palestinian Syriac מה חביבין משכנך (= מה אהובים משכנותיך; see Black 1954:244). This translation is identical to the translation offered to the verse in the *Peshitta* (see below § 5), however, it was not taken from there, but rather straight from the LXX to standard Palestinian Syriac. On the other hand, it appears that the *Peshitta* translated directly the Hebrew מה ידידות משכנותיך.

27 The translation in the Vulgate is also the formulation of the LXX (as is known, within the Psalms in the Vulgate are translations directly from the Hebrew as well as translations made from the LXX).

28 However, in translation, in the formulation of LXX in the Vulgate we find the translation canticum pro dilecto (= a song for the beloved).

§ 8 Here is a sampling I collected from medieval exegesis. Saadia[29] translates the expression ידיד ה' (Deut. 33:12)[30] – ודיד אללה "friend of God." He used a similar expression in one place in his Tafsīr to Psalms – ידידיך (60:7)[31] – ודידיך "your friends." However, in the translation of מה ידידות משכנותיך (84:2), he altered the syntax and rendered, מא אכת'ר ודנא מסכנך "how great is our love for your home!"[32] It is worth noting that in his translation of the expression שיר ידידת (45:1), Saadia chose the translation פי וצף מחבי אללה "in a description of those who love God,"[33] and in his commentary there, he writes: פסרת שיר ידידות, וצף פצ'איל מחבי אללה, לאן לפצ'ה' ידיד וידידות כד'אך מענאהא "I interpreted שיר ידידות as a description of the merits of those who love God, because this is the meaning of the words ידיד and ידידות."[34]

As is known, the noun ודיד, which Saadia uses in his translation to the verse in Deuteronomy, may indicate either an active meaning "one who loves" or a passive meaning "beloved," as is the case with all Arabic nouns of the pattern *faʿīl*. However, in his translation to Ps. 45:1, and even more explicitly in his commentary on that verse, Saadia revealed his view that ידיד is active in meaning: "one who loves" (as is ידידות[35], which he takes to mean "those who love"). Nevertheless, in two psalms he uses a form which is passive either in morphology or meaning: he translates ידידיך in Psalm 108:7 as מצטפיוך "your chosen ones"[36] or "your choice ones,"[37] and he translates לידידו in Psalm 127:2 as אוליאה "(to) his beloveds."

§ 9 On Isaiah 5:1, Radaq writes:

> אשירה נא – דברי הנביא, עושה משל בין האל יתברך ובין ישראל ... וקורא זה המשל שירה ... לפי שזה שבח האוהב ואהבתו עם האהוב ... וקורא הנביא האל יתברך 'ידידי' ו'דודי' על דרך 'כי בי חשק'.
>
> "I will sing" – these are the words of the prophet, who crafts a parable between God, may He be blessed, and Israel ... and he calls this parable a 'song' (שירה) ... since this is praise for the one who loves and for his love for the beloved ... and the prophet calls

---

29 For specific details in Saadia's translation I was advised by Prof. Joshua Blau and with my brother Meir Michael. I thank them for their assistance.

30 The text of Saadia's *Tafsīr* on the Torah is based on A. Hasid's printing of the Tāj, and for Psalms they are based on the edition of Rabbi Yosef Qafiḥ.

31 However, in Psalm 108:7, he translates in a differently (see below at the end of this paragraph).

32 See the remarks of Qafih *ad loc.*

33 Thus Qafih translates the *Tafsīr* into Hebrew.

34 See Qafih there.

35 Note that he is speaking of the form in the collocation שיר ידידות.

36 This is Qafih's translation.

37 As stated above (next to n. 31 mark), this is not the translation he used in the first appearance of the verse (in Psalm 60:7).

God, may He be blessed, "my love" (ידידי) and "my beloved" (דודי), similar to "for he desired me" (Psalm 91:14).

That is to say, "the one who loves" is the prophet who recites the poem, and "the beloved" is the "loved," namely, God. Commenting on Jeremiah 11:15, Radaq writes:

מה לידידי – אמר הנביא 'מה לידידי בביתי', קרא האל ידידי לפי שהוא [= הנביא] היה מאוהבי האל; אמר, מה לו עוד בביתי, ר"ל בבית המקדש.

"What, my beloved" – the prophet said, "what does my beloved want in my house?" He called God "beloved" because he (i. e., the prophet)[38] was among those who loved God; so he said, "What is there for him in my house," namely, in the Temple.

In other words, if the prophet is a lover of God, then God, who is his love (ידיד), is his beloved.[39] In the verse from Psalm 84:2, we find that Rashi interpreted: כמה אהובות וחביבות משכנותיך "how beloved and treasured are your tents." So, too, in the commentary of Ibn Ezra: "ידידות – אהובות beloved, an adjective describing the tents," and so, too, according to Radaq: "מה ידידות משכנותיך – how loved are your tents, and how greatly I love and desire to be in them."

§ 10 In order to arrive at a final definition of the word ידיד, there are four additional sources I would like to consider. One of them is very ancient – it is from the Bible itself. These are they:

1. An inner-biblical interpretation of the word ידיד. This interpretation is both earlier and more important than all the translations and interpretations mentioned above.
2. An implied – but unambiguous – interpretation of the word in a homily in Rabbinic literature.
3. The use of the word ידיד in a blessing formulated by the Rabbis. Minimally, this provides evidence for how the word was understood by those Rabbis.
4. The various interpretations given to the word ידיד by the medieval commentators in the blessing recited at a circumcision, and the way in which each interpretation is supported.

---

38 This explanatory words in brackets are my own addition (MBA).

39 There is reason to assume that Rashi also glossed ידידי as "beloved," "treasured." However, in his opinion, the beloved and treasured ידיד is the People of Israel. Allow me to explain. Rashi says: "מה לידידי בביתי" – מה לעם סגולתי לבוא בביתי. We know that Onqelos translated the word סגולה with the words חֲבִּיב/חֲבִּיבִין. Thus, in the verse והייתם לי סְגֻלָּה מכל העמים (Ex. 19:5), Onqelos has ותהון קדמי חֲבִּיבִין מכל עממיא, and the collocation עם סגלה (Deut. 7:6, 14:2, 26:18) he translates עם חֲבִּיב. Rashi, in his commentary to the verse in the Book of Exodus, accepts this explanation of Onqelos'; he writes: 'סגלה' – אוצר חביב. It is not unreasonable to suppose that his explanation in Exodus echoes his commentary to Jeremiah (11:15), namely, when he explains 'לידידי' – לעם סגולתי as if to say: לעמי החביב, עמי אהובי.

The first two sources provide direct and explicit evidence for the position that the word ידיד means “beloved,” and with the third given there is implicit evidence for this opinion. The fourth source only provides indirect evidence for this understanding of ידיד, but should not be discounted. Allow me to elaborate.

§ 11 1. Long before all the ancient translations (in Jewish Aramaic, Syriac, Greek, and Latin), and before all the medieval exegetes, the word ידיד was already interpreted within the Bible itself. We read: וינחם דוד את בת שבע אשתו ויבא אליה וישכב עמה ותלד בן ויקרא (קרי: ותקרא) את שמו שלמה וה' אֲהֵבוֹ “David consoled his wife Bathsheba, and came to her and lay with her. She bore a son and named him Solomon, and the Lord loved him” (2 Samuel 12:24). The following verse says: וישלח ביד נתן הנביא ויקרא את שמו יְדִידְיָהּ[40] בעבור ה' “He sent by the hand of Nathan the prophet and named him Yedidya, because of the Lord” (12:25). In other words, v. 24 (וה' אֲהֵבוֹ), despite appearing before v. 25 (יְדִידְיָהּ – בעבור ה'), actually interprets the latter verse. Indeed, this observation was already made in the Tannaitic sources: שלמה נקרא ידיד, שנאמר "וישלח ביד נתן הנביא ויקרא את שמו יְדִידְיָהּ", ואומר "וה' אהבו" “Solomon was called ידיד, as it says, ‘He sent by the hand of Nathan the prophet and named him Yedidya,’ and it says, ‘the Lord loved him” (Sifre Devarim § 452[41]).[42]

---

40 This is the precise text, as found in the edition of R. Mordechai Breuer (1977). Likewise in MS Leningrad (St. Petersburg; see edition of Tanakh edited by Aron Dotan), and in MS Cairo of the Prophets. However in the edition of the Miqraot Gedolot published in Venice, 1523–1525, the form יְדִידְיָה appears without a *mappiq* in the *heh* (see the details on “The Text and its Sources,” by Rabbi Mordechai Breuer *apud* Kil 1981:175). In the standard editions of Tanakh, too, the form is found without the *mappiq*, almost certainly following the edition of Miqraot Gedolot just mentioned (see also the Minhat Shai *ad loc.*, who notes a tradition of this word without a *mappiq* and what is written about this by the author of the Terumat ha-Deshen). Evidence of this disputed reading is already found in the Talmud Bavli: there we find that this is one of the words disputed by the Amoraim (b. Pesahim 117a) as to whether it is one word or two. Apparently the reading without the *mappiq* relies on the understanding that it is one word, so that there is no divine name. According to the second opinion, which holds that ידידיה is two words, the *mappiq heh* is necessary. It goes without saying that the text of the Bible was fixed by the sages of the *mesorah* and not by the sages of the Talmud.

41 See the complete quote below in footnote 56. It should be noted that the explanatory expression ואומר: וה' אהבו is also cited in Yalqut Shimoni (ed. Mossad ha-Rav Kook, § 955 p. 691). Perhaps it is worthwhile to mention that the meaning of ואומר can be “as the verse says (אומר),” equivalent to שנאמר.

42 Apparently it is understood that the newborn – called יְדִידְיָה at the time of birth – could be “the beloved of God,” but he cannot yet express emotions and thus cannot be called “one who loves God.” However, one must not err with arguments like this, since the epithet is likely expressing a hope for the future, similar to, ויקרא את שמו נֹחַ, לאמר: זה ינחמנו ממעשנו ומעצבון ידינו מן האדמה אשר אררה ה'. “He named him Noah, saying, ‘he will comfort us

§ 12 2. In the same passage from Sifre Devarim,[43] we read: "לבנימין אמר ידיד ה'", חביב בנימין שנקרא ידיד למקום, שהרבה אוהבין למלך וחביב מכולן מי שהמלך אוהבו "'To Benjamin he said, "*yedid* of the Lord"': Benjamin is treasured since he is called the *yedid* of God, for there are many who love the king, but the most treasured of all is he whom the king loves."[44] The homily replaces the Scriptural word ידיד with the rabbinic word חביב "treasured, beloved," and thus clarifies it. The midrash continues and says that of the many people who love the king, dearest (חביב "beloved") of all is the one beloved by the king. Perhaps it is not superfluous to note that in the Midrash ha-Gadol, in place of וחביב מכולן we find the expression האהוב שבכולם "the most beloved of all of them."[45]

§ 13 3. As is known, the language of prayer often uses phrases made of a word and its synonym. Sometimes the synonymous words occur in sequence, as in חי וקים[46], אמת ואמונה,[47] אמת ויציב,[48] אהוב וחביב, and others. In other cases, the synonymous words come in parallel lines, such as סלח לנו אבינו כי חטאנו / מחול[49] לנו מלכנו כי פשענו "forgive us, our Father, though we have sinned/pardon us, our King, though we have transgressed" (from the blessing for "forgiveness" in the *'amidah*), (על כן זכרונו בא לפניך ה' אלוהינו להרבות) זרעו כעפרות תבל / וצאצאיו כחול[50] הים "(therefore his remembrance comes

---

from our labor and the painful toil of our hands caused by the ground the Lord has cursed'" (Genesis 5:29).

43 The text (§ 352) is cited according to Ma'agarim; variants will be cited from Finkelstein's edition (1969:409) as needed.

44 In place of the phrase זה עוזיהו, Finkelstein's edition has מי שהמלך. This is a correct proposal, since Uzziah could not be called "loved by God".

45 See the variants recorded in Finkelstein (*ibid.*). The text in the Midrash ha-Gadol in full is, אשריך בנימין שנקראת ידיד למקום, הרבה אהובים למלך, האהוב שבכולן מי שהמלך אוהבו (see ed. R. Solomon Fish 1973:765).

46 In these structures, the liturgy sometimes utilizes specifically Mishnaic Hebrew words, or words borrowed into Mishnaic Hebrew from Aramaic, as one of the two synonymous words. Here, for example, חי is Biblical and קים is Mishnaic; אהוב is Biblical and חביב is Mishnaic.

47 The parallelism and identicality of meaning of the words אֱמֶת וְיַצִּיב is also seen in Aramaic, as seen in the Biblical Aramaic adverbial phrases מִן קְשֹׁט (Dan. 2:47, equivalent to Hebrew באמת, מן אמת) and מִן יַצִּיב (*ibid.* 2:8); both expressions mean one thing: "in truth." There are other examples like this, as well.

48 See above § 3–5, and the details in § 12.

49 סְלַח is a Biblical Hebrew verb, and מְחוֹל is Mishnaic Hebrew, both lexically (מְחַל is a new verb in Rabbinic Hebrew; cf. Kutscher 1972:5) and grammatically (מְחוֹל rather than מְחַל). Those who "corrected" the siddur and its language changed מְחוֹל to מְחַל in the Ashkenazi version hundreds of years ago.

50 Here there are two pairs of synonyms in two parallel hemistichs: זרעו/צאצאיו, כעפרות/כחול.

in front of you, O Lord, to increase) his seed like the dusts of the earth/and his descendants like the sand of the sea" (from the paragraph אתה זוכר מעשה עולם in the benediction of זכרונות in the Musaf of Rosh Hashannah). Indeed there is an additional parallel line relevant to our subject: על זאת שִׁבחו אהובים ורוממו לאל / ונתנו ידידים זמירות שירות ותשבחות ברכות והודאות למלך אל חי וקים "Therefore the beloved ones praised and exalted God / and the dear ones offered songs, hymns, and praises, blessings, and thanks to the King, living and existing God."[51] It is easy to see that "dear (beloved) ones" (ידידים) in the second half of the line is parallel to – indeed, synonymous with – "beloved ones" (אהובים) in the first half of the line.

§ 14 4. In the blessing on circumcision there is a series of three lines, which refer to three stages in fulfilling the commandment of circumcision: sanctification of the "beloved" (ידיד), establishment of the law, and the inscribing of the descendants with the "sign of the sacred covenant."

אשר קידש ידיד מבטן
וחוק בשארו שם
וצאצאיו חתם באות ברית קודש.[52]

Scholars over the generations have debated the question of the identity of the "beloved" (ידיד)[53] alluded to in the first line. The major views are as follows:

Abraham: Rabbenu Jacob Tam says that the ידיד is Abraham (on b. Shabbat 137b, Tosafot s. v. ידיד מבטן): "Rabbenu Tam says, Abraham is the one who is called ידיד,[54] as it says, 'What is my beloved doing in my Temple' (Jeremiah 11:15), as we learn in b. Menahot (53a–b)."[55] Indeed, in Menahot we find a *beraita*: "Let the 'beloved' (ידיד) son of the 'beloved' (ידיד) and build a

51 We should not be surprised that the hemistichs are of unequal length; this phenomenon is common in prayer to such an extent that it needs no demonstration.

52 Here, too, the lines are of unequal length; it is worth mentioning here that Menachem Kister is of the opinion that the words ברית קודש were added to the blessing at a later time (see his article quoted in the following footnote).

53 It is clear that the straightforward reading of the designation ידיד is to take it to refer to Abraham, as already established by M. Z. Segal on the basis of Ben Sira (44:23–25): "אברהם אב המון גוים [...] ובא בברית עמו, בבשרו כרת לו חק" (see Segal 1953:306,308; the version mentioned above is found also in the Academy of the Hebrew Language edition, Ben-Sira 1973:54). M. Kister further strengthened this claim, and gave it further support, in two excellent articles on Ben Sira. This idea is propounded briefly in his first article (1983:125–126), and at length in his second article (1989:36–39). However, our concern here is with the interpretations provided by the medieval interpreters and the evidence they cite for their positions.

54 Rabbenu Tam's interpretation is also quoted in b. Men. 53b in Tosafot s. v. בן ידיד.

55 Rabbenu Tam continues (Tosafot Shabbat *ibid.*): ושלושת האבות נזכרים שם: "חוק בשארו שם" – הוא יצחק, "וצאצאיו חתם באות ברית קדש" – הוא יעקב וצאצאיו הוא ובניו.

'beloved' (ידיד) for a 'beloved' (ידיד) in the territory of a 'beloved' (ידיד) and let the 'beloveds' (ידידים) be thus atoned. Let the beloved come – this is King Solomon, as it says ... 'he shall be called Yedidya, because of the Lord'; son of the beloved – this is Abraham, as it says, 'What is my beloved doing in my Temple?'"[56]

Isaac: Rashi (on b. Shabbat 137b, s. v. אשר קידש ידיד מבטן) identifies the "beloved" with Isaac: "Isaac is called 'beloved' because of the verse, [קח נא את בנך את יחידך] אשר אהבת '[Take your son, your only one,] whom you love' (Gen 22:2)."

Jacob: Sherira Gaon (cited in the Arukh, ed. Kohut, 4:110), s. v. ידיד:[57] "אשר קידש ידיד מבטן Who sanctified the beloved from the womb: 'From the womb,' R. Sherira Gaon explained that this is Jacob our father, as it says about him, וָאֹהַב אֶת יַעֲקֹב 'I loved Jacob' (Malachi 1:2). He is the one who was sanctified while still in his mother's womb, as it said, וְרַב יַעֲבֹד צָעִיר 'the older shall serve the younger.' That is to say, you will find the sanctity of the descendants of Abraham within him, and it was already said (in a blessing) להכניסו בבריתו של אברהם אבינו 'to bring him into the covenant of our father Abraham'."

From the biblical texts upon which Rav Sherira and Rashi based their explanations of the epither ידיד, it is clear that they understand ידיד as "one loved by God." On the other hand, from Rabbenu Tam – who identified the ידיד in the benediction with the ידיד in the verse in Jeremiah, taken to be Abraham in the passage from Menahot – we know his view about the identity of the ידיד, but not its exact meaning.

---

56 As was said earlier, this is a *baraita* whose full source is found in Sifre Devarim: ששה נקראו ידידים, הקב"ה נקרא ידיד, שנאמר "אשירה נא לידידי", בנימין נקרא ידיד, שנאמר "ידיד ה' ישכן לבטח", שלמה נקרא ידיד שנאמר "וישלח ביד נתן הנביא ויקרא שמו ידידיה", ואומר "וה' אהבו", ישראל נקראו ידידים, שנאמר "נתתי את ידידות נפשי בכף אויביה", בית המקדש נקרא ידיד, שנאמר "מה ידידות משכנותיך", יבא ידיד בן ידיד ויבנה בית ידיד לידיד, ויבואו ישראל שנקראו ידידים, בני אב שנקרא ידיד, ויבנו בית המקדש שנקרא(ו) ידיד, להקב"ה [שנקרא ידיד] לכך נאמר, "ידיד ה'" (Sifre Deut., § 352, according to the Ma'agarim. And see Finkelstein's edition, p. 409). In the enumeration of the attestations of ידיד in Ma'agarim, one was dropped [the second in the list]: "אברהם נקרא ידיד, שנאמר "מה לידידי בביתי" (see Finkelstein *ibid.*). However, later on in the *baraita* Abraham is referred to in the phrase בני אב שנקרא ידיד. It should be mentioned that the explanatory phrase ואומר "וה' אהבו" is not found in the main text in Finkelstein's edition, but only among the variant readings given there.

57 This fact is cited by S.Y Fein in his dictionary s. v. ידיד (see below § 16, footnote 68). In his short comment gloss on t. Berakhot 6:13 (p. 37), Saul Lieberman cites the opinion of Sherira Gaon alone, but in *Tosefta ki-fshutah* (1955, 1:114), he cites the three opinions and references to the literature. (Note that there is a typo there: at the end of his discussion, he writes ויש מפרשים שהכוונה ליעקב instead of שהכוונה לאברהם, since he already cited Jacob and Isaac previously). A summary of the opinions can be found in the entry ברית מילה in the *Encyclopedia Talmudit* (4:255).

§ 15 For a long time I wondered why Rabbenu Tam did not follow Sherira Gaon[58] and Rashi. Those two earlier scholars both cited appropriate biblical prooftexts, which explicitly use the verb אהב is with regard to one of the Patriarchs. Why, then, does Rabbenu Tam not also cite such a verse? After all, this verb is used about Abraham twice: זרע אברהם אֹהבי "the offspring of Abraham who loves me" (Isa. 41:8), ותתנה לזרע אברהם אֹהבך לעולם "you gave it forever to Abraham who loves you" (2 Chron. 20:7). Naturally, it is possible to say that Rabbenu Tam preferred to prove his point by citing a text which used the word ידיד about Abraham, as it was interpreted in Menahot. It does seem obvious, however, that a proof from a biblical verse, if one exists, is superior to evidence from a rabbinic text which is in turn interpreting a biblical text. However, it is possible that Rabbenu Tam refrained from citing the verses mentioned above that discuss Abraham, since in those Abraham is the *subject* of the verb אהב; in other words, he is the lover – and not the beloved[59] – of God. Put differently, it may be that Rabbenu Tam thought that the meaning of ידיד was "the one who is loved," not "the one who loves," and that he therefore did not rely on the verses from Isaiah and Chronicles, which present Abraham as the *lover* of God.

§ 16 It should be noted that also most modern dictionaries defined the word ידיד as "beloved," although there are others that chose to define it "lover." We may begin with the Hebrew dictionaries. Y. L. Ben-Zeev[60] defines

58 Of course, there is no way to know if Rabbenu Tam saw the Arukh, or if he knew Sherira Gaon's opinion from some other source. I learned from Dr. Rami Reiner that Rabbenu Tam does mention Sherira a few times, and makes regular use of the Arukh. It may still be appropriate to inject a note of caution here, since it is possible that he knew of them only second-hand.

59 Nevertheless, it should be remarked that in one verse Abraham, as one of the Patriarchs, is implicitly called the beloved of the Deity: ותחת כי אהב את אבתיך ויבחר בזרעו אחריו "because he loved your fathers he chose their offspring after him" (Deut. 4:37), which implies that "your fathers" (Abraham, Isaac, and Jacob) are beloved by God. However this verse uses the plural, as if to say that the *three* of them are beloved to God, and the singulars "his offspring ... after him" are not necessarily referring to Abraham specifically, but to each of the three and the three as one, as the exegetes understood. For example, Onqelos translated ואתרעי בבניהון בתריהון "he was pleased with their descendants after them," and, similarly, Neofiti reads, ויתרעי בבניהון מן בתריהון "he was pleased with their descendants after them." So, too, Saadia: ואכ'תר נסלהם מן בעדהם. However, I did find one source that saw in the 3ms pronominal suffix on בזרעו a hint specifically to Jacob: Targum Pseudo-Jonathan reads, וחולף דרחים ית אבהתכון אברהם ויצחק ואתרעי בבני דיעקב, and Ibn Ezra comments (s. v. ויבחר בזרעו): רמז ליעקב כי אם אמר 'בזרעם', יכנסו עמנו [לארץ] שמנה גוים "a hint to Jacob, for if it said 'to *their* offspring, eight other nations would go into the land with us."

60 See Ben-Ze'ev 1807, s. v.

ידיד: "an adjective referring to one loved with a spiritual and desirous love."[61] Y. Grazovsky and D. Yellin provided a similar definition:[62] "beloved, treasured, deserving of love," although they also added the definition "friend."[63] Grazovsky defined the word similarly (although with a slight addendum) in the dictionary he authored alone:[64] "beloved, treasured, deserving of affection and friendship." S. Y. Fein, on the other hand, gives two definitions.[65] The first is given explicitly – "beloved and treasured."[66] The second is by implication, when he interprets the expression אשר קידש ידיד מבטן – which refers, in his opinion, to Abraham[67]– he chooses the word "lover" (אוהב): "as we found, that he is called 'one who loves God'" – and cites the verse from Isaiah 41:8, "Abraham who loves me."[68] In Ben-Yehuda's dictionary, the definition "one who loves" is the primary one: "one who loves his friend, desires good for him, and is inclined towards him."[69] For a first example he cites the verse from Deuteronomy 33:12 (לבנימין אמר ידיד ה'). However, for the verse from Psalms 84:2 (מה ידידות) he proposes the definition "treasured, fit to be loved."[70] In Even-Shoshan's dictionary,[71] the definition "faithful friend, good friend," is cited at the beginning, and only regarding the verse מה ידידות משכנותיך did he follow his predecessors and cite the definition "beloved, treasured." The מילון ההווה, too,[72] writes: "friend," and we find something

---

61 Ben-Ze'ev cites the word ידידות in the verse מה ידידות משכנותיך (Ps. 84:2), with the expression שיר ידידות (*ibid.* 45:1), and with the expression ידידות נפשי (Jer. 12:7) in a separate entry (see what I said above, n. 13).

62 See Grazovsky and Yellin (1919), s. v.

63 Grazovsky and Yellin also combined ידידוֹת and ידידוּת (see above, n. 61, although they do not include source citations), which is defined by them as "a lovely thing, delight; friendship; love."

64 See Grazovsky 1934, s. v. ידיד. In this edition he cites in this entry the form from the verse in Psalms 84:2 (מה ידידות משכנותיך) and defines it, "treasured and pleasant." Essentially the same definition appears, almost without any change, in the 1945 edition of the dictionary.

65 See Fein 1904, s. v. ידיד.

66 See below, n. 69, for the synonyms cited by Ben-Yehuda.

67 There he rejects the opinion cited in the Arukh (in the name of Sherira Gaon) that the designation ידיד refers to Jacob.

68 S. Y. Fein also combines the form ידידוֹת of Psalm 84:2 together with ידידוּת of Psalm 45:1, and cited them as a separate entry in the lexicon (see above, n. 61); for the form ידידוּת of Jer. 12:7, on the other hand, he proposes a third entry.

69 He also gives translations in modern European languages: *Freund; ami; friend.*

70 Again, he gives the translations into German, French, and English: *lieblich; aimable; lovely.*

71 This dictionary is cited according to the Moshe Azar 2003 edition.

72 See Bahat and Mishor 1995.

similar in the dictionary רב מילים:[73] "a friend, someone with whom one is on good and close terms with."

§ 17 There are three scientific dictionaries we will mention here. Kaddari's dictionary of Biblical Hebrew, the most recent to be written in Hebrew,[74] gives the definition "one who loves" for the majority of the occurrences of the word ידיד in Scripture, although for Psalms 84:2 does it uses the gloss חָבִיב "treasured."[75] The two most important English dictionaries of Biblical Hebrew are BDB and HALOT. BDB lists three definitions: (1) beloved – and under this definition are cited most of the biblical attestations of the word; (2) lovely – here the aforementioned verse from Psalms (84:2) is cited; (3) fpl. as abstr. subst – here BDB cites שיר ידידות (Ps. 45:1) and defines it "love song." HALOT follows BDB completely, with only a slight change: what was cited as meaning #3 in BDB is a separate lemma in HALOT.

In short, most dictionaries understood ידיד as "beloved," but a few understood it to mean "the one who loves" (Ben-Yehuda says this explicitly, and in the dictionary of S. Y. Fein this is implied), and there are those who were content with the definition "friend," or at least added that on to other definitions.

§ 18 The views found in the dictionaries are also reflected in the modern commentaries. I will not discuss many commentaries, but only mention the interpretations found in the *Daat Miqra* series.[76] The essence of what is found here is also what is found in other modern commentaries. In explaining the verse from Deuteronomy, Aaron Mirsky writes:[77] "Because the Divine Spirit dwells next to [Benjamin], he is called the ידיד of God. Something similar is found in Psalm 69:37: 'the lovers of His name (אֹהֲבֵי שְׁמוֹ) will dwell in the Lord.' Therefore he says: 'he will dwell on him forever' – meaning, *next to* him, *next to* the Divine Presence." We can infer that Mirsky understood ידיד as "one who loves" (since he connects ידיד in this verse to the verse from Psalm 69, "lovers of His name"). On the other hand, Menachem Bolle,[78] in his interpretation of Jeremiah 11:15, explains ידיד as "beloved." Here are the most important of what he has to say: "ידידי is 'my beloved'. Moses calls the tribe of Benjamin

---

73 See Chveka 1996.

74 See Kaddari 2005.

75 First, one should remember that חביב in contemporary Hebrew, which is given as the definition in Kaddari's dictionary, does not mean "beloved"; a better definition for it would be "likable". Second, Kaddari says nothing about the grammar of the word ידידות in this verse, as would have been appropriate (see above, n. 13).

76 This is in deference to Amos Hakham, in whose honor this study was originally published, and who is, as already mentioned, the series' finest commentator according to many.

77 See Mirsky 2002:485.

78 See Bolle 1985:103.

by this epithet, 'beloved of the Lord' (Deut 33:12). Here, however, the epithet 'beloved of the Lord' is being used in a mocking way, as if to say, they used to be the beloveds of God, but now there are his enemies."

We now turn to the chief of the *Daat Miqra* commentators, Amos Hakham. The word ידיד occurs both in Isaiah and in Psalms, both of which were interpreted by Hakham in the series, and Hakham comments on the word in each of its occurrences in the two books. When it appears in Isaiah 5:1,[79] he explains it as "beloved," as emerges clearly from the formulation of his commentary: "the prophet means God when he says 'ידידי', for the prophet clings to him and **loves** him."[80] ידיד is therefore he who is loved, that is to say, "beloved." Something similar emerges from his commentary on Psalms 84:1. There he writes:[81] "מה ידידות משכנותיך ... how treasured and beloved are the places where you dwell! In other words, how treasured and **beloved** is the Temple!" On the other hand, in Psalm 127:2, he understands it as an active form and glosses "the one who loves": "יתן לידידו שנא – God gives sleep to the one who **loves** him, and does not compel him to go without sleep ..." Finally, in his comment on the phrase that appears in two psalms, למען יחלצון ידידיך (Psalms 60:7 and 108:7), he combined "beloved" and "lover" in explaining the word. In the first occurrence he writes: "In other words, Israel, **who are loved by you and who love you**, will be saved from their troubles." In in the second appearance: "Because your ידידים, Israel, who are beloved and who love you, will be saved from their troubles." In short, Amos Hakham explains the word ידיד with the help of the verb אהב, and glosses it in all possible ways – "beloved" (אהוב) or "one who loves" (אוהב), as well as a combination of the two, "who loves him and who is loved by him," together.

§ 19 Let us summarize what we have seen so far.

(a) It is entirely clear from both direct and indirect evidence that most ancient interpreters understood ידיד as "beloved, treasured." We found that the Bible itself already provided this explanation (2 Sam. 12:24–25: – יְדִידְיָהּ וה' אהבו), and that the word is thus explained in the rabbinic midrash from Sifre Devarim, where biblical ידיד interchanges with rabbinic "treasured" (חביב), or "beloved" (אהוב) according to the Midrash ha-Gadol. It is also translated this way in the LXX,[82] in Targum Onqelos, and (in most of its occurrences), in the remaining Jewish Aramaic Targumim (except for once in Targum Psalms),[83] and so, too, also in the Peshitta. The same is true, generally speak-

---

79 See Hakham 1984:48.

80 All the emphases in the citations from Hakham's commentary are mine.

81 See Hakham 1979 and 1981.

82 This understanding also passed to the Palestinian Syriac translation (as mentioned above, n. 26), whose formulation is just an Aramaic translation of the LXX.

83 If the extant text that we have is correct (see above the end of § 3).

ing, for the Vulgate, although it did explain the word once as meaning "one who loves," and once as "friend." We should mention that in the Latin translation of the text of the LXX Psalms, the Vulgate followed in the LXX and translated ידיד in every instance with a word meaning "beloved."[84] The same emerges, again, from the commentaries of most of the medieval Jewish biblical exegetes (Rashi, Ibn Ezra, Qimhi), although Saadia did explicitly saw that the meaning of the word in every occurrence is "one who loves."[85] In two verses, however, he used a word with a passive meaning, "beloved" or "chosen," to translate ידיד.[86]

(b) The interpretation of ידיד as "beloved" also emerges from the use of ידיד in the language of prayer as synonymous with אהוב "beloved" (נתנו **ידידים** זמירות ... / שבחו **אהובים** ורוממו ...). This is also indirectly reflected in the interpretations offered by Sherira Gaon (וְאֹהַב את יעקב) and of Rashi (את בנך [...] אשר אהבת את יצחק) of the epithet ידיד in the blessing recited at a circumcision. This may also have been the intention of Rabbenu Tam, who refrained from supporting his alterantive interpretation with biblical texts – perhaps because those indicate that Abraham is the lover of God.[87]

(c) This is also, as already mentioned, the position of the most modern scholars, who define ידיד as "beloved"; only a small minority of them offer the definition "lover." And there is also a distinct minority that combines the active and the passive.

(d) It seems to me that the combination of the active and the passive also finds expression in the definition, employed by a few, beginning with Jerome in the Vulgate, of ידיד as "friend." A "friend" is precisely both one who loves and one who is loved, simultaneously. In fact, this is how the word is used today: my ידיד is someone whom I love and by whom I am also loved[88] – in other words, he is my friend. Indeed, someone whom I befriend (מתחָבֵּר[89]), or with whom I become friends, is a person that shares with me a reciprocal

---

84 As mentioned above, Greek words meaning "beloved, treasured," are the standard translations of ידיד in the LXX. See above § 7.

85 We have already said that the word Saadia uses, ודיד, expresses both an active sense ("the one who loves") and a passive sense ("beloved"), following the pattern of Arabic *faʿīl* forms.

86 See above, at the end of § 8.

87 See above, at the end of § 15.

88 It is hardly necessary to point out that today, אָהַב "loved" indicates a deeper relationship than חִבֵּב "liked". In fact, in contemporary Hebrew, the intensity of the relationship denoted by the word ידיד has been reduced; there is a difference between a ידיד and a חבר. When speaking of relationships between the sexes, חבר and חברה indicate "boyfriend" and "girlfriend," whereas one can have many ידידים and ידידות.

89 In contemporary spoken Hebrew many people (and not just children) say מִתְחָבֵר אליו (and note the fricative *bet*!).

loving relationship. In other words: it seems reasonable to suggest that initially the word ידיד meant a "beloved" person, but over time the active meaning "one who loves" also became attached to it, and it thus became an appropriate synonym for the other words for friend (חָבֵר and רֵעַ).

2.3 On the Morphology of the Word

§ 20 From all the examples that were cited in the previous sections it can be seen that in the singular absolute form is not attested in the Bible. Al that appears there are the construct form of the singular (יְדִיד ה'), and the plural form (יְדִידוֹת[90] [משכנותיך]), and the forms attached to singular and plural pronouns (יְדִידִי, יְדִידוֹ, יְדִידֶיךָ). Grammatically, these forms could all be derived from either יָדִיד, in the *pāʿīl* form, or יְדִיד in the *pəʿīl*.[91]

In post-biblical literature the absolute form occurs, both in the blessings formulated by the Sages – אשר קידש **ידיד** מבטן – and also in the passage from b. Men 53a, no less than ten times: יבא ידיד בן ידיד ויבנה ידיד לידיד בחלקו של ידיד [...] יבוא ידיד זה שלמה ... בן ידיד זה אברהם [...] ויבנה ידיד זה בית המקדש [...] לידיד זה הקב"ה [...] בחלקו של ידיד זה בנימין.[92]

§ 21 A thorough investigation of the data reveals that we have evidence of two forms – יָדִיד and יְדִיד.

(a) The absolute form יָדִיד is found, for example, in a vocalized Geniza fragment of a *piyyut* by Shemuel ha-Shelishi (who lived around 1000 CE): יָדִיד[93] בצדק עמות / כלול ענוה ותמות.[94] The Yemenites read the blessing at the

90 See above §§ 3, 5–7, and nn. 13 and 26.

91 Ibn Ezra already realized this. In his discussion of these two patterns, he cites, in the absolute form ("מוכרת" in his terminology), the forms פָּקִיד, שָׂרִיד on the one hand, against גְּבִיר, כְּפִיר, and מְרִיא on the other hand. And he notes: "And there are some whose construct and absolute forms are identical. ... See, for instance, the word יְדִיד ה': we are unable to know what its absolute form is" (1868:26b; 1827:39a). From Ibn Ezra this point made its way to Avineri 1976:237, who illustrates it with nouns like יְדִיד, שְׁבִיב, and נְקִיק, which are not attested in the Bible in the absolute, but only in the construct or declined forms. It is therefore difficult to decide what their singular forms are, whether they are פָּעִיל or פְּעִיל pattern nouns.

92 As mentioned, the source of this *baraita* is Sifre Devarim § 352 (see above, n. 56). I cite it here from the Bavli (as mentioned by Rabbenu Tam; see above § 14) primarily because we have the Yemenite tradition given by Rav Yosef ʻAmar of the passage.

93 This is the vocalization in the fragment according to my friend Dr. Benjamin Elitzur, who provided me with this information.

94 The citation is taken from Ma'agarim. Is this the primary evidence based on which it was decided that the lemma should be יָדִיד? Or did Ma'agarim decide to follow the vocalization employed by the modern dictionaries (see below § 29)?

circumcision this way, too: אשר קִדַּשׁ[95] יָדִיד[96]. R. Yosef Qafiḥ vocalized the word this way in his *siddur*,[97] and R. Yosef ʿAmar also vocalized it יָדִיד in all ten appearances of the noun in the absolute in Menahot 53a–b[98] in the Talmud he published.[99]

(b) On the other hand, the Sephardim and Ashkenazim read יְדִיד when the form is attested in the circumcision benediction (אשר קידש יְדִיד):[100] I found this vocalization in dozens of Sephardic and Ashkenazi siddurim.[101] H. Y. Kosovsky in his concordance to the *Tosefta* vocalized אשר קידש יְדִיד, apparently according the tradition of his fathers.[102] The Ashkenazi tradition is apparently also reflected in the vocalization of the word in one poem of Bialik's: he begins his poem גָּדִי גְּדִיי[103] with the two lines, אבא שב מן הַיָּרִיד[104] / קנה רע לי וִידִיד. Finally, the family name ידיד, which is very common among Mizrahi Jews – for example, among Aleppan Jews – is pronounced with *shewa* under the *yod* (יְדִיד).[105]

§ 22 It is important to note that the reading יְדִיד is the one that is reflected in the rhythms of poems written according to the Spanish poem patterns in various communities in the Diaspora. Here is a representative sampling of the evidence gathered by my friend Dr. Uri Melamed at my request:[106]

---

95 Thus: קִדַּשׁ, with a *pataḥ* under the *dalet*, as is usual in the Yemenite tradition for the פִּעֵל verbs in Mishnaic Hebrew.

96 I learned this from a number of reliable witnesses: Prof. Isaac Gluska, Prof. Judah Ratzhabi, Dr. Uri Melammed, and Dr. Yehiel Qara.

97 See Qafih 2000:289.

98 See above, § 14 with n. 93.

99 In Yemenite poetry, however, the form יְדִיד is found (see below § 23).

100 The Jews of Aden, too, read יְדִיד (אשר קידש יְדִיד). Mr. Doron Jacob, a descendant of a family from Aden, told me this. He even added, emphatically: "I know that the word is read differently in Aden and Yemen; my grandfather has been a *mohel* for over sixty years, and I always heard him say אשר קידש יְדִיד!" In Dr. Uri Melammed's opinion, the Jews of Aden were influenced by Sephardic traditions, and adopted the reading יְדִיד from them. It is clear that this subject requires some fundamental research. One can hope that this issue will be clarified in the doctoral work of Mr. Doron Jacob, who is dealing systematically with the traditions of the Jews of Aden.

101 I checked more than twenty Sephardic prayer books and more than twenty Ashkenazi prayer books that were printed in last three centuries.

102 However, his son, Moshe Kasovsky, vocalized in the concordance to the Talmud Yerushalmi יָדִיד. (Moshe Kasovsky saw himself as less compelled by the vocalizations of his father, even when those vocalizations reflected faithful Ashkenazi reading traditions, and followed modern dictionaries and grammars instead; see Ryzhik 1998 for discussion of this difference between the practices of the two.)

103 See Bialik 2001:237 (here גְּדִּי is vocalized with a *dagesh* in the *dalet*), 295.

104 An alternative reading, הַיְרִיד, is cited there, too.

105 I have heard many people with this family name pronounced it this way.

106 As mentioned, Dr. Melammed went out of his way to search for and collect examples from many places on my behalf. I cite here only a fraction of them.

וְאֵיךְ אֶזְכֹּר יְדִיד לֹא יִזְכְּרֵנִי וְלָמָּה יִרְבְּיוּן תִּנָּם פְּצָעַי (רבי יהודה הלוי).[107]
חֵי הַיְּדִיד אִם יֵשׁ תְּעָלָה אַחֲרָיו עַד שֶׁיְּהֵא פִגְעוֹ לְפֶגַע נוֹד (הנ"ל).[108]
לְךָ שָׁלוֹם יְדִיד הָלַךְ לְדַרְכּוֹ וְעָבַט הַנְּפָשׁוֹת כַּעֲבֹטִים (רבי משה אבן עזרא).[109]
לְכָה אִיעָצְךָ עֵצָה וּמַה-טּוֹב יְדִיד יוֹעֵץ בְּתָם-לֵבָב תְּמִימָיו (הנ"ל).[110]
עַל כֵּן, יְדִיד, אַל תַּאֲשִׁימֵנִי וּמְחַל וְאַל תִּקְצֹף וְתִתְעַבָּר (יהודה אלחריזי).[111]
יְדִיד קָדַח בְּעַד לִבִּי בְּעֵת נָד אֶת שְׁבִיב הַבְּהַב (אלעזר בן יעקב הבבלי).[112]
זָרְחָה בְנֶפֶשׁ יְדִיד[113]נַפְשִׁי אֲהוּבִי אֲשֶׁר נָטְעָה יְמִינִי וְהוּא חֶמְדַּת שְׁתִילֶיהָ (סעדיה בן דנאן הראשון).[114]

It is very possible that the form יְדִיד is preferred in poetry in the Spanish pattern, since it offers a foot, and the poets in this tradition needed both full vowels and feet, in the same way that they preferred the form זְמִיר "song" over the form זָמִיר.[115] The use of the particle הֲכִי is known to have been common for similar reasons ("a filler word in medieval poetry for the needs of the rhythm").[116]

§ 23 It should also be mentioned that in the poetry of the Yemeni Jews written in the Spanish pattern, the word is vocalized יְדִיד, as can be seen in the following examples:

יְדִיד, קוּמָה   יְרוּשְׁלַיְמָה   וְשָׂא מִנִּי כְּתָב (יוסף סעיד).[117]
יְדִיד, קוּמָה   קְנֵה חָכְמָה   וְשֵׂו לִבָּךְ לְמוּל (ישועה).[118]
יְדִיד, בִּינָה   בְּהֶגְיוֹנָה   צְעִיר נִבְזֶה בְּכֹל (אברהם צנעאני).[119]
יְדִיד, הַבֵּט בְּרֵאָה   נִמְצְאוּ בָהּ   אֲבַעְבּוּעוֹת אֲבַעְבּוּעוֹת וְכַמָּה (דוד).[120]
יְדִיד, עוּרָה   וְהַזְכִּירָה   שְׁבָח שׁוֹכֵן זְבוּל (אברהם צנעאני).[121]

§ 24 But again, it bears repeating that in the Yemenite tradition, it is the form יָדִיד which is the usual one in the blessing at the circumcision and in

107 Halevi 1945 3.27 (Poem 10 line 8).
108 *Ibid.* p. 362 (9:1).
109 Ibn Ezra and Brody 1935 1:82 (song 79:23).
110 *Ibid.* p. 132, 127:23.
111 Hariri 1950:41.
112 Brody 1935:116 (258:1).
113 This is not necessarily a construct phrase ידיד נפשי.
114 Sa'adia ben Denan I, in *Diwān Abraham b. Zimra*, MS 6 in the collection of Moshe 'Amar, page 4b, poem 17:3–4.
115 I thank Dr. Uri Melammed who reminded me of this example.
116 For instance, וְאִם נשאר כשערה מבריתו / הֲכִי לא יחטיאוה קלעי (from a poem of Judah HaLevi, cited in the Evan-Shoshan dictionary s. v. הכי); the particle הֲכִי is patterned like the particle וְאִם.
117 Shabazi 1966:385(1).
118 *Ibid.*, 386(1).
119 See Tobi and Seri 1988:350–51, § 1964.
120 *Ibid.*, § 1966.
121 *Ibid.*, § 1973.

the *baraita* in Menahot, as vocalized by Yoseph Amar (10 times!). יָדִיד is also the form found in the poems for circumcision written Rabbi Shalom Shabazi. Here are two examples from his poetry:

שָׁמַעְתִּי, מִפַּאֲתֵי תֵימָן \ קוֹל יָדִיד קִיֵּם בְּרִית נֶאֱמָן
זְכוּת מִילָה, תַּגִּין עֲלֵי יָדִיד \ מִשָּׂטָן רָשָׁע שֶׁהוּא מַמְרִיד.[122]

In Yemen, only in poetry on the pattern of feet and vowels is the form יְדִיד attested. Dr. Melammed suggested that the vocalization of the noun in the absolute as יְדִיד was brought to Yemenite poetry by Rabbi Yaḥya al-Ḍahari (1531–1608).[123] According to Dr. Melammed, R. Yaḥya got the vocalization יְדִיד from Radaq,[124] who claimed that יְדִיד is the absolute form of the word.[125] It should be said that Rabbi Yaḥya himself uses both independent forms in metrical poetry[126] – יָדִיד and יְדִיד. He even included the two of them together in a *piyyut* on the Spanish pattern, in two adjacent stanzas:[127]

וְלֹא אֶמְצָא לְדִמְיוֹן **הַיְּדִיד** זֶה — וְכָלִיל הוּא יְדִידִי בַּהֲדָרוֹ.
וּמִי יִתֵּן וְאָעוּפָה כְּנֶשֶׁר — אֱלֵי **יָדִיד** לְמוֹלַדְתּוֹ וְעִירוֹ.

If we accept the very reasonable suggestion of Dr. Melammed, we understand the double vocalization of R. Yaḥya al-Ḍahari: he utilizes both יָדִיד, as in the Yemeni tradition, as well as יְדִיד, under Radaq's influence.

§ 25 To summarize, there is evidence within the reading traditions for both forms, יָדִיד and יְדִיד. The Sephardic and Ashkenazi traditions uphold the second reading, יְדִיד, consistently. This form is the one employed in the poetry patterned in Spain, North Africa, in the East, and in Yemen according to the needs of the meter. Nevertheless, one should be cautious and say that the

---

122 Tobi and Seri 1988:69, lines 1,10.
123 On him, see Amir 2005.
124 Rabbi Yaḥya al-Ḍahari was a great admirer of Radaq's, and even composed a poem in praise of him. This poem can be found in Fascicle 17 of his *Sefer ha-Musar* (see Ratzahbi 1964:203–04). This poem opens, לִפְנֵי אֱלֹהִים אֶעֱרֹךְ שִׂיחִי / אָשִׁיר בְּמַהֲלָלוֹ כְּפִי כֹחִי (and see the notes of the editor, Ratzhabi, in the introduction on page 38, near n. 23, as well as on p. 55 – in the list of the contents of the various fascicles – near n. 80; on p. 85, in a note to poem 167, the editor relies on Radaq's commentary on Psalms 12:9).
125 See below § 30.
126 Here are Dr. Melammed's own words: "I believe that I will not be a mistake to say that Rabbi Yaḥya al-Ḍahari, who was much influenced by the writings of Radaq (from his biblical commentaries and his grammatical compositions, and even dedicated a poem of praise to him), and who also knew the 'Sephardic' traditions of pronunciation, was the one who brought the pronunciation of יְדִיד to Yemen. The proof is that he preserves these two forms alongside each other."
127 See Ratzhabi 1964:235 (above, n. 124), stanzas 119, 122.

consistency of its use in poetry shows that we should not view it as an arbitrary form which is produced only by the exigencies of the meter; it is, after all, in agreement with the readings of the Sephardic communities and other communities connected to Spain. Therefore, it does not seem reasonable to argue that it is only the fact that the noun is not found in the absolute form in the Bible which encouraged the spread of the form with a *shewa*(attested are only the construct form יְדִיד and the declined forms יְדִידַי, etc., as mentioned). Nevertheless, the reliability of the first reading – יָדִיד – is secure. It is found in the Geniza fragment of the hymn by Shemuel ha-Shelishi mentioned above, and in the Yemenite reading tradition in the blessing at circumcision and ten times in Menahot, and also in the *piyyutim* of R. S. Shabazi for circumcision. Even R. Yaḥya al-Ḍahari did not forsake it in his metrical poetry. Consequently, it is clear that it has great weight in the history of the language.

§ 26 Moreover, it is possible that the reading יָדִיד is what stands behind the early interpretations of the word within the Bible, in Rabbinic literature, and in most of the ancients – beginning with the LXX and continuing through the Middle Ages, all of which take the word to mean "beloved." It cannot be excluded that that they understood the form יָדִיד to be comparable to the many other words on the pattern פָּעִיל. These include adjectives and nominalized adjectives, and of course also passive participles of *binyan* Qal verbs, both in Biblical and Mishnaic Hebrew; some of the adjectives and nominalized adjectives were, indeed, derived from these participles. It is possible that the ancients interpreted יָדִיד as a passive participle, similar to the participle קָרִיא – an alternative of קָרוּא[128] – which is found in the expression קְרִאֵי מועד/קְרִיאֵי העדה (Num. 16:2; 26:9), the participle שָׂנִיא – an alternative of שָׂנוּא[129] – found in the feminine form (לַ)שְּׂנִיאָה (Deut. 22:15), and the participle שָׁלִיחַ (Git. 3:6) – an alternative of שָׁלוּחַ[130] – and similar forms.

§ 27 And there are, as is known, nominalized פָּעִיל forms (more precisely: nouns, in the full sense of the word) which have no corresponding verb in the Qal, such as נָבִיא, which is the nominal form related only to participles in the Nip'al and the Hitpa'el. Moreover, among forms like these are also examples that have no corresponding verbs at all within Hebrew, such as יָדִיד and שָׂעִיר. It is true that there is no root יד"ד used in the Qal, or in any other *binyan*, in

128 As is well known, קָרִיא and קָרוּא interchange: for the *ketiv* קריאי העדה, the *qere* is קְרוּאֵי העדה (Num. 1:16); the interchange is also found in Num. 26:9.

129 As is well known, the two forms occur within a single context: שְׂנוּאָה (four times) and שְׂנִיאָה (one time) within Deut. 21:15–17.

130 In this mishnah itself the two forms שָׁלִיחַ and שָׁלוּחַ are found: אין הַשָּׁלִיחַ האחרון צריך שיאמר בפניי ניכתב ובפני נתחתם, אלא אומ' שָׁלוּחַ בית דין אני (m. Gittin 3:6; this is the text according to MS Kaufman!).

Hebrew,[131] but a word on the פָּעִיל pattern which describes people (although not only people), could certainly be understood as an passive participle of the Qal. Something like this is reflected, as is well known, in the form שָׂעִיר (איש שָׂעִיר [Gen. 27:11]; כידי עשו אחיו שְׂעִרֹת [*ibid.*, 23]), which means מכוסה שֵׂעָר. It is understood to be comparable to an unattested form, שָׂעוּר, which has no corresponding verbal root שׂע"ר in any of the *binyanim*. Both forms, then – יָדִיד[132] and שָׂעִיר – could be understood, and apparently *were* understood, as passive participle forms ("beloved," "covered with hair"). Forms like these – יָדִיד and שָׂעִיר – could undergo a process of nominalization and to turn into adjectives and even into full nouns.

§ 28 One could say that the form יְדִיד could also be understood as an Aramaic passive participle – פְּעִיל. But this is difficult to accept, since for all intents and purposes, the word יְדִיד is not attested in Aramaic. It is very doubtful that the ancients (certainly the majority of them) knew about the existence of the Syriac יַדִּידָא. In Hebrew itself, the pattern פְּעִיל is not understood as an intermediate passive form. The forms בְּדִיל, בְּרִיחַ, מְעִיל, and the others in the Bible, and צְרִיךְ, סְכִין,[133] גְּלִיד, שְׁפִיר and comparable forms in rabbinic literature are fully nouns. The vast majority are not related to people at all. On the other hand, there are the nouns אֱוִיל, כְּסִיל, גְּבִיר, and נְצִיב in the Bible, and שְׁלִישׁ (= a third person)[134] in Rabbinic literature, which describe people in terms of their characteristics (אֱוִיל, כְּסִיל) or in terms of their positions or functions (שְׁלִישׁ, נְצִיב, גְּבִיר), and it is possible that one or two of them[135] is a passive participle form of a *binyan* Qal verb. But this is not a serious possibility with regard to the word יְדִיד.

---

131 The verb התיידד "to associate" attested in later Hebrew was obviously derived from the noun ידיד.

132 However, in Arabic, a verbal root וד"ד actually is used, alongside the word ודיד; in Syriac, too, are found the forms יַדֵּד (Pa'el) and אֶתְיַדַּד (Etpa'al), which were apparently derived from the noun יַדִּידָא (see the dictionary of Margoliouth s. v., and the sources cited above, n. 6).

133 This noun is more usually known with the vocalization סַכִּין, but is cited here according to the vocalization in the reliable manuscripts of Rabbinic literature.

134 For the form שְׁלִישׁ we have only weak evidence. According to the tradition of the scribe of MS Kaufmann, the Mishnah calls "a reliable third party" a "שלישי". The vocalizer, however, erased the final *yod* and read once שָׁלִישׁ in the פָּעִיל pattern, and once שְׁלִישׁ in the פְּעִיל pattern: המשרה את אשתו על ידי שָׁלִישׁ(י) (m. Ketubbot 5:8), and [...] המשליש מעות לבתו יעשה שְׁלִישׁ(י) (m. Ketubbot 6:7). This shows neatly that the vocalizer of MS Kaufmann did not have a reliable tradition on this word.

135 This is possible, for example, with regard to the word נְצִיב (see HALOT s. v. נְצִיב I, p. 716; they connect the word to Aramaic נצ"ב, although they do not go so far as to claim that it is a Qal passive participle).

§ 29 Some of the modern dictionaries[136] cite only one form of the singular absolute form: יָדִיד. This is true for the two scientific dictionaries of Biblical Hebrew familiar to every researcher, BDB and HALOT. The situation is similar in the dictionaries of Ben-Yehuda, Grozowsky & Yellin, and Grozowsky's 1945 edition, as well as in the recent dictionaries: Even-Shoshan,[137] the Millon ha-Hoveh, Rav Millim and the Sapir dictionary.[138] And there are dictionaries that cite two forms for the singular absolute, יָדִיד and also יְדִיד; Kaddari showed both vocalizations in his dictionary, as do the dictionaries of Ben-Ze'ev, Fein, and Grozowsky's 1934 edition.

§ 30 The vocalization of יְדִיד as an independent form is already known for centuries. Isaac Avineri already pointed out that Radaq cited the form in this way in his *Mikhlol* and in his *Sefer ha-Shorashim*.[139] R. Abraham de Balmes followed Radaq in this regard,[140] as did Avineri himself.[141] Others remained silent about the noun ידיד altogether, and did not cite it either as a פָּעִיל or as a פְּעִיל form: Bauer and Leander's Hebrew grammar, for example, does not mention it at all.[142] But as mentioned, not only did most dictionaries not omit the noun, as detailed above, but most preferred the vocalization יָדִיד as the absolute form. It seems that recent dictionaries are merely following in the footsteps of the older dictionaries, but why did those earlier dictionaries prefer the vocalization יָדִיד? Apparently they interpreted the construct form יְדִיד and the declined forms יְדִידִי and so on as analogous to שְׁלִיחַ-, שְׁלִיחִי, etc. As said above, the early sources probably analyzed the word as a passive participle, and thus connected between form and meaning ("beloved").

2.4 Concluding Remarks

§ 31 Regarding the *meaning* of the word ידיד, it has been clearly seen that the definition "beloved" is the one indicated by the vast majority of the early sources, most importantly the Bible itself. However, already in the first millennium there are sources that take it to mean "one who loves." It was this under-

136 See the details in §§ 16–17 above.

137 But in his biblical concordance, Even-Shoshan cites the absolute singular form as יְדִיד.

138 See Avneyon 1998.

139 See Avineri 1976:228, 233; and Avineri 1964:468, 506.

140 See De Balmes 1523:142, who cites the noun in the פָּעִיל pattern, and comments: "Some put this word in a row of words with a *shewa* under the first consonant, like כְּסִיל, יְדִיד, רְצִין, גְּבִיר – these are unchangeable."

141 See above, n. 139.

142 See Bauer and Leander 1922 (see the פָּעִיל pattern on pg. 470 and the פְּעִיל pattern on pg. 471).

standing that we found once in the Vulgate, once in Targum Tehillim, and explicitly in R. Saadia's *Tafsīr* in his commentary on Psalms. What these three sources have in common is that they all understand that the word contains both senses, "the one who loves" and "the one who is loved." It appears that pragmatics – in other words, the realities of life – provided an important consideration here: usually (but not always!) someone whom I love (that is to say, he is my beloved) also reciprocates and loves me (that is to say, I am his beloved). There is, therefore, justification for the definition "friend."[143] Contemporary speakers, who of course have inherited the language from previous generations, use ידיד in this sense: for us, a ידיד is friend.[144]

§ 32 Regarding the *morphology* of the word, we saw that there is evidence for two forms – both יָדִיד and יְדִיד. It seems that the meaning most ancient authorities attributed to the word – "beloved, treasured" – can be more transparently related to the form יָדִיד (taken to be a passive participle) than to the form יְדִיד. Therefore, if I had to choose one of these forms, I would prefer יָדִיד over יְדִיד in terms of the *history of the language*; this best accounts for the interpretation of the word found already within the Bible, and which is widespread among the ancient interpreters. Indeed, this was the decision made, perhaps unwittingly, by the majority of modern dictionaries, academic and practical.[145]

§ 33 One more word is appropriate in conclusion. We are not always able to establish the precise meaning of a word in ancient texts. Sometimes, even meticulous research and careful analysis can only reveal the meaning (or meanings) attributed to a word by the ancient interpreters. Their proximity, chronologically speaking, to the time when the language was a living one is a very important fact to consider. Their exegetical traditions, too, are often more reliable than the conclusions reached by modern scholars, despite the great learning and depth of wisdom attained by the latter group. It is this type of analysis that I have tried to carry out here, in clarifying the meaning and establishing the form of the word ידיד.

---

143 Of course, in Mishnaic Hebrew, the primary meaning of חבר is not "a friend," but someone who accepted upon himself to eat non-sacred food in a state of purity and who is meticulous in the laws of *terumah* and tithes. For "friend," the word אוהב is normally used; e.g., מי שזכה זכה בקטורת היה נוטל את הבזך מתוך הכף ונותנו לאוהבו או לקרובו (m. Tamid 6:3). But it should be emphasized that the word חבר with the meaning "friend" is not entirely gone from Mishnaic Hebrew; cf., e.g., m. Avot 1:6: וקנה לך חבר. There are also examples outside of Avot, but this is not the place to elaborate on this issue.

144 And see above, n. 89.

145 Inspired by this study, my son and daughter-in-law gave the name Yadid Baruch to one of their twin boys, born April 6, 2009. (The other one is Nataf Moshe.)

3 The Bible Interpreting Itself

3.1 Introduction

§ 1 In this chapter I would like to comment on a phenomenon which can be called "the Bible as the interpreter of its own language."[1] Certain aspects of this phenomenon have been well known for a long time, while others less so. The best known type of such interpretation is when synonymous terms are used in parallel hemistiches within Biblical poetry. Obviously, the same type of interpretation is possible outside of poetry, as well, and this can assist us in interpreting many words.[2] I will offer a few short comments about this phenomenon.

---

1 Various aspects of internal commentary in the Bible have been discussed in studies conducted in the previous generation; I will mention only a few: Fishbane 1985; Zakovitch 1986–1987 (a review of Fishbane's book) and Zakovitch 1992 (his own book on the subject). Occasionally, linguistic topics are dealt with in these studies (example 19 on p. 25 in Zakovitch 1992 is discussed below in § 12; see also n. 40, below, for examples discussed by David Yellin). However, I have not seen anyone who has presented the issues in the way that they are presented here. I have tried to present a linguistic explanation of words and expressions, divided into four different types, with explicit examples. Beyond the others, there is the comprehensive and instructive study by Kariv 1970:239–263. His exegetical comments on the verses he deals with come in the course of his commentary, that is the word being explained and its explanation appear in one sequence (in sort of glosses). For example, in the verse "he called up his retainers, born into his household" (Genesis 14:14) the phrase "born into his household" explains "his retainers". Many good, sensible examples appear in this study, but there are also some unconvincing, and even baseless, ones. In any event, my study differs from his. I almost never deal with the many small details of a running commentary in this study. Two examples deal with synonyms that appear consecutively in the text: "in troughs-the water receptacles" (Genesis 30:38; Kariv 1970:240); "then is the prey of a great spoil divided" (Isaiah 33:23, p. 262 in Kariv's study). In his study these examples are two of many, whereas in my study this type is mentioned only in passing (see below, § 15). We disagree about the explanation of the third example. In the sentence ויהי רֹבֶה קַשָּׁת "and [he] became a young man, an archer" (Genesis 21:20; cf. Kariv 1970:239), Kariv takes the word קַשָּׁת to explain the word רֹבֶה, implying that he understood the word רֹבֶה to be equivalent to "shooting [arrows]." I am of the opinion that the word רֹבֶה means "young man," and that the word הַנַּעַר (*hanna'ar*) that appears in the first part of the verse clarifies the meaning of רֹבֶה that appears in the second part (see below §§ 19–21 and footnote 37). It should already be clear that I will argue that Biblical style assists in the linguistic inquiry of these matters.

2 In recent decades a number of scholars have researched biblical parallelism. Two must be singled out. The first is Kugel 1981, whose seven chapters are replete with examples and extremely important discussions; Kugel concentrates especially on the texts usually understood to be poetic. The second is the important work by Adelel Berlin 1985. The six chapters of this book focus on linguistic issues. Both of these books are fundamental for discussion of parallelism, and anyone interested in the topic must consult them. My study on the subject here is a short, preliminary study of a topic that deserves much fuller treatment: the Bible interpreting its own words.

§ 2 One of the more interesting types of this phenomenon is when a word's meaning is clarified through something else in the immediate context. This can occur with, for example, Aramaic loanwords, or with uncommon usages of standard Hebrew words. Clearly not every time that the meaning of a word becomes clear in context did the author *intend* to explain the word this way. It is very possible that in most cases the meaning is expressed unintentionally. Often, in order to create stylistic variety within a context, an author will employ a rare word. In close proximity, he uses more common word or expression, parallel to the rare word; the meaning of the rare word thus becomes clear. I shall deal with a number of examples of different types where the Bible interprets itself in a given context. The discussion will begin with some better-known examples, and then proceed to those which are less well known. I believe that both kinds of examples will clarify an important phenomenon in biblical literature and language.

3.2 Words that Explain and Words that are Explained

3.2.1 Parallelism and Parallel Verses

§ 3 I shall begin with the well-known phenomenon of synonyms and expressions that appear parallel to each other in a Biblical verse. This is especially characteristic of the language of Biblical poetry, whether the parallelism is synonymous or complimentary, or whether it is antithetical or otherwise. For example, אַף and עֶבְרָה, עַז and קָשָׁה in the verse אָרוּר אַפָּם כִּי עָז, וְעֶבְרָתָם כִּי קָשָׁתָה "Cursed be their fury so fierce, And their wrath so relentless!" (Genesis 49:7), or the pairs עַיִר and בֶּן אֲתוֹן, יַיִן and דַּם עֲנָבִים in the verse אֹסְרִי לַגֶּפֶן עִירֹה וְלַשֹּׂרֵקָה בְּנִי אֲתֹנוֹ, כִּבֵּס בַּיַּיִן לְבֻשׁוֹ וּבְדַם עֲנָבִים סוּתֹה "He tethers his ass to a vine, His purebred to the choicest stem; In wine he washes his garments, His robes in the blood of grapes" (Genesis 49:11). In all of these pairs, each word clarifies the meaning of the other.[3] Of course, for the reader of the text, the clarification of the less common word by means of the more common one is of greater importance.

3 I did not mention the two words גֶּפֶן and שׂוֹרֵקָה, which are parallel to each other in the two first hemistiches of this verse. This is because based upon evidence from Ugaritic, Syriac and other sources scholars have explained these words in ways which differ from the traditional explanation (see Greenfield 2001:2.847 n. 2), citing H. L. Ginsberg 1933:83, as well as the comments of J. N. Epstein, the then-editor of *Tarbiz*, there. Greenfield also added some important observations of his own; I wish to thank Steven Fassberg who brought Greenfield's article to my attention. I should add that Yitshak Avishur extensively studied the topic of word pairs in the Bible in his articles and books and made important contributions in this

§ 4 This is also true in the case of the pair of common nouns שֵׁם and זֵכֶר. These appear in the same verse in antithetical parallelism: זֵכֶר צַדִּיק לִבְרָכָה, וְשֵׁם רְשָׁעִים יִרְקָב "The name of the righteous is invoked in blessing, But the fame of the wicked rots" (Proverbs 10:7), or in synonymous parallelism: זֶה שְּׁמִי לְעֹלָם, וְזֶה זִכְרִי לְדֹר דֹּר "This is my name to eternity, and this is my designation (by) age" (Exodus 3:15).[4] In fact both שֵׁם and זֵכֶר have the same meaning ("name"). Sometimes the two synonymous nouns could come one after the other in one utterance with the same syntactical function. For example, the two nouns come one after the other in the verse לְשִׁמְךָ וּלְזִכְרְךָ תַּאֲוַת נָפֶשׁ "To invoke your name is the soul's desire" (Isaiah 26:8).[5] From the three aforementioned verses we can understand parallel uses of the pair שֵׁם and זֵכֶר in other portions of the Bible. For example in the verses כִּי מָחֹה אֶמְחֶה אֶת זֵכֶר עֲמָלֵק "I will eradicate, eradicate the *zēḵer* of Amalek" (Exodus 17:14), תִּמְחֶה אֶת זֵכֶר עֲמָלֵק "you shall blot out *zēḵer* of Amalek" (Deuteronomy 25:19) on the one hand, compared to וְלֹא יִמָּחֶה שְׁמוֹ מִיִּשְׂרָאֵל "that his *šēm* may not be obliterated in Israel" (Deuteronomy 25:6), בְּדוֹר אַחֵר יִמַּח שְׁמָם "From the age to come their *šēm* erased" (Psalms 109:13). This comparison shows that the obliteration of the זֵכֶר is equivalent to the obliteration of the שֵׁם.

§ 5 The occurrence of a pair of words parallel to each other can assist in clarifying the exact meaning of the rare word. I would like to mention the example of one word of a pair of words that is explained with two meanings. It seems to me that the parallel helps favor one meaning over the other. For example in the verse כְּחוּט הַשָּׁנִי שִׂפְתוֹתַיִךְ וּמִדְבָּרֵךְ נָאוֶה "Like a scarlet fillet your lips, Your mouth comely" (Song of Songs 4:3). The *hapax legomenon* מִדְבָּר, derived from the root ד-ב-ר I, means "the production of speech from the mouth." This word has no connection with the common noun מִדְבָּר, derived from the root ד-ב-ר II and referring to "an unsettled area" or "pasture."[6] There are two possible interpretations of the word, however.

---

matter. He began his research into this subject in his comprehensive doctoral dissertation (1974), and published many studies; see the bibliography in Heltzer and Malul 2004:15–37.

4 It is not superfluous to state that while this verse is in a prose context, it is built in the structure of Biblical poetry.

5 See § 15 below.

6 This is apparent from the verse וַיִּנְהַג אֶת הַצֹּאן אַחַר הַמִּדְבָּר "He led the flock along the side of the *pasture*" (Exodus 3:1) and is reflected in the adjective מִדְבָּרִי which appears, for example, in the Mishnah אֵין מַשְׁקִין וְשׁוֹחֲטִין אֶת הַמִּדְבָּרִיּוֹת, אֲבָל מַשְׁקִין וְשׁוֹחֲטִין אֶת הַבַּיְתִיּוֹת. אֵלּוּ הֵן הַבַּיְתִיּוֹת? הַלָּנוֹת בָּעִיר; הַמִּדְבָּרִיּוֹת? הַלָּנוֹת בָּאֲפָר. "They may not give drink to animals of the pasture or slaughter them, but they may give drink to household animals or slaughter them. Which are deemed household animals? Such as spend the night in a town. And animals of the pasture? Such that spend the night in [more distant] pasturage" (m. Beṣah 5:6).

(A) Some explain מִדְבָּר in the above verse as speech, that is, the verbal noun of the verb דָּבַר[7] (similar to דִּבֵּר) in the nominal pattern *miqtāl*, like מִשְׁפָּט from the verb שָׁפַט. For example, the Aramaic Targum to Song of Songs translates the pair of words שִׂפְתוֹתַיִךְ/מִדְבָּרֵךְ as שִׂפְתְוֹי/מִילּוֹי. Rashi also explains this way (מדברך – דבורך "your speech"), as does Kaddari in his dictionary ("דיבור").[8]

(B) On the other hand, BDB[9], HALOT[10] and others explain it as 'mouth'.[11] It seems to me that from the parallel to שִׂפְתוֹתַיִךְ (your lips) in the first hemistich, it would be more logical to assume that the noun מִדְבָּר signifies "mouth," and that מִדְבָּרֵךְ would therefore mean "your mouth." In the two hemistiches there appear nouns which signify "speech organs."[12] As is well known, the nominal pattern *miqtāl* signifies various objects such as מִזְרָק "basin" (Numbers 7:13), מִכְמָר "net" (Isaiah 51:20).[13]

---

7 As is known, the verb דָּבַר (in the Qal stem) is attested in the Bible only in the participle (and once in the verbal noun), for example דֹּבֵר "[I] speak" (Exodus 6:29), דּוֹבְרֵי שָׁקֶר "those telling lies" (Psalms 63:12), and in בְּדָבְרֶךָ "when you sentence' (Psalms 51:6). Forms such as דָּבַר, יִדְבֹּר where switched in an ancient period to their parallel forms in the Pi'el stem (דִּבֵּר, יְדַבֵּר), just as happened to other verbs which shifted from the Qal stem to the Pi'el stem during the period of the Second Temple and in Mishnaic Hebrew. When the Pi'el forms replaced the Qal forms, the Qal participle (דֹּבֵר) continued to be used in the Biblical text. This is because the use of the Pi'el participle would not only require changes in vocalization but also changes to the consonantal text: the addition of the letter *mem* – דֹּבֵר > [מְ]דַבֵּר; and also the removal of the *waw* when used as *mater lectionis* – ד(וֹ)בֵר > [מְ]דַבֵּר. Those who switched the first reading (דָּבַר, יִדְבֹּר) for the second reading (דִּבֵּר, יְדַבֵּר), almost never touched the consonantal text.

8 However he comments that one of the commentators explained this as "the point of the tongue" (see Kaddari 2006:580). I will not deal with the question of the alternate orthographic form מדבריך on which Kaddari bases his comment that this is a plural form. (This orthographic form appears in the Leningrad [St. Petersbeug] MS as it appears in A. Dotan's edition of the Bible, but not in M. Breuer's edition.) Even-Shoshan, in his *Concordance*, also gives the definition דִּבּוּר.

9 See BDB, p. 184. BDB indicates the parallel to שִׂפְתוֹתַיִךְ (your lips).

10 HALOT, p. 547. (This dictionary also cites the orthographic form מדבריך).

11 See the next footnote.

12 Ben Yehuda 1960: 2795 gives the definition דִּבּוּר "speech" but comments "most of the modern [scholars] explain this word to have the meaning 'speech organs,' i.e. 'the mouth'." The editor rejects this explanation, however, strangely claiming that "after describing the lips there is no need to describe the mouth." If that is the case, all parallels present difficulties. The editor ends his comment by saying that "the early [scholars] explain this word to have the meaning 'speech' and this [meaning] has spread throughout the literature."

13 Clearly, we need not take from parallelism more than it contains. For example, in the verse מֵסִיר שָׂפָה לְנֶאֱמָנִים, וְטַעַם זְקֵנִים יִקָּח "The confident he deprives of speech, takes away the reason of elders' (Job 12:20). Some explained this verse as referring to the removal of language, i.e. the power of speech from the נֶאֱמָנִים "confident", the meaning here is that the נֶאֱמָנִים

§ 6 There are also synonyms that do not appear in parallel hemistiches of one verse but rather in two parallel verses from different portions of the Bible while having an identical or very similar structure. Such a case is the verb שָׁמַר with the meaning 'remember' in a few Biblical verses, for example in the fourth commandment in the two parallel versions of the Decalogue; זָכוֹר את יום השבת לקדשו "Remember the Sabbath day to sanctify it" (Exodus 20:8) as opposed to שָׁמוֹר את יום השבת לקדשו "Observe the Sabbath day to keep it holy" (Deuteronomy 5:12). The Rabbis gave a beautiful homiletic commentary to this parallel: "Remember" and "Observe" were both spoken at one utterance (Mekhilta de-Rabbi Ishmael, BaHodesh § 7).[14] However, the Biblical text is to be understood according to its plain meaning. From this parallelism we learn that there are verses in the Bible wherein the meaning of שָׁמַר is "remember" (namely: שָׁמוֹר את יום השבת לקדשו "*Remember* the Sabbath day to keep it holy"). From this we can understand the verse וְאָבִיו שָׁמַר אֶת הַדָּבָר "and his father שָׁמַר the matter" (Genesis 37:11) which is said of Jacob after he hears Joseph's dreams, which should be understood as "his father remembered the dreams."[15]

§ 7 As is well known, from two parallel verses not in the same context but expressing the same content and having a similar structure we can understand many words and expressions. For example, by comparing the two clauses לֹא תַחְמֹד בֵּית רֵעֶךָ "don't covet your fellow's house" (Exodus 20:14) and לֹא תִתְאַוֶּה בֵּית רֵעֶךָ "you shall not covet your neighbor's house" (Deuteron-

---

here are הנואמים, i.e. "the speakers"; נֶאֱמָן here is a noun in the nominal pattern *pa'lān* with the root נ-א-ם and not the participle of the root א-מ-ן in the *Nif'al* stem. If that is the case, this would be a new noun to add to what is thought to be the only noun in Biblical Hebrew in the nominal pattern *pa'lān* – רַחֲמָנִיּוֹת "kindly [women]" (Lamentations 4:10). However, this insightful suggestion is not supported by the parallelism. While the verbs מֵסִיר and יִקָּח in the parallel hemistiches are equivalent in meaning, this is not the case with the nouns נֶאֱמָנִים (= speakers) and זְקֵנִים. In fact, this is an example of complimentary parallelism and not synonymous parallelism (See Hakham 1970 *ad loc.*, with n. 20b). I am not entirely convinced by Hakham's reasoning, but as I have already said, we need not take from parallelism more than it contains.

14 See Horovitz and Rabin, 229. Rashi quotes this homily but changes the order of the words in his commentary to Exodus 20:7; in his commentary to Deuteronomy 5:19 he quotes the original and adds: "both [words] were spoken in one utterance and in one word and were heard together." What did Rashi mean by his addition? Could he have meant that זָכוֹר and שָׁמוֹר are two words that are one in respect of their meaning? It is hard to say.

15 Especially appropriate is Rashi's comment on this verse: "He awaited the matter with anticipation for when it would be fulfilled". Is it possible to understand from this comment that the verb שָׁמַר is to be understood 'remembered the dream and awaited with anticipation its fulfillment'? If so, then my explanation has been anticipated by Rashi, but I fear that I may be looking in his words for what is missing.

omy 5:18), we can understand that from the point of view of the verse in Deuteronomy, חָמַד and הִתְאַוָּה have the same meaning. From two verses with a similar structure and content we can understand that נִשְׁבַּע בְּשֵׁם and נָשָׂא שֵׁם have the same meaning. This is clear from the verses: לֹא תִשָּׂא אֶת שֵׁם ה' אֱלֹהֶיךָ לַשָּׁוְא "Don't raise God's name for nothing" (Exodus 20:7), וְלֹא תִשָּׁבְעוּ בִשְׁמִי לַשָּׁקֶר "And you shall not swear falsely by my name" (Leviticus 19:12). Onkelos, for example, translates לֹא תִשָּׂא אֶת שֵׁם ה' as לָא תֵימֵי בִשְׁמָא דה' (Do not swear in the Lord's name). This is similar to the translation וְלָא תִשְׁתַּבְעוּן בִּשְׁמִי of the words וְלֹא תִשָּׁבְעוּ בִשְׁמִי from the aforementioned verse in Leviticus.

§ 8 Certainly, the use of different words, one Hebrew and one foreign, in parallel verses in contexts far removed from each other in the Biblical text is also a known phenomenon. For example, when the reader encounters the unusual word פַּדָּן, like in the verse אֲשֶׁר רָכַשׁ בְּפַדַּן אֲרָם "[the property in his possession] that he had acquired in *Paddan-Aram*" (Genesis 31:18),[16], the Bible provides the explanation in another context. The verses state קום לך פַּדֶּנָה ארם [...] וילך פַּדֶּנָה ארם [...] וְשִׁלַּח אתו פַּדֶּנָה ארם "Go at once to Paddan -aram ... and he went to Paddan-aram ... he sent him to Paddan-aram" (Genesis 28:2, 5–6). Already at the beginning of this portion of the narrative, the action of "going" is called "flight": וְקוּם בְּרַח לְךָ אֶל לָבָן אָחִי חָרָנָה "flee at once to my brother Laban in Haran" (Genesis 27:43). The narrative of Jacob's flight is echoed in another story in the Bible: וַיִּבְרַח יַעֲקֹב שְׂדֵה (אֲרָם) "Jacob fled to the field of Aram" (Hosea 12:13). We learn from this that פַּדַּן (ארם) in Genesis is expressed as שְׂדֵה (ארם) in the language of Hosea.[17] Hence, שָׂדֶה and פַּדָּן are synonyms in Biblical Hebrew.[18]

3.2.2 The Explicit Suggestion of the Explanation

§ 9 In addition to parallelism in the same verse or parallel verses in different contexts as already mentioned, sometimes two words appear in the same

---

16 This noun occurs 11 times in the Bible – only in the book of Genesis. 10 times it comes in *status constructus* in the phrase פַּדַּן אֲרָם, including with *he locale* פַּדֶּנָה אֲרָם, except in the final occurrence in Genesis. In this case without the *nomen rectum* (48:7).

17 In cognate languages the noun פַּדָּן has different meanings: "garden," "field," "yoke," "span of oxen" (see BDB and HALOT in this entry).

18 In Arabic the meaning of فدان is 'a sown field'. I wish to point out that the meaning "field" for the noun فدان is the meaning that I have known since my youth from both the Jewish and Muslim dialects of Moroccan Arabic. This noun signifies especially "a field for growing cereal grains." This meaning is brought by Georges Sêraphin Colin in his dictionary (see Sinaceur 1993:6.1431).

context – one word more common than the other, or a common word that appears in parallel to a common word with a rare meaning, or a Hebrew word or expression in parallel to a foreign word or expression – and from the parallelism in context the meaning becomes apparent without need of external commentary. I shall bring two examples and offer some short comments.

§ 10 A well known example of this phenomenon is the explanation given for the two Aramaic words in Genesis וַיִּקְחוּ אֲבָנִים וַיַּעֲשׂוּ גָל [...] וַיִּקְרָא לוֹ לָבָן יְגַר שָׂהֲדוּתָא וְיַעֲקֹב קָרָא לוֹ גַּלְעֵד "They got stones and made a mound ... Laban named it *Y^e^gar-sāh^a^ḏūṯā*, but Jacob called it *Gal'ēḏ*." (Genesis 31:46–47). The Hebrew noun גַּלְעֵד (which is a compound word made of גַּל "mound" and עֵד "testimony"), clarifies the parallel Aramaic expression יְגַר שָׂהֲדוּתָא. The Aramaic יְגַר is semantically equivalent to Hebrew גַּל, and שָׂהֲדוּתָא is equivalent to עֵד.

§ 11 It is important to note that this example also shows how two phrases can be mutually illuminating. Biblical Hebrew עֵד usually means "witness, one who gives testimony," for example in the verse לֹא יָקוּם עֵד אֶחָד בְּאִישׁ "A single witness may not validate against a person" (Deuteronomy 19:15). It does, however, also refer to "testimony," as earlier scholars understood in some Biblical verses. For example, Onkelos translates the phrase עֵד שָׁקֶר in the verse לֹא תַעֲנֶה בְרֵעֲךָ עֵד שָׁקֶר "Don't testify against your fellow as a false witness" (Exodus 20:13) as סָהֲדוּתָא דִשְׁקְרָא (false testimony). The Peshitta also translates this way – סָהדותָא דַגָלתָא. Other occurrences of the noun עֵד are translated this way in the Peshitta: the expression יְבִאֵהוּ עֵד "let him bring it, evidence" (Exodus 22:12) is translated into Syriac as ונַיתֵוהי לסָהדותָא. The verse וְהָיָה לְאוֹת וּלְעֵד לַה' צְבָאוֹת "It will serve as a sign and testimony to the Lord of hosts" (Isaiah 19:20), as well, is translated in the Peshitta as ותהוא לאָתָא ולסָהדותָא למריא חילתנא. We can add our verse from Genesis 31 to this evidence, since Aramaic שָׂהֲדוּתָא means "testimony." Therefore, both גַּלְעֵד and יְגַר שָׂהֲדוּתָא should be understood as "The Hill of Testimony."[19]

§ 12 Similarly, there is the case of a Hebrew word which is used in one chapter in the Bible with an unusual meaning. 1 Samuel 9:9 reads כֹּה אָמַר

---

19 There are other participial forms which function as verbal nouns or as abstract nouns. For example, the participle פּוֹתֵחַ in the common Mishnaic phrase פּוֹתֵחַ טֶפַח (for example in Shabbat 24:5; Ohalot 3:7) means 'the opening of one square handbreath'. Another example would be the word עָז in the expression יתר שְׂאֵת ויתר עָז "Exceeding in rank and exceeding in honor!" (Genesis 49:3); עָז is equivalent to עֹז, in the same position as שְׂאֵת in the first portion of the expression. Similarly the form קַל in the expression קַל וָחוֹמֶר, which is equal to קֹל like in the expression קוֹל וָחוֹמֶר which appears in reliable manuscripts of Mishnaic Hebrew (see Kutscher 1972b:32-33), and see additional material and a short discussion of this phenomenon in Bar-Asher 2009a:169–170.

הָאִישׁ בְּלֶכְתּוֹ לִדְרוֹשׁ אֱת אֱלֹהִים: "לְכוּ וְנֵלְכָה עַד הָרֹאֶה" – כִּי לַנָּבִיא הַיּוֹם יִקָּרֵא לְפָנִים הָרֹאֶה "Formerly in Israel when a man went to inquire of God, he said, 'Come let us go to the seer!' For someone who would be called today the prophet was formerly called the seer". The word הָרֹאֶה appears a number of times in this story (in verses 11, 18 and 19 of this chapter) but since it is not used in its usual meaning, it is explained after the first occurrence in verse 9.

In these two examples the clarification of the word in question is explicit. The first example involves translation between two languages. In the second example the Bible gives the reader a diachronic lexical definition; a short lesson, as it was, in the history of the Hebrew language.

3.2.3 The Use of an Explanatory Word or Expression

§ 13 I shall now present examples of a different kind and analyze them. I have already shown elsewhere that the Bible sometimes employs partially concealed explanatory language (or to be more exact: partially revealed explanatory language) while explaining itself in context. I am referring to my study of the meaning of the word יָדִיד in the Bible. In one place the Bible explains this word, without explicitly stating that it does so. When this noun appears in the context of Solomon's names, the author of the text shows from context that יָדִיד means "beloved."[20] The text explicitly states ויקרא את שמו יְדִידְיָהּ[21] בַּעֲבוּר ה' "he was to be called Yedidyah by the grace of God" (2 Samuel 12:25). In the preceding verse, while presenting the other name, Solomon, which is the more common name of יְדִידְיָהּ, even before the less common name is mentioned, it states וַיִּקְרָא את שְׁמוֹ שְׁלֹמֹה וה' אֲהֵבוֹ "He called him Solomon and God loved him" (2 Samuel 12:24). The verse explicitly states that God loves him, implying that יְדִידְיָהּ is a child "beloved of God." I already showed that nearly all of the early commentators understood יָדִיד to mean "beloved."[22]

§ 14 A similar example to what has been said about יְדִידְיָהּ can be found in a text about sacrifices. The verse states זאת תּוֹרַת הָעֹלָה הִיא הָעֹלָה על מוקדה על המזבח כל הלילה עד הבקר ואש המזבח תוקד בו "This is the ritual for the

---

20 See Chapter Two § 11 above.

21 The name יְדִידְיָהּ also appears without the *mappiq:* יְדִידְיָה (see ibid., n. 40).

22 The authorities who explain יָדִיד to mean 'beloved' appear in §§ 3–14 of the aforementioned study (It can be clearly seen that the number of authorities not explaining יָדִיד as 'beloved' is negligible). In the discussion in Chapter Two above, I explain why I prefer to vocalize this word as יָדִיד (and not יְדִיד) in the absolute state (see the summary in § 32 there).

burnt offering – that is, the burnt offering which stays on the altar hearth all night until the morning, while the altar fire is kept burning on it." (Leviticus 6:2). There is a difference of opinion as to the etymology of the noun עוֹלָה[23] (*'ōlā*), which signifies the type of sacrifice. Some derive עוֹלָה from the root ע-ל-י, with the basic meaning of "to ascending" (equivalent to Aramaic ס-ל-ק). BDB and HALOT state this explicitly.[24] However, some derive this noun from the root ע-ל-י with the Hebrew consonant *'ayin* as representing a voiced velar fricative (ɣ) corresponding to the Arabic غ, with the meaning "cook, boil," like in the Arabic root غلي. This opinion was recently cited by Kaddari in his dictionary.[25] What has not been noted is that in context, the Bible explains the meaning of עוֹלָה as "a sacrifice burnt on the altar throughout the night until entirely consumed." This is reflected in the verse concerning the sacrifice of Aaron and his sons כָּלִיל תָּקְטָר,[26] כָּלִיל תִּהְיֶה לֹא תֵאָכֵל "it shall entirely go up in smoke ... shall be a total offering; it shall not be eaten." (Leviticus 6:15–16). It may well be that the verse זֹאת תּוֹרַת הָעֹלָה הִוא הָעֹלָה (Lev 6:2) reflects a folk

23 Henceforth the noun עֹלָה will be written with *plene* spelling (עוֹלָה).

24 See BDB p. 750 which mentions explicitly the notion of "ascending." HALOT also derives עוֹלָה from the root ע-ל-י and mentions as a possibility Koehler's opinion that עוֹלָה is "probably an abbreviation for מִנְחַת עוֹלָה 'tribute rising (in the fire)'". There is a similar, interesting remark in a homiletical interpretation of the Sages: "If the altar has not acquired the right to the flesh of an offering the priests have not acquired the right to its hide, for it is written, *A man's whole offering* (Leviticus 7:8) – a Whole-offering (עוֹלָה) that has been offered up (שֶׁעָלַת, in the printed editions שעלתה) for a man ... although it does not count (שֶׁלֹּא עָלַת, in the printed editions שלא עלתה) to its owner [in fulfillment of his obligation]" (m. Zebahim 12:2). The Mishnah clearly states that the noun עוֹלָה is an inflected form of עָלָה ('to ascend'). Also worthy of note is the statement in the Babylonian Talmud (Zebahim 27b): "From the phrase, '*the law of the burnt-offering*', which intimates one law for all burnt-offerings: if they ascended, they do not descend." Rashi there comments "... because this verse comes to teach us that disqualified offerings, once they have ascended to the altar they do not descend. We derive this from the verse (Leviticus 7:2) the *burnt offering that stays on the altar hearth all night* (implying) once it has ascended to the altar let it remain there all night." The Talmud follows the wording of the verse that the offering called עוֹלָה is called thus since it ascends (עוֹלֶה) to the altar.

25 See Kaddari p. 801. He adds the definition "it ascends 'burnt by fire' as the burnt offering."

26 It is interesting to note that the two nouns עוֹלָה and כָּלִיל come together in the same syntactical position: ויעלהו עוֹלָה כָּלִיל לה' "offered it whole as a holocaust to God" (1 Samuel 7:9), אז תחפץ זבחי צדק עוֹלָה וְכָלִיל, אז יעלו על מזבחך פרים "Then will you wish legitimate sacrifices, holocaust and whole offering; Then will young bulls mount your altar." (Psalms 51:21). See below in § 15.

etymology, equating the עוֹלָה sacrifice with the participle עוֹלָה "ascending."[27] Indeed, the following verse states explicitly וְהֵרִים אֶת הַדֶּשֶׁן אֲשֶׁר תֹּאכַל הָאֵשׁ אֶת הָעוֹלָה עַל הַמִּזְבֵּחַ (Lev 6:3).

§ 15 À propos the aforementioned explanation, a study of synonyms that appear in succession in the same clause while in the same syntactic position and having the same syntactic function should be undertaken. This matter requires comprehensive study since the appearance of synonyms in pairs could be the result of various factors. For example, when the author of the text chose the pairs of synonyms שֵׁם and זֵכֶר, עוֹלָה and כָּלִיל in the verses לְשִׁמְךָ וּלְזִכְרְךָ תַּאֲוַת נָפֶשׁ "To invoke your name is the soul's desire" (Isaiah 26:8)[28] or אָז תַּחְפֹּץ זִבְחֵי צֶדֶק עוֹלָה וְכָלִיל "Then will you wish legitimate sacrifices, holocaust and whole offering" (Psalms 51:21), and chose to connect them by means of a *wāw*, he probably intended to stress the meaning of one noun by having it appear together with its synonym. Perhaps this is also the case in the verse וַיַּעֲלֵהוּ עוֹלָה כָּלִיל לה' "offered it whole as a holocaust to God" (1 Samuel 7:9) even though the *wāw* is absent. On the other hand, in some instances one of the synonyms is in Aramaic or is a rare word. For example, in the verses בָּרְהָטִים בְּשִׁקֲתוֹת הַמָּיִם "in troughs – the water receptacles" (Genesis 30:38), אז חֻלַּק עַד שָׁלָל[29] מַרְבֶּה "then is the prey of a great spoil divided" (Isaiah 33:23). One of the nouns in these pairs is probably an explanatory gloss. The first word of each pair is either in Aramaic (רְהָטִים[30]) or is a rare Hebrew word (עַד[31]) while the second word is a common Hebrew word (שִׁקֲתוֹת המים and שָׁלָל). Other factors may have influenced the choice of words, but more study is needed.

3.2.4 Explanatory Words in Similar Structures

§ 16 Another example of one word explaining another in the same context is evident in the case of a common word occurring in the same context

27 If we accept Kaddari's opinion that the noun הָעוֹלָה and the participle הָעוֹלָה that qualifies it (in verse 2) are derived from two different roots, then the explanation seems to reflect popular etymology. However, if the noun and the participle are derived from the same root (ע-ל-י with the standard *'ayin* having the connotation "ascend"), as brought in BDB and HALOT, then the verse does not reflect popular etymology.

28 See above § 4.

29 As is well known, in the Blessings of Jacob the nouns עַד and שָׁלָל appear in parallel hemistiches of the same verse: בַּבֹּקֶר יֹאכַל עַד וְלָעֶרֶב יְחַלֵּק שָׁלָל "Mornings he devours the prey, And evenings he distributes the spoils." (Genesis 49:27).

30 רְהָטִים is a noun derived from the Aramaic root ר-ה-ט (cognate of the Hebrew ר-ו-ץ), but its form – the plural pattern פְּעָלִים – is Hebrew.

31 The Hebrew noun עַד has been shown to have parallel forms in Targumic and Galillean Aramaic (see Kaddari in entry עַד II p. 774).

with a rare synonym in similar or identical structures. I shall analyze three interesting examples.

§ 17 The noun עֶלֶם is rare in the Bible, appearing only twice, and only in the book of Samuel: וַיֹּאמֶר הַמֶּלֶךְ שְׁאַל אַתָּה: בֶּן מִי זֶה הָעָלֶם "The king said: Then inquire whose son the youth is" (1 Samuel 17:56), and וְאִם כֹּה אֹמַר לָעֶלֶם: הִנֵּה הַחִצִּים מִמְּךָ וָהָלְאָה "But if I say to the lad, The arrow is on the far side of you!" (1 Samuel 20:22).[32] In both of these instances appear verses parallel to the aforementioned examples with nearly identical structures.

(A) Before the verse containing the word עֶלֶם (1 Samuel 17:56) the text reads וְכִרְאוֹת שָׁאוּל אֶת דָּוִד [...] אָמַר אֶל אַבְנֵר [...]: בֶּן מִי זֶה הַנַּעַר "When Saul saw David ... he said to Abner ... Whose son is that lad?" (v. 55). In a later verse, the text reads וַיֹּאמֶר אֵלָיו שָׁאוּל: בֶּן מִי אַתָּה הַנָּעַר "Saul asked him: Whose son are you, lad?" (ibid 58). In these three verses Saul poses the same question. The first two times it is addressed to Abner, and in the third to David. In all three verses the questions are similar or identical in all respects, excluding the last word in the second question: בֶּן מִי זֶה הַנַּעַר, בֶּן מִי אַתָּה הָעָלֶם, בֶּן מִי זֶה הַנָּעַר. The use of the word נַעַר in verse 55 clarifies the word עֶלֶם in the following verse (56). The text then reverts to נַעַר in v. 58.

(B) Something similar is true regarding the second example, וְאִם כֹּה אֹמַר לָעֶלֶם: הִנֵּה הַחִצִּים מִמְּךָ וָהָלְאָה "But if I say to the lad, The arrow is on the far side of you!" (2 Sam 20:22). Preceding this verse is a nearly identical one: אִם אָמֹר אֹמַר לַנַּעַר, הִנֵּה הַחִצִּים מִמְּךָ וָהֵנָּה "if I say to him The arrow is on the near side of you!" (v. 21). Here too the word לַנַּעַר in verse 21 clarifies the meaning of לָעֶלֶם in the following verse. Some may try to see in thrice-mentioned question in chapter 17, and in the parallelism of chapter 20, evidence for parallel versions which served as sources for the text's editor and not as statements pronounced multiple times from the outset. Even were one to make such a claim, justified or not, this does not take away from the fact that in the Biblical text, in its present form, common words clarify rare words.

§ 18 This is also the case concerning the feminine form עַלְמָה in the narrative of Rebecca being taken by Abraham's servant to be his son's bride in Genesis. The noun עַלְמָה is not a common word in the Bible. It occurs only

32 Some claim to have recognized a third occurrence of the noun עֶלֶם in the narratives of David in the book of Samuel: the problematic verse, describing David as a young man, says וְהוּא אַדְמוֹנִי עִם יְפֵה עֵינַיִם וְטוֹב רֹאִי "he was ruddy and attractive, with (עִם) handsome to the eye and of good appearance" (1 Samuel 16:12). The suggested reading is וְהוּא אַדְמֹנִי עֶלֶם יְפֵה עֵינַיִם וְטוֹב רֹאִי (cf. HALOT s.v. עֶלֶם, p. 835, end). This is a sharp suggestion, but remains a conjectural reading and not a linguistic fact.

seven times. Its synonym נַעֲרָה,[33] however, occurs a total of sixty-three times. In its first appearance in the singular form in the Bible, נַעֲרָה occurs four times in Genesis 24 (vv. 14, 16, 28, 55). In his prayer, Abraham's servant asks והיה הַנַּעֲרָה אֲשֶׁר אֹמַר אֵלֶיהָ הַטִּי נָא כַדֵּךְ וְאֶשְׁתֶּה וְאָמְרָה שְׁתֵה וְגַם גְּמַלֶּיךָ אַשְׁקֶה "let the girl to whom I say 'Please lower your jug that I may drink' and who answers 'Drink, and I will also give water to your camels!'" (Genesis 24:14). However, when he meets with her family and speaks with them he says וְהָיָה הָעַלְמָה הַיֹּצֵאת לִשְׁאֹב וְאָמַרְתִּי אֵלֶיהָ: 'הַשְׁקִינִי נָא מְעַט מַיִם מִכַּדֵּךְ'. וְאָמְרָה אֵלַי: 'גַּם אַתָּה שְׁתֵה וְגַם לִגְמַלֶּיךָ אֶשְׁאָב'. "let the young woman who comes out to draw water, to whom I say, 'Please give me a little water from your jug,' and who answers, 'Not only may you drink, but I will also water your camels'" (vv. 43–44). Rebecca is referred to as הַנַּעֲרָה three times in the narrative (in verses 14, 15 and 28), but the fourth time as הָעַלְמָה (in verse 43). Clearly, the meaning of the word הָעַלְמָה is made plain from the context by the use of its more common synonym הַנַּעֲרָה in parallel.

§ 19 The third example that I wish to present is also from the book of Genesis. The text refers to Ishmael and states וַיְהִי אֱלֹהִים אֶת הַנַּעַר וַיִּגְדָּל, וַיֵּשֶׁב בַּמִּדְבָּר וַיְהִי רֹבֶה קַשָּׁת "God was with the boy as he grew up. He lived in the desert and became a young man, an archer." (Genesis 21:20). In the first part of the verse (as in verses 12, 17 [twice], 18 and 19) Ishmael is called הַנַּעַר while in the second part he is called רוֹבֶה.[34] רוֹבֶה is a *hapax legomenon* and appears only in this instance. In this case, too, the Biblical verse explains itself: Ishmael is first called נַעַר and then afterwards רוֹבֶה. Thus, נַעַר and רוֹבֶה have the same meaning.

§ 20 Indeed, many of the early exegetes also understood רוֹבֶה in this way. For example, Onqelos translated וַיְהִי רֹבֶה קַשָּׁת as וַהֲוָה רָבֵי (רָבְיָא) קַשָּׁתָא. The Aramaic words רָבֵי/רָבְיָא mean "lad." Similarly Saadia Gaon translated וכאן ג'לאם ראם. The Vulgate gives the translation "iuvenis sagittarius". This is also implied in the words of the Midrash in Bereshit Rabbah (LIII 15) ויהי רבה קשת ... רבה (= רוֹבֶה) [הוא] מתלמד בקשת "And [he] became an archer ... while a lad (רובה), a trainee in the use of the bow." The midrash takes מתלמד as a reflexive verb, so רובה קשת means a lad who trained himself in archery.

§ 21 The word רוֹבֶה is rare not only in the Bible but also in the Mishnah. It occurs only once in the Mishnah as the plural form רוֹבִים: וְהָרוֹבִים שׁוֹמְרִים שָׁם

---

33 As is well known, in most of its occurrences in the Pentateuch this word, in its singular form, is written defectively, without *he*: נער/הנער. This form reflects the ancient use of נַעַר as referring to both masculine and feminine genders. In only one occurrence in the Pentateuch this word is written *plene* (נערה), in Deuteronomy 22:19. The *plene* form is used throughout the rest of the Bible. However, there are distinct plural forms for the masculine and feminine, even in the Pentateuch; נְעָרִים for masculine: הַנְּעָרִים "the boys" (Genesis 14:24; 25:27), and נְעָרוֹת for feminine: וְנַעֲרֹתֶיהָ "and her maids" (Genesis 24:61; Exodus 2:5).

34 Henceforth I shall bring this word with *plene* spelling.

"and there the young men kept watch" (Tamid 1:1). The "young men" (רוֹבִים) mentioned in the Mishnah are young priests who have not yet begun to perform the sacrificial service in the Temple. However, they served in the capacity of watchmen. The meaning of the word רוֹבֶה is clear;[35] this is the participle of the verb רָבָה, "grow." In other words, רוֹבֶה in Hebrew and רָבֵי in Aramaic mean "a growing child,"[36] that is a "youth."[37]

§ 22 One can not fail to notice the interesting phenomenon apparent from the three examples mentioned above. In all three narratives, the Biblical text initially employs a common word – נַעַר (1 Samuel 17:55), נַעֲרָה (Genesis 24:14, 16, 28), נַעַר (Genesis 21:12, 17–20). In the following verses a less common word is employed – עֶלֶם (1 Samuel 17:56), עַלְמָה (Genesis 24:43), רוֹבֶה (Genesis 21:20). In other words, once the reader knows who is the subject of the narrative, this character is first introduced in the text by a common and frequent word – נַעַר or נַעֲרָה – and afterwards, this same character is introduced in the text by a rare word – עֶלֶם, עַלְמָה, רוֹבֶה. The use of the rare word entails no difficulty because the subject of the narrative is known. Another linguistic point worthy of note is that in the first example, after the text uses the word עֶלֶם (1 Samuel 17:56) it reverts to the word נַעַר (1 Samuel 17:58). In the second example the text employs the word עַלְמָה (Genesis 24:43) but then reverts to נַעֲרָה (Genesis 24:55).

3.3 Conclusion

§ 23 I shall summarize the main points of this study.

A. Certainly, exegesis of the Bible based on parallelism, whether in one verse or in verses appearing in different contexts or even in different Biblical

35 The feminine form רוֹבָה (also רובא) has been preserved only in reliable manuscripts of Rabbinic literature. Less reliable manuscripts have the form ריבה which is a result of the *wāw* having been replaced by *yod* in error. See my article "On Words that have been Uprooted from Mishnaic Hebrew," in the *Festschrift* in honor of Dr. Yitzhak Sappir §§ 16–23 [in press].

36 It should be noted that a נַעַר is sometimes called יֶלֶד. For example, אַל יֵרַע בְּעֵינֶיךָ עַל הַנַּעַר "Do not be distressed about the boy," וַיִּתֵּן אֶל הָגָר שָׂם עַל שִׁכְמָהּ וְאֶת הַיֶּלֶד "and he gave to Hagar. He placed them on her back ... with the child," וַתַּשְׁלֵךְ אֶת הַיֶּלֶד "she abandoned the child," אַל אֶרְאֶה בְּמוֹת הַיָּלֶד "Let me not look on the child as he dies," וישמע אלהים את קול הנער [...] כִּי שָׁמַע אֱלֹהִים אֶל קוֹל הַנַּעַר "God heard the boy's cry ... for God has heard the cry of the boy" (Genesis 21:12, 14, 15, 16, 17).

37 Incidentally, some have interpreted the word רוֹבֶה in the phrase רוֹבֶה קַשָּׁת referring to Ishmael to mean 'an archer shooting arrows'. They understand the word רוֹבֶה to be derived from the root ר-ב-י, an alternate of the form derived from the root ר-ב-ב, also meaning "shoot." This meaning is reflected in the verse וַיְמָרְרֻהוּ וָרֹבּוּ וַיִּשְׂטְמֻהוּ בַּעֲלֵי חִצִּים "The archers have sorely grieved him, and shot at him, and hated him" (Genesis 49:23). Based on this

books, is a well known phenomenon. This study offers some comments (presented above in sections 3.2.1–3.2.2) that add to our understanding of this phenomenon and presents varied examples to show that the Bible interprets itself. These comments also serve as the basis for the exegetical remarks offered in the latter part of the study (sections 3.2.3–3.2.4).

B. Not in all places where I spoke of the act of explanation as an implicit action need we assume that this was the express intention of the author. The explanatory comment כִּי לַנָּבִיא הַיּוֹם יִקָּרֵא לְפָנִים הָרֹאֶה in the book of Samuel is not to be compared to the comment explaining the name וַיִּקְרָא – אֶת שְׁמוֹ יְדִידְיָהּ וה' אֲהֵבוֹ in the same book. Neither are the clarified words in these verses to be compared to the use of the synonyms נַעַר and עֶלֶם which also appear in the very same book.[38] In the first example it is clear that when the text states that the נָבִיא was formerly referred to as רוֹאֶה, this is an intentional explanatory remark.[39] However, in the second example, the use of the expression וה' אֲהֵבוֹ to clarify the name יְדִידְיָהּ is less direct yet still clear. In the third example, the positioning of עֶלֶם in parallel to נַעַר in similar or identical syntactical structures can be considered a stylistic device with the exegetical aspect expressed unintentionally. In our case, all of the types mentioned herein lead to one conclusion: the Bible interprets its own words and this phenomenon takes on different forms in the various books of the biblical canon. That is the main point that I wished to present in this study.

C. I have amassed additional information on this subject over the years. However, I have decided to limit the presentation to the examples brought here. The important point is not the number of examples but rather the phenomenon itself. My intention in this study was to present the phenomenon by means of various examples and to provide a short discussion of those examples. The many additional examples that I have amassed reflect different aspects of this phenomenon[40] that are worthy of discussion in

understanding of the form וָרֹבוּ, the word רוֹבֶה has come to mean a type of firearm in Modern Hebrew (see § 23 footnote 35 in the aforementioned article).

38 It should be noted that many important and interesting linguistic issues lie hidden in the book of Samuel.

39 This can also be said of parallel hemistiches in the same verse. Similarly, the use of a pair of synonyms, with one appearing in the first hemistich and the other in the second, can be considered an intentional explanatory note.

40 One of the additional aspects of the Bible interpreting its own words is when the meaning of words in context is expressed implicitly, or nearly explicitly, and the Biblical text uses two or three times a word with two meanings or uses two homonyms. In this case, the Biblical text will sometimes employ explanatory words to clarify the uncommon word or meaning. A well known example of this aspect is from the book of Numbers (15:38–39). The Biblical text employs the word צִיצִת with two different meanings: (A) tassel: וְעָשׂוּ לָהֶם צִיצִת עַל כַּנְפֵי

their own right. I hope to present these at a later occasion. In conclusion, I wish to state that not every comment on a Biblical word is linguistic in nature. Sometimes the clarification of a word comes to clarify the content of the text.[41]

בִּגְדֵיהֶם ... וְנָתְנוּ עַל צִיצִת הַכָּנָף "when they fashion tassels for themselves on the corner of their garments ... they must join ... to the tassels, at each corner.", similarly, וַיִּקָּחֵנִי בְּצִיצִת רֹאשִׁי "seized me by a lock of my hair" [Ezekiel 8:3]; (B) something that protrudes and is visible: וְהָיָה לָכֶם לְצִיצִת וּרְאִיתֶם אֹתוֹ "It shall serve you as a visible garment, and when you see it ...". The text in Numbers 15 employs צִיצִת twice with one meaning (tassel), and afterwards employs the word with its other meaning (something visible). Having done so, the text adds an explanatory gloss to the second meaning – וּרְאִיתֶם אֹתוֹ. This gloss draws the reader's attention to the new meaning (see the commentaries of Rashi and Rashbam loc. cit.). This is also the case in the verse ,וַיְהִי לוֹ שְׁלֹשִׁים בָּנִים רֹכְבִים עַל שְׁלֹשִׁים עֲיָרִים; וּשְׁלֹשִׁים עֲיָרִים לָהֶם לָהֶם יִקְרְאוּ חַוֹּת יָאִיר "Now he had thirty 'sons' who rode thirty donkeys. Thirty towns belonged to them. Their towns are called Havvoth-Yair" (Judges 10:4). The verse twice employs the word עֲיָרִים but these are two completely different words. In the first instance עֲיָרִים is the plural form of the word עַיִר 'male donkey'; in the second instance it is the plural form of the word עִיר ('a small village'. עֲיָרִים is an alternate form of עָרִים in Biblical Hebrew and of עֲיָרוֹת in Rabbinic Hebrew). When the text employed the second meaning, it added an explanatory gloss (חַוֹּת יאיר). These two examples were cited and interpreted by David Yellin and explained by him (Yellin 1972– vol. 8, pp. 280–282, as well as other examples on pp. 272–273 and 281). These are only a few examples of another aspect of the Bible explaining itself. As stated, there are additional examples of additional aspects.

41 Even so, not included is another type that clarifies the content and even has a poetic element but does not include an explanation of a word or expression. I am referring to an interesting example brought by S.D. Luzzatto 1871. The verse states ,כִּי יַבְעֶר אִישׁ שָׂדֶה אוֹ כֶרֶם וְשִׁלַּח אֶת בְּעִירֹה (בְּעִירוֹ) וּבִעֵר בִּשְׂדֵה אַחֵר "When a man clears a field or vineyard, and he releases his cattle and it clears in another's field" (Exodus 22:4). Luzzatto says that the clause וְשִׁלַּח אֶת בְּעִירֹה וּבִעֵר בִּשְׂדֵה אַחֵר explains the general rule כי יַבְעֶר אִישׁ שָׂדֶה אוֹ כֶרֶם which appears at the beginning of the verse. The act of destruction which is stated generally is specified as having been carried out by an animal that performed the damage. Luzzatto 1965 explains that [the verse] "states בְּעִירוֹ to act as a pun with the expression כי יַבְעֶר and the expression וּבִעֵר and these verses where said as a kind of poem in order that they should be impressed upon the minds of simple people. Similarly, the text states below ,וְחָדַלְתָּ מֵעֲזֹב לוֹ עָזֹב תַּעֲזֹב עִמּוֹ "and [you] would refrain from leaving (it) to him, you must help, help (it) with him." (Exodus 23:5). Indeed, this comment does employ the use of two close roots: (A) ב-ע-ר meaning 'destruction', (B) ב-ע-ר from which is derived the noun בְּעִיר ("an animal"). While the clarification of the general rule by the detail explains the content of the verse, it does not explain any word and is only a stylistic device. Luzzatto correctly brought a similar example of this stylistic device: the use of the two verbs עָזַב, once meaning "to abandon" and once meaning "to aid" in Exodus 23:5. Here also, no word is explained. I also wish to mention Abraham Kariv's important study (above, n. 1).

4 Gesenius' *Thesaurus* and Mishnaic Hebrew Studies

4.1 Introductory Remarks

§ 1 Without a doubt, the modern era of research into biblical Hebrew is tied up with the immense work of Wilhelm Gesenius, both in grammar and lexicography. Prior to his time, the medieval Jewish scholars had made much progress in the study of biblical Hebrew, and Gesenius used this accumulated knowledge, especially as found in the works of R. David Qimhi (Radaq) to great benefit in his grammar and his dictionaries. By Gesenius' time, great strides had been made also in the study of other Semitic languages, and these too were utilized profitably in his works – especially in his dictionaries, and most especially in his great *Thesaurus*. He paid particular attention to comparisons with Aramaic, which was then called (by Gesenius, as well) "Chaldean." The Aramaic data was drawn from the Targumim, the Talmudim, and the Midrashim, in the printed editions then in circulation, as well as many citations from Syriac, which was already a well-studied language.

§ 2 Undoubtedly, Gesenius paid careful attention to findings regarding Mishnaic Hebrew and utilized this information in all of his books – his dictionaries, his grammar, and his book on the history of the Hebrew language. For him this was reasonable, since he believed that a significant amount of the ancient Hebrew lexicon from biblical times was preserved only in rabbinic literature, and especially in the Mishnah. He believed this to be true especially in fields such as names of animals and plants, words such as אגס, חרדל, דלעת, and חזרת. In his view, these words were very ancient, and are only accidentally not preserved in earlier biblical language and instead make their first appearances in the Mishnah.[1] He also drew attention to linguistic phenomena whose origins were in the spoken language in biblical times, which were well preserved in Mishnaic Hebrew that their traces were found in the Bible, such as the particles שֶׁ and שֶׁל.[2] In the introduction to the second edition of his German dictionary,[3] he speaks explicitly of the biblical lexemes whose meanings can be ascertained with the help of Mishnaic Hebrew, such as

1 Cf. Gesenius 1815:52–53.
2 Cf. *ibid.*, p. 56.
3 Gesenius 1823:XXXI and n. 61.

אָבַס[4], אַשְׁפָּה[5], גִּבְעֹל[6], and more. The fact is that in his great Thesaurus there are a good number of citations of Mishnaic Hebrew, which he calls "Rabbinic [Hebrew]." There are, however, instances in which he suffices with a citation from Aramaic, omitting any mention of the Mishnaic data. Such is the case, for example, in the entry for בִּזָּיוֹן, in which he cited the Babylonian Aramaic cognate בזיונא but not its parallel from Mishnaic Hebrew.[7] Sometimes, Gesenius' discussion of details within an issue in biblical Hebrew foreshadows the findings of contemporary scholarship on Mishnaic Hebrew, although he did not intend these contributions and often did not make his points explicitly.

§ 3 As is known, research into Mishnaic Hebrew has made tremendous strides since the nineteenth century. The most dramatic changes in the field took place only in the twentieth century, due to the work of a few generations of researchers. The paradigm shift occurred under the watch of the first and second generation of scholars. In the realm of grammar, these were Moshe Zevi Segal and his incisive disputant Hanoch Yalon, followed by Yehezkel Kutscher and Zeev Ben-Ḥayyim. In the realm of lexicography, major achievements belonged to Jacob Nahum Epstein and his outstanding student, Saul Lieberman. Contributions of no lesser magnitude were made by Eliezer Ben-Yehuda and his collaborators on his dictionary. The concordance-writing Kasovsky family – the father Yaakov Hayyim and his sons Moshe and Binyamin – also contributed important work. After these, three generations of scholars arose who advanced our knowledge of Mishnaic Hebrew.[8]

§ 4 In this study I will concentrate on three issues relevant to Mishnaic Hebrew based on the three-volume *Thesaurus*, which is without a doubt Gesenius' most ambitious project and most impressive accomplishment. Occasionally I will make reference to other works of his, as has already been seen in the preceding and as will be seen below, and at times I will also refer to other lexicons in circulation today – especially BDB – with an eye to their relationship to Gesenius' work. This is not just to investigate the degree to which they

4 In fact, in the *Thesaurus* s. v. אָבַס (p. 17) a citation from the Mishnah is brought: אין אבסין את הגמל ולא דרסין אבל מלעיטין (m. Shabbat 24:3). Incidentally, Gesenius' practice in the *Thesaurus* is to cite active participles from biblical and post-biblical texts defectively, without a *vav*.

5 Included in the entry for שָׁפַת (*ibid.*, pp. 1470–1472) is the Mishnaic noun אַשְׁפָּה (p. 1471), and a number of Mishnaic sources are cited there, e.g., מכר את הָאַשְׁפָּה מכר זִבְלָהּ (m. Baba Batra 5:3).

6 In the entry גִּבְעֹל (*ibid.*, p. 201), he cites examples of this noun from Mishnah Parah (11:7; 11:9). At the very beginning of this entry, he mentions Radaq and J. Buxtorf by name.

7 See example A in § 13 below.

8 See Bar-Asher 2009a:1.58–75.

have remained loyal to or broken free of Gesenius' conclusions, but rather to show the degree to which the data he collected has provided the framework for all who worked after him. Clearly I will not be able to exhaust this topic here, and I will have to suffice with illustrative examples of the three issues.

§ 5 These are the issues I will discuss:

A. **Data in need of correction.** In some entries, Gesenius cites data from Mishnaic Hebrew, without citing specific sources, based on what he found in his predecessors such as Elia Levita (i.e., Eliyahu Bachur) and Johannes Buxtorf. Scholars have since found, however, that these data are sometimes inaccurate, at least in part. On occasion it can even be seen that in Gesenius' own day he could have prevented some of the inaccuracies had he checked the printed editions of the Mishnah in circulation then in Europe.
B. **Augmentation of incomplete data.** In some entries, Mishnaic Hebrew data is cited, but further facts can now be cited which flesh out and complete the picture.
C. **Early signs of MH scholarship.** In some entries Gesenius anticipates modern scholarship on Mishnaic Hebrew by more than a century. Although his primary concern was Biblical Hebrew, and most of his conclusions relate directly only to the Bible, they are sometimes valid also with regard to what is now known about Mishnaic Hebrew. In such cases, Gesenius can be said to prefigure such research by a number of generations.

4.2 Data in need of correction

§ 6 One who reads large sections of Gesenius' *Thesaurus* will find that there are entries in which Mishnaic Hebrew data is cited, but that the data is distorted and in need of correction. In the entry אִי (pp. 79–80), under which the *Thesaurus* cites the expressions אִי-נָקִי (Job 22:30), אִי-כָבוֹד (1 Samuel 4:21), the particle אִי is defined as an adverb and explained by Gesenius – as it was explained by a number of his medieval and early modern predecessors – as a negative particle. To buttress this interpretation he cites parallels from "Rabbinic" Hebrew: אִי אֶפְשַׁר, אִי הֶכְרֵחַ, and אִי אַתָּה יָכוֹל (these vocalizations are found in the *Thesaurus*). Immediately one recognizes that his category of Rabbinic Hebrew includes not only the language of the Mishnah, but much later strata, as well, since the phrase אִי הֶכְרֵחַ is attested only in very late sources, as will soon be seen.

§ 7 It should be noted that medieval sources, too, interpreted אִי as a negative particle, but they did not connect it to phrases in Mishnaic Hebrew.

Radaq, for example, presented two interpretations of this particle in both his *Sefer ha-Shorashim* (Book of Roots) and his commentary to 1 Samuel 4:21. The first interpretation cited for the particle in the phrase אִי-כָבוֹד is as a negative particle, and he glosses the phrase, אֵין כָּבוֹד "there is no honor."[9] Gesenius actually cites Radaq by name at the end of the entry, based on the latter's commentary on Samuel.[10] It is worth mentioning, too, that Gesenius' interpretation is still found in the BDB lexicon (including the citation of the phrase אִי אפשר). I will also point out that this interpretation of the particle in the expression אִי-נָקִי is one possibility found in Kaddari's dictionary,[11] and is the only possibility cited in Even-Shoshan's concordance.[12]

§ 8 One could quibble regarding the correct interpretation of the particle in the two biblical expressions mentioned, but the evidence from Mishnaic Hebrew is without any foundation, since the negative particle there is not אִי at all, but אֵי – the *aleph* is vocalized with a *tsere*: אֵי אפשר. In fact, this particle is simply a form of אֵין with the loss of the final *nun*, and the same is true in expressions such as אֵי אפשי, אֵי אתה, and more. Clearly Gesenius is not responsible for the citation of this mistaken form, since he relied on his predecessors for it. For example, Elia Levita in his *Sefer ha-Tishbi* cited the form with the same vocalization; he writes: "אִי is like אין, but it is [vocalized] with a *hiriq*, [the same] as in [the biblical expressions] אי כבוד and ימלט אי נקי. It is also proper to say אי אפשר with a *hiriq*, and those who pronounce it with a *tsere* are mistaken, for [pronounced that way] it means 'where'."[13] Buxtorf, too, vocalized אִי, in the expression אִי אפשר, with a *hiriq*.[14]

§ 9 Had Gesenius checked the vocalized Mishnayot in circulation in his time in Europe – such as the Amsterdam edition of 1644,[15] the Venice edition

9 See Radaq, *Sefer ha-Shorashim*, p. 11: אי כבוד ... its meaning is 'there is no honor', despite its being with a *hiriq*." Later, however, he proposes a second interpretation: "it is also possible to explain it ... like אַיֵּה 'where'." On the other hand, he interprets אִי in the expression אִי נָקִי as a noun – an island (or peninsula).

10 There, too, Radaq suggests the two interpretations found also in his *Sefer ha-Shorashim*, and Gesenius cites both.

11 Cf. Kaddari 2006:31.

12 Cf. Even-Shoshan 1988:44.

13 See Levita (1541:9). Dr. Michael Ryzhik pointed something interesting out to me: David de Pommes ("of the apples"), in his dictionary *Tsemah David* (Venice, 1587), who generally follows Eliyahu Bachur, vocalized אֵי אפשר (on p. 3b) with a *tsere* under the *aleph*.

14 See Buxtorf 1639 p. 39.

15 In this edition the expressions אי אפשי (5×), אי אפשר (4×), אי אתה (5×), and אי אתם (1×) were checked; all are vocalized with a *tsere*.

of 1706,[16] the Venice edition of 1737 (the first one vocalized by David Altaras),[17] and the Mantua edition of 1777[18] – he would have found that the particle אֵי was consistently[19] vocalized with a *tsere*.[20]

§ 10 A further incidental remark: the expression אֵי הכרח is not a phrase from Mishnaic Hebrew. Consulting the databases (Ma'agarim) of the Historical Dictionary of the Hebrew Language reveals that there is no attestation of the noun הֶכְרַח on its own until the eleventh century, and the expression אי הכרח does not appear in the archives at all. It appears only in later texts: it is found, for instance, in the work of Moses Zacuto (1625–1697) in his book קול הרמ"ז.[21] In his comments on Pesahim 5:9, he writes: דדלמא שאני הכי דאפשר בלא מקלות אבל אי הכרח "Perhaps here is different, since it is possible without sticks, but this is not certain (אבל אי הכרח) ...". It is impossible that from here the phrase found its way into Buxtorf's dictionary,[22] and from there into Gesenius' work, since קול הרמ"ז was published after Buxtorf's Dictionary. Buxtorf did not reveal where he took the phrase from or on what basis his corrupt vocalization הֶכְרַח rested. Clearly complaints cannot be lodged against a researcher like Gesenius, who cited the forms uncovered by others based on the works he had in front of him, especially if the authority on which he was relying was someone known to him to be generally reliable. On the other hand, one may reasonably question the latest editions of BDB, which still rely on these erroneous data.

§ 11 Incidentally, a full study of Gesenius' reliance on his predecessors, early and late, would be worthwhile. Often his dependence on Radaq is evident, but this has escaped the attention of many researchers who have placed the beginnings of Biblical Hebrew scholarship in Europe of the eighteenth and nineteenth centuries, and have forgotten that the foundations were built in the Middle Ages. Great scholars like Gesenius knew how to utilize the earlier works, and certainly publicly declared their reliance on earlier scholars.[23] The

16 Here, too, the expressions אי אפשי (2×), אי אפשר (1×), אי אתה (1×), and אי אתם (1×) were checked, and in all cases the vowel is a *tsere*.

17 In this edition the expressions אי אפשר (4×) and אי אתה (5×) were checked. In eight of the instance אֵי is vocalized with a *tsere*, but once it appears with a *hiriq*: אִי אתה (BQ 9:10).

18 Here, too, the expressions אי אפשי (2×), אי אפשר (2×), אי אתה (1×) and אי אתם (1×) were checked, and all are vocalized אֵי.

19 The single exception is mentioned above in n. 17.

20 This is also the vocalization in the Livorno editions of the nineteenth and early twentieth centuries.

21 This is a supercommentary on the Mishnaic commentaries of R. Overdiah Bertinoro and the Tosafot Yom Tov (Amsterdam, 1714).

22 See Buxtorf 1639:39.

23 As was mentioned above in § 7, at the end of the entry of אֵי, Radaq's commentary on the word in 1 Sam 4:21 is cited explicitly. See also above, n. 6.

degree to which Gesenius was dependent on early modern scholars such as Johannes Buxtorf[24] is worth investigating, although clearly this is an issue which belongs to the history of scholarship, rather than to scholarship itself. This type of research is properly secondary, and few would find it of substantial interest.

4.3 Augmentation of incomplete data

§ 12 Naturally, many entries in the *Thesaurus* would be further supported by the data from Mishnaic Hebrew. I am not referring only to data from the best manuscripts of Mishnaic Hebrew, the essential work on which was done only in the twentieth century; even the materials which were printed and in circulation in Gesenius' time would have contributed significantly to what was written in the Thesaurus, but of course, the data was not always known to the author of the dictionary when he was writing. One could discuss many such examples, but I will suffice here with only illustrations.

§ 13 Here is a brief selection of examples. These are words which are hapax legomena or rare words in Biblical Hebrew, but for none of them is the relevant Mishnaic Hebrew data cited in Gesenius' *Thesaurus*:

A. In the entry for the hapax noun בִּזָּיוֹן (p. 197), found in the verse וכדי בזיון וקצף (Esther 1:18), the Aramaic cognate בזיונא (found in Bavli Sotah 8b) is cited, but none of the Mishnaic Hebrew examples, such as מנהג ביזיון (Bavli Berakhot 18a) and many others, is mentioned. It is worth pointing out that in his citation of בזיונא from Sotah, Gesenius is following Buxtorf, who also cited only this example.[25]

B. In the entry גֹּמֶד (p. 292) – also a hapax – from the verse ויעש לו אהוד חרב ... גֹּמֶד ארכה "Ehud made for himself a sword ... a *gomed* in length" (Judges 3:16), parallels are cited from Syriac (גורמיזא and גַּוְרְמִידָא), but the example from Mishnah Kelim is not cited. There the word is used with a slightly different meaning: והגומדין של ערביין "and the *gomedin* of the Arabs" (Kelim 29:1), where it means "a scarf whose length and width are a *gomed*, and the Arabs used to wear them on their heads."[26]

C. In the discussion of the noun דִּבֵּר (p. 317), found in the verse והנביאים יהיו לרוח וְהַדִּבֵּר אין בהם "and the prophets will be wind, and the *dibber* is not in them" (Jer 5:13), the word's later attestations go unmentioned. In

---

24 See above, § 10 and n. 6 above and n. 25 below.

25 See Buxtorf, *ibid.* (above, n. 14), p. 279. Buxtorf mistakenly referred to Sotah 8**a** instead of 8**b**, and the mistake was repeated by Gesenius.

26 See Bar-Asher 2009a:2.166–167.

fact, this word is found in Mishnaic Hebrew in the phrase עשרת הדיברות (the Ten Commandments),[27] and in another Rabbinic text – the Passover Haggada, where the texts throughout the generations was אנוס על פי הַדִּבֵּר "forced by the *dibber*" – "corrected" in modern times to *ha-dibbur*.[28]

D. We may have expected that the entry for עֲצֶרֶת (pp. 1059–1060) would mention the fact that in Mishnaic Hebrew this word came to be the name of the festival of Shavuot. In the Mishnah alone, this name appears more than twenty times, for example, אין מביאים ביכורים קודם לעצרת "one may not bring the first fruits (*bikkurim*) before *Atzeret*" (Bikkurim 1:3).

E. In the entry for the word שַׂכִּין (p. 1329), attested only once in the verse ושמת שַׂכִּין בלעך (Proverbs 23:2), Gesenius cites Aramaic examples of סַכִּין with a *samekh*, but no examples from the Mishnah. It would have sufficed to cite the form in its conventional vocalization as found in the printed editions – סַכִּין (for example, Sheqalim 8:3). It is superfluous to add here that only in the mid-twentieth century did it become known that in the reliable manuscripts of the Mishnah, the vocalization was סְכִּין.[29]

F. An interesting example relates to the entry for the Aramaic words נְוָלִי, נְוָלוּ (p. 862), which appear in the verses וּבַיְתֵהּ נְוָלוּ יִתְעֲבֵד (Ezra 6:11) and וּבָתֵּיכוֹן נְוָלִי יִתְּשָׂמוּן (Daniel 2:5). Gesenius points out a Hebrew cognate from the root נו"ל from a citation of Saadia: יש אמרים לשון מנוול כדומן וכצואה לאיבוס בהמות "some say it has the sense of מנוול 'disgusting', like dung or excrement for the trough of animals."[30] But no citation from the Mishnah or any other text of rabbinic literature is cited, although they are readily available: for example, בנות ישראל נאות הן אלא שהעניות מנוולתן "the daughters of Israel are beautiful, but poverty makes them unattractive (מנוולתן)" (Nedarim 9:10).

§ 14 The purpose here is not, of course, to enumerate the deficiencies in Gesenius' dictionary, but rather to draw attention to the changes which have occurred in Hebrew scholarship since Gesenius' time. In particular, since then research into Mishnaic Hebrew has come into its own as an important stream of Hebrew research. When it was common to conceive of Mishnaic Hebrew as

---

27 As is known, it is also attested in the blessing "Shofarot" in the Musaf prayer of Rosh ha-Shana: וְדִבְרוֹת קדשך. See also Steiner (1992).

28 Cf. Berggrün 1995:77–79.

29 See Yalon 1964:30, Kutscher 1977a:449; Bar-Asher 2009a:1.147, 156, 224.

30 The source of this citation is not given. R. Joseph Qafiḥ, in his edition of Saadia's translation of Daniel (1981), observes that in the word's first occurrence in Daniel 2:5, Saadia translates צואפי "abandoned," but in its second occurrence in Dan 3:29, he translates it נכאלא "punishment."

an artificial literary language, it made good sense to cite Aramaic examples instead. Aramaic was believed to be the primary language of the Jews for both speech and literary production, beginning already in Second Temple times and continuing for centuries afterwards; Mishnaic Hebrew, on the other hand, was believed in the nineteenth century to be an artificial creation. Despite this, Gesenius used Mishnaic Hebrew fairly often.[31]

4.4 Early signs of MH scholarship

§ 15 I would like now to discuss another important aspect of Gesenius' work. When we ask what the relationship is between the *Thesaurus* and modern scholarship on Mishnaic Hebrew, the question need not be limited to his use of data from that dialect. Even when he does not mention anything from the Mishnah or the Talmud in a particular entry or series of interconnected entries, it is possible to discern his involvement with issues which would later be discussed in the context of the modern study of Mishnaic Hebrew. Sometimes this is not limited to a single word, but relates to a general grammatical issue, although the *Thesaurus* itself is, of course, a dictionary which presents words individually and in alphabetical order.

§ 16 Allow me to discuss an example where there is involvement with a larger grammatical issue within Biblical Hebrew, which has implication for Mishnaic Hebrew, as well. More specifically, it can be said that it turns out that Gesenius in his *Thesaurus* reached conclusions which were later to be revealed in Mishnaic Hebrew research. I have no better example of such an issue than the way the *Thesaurus* deals with the secondary entries devoted to words on the pattern *pā'ōl* (פָּעוֹל), which are called *nomen agentis*. In my view, the basic conclusions which would be reached in the mid-twentieth century are already contained in kernel form in the *Thesaurus*, although they are distributed throughout the work, primarily in the definitions given in the relevant entries. When these definitions and interpretations are collected, it is possible to see the linguistic theory animating them. I turn now to the details.

§ 17 In the Bible there are at least eight words on the pattern פָּעוֹל, with a stable *qamets*: בָּחוֹן "one who checks metals," חָלוֹם* "dreamer," חָמוֹץ "one who robs and oppresses," עָשׁוֹק "one who steals and robs," צָרוֹף "one who refines gold and other precious metals," רָזוֹן (which interchanges with רוֹזֵן) "ruler, prince"; and there is one word attested in the feminine form: בָּגוֹדָה "one who habitually betrays." There is one further word in Biblical Aramaic:

31 See above, nn. 4–6.

כָּרוֹז "one who announces on behalf of the rulers." First it is worth mentioning that the word חָלוֹם is a form restored by M. Z. Segal over seventy years ago;[32] the Masoretic text is vocalized with a *hatef-patah*: חֲלֹמֹתֵיכֶם (Jer 27:8; 29:9), but the contexts make it clear that the reference is to dreamers, and not the dreams themselves.[33]

§ 18 Of the eight words just mentioned, Gesenius has secondary entries for just six of them: בָּחוֹן, חָמוֹץ, עָשׁוֹק, רָזוֹן, בָּגוֹדָה, and כָּרוֹז. Here are the details:

A. Gesenius defines בָּגוֹד (p. 178), which is reflected in the feminine form בָּגוֹדָה, in the phrase בָּגוֹדָה אחותה יהודה (Jer 3:7, 10), as an adjective, and notes that the *qametz* is irreducible like in the Aramaic קָטוֹל pattern and Arabic *qātūl*.
B. He classifies בָּחוֹן (p. 198), in the verse בָּחוֹן נתתיך בעמי מבצר (Jer 6:27), as "adj. verbale," and notes that it is equivalent ("i.q." = idem quo) as the participle בֹּחֵן.[34]
C. Similarly, with regard to עָשׁוֹק (p. 1080), attested in the verse והצילו גזול מיד עָשׁוֹק (Jer 22:3), Gesenius writes that this form is equivalent to the active participle עוֹשֵׁק found in the parallel והצילו גזול מיד עוֹשֵׁק (Jer 21:12).
D. In speaking about חָמוֹץ (p. 712) in the verse דרשו משפט אשרו חָמוֹץ (Isa 1:17), Gesenius writes at length. He never actually specifies a grammatical analysis of the word, but he does mention that it is equivalent to the participle חוֹמֵץ in the verse פלטני מיד רשע, מיד מְעַוֵּל וחוֹמֵץ (Psalm 71:4). Furthermore, he compares it to the word חַמְצָן, which is attested in the Babylonian Talmud,[35] referring to the phrase found twice, והיו קורין אותו בן (בר) חמצן עד יום מותו "they would call him 'son[36] of a thief (חמצן)' until the day of his death" (b. Yoma 39b; Qiddushin 53a).[37] Especially worthy of note is the important comment he appends in parentheses: "Compare עָשׁוֹק and עֹשֵׁק, רָזוֹן and רֹזֵן, בָּחוֹן and בֹּחֵן."

32 See Segal 1939–1940:154–156. The context is unambiguous in pointing to the meaning dreamers.

33 See Chapter Seventeen below, with n. 13 there, and Bar-Asher 2009a:1.137–139, where I explain how חֲלוֹמוֹתֵיכֶם became חָלוֹמוֹתֵיכֶם.

34 As mentioned (above, n. 4), all participles are cited in the *Thesaurus* without a *vav*, even when the word is spelled with a *vav* in the biblical text.

35 This was apparently drawn from Buxtorf's dictionary (see there, p. 785). Buxtorf cites the example from Yoma, cited below.

36 It appears with בן in Yoma and with בר in Qiddushin.

37 He sees the root חמ"ץ as a biform of the root חמ"ס.

E. Similar views, although presented in abbreviated form, are found in his discussion of רָזוֹן (p. 1280), attested in the verse ברב עם הדרת מלך, ובאפס לְאֹם מחתת רָזוֹן (Prov 14:28). Here, too, Gesenius observes that רָזוֹן is equivalent to רֹזֵן,[38] and parenthetically compares the pair עָשׁוֹק and עֹשֵׁק.[39]
F. Gesenius also devoted a discussion to the Aramaic noun כָּרוֹז (p. 712), attested in the determined state in the verse וְכָרוֹזָא קרא בחיל (Dan 3:4).

§ 19 I have no intention of taking the *thesaurus* writer to task for not including entries for the other two nouns on this pattern, צָרוֹף and חָלוֹם. For our purposes what is significant is that Gesenius presents a correct understanding of this linguistic phenomenon nearly every time the issue arises. He does not suffice with merely identifying a word as a noun or an adjective, but compares it in a number of instances to the Qal active participle – the פּוֹעֵל pattern. More than this, he even enumerated the four examples of פּוֹעֵל – פָּעוֹל interchanges: as mentioned, in the discussion of חָמוֹץ he pointed to חוֹמֵץ and then cited the three other pairs.[40] No less significant is his citation from the Babylonian *Talmud* of the word חַמְצָן, in the פַּעְלָן pattern, as equivalent to חָמוֹץ/חוֹמֵץ.

§ 20 In fact, Mishnaic Hebrew research later revealed a complete picture of the relationship between the patterns פּוֹעֵל, פָּעוֹל, and פַּעְלָן: alongside the participle פּוֹעֵל, which had both verbal and nominal uses, there were also two patterns whose usages were primarily nominal (adjectival or true nouns) – פָּעוֹל and פַּעְלָן. Of course, there is no reason that the *Thesaurus* would be expected to cite the Mishnaic forms on this pattern, since the words attested on this pattern in Biblical Hebrew do not appear in the Mishnah. Purely Mishnaic forms, such as גָרוֹסוֹת (Kelim 12:4) "makers of grits," דָרוֹכוֹת (Terumot 3:4) "those who tread on grapes to make wine," לָקוֹחוֹת (Ketubbot 8:1) "regular purchasers," and מָשׁוֹחוֹת (Eruvin 4:11) "measurers of land," also do not belong in the *Thesaurus*, since they are not attested in the Bible.

§ 21 The classification "adj. verbale" Gesenius gives to בָּחוֹן is interesting. Apparently this is based on the fact that בָּחוֹן is in free variation with בּוֹחֵן,

---

38 The form רוֹזֵן appears in the Bible six times, all in the plural, for example, הנותן רוזנים לאין (Isa 40:23). Ben-Yehuda's *Thesaurus* compares the interchange between singular רָזוֹן and plural רוֹזְנִים to the interchange between singular בֵּן and plural בָּנִים, and other such pairs in which the two forms appear in different patterns. In my opinion, the cases are not comparable.
39 We can add a few פָּעוֹל forms to his list: אָמוֹן (Prov 8: 30) and יָקוֹשׁ (Hos. 9 8). Gesenius (1810:403) defines יָקוֹשׁ as a participle like בָּחוֹן, חָמוֹץ, עָשׁוֹק, but in the *Thesaurus* he cites it along with the passive participle יָקוּשׁ. (Ps 91:3). Does he assume that יָקוֹשׁ is a variant of יָקוּשׁ?
40 In the discussion of רָזוֹן, on the other hand, he mentions only one other example.

and this gave Gesenius the clue to properly understand the connection of the פָּעוֹל pattern to the verbs in the Qal. It should still be said that פָּעוֹל only interchanges with the *nominal* use of the participle. It goes without saying that one would not expect to find in the *Thesaurus* other insights uncovered by modern scholars working on Mishnaic Hebrew regarding any of the patterns just discussed. In particular the findings of Ben-Zion Gross in his book on the patterns ending in *nun*, such as the difference between the Eretz Israel form פָּעְלָן and the Babylonian form פַּעְלָן, and other conclusions which he reached: these would be out of place in Gesenius' *Thesaurus*.[41]

§ 22 In sum, when one combines all that Gesenius said about the six words on the pattern פָּעוֹל which have their own entries, it becomes clear that his work contains the core of the findings of more recent scholarship on Mishnaic Hebrew.

On a related point, however, it should be observed that in discussing the word רַחֲמָנִיּוֹת (Lament. 4:16) on p. 1283, Gesenius determined that the singular form was רַחֲמָנִי, instead of רַחֲמָן (although he did cite the Arabic form *raḥmān* in that context). Was he unaware of the fact that the feminine form of nouns on the פַּעְלָן form in Mishnaic Hebrew was פַּעְלָנִית, and that therefore the masculine equivalent of פַּעְלָנִית is פַּעְלָן? Buxtorf's lexicon (p. 498) did, in fact, cite the pair דַּבְּרָן and דַּבְּרָנִית.[42]

§ 23 I will conclude with a brief remark: sometimes a particular entry in Gesenius' *Thesaurus* is silent with regard to Mishnaic Hebrew, and yet it is discussed explicitly in his grammar. A relevant example is the *binyan* Nitpa'el in Biblical Hebrew: on p. 207 of the *Thesaurus* he cites the form נִכַּפֵּר, and on p. 605 he cites the form נִוַּסְּרוּ, and in both occurrences he suffices with the note that these are from the *binyan* Nitpa'el. In his grammar, published in 1817,[43] however, he points out that these are from the binyan Nitpa'el, which, he says, is the passive of the Hitpa'el. The relationship between these two *binyanim* is not the issue now, but it is important to note that in the discussion, Gesenius compares these words to Mishnaic Hebrew נִתְאַשֵּׁשׁ and נִזְדַּקֵּן (and it would be superfluous to note that there is nothing surprising in the vocalization of these forms with a *tsere* under the second root letter, נִתְאַשֵּׁשׁ and נִזְדַּקֵּן, to match the vocalization familiar from Biblical Hebrew).[44]

---

41 Gross' book (1993) contains a thorough discussion of these patterns in the dialects of the Tannaim and Amoraim.

42 It is true, however, that Buxtorf 1639 gives עַסְקָנִי as the masculine equivalent of עַסְקָנִית (p. 1639). Of course, he cites other nouns on this pattern, as well, such as נַפְקָנִית (p. 1374) and רַחֲמָנִית (p. 2239).

43 See Gesenius 1817:249–250.

44 See Yalon 1964:16-17; Yalon shows that the original *patah* in the נִתְפַּעַל was replaced in late printings by the biblically-inspired *tsere* (and sometimes even spelled with נתפעיל).

4.5 Summary remarks

§ 24 Two centuries after Gesenius' first publications in Hebrew scholarship, the field has achieved much beyond what was done in the early nineteenth century. Invaluable Hebrew documents have been uncovered, "new" Semitic languages have been discovered and deciphered, and the research itself has gotten stronger. Study of living languages and dialects have also earned their proper place within the field. In this new path of scholarship, we approach the transmitters of all of world literature, including Jewish literature, with great respect; we refrain as much as possible from correcting the texts transmitted and instead work hard to explain the transmitted forms. Within this approach, the work of Gesenius is of great importance, and even in the few examples I have cited this should be evident.

§ 25 The corrections that need to be made to Gesenius' work and what remains to be added to what he produced are grist for every scholar's mill. Later generations always add to what their predecessors did, and strip away what are perceived as excesses. Our own generation will be judged by those who come after us, and will no doubt criticize, to a greater or lesser extent, the work we are producing. It is true that there are always scholars of such reduced stature that even in their own lifetimes they are forgotten. But there are those whose work is valued hundreds of years after their own lives, to whom scholars for generations will return, and from whom future scholars will always learn. Wilhelm Gesenius is certainly one of these.

5 איש יהודי היה בשושן הבירה: When did יהודי Come to Denote 'Jew'?

§ 1 The verse, אִישׁ יְהוּדִי הָיָה בְּשׁוּשַׁן הַבִּירָה וּשְׁמוֹ מָרְדֳּכַי ... אִישׁ יְמִינִי "there was Jew (איש יהודי) in the fortress Shushan by the name of Mordechai ...a Benjaminite (איש ימיני)," (Esther 2:5) could not possibly have been written in a book from the First Temple Period. This is not only due to its content, as the verse describes a man who lived during the time of the Second Temple, but also due to the language employed. In Hebrew of the First Temple Period, someone who is a *yehudi* (יְהוּדִי) could not also be an *yemini* (יְמִינִי), just as someone who is an *yemini* could not be a *yehudi*. *Yehudi*, in the language of the First Temple Period describes one who is "a member of the tribe (or of the family) of Judah," or "an inhabitant of the land of Judah."[1] For example, we find, "Likewise all of the *yehudim* (Judeans) who were in Moab" (Jeremiah 40:11; in other words, "all of the members of the tribe of [or inhabitants of the land of] Judah who were in Moab"). Similarly, *yemini* or *ben-yemini* describes one who is a "member of the tribe of Benjamin" or "a man from the land of Benjamin," such as "Sheva the son of Bikhri a Benjaminite (*ish yemini*)" (2 Samuel 20:2).[2] This is true for all genealogical names derived from the names of the other tribes, or from names of other people, for example, "the Reubenites, the Gadites, and the Menashites" (2 Kings 10:33), "Canaanite," whether derived from Canaan the person (mentioned in Genesis 10:6, 15) or Canaan the land, and *misṛī* (Egyptian), whether derived from Mitzrayim the person (Gen 10:6, 13) or Mitzrayim the land. This is well known.

§ 2 There are scholars of the Hebrew Language, as well as Biblical exegetes, who paid attention to the fact that the meaning of word *yehudi* changed after the exile of the 10 tribes, and from then on referred to anyone from the nation of Israel. While it is true that this change could not have come about before the exile of the Ten Tribes, nevertheless, it is necessary to add certain details to the description of the semantic change which came about only at

1 Of course, we need to exclude the personal names *yehudi* and *yehudit*: *yehudi ben netan'el* (Jeremiah 36:14), *yehudit bat be'eri* the Hittite (Gen. 26:34) as well as *Yehudit*, the language spoken in the land of Judah (2 Kings 18:26, 28; Neh. 13:24).

2 This is the view which still echoes later on, regarding the verse from Esther, in a passage from b. Megillah 12b: קרי ליה יהודי, אלמא מיהודה קאתי; וקרי ליה ימיני, אלמא מבנימין קאתי "He is called *yehudi* – so he must have been from Judah, but he is called *yemini* – so he must have been from Benjamin." Or, as in the understanding of Rabbi Joshua ben Levi, who tries to harmonize the two later in that passage: אביו מבנימין ואמו מיהודה "his father was from Benjamin, and his mother was from Judah."

the beginning of the Second Temple Period. *Yehudi* is a resident of the province of Judah (*yehud medinta* in Aramaic, as in Ezra 5:8), the Persian province which was the dwelling place of those who returned from Babylonia to Zion, and to which members of other tribes joined as well (with Judah, of course, leading the group). Another substantial change occurred with regard to the name *yehudi*; from then on, "the noun *yehudi* does not indicate the tribe [...] or the religion alone, but rather the nation and the religion, which are together a single unit which cannot be divided."[3] This nation does not only dwell in the Land of Judah or in the province Yehud, but is ... מְפֻזָּר וּמְפֹרָד בין העמים ודתיהם שֹׁנוֹת מכל עם "scattered and dispersed among the nations [...] and their laws are different from those of any other people" (Esther 3:8).[4] It is important to note that these words come from (or are attributed to) a foreigner (Haman).

§ 3 Henceforth, an *ish yehudi* (= "member of the Jewish nation") could be from the tribe of Judah or from any other tribe, such as Benjamin; he could be an *ish yemini*, as was Mordechai. The double description, איש יהודי... איש ימיני *ish yehudi* [...] *ish yemini* (Esther 2:5), which first gives the general affiliation and then the specific tribal connection, parallels a verse in Leviticus (24:11), בֶּן-הָאִשָּׁה הַיִּשְׂרְאֵלִית ... לְמַטֵּה-דָן "son of an Israelite woman ... of the tribe of Dan." Here, too, the woman is first introduced by the nation to which she belongs, and then comes her familial/tribal pedigree (למטה דן).

§ 4 This new meaning of the term *yehudi* – as a noun which refers not to a geographical origin or tribal identity, but rather one which expresses an idea with a broad definition, which identified one called by this term with a particular nation and a particular religion – is confirmed both by the story of Esther and by its language: later, a reality is created wherein people wish to join the community of *yehudim*, without being descendants of Judah or residents of the province Judah, as the verse specifically states, ורבים מעמי הארץ מִתְיַהֲדִים כי נפל פחד היהודים עליהם "and many of the people of the land were becoming *yehudim* (מִתְיַהֲדִים), for the fear of the Jews had fallen upon them" (Esther 8:17).

§ 5 The word for "becoming Jews" (מִתְיַהֲדִים) is a verb derived from the noun *yehudi* in its new meaning: "a member of the Jewish nation, according

---

3 See Hirschler 1930:257.

4 This is perfectly in line with the view in the Talmud (see note 2): רבי יוחנן אמר: לעולם מבנימין קאתי; ואמאי קרי ליה יהודי? – על שם שכפר בעבודה זרה; שכל הכופר בעבודה זרה נקרא יהודי "Rabbi Yohanan said, "In truth, he was from the tribe of Benjamin. Why is he called a *yehudi*? Because he repudiated idolatry, and anyone who repudiates idolatry is called a *yehudi* ..." (b. Megillah 13a).

to its religion (its beliefs and practices)."[5] Just as with all verbs in the Hitpa'el, the word מִתְיַהֲדִים can mean "becoming Jewish," "converting": מתגיירים in Mishnaic Hebrew (and indeed, both *Targum Rishon* and *Targum Sheni* on Esther translated as מתגיירין)[6]. However, it is possible that the meaning of מתייהדים is to be understood with a mood of pretentiousness, a concept often expressed by verbs in the Hitpa'el; then it would mean "made themselves appear to be Jewish,"[7] similar to what is said of Amnon: שכב על משכבך וְהִתְחָל "lie down in your bed, and pretend to be sick (וְהִתְחָל)" (2 Samuel 13:5), and וישכב אמנון וַיִּתְחָל "Amnon lay down and pretended to be sick (וַיִּתְחָל)" (2 Samuel 13:6).

§ 6 It seems that the text of the book of Esther supports the first possibility ("became Jews," "converted"); it would appear that the מתייהדים are the people who are described later as נִלְוִים "joined": קימו וקבלו היהודים עליהם ועל זרעם ועל כל הַנִּלְוִים עליהם ... להיות עֹשִׂים את שני הימים האלה ככתבם וכזמנם בכל שנה ושנה "The Jews undertook and irrevocably obligated them-

5 The comments of Rabbi Jonah ibn Janaḥ in his Sefer ha-Riqmah (according to the translation of Judah ibn Tibbon, in Wilensky and Téné [1964:21–22]): כי כאשר רב שמושם ב"יהודים" ורצו לגזור ממנו פועל, שמו היו"ד שלו כשרשיה ואמרו "מתיהדים" על משקל "מתפעלים" ... הנהיגו היו"ד ב"מתיהדים" מנהג פ"א הפעל, והנהיגו הה"א ... מנהג עי"ן הפעל, והנהיגו הדל"ת מנהג הלמ"ד [= ל' הפעל] וכן עשו בעלי המשנה ב ... יתרום ... תרם ... כי כאשר רב שמושם ב"תרומה" אמדוהו אומד ... ואמרו תרם ויתרום ... וזאת היתה דעתם ב"מתריעין" ו"מתחילין" ו"יתריעו" ו"יתחילו" [מן תרועה ומן תחילה] ... כי דעת אנשי המשנה ב"תרם" ו"יתרום" וזולתם הדומים להם היא דעת העברים ב"מתיהדים" בשוה "For when the use of the term *yehudim* became commonplace, and they wanted to derive a verb from it, they used its *yod* as part of its root, and said that מתיהדים was based on the paradigm of מתפעלים [...] they used the *yod* of מתיהדים as the first radical, and used the *heh* [...] as the second radical, and they used the *dalet* as the third radical. The Tanna'im did the same with the word [...] יתרום [... and] תרם [...], because when the use of the word תרומה became commonplace, they assessed it [...] and said, תרם and יתרום [...] and this was their understanding with מתריעין and מתחילין and יתריעו and יתחילו [from תרועה and תחילה] [...]. The intention of the Tanna'im with regard to תרם and יתרום and similar words, is the same as the intention of the Hebrews (עברים!) [= speakers of Biblical Hebrew and those who wrote it, in the Bible] with regard to the word מתיהדים.

6 This is also how Rashi understood it. However, according to Abraham Ibn Ezra: ויתכן היות מתיהדים שיתיחסו על שבט יהודה "it seems as if the meaning of מתייהדים is that they associated themselves with the tribe of Judah," but from the Hebrew that Ibn Ezra himself uses, it is clear that he uses התייהד with the meaning "to become Jewish" > "to convert" (sincerely or not?), as is attested in two places in his commentary on the Pentateuch: **בן איש מצרי:** מתיהד "the son of an Egyptian man: a convert" (Lev. 24:10); **וישבה בביתך ובכתה** [...] כי זה הבכי על אביה ועל אמה שלא התיהדו "and she shall dwell in your house, and shall cry: this crying is with regard to her father and her mother who did not convert."

7 This is how Gersonides understands the phrase, as do many of the moderns (see Hirschler's commentary, mentioned in note 3).

selves and their descendants, and all who had joined them [...] to observe these two days in the manner prescribed and at the proper time each year" (9:27). The same rule applies to both the Jews (and their descendants), and to those who had joined them.[8]

§ 7 The status of the people of the land who had "became Jewish, converted" (מתייהדים), and "those who had joined" (הַנִּלְוִים), is mentioned in a *baraita* quoted in b. *Yebamot* 24b, where it is stated explicitly that they are converts: שהיה רבי נחמיה אומר: אחד גירי אריות ואחד גירי חלומות ואחד גירי מרדכי ואסתר אינן גרים עד שיתגיירו בזמן הזה "as Rabbi Nehemiah would say, 'Neither the lion converts, nor the dream converts, nor the converts of Mordechai and Esther[9] are proper converts unless they become converted at the present time'." They are called converts even though they converted מחמת שררה "due to [fear of] authority" (Rashi *ibid.* s. v. כבזמן הזה). An even earlier source, the Greek translation of Esther, already stated that those who had joined (הַנִּלְוִים) were circumcised;[10] when this translation was composed, ritual circumcision was ultimate symbol of the convert who wished to attach himself or herself to the "inheritance of God."

§ 8 In summary, the name *yehudi* changed in meaning in the Second Temple Period, and no book better shows the transition than Esther. Esther shows this transition quite clearly: *yehudi* no longer signifies a geographical or familial/tribal origin alone, but designates one who belongs to a group, bound by bonds faith and beliefs, and who are connected by law and custom.

---

8 The word נִלְוָה implies a connection to the one being joined, without specifying the level of connection; however, in this instance, the mandate that both the Jews and their descendants and those who had joined them (הנליום) have the same obligation, seems to demonstrate that we are dealing with a complete unification – meaning, conversion. However, it is unclear if the נִלְוים mentioned in Isaiah have the same status: ובני הנכר הנלוים, בן הנכר הנלוָה (Isaiah 56:3, 6). It is true that the concern that הבדל יבדילני ה' מעל עמו "God shall surely separate me from upon His nation" is rejected, for, as it is said there כל שומר שבת מחללו ומחזיקים בבריתי "all who keep the Sabbath from profaning it, and those who hold strong to my covenant" (ibid., 6) will ultimately be brought to the house of God, and will rejoice in His house of prayer. However, this is done with the notice that the house of God will be a כי ביתי בית תפִלה יקרא לכל העמים "house of prayer for all of the nations." This needs to be studied further.

9 According to Rashi, **גירי אריות**, כגון כותים דכתיב בספר מלכים "וישלח ה' בהם את האריות" ונתגיירו, כדכתיב התם בגלות שומרון, **גירי חלומות** – בעל חלומות אמר להם להתגייר; **מרדכי ואסתר** – ורבים מעמי הארצות מתיהדים "the lion proselytes: for example, the *Kuthim* (Samaritans), as it says in 2 Kings (17:25), 'the Lord sent lions among them' and they converted, as it says by the exile of Samaria; the dream proselytes – the interpreter of dreams told them to convert; the proselytes of Mordechai and Esther – *and many of the people of the land professed to be Jews.*"

10 See Hirschler (note 3), who quotes the Septuagint version of this verse, but rejects it.

One who wishes to present a *yehudi* in terms of his tribal affiliation as well must now provide further details, when it presented Mordechai's genealogy: "*ish yehudi* [...] *ish yemini*" (with the general description given first, followed by the specific description). Had this man been from the tribe of Levi or from the tribe of Judah, the writers would presumably have indicated that he was a *yehudi* מבית לוי or *yehudi* ממטה יהודה.[11]

11 The name Levi (לֵוִי), in morphological terms, is derived from its genealogical name, and we therefore use it in the way it is found in the Bible: וילך איש מבית לוי ויקח את בת לוי (Exod 2:1). We also find לוי and הלוי used similarly, for example, הנער הלוי (Judg 18:3), האיש הלוי (ibid. 20:4). Furthermore, we used the phrase ממטה יהודה and not יהודי because, as mentioned, the word יהודי had already changed its meaning.

6 Biblical Language in Mishnaic Texts

6.1 Introductory comments

§ 1 From the moment that the spoken language within Eretz Israel became a literary language in the first century CE,[1] we find a Hebrew different from the language of the Hebrew Bible,[2] with its own distinctive features. This is the language in which Tannaitic literature (the Mishna, Tosefta, Halakhic Midrashim, and Seder ʿOlam Rabba) were composed. Because this language is known to us primarily from rabbinic literature,[3] it is known as "Rabbinic Hebrew," or "Mishnaic Hebrew" (= MH), based on the primary and exemplary Tannaitic composition.

§ 2 Many features in all areas of the language – lexicon, semantics, and all types of grammar (phonology, morphology, morphosyntax, and syntax)[4] – distinguish between MH and the layer that preceded it, Biblical Hebrew (= BH). The scholarly literature on MH from the outset until today consists in large part of analyses of these various differences between the two layers of the language.[5]

For our purposes, the mention of two very brief examples will suffice. First, in BH the Puʿʿal stem is used as the passive of the Piʿʿel, whereas in MH the Nitpaʿʿal is used for the same purpose.[6] Second, in the realm of the lexicon,

---

1 Conventional wisdom holds that the Mishna was edited in approximately 200–220; there are, however, many earlier literary units ("משנה ראשונה"), which were edited close to the date of the destruction of the Temple in 70 CE (Epstein [1957:25 ff.]).

2 Even Prof. Ben-Ḥayyim, who was of the opinion that the morphological system of MH is identical in all details to that of BH, does not deny that in other linguistic realms the two layers are clearly distinguished; cf. Ben-Ḥayyim (1985:3–25, esp. § 5 on pp. 18–21), and my response in Bar-Asher (1985:75–99, esp. §§ 4–13 on pp. 77–86).

3 The non-rabbinic literature composed in this language (or something similar) is limited, but its importance is great; I have in mind especially the Copper Scroll from Qumran and the Hebrew letters of Šimʿon Bar Koseba, as well as other texts; cf. Mishor (2000–2001:327–332).

4 It may be appropriate to point out that the differences between BH and MH are not of equal scope in the various areas of the language. Within morphology, the differences are slight, but with regard to the lexicon and semantics, the differences between the two are naturally far greater.

5 One who reviews all that has been written, from the justifiably renowned article by Segal (1908) until today, will find that a clear majority of the literature on MH discusses facts and hypotheses about the difference of this language from BH.

6 Note, too, that morphologically the Mishnaic form נִתְפַּעֵל is a late development from BH הִתְפַּעֵל/הִתְפַּעַל; the initial *nun* of the Nipʿal stem was transferred analogically to this stem, as well.

Biblical and Mishnaic Hebrew differ on the word for a person sent to perform a mission: מַלְאָךְ in BH, but שָׁלִיחַ in MH.[7]

6.2 Relationship of the Mishna to Biblical Hebrew

§ 3 Alongside these observations, it is important to emphasize that the Tannaim wove words, phrases, and expressions drawn from the Bible into their compositions, in many different texts and contexts, or, more subtly, utilized BH grammar. This Tannaitic relationship to the language of the Bible has been appropriately clarified in a number of studies.[8] This research has identified a number of specific aspects of this relationship. Some of the most notable are the following:

1. There is a close connection to BH in the early mishnayot, which deal closely with the Temple and the Temple service, and which were apparently composed in the second half of the first century CE, close to the destruction of the Temple.[9]
2. There is more of a connection to the language of the Bible in non-halakhic material; for our present purposes all non-halakhic material will be called the *aggada* within Tannaitic literature.
3. There are conscious or unconscious echoes of biblical language in Tannaitic texts in which a biblical verse is invoked; in these cases the connection is clearly textual.

I will now elaborate on these points in brief with examples from the Mishna. It will not be difficult to see that there are examples that relate to a number of the different types of connections.

§ 4 It is known that the tractates Tamid, Middot, and Šeqalim, as well as chapters and individual *halakhot* in other tractates, are what as known as משנה ראשונה "early Mishna," i.e., mishnayot which preceded the canonical Mishna of R. Judah ha-Nasi by a number of generations, and some were composed adjacent to the destruction of the Temple in 70. It is, first of all, important to note that the language of these early mishnayot, as well, is MH like the rest of the Mishna in all its sixty tractates, but the early mishnayot reveal here and there a connection to the Bible in grammar and lexicon. Here are two examples:

---

7 I owe this point to Dr. Yoḥanan Breuer.

8 See, for example, Haneman 1980a, in which Haneman ably and succinctly set forth most types of loans from the Bible. Cf. also Bar-Asher 1985:96–98 and Brawerman 1994.

9 See, for example, Epstein 1957:27–28, and Ginzberg 1919.

1. In all of MH the secondary verb הִתְחִיל, which was derived from the nominal form תְּחִלָּה,[10] but in Tamid we find three times the verb הֵחֵל, as is proper in BH grammar:[11] החלו מעלין באפר "they began to pile up the ashes" (Tamid 2:2); החלו מעלין בגיזרין לסדר אש המערכה "they began to bring up faggots to set in order the fire of the altar" (2:3); and החלו עולין במעלות האולם "they began to go up the steps of the porch" (6:1).[12]
2. In mRH 1:9, we read, מי שראה את החודש ואינו יכול להלך מוליכין אותו על החמור אפילו במיטה. ואם צודה להן לוקחין בידן מקלות, ואם היתה הדרך רחוקה לוקחין בידן מזונות, שעל מהלך לילה ויום מחללין את השבת ויוצאין לעדות החודש "One who saw the new moon but cannot walk, they may bring him, even on a donkey [on the Sabbath] or even on a bed. And if any lie in wait for them, they may take (לוקחין בידן) staffs, and if the distance was great, they may take (לוקחין בידן) food with them, because we desecrate the Sabbath for a journey lasting a day and a night, in order to travel to testify about the new moon." It is well known that in BH the verb לָקַח is used for picking up an object with one's hands, but in MH the verb נָטַל is used in its place; the meaning of לָקַח changed, and in MH it means "to acquire." But in this early mishna we find לוקחין בידם twice, in biblical style, and not נוטלין בידם, as is expected.[13]

§ 5 The second avenue of connection is the relationship to biblical language seen in non-halakhic (aggadic) passages. Here, too, one must emphasize that aggadic texts are composed for the most part in good MH, but one finds within them elements drawn from the language of the Bible, as well. Again, here are two examples:

1. We read in mSan 10:10: 'וְלֹא-יִדְבַּק בְּיָדְךָ מְאוּמָה מִן-הַחֵרֶם לְמַעַן יָשׁוּב ה' מֵחֲרוֹן אַפּוֹ' (דב' יג, יח) – שכל זמן שהרשעים בעולם חרון אף בעולם; אבדו רשעים מן העולם, נסתלק חרון אף מן העולם "Let nothing of the ban stick

---

10 Cf. Ibn Janah 1964:21–22, and Maimonides in the beginning of his commentary on Tractate Terumot.

11 See Epstein 1957:27 and Ginzberg 1919:201 and 273–274. Support for the connection between the tractates composed adjacent to the Destruction and biblical language can be found in the excellent article by Mishor 2000–2001: in the texts discussed by Mishor, the lexeme עץ "tree" is used in place of MH אילן; זות is used in place of זו; and there are direct borrowings from the Temple description in Ezekiel.

12 Within Tamid we also, however, find the verb הִתְחִיל, in agreement with the language of the Mishna as a whole: שמא תתחיל לפניך ... התחיל מרדד ויוצא "lest you begin before you ...began to smooth it down and go out" (6:3), just as we find the lexeme אילן "tree" in another document from the era of the Great Revolt (Mishor 2000–2001).

13 Cf. Bar-Asher 1985:97. It is possible that the expression ואם צוֹדֶה להם לוֹקְחִין בידם is dependent on the explicit biblical verse, וְאַתָּה צֹדֶה אֶת-נַפְשִׁי לְקַחְתָּהּ (1 Sam 24:11).

in your hand, so that the LORD may turn from his blazing anger (חֲרוֹן אַפּוֹ)' (Deut 13:18) – for whenever the wicked are in the world divine anger (חרון אף) is in the world; if the wicked cease from the world, divine anger (חרון אף) disappears from the world." Beside the biblical verse cited the entire passage is in MH, but the biblical phrase חרון אף "(divine) anger," which appears nowhere in the Mishna but here, has been embedded twice within it.

2. In the aggadic passage in mSoṭa 9:6, we read: זקני אותה העיר רוחצין את ידיהם במקום עריפתה של העגלה ... לא היו צריכין לומר 'וְנִיכַּפֵּר לָהֶם הַדָּם' (דב' כא, ח), אלא רוח הקודש מבשרתן: אמתיי שתעשו ככה, מתכפר לכם הדם "The elders of that city wash their hands in the place where the calf's neck's was broken ... they do not need to say 'they will be purged of bloodguilt' (Deut 21:8), but rather the divine spirit informs them: whenever you do this, you will be purged of the bloodguilt." Here, too, the entire passage is written in MH, but the tell-tale biblical word כָּכָה, as opposed to Mishanic כך, has been embedded within. Additionally, כָּכָה appears in the Bible 37 times, 18 of which are in conjunction with the verb עָשָׂה, and it appears that it was dragged into the mishna in Soṭa along with the word adjacent to it – שתעשו.[14] It is also worth noting that there is a version אמתיי שתעשון ככה (so in MS Kaufmann and a fragment from the Geniza), and according to this version, it is not just the word כָּכָה that is biblical in this phrase; the form תַּעֲשׂוּן, with the final *nun*, is also biblical, since the imperfects with final *nun* (יפעלון, תפעלון, תפעלין) are entirely nonexistent in MH. It is not possible to suggest that this is the common Aramaic form תפעלון, because the verbal root עש"ה does not exist at all within Aramaic. On the other hand, תעשון appears fourteen times in the Bible, e.g., וְהוֹרֵיתִי אֶתְכֶם אֵת אֲשֶׁר תַּעֲשׂוּן (Exod 4:15).

§ 6 Now let us turn to an example of the third category – a connection to BH in a context in which a biblical verse is present explicitly or implicitly. In the Mishna, one who lacks material possessions, a poor person, is known as an עָנִי. This word occurs more than 225 times in the Mishna, but its lexical equivalent דַּל is exceedingly rare in that corpus: it appears but three times.

One occurrence is in Kil'ayim 5:1: כרם שחרב אם יש בו ללקט עשר גפנים לבית סאה ונטועות כהלכתן, הרי זה נקרא כרם דל "a vineyard that was destroyed, if it has enough from which to harvest ten vines within a *bēt se'āh*, planted according to custom, this is known as an impoverished vineyard' (כרם דל)." In this context דַּל appears as an adjective modifying something

14 Cf. Haneman 1980a:6.

non-human – a vineyard[15] – and is therefore not germane to our discussion. The other two occurrences, on the other hand, do refer to poor people:

1. mŠeq 5:3: ארבעה חותמות היו במקדש וכתוב עליהן, עגל, זכר, גדי, חוטא. בן עזאי אומר חמישה היו וארמית כתוב עליהן: עגל, דכר, גדי, חוטא דל, וחוטא עשיר ... עגל משמש עם נסכי צאן גדולים וקטנים, זכרים ונקבות ... חוטא משמש עם נסכי שלוש בהמות של מצורעין "There were four seals in the Temple, and written on them were 'calf,' 'ram,' 'kid,' 'sinner.' Ben Azzai said there were five, and Aramaic was written on them: 'calf,' 'ram,' 'kid,' 'poor sinner,' and 'rich sinner' ... *calf* serves also for drink-offerings of small livestock, adult and young, male and female ... *sinner* serves for the drink-offerings of the three animals of lepers." Ch. Albeck noted in his commentary *ad loc.* that "'poor sinner' (חוֹטֵא דַל) is shorthand for the drink-offerings of a poor leper, who brings only one sheep (כֶּבֶשׂ אֶחָד), and its libations, and another *log* of oil" (based on Lev 14:21).
2. mNeg 14:7: ביום השמיני מביא שלוש בהמות: חטאת ואשם ועולה, והדל מביא חטאת העוף ועולת העוף "On the eighth day, he brings three animals: a purgation offering (חטאת), a guilt offering (אשם), and a burnt offering, and the poor man (והדל) brings a purgation offering of fowl and a burnt offering of fowl."

It is clear that these two mishnayot utilize the noun דַּל rather than עָנִי because they are attached to the verse (Lev 21:14) dealing with an impoverished leper: וְאִם-דַּל הוּא וְאֵין יָדוֹ מַשֶּׂגֶת וְלָקַח כֶּבֶשׂ אֶחָד אָשָׁם לִתְנוּפָה לְכַפֵּר עָלָיו ... "and if he is impoverished and he does not have the means, he shall take one sheep as a guilt offering to be waved to atone for himself ..." The power of this verse was great enough that it was able to attract the biblical word דַּל, which is central to the topic under discussion, and to push aside mishnaic עָנִי.[16] The semantic range of the lexeme דַּל, then, has been limited within MH; it is now a technical term within the discourse of sacrifices.[17]

---

15 This was insightfully pointed out to me by Ch. E. Cohen, who also directed my attention to an associated verb: הַמֵּדֵל בגפנים (m. Peah 7:5); הַמֵּדֵל בזיתים (m. Ševi'it 4:4). Maimonides explained that the verb is denominative, "to impoverish," from the word דל (*ad* m. Peah 7:5 and *ad* m. Ševi'it 4:4).

16 I will add that in the example from m. Šeqalim, there is the additional factor of an early mishna, which deals with the Temple. The topic is a reality that existed in the Temple – seals that related to the sacrifices, and the Temple was closely connected to the biblical text. It is interesting that Ben 'Azzai testifies that the words 'calf,' 'male,' 'goat,' 'poor sinner,' and 'rich sinner' were written in Aramaic, in the language people regularly spoke – but in formulating his position, the author of the mishna utilizes Hebrew, and in this formulation he appeals to the biblical word דל and not the colloquial עני.

17 Compare what I wrote about the use of the word הָלְאָה in Mishna Para in Chapter Seventeen, below, § 14.

§ 7 Especially numerous are the expressions that were lifted from the Bible and embedded as they were within rabbinic literature. One example is the expression ראשית הגֵז, which appears nine times in the Mishna (e.g., mḤul 11:1 [3×]). This is essentially a quotation drawn from Deut 18:4, וְרֵאשִׁית גֵּז צֹאנְךָ תִּתֶּן-לוֹ, whose topic is discussed in rabbinic literature. Another example of a different type: when the Tanna discusses women's ornaments, he draws inspiration from Isa 3:18–23. When he says – עיר שלזהב קטליות נזמים וטבעות וטבעת בין שיש עליה חותם בין שאין עליה חותם – וניזמי האף "a [crown in the shape of a] city of gold, necklaces, rings, signet rings – and a ring whether or not it has a seal attached to it – and nose rings" (mKel 11:8),[18] he is following the verse, הַטַּבָּעוֹת וְנִזְמֵי הָאָף (Isa 3:21), and specifically uses the expression וְהַטַּבָּעוֹת ... וְנִיזְמֵי הָאָף despite the fact that nose, to which rings may be attached, is known in MH as the חֹטֶם.

6.3 Substantive changes due to biblical influence

§ 8 All the examples discussed up to this point – whether drawn from the work of others or presented for the first time here – relate to clear connections between rabbinic literature and the language of the Bible, in linguistic matters alone. We have cited examples in which one sees replacements of normal Mishnaic lexical or grammatical items with their biblical counterparts, in some instances in clear cases of borrowing and in others merely allusions to biblical verses. Now I would like to point to an interesting phenomenon related to this issue: the few places in the Mishna in which detailed analysis reveals a flaw in the internal coherence of the text, but further probing shows that overt or covert reference to a biblical text is the cause for the apparent disruption. I will discuss one very clear example, and another that is less transparent.

6.3.1 בין האולם ולמזבח

§ 9 In mKel 1:6–9, we read:

> עשר קדושות הן: ארץ ישראל מקודשת מכל הארצות ... עיירות מוקפות חומה מקודשות ממנה ... לִפְנִים מן החומה מקודש מהן ... הר הבית מקודש ממנו ... החיל מקודש ממנו ...

18 Note that there is clearly continuity within the phrase הַטַּבָּעוֹת וְנִזְמֵי הָאָף, and the words וטבעת בין שיש עליה חותם בין שאין עליה חותם are an explanatory addition which explain the word טבעות, added at a late date to the list of ornaments (עיר שלזהב ... וטבעות ונזמי האף). This example is studied in Chapter Twenty-Three below, § 12.

עזרת הנשים מקודשת ממנו ... עזרת ישראל מקודשת ממנה ... עזרת הכוהנים מקודשת ממנה ... בין האולם ולמזבח מקודש ממנה ... ההיכל מקודש ממנו ... בית קודש הקודשים מקודש מהן.

There are ten levels of sanctity: the land of Israel is more sanctified than all other lands ... walled cities are more sanctified than [the rest of] it ... within the wall [of Jerusalem] is more sanctified than them ... the Temple Mount is more sanctified than it ... the Rampart is more sanctified than it ... the Court of the Women is more sanctified than [the rest of] it ... the Court of the Israelites is more sanctified than it ... the Court of the Priests is more sanctified than it ... between the porch and the altar (בין האולם ולמזבח)[19] is more sanctified than it ... the sanctuary is more sanctified than it ... the Holy of Holies is more sanctified than [all of] them.

One should note, first of all, that the Mishna actually lists 11 levels of sanctity, each one greater than the previous one. It appears that the introduction, "ten levels of sanctity," was formulated according to the view of R. Yose, who is cited at the end of the mishna: בחמישה דברים 'בין האולם ולמזבח' שוה להיכל ... ופורשים מ'בין האולם ולמזבח' בשעת ההקטרה "In five respects 'between the porch and the altar' (בין האולם ולמזבח) is equal to the sanctuary ... and all must separate from [= leave] 'between the porch and the altar' (בין האולם ולמזבח) during the time of the burning of the incense."[20] Albeck already noted as much in his commentary (following Maimonides in his commentary on this mishna): "according to R. Yose there were only ten levels of sanctity, but according to the first Tanna, there were eleven."

§ 10 In detailing the varying levels of sanctity that existed within the Temple Mount, the Mishna proceeds in a clear and logical order: from the outside in, from east to west: the חֵיל "Rampart," the Court of the Women, the Court of the Israelites, the Court of the Priests, between the porch and the altar (בין האולם ולמזבח), the sanctuary, and the Holy of Holies.[21] But this structure is tarnished by the phrase "between the porch and the altar" (בין האולם ולמזבח): following geographically with the outside in and from east to west, the expression should have been "between the altar and the porch" (בין המזבח ולאולם), since, after all, the porch is to the west of the altar and on the way to the sanctuary, and yet the Tanna reversed the order and mentioned the porch first. This point was raised already by R. Yo'el Ḥasid in his novellae,

19 The phrase בין האולם ולמזבח in all three of its attestations in this mishna (the one cited here and two, cited later, from the final line of the mishna) appear in all the reliable textual witnesses (MS Kaufmann, Parma A [De Rossi 138], Parma B [De Rossi 497], MS Cambridge [published by Lowe], and the first printed edition [Napoli 1492]).

20 Here too, as mentioned, all textual witnesses show the relevant phrase.

21 See the attached drawing (p. 94), "The Plan of the Temple Mount and the Temple," taken from Ch. Albeck's commentary on Middot.

who suggested two explanations for the aberration. Here is his formulation of the question:[22]

> לא יכולתי להתאפק מה שקשה לי, בכל מקום הוא "בין האולם ולמזבח", ואיפכא מיבעי ליה, "בין המזבח ולאולם", דהא כל מסכת מדות השיב כסדר מן המזרח ולמערב, ע"נ עד המזבח אחר כך האולם, ופשיטא כאן נכנסין מן החוץ [פנימה], והל"ל "בין המזבח ולאולם".
>
> I could not resist [asking] what bothers me: every time[23] it says "between the porch and the altar" (בין האולם ולמזבח), but it should have said the opposite: "between the altar and the porch" (בין המזבח ולאולם), since the entire tractate Middot teaches in the order from east to west, properly until the altar, and then the porch, and it is obvious that here [in Kelim] we are entering from the outside [inwards],[24] and it should have said "between the altar and the porch" (בין המזבח ולאולם).

§ 11 Ḥasid offers, as mentioned, two explanations. The first offers the farfetched claim that all occurrences of the phrase are based on mMid 3:6 (הכיור היה בין האולם ולמזבח "the basin was between the porch and the altar"), in which, he suggests local contextual requirements forced the reversal of the order. The second explanation suggests that the order is based on Ezek 8:16, וַיָּבֵא אֹתִי אֶל-חֲצַר בֵּית-ה' הַפְּנִימִית וְהִנֵּה-פֶתַח הֵיכַל ה' בֵּין הָאוּלָם וּבֵין הַמִּזְבֵּחַ "He brought me to the inner courtyard of the House of the Lord, and at the entrance to the sanctuary of the Lord, between the porch and the altar ...," where, Ḥasid suggests, the porch was mentioned first because the prophet first encountered the porch and then turned to arrive at the altar. He concludes, לכן מתניתין לישנא דקרא נקט בכל מקום "therefore the Mishna specifically used the language of Scripture in every instance."

§ 12 Although the direction taken by Ḥasid in his second explanation is the correct direction, he chose the wrong path. He is correct to say that the Mishna was formulated to mimic the language of Scripture, and in fact it was the biblical idiom that influenced the formulator of our mishna, but it was not the unique Ezek 8:16 that he had in mind. Instead, it was Joel 2:17, בֵּין הָאוּלָם וְלַמִּזְבֵּחַ יִבְכּוּ הַכֹּהֲנִים "between the porch and the altar will the priests cry,"[25]

---

22 The text is as printed in ששה סדרי משנה עם פירושי הראשונים והאחרונים (Jerusalem: 'El ha-Meqorot, 1957); I have added punctuation to ease the reading.

23 By "every time," Ḥasid means all ten attestations of this phrase in the Mishna: 'Eruvin 10:15; Yoma 3:8; Tamid 5:6 (2×); Middot 3:6 (2×); 5:1; here in Kelim 1:9 (3×).

24 I have added this word for clarity.

25 My son, Elitzur Avraham, pointed out to me that in the parallel rabbinic text that deals with the ten levels of sanctity (Sifre Zuṭa Nāso' 5:2 [ed. Horovitz, p. 228]), the editor noted that the author of Sefer Ḥasidim נתן רמז והא דאין בעלי מומין נכנסין 'לבין האולם ולמזבח' מן הכתוב בֵּין הָאוּלָם וְלַמִּזְבֵּחַ יִבְכּוּ הַכֹּהֲנִים מְשָׁרְתֵי ה' "offered a mnemonic for the fact that those with blemishes are not permitted to enter 'between the porch and the altar' (בין האולם ולמזבח) from the verse 'between the porch and the altar cry the priests, servants of the Lord." Beside this comment, though, Sefer Ḥasidim does not mention anything about the connection. In

that served as the mishna's source. The formulation of this verse forced itself into the Tannaitic text at every opportunity,[26] including in the list of "ten levels of sanctity," in which its order disrupted the otherwise logical presentation of the ascending ranks of sanctity.

§ 13 We can conclude, therefore, that the adherence to the language of the biblical verse overpowered, consciously or unconsciously, the logical order required by the context. It should also be pointed out that the formulation בין ... ול ... is attested in classical Hebrew only once in the Bible, in the verse from Joel discussed here,[27] and it is unattested in the Mishna, as well, with the singular exception of our phrase, which was borrowed entirely – both with regard to its lexemes (אולם and then מזבח) and with regard to how they are joined (בין ... ול ...), yielding בין האולם ולמזבח instead of the expected בין המזבח והאולם.

6.3.2 הזורע והחורש והקוצר

§ 14 The thirty-nine activities prohibited on the Sabbath are listed in the mishna in Shabbat 7:2. The list opens with the "process of bread-making":

> אבות המלאכות ארבעים חסר אחת: הזורע והחורש והקוצר והמעמר והדש והזורה, הבורר והטוחן והמרקד והלש והאופה.
>
> The main classes of work are forty minus one: sowing, plowing, reaping, binding sheaves, threshing, winnowing, cleansing crops, grinding, sifting, kneading, baking.

This is the version of the mishna in our texts, and it is the same as the text studied by the Babylonian Amoraim, who ask (bŠab 73b) about the illogicality of listing זורע "sowing" before חורש "plowing." As Tosafot (s. v. מכדי מכרב) put it: דהכא כל סידורא דפת נקט כסדר, לבד מחרישה "since here the entire process of [making] bread is given in sequence, except for plowing." This is how the Talmud puts it: מכדי מכרב כרבי ברישא, ליתני חורש והדר ליתני זורע! "Since one plows first, it should teach 'plow' and then teach 'sow'!" The Talmud answers: תנא בארץ ישראל קאי, דזרעי ברישא והדר כרבי "the Tanna was in Eretz Israel, where they sow first and then plow." Rashi explains: בארץ ישראל – קשה היא, ואין יכול לכסות בלא חרישה, ואשמעינן דהא נמי חרישה היא "in Eretz Israel – [the land] is tough, and one cannot cover without plowing;

---

modern times, the connection between this mishna and the verse from Joel has been noted by Haneman, in his excellent article (1976). Neither Sefer Ḥasidim nor Haneman mentioned the distortion within the order of m. Kelim 1:9 caused by this allusion, however.

26 See the list in n. 23 above.

27 Cf. Haneman 1976:47.

[the Mishna] teaches us that this [secondary plowing] is also [legally] considered plowing." The procedure, then, is as follows: the farmers plow, then sow, then plow again in order to cover the seed, and that secondary plowing is legally considered plowing, as well. The primary plowing, however, is of course still the first one, and it remains strange that the mishna failed to mention this plowing in its enumeration of the actions involved in preparing bread.

§ 15 It is interesting that another Tannaitic – i.e., Palestinian – source, also quoted in the Bavli, also discusses the process of making bread, and presents them in their logical order, with plowing prior to sowing. We read thus in bBer 58a:

> בן זומא ראה אוכלוסא על גב מעלה בהר הבית אמר: "ברוך חכם הרזים וברוך שברא אלו לשמשני". הוא היה אומר: "כמה יגיעות יגע אדם הראשון עד שמצא פת לאכול: חרש וזרע וקצר ועמר ודש וזרה וברר וטחן והרקיד ולש ואפה, ואחר כך אכל. ואני משכים ומוצא כל אלו לפני!"
>
> Ben Zoma saw a crowd on top of the step of the Temple Mount, and said: "Blessed is the one Wise of secrets, and blessed is He who created all these to serve me!" He used to say: "How much Adam had to exert himself in order to eat bread! He plowed and sowed and reaped and bound sheaves and threshed and winnowed and cleansed crops and ground and sifted and kneaded and baked, and only then did he eat. And I get up and find all this before me!"

Note: חרש וזרע "plowed and sowed," in accord with their logical order.[28] This is the text also in the parallel (yBer 9:2 [Venice printing p. 13c; and MS Leiden ed. Academy of the Hebrew Language, p. 69]), but there additional activities are included (ניכש "weeding," עידר "hoed," and קיטף "picked"):[29] חרש וזרע ניכש עידר קצר עימר דש זרה בירר טחן הרקיד לש וקיטף ואפה.

In the parallel in the Tosefta, however, (tBer 9:2), we find עד שזרע וחרש וקצר ועמר ודש וזרה וברר וטחן והרקיד ולש ואפה. Saul Lieberman showed that the version זרע וחרש is attested in MS Vienna and MS Erfurt,[30] and he commented, וזו היא 'נוסחת א"י' על פי מה שיש בידינו במסכת שבת פ"ז מ"ב ובבלי שם [דף] עג ע"א וכן במכילתא דרשב"י עמ' 67 "and this is the 'Palestinian version,' based on what we have in mŠab 7:2 and bŠab 73a, and in the Mekhilta de-RŠBY p. 67." Later, however, Lieberman pointed out, אבל בד [דפוס] ראשון של התוספתא] שחרש וזדר (צ"ל וזרע) וכן במשניות של שבת מטיפוסי א"י (ירושלמי לו, קויפמן, פרמה ועוד): החורש והזורע, וכן הוא הסדר בסוגיית

28 This is the text of the MSS (Florence I.II.7 and Paris 4:671) of Bavli Berakhot.

29 Saul Lieberman 1955–1983:1.105 referred also to the version that included these three in MS Rome.

30 Lieberman 1955–1983:1.105.

הירושלמי שם וכ"ה בירושלמי כאן ובשקלים פ"ה מ"א "but in the first printed edition [of the Tosefta, we read] [וזרע] (וזדר) שחרש 'who plowed and sowed', and so, too, in the Mishna Shabbat of Palestinian type (Yerušalmi, Lowe, Kaufmann, Parma, etc.): החורש והזורע 'one who plows and one who sows', and this is also the order in the *sugya* in the Yerušalmi there, and so, too, in the Yerušalmi here, and in yŠeq 5:1."

§ 16 If so, the version הזורע והחורש והקוצר is attested in our texts of the Mishna, and to which the discussion in the Bavli testifies, as well, stands against the version found in Palestinian-type Mishnayot (Kaufmann, Parma A, Cambridge [ed. Lowe]) and the discussion in the Yerušalmi, all of which show החורש והזורע והקוצר. The *baraita* of Ben Zoma, as quoted in both the Bavli and the Yerušalmi, is in accord with the Palestinian version, whereas the Tosefta in Shabbat agrees with the version assumed in the Bavli.[31]

As mentioned, the Bavli explicitly states that the illogical order is based on practices common in Palestine: there they plowed, sowed, and plowed again in order to cover the seed. Lieberman, too, accepted this claim, and writes, כנראה שבא"י חרשו פעמיים "apparently in Palestine they plowed twice."[32] But one may ask, does the assumption that "in Palestine they plowed twice" justify the illogical order of activities in our text of the Mishna?

§ 17 I would suggest that it is worth weighing an alternative approach to explain the disruption in the order of activities – הזורע והחורש והקוצר instead of החורש והזורע והקוצר. It should first be noted that of the 39 prohibited activities listed in the Mishna in Shabbat, only four are found explicitly in the Bible: המבעיר "lighting a fire" (לֹא-תְבַעֲרוּ אֵשׁ בְּכֹל מֹשְׁבֹתֵיכֶם בְּיוֹם הַשַּׁבָּת [Exod 35:3]); החורש והקוצר "one who plows and one who harvests" (שֵׁשֶׁת יָמִים תַּעֲבֹד וּבַיּוֹם הַשְּׁבִיעִי תִּשְׁבֹּת בֶּחָרִישׁ וּבַקָּצִיר תִּשְׁבֹּת [Exod 34:21]); המוציא (מרשות לרשות) "one who carries from one domain to another" (וְלֹא-תוֹצִיאוּ מַשָּׂא מִבָּתֵּיכֶם בְּיוֹם הַשַּׁבָּת [Jer 17:22]). It seems to me fair to assume that when the list of prohibited activities was formulated, the combination החורש והקוצר was already well-established, formulated on the basis of the verse in Exodus, בֶּחָרִישׁ וּבַקָּצִיר תִּשְׁבֹּת.

Allow me to explain. When the Rabbis decided to formulate the list of thirty-nine prohibited activities, beginning with the eleven which constitute the process of bread-making, the expression החורש והקוצר was already a stock

---

31 Further data on rabbinic sources which read חרש וזרע (or חורש וזורע or חרישה וזריעה) as opposed to those which read זרע וחרש (or זורע וחורש or חריעה וחרישה) can be found in David Rosenthal's important article (1999:n. 89). Rosenthal concludes his discussion: "נניח למשנת שבת ולפתרון גרסתה."

32 Lieberman 1955–1983:1.105.

phrase, based on the biblical verse. The Rabbis had to add the other nine activities to the list (זורע, מעמר, דש, זורה, בורר, טוחן, מרקד, לש, and אופה), there was no difficulty in adding the last eight, from עימור "binding sheaves" to אפייה "baking," since their rightful place was following קוצר, but inserting זורע into the list presented a problem. It could not be placed after קוצר, but the Rabbis did not want to break up the set phrase החורש והקוצר,[33] so they placed הזורע before the pair.

§ 18 This was the version that stood in front of the Babylonian Amoraim, and it was apparently a "first edition" of the Mishna. But already in the first few generations after its publication, a new edition was put out, which listed the prohibited activities in their logical order, החורש והזורע והקוצר, as is found in the Yerušalmi, MS Kaufmann, Parma A, Cambridge, and other MSS related to these. The *baraita* of Ben Zoma, which simply describes a reality and bears no strong connection to any biblical text, was most likely formulated with חרש זרע קצר in their proper order to begin with, since when one describes the procedure of bread-making, it is natural to list them in that order, with plowing preceding sowing. The Toseftan version of Ben Zoma's statement, on the other hand, appears to have been altered to bring it in line with the Bavli's version of the Mishna.

We can point out that Maimonides, too, lists the prohibited activities in their logical sequence in his code (*Laws of Shabbat* 7:1; he replaces the participial forms with verbal nouns):

> ומניין כל אבות מלאכות ארבעים חסר אחת. ואלו הן: החרישה והזריעה והקצירה והעימור והדישה והזרייה והברירה והטחינה וההרקדה והלישה והאפייה.

---

33 It is worth noting that the eleven activities within the bread-making process can be divided into two groups: the six done by the farmer (חורש to זורה), and the five done in the home or by the baker (בורר to אופה). When the subject is the labor of the farmer, who works his land, the Bible employs a synecdoche and mentions only the two most important activities to refer to all his labor: it opens with חורש and ends with קוצר, or opens with זורע and ends with קוצר. The first option is employed in these verses: אֲשֶׁר אֵין-חָרִישׁ וְקָצִיר (Gen 45:6); וְלַחֲרֹשׁ חֲרִישׁוֹ וְלִקְצֹר קְצִירוֹ (1 Sam 8:12); וְנִגַּשׁ חוֹרֵשׁ בַּקֹּצֵר (Amos 9:13); חֲרַשְׁתֶּם רֶשַׁע, עַוְלָתָה קְצַרְתֶּם (Hosea 10:3). The second option is adopted in these: זֶרַע וְקָצִיר (Gen 8:22); וּבַשָּׁנָה הַשְּׁלִישִׁית זִרְעוּ וְקִצְרוּ (2 Kgs 19:29 = Isa 37:30); זָרְעוּ חִטִּים, וְקֹצִים קָצָרוּ (Jer 12:13); כִּי רוּחַ יִזְרָעוּ וְסוּפָתָה יִקְצֹרוּ (Hosea 8:7); זִרְעוּ לָכֶם לִצְדָקָה, קִצְרוּ לְפִי־חֶסֶד (ibid 10:12); אַתָּה תִזְרַע, וְלֹא תִקְצוֹר (Micah 6:15); הַזֹּרְעִים בְּדִמְעָה, בְּרִנָּה יִקְצֹרוּ (Ps 126:5); זוֹרֵעַ עַוְלָה, יִקְצָר אָוֶן (Prov 22:8). As an aside, I will note that in one verse, the three actions are mentioned sequentially and in their logical order: חֹרְשֵׁי אָוֶן וְזֹרְעֵי עָמָל יִקְצְרֻהוּ (Job 4:8).

The verse regarding the laws of the Sabbath, בֶּחָרִישׁ וּבַקָּצִיר תִּשְׁבֹּת (Exod 34:21), follows the first of these routes, and so whoever formulated the phrase החורש והקוצר did not only align himself with this particular verse regarding the Sabbath, but, as it turns out, followed a well-trodden path within biblical stylistics.

> The sum total of all the prohibited activities is one less than forty, and these are they: plowing, sowing, harvesting, binding sheaves, threshing, winnowing, cleansing crops, grinding, sifting, kneading, and baking.

§ 19 The upshot of all this is that if our suggestion is correct, we have an example in which the influence of the biblical text (בֶּחָרִישׁ וּבַקָּצִיר תִּשְׁבֹּת) was powerful enough to alter the expected order of presentation within the mishnaic text.[34]

6.4 Concluding comment

§ 20 The majority of biblical influences detected in the Mishna remain examples of linguistic embeddings: the Tanna embedded within his text a biblical expression in place of its normal rabbinic counterpart.[35] In the mishna of "ten levels of sanctity," too, there is a biblical phrase embedded in the rabbinic text (בין האולם ולמזבח), but here the expression ruptures the logical procession of the text. This shows the strength of the biblical influence within rabbinic literature: the Bible's presence in the background shows through even when the use of a biblical expression does not entirely fit the rabbinic context. It is possible that this is the phenomenon seen in the mishnaic list of activities prohibited on the Sabbath, as well (הזורע והחורש והקוצר). It must be admitted, however, that the first example if far clearer and unproblematically identified, since the language of the biblical idiom remained unchanged in its rabbinic citation, whereas the example of plowing and sowing is less transparent.[36]

---

34 Yedidyah Kohen dealt with this mishna in his book (1992: 242–243). He suggested seeing in the Bavli's version an early formulation originating in Judea, as in Judea the sowing in fact preceded the plowing (a conclusion he reached based on the modern practices of the Arab residents of the Judean Hills), whereas the Palestinian-type mishna (MS Kaufmann, Parma A, etc.) and that attested in the Yerušalmi derived from a version edited in the Galilee, where the plowing always preceded the sowing. If this is true, it was not biblical influence that made the difference, but varying agricultural realities. One may ask, however, if it is true that in ancient times Judean farmers plowed only after sowing; and what of the ancient sources that testify to plowing both before and after sowing the seeds, which were collected by Lieberman (תוספתא כפשוטה לברכות, 105; e.g., t. Bava Metsia' 11:9: כדי שיהא איכר אומן חורש ושונה)? If these sources reflect reality, then even where plowing followed sowing, that was a secondary plowing; what did farmers do in the Galilean hills? The basic question, then, remains unaltered: why was plowing not mentioned before sowing?

35 For example, those mentioned above in §§ 4–7.

36 In simple embeddings of biblical expressions, which do not disturb the order of the mishnaic text (such as those mentioned above, §§ 4–7), we also encounter examples that are not entirely clear.

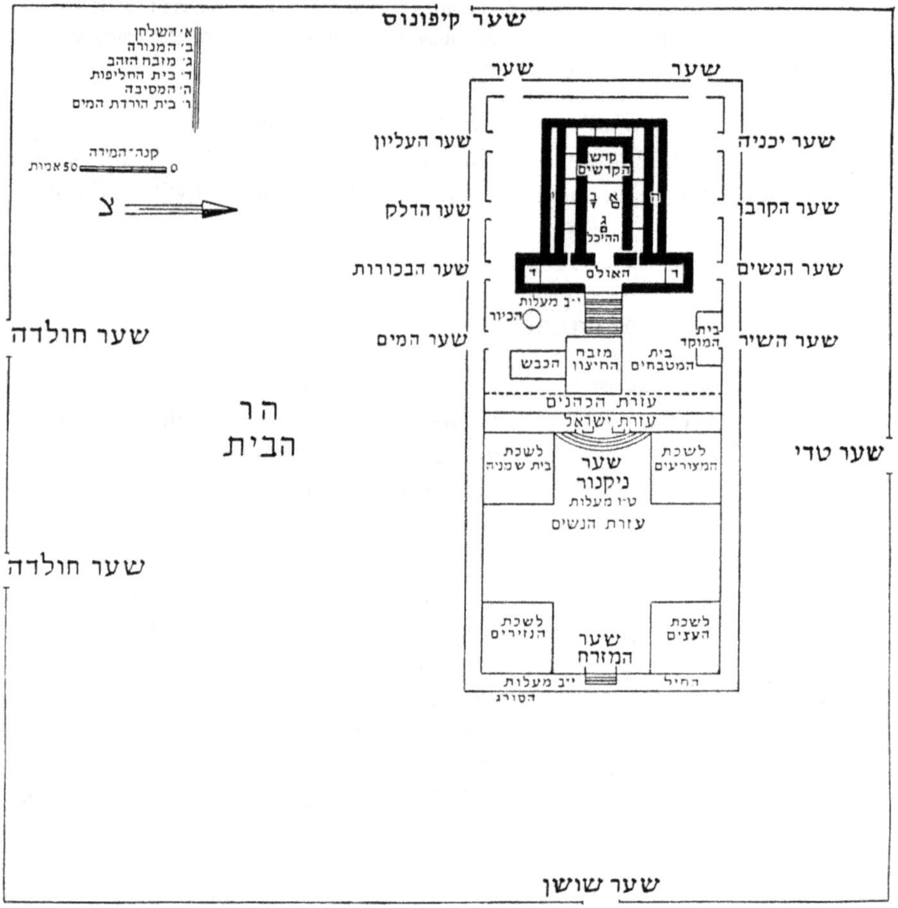

תכנית הר־הבית ובית־המקדש

Fig.: Plan of Temple and Temple Mount.

7 וְצִוִּתְךָ אַל יִכְבַּד לְבֶּךָ: Regarding One Sentence from the Letter to Pelatyahu

§ 1 The discovery of Hebrew texts from early periods in the history of the Hebrew language is always a uniquely important cultural event. Material that has not been touched by human hands for thousands of years introduces us to linguistic phenomena in their original forms. While there are various limitations that come along with these texts – both in terms of damage to the texts themselves that occurred over time, or in terms of the limitations of Hebrew orthography, which does not convey a full picture of many words until the system of vocalization came into use – Hebrew scholars often have much to gain from discoveries such as these. This is even more true with regard to texts from the First Temple Period, which bring us back at least 2,600 years. This short study is a further example of this.

§ 2 An important book edited by Steven Fassberg and Avi Hurvitz was recently published regarding Biblical Hebrew, containing 20 articles on various topics.[1] Two of the articles were written by André Lemaire; one he wrote alone, and the other he wrote together with Ada Yardeni. In this second article, Yardeni and Lemaire published a series of ostraca from the Shephelah from the end of the First Temple Period. The publication was accompanied, as expected, by photographs and drawings of the texts.[2] In fact, it is easy to see the linguistic similarities between these documents and others from the same period, such as the shards from Lachish, texts from Arad, and the Biblical books of the First Temple Period.[3] The first collection of texts includes letters; the most easily read text is the first one, the letter "to Pelatyahu," but it is also incomplete, and has some questionable readings.

§ 3 I wish to focus on one line from the letter "to Pelatyahu,"[4] and to progress from there to the Bible, the book of Ben Sira, and to a text from Qumran.

1 Fassberg and Hurvitz 2006.

2 See Lemaire and Yardeni 2006.

3 This can be seen both from the onomasticon, e.g., פלטיהו (Text A; p. 197 line 1), עזיהו, צדקיהו (p. 201, lines 4, 6), גדליהו (p. 204, line 1), שבנא (p. 207, line 4), etc., as well as from the general lexicon and from grammar (the use of similar forms and syntax), e.g. עת כים (= עַתָּה כַּיּוֹם; p. 197, lines 2–3), תשבני דבר (= תְּשִׁיבֵנִי דָּבָר; ibid., line 2), אשר לקח צדקיהו עבד המלך (p. 201, lines 6–7), among others.

4 Lemaire and Yardeni 2006:197–200.

At the end of line 3 and the beginning of line 4, the editors propose the following text:

וצוי/תך: אל נ/תכבד[5] לבך.

The line that is placed in between two letters – in this passage in the aforementioned text, it appears twice, in the words וצוי/תך and נ/תכבד – indicates that the letter cannot be read, and the editors are unsure whether to read it as the letter before the line or the letter after it; in other words, the words may be וצויך or וצותך, and נכבד or תכבד. Indeed, both in the photograph and the drawings that accompany the text, there is no support for either the *yod* or the *tav* in the first word. Despite that, their decision to read וצותך (= וְצִוִּיתִיךָ with defective spelling, without the two *yod*-s), is more likely than the first possibility (וצויך)

§ 4 As was said, in the continuation they also offer two alternative readings: נכבד or תכבד, meaning אל נכבד לבך or אל תכבד לבך. The editors first give the second reading, אל תכבד לבך, and suggest understanding תכבד as either the *pi'el* form (תְּכַבֵּד) or a *hif'il* form (תַּכְבֵּד). Both suggestions are reasonable in light of the biblical evidence, which is well presented by the editors: stubbornness (כובד הלב) is attested in the Bible (according to the Tiberian vocalization) with both the *pi'el* form of the verb, as in ולמה תְכַבְּדוּ את לבבכם כאשר כִּבְּדוּ מצרים ופרעה את לבם (2 Samuel 6:6), and with the *hif'il* form, as in וַיַּכְבֵּד פרעה את לבו (Exod 8:28 and others).[6] It is important to note that the Samaritans, too, read the verse in Exodus in the *hif'il* form as well: *wyakbəd*.[7]

§ 5 However, I question whether there is room to read what is left of the first letter of the verb in the letter to Pelatyahu as a *tav*. A diagonal line remains, descending from right to left, and it is longer than all of the other right-to-left diagonals in the text's other *tav*-s; compare those in ועת (= וְעַתָּה; p. 197 l. 1), שלחתיך (*ibid.*, ll. 1–2), תשבני (= תְּשִׁיבֵנִי; *ibid.*, l. 2), עת (= עַתָּה; *ibid.*, l. 2), אמרתי (*ibid.*, l. 4), עשת (= עָשִׂיתָ; *ibid.*, ll. 5–6).

§ 6 Their other suggestion, to read נכבד with a *nun* at the beginning of the word: אל נכבד לבך, should not have been proposed, not only paleographically (the line right-to-left diagonal does not look like the letter *nun*), but also grammatically. The word would have to be a *nif'al* past or participle (נִכְבַּד or

5 The letters כבד in this word begin the 4th line.

6 See Lemaire and Yardeni 2006:199.

7 See Ben-Ḥayyim 1957–1977:4.133. In the book of Ben Sira, we find הכבד in the *hif'il* form alone in connection with other nouns: הכבד את רעתך (8:15) and והכבד עולו (13:30). The text of Ben Sira is quoted from ספר בן סירא: המקור, קונקורדנציה וניתוח אוצר המילים (Jerusalem: Academy of the Hebrew Language, 1973).

נִכְבָּד), but the grammar of Hebrew does not allow a past tense verb or a participle in the present construction. Had the word indeed been in the *nif'al* form, we would have had to find a *yif'al* form, אל יכבד (= יִכָּבֵד) לבך, since the verb following the negative particle אַל is always the *yif'al* form; the form נכבד would be out of place.

§ 7 In my opinion, what descends from the first letter in the word resembles more the letter *yod*, and is similar to the line that descends from the right side to the left side in the words פלטיהו (p. 197, l. 1), תשבני (*ibid.*, l. 2), כי אני אמרתי (*ibid.*, l. 4), דברי (*ibid.*, l. 6). The angle that cuts the right-to-left diagonal in order to write the *yod* was erased in this word. Consequently, one should read here אל יכבד לבך.[8]

I suggest reading יכבד as a form in the *binyan* Qal: אל יִכְבַּד לבך. This is similar to the biblical verse וַיִּכְבַּד לב פרעה (Exod 9:7); here the Samaritans read the word this way as well: *wyikbad*.[9] The participle form of the *binyan Qal* in the *pa'el* form is also attested: כָּבֵד לב פרעה (Exod7:14) in the Tiberian vocalization; again, this is the same reading that the Samaritans have: *kabəd*.[10] In Ben Sira, too, the phrase לב כבד is attested (3:26–27).

§ 8 It is important to note that the editors do mention the existence of this *nif'al* form in one of the Dead Sea Scrolls. They refer to a passage from the Qumran text of the Book of Mysteries (4Q301), published by Lawrence Schiffman:[11]

1. משפטי כסיל ונחלת חכמ<ים>
2. מה נכבד לבב והוא מ֯מ֯ש֯<ל>

Schiffman understands מה נכבד in this text as "how honored," but Lemaire and Yardeni rightly question this understanding and suggest understanding the phrase with the sense of "stubbornness" (כובד הלב).[12] From here Lemaire and

8 I was pleased to hear that Dr. Ada Yardeni found my reading to be paleographically reasonable.

9 See Ben-Ḥayyim 1957–1977:4.133.

10 *Ibid.*

11 See Schiffman 1997:115–116.

12 See § 10 below. We also find the nominal phrasal idiom וכובוד לב in the DSS (the Manual of Discipline 4:11; cf. Licht 1965:98). כובוד is a phonetic variant of Tiberian כֹּבֶד (cf. Kutsher 1959, p. 397; he mentions the idiom כובוד לב; see also the detailed study by Elisha Qimron 1976:277–281; the noun כובוד is mentioned in various places in a recent article of his, as well: Qimron 2003:333, for example). It seems that this is how we should understand the phrase from 4Q487, frg. 24 line 2: <כי>בוד לב (Baillet 1982:8). In light of the example from the Manual of Discipline, it seems appropriate to suggest reading here a *waw* (and not a *yod*), as the second letter in <כו>בוד לב.

Yardeni arrive at the reading in our text, אל נכבד לבך, without noting that the differing syntactic constructions necessitate different forms. In the Book of Mysteries the use of the participle נכבד is appropriate. In Hebrew, the word מה can be followed either by a past tense form (נִכְבַּד), as in, for example מה פָּרַצְתָּ (Gen 38:29), מה יעצת (Job 26:3), מה נִכְבַּד היום מלך ישראל (2 Sam 6:29), or by a participle, with the subject coming after the participle, as in, for example מה נורָא[13] המקום הזה (Gen 28:17), מה יָקָר חסדך (Ps 36:8), מה נורָא מעשיך (*ibid.* 66:3).[14] However, when the negative article אַל begins the clause, it will not be followed by a past tense verb or by a participle, but by a *yif'al* form verb. Therefore, in the letter to Pelatyahu, one may read אל יִכְבַּד לבך or אל יִכָּבֵד. For reasons to be explained immediately, I am inclined towards the first possibility, אל יִכְבַּד.

§ 9 In Biblical Hebrew, כובד הלב, stubbornness, expressed with an intransitive verb, appears in the *Binyan Qal* (וַיִּכְבַּד לב, כָּבֵד לב[15]), but not in the *nif'al*. Most of the connotations of הִכָּבֵד and נִכְבַּד in the *nif'al* are connected to honor and value; see, for example, והוא נכבד מכל בית אביו "he is **honored** above all those in his father's household" (Gen. 34:19), בהכבדי בפרעה "when I gained **honor** through Pharaoh" (Ex. 14:18).[16] The first evidence of the *nif'al* being used in connection with stubbornness is found only in the aforementioned text from Qumran, מה נכבד לבב והוא ממש<ל>.[17]

However, in the transition from the Biblical books of the First Temple Period to the Second Temple Period, and of course to the texts at Qumran and Rabbinic literature, many intransitive verbs went from the *binyan Qal* to *nif'al*, as a few scholars have noted, including H. L. Ginsberg, who wrote: "the shift from the intransitive Qal verbs to *nif'al* is a general shift that takes place in front of our eyes in the Bible and the books which follow it."[18] He substantiated this claim with his analysis of the shift of כָּשַׁל > נִכְשַׁל, as well as other verbs.[19]

---

13 The form נורא can also be understood as a past tense verb, but I prefer to understand it as a participle, as it was understood by the earliest interpreters. Onqelos, for example, translates the verse from Genesis, מא דחילו אתרא הדין. The word דחילו is a contraction of דְּחִיל הוּא, as I have shown elsewhere (Bar Asher 1979:190–193). דְּחִיל is a passive participle.

14 Here too, I understand נורא as a participle, in light of the *Targum* of Psalms, which renders it מא דחילין אינון עובדיך (see the previous note).

15 See § 7.

16 We do however find a use of the *nif'al* כבד meaning the abundance and power of water, באין מעינות נכבדי מים (Prov 8:24).

17 Perhaps it is not superfluous to remark that the combination כב"ד + לב (לבב) is not attested in Rabbinic literature. The latest evidence we have of its use in the Hebrew Classical Period is in the book of Sirach, and the Dead Sea Scrolls.

18 See Ginsberg 1934:216.

19 His comments regarding this issue can be found there on p. 215 (see footnote 4 there as well). Ginsberg himself noted that Lambert (1900) preceded him with regard to this comment. It is important to emphasize that most of the theories found in Lambert's important article

§ 10 This is what we find in the Book of Mysteries: מה נכבד לבב והוא מ<ל>ממש. The context affirms Lemaire and Yardeni's suggestion that we are dealing here with stubbornness, and not honor or value. In other words, כָּבֵד לֵב of Exodus has been transformed into נכבד לבב at Qumran. However, the form נכבד is not written, and is indeed impossible, in the letter to Pelatyahu. There we find אל יכבד לבך, and the word יכבד can be read either as יִכְבַּד (Qal) or as יִכָּבֵד (Nif'al). However, as the text is very early – the end of the First Temple Period – I prefer the form of the Qal, אל יִכְבַּד לבך, as one would find in both the Tiberian tradition and in the Samaritan version of the Bible.[20]

§ 11 It is also important to comment on another small detail. We read in the letter to Pelatyahu: וצותך [= וְצִוִּיתִיךָ] אל יכבד לבך. One may ask: when dealing with an active command, it is possible to command someone not to "harden" (יְכַבֵּד or יַכְבִּיד) his heart, but how can one command someone that their heart not *be hardened* (by itself)? Indeed, we find in the editors' translation, "I ordered you: may you not harden your heart,"[21] but this is not precise. While the basic meaning of the verb ציווה is to give a command (like وصى in Arabic), ציווה took on another connotation, that of the general idea of saying, rather than a command specifically. A good example of this in Biblical Hebrew is the verse, הלא **צויתיך** חזק ואמץ אל תערץ ואל תחת (Josh 1:9). The verses inform us, ויאמר ה' אל יהושע בן נון משרת משה לאמר [...] ועתה קום עבר את הירדן [...] חזק ואמץ כי אתה תנחיל את העם הזה את הארץ [...] רק חזק ואמץ מאד לשמר לעשות ככל התורה [...] לא ימוש ספר התורה הזה מפיך "The Lord said to Joshua b. Nun, the attendant of Moses, ... 'Now get up and cross the Jordan ... be strong and bold, for you will give the land to this nation ... only be very strong and bold, to carefully observe all this instruction ... let this book of instruction never cease form your mouth'" (Josh 1:1–8), and afterwards add, הלא **צויתיך** חזק ואמץ אל תערץ ואל תחת. "Lo, I have told you to be strong and bold, do not fear and do not be afraid." It is clear that this is not

---

written more than 100 years ago are still valid, despite some broad generalizations. So, too, Ze'ev Ben-Ḥayyim, in his famous article from 1953, לשון עתיקה במציאות חדשה, demonstrated the shift of intransitive verbs from the *binyan Qal* to *nif'al* (see Ben-Ḥayyim 1992:62, bottom). Characteristics of the Classical Period of the Hebrew language (meaning Biblical Hebrew and Rabbinic Hebrew) are scattered across his first book of the Samaritan Pentateuch (Ben-Ḥayyim 1961, e.g. in comments on Exod 15:8 [נצבו], and on Deut 20:2 [ונגש]; in both cases the *binyan Qal* in the Samaritan tradition retains its earlier meaning, and *nif'al* in the Tiberian tradition illustrates its subsequent meaning. There are other examples similar to this.) See also what he wrote in his grammar (Ben-Ḥayyim 1957–1977:5.77). Recently, David Talshir contributed important observations on this issue, as well (Talshir 2004:5–6).

20 See § 7.

21 See Lemaire and Yardeni 2006:198.

a command, rather speech in general. One could say with more precision that this is speech of urging and encouragement.

§ 12 In short, the verb ציווה in Biblical Hebrew does not only convey the giving of a command, rather sometimes is just connotes talking, or urgent speech. The Rabbis understood it as urging, as well. In a short midrashic comment, we find that the first word in the verse, צו את אהרן ואת בניו לאמר (Lev 6:2), is explained in the Sifra (96:1) thus: "צו" – אין צוואה בכל מקום אלא זירוז מיד ולדורות "*tsav*, every time it appears, is not a command, but rather an urging for now and for generations."[22] In an expanded midrash, we find that the use of the צו in a different verse is also understood this way. The verse I refer to is צו את בני ישראל וישלחו מן המחנה כל צרוע וכל זב וכל טמא לנפש (Num 5:2). "צו" – רבי יהודה בן בתירה אומר אין הציווי בכל מקום אלא זירוז, שנאמר "וצו את יהושע וחזקהו ואמצהו," לפי דרכנו למדנו שאין מחזקין אלא המוחזקין ואין מזרזין אלא למזורזין '*tsav*, says Rabbi Judah ben Beteira, is not a command but a repeated encouragement, as is says וצו את יהושע וחזקהו ואמצהו (Josh 3:28). By the way, we learn that one only encourages he who has already been encouraged, and one only urges he who has already been urged" (Sifre Numbers 1).[23]

§ 13 It is characteristic that the verse with which Rabbi Judah ben Beteira supports his explanation concerns the "command" to Joshua bin Nun, וצו את יהושע וחזקהו ואמצהו, and this is the very same verse which is echoed, almost verbatim, in the verse we were discussing, הלא צויתיך חזק ואמץ (Josh 1:9). In this verse from Joshua, the verbs that follow the verb צויתיך do not connote actions that the one who was commanded can do, so that we can say that there was an actual command given by someone for the subject to carry out, rather we are dealing with stative verbs. These can be presented either as a positive obligation (e.g., חזק ואמץ), or as a negative prohibition (e.g., אל תערץ ואל תחת). In either case, צויתיך should be understood as "I said to you" or "I urged you."[24]

---

22 As it is widely known, this interpretation is found in Rashi's commentary there, s. v. צו את אהרן (see the comments of Nahmanides and Hizquni as well; it is beyond the scope of this study to discuss the dispute between Rashi and Nahmanides).

23 The text of MS Vatican 32 of Sifre Numbers is almost identical to the text presented by Horovitz; however, there are two important differences that should be noted here. Instead of המוחזקין, MS Vatican has מן המחזיקין, and instead of למזורזין, it has מן המזורזין.

24 It seems that this is what HALOT mean (p. 1010), when they presented the definition "urge" and "place in someone's care." Radaq, too, in his commentary on this verse in Joshua speaks of urgency, but he sees the word הלא as the indicator of this urgency, as can be seen clearly from his comments and from the examples that he brings: "הלא צויתיך, a word connoting urgency, so too הלא שמעת בתי (Ruth 2:8), הלא שלחתיך (Judg 6:14), and others." All of the examples brought by Radaq begin with the word הלא, connoting urgency. This comment of Radaq found its way into later commentaries (see for example מצודת ציון: "הלוא: this word designates urgency and encouragement, for example הלוא שלחתיך").

§ 14 It can be said that the Hebrew verbs אמר and ציווה both originally meant "to give a command," like their Arabic parallels امر and وصى. In the verb אמר, the general meaning of speech became the primary one, and the meaning of "the giving of a command," became secondary, but it can still be found in Biblical Hebrew in passages such as, for example, דבר אל בני ישראל ואמרת אליהם ועשו להם ציצת (Num 15:38), ויעש להם יהושע כאשר אמר לו ה', את סוסיהם עקר ואת מרכבתיהם שרף באש (Josh 11:9), אמר להביא את ושתי המלכה לפניו ולא באה (Esth 1:17), אמר אל הכהנים בני אהרן ואמרת אלהם לנפש לא יטמא בעמיו (Lev 21:1),[25] and others. In the verb ציווה, the primary definition "to give a command" is most common (and therefore needs no documentation here), and the more general meaning of the word "to talk," "to urge," is less common, especially in the First Temple Period. It is used sporadically in the Bible (for example, the use of צויתיך in the verse from Joshua we have been discussing), and there are extra-biblical attestations, as now demonstrated in the letter to Pelatyahu: צותך (= צִוִּיתִיךָ).[26]

§ 15 To summarize this brief study, it can certainly be said that the letter to Pelatyahu, like other extra-biblical texts from the Biblical Period, adds important data to what we already know from Biblical texts and other documents written in later periods (the book of Ben Sira and the Dead Sea Scrolls). Both the idea that כובד הלב "stubbornness," and more precisely, the verbal expression כבד לב, as well as the definition of ציווה as "to urge" or "to speak urgingly" rather than "to give a command," are reinforced and put in their proper historical perspectives by the letter to Pelatyahu from the Shephelah.

---

25 For a list of examples, see BDB, p. 56 § 4, HALOT, p. 66 § 6.

26 It would appear at first that the sequence וצותך אל יכבד לבך can also be read as two sentences. The first sentence, consisting only of וצותך, would refer to the earlier giving of a command, perhaps given to Pelatyahu at the beginning of his mission, but which is not specified here (ועת [= ועתה] הנה שלחתיך הלא תשיבני דבר עתה כים [= כיום]). The second sentence, אל יכבד לבך, would then be an independent clause meaning, "do not refuse stubbornly." However, this reading seems problematic in my eyes; it is based on an assumption and not on fact. Therefore, I prefer to accept the suggestion of Lemaire and Yardeni: by placing a colon after their translation of the word וצותך (p. 198), they correctly indicated that the following clause was the substance of the command. However, as opposition to their view, in my opinion, this "imperative" carries with it a sense of (urgent) speaking, and not an actual command.

8 The verse שְׁמַע יִשְׂרָאֵל ('Hear, O Israel') in Greek transcription on an ancient amulet

§ 1 In a lecture at a conference in Vienna in February, 2008, Hans Taeuber presented an amulet which had been found in a child's grave.[1] The grave had been excavated in the course of excavations of an ancient cemetery in the town of Halbturn, in eastern Austria near the Hungarian border. The amulet is a small golden plaque (2.5 cm long and 1.2 cm wide) found in a circular silver box. The amulet was apparently written originally for a Jewish child, and is engraved in Greek script with the verse, שמע ישראל ה' אלהינו ה' אחד (Deut 6:4). According to Taeuber, the text can be dated paleographically to the 2nd or 3rd century CE, when the area was a Roman settlement, and thereby provides evidence for a Jewish presence there at this time. The amulet was first published, by Armin Lange and Hans Taeuber, in a catalog of one of the museums of Vienna.[2]

§ 2 Following Taeuber's lecture, there were scholars who dismissed the find's significance, based on what they called the "grave errors" in the transcriptions, which allegedly showed that the scribe was an ignorant non-Jew. At the time, however, I contended that these were not "errors," but reflexes of linguistic phenomena either known or explicable (some detailed by me on the spot), and that the amulet should be taken seriously. Taeuber's view that the scribe was Jewish is to be accepted.[3]

At the conference, I agreed with Prof. Lange that I would put my comments into written form after the formal publication of the amulet in the catalog, and this is the promise I am keeping here.

---

1 The conference, convened by Armin Lange of the University of Vienna and Emanuel Tov of the Hebrew University in Jerusalem, took place 11–14 February, 2008, and was entitled "The Dead Sea Scrolls in Context." Lectures regarding topics other than Qumran itself, such as Taeuber's, were also included.

2 Lange and Taeuber 2008:177–179. A detailed description of the excavations at Halbturn is available on the website of the University of Vienna. I am indebted to Prof. Lange for sending me a copy of the article mentioned, and (since slight errors crept into the printed text) a copy of the article as submitted to the editors of the catalog.

3 I wish to thank Cordelia Hesterman, of the staff of the Historical Dictionary of the Hebrew Language, for her assistance with information regarding Halbturn, the excavations there in general, and the article about the amulet (in the previous note) in particular.

8.1 The text

§ 3 First I will cite the text of the amulet, and then turn to the comments on the linguistic phenomena underlying it.

Text	Transliteration
ΣΥΜΑ	שְׁמַע
ΙΣΤΡΑΗ	יִשְׂתְּרָאֵ
Λ ΑΔΩ	ל אֲדוֹ
ΝΕ ΕΛΩ	נֵי אֱלוֹ
Η ΑΔΩ	[הֵ]י אֲדוֹ
Ν Α	נ 41

8.2 Linguistic comments

§ 4 The verb שְׁמַע is transcribed συμα, with the realization of the *shewa* (as found in both the Tiberian and Babylonian masoretic vocalizations) as a vowel. It should be noted that this very word (in Ps 30:11) is transcribed in the second column of Origen's Hexapla as σμα.[5] This transcription shows that the *shewa* was elided and that a consonant cluster appeared at the beginning of the word.

In practice, based only on the transcriptions of Origen, it can be established that in this era (the second and third centuries CE) three different methods – which can be reduced to two – of representing a *shewa* under a word's initial consonant:

1. As a vowel,[6] as in σεμω for שְׁמוֹ (Ps 29:2 [Brønno, 110]); βεσαυει for בְּשַׁוְעִי (Ps 31:23 [Brønno, 81]); μαλαμμεδ for מְלַמֵּד (Ps 18:35 [Brønno, 84]);

4 It is well known that the letter α in Greek represents the number 'one' (cf. LSJ s. v. α, ἄλφα). This usage is known from rabbinic literature, as well: בשלוש קופות של שלוש סאין תורמין את הלשכה, וכתוב בהן: אל"ף, בי"ת, גימ"ל. ר' ישמעאל אומר: יוונית כתוב בהן: אלפ"א, בית"א, גמ"א (גמל"א) "They pay out of the bureau with three boxes of three *se'ah*s each, on which was written: *aleph*, *bet*, *gimel*. R. Ishmael says, they were written in Greek: *alpha*, *beta*, *gamma*" (m. Sheqalim 3:2). See below, §§ 8–9.

5 Cf. Brønno 1943:222. More recently, the excellent article by Yuditsky 2005 has provided a thorough survey of the data and the history of scholarship.

6 I am avoiding the question of whether this represents a reduced vowel, matching the original pronunciation of the *shewa*, or a full vowel – as it was pronounced in the Hebrew and Aramaic of the Samaritans in Eretz Israel. The analysis and conclusions of Yuditsky need to be further studied.

λαμαλχη for לְמַלְכֵי (Ps 89:28 [Brønno, 126]); μοσαυε[7] for מְשַׁוֶּה (Ps 18:34 [Brønno, 84]); χισουσ for כְּסוּס[8] (Ps 32:9 [Brønno, 115, 220]).

2. A. Elision of the *shewa* and the appearance of a consonant cluster at the beginning of the word, as in σμα for שְׁמַע cited above, as well as ζχορ for זְכָר- (Ps 89:48 [Brønno, 46]); βχορ for בְּכוֹר (Ps 89:28 [Brønno, 161]), βριθ for בְּרִית (Ps 89:40 [Brønno, 183]); θβουνωθ for תְּבוּנוֹת (Ps 49:4 [Brønno, 181]).
   B. Elision of the *shewa* and resolution of the consonant cluster by the addition of a prosthetic vowel. There are not very many examples, but the significance of those that do appear should not be minimized: ηζχορ for זְכֹר (Ps 89:51 [Brønno, 46]); αρσαειμ for רְשָׁעִים (Ps 1:1 [Brønno, 151]).[9]

It is possible that the difference between many of the words in category (2a), such as זְכָר-/ζχορ, and words in category (2b), such as זְכֹר/ηζχορ, is a difference in spelling alone: in some of the words, the prosthetic vowel found in the pronunciation was simply not recorded in the writing. This should not be facilely assumed, however, since Hebrew tolerated consonant clusters in some words; compare, for instance, זְרוֹעַ with אֶזְרוֹעַ and the like.[10]

§ 5 The transcription συμα of the Austrian amulet belongs, of course, to the first category; it is slightly suprising in that it shows the use of υ for the

7 It would appear that the [m] caused the vowel to shift to an [o], as Yuditsky 2005:134 correctly surmised.

8 There was also a *shewa* under the initial consonant in the 2mp imperative forms of the binyan Qal, as well as the 2ms lengthened imperative forms or the forms that end with a vowel or with the pronominal suffixes, in various traditions of Hebrew. See, for example, for MT שִׁרְצוּ in Gen 9:9, the Samaritans read *šerēṣu* (< שְׁרצו). Within the MT, cf. רְפָאָה (Ps 41:5) and וּקְרָאֵנִי (Ps 50:15). In the Babylonian vocalization we find מְלֹכִי (Jud 9:10; Tiberian מָלְכִי); מְשֹׁכֵנִי (Song 1:4; Tiberian מָשְׁכֵנִי); and many others, collected by Yeivin 1985:479 ff. A penetrating analysis can be found in Ben-Ḥayyim 1957–1977:5.136, but this issue remains beyond the parameters of our note. A new investigation of the G-stem imperatives, which suggests a new interpretation of their development and history, can be found in Bar-Asher 2008.

9 This example is from Codex Vatican. One could presumably claim that as opposed to MT אַשְׁרֵי הָאִישׁ אֲשֶׁר לֹא הָלַךְ בַּעֲצַת רְשָׁעִים, the transcriber had a version which read הָרְשָׁעִים, and that the [a] which begins the word reflects the a-vowel of the definite article. However, we have no serious support for the claim of a text other than the Masoretic one here.

10 For the two major paradigms – either a full vowel following the first consonant or an initial consonant cluster following the elision of the *shewa* – a parallel can be cited from the Samaritan tradition, of Aramaic in particular (since the phonological processes which governed Samaritan Hebrew governed Samaritan Aramaic, as well). Two examples of nouns of the form פְּעָל* are relevant: qēråb (< קְרָב) vs. aktåb (< כְּתָב); the two are taken from Ben-Ḥayyim 1957–1977:3/2.46, 50. The same phenomenon is attested in Syropalestinian Aramaic (Bar-Asher 1977:435).

shewa.[11] This would seem to be worthy of note, and demand some sort of analysis of the quality of the vowel being represented by υ. May this be an indication of a realization of the vowel as a rounded [u] or [ü], caused by the proximity to the מ [m]? Such a conclusion is certainly possible; as is known, the υ was pronounced in classical Greek as a back rounded vowel [u], and when its pronunciation changed, it remained still a central rounded vowel [ü], and it was thus pronounced for the last centuries BCE and the first centuries CE.[12] There is no reason not to assume that the transcription found in our amulet became established at a time when the u still retained its original pronunciation as a rounded back vowel, [u], or at least its later pronunciation, [ü].[13]

§ 6 The transcription Ιστραηλ (ישתראל) for the name יִשְׂרָאֵל is further evidence for what has already been found in other epigraphic texts. Only recently, Yitzhak Sapir has studied a similar transcription:[14] the form Ιστραελ found in a text from Tell Qasile, as well as an inscription from Jaffa and in the writings of some Church Fathers.[15] For our present purposes, the difference between the η and the ε (in the two inscriptions and the Church Fathers) is secondary; far more important is the appearance of the τ as a glide between the σ (שׂ) and the ρ (ר).[16]

---

11 Dr. Alexey Yuditsky informed me that in the manuscript of the second column of the Hexapla (MS O39) in the Ambrosian Library in Milan, there is not even a single example of the use of υ (its appearance in the digraph ου is irrelevant here). Indeed, the examples cited above (§ 4) showed that when the *shewa* was transcribed as a vowel, e, a, o, and i were all used, but not u (cf. also Yuditsky, § 2, pp. 124–125).

12 See, for example, Allen 1974:62–66. Allen points out that there were regions in which the pronunciation [u] (back rounded vowel) was retained even as late as the second century CE, but the evidence for the shift [u] > [ü] begins already in the last centuries BCE. The further shift of the vowel to a front [i] is notably late – beginning only in the late first millennium CE (although the pronunciation [i] is attested in Egypt occasionally in the second and third centuries CE already). Similar conclusions are found also in Sturtevant 1968:41–44. He establishes that the shift [u] > [i] is consistently either late or took place in regions where there was no background of Greek use (Egypt and Armenia).

13 Realization of the *shewa* (which had become a full vowel) as a back vowel – [u] – is known also from the Syro-Palestinian Aramaic (SPA) dialect. For example: שומין, pronounced apparently *šumayən* < שְׁמַיִן; שומיא (*šumayya*) < שְׁמַיָּא; תומניא (*tumanya*) < תְּמָנְיָא; תומנין (*tumanən*) < תְּמָנִין, and more (cf. Bar-Asher 1977: 421, 425, 430, 433, 435, 453, 491). In the four words just cited from SPA, I transliterated the vowel marked by the *waw* a [u], not [o], because they are found in open syllables, in accordance with the conclusions I reached years ago (*ibid.*, 483–505, and esp. the summary on pp. 504–505).

14 Sapir 2007.

15 See Kaplan 1978:78–80.

16 Sapir 2007 also mentioned (p. 266) the name סטרול, which is a development from יִשְׂרָאֵל, and the names Strolovitz, Strolov, and the like, which mean 'son of Israel'. See also Samuel 2011.

§ 7 The transcription Αδωνε for the name of God (pronounced as from the stem אד"ן) is most interesting; it is not αδωναι (אֲדוֹנָי), as found in the transliterations of Origen (Brønno, 162),[17] reflected here, but rather αδωνε, which shows the contraction of the diphthong [ay] to [e] in a stressed syllable. Is this evidence that the contraction took place within Hebrew, or is this a reflex of the [ay] > [e] shift known to have taken place within Greek?[18] My own view tends towards the second option. We can assume that the sentence שמע ישראל, including the pronunciation of the name of God, was known to Jews in the region in which the amulet was written in their original pronunciations – generations prior to the amulet's writing. One the divine name was integrated into their own Greek language, however, it is reasonable to assume that they pronounced it like every other Greek word with an original [ay] diphthong in it, and the diphthong contracted to [e].[19]

§ 8 For three words the amulet does not provide a full transcription:

1. For אֱלֹהֵינוּ we find only ελωη (ll. 4–5), with nothing corresponding to the final syllable.
2. In the second occurrence of the name of God, the transcribed form is only Αδων (אֲדוֹן), with no final vowel (but see below, § 9).
3. I already mentioned that instead of a full transliteration of the Hebrew word אֶחָד, the Greek letter α appears.[20] (Might the scribe have feared that he would not have sufficient space for the entire verse, and therefore abbreviated these words?)

§ 9 It is also possible that in the second instance of the name of God (ll. 5–6 in the amulet), the fact that the final vowel was not indicated – and, as mentioned, the name was written Αδων rather than Αδωνε – is due to the juxtaposition of the name to the following word אֶחָד, pronounced εαδ. It is very likely that the two contiguous vowels ε (Αδωνε εαδ) became a single [e]. Since the noun אֶחָד was actually not transliterated, however, but represented

17 It should be noted that when the Tetragrammaton is written according to its etymology, from the root הי"י, Origen does not preserve the pronunciation. The pronunciation is transcribed only when the name is written as it is read – אֲדוֹנָי.

18 See Allen 1974:75–76, who points out that evidence for this contraction appears already in the first century CE. Sturtevant 1968:49, on the other hand, speaks of the beginnings of this shift already in the second century BCE, as reflected in papyri of that time. It is important to note that Sturtevant does say that Jewish gravestones inscribed with Greek in Rome show the contraction of the diphthong in the second century CE.

19 It is well known that the Hebrew phonology of the Jews in various countries was influenced by the colloquial languages spoken by them.

20 See above, n. 4.

by the letter α alone, this pronunciation is not explicitly indicated, and so this claim must remain nothing more than speculation.

8.3 Summary

§ 10 This discovery is truly of great significance:

A. It testifies to the presence of Jews in what is today Austria already in the first centuries of the common era.
B. It reveals the central role played by the *Shema* in the lives of those Jews.
C. It provides echoes of the pronunciation of Hebrew current among the community:
   1. The *shewa* was pronounced by them as a vowel (συμα), in contradistinction to other communities, in which it was elided (σμα).
   2. The amulet provides supporting evidence for the realization of the name Israel with a [t] between the *śin* and the *resh*.
   3. The transliteration of the name אֲדֹנָי (*αδωναι) with a contracted diphthong (αδωνε) shows the effect of the colloquial speech on the pronunciation of Hebrew.
   4. Finally, the use of the Greek α for the number 1 in a Hebrew text is seen here.
   5. Probably, we have an echo here of Αδωνε εαδ > Αδωνεαδ, the two contiguous ε vowels becoming a single ε.

Presumably folklorists and scholars in other fields will also judge this to be a significant find, but discussions of these issues would take us too far afield here.

§ 11 It is now evident that this text is far from insignificant. This should not surprise us; we certainly know that even remarkably short texts can contain important historical and linguistic data. Such data is to be found in the amulet from Halbturn, Austria, and have been detailed above. It is to be hoped that scholars, including linguists, will continue to study this amulet.[21]

21 See Samuel 2011.

B Qumran Hebrew

9 A Few Remarks on Mishnaic Hebrew and Aramaic in Qumran Hebrew

§ 1 This short paper aims to make several short observations on the affinity of Mishnaic Hebrew and Aramaic to Qumran Hebrew. Two preliminary points are in order. First, the goal is not so much to learn about Qumran Hebrew from Aramaic and Hebrew as to learn about grammatical phenomena in Mishnaic Hebrew from Qumran Hebrew. Second, I have no intention to analyze any particular phenomenon within Aramaic, but rather to present a hypothesis regarding the source of several of the Aramaic elements which we find in the Hebrew texts from Qumran.

9.1 Mishnaic Hebrew and Qumran Hebrew

§ 2 To my mind a major contribution of Qumran Hebrew to the study of Mishnaic Hebrew inheres in the light QH sheds on linguistic phenomena found in MH that are sometimes suspected as late or even as medieval scribal innovations. Evidence from Qumran Hebrew enables us to identify these linguistic phenomena as authentic representatives of a living Hebrew in use at Qumran. I would like to cite two different examples. The first one deals with a linguistic detail that exemplifies the more widespread phenomenon and the second with an entire grammatical noun pattern. The existence of these linguistic details in Mishnaic Hebrew is beyond doubt and the Qumran material simply adds historical depth to it.

9.1.1 Example 1

§ 3 In Biblical Hebrew, the verbal root *q-r-*^{c} (√קרע) is attested only in *pāʻal* and *nifʻal*, both in the consonantal and vocalized text, e.g. הנני קֹרֵעַ את הממלכה מיד שלמה (I Kgs 11:31), קְרוּעֵי בגדים (Isa 36:22), וְקָרַע אותו מן הבגד (Lev 13:56); והמזבח נִקְרָע וישפך הדשן (I Kgs 13:5), לֹא יִקָּרֵעַ (Exod 28:32, 39:23). No cases of this root are attested in *piʻel*, *puʻal* or *hiṯpaʻel* in spite of the suggestion in the editions of KB to emend a verse in Proverbs and to discover a *hiṯpaʻel* form in it as a result of this emendation. This is said with regard to Proverbs 27:9: שֶׁמֶן וּקְטֹרֶת יְשַׂמַּח לֵב וּמֶתֶק רֵעֵהוּ מֵעֲצַת נָפֶשׁ. The 1953 edition of KB (p. 857) suggests reading the second part of the verse as: וּמִתְקָרְעָה עַצֶּבֶת

נָפֶשׁ, and in the latest edition from 1983 (p. 1070)[1] this suggestion is repeated with a slight change: וּמִתְקָרְעָה מֵעַצֶּבֶת נָפֶשׁ. The second possibility is more ingenious than the first, but still all in all introduces into the biblical text a reading and grammatical form that is completely foreign to it.

§ 4 On the other hand, in Mishnaic Hebrew, besides numerous examples of the usual forms in *pāʿal* and *nifʿal*, we also find examples of *piʿel*, *puʿal* (participle)[2] or *nitpaʿal*, e.g. מקרע את כסותו (*t. Ter.* 1:3), לבש שתי כותנות ושתי מכנסים ושני אבנטים או שהיו מקורעין (*t. Men.* 1:8), נתקרע הגט (*t. Giṭ.* 7:6). This is a well-known development in Mishnaic Hebrew as opposed to Biblical Hebrew, as Z. Ben-Ḥayyim clearly demonstrated many years ago: many verbs, both transitive and intransitive that were used in Biblical Hebrew in *pāʿal* and *nifʿal* pass into *piʿel*, *puʿal* (participle) and *nitpaʿal* in Mishnaic Hebrew.[3] As is well known, this contrast also occurs in differences between the Tiberian and Samaritan tradition of the Pentateuch, as pointed out by Ben-Ḥayyim[4] and treated as well in an article by T. Zurawel.[5] The same is the case with the root *q-r-ᶜ* (√קרע). The five occurrences of the *pāᶜal* of this root in the Tiberian traditions appear in *paᶜᶜəl*[6] in the Samaritan Pentateuch. For example the form *qārəʿū* (קָרְעוּ Num 14:6) is pronounced *qarraʿu* by the Samaritans in the *paᶜᶜəl* verbal stem and the *nifʿal* form *iqqārēᵃʿ* (יִקָּרֵעַ Exod 28:32; 39:23) is pronounced *yiqqarra* by the Samaritans, which can only be interpreted as a *nitpaᶜᶜal* form (> *nippaᶜᶜal*).[7]

§ 5 A text which was recently discovered provides us with evidence that anticipates that which we find in tannaitic literature and the Samaritan Pentateuch for the existence of *q-r-ᶜ* in *nitpaʿal* / *hitpaʿel*: ויתקרע ישראל בדור הה[וא] להלחם א[י]ש ברעהו על התורה ועל הברית (4Q387, 3). We have here confirmation of the existence from the Second Temple Period, i.e. at least 100 BCE, of forms of a verbal stem whose middle consonant is doubled.

---

1 In this entry there is a cross-reference to the entry III עֵצָה for a further suggestion.
2 As is well-known, in Mishnaic Hebrew the *puᶜᶜal* pattern disappeared and all that remains thereof are the participial forms which may be seen as representing the passive participle of the *piᶜᶜel* verbal-stem (see Bar-Asher 1999b:66-72, §§ 6–9 and below, Chap 20, § 6).
3 Cf. Ben-Ḥayyim 1958:236–241.
4 Ben-Ḥayyim, *ibid*.
5 Cf. Zurawel 1984.
6 *Piᶜᶜēl* in the Tiberian tradition = *paᶜᶜəl* in the Samaritan tradition.
7 Cf. Ben-Ḥayyim 1957–1977:254; Zurawel 1984:139.

9.1.2 Example 2

§ 6 The second example I have in mind is the *pa'lān* pattern used as a *nomen agentis* in Mishnaic Hebrew, identified by B. Z. Gross as a Babylonian tradition, in contrast to the *po'lān* pattern, which he views as an authentic Palestinian form.[8] Yohanan Breuer also discussed the noun-pattern *pa'lān*, e.g. גַּזְלָן, גַּרְגְּרָן, דַּרְשָׁן, רַחֲמָן, etc. It is true that he identifies a few examples of *po'lān* (פועלן) which occur, perhaps due to special phonetic changes: a > o/u before *resh* or a labial (e.g. עובדן, דורשן) or in a loanword that preserves the original phonological shape of the source language, e.g. פורקדן (< *purqidam* in Akkadian as pointed out by Kutscher).[9] He sums up his conclusions by saying: "The noun pattern qatlān (קטלן) is obviously the dominant one in these texts."[10]

§ 7 Two sentences from a text recently shown to me by Devorah Dimant attest to the occurrence of the *pa'lān* pattern in Qumran Hebrew; the sentences in question read as follows:

1. 4Q387a 2 [olim 3] II 7–9: וממלכת ישראל תאבד בימים ההמה [י]ה[י]ה מלך ה]וא גדפן[11] ועשה תעבות וקרעתי [את] ממלכ[תו].
2. 4Q389 8 [olim 1] II 7–9: והפרו את הברית אשר כרתי עם אברה[ם] וע[ם]י יצחק ואם [יעקב בימים ההמה י]קום מלך לגוים גדפן [וע]שה רעות.

What is significant for our discussion is the occurrence of the noun *gadfān* 'blasphemer', derived from *giddef*, which follows the pattern of *pa^{c}lān* like *sarvān/gazlān/daršān*, etc. These witnesses of the *gadfān* form precede by cen-

---

8 Cf. Gross 1993:57–103, 256–265, for a presentation of the data in great detail and an in-depth discussion of the details, as well as the development of the *po'lān/pa'lān* pattern, and other patterns. He makes a distinction between names pertaining to the *pā'al* verbal stem and those pertaining to other verbal stems. For our discussion a reference to what he wrote will suffice. See also Bar-Asher 1987:19–20.

9 Cf. Breuer 1993:226–227.

10 Breuer 1993:226. Blau 1996:75–78 presents a different approach to the relation between the *pa^{c}lān* and *po^{c}lān* forms. In his opinion, *pa'lān* became *po'lān* in Eretz-Yisrael due to the sound change (*a* > *o*), and later returned to being *pa'lān* in Babylonia under the influence of Babylonian Aramaic, in which the *a* > *o* shift did not apply.

11 The spelling without *waw* after *gimmel* demonstrates that the form follows the *pa'lān* pattern and not the *po'lān* pattern, as in Qumran *o/u* short or long vowels are usually written with a *waw*. Even though the word תועבות is written here without a *waw*, an ancient literary text was apparently of influence here, possibly the spelling of the Massoretic text of the Bible. There we find תועבות often (for example Gen 47:32) but also תעבות rarely (5×; for example in Ezra 9:1).

turies the examples from the Jerusalem Talmud cited by Gross in his book: הגדפנין, הגודפנין, הגודפנים etc.[12]

§ 8 This example of *gadfān* argues for the early origin of the Mishnaic Hebrew *pa'lān* form, hitherto believed to be late. This new evidence from Qumran indicates that the antecedents of this noun pattern lie in the Second Temple period, centuries before the redaction of the Mishna. The Qumran witness obviates the need to seek the origins of this phenomenon in Babylonian influence. The example of גדפן [*gadfān*] (2×) found in Qumran also strengthens the reliability of the biblical vocalization רַחֲמָנִיּוֹת (Lam 4:10), as רַחֲמָנִית is the feminine form of רַחֲמָן (in the *paᶜlān* noun pattern).[13] More remains to be said regarding this noun pattern and its usage.

9.2 Aramaic at Qumran

§ 9 Having given examples of how Qumran Hebrew can elucidate the origins of Mishnaic Hebrew Forms, I now come to some observations on Aramaic at Qumran. With the early discoveries of the Dead Sea Scrolls came the discovery of Aramaic works; including such important Aramaic texts as the *Genesis Apocryphon* and the *Targum* to Job. Moreover, eminent scholars have shown that even Hebrew works composed or transmitted at Qumran display varying degrees of affinity to Aramaic.[14]

§ 10 Nonetheless, I would like to suggest that a distinction be drawn between the elements shared by Qumran Hebrew and Mishnaic Hebrew on the one hand, and the Aramaic elements found in Qumran Hebrew on the other. The Hebrew elements from MH now attested at Qumran certainly belonged to a living dialect or perhaps dialects of Hebrew. We must inquire, however, if this also holds for the origins of the Aramaic elements at Qumran. Were they, like Mishnaic Hebrew elements, part of a living spoken dialect, or should we perhaps explore the possibility that Qumran Hebrew possesses affinities to written Aramaic literature?

§ 11 What I present here is a tentative hypothesis. I would like to suggest that we consider the second possibility, namely, that the Hebrew authors at Qumran, and perhaps their predecessors in Jerusalem, drew Aramaic elements from written sources, taking literary inspiration from Aramaic biblical *targumim* or from related works, such as the *Genesis Apocryphon*. By *targumim* I

12 Cf. Gross 1993:82. The Ben Yehuda dictionary presents only the גַּדְפָן form without *waw* after the *gimmel*.

13 Cf. Gross 1993:97–98, 258.

14 Cf. Kutscher 1974:187–215.

mean Aramaic targumic works dated earlier than what is usually referred to as the "*targum* literature", whose classic representatives are the second century CE works, *Onqelos* to the Pentateuch and *Jonathan* to Prophets, as well as later *targumim* such as the *Targum Neofiti*, and the Fragmentary *Targum*, which themselves contain earlier material. What I am arguing here is that an earlier *targum* literature, which was used by the Qumran community, preceded these classic works. While the extant Aramaic *targumim* corpus from Qumran is extremely limited, consisting solely of the *Targum* to Job and some fragments from the *Targum* to Leviticus, I believe that their very presence suffices to allow us to conjecture that the entire biblical corpus or a large part of it was extant in Aramaic at Qumran. Certainly I know of no evidence to the contrary. As texts that were read and studied alongside the Hebrew original, these *targumim* could well have been the source for Aramaic linguistic variants, variants readily understood by the Qumran authors. I see no reason why the Qumranites should not have utilized words or phrases from this presumed Aramaic corpus.

§ 12 I would now like to cite two examples, which I believe substantiate this hypothesis, both taken from texts already published.

9.2.1 Example 1

§ 13 A text published by Devorah Dimant in the *Sarah Kamin Memorial Volume*[15] contains a citation from Nah 3:8–10. The relevant lines of the text, 4Q385-6 II ll. 6–7, read as follows (vv. 9–10): [16]כוש מצר[ים עצמה] אין קץ [לבריח]יך לוב בסעדך והיא בגולה תל. The similarities to MT are readily apparent: כּוּשׁ עָצְמָה וּמִצְרַיִם וְאֵין קֵצֶה פּוּט וְלוּבִים הָיוּ בְּעֶזְרָתֵךְ גַּם הִיא לַגֹּלָה הָלְכָה בַשֶּׁבִי "Ethiopia and Egypt were your strength, and it was infinite; Put and Lubim were your helpers. Yet she was carried away, she went into captivity."[17] The most striking difference, and the one relevant to my thesis, is the Qumran text's use of בסעדך for MT's בעזרתך.

§ 14 On what basis can we surmise that this Qumran author, who cited Nahum, substituted an Aramaic word for a Hebrew one? It seems improbable that it was his intent here to replace an incomprehensible Hebrew word with a more accessible Aramaic one. Rather, I would like to explain differently what may have happened. It seems to me more likely that the writer of the Hebrew text at Qumran, who I propose was evidently conversant with an Aramaic

15 Dimant 1994.

16 Dimant 1994:32.

17 The English translation is taken from the old translation of the Jewish Publication Society.

targum to Nahum, inserted the Aramaic equivalent for the Hebrew בעזרתךְ under its subliminal influence. Like the second-century witness to Nah 3:9 from *Targum Jonathan*: ולובאי הוו בסעדיך, I conjecture that the Qumran author, who cited this verse, was familiar with a similar reading found in some early *targum* to Nahum. To my mind, this conjectural assumption of the existence of a corresponding Aramaic *targum* perhaps better explains the interpolation of an Aramaic word in the Hebrew text than the surmise that it was a loanword from spoken Aramaic.[18]

9.2.2 Example 2

§ 15 This brings us to our second example: In the Pseudo-Ezekiel text published by Devorah Dimant, we find the following clause: כאשר יאמרו היה השלום והשדך (4Q386 II, 7). In her article,[19] Dimant first publishes the text in its entirety, noting in the linguistic discussion that follows that this is the sole known occurrence of the noun הַשֶּׁדֶךְ in a Qumran text. Following a comment on this word's Aramaic origins, including a *piyyuṭ* by Yannai in which שדך is paired with שקט: שדך לעמילים שקט לאבילים, noting in addition that the Aramaic *targumim*, *Jonathan* in particular, use Aramaic √שדך to translate the Hebrew root שקט. For example, *Jonathan* translates ושלות השקט (Ezek 16:49) as ושלויא וּשְׁדוֹכְיָא (variant: וְשִׁידּוּכַיָּא) and ותשקט הארץ (Judg 3:11, 3:30, 5:31, 8:28) is consistently translated into Aramaic as ושדוכת ארעא. Dimant also notes the occurrence of the phrase שודכה ושלמה in an Aramaic-Palestinian *piyyut* published by M. Sokoloff and J. Yahalom.[20] In addition, Dimant notes that the expression השלום והשדך found in Pseudo-Ezekiel has a Hebrew parallel at Qumran: שלום והשקט (4Q418, 55 7) which is similar to the biblical שלום ושקט (1 Chr 22:9).

§ 16 Essentially, both the Hebrew השקט/שקט and the Aramaic שדך appear in the Qumran lexicon. It appears that whereas the former derive from

18 Prof. M. Kister directed my attention to a fragmentary text from Qumran published in DJD XIX (1995), pp. 198, in which the expression עם החביב (4Q462) appeared. Kister correctly pointed out that in the *Targum Onqelos* (and likewise in the *Targum Neofiti*, the *Fragmentary Targum* and *Targum Pseudo-Jonathan*), the expression לְעַם סְגֻלָּה (Deut 7:7, 14:2, 26:18) is translated לְעַם חֲבִיב. Is it possible that the usage of this expression in Qumran derives from an ancient Aramaic translation of the Book of Deuteronomy?

19 Dimant 1998:512, 517–518.

20 Cf. Sokoloff-Yahalom 1999:280, poem 50. Dimant mentions also the phrase שלמה ושודכה (with the two nouns transposed) from poem 49, but there is no such phrase in this poem in the above-mentioned edition. The index of the book refers us only to poem 50.

the biblical corpus, the latter perhaps come from the Aramaic targumic corpus. We should note, however, that in the course of its absorption the Aramaic word assumed a Hebrew form marked by the Hebrew definite article: not שודכא but השדך.[21]

§ 17 To sum up my venture into the realm of conjecture: it has been long recognized that the Qumran sectarians mainly derived their words and idioms from Biblical Hebrew, using these elements to express their historical and ideological interpretation, and even more so to meet the needs of current linguistic usage. The biblical corpus undeniably served as the Qumranites' main literary pool. What I have suggested here is that alongside this Hebrew corpus there existed a literary Aramaic corpus, which was more randomly utilized, perhaps only involuntarily.

§ 18 Naturally, we must also recall that the Qumranites authored independent works, that their corpus of independent literary creations witnesses linguistic innovations that gave written expression to their language and concepts, but this is not our topic.

§ 19 I would like to take the conjecture I have presented a step further. If it could somehow be better substantiated, this hypothesis would then document an early stage, as early as the Second Temple period, during which Hebrew writers drew upon Aramaic *targumim*, centuries before the crystallization and redaction of tannaitic literature. Regarding the affinity of tannaitic literature to the Aramaic targumim, there is no dispute, as M. I. Kahana's recent work on the *mekhiltot* has definitively shown. He notes, for example, the substitution of the Aramaic ארנונה for the Hebrew place name[22] ארנון. Of special relevance to our discussion is Kahana's observation regarding the interpolation of the expression נסין וגבורן from the Aramaic *targum* into the text of the *mekhilta*:[23] "Given the affinity between the *derashot* in the *mekhilta* and the Aramaic *targumim*, we cannot rule out the possibility that the *Geniza* fragments here contain an expression penned by the redactors of the *mekhilta*."[24] Menachem Kahana cites a fine example pertaining to a *midrash* on the verse והיה כאשר ירים משה ידו וגבר ישראל וכאשר יניח ידו וגבר עמלק (Exod 17:11) in the *Parasha* (portion) "Amaleq". He demonstrates the close connection between this *midrash* and the biblical *targumim* of the verse.[25] I argue here that, if my hypothesis be correct, a similar process occurred during the Second

21 Nor do we find any evidence at Qumran for the Hebrew verbs שתק, נשתתק, or the שתיקה, known from LBH (e.g. Jon 1:11) and Mishnaic Hebrew.

22 Cf. Kahana 1999:86.

23 Kahana 1999:75–76.

24 Kahana 1999:76.

25 Kahana 1999:255–257.

Temple Period, in Qumran literature, long before the crystallization of tannaitic literature.

§ 20 I would like to comment on the potentially strong influence of a coexisting source and translation, which creates a strong link in the user's mind, and leaves its impression on both written and spoken expression. This, in my opinion, underlies the appearance of locutions of the באש ישרף ובנורא יתוקד type in the speech of Arabic-speaking Jews. Any individual making constant use of a Hebrew original and its translation may draw equally upon either or both, as in the case of this expression, which derives from Lev 7:17 בָּאֵשׁ יִשָּׂרֵף and its Aramaic targum (*Onqelos* בְּנוּרָא יִתּוֹקַד).[26] Perhaps the embryonic form of this phenomenon in the history of Hebrew literature should be sought at Qumran.

9.3 Summary

§ 21 The two examples pertaining to Mishnaic Hebrew are derived from solid facts and the explanations we offer here have strong and substantial supporting evidence. The two examples pertaining to Aramaic are likewise solid but the explanations we offer remain hypothetical and only further data can confirm our thesis. Future findings could substantiate the hypothesis I have presented here.[27]

26 See Bar-Asher 1999a: 153–154.
27 For more on the issues discussed here in §§ 19–21, see Bar-Asher 2012, pp. 97–99 (§ 24–29).

10 On Several Linguistic Features of Qumran Hebrew

§ 1 In this study I intend to examine various grammatical and lexical features of *4QNarrative* Cª (4Q462) fragment 1, a text dealing with the Israelites' sojourn (or more precisely sojourns) in Egypt, and to place them in a broader context.[1] It must be borne in mind from the outset that the fragmentary state of many Qumran texts does not enable us to interpret them unequivocally within their given context. Therefore, much of what I present here necessarily remains within the realm of conjecture.

10.1 ריקמה

§ 2 The text of 4Q462 1:5 reads [ ]ים ריקמה הלכנו כי לוקח[ ]. Smith considers both the readings רוקמה and ריקמה, but prefers the former. In the notes to his commentary he expands on his discussion, stating that רוקמה is a variant of רִקְמָה. He provides several citations from the Qumran Scrolls and points at relevant discussions in scholarly literature,[2] eventually arriving at the translation of ריקמה הלכנו as "with embroidered robe we went." However, Smith also suggests interpreting the word as ריקמה, to be pointed רֵיקָמָה, a longer form of רֵיקָם. He links the sentence in question to verse Exod 3:21, in which the verb הָלַךְ and the adverb רֵיקָם appear together: והיה כי תלכו לא תלכו ריקם "and it will come to pass that, when you go, you will not go empty."

In the morphological analysis of the word Smith states that רֵיקָמָה is constructed of three morphemes: (a) רֵיק,[3] (b) the adverbial suffix ָם-, and (c) the suffix ָה-. He also compares this word to מאודה (מאדה, מואדה), an expanded form of the adverb מאוד used in Qumran Hebrew.[4] Smith is of the opinion that

1 For the edition of 4Q462 see Smith 1995:198. Smith 1995:195 mentions two previous discussions of this text: Smith 1991 and Eisenman and Wise 1993:267–269.

2 See Smith 1995: 201.

3 Smith 1995:201 marks this word with an asterisk, as if it were a reconstructed form: "**rêq* (spelled *rîq* without sufformatives < **ryq*)." He did not notice that the base form of the adjective רֵיק/רֵק is actually attested (cf. Deut 32:47 כי לא דבר רֵק הוא מכם "for it is not a vain thing for you"; Judg 11:3 אנשים רֵיקים "vain men"), as was correctly noted by others (cf., e.g., Ben-Yehuda 1960 s. v. רֵיק).

4 See Kutscher (1959:216–317, 393), and additional references according to the index on p. 515. The variant הִנָּם (Isa 41:27) in comparison with הנומה (1QIsaª 35:7) mentioned by Smith in this context is irrelevant here. Apparently the word הנומה is a transformation of הִנֵּמָּה (הִנֵּה + third person plural pronoun); the [e] vowel found in a closed syllable became [u] under the influence of the *mem*.

this explanation can be accepted even if the version is רוקמה written with a *waw*, namely רוֹקָמָה, a variant of רֵיקָמָה.

§ 3 Personally, however, I prefer to interpret the form as ריקמה (= רֵיקָמָה). This possible reading is well substantiated by the remnants of the word preceding ריקמה. Smith correctly states that ים[ ] is found before the word. Although the upper part of the letter *yod* is clearly evident from the photograph, somehow in the interpretation suggested first he comes to translate it: "with (...) we went", as noted above. He unintentionally ends up reading [עִ]ים, whereas the text should be read [למצר]ים ריקמה הלכנו,[5] and thus the affinity to the verse לא תלכו ריקם "you will not go empty" cited from Exod 3:21 becomes even more pronounced. The contrast is a poignant one: at the exodus from Egypt (predicted in Exodus 3), the Israelites were told that they would not go empty-(-handed), whereas the speaker or speakers in this passage remark that the Israelites *did* go empty-handed on their way *down* to Egypt.

It must also be mentioned that, like any other adverb, רֵיקָם can come either before or after the verb being described. Hence we find לא תלכו רֵיקָם in the verse just quoted from Exodus, Ps 25:3 יבושו הבוגדים רֵיקָם "let them be ashamed which transgress without cause", as well as Gen 31:42 רֵיקָם שִׁלַּחְתָּנִי "you would have sent me away empty", and Ruth 1:21 וְרֵיקָם השיבני ה' "and the Lord has brought me home again empty". This is comparable to the adverb חִנָּם found for instance in Ps 119:161 רדפוני חִנָּם "they pursued me without cause" and Isa 52:3 חִנָּם נמכרתם "for nought were you sold."

§ 4 Nevertheless, it must be emphasized that a comparison of the רֵיקָם > רֵיקָמָה interchange with that of מְאוֹד > מאודה (מואדה) provides only a partial explanation and does not fully elucidate this matter. It is known that the word מְאֹד is used as a noun in Biblical Hebrew, where the following two occurrences of it are found: Deut 6:5 מְאֹדֶךָ "with all your resources" and 2 Kgs 23:25 מְאוֹדוֹ "with all his resources". However, for the most part מְאֹד serves as an adverb or as an intensifier of an adjective or the present participle. There are hundreds of occurrences of מְאֹד functioning as such, without any grammatical mark added to indicate their role, for example: Gen 4:15 ויחר לקין מְאֹד "Cain was annoyed exceedingly", Exod 11:3 גם האיש משה גדול מְאֹד "the man Moses was very great". In Qumran Hebrew, on the other hand, the addition of the ָה-, suffix, as in מאודה, clearly defines the word as an adverb with such a grammatical mark. This can be compared to the role of ָה- indicating an orientation (termed the directional *he*). For example: אַרְצָה "to the land", הַנֶּגְבָּה "to the Negev", שָׁמָּה "thither, there," which is also comparable to the ָה- in the word לַיְלָה when it is used adverbially, e.g., Gen 14:15 ויחלק עליהם לילה "and he

5 The reading [ממצר]ים ריקמה הלכנו could be considered.

divided himself, by night."[6] However, רֵיקָם already has the adverbial suffix ־ָם (*-ām*); this is a remnant of the adverbial *ā* case with the addition of the ancient *tamyim* (*-m*), as found in the adverbs אָמְנָם, חִנָּם.[7] Hence the question arises why the adverbial suffix ־ָה, is added to a word already having the ־ָם, adverbial suffix.

§ 5 Apparently it can be assumed that the ־ָם suffix in רֵיקָם was no longer felt to be an adverbial suffix in Qumran Hebrew, and that the suffix ā was added in order to mark clearly the syntactical status of the word as adverbial. This is worth some further explanation. I will begin by examining the relevant data from Mishnaic Hebrew, and then return to reappraise the situation in Qumran Hebrew.

The form רֵיקָן functioning as an adjective or a substantivized adjective is well known in Tannaitic Hebrew. We have here a juxtaposition of two elements: רֵיק + ־ָן. Ben-Zion Gross assumes that ריקן is a word borrowed from Aramaic; he bases his assumption on findings from *Targum Onqelos*, Syriac and Mandaic.[8] Yet I believe there is room for a reevaluation of Gross' supposition on the Aramaic origin of ריקן.

For our discussion, it is important to emphasize that the singular form of the word רֵיקָן is mostly written רֵיקָם in Tannaitic language, even though clearly in the vast majority of its occurrences in this language it functions as an adjective or the substantivized adjective רֵיקָן, pronounced mainly with a final *nun* and not as the adverb ריקם. Indeed, the feminine form of this adjective/noun is רֵיקָנִית (e.g. t. Baba Qamma 3.7) and its plural form is רֵיקָנִים/רֵיקָנִין (e.g. m. Shabbat 16.5). In other words, the last consonant in the word is originally a *nun*. This is also attested decisively by the denominative verb רִקֵּן and נִתְרוֹקֵן derived from רֵיקָן; for example רִיקְּנוֹ (m. Uqṣin 1.5), רִיקְּנָה (ibid., 1, 3, 5) in the MS Parma B tradition[9] and in other sources, נִתְרוֹקְנָה (m. Nedarim 10.2).[10]

§ 6 Nevertheless, the singular form of ריקן is for the most part written as ריקם in the most reliable sources of Mishnaic Hebrew, as noted. Ben-Zion Gross

6 Indeed Kutscher 1959:316 (in the title of his discussion there) correctly juxtaposes "the locative ־ָה and the adverbial ־ָה".

7 As is known, we also find [ā] > [ō]: פִּתְאֹם.

8 See Gross 1993:112–113, and Gluska 1988:1125–1126, who presents extensive data from Aramaic. However, Gluska is more cautious in stating that the form רֵיקָן in Mishnaic Hebrew may have been borrowed from Aramaic.

9 The second hand of MS Kaufmann (who copied and vocalized one folio from tractate *Niddah* and the last seven folios of Seder *Toharot*) and the *Geniza* fragment with Babylonian vocalization read רֵיקְנוֹ, רֵיקְנָה in the Pēʿēl stem, the parallel of Piʿel (see Chapter Twenty below, § 18).

10 See below, Chapter Twenty § 27.

has already indicated the spelling רֵיקָם in MS Kaufmann, MS Cambridge (published by W. H. Lowe) and in MS Parma B.[11] Moreover, the word is also written this way in most of the other manuscripts of the Mishnah, in all six of its occurrences: וביתו רֵיקָם (Ta'anit 2.2)[12]; כלי רֵיקָם (Parah 9.6[13]; 10.5[14]; 11.6[15]), המלא (...) הָרֵיקָם[16] (Pesahim 5.6), המלא בְּרֵיקָם[17] (Yoma 5.4). Likewise, we find ריקם instead of ריקן in Sifra: לעשותו רֵיקָם כמלא (Zabim 2.2; MS Vatican 66).[18] We also find the ריקן spelling, as cited in the notes accompanying the above-mentioned examples from the Mishnah,[19] and as found in the Vienna manuscript of the Tosefta, for example: מלא (...) ריקן[20] (Haggiga 2.10), אחד רכוב ואחד ריקן[21] (Baba Qamma 2.10 and so on).

It is clear to me that the spelling רֵיקָם instead of רֵיקָן may be contingent upon two factors, namely, the influence of the spelling of the biblical adverb ריקם and alternation[22] of the consonants *n/m* at the end of a word.[23]

§ 7 Furthermore, we may have evidence of the existence of the adjective ריקן in Qumran Aramaic. In the Targum to Job 6:9 we find [רי]קנה, as a translation of Job 22:9 רֵיקָם.[24] We are aware of the final *-m/-n* alternation in Qumran

11 Gross 1993:113.

12 This is also the spelling found in MS Parma A and in the Naples edition 1492, although MS Rambam (Qafih edition) and MS Paris 328–329 read ריקן. Qafih gives also the variant ריקם.

13 MS Antonin, MS Parma A and MS Paris, as well as the Naples ed., also read ריקם, and this is what is recorded in Yeivin 1985:1047 from a fragment of the Mishnah in Babylonian vocalisation. However, in MS Rambam (Qafih ed.) we find ריקן (but he gives the variants רקם and ריקם as well).

14 MSS Paris, Antonin and Rambam (Qafih ed.) also read ריקם, but MS Parma A reads ריקן.

15 MSS Antonin, Paris and Parma A as well as the Naples ed. read ריקם, but MS Rambam (Qafih ed.) reads ריקן (he also gives the variant ריקם).

16 However MSS Parma A, Rambam (Qafih ed.) and Paris as well as the Naples ed. read הריקן.

17 MS Paris and the Naples ed. also have this reading, but MSS Parma A and Rambam (Qafih ed.) read ריקן.

18 See Yeivin 1985:1047; Gross does not mention the witness from Sifra either.

19 See nn. 12–17 above.

20 However MSS Erfurt and London read ריקם.

21 Here too MS Erfurt reads ריקם.

22 Gross 1993:113, attributes decisive importance to the influence of the biblical spelling ריקם and dismisses the possibility of final *-m/-n* alternations. Gluska 1988:1126 is more cautious in stating that the spelling of the singular ריקם may constitute a historical spelling, influenced by the biblical adverb ריקם.

23 It is irrelevant for our purpose whether this is attributed to *-n/-m* alternations or to a shift of final *m* to final *n*. The fact that *mem* is written instead of *nun* does not contradict this change, and this is not the place to discuss this further.

24 Sokoloff 1974:38, 113.

Hebrew, similar to the instances presented by E. Qimron in his grammar.[25] In fact, this phenomenon was already demonstrated by E. Y. Kutscher over fifty years ago. He noted the spelling מדים in 1QIsa^a (Isa 9:3; 60:6) instead of מִדְיָן appearing in the Masoretic text.[26] We may also have evidence of the adverb רֵיקָם in Qumran Hebrew, ריקם ה°°[ ] (4Q418 96:4),[27] which could have been pronounced רֵיקָן. If this is the case, the pronunciation of the adjective רֵיקָן, possibly known from the Aramaic of Qumran, would have the same pronunciation as the adverb רֵיקָם (> רֵיקָן).

On the basis of this information I believe we would not be mistaken in stating that the appearance of the form רֵיקָמָה serves to distinguish the adverb רֵיקָן/רֵיקָם from the nominal form (i.e. the adjective or the substantivized adjective) רֵיקָן, just as the *-a* suffix in the adverb מאודה serves to distinguish it from the noun מְאֹד.

§ 8 Furthermore, there is no reason to doubt that the appearance in Qumran Hebrew of the adverbs מאודה and רֵיקָמָה with penultimate stress could have come about under the influence of their Aramaic parallels. For example, in Egyptian Aramaic we find the adverbs כלא (כֹּלָּא "entirely, absolutely"), ברא (בָּרָא "going outside, outside"), עלא (עֵלָּא "upward, above") etc.,[28] and in Biblical Aramaic we find adverbs with penultimate stress: כֹּלָּא (Ezra 5:7), עֵלָּא (Dan 6:3). This is apparently how אֲרַע מִנָּךְ (Dan 2:39), written ארעא should be understood (W. Baumgartner is not alone in suggesting the vocalization אַרְעָא[29]).

§ 9 As a parenthetical remark I should like to add that the biblical adverb רֵיקָם continues to appear in the Amoraic Hebrew of Palestine and Babylon as a biblical borrowing.[30] For example: סופו לצאת ריקם "he will become empty in the end" (Pesiqta on the Ten Commandments 113:2); אין תפילתו חוזרת ריקם "his prayer does not return empty [unanswered]" (b. Berakhot 32b),[31] etc. Moreover, we must note that ריקם occurs once as an adverb in Tannaitic litera-

25 Qimron 1986:27, and the references cited there.

26 See Kutscher 1959:82, who also mentions two instances of the historical spelling מדין.

27 "418. 4QInstruction^d (*Mûsār l^{e}Mēvîn^d*)", in *Qumran Cave 4 .XXIV, Sapiential Texts II* (ed. J. Strugnell and D. Harrington; DJD 36; Oxford: Clarendon, 1999), 323 (an extremely fragmented text without context).

28 See Muraoka and Porten 1998:93, 94.

29 See this entry in Koehler-Baumgartner's dictionary.

30 This conclusion can be reached easily based on the data in Ben-Yehuda (1960), s. v. רֵיקָם.

31 Note that the spelling ריקם for the adjective ריקן occurs also in Amoraic literature, e.g. שלא יהא שולחנך מלא ושלחן רבך ריקם (b. Beṣah 20b, as can be gathered from the database of the Historical Dictionary of the Hebrew Language Academy. The text of the tractate Beṣah is based on the MS Göttingen 3 in the National and University Library of Lower Saxony). Nevertheless, in the common editions of the Talmud we find ריקן.

ture as well: שהוא מחזירה ריקם "that he returns it empty" (Mekhilta 15.3).[32] In my evaluation of this data I share Gross' view that the documentation of ריקם as an adverb is insignificant, and it is doubtful whether it really held sway in the living language.[33] Gross argues that all of the examples, from Tannaitic literature (the Mekhilta) and Amoraic literature (Genesis Rabbah), should be seen as borrowings from Biblical Hebrew.[34]

§ 10 The living usage of the adverbial suffix ־ָה in Qumran Hebrew is evident in another adverb as well. It is easy to discern that the writers of Qumran Hebrew apply the adverb שמה more frequently than the form שם without the suffix ־ָה. It should be noted that in many of the occurrences שמה is an adverb of location, exactly like שם "there", and does not necessarily denote direction "to there". For example, the Temple Scroll exclusively uses the adverb שמה (14 times in all), as E. Qimron informs me. For instance 11QT 45:6–7 ולוא תהיה שמה תערובת "and there shall not be a mixture there", 11QT 37:14 אשר יהיו מבשלים שמה "which will be used to cook there".[35] In this context, it is important to mention the use of שם and שמה in 4QRP[a] (4Q158).[36] The first part of this text is a reworking and an elaboration of the story of Jacob's encounter with the angel in Penuel (Gen 32:25–32). Here (4Q158 1–2:7) we find [ויבר]ך אותו שם "and he blessed him there" (= Gen 32:29). Then, in line 10 we find a sentence alluding to this citation as follows: וילך לדרכו בברכו אותו שם "and he went on his way having blessed him there." But where this word does not occur in a biblical verse, the author writes וי[ותר י]עק[וב ל]בדו שמה "and he was left alone there" (line 3).

Furthermore, the data from the Samaritan version of the Pentateuch reveals a clearly defined and distinct preference for the שמה form. The Samaritan reading tradition knows only the form *šamma* (i.e. שָׁמָּה "there"), even when the writing of the word is שם in their Pentateuch, so they read, for example, לגור שם "to sojourn there" (Gen 12:10) as *algor šamma*, ויבן שם "(and Abraham) built (an altar) there" (Gen 22:9) as *wyibni šamma*,[37] and so on.

---

32 Mekhilta Shirata 4, line 4, Ed. Horowitz-Rabin, 130 l. 18.

33 See Gross 1993:112–113, esp. nn. 68–69.

34 It should be borne in mind that when a specific form in Tannaitic Hebrew is documented only in the *Mekhilta* as against all other Tannaitic literature, we must determine whether the form is due to the influence of Biblical Hebrew or Amoraic Hebrew.

35 These citations are according to Qimron 1996.

36 Allegro 1968:1–6)

37 See Ben-Ḥayyim 1957–1977:3/2.290; all the occurrences of this word in the Samaritan version of the Pentateuch are given there. In a survey of the first twenty occurrences in the Samaritan Pentateuch in a passage from Gen 12:7–22:9 in MS C in Abraham Tal's edition (Tal 1994). I discovered that this word was always written שם, although we also find the writing שמה, such as לנוס שמה (Gen 19:20) "to flee thither."

§ 11 In concluding this matter, I should like to adduce several grammatical parallels which illustrate linguistic transparency, similar to the way I suggest the shift from מְאֹד to מאודה and from ריקם to רֵיקָמָה should be viewed:

A. The demonstrative pronoun for the feminine form זאת is composed of two morphemes: זא/זוֹ[38] with the addition of ת-.[39] Addition of the *taw* attaches a feminine morpheme to the pronoun, and thus the feminine demonstrative pronoun becomes clearly distinguishable from the masculine form זֶה.

B. The definite pronoun הַזֹּאת is written as הזאתה once in the Bible: ונתתי את הבית הזה כשילה ואת העיר הזאתה אתן לקללה "I shall make this temple like Shiloh and I will make this city the epitome of a curse" (Jer 26:6). We find here הזאתה (*ketib*), הַזֹּאת (*qere*). It is possible that the spelling הזאתה alludes to an additional form of feminine demonstrative pronoun. Apparently, speakers who no longer sensed the feminine mark ת- present in the pronoun הַזֹּאת, attached a more distinct feminine suffix ָה- to it, thus creating הַזֹּאתָה.[40] This means that הזאתה contains two feminine morphemes: ָה- + ת-. So too the adverb רֵיקָמָה comprises two adverbial morphemes: ָם- and ָה-. Both these examples indicate that when the first morpheme ceased to be prominent, a second one was added to the word.

C. In the transition from Biblical to Mishnaic Hebrew, the final vowel of the near demonstrative pronoun of the plural changes: אֵלֶּה > אֵלּוּ. Indeed, M. H. Segal has already recorded the form אֵלּוּ in the language of Ben Sira.[41]

38 Several years ago, David Talshir 1987:165 conjectured that the *aleph* in the word זאת was consonantal, like the Phoenician parallel זא. Indeed, in the Mesha' inscription we also find זאת (הבמת זאת; l. 3) and not זות. For the time being a presentation of the accepted opinion will suffice. This view holds that the *aleph* indicates the vowel *o* like the *waw* of the pronoun זוֹ, which is common in Mishnaic Hebrew and can also be found in the Bible in the זֹה/זוֹ spelling (לא זה הדרך ולא זה העיר "this is not the way, neither is this the city" [2 Kgs 6:19], ועדותי זו אלמדם "my testimony that I shall teach them" [Ps 132:12]). This is also deduced from the Aramaic parallel דָא/דָה.

39 Cf. the use of דת in Old South Arabic.

40 I heard this explanation from Ze'ev Ben-Ḥayyim in 1965. Prof. Jan Joosten brought to my attention that the word הזאתה occurring in the version of the *Massorah* is missing in the original version of the Septuagint, in which we find καὶ δώσω τὸν οἶκον τοῦτον ὥσπερ Σηλωμ καὶ τὴν πόλιν δώσω εἰς κατάραν "I shall make this Temple like Shiloh and I make the city (the epitome) of a curse." In his opinion, this word is like other elements (from late Hebrew) that exist only in the Masoretic version of Jeremiah and are missing in the Septuagint. This may substantiate the hypothesis that the extensions in the Masoretic version of Jeremiah are of late origin.

41 Segal 1936:50; I refer to the following verse: עד מתי תחסרון מן אילו ואילו ונפשכם צמאה מאד תהיה (51:24).

Here too it is evident that substitution of [ē] by [ū] is intended to provide the demonstrative pronoun with a transparent plural suffix.[42] Moreover, we also have evidence of this elsewhere.[43]

D. In spoken Israeli Hebrew, the present participle form נוֹרָא has been replaced by the נוֹרָאִי form. The suffix -ī, which clearly defines adjectives, has been added to the present participle form נוֹרָא. Evidently, a combination of several factors is at work here expediting the derivation of the form נוֹרָאִי. It is possible that since usage of the יר"א root in the Nif'al pattern was absent in living Hebrew, speakers became unaware of the present participle form נורא, which led to its severance from the Nif'al pattern and hastened its integration in the derivation of the adjective נוראי. However, this process did not take place in the present participle forms of other verbs in the Nif'al, for instance: נוֹלָד, נוֹצָר, etc., since these verbs are fully inflected in the Nif'al paradigm in all tenses. Moreover, the present participle forms of other Nif'al verbs are still used with verbal significance.[44] Furthermore, we must not ignore the common contemporary usage of נורא as an adverb in spoken Hebrew, for example: התחשק לי נוֹרָא לבוא "I really felt like coming", הבגד נורא יפה "the garment is really beautiful". Addition of the suffix -ī clearly distinguishes between the adjective (נוֹרָאִי) and the adverb (נוֹרָא).[45]

---

42 Cf. Segal 1936:49–50: "In these forms the *segol* of the biblical אֵלֶּה changed into *shuruq* due to the popular tendency to emphasize the plural meaning of the pronoun, by analogy of other plural pronouns such as אנו, ממנו etc."

43 A parallel phenomenon occurred in the Arabic dialects of the Maghreb. The singular pronouns have been derived from the plural demonstrative pronouns (near and far), and the vowel *u* indicates their plural form:

hada (m.)	"this"	*hadak* (m.)	"that"
hadi (f.)	"this"	*hadik* (f.)	"that"
hadu (c.p.)	"these"	*haduk* (c.p.)	"those".

44 The adjective נוכחי should also be mentioned in this context. Ben-Yehuda 1960, s. v. /נוכחיי נֹכְחִי we find מה שהוא נֹכַח לדבר, נגדו "what is the opposite (נֹכַח) to s.th." apparently derived from נֹכַח. The Even-Shoshan dictionary also gives נוֹכְחִי from נוֹכֵחַ "of the present, actual, contemporary", as well as נָכְחִי from נֹכַח "in front of, opposite, facing". See also Bahat and Mishor 1997, s. v. נוֹכֵחַ and נוֹכַח.

45 There are many instances of the addition of such "redundant" morphemes for reasons of linguistic transparency. This is definitely how the phenomenon of doubled plurals should be explained. We know of several nouns comprising two plural morphemes, like סַם, the plural form of which is סַמִּים, but סַמְמָנִים in Mishnaic Hebrew. Alternatively we find בִּירָה, the plural form of which is בִּירָנִיּוֹת (2 Chron 17:12). It seems that speakers who were unaware of the plural morpheme ָן- (*-ān*) supplemented it with a more common Hebrew plural morpheme: ִים- (*īm*)-וֹת (*-ōt*), or ִיּוֹת- (*iyyōt*). It is known that the phenomenon of double plural morphemes is common in loan words. Speakers who did not sense the plural morpheme of the lending language, supplemented the loan word with a plural morpheme used in their own language.

§ 12 To sum up, it appears that a wish to create grammatical transparency was the driving force behind the changes from רֵיקָם to רֵיקָמָה and from מְאֹד to מאודה in Qumran Hebrew, as in the change from שָׁם to שמה in Qumran and in the Hebrew of the Samaritan Pentateuch. Moreover, the occurrence in Qumran Hebrew of adverbs suffixed with ־ָה may have come into being under the influence of the parallel phenomenon in the Aramaic of that period, in which such adverbs (כֹּלָא, עֵלָּא etc.) were common.

10.2 מאחד

§ 13 The text of 4Q462 1:8 reads כבודו אשר מאחד ימלא את המים ואת הארץ, which Smith translates as "his glory which secretly will fill the waters and the earth".[46] In the notes on the translation, Smith states that the meaning of מאחד is problematic ("a crux").[47] He suggests three possible explanations of the word: (a) מאחד is an elliptical prepositional phrase, in which case the word should be interpreted as if the word טיפה or some such form precedes it; the sentence should be understood as כבודו אשר (מטיפה) אחד ימלא (...);[48] (b) מאחד serves as an adverb modifying the verb ימלא (however, Smith does not give the meaning of the adverb in this context nor does he provide us with the basis for his explanation); (c) מאחד may be read as מְאַחֵד, an active participle Pi'el derived from the Aramaic root אחד, similar to what we find in Tg.

For example, this is what happened to the plural form of the noun כְּתֻבָּה in the Spanish or French spoken by the Jews of Southwestern France. Here *ketubboths*, with the addition of the plural pronoun –*s*, can be found instead of *ketubboth* (see Bar-Asher 1998:60–86, esp. 62 n. 23 and 73 n. 90). It is not surprising, therefore, that these forms were often interpreted incorrectly, as was the case with סְלִיחוֹת in the French vernacular of the Jews of Southwestern France; here the plural form is *les selixots* and the singular *le selixot*. Furthermore, lexicographers and compilers of concordances as well as everyday speakers have done likewise with several Hebrew words. For example, they derived the singular form סַמְמָן, נִצָּן, בִּירָן from סַמְמָנִים, נִצָּנִים, בִּירָנִיּוֹת. Perhaps we should mention that instances of triple plural morphemes being applied to a word have also been discovered occasionally. Speakers who were no longer aware of both plural morphemes in a certain noun supplemented them with a third one. For instance, in the Spanish vernacular of the Jews of Southwestern France we find the form *rummanims*, "pomegranates, finials for the Torah scroll". Here the Arabic (broken) plural form *rummān*, was supplemented with the Hebrew plural *-im*, since it was not perceived as a plural form. Subsequently, it was supplemented with the Spanish plural morpheme *-s* (for further details, see Bar-Asher 1998:78–79).

46 Smith 1995:200.

47 Smith 1995:202.

48 Smith makes no mention of the lack of syntactical concord in gender between טיפה and the numeral אחד.

Job, where the clause מְאַחֵז פְּנֵי-כִסֵּה "he holds back the face of his throne" (Job 26:9) was translated as מְאַחֵד (...) דמן כורסיה, whereby מְאַחֵד is interpreted as "conceals".[49] It seems that Smith's translation is based on the third explanation.

§ 14 In my opinion, the second explanation, according to which מאחד is interpreted as an adverb, is to be preferred. In other words, מאחד is מִן אֶחָד and means "simultaneously" or "jointly, together." Thus the whole sentence כבודו אשר מאחד ימלא את המים ואת הארץ should be translated as "his glory, which will simultaneously fill the waters and the earth" or "his glory, which will fill the waters and the earth together". If this hypothesis could be substantiated, it would mean that the usage of מאחד found here is parallel to the usage of the adverbial phrase כְּאֶחָד "as one" found in Biblical and Mishnaic Hebrew in the sense of "together", e.g., (...) כל הקהל כאחד ארבע רבוא אלפים "The entire congregation together numbered forty-two thousand (...)" (Ezra 2:63–64); השוחט שני ראשין כאחד "if one slaughtered two heads simultaneously" (m. Hullin 2.2). By the same token, Aramaic כַּחֲדָה is used in the sense of "simultaneously", "jointly", "together", e.g., באדין דקו כַּחֲדָה פרזלא חספא נחשא כספא ודהבא "then they crumbled together: the iron, the earthenware, the bronze, the silver and the gold" (Dan 2:35). Moreover, מאחד can be related to Syriac ܡܢ ܚܕܐ, ܡܚܕܐ "immediately."

§ 15 It is noteworthy that there are parallel forms in Aramaic with the same structure as the adverb מֵאֶחָד in Qumran. Indeed, in Biblical Aramaic we find a similar form, in which מִן may exert the same function whether before a noun or an adjective. For example, in Dan 2:47 ענה מלכא לדניאל ואמר מִן קְשֹׁט די אלהכון הוא אלה אלהין the phrase מִן קְשֹׁט "in truth" serves as an adverb meaning "certainly". Similarly, in Dan 2:8 ענה מלכא ואמר מִן יַצִּיב ידע אנה the phrase מִן יַצִּיב[50] has the meaning "certainly".[51] But in these Aramaic

---

49 In passing we should mention that Jastrow's dictionary (I, 39), to which Smith refers, does not give an active participle from the Tg. Job, but rather a passive participle form מְאַחַד "concealed".

50 The expression מִן בָּרוּר meaning "certainly, clearly, without doubt, unquestionably" was derived in a similar fashion, as in השוא הנע הופך שוא נח כפי שהראנו מן ברור ח' ילון "the mobile *shewa* becomes quiescent as H. Yalon showed us clearly" (1977:87). To the best of my knowledge, this was the first usage of this phrase in Hebrew. It was neologized by the author shortly before its appearance here, inspired by מִן יַצִּיב and מִן קְשֹׁט. It was adopted by others and has struck roots since then, cf. the recent example דומה כי שלושת המקורות שהוצגו לעיל חושפים מן ברור את נסיונותיהם של חכמי הדורות ליישב את חידת האקרוסטיכון המקראי האלפביתי "it seems that the three sources presented above unquestionably reveal the attempts of modern scholars to solve the riddle of the alphabetic biblical acrostic" (Melammed 2001:18).

51 An additional example is the phrase מן האמנו "certainly" found in the Samaritan translation of the Pentateuch.

expressions מן stands independently, whereas in Hebrew it is attached to the succeeding word, with assimilation of the final *nun*.

In my opinion, we cannot detach this feature from the usage of the structure מן + present participle found in Palestinian Aramaic and Mishnaic Hebrew, e.g., מְעוֹמֵד, מְיוֹשֵׁב, מְיָּתֵב/מִן יָתֵב as was convincingly demonstrated by E.Y. Kutscher. As we know, this structure serves as a circumstantial clause.[52]

10.3 עם החביב

§ 16 4Q462 1:11 reads as follows: כי היה בתוכנו עם החביב. Elsewhere I have referred to a remark by M. Kister, who pointed out that the phrase לעם סגולה (Deut 7:6, 14:2, 21:18) is rendered in Onqelos as לְעַם חֲבִיב.[53] It is possible that the phrase עם החביב documented in Qumran was taken from an Aramaic translation of the Pentateuch, which preceded by centuries the translation we know as Targum Onqelos.[54] For example, we find the word בסעדך in a citation from a Qumran text instead of בעזרתך (Nah 3:9). It is possible that this word was also taken from an Aramaic translation long preceding Targum Jonathan to the Prophets.[55]

§ 17 At this point in our discussion, several comments on the syntactical relation between the noun (עם) and the adjective (החביב) should be made. This phrase can be viewed as a further example of the well-known structure יום הששי "the sixth day" (Gen 1:31), שער העליון "the upper gate" (Ezek 9:7; 2 Chr 23:20), לולב הגזול "the stolen Lulav" (m. Sukkah 3.1), דם הירוק "greenish blood" (m. Eduyot 5.6). Indeed, we have found phrases like these in Qumran, although to date only in the pattern: *day* + ה- + *ordinal number*. Alexander Borg has presented examples from Qumran scrolls,[56] where we find: יום הרביעי ויום החמישי ויום הששי (4Q252 1:9–10).[57] The example of עם החביב can now be added to these.

§ 18 I believe that we should propose a different explanation as well. Could the phrase עם החביב reflect a phonetic transformation of העם החביב?

---

52 See Kutscher 1959:199–203, Ben-Ḥayyim 1957–1977.

53 Chapter 9 above, n. 18; Kister 2000:137–165, esp. 137.

54 Ibid.

55 Chapter 9 above, §§ 13–14.

56 Borg 2000:26–39, esp. 26, 33.

57 The example in 11Q20 14:2 יום השביעי "the seventh day" (DJD 23, p. 396) cited by Borg 2000:33 is extremely questionable. There we find [יו]ם השביעי, and I know of no evidence preventing us from assuming that היום or ביום השביעי was written there. Furthermore, the example 4Q225 1:7 יום הרביעי (DJD 13, p. 143) cited by Borg (ibid.) does not exist; Prof. E. Qimron informs me that the correct reading is יום הבריאה.

By a process of haplology, the הָ was dropped in the word עם in both pronunciation and spelling (הָעם > עם) due to the contiguity of [*hā*] with [*'ā*]?[58] Indeed, the dropping of the הָ could have taken place in the adjective החביב as well and there is no evidence to contradict such a supposition. In any case, here the historical spelling conceals this fact.

The phenomenon of dropping the definite article ([*ha*-]) preceding a laryngeal or pharyngeal consonant is well known in Mishnaic Hebrew, and is attested in "the most reliable Rabbinic text,"[59] viz. the Rehov inscription. This is well known also from manuscripts of the Mishnah. In the Rehov inscription we find: העיירות אסורות (line 11) in contrast to העיירות האסורות (line 9), as was noted years ago by E. Qimron.[60] It is not difficult to discern that in the first citation (from line 11) the letter *he* remains in the noun העיירות and was dropped only in the adjective אסורות, in a similar fashion to what occurred in the phrase עם החביב, in which the *he* is dropped before עם but remains in the adjective החביב. I shall cite one example of many from the Mishnah according to MS Kaufmann: הירבוזין השוטין וחלגלוגות[61] "the goosefoot and purslane" (m. Shebi'it 9.1).[62]

§ 19 The value of both proposed explanations is more or less identical. Some may claim that עם החביב cannot be interpreted like יום הששי since in Qumran this structure is found only when indicating a date. They suggest that the presence of this structure in the Qumran scrolls does not necessarily reveal an actual living usage, but rather may indicate a deliberate imitation of Biblical Hebrew in the phrases יום הששי (Gen 1:31), יום השביעי (Exod 12:15), etc. In my opinion, however, this is not a substantial claim, since what is important here is the structural identity. The phrases עם החביב and יום הששי have the same syntactical structure, which cannot be limited to a single semantic group. Hence I see no reason preventing us from assuming that these forms reflect a living usage.

In contrast to this conjecture, one may claim that the dropping of the definite article (העם > עם) due to its contiguity with a laryngeal or pharyngeal consonant is not likely. After all, one might claim, why would the article drop before the noun beginning with an ע, but not drop before the adjective, which

58 This suggestion was presented briefly by Kister 2000:137 n. 6, following Qimron. Kister himself conjectured that החביב might be associated with the succeeding word יעק[ב], as in the construction המלך דוד.

59 This is how Yaacov Sussman termed the *Rehov* inscription (1974:88–158, esp. 148).

60 See Qimron 1975–1976:154–156, esp. 156.

61 The vocalizer of MS Kaufmann added the definite article ה held to be absent in this noun, as he did elsewhere.

62 See Bar-Asher 1980a:103–104.

itself begins with a ח (החביב)? However, this is precisely what we find in העיירות אסורות from the Rehov inscription (line 11), although here the *he* dropped only in the spelling of the adjective and not in that of the noun. In actual pronunciation, however, the *he* was dropped in העיירות as well. Therefore, we may assume that in the first appearance (line 9) the *he* continued to be realized only in the orthography of both elements of the phrase העיירות האסורות.

At this stage, I consider both of these explanations to be possible, without a strong preference for either one.[63]

10.4 התקיים

§ 20 In 4Q462 1:12 we read ויעבודו ויתקימו ויזעקו אל ה',[64] which Smith renders as "and they will serve and they will endure and they will cry to YHWH". It appears that the verb התקיים reoccurs at the end of line 13: והנה נתנו במצרים שנית בקץ ממלכה ויתקי̊[מו], which Smith translates as follows: "and then they were delivered into Egypt a second time in a royal period and they endur[ed]."

Even though we do not have the full context, as is the case with most of the Qumran documents published recently, what context is provided in line 12 is enough to indicate the usage (or diverse usage) of the verb התקיים in the given passage.

10.4.1 קם = התקיים

§ 21 Smith's translation of line 12 shows that he discerns two actions of the children of Israel mentioned in line 11 (עָבַד "serve" and זָעַק "cry"), while the verb in between describes a state (התקיים "endure, suffer" or "survive"). If this is indeed the case, our text is probably the first witness in Hebrew of

---

63 In this context a different category of example appearing in 4QDiscourse on the Exodus (4Q374) published by C. Newsom (DJD 19 [1995] 99–110) should be mentioned. In 4Q374 2 ii 5 we find כל הארצות, as against כל הרצות in 2 i 4. Apparently the editor is right in stating that הרצות is the phonetic spelling of הארצות. However the background to this deletion is different. Here we find a weakening of the *aleph* that occurs in Biblical Hebrew, like הָאֲזִקִּים (< הָאֲזִקִּים; Jer 40:4) and in Qumran Hebrew, such as נֶאֱסָפִים (MT, Isa 13:4) as against נספים (1QIsa^a 11:14). See Kutscher 1959:398–399.

64 There are four dots in the manuscript, indicating the tetragrammaton (see Smith's notes on lines 7 and 12; 1995:199).

the verb התקיים in the sense "endure,"[65] which is used in Mishnaic Hebrew, e.g. אם נתקיימת שלושים יום בידוע שאינה טרפה "if [the animal] survives thirty days, it is well known that it is not *taref*" (t. Hullin 3.19). This Nitpa'al/Hitpa'el form replaces קָם (Qal), which in the Bible also has the meaning "endure, continue to exist",[66] e.g., בשומו כל אבני מזבח כאבני גר מנפצות לא יקמו אשרים וחמנים "When he makes all the altar stones like chalk stones ground to pieces, no *asherah*-trees or sun-idols shall arise anymore" (Isa 27:9); ועתה ממלכתך לא תקום "but now your kingdom shall not endure" (1 Sam 13:14).

§ 22 I propose a different explanation, however. It seems feasible to assume that we have here three verbs depicting three Israelite actions whilst under Egyptian servitude: first they served[67] Egypt, then they arose, and finally they cried to God. I agree that in this context התקיים replaced Qal קָם. However, I propose that התקיים serves as a substitute for the conventional meaning of קָם and does not denote "endurance."

In Biblical Hebrew it is common for the verb קָם to appear in one sequence with another verb in the pattern קם ופעל "arise and act."[68] We encounter this mostly in the narrative texts in the form ויקם ויפעל "he arose and acted", e.g., הוא קם ויך בפלשתים "he rose up and struck the Philistines" (2 Sam 23:10), ויקם וילך אל ארם נהרים "and he arose and went to Mesopotamia" (Gen 24:10), ויקם ויעבר את הנהר "he arose and crossed the river" (Gen 31:21), ויקם דוד ויברח "David arose and fled" (1 Sam 21:11), ויקומו ויעלו בית אל "they got up and went to Bethel" (Judg 20:18). Of course, we also know of many examples of such constructions in which the second verb is not necessarily a verb expressing movement, e.g., ויקמו משם האנשים וישקִפו "so the men got up from there and gazed down" (Gen 18:16), ויקומו (...) ויקראו "and they stood up (...) and read" (Neh 9:3), ויקמו (...) ויברכו את העם "(...) got up and blessed the people" (2 Chr 30:27), ויקם (...) ישוע ובני (...) ויזעקו[69] בקול "then Jeshua and Bani (...) stood up (...) and cried with a loud voice" (Neh 9:4). In these last three instances we find a verb of speaking as the second verb in the sequence.

---

65 Ben-Yehuda 1960:5916, s. v. קִיֵּם.

66 Ben-Yehuda 1960:5841, s. v. קום, sixth definition.

67 Smith assumes these verbal forms to be in future tense, whereas I prefer to take them as narratives expressing past tense.

68 Note that פָּעַל and וַיִּפְעַל also stand for all parallel forms in other stems and tenses.

69 Here the verb occurs in the singular (וַיָּקָם) before a singular personal noun (the first name יֵשׁוּעַ), and is part of a clause in which a series of proper names forms the subject. However, the second verb (וַיִּזְעֲקוּ) which follows the names is in the plural, just as in ותדבר מרים ואהרן במשה (...) ויאמרו הרק אך במשה דבר ה' "And Miriam and Aaron *spoke* against Moses (...) and they *said*, has the Lord indeed spoken only by Moses?" (Num 12:1–2). Cf. Zer-Kavod 1980, *ad loc.*: "ויקם – in the *Targumim* ויקומו".

This verb can be interpreted as indicating a second action after the initial rising: at first whoever arose, and after that he went, fled, gazed, read, blessed, or cried. In all these clauses, קם serves as an auxiliary verb indicating the beginning of an action.[70] It can also be explained as part of an expanded predicate: "he arose (in order to) go/escape/... etc., as in ויקמו (...) להלל לה'[71] אלהי ישראל "and (...) stood up (in order) to praise the LORD God of Israel" (2 Chr 20:19).

§ 23 Parallel to this construction we find in our Qumran fragment (4Q462 1:12) ויתקימו ויזעקו and not ויקומו ויזעקו,[72] that is to say a Hitpa'el is used here instead of a Qal in Biblical Hebrew. This shift is not difficult to account for. The verb קָם belongs to the category of intransitive verbs.[73] We have seen that in the transition from Classical Hebrew to later phases of the language both Nif'al and Hitpa'el/Nitpa'al can substitute for Qal forms. Ginsberg mentions נִרְעַשׁ > רָעַשׁ, נִסְעַר > סָעַר, נִקְדַּשׁ > קָדַשׁ, נִטְמָא > טָמֵא, נִכְשַׁל > כָּשַׁל in Biblical Hebrew.[74] When referring to the shift from intransitive Qal to Hitpa'el/Nitpa'al, he mentions the examples נִתְחַזֵּק > חָזַק, נִתְמָעֵט > מָעַט, נִתְרַבָּה > רָבָה, נִזְדַּקֵּן > זָקֵן in the transition from Biblical to Mishnaic Hebrew.[75]

§ 24 We may therefore assume that our Qumran passage reflects this shift, and instead of the instransitive verb ויקומו we find ויתקימו. If indeed this is the case, our conclusion is of lexical significance as well. We know of קִיֵּם in the Pi'el in the sense of "confirm, perform, strengthen, validate," found in Biblical Hebrew[76] already in books from the end of the First Temple period, and thereafter in the books actually composed during the Second Temple era, as illustrated by the following examples: ויחלו לְקַיֵּם דבר "and they would be able to confirm the word" (Ezek 13:6), לְקַיֵּם כל דבר "to confirm all things" (Ruth 4:5), קַיְּמֵנִי "strengthen me" (Ps 119:28), וָאֲקַיֵּמָה "and I will perform" (Ps

70 This is what Tal 2000:764 correctly gives as definition no. 13 s. v. קום in Samaritan Aramaic, e.g. וקם פרעה וצמת אכלסין רברבין, which he rendered as "and Pharaoh arose and gathered large assemblies."

71 Rashi provides a similar explanation regarding other sequences in which the first verb denotes movement, like ויצא וילך in the verse ויצא יעקב מבאר שבע וילך חרנה "And Jacob went out from Beer-Sheba and went towards Haran" (Gen 28:10). Rashi notes that וילך חרנה means יצא ללכת לחרן, i.e. "he went out (in order) to go to Haran". This is based on an interpretation of Genesis Rabbah.

72 See note 68 above.

73 See Ginsberg 1934:208–223, esp. 216 with n. 1.

74 Ibid., 216. In passing we should note Ginsberg's conjecture regarding the root כשל; he suggests that the switch may also be from passive Qal (*כֻּשַּׁל) to Nif'al.

75 Ibid., 216 n. 1. See also Ben-Ḥayyim 1985:206, § 150a n. 2 regarding the situation in Samaritan Aramaic (as well as the reference to his earlier article, 1971:249).

76 Ben-Yehuda 1960:5910.

119:106); כאשר קִיַּם עליהם מרדכי "as Mordecai (…) had enjoined them" (Esth 9:31 and six further occurrences in this book). The reflexive-passive Nitpa'al is recorded in Mishnaic Hebrew in the sense of "withstand, continue, persist, prevail, survive"[77] (and in other meanings, as will be demonstrated in the course of our discussion[78]). However, if accepted, this explanation shows that התקיים in the fragment from Qumran is nothing but a variant of קָם with the basic meaning of "rising." In other words, התקיים ופעל denotes "arose and acted" (קם ופעל) or "arose to act" (קם לפעול).

§ 25 In this context a related usage of נתקיים in Mishnaic Hebrew must be mentioned. I refer to the sense of נתקיים as "stand over him as a guard to save him" as defined in Ben-Yehuda's dictionary.[79] This is the meaning that clearly arises from the interpretation of the verbs נִצָּב and עוֹמֵד in Genesis Rabbah:

> "והנה ה' נצב עליו". רבי חייא ורבי ינאי, חד אמר "עליו" – על סולם, וחרנא אמר "עליו" – על יעקב. מאן דאמר "עליו" על סולם – ניחא, מאן דאמר "עליו" על יעקב – מתקיים עליו. אמר רבי יוחנן הרשעים מתקיימין על אלהיהם, שנא' "ופרעה חולם והנה עומד על היאור", אבל הצדיקים אלהיהם מתקיימים עליהם, שנאמר "והנה ה' נצב עליו".
>
> והנה ה' נצב עליו "And behold the Eternal stood above him/it" (Gen 28:13). Rabbi Hiyya and Rabbi Yannai – one held that עליו refers to the ladder, the other held that עליו refers to Jacob. Whoever claims that עליו refers to the ladder – very well! But whoever holds that עליו refers to Jacob, means that God stood over Jacob to guard him. Rabbi Yohanan says, that the wicked guard their gods, as it is said ופרעה חולם והנה עומד על היאור "Pharaoh dreamed: and, behold, he stood by the river" (Gen 41:1), but God guards the righteous, as it is said והנה ה' נצב עליו.[80]

All the occurrences of התקיים על in this section denote "stood over him to guard him". Thus מתקיים עליו means "(God) stands over him (to guard him)". In the opinion of the Midrash, the meaning of הרשעים מתקיימים על אלהיהם is that the evil stand over their gods to protect them, and in a similar fashion הצדיקים אלהיהם מתקיימים עליהם means "God stands over the righteous to guard them."[81] If this is the case, then in Mishnaic Hebrew we have a continua-

---

77 See § 21 above and the citation from Ben-Yehuda 1960, referred to in nn. 65–66 above.

78 See § 25 below.

79 Ben-Yehuda 1960:5918.

80 Gen. Rab. 69:3 (ed. Theodor-Albeck, 792–793). The text is cited here with minor alterations in punctuation.

81 Cf. also the citation from y. Berakhot 9:1 (fol. 13a in the Venice ed., and p. 67 in the edition of the Jerusalem Talmud based on Leiden manuscript published by the Hebrew Language Academy [Jerusalem 2001]): בשר ודם יש לו פטרון (…) הרי אני מתקיים עליו. See also Lieberman 1962:49–50 (I am grateful to M. Kister for this reference). Lieberman's comment on מתקיים עליו meaning "guard him" when indicating the role of the Patron – קיומה in the language of the Jerusalem Talmud – in Galilean Aramaic (and the Syro-Palestinian parallel) does not undermine the assertion that התקיים is equivalent to "stood" in a slightly extended sense.

tion of the usage of התקיים found in Qumran, albeit with an extended meaning.

§ 26 It should be noted in passing that the shift from Qal to reflexive-passive Hitpa'el in the verb קום denoting "rising, standing over" has already been documented in the book of Ben Sira. There we find the verse: מהתעשק עם[שפ]חה לך ומהתקומם על יצעיה (41:22) in the version of the *Masada* scroll. One could easily assume, as was done by the Septuagint translators, that the verbs הִתְקוֹמֵם and הִתְעַשֵּׁק denote "fighting, disputing". However, I think that Kister's interpretation is more feasible. He convincingly demonstrates that in this context התעשק denotes "making love"[82] and התקומם probably stands for "arose, stood over the maidservants' couches".[83] If indeed this is the case, we have here in Ben Sira הִתְקוֹמֵם instead of קָם/עָמַד, whereas in Qumran Hebrew the late variant התקיים appears as an equivalent of קָם/עָמַד.

10.4.2 התקומם = התקיים

§ 27 Furthermore, an additional explanation may be considered. It is known that the verb קָם also means "rebel, resist, be against," "dispute" and even "behave wickedly," or "behave like an enemy". An example of this can be found in the words of Jotham the son of Gideon: ואתם קמתם על בית אבי היום ותהרגו את בניו שבעים איש "and you are risen up against my father's house this day, and have slain his sons" (Judg 9:18). Moreover, the present participle קָם used as a noun in the sense of "adversary, foe, enemy" is especially well known, e.g. תהרס קמיך "Thou hast overthrown them that rose up against thee" (Exod 15:7), שפתי קמי "the lips of those that rose up against me" (Lam 3:62). Forms derived from the biblical Hitpolel (הִתְקוֹמֵם) also pertain to this semantic field.

All these forms occur in the Bible in the present participle, as in the following examples: (a) יגלו שמים עונו וארץ מתקוממה לו "The heaven shall reveal his iniquity; and the earth rises up against him" (Job 20:27); (b) יהי כרשע איבי ומתקוממי כעול "Let my enemy be as the wicked, and he that rises up against me as the unrighteous" (Job 27:7); (c) הפלה חסדיך מושיע חוסים ממתקוממים בימינך "Demonstrate clearly Your kindness, (You) Who saves with Your right hand those who seek refuge (in You) from those who arise (against them)" (Ps

---

82 See Kister 1989–1990:303–378, esp. 351.

83 Kister (ibid.) applies greater caution concerning the meaning of הִתְקוֹמֵם. In my opinion, the citation he mentions there from Midrash Gen. Rab. 87:5 (העמידתו לפני מיטתה; ed. Theodor-Albeck, 1068) substantiates the interpretation of הִתְקוֹמֵם as meaning עמד "stood over."

17:7); (d) הצילני מאיבי אלהי ממתקוממי תשגבני "Deliver me from my enemies, O my God; defend me from them that rise up against me" (Ps 59:2); (e) הלוא משנאיך ה' אשנא ובתקוממיך[84] אתקוטט "Do not I hate them, O Lord, that hate You? And am not I grieved with those that rise up against You?" (Ps 139:21).

In example (a), מִתְקוֹמָמָה is a verbal participle, which is possibly also the case in (c). In the remaining instances we have to do with participles functioning as nouns. In all these examples, intransitive Qal (קָם) is replaced by Hitpolel (הִתְקוֹמֵם), with the meaning "to rise up against."

It might seem that the verb התקיים in our Qumran texts is to be understood in the sense of "rise up against, to rebel". We could thus interpret the content of line 12 as follows: at first they served Egypt, and after that they rebelled and cried out against Egypt. This may also be the case in line 13: והנה נתנו במצרים פעם שנית בקץ ממלכה ויתקי[מו] should be understood as "and then they were delivered into Egypt a second time in a royal period, and after that they rebelled". As noted before, קָם "rebel" was already substituted with הִתְקוֹמֵם in Biblical Hebrew.[85]

Moreover, it is known that Biblical Hebrew Polel and Hitpolel stems were replaced in Mishnaic Hebrew with Piyyel/Piwwel or reflexive-passive Nitpayyal/Nitpawwal respectively; קוֹמֵם > קִיֵּם, כּוֹנֵן > כִּוֵּן; הִתְקוֹמֵם > נִתְקַיֵּם, הִתְכּוֹנֵן > נִתְכַּוֵּן . We have come across this form in our Qumran fragment: ויתקימו in the Nitpa'al (Nitpayyal) stem instead of the Biblical form הִתְקוֹמֵם. Yet this interpretation is to be dismissed for the simple reason that nowhere have we heard of the Israelites rebelling in Egypt.

§ 28 We shall now examine some biblical verses that may have set the stage for what we find in the passage from Qumran. I refer to two sections appearing in the book of Exod 1:13–14; 2:23–25. The issue of servitude (עבד) is alluded to in the first passage:

> ויעבִדו מצרים את בני ישראל בפרך: וימררו את חייהם בעבודה קשה בחומר ובלבנים ובכל עבֹדה בשדה, את כל עבודתם אשר עבדו בהם בפרך.
>
> And the Egyptians *made* the children of Israel *serve* with rigour. And they made their lives bitter with hard *service*, in slime and in bricks, and in all *manner of service* in the field: all *their service* wherein *they made* them *serve* was with rigor (Exod 1:13–14).

The service is mentioned again in the second passage:

> ויהי בימים הרבים ההם וימת מלך מצרים ויאנחו בני ישראל מן העבֹדה ויזעקו ותעל שועתם אל האלהים מן העבֹדה.

84 This is a transformation of וּבְמִתְקוֹמְמֶיךָ; the first *mem* was dropped due to haplology.

85 This is how the Septuagint perceived התקומם in Sir 41:22 (see § 26 above). Moreover, קוֹמֵם with a similar meaning does indeed occur in Sirach: בין זקנים אל תקומם ושרים אל תרב לטרד (35:9).

> During those many days, it happened that the king of Egypt died: and the children of Israel sighed by reason of the *service*, and they cried, and their cry for help came up unto God by reason of the *service* (Exod 2:23).

It appears that the Qumran author based himself on these verses, when he wrote ויעבודו ויתקימו ויזעקו (4Q462 1:12), in which he meant that after the service they cried out. Evidently, the author wrote ויתקימו (= ויקומו) ויזעקו in order to elucidate his description. This interpretation, which suggests an affinity between the aforementioned verses from the book of Exodus and our Qumran passage, would imply that the form ויתקימו refers neither to "endurance"[86] nor "rebellion," but rather should be translated as "they arose and cried" or "they arose to cry."

10.5 Concluding remarks

§ 29 Our survey of 4Q462 fragment 1 has led us to explore various linguistic issues, all of which pertain to words or phrases occurring but once in texts from Qumran. Evidently, the meaning and interpretation of רֵיקָמָה and מֵאֶחָד are sufficiently clear; both are adverbs, one having a distinct morphological morpheme, the other a distinct syntactical structure. It is evident from both that the influence of Aramaic upon writers of Qumran Hebrew cannot be easily dismissed. The phrase עם החביב can be interpreted in two different ways, neither of which can take decisive preference over the other. The function of the verb ויתקימו is less clear. The existence in Qumran of this verb provides an early attestation of קום Hitpa'el, which until now was known only in Mishnaic Hebrew. The semantic value of this verb has not been determined with certainty, although we believe that ויתקימו means "rise." The passage 4Q462 1:12 ויתקימו ויזעקו should be translated as "they arose and cried" or "they arose to cry."

---

86 One might be inclined to agree with Smith's assessment that the author of our Qumran fragments refers to endurance and survival of the children of Israel in view of the fact that, despite the hard service and the decree against the children, they פרו וישרצו וירבו ויעצמו במאד מאד "were fruitful and prolific; they multiplied and grew exceedingly strong" (Exod 1:7); that is to say, they continued to endure and only cried out afterwards. I am however of the opinion that more decisive importance should be attributed to the literary interdependence of the text in the passages quoted, esp. to 2:23 ויאנחו בני ישראל מן העבֹדה ויזעקו, "the children of Israel sighed because of the service and cried". It should be noted that we might have expected the verb between ויעבדו and ויזעקו to express the sigh (ויאנחו), i.e. the suffering of the children of Israel, yet it is obvious that ויתקימו does not have this function.

It must be remembered that lack of solid evidence leaves us in doubt as to the precise grammatical and lexical interpretations of the expressions discussed. Our present study is only the first step towards a better understanding.[87]

87 See also the appendix in Bar-Asher 2012, pp. 117–121, §§ 30–36.

11 Qumran Hebrew Between Biblical and Mishnaic Hebrews: A Morphological Study

11.1 Introductory Comments

§ 1 The history of Qumran Hebrew (QH) studies is like that of Qumran studies in general. From the publication of the first scrolls, linguistic inquiry has accompanied the study of the scrolls' contents and other aspects of research. The study of QH encompassed all areas of language: orthography, all aspects of grammar (phonology, morphology, and syntax), and the lexicon. Many of the linguistic studies from first generation of Scrolls research remain reliable, because they were fundamental works done by some of the best scholars, such as Hanokh Yalon, Yehezkel Kutscher, and Ze'ev Ben-Ḥayyim, among others.

§ 2 Pride of place in the study of QH grammar is reserved for Yehezkel Kutscher and also to Elisha Qimron. Kutscher's profound and comprehensive study of the language of the Great Isaiah Scroll and Qimron's grammar in its Hebrew (1976) and abridged English (1986) editions are the two widest-ranging works produced in the study of QH grammar. However, there are, still, aspects of the grammar that require further study to fill in and correct earlier work. This is true even with regard to some issues treated in the works of Kutscher and Qimron and studied by others. At times such questions need to be raised again in order to clarify and present again the QH data themselves; alongside such work comparative analysis is required. Such comparison has to take into account the earlier layer – biblical Hebrew (BH), and the later one, namely Mishnaic Hebrew (MH), and of course the Hebrew of Ben Sira (BSH), which overlaps with QH. Diachronic analysis is also necessary, situating QH within the three-fold periodization of Hebrew just mentioned: BH, QH and BSH, and MH.

§ 3 It is such an issue I would like to discuss here. Although it has been described and analyzed, there are both details and general conclusions yet to be added, with regard to the data from each of the aforementioned strata of Hebrew and with regard to the evaluation of the material as a whole. The issue I have in mind is the third-person plural suffixes, masculine and feminine, attached to plural nouns ending in וֹת-, forms such as משפחותם "their families" and שמותן "their names" as against משפחותיהם and שמותיהן.

11.2 Third-person Pronominal Suffixes on Plural Nouns with the Ending ־וֹת

11.2.1 Biblical Hebrew

§ 4 It is known that in the grammar of BH, two forms of the 3p suffixes appear with nouns whose plural is formed with ־וֹת, such as אָבוֹת, דּוֹרוֹת, מִשְׁפָּחוֹת:

A. The forms that appear on singular nouns, ־ָם and ־ָן, such as אֲבוֹתָם and שְׁמוֹתָם,[1] similar to מַלְכָּם, מַלְכָּתָם, בֵּיתָן, and יַלְדָּתָן. Henceforth these will be called the short forms.

B. The forms that appear on plural nouns, ־ֵיהֶם and ־ֵיהֶן,[2] such as אֲבוֹתֵיהֶם and תּוֹעֲבוֹתֵיהֶן,[3] similar to מַלְכֵיהֶם and בָּתֵּיהֶן; henceforth these will be called the long forms.

As was already noted by Jonah ibn Janah,[4] the short forms are the more common ones in BH:

> ואם יתחבר עם השמות המקובצים בוו ובתו יהיה מם, כמו: ידותם [מלכים א ז 33] ... וגבותם [יחזקאל א 18] ... בשדותם [נחמיה 25], למשפחותם [בראשית י 5] ... ויש שיהיה הא ומם כאמרו: ... ותועבותיהם [יחזקאל יא 21], למשפחותיהם [בראשית ח 19] ... חרבותיהם ... וחניתותיהם ... [מיכה ד 3].
>
> If it is attached to nouns pluralized with a *waw* and a *taw*, it [the suffixed pronoun] will be *mem*, such as יְדוֹתָם (1 Kgs 7:33),[5] ... וְגַבֹּתָם (Ezek 1:18) ... בִּשְׂדֹתָם (Neh 11:25) ... לְמִשְׁפְּחוֹתָם (Gen 10:5) ... and occasionally it is *hē* and *mem*, as is found ... וְתוֹעֲבוֹתֵיהֶם (Ezek 11:21), לְמִשְׁפְּחֹתֵיהֶם (Gen 8:19) ... חַרְבוֹתֵיהֶם ... וַחֲנִיתוֹתֵיהֶם (Micah 4:3).

---

1 It should be noted that the majority of forms attested in the Bible are 3mp forms, but a number of nouns are attested in 3fp forms as well, e.g., וּשְׁמוֹתָן (Ezek 23:4 2×).

2 According to some analyses, the pronominal morpheme is only הֶם and הֶן, and the ־ֵי that precedes it is part of the plural morpheme (see the discussion of Ibn Janah, quoted immediately below).

3 תּוֹעֲבוֹתֵיהֶן with the 3fp pronominal suffix is attested twice (Ezek 16:47; 23:36). I should also mention that longer forms with a final *ā* are also attested occasionally, such as גְּוִיֹּתֵיהֶנָה (Ezek 1:11). There are also 3fp forms that end with ם-, such as גְּוִיֹּתֵיהֶם (Ezek 1:23). The use of ם- for feminine forms (alongside ן-) is also found in other contexts, such as לָהֶם and אֲבִיהֶם, alongside לָהֶן and אֲבִיהֶן in Num 27:7.

4 Cf. Ibn Janaḥ 1964:381.

5 The sources cited in the Academy's edition in footnotes have here been incorporated within the text.

As Wilensky noted in his editorial notes there, “he means to say ... the basic form is ם, and only occasionally does it appear as ה and ם.”[6]

§ 5 It is also well known that the short forms are by far more common in the early books of the Bible, as scholars established long ago.[7] It has also been noted that the minimal pair אֲבוֹתָם/אֲבוֹתֵיהֶם nicely reflects this distribution:[8] only the short form אֲבוֹתָם appears in the early books (for example, 46 times in the Pentateuch), and the long form אֲבוֹתֵיהֶם appears only in books dating from late First Temple times and later (Kings [1×], Jeremiah [3×], Ezra and Nehemiah [3×], Chronicles [26×]), altogether 33 times.[9] The same distribution seems to lie behind the difference between מִסְגְּרוֹתָם in the early version of David’s Song (2 Sam 22:46) and מִסְגְּרוֹתֵיהֶם in the later version (Ps 18:46).[10]

§ 6 It is also possible to add further facts, both of a general nature[11] and regarding certain details, that confirm the picture just sketched. Here are just two examples.

---

6 Ibn Janah distinguished between ם- and הם-, because he takes the syllable preceding הם- (i.e., ֵי-) to be part of the pluralizing morpheme, not part of the pronominal suffix. For our purposes, nothing needs to be added to this. I am also avoiding the question of diachronic precedence, namely, whether the short forms or the long forms are earlier within Hebrew (cf. Kutscher 1959:355, following Barth). I will also not discuss the question of whether the long forms developed under Aramaic influence, or were the result of inner-Hebrew analogy to forms such as דִּבְרֵיהֶם; this question was mentioned briefly in Hurvitz 1982:25. I tend to prefer the second possibility, but this is not the place to elaborate on the considerations involved.

7 See GKC § 91n (p. 259) and Hurvitz 1982:24–27, which is a fundamental discussion of the phenomenon.

8 HALOT s.v. אב notes that the plural form אֲבֹ(וֹ)תָם is attested 107× in the Bible, and אֲבֹ(וֹ)תֵיהֶם 33×, only in the later books (see immediately below).

9 It should be stressed, however, that the short form אֲבוֹתָם also appears 34× in these later books (9× in Kings, 10× in Jeremiah, 3× in Ezra and Nehemiah, 12× in Chronicles).

10 GKC § 91n.

11 My friend Dr. David Talshir allowed me to use his collection of information regarding the distributions of the short and long forms. This was not a complete list, however, and for that reason in the presentation of some of the facts that follow I do not give absolute numbers.

11.2.1.1 Distribution patterns in some biblical books

	Short Forms	Long Forms
Pentateuch	Over 210	c. 110[12]
Hosea	10	1
Ezra – Nehemiah	6	c. 20

But Chronicles, which is clearly dependent on First Temple literature, the distribution is approximately equal: 43 short; c. 40 long.

Some of the more specific details are also revealing. Of the 43 attestations of the short forms in Chronicles, the vast majority are found in those forms in texts of First Temple times (such as אבותם, מושבותם, מחלקותם, משמרותם, and משפחותם). Only תּוֹצְאוֹתָם (1 Chron 5:16) is unattested in earlier biblical texts. On the other hand, there are cases of the short forms in First Temple books that appear in Chronicles with the long forms of the pronominal suffixes (אבותיהם more than 25×, מחלקותיהם, משמרותיהם, משפחותיהם). And most of the nouns which do not appear in the earlier books are attested in Chronicles with the long forms of the pronominal suffixes, as expected (דלתותיהם, נֵרֹתֵיהֶם, קינותיהם, תְּחִנֹּתֵיהֶם), except for תּוֹצְאוֹתָם, as already mentioned.

11.2.2.1 Analysis of one late biblical text

Within Ps 107, which shows several signs of dating from late First Temple times or even later (it contains the line הֹדוּ לַה' כִּי-טוֹב כִּי לְעוֹלָם חַסְדּוֹ [107:1], and contains the root שת"ק [107:30: יִשְׁתֹּקוּ]),[13] the long forms are found six times: מִמְּצוּקוֹתֵיהֶם (6); מִמְּצֻקוֹתֵיהֶם (13, 19); וּמִמְּצוּקֹתֵיהֶם (28); וּמוֹסְרוֹתֵיהֶם (14);

12 But note the form מְכֵרֹתֵיהֶם (Gen 49:5) – and not מְכֵרֹתָם* – in the early text of the Blessings of Jacob. It should be noted, however, that the Samaritan tradition reads here *makrētiyyimma* (= Tib. vocalization: מַכְרְתֵיהֶם), from a singular form מַכְרֵת, understood by the Samaritans to mean "their swords" or "their covenants", as was shown in a penetrating study by Florentin 2001. It is self-evident that according to this reading this is not an example of the ending וֹת.

13 It is true that the word מָחוֹז is found here, as well (מְחוֹז חֶפְצָם in v. 30 itself), but this is apparently a word originally Canaanite which entered Akkadian and then, through Aramaic, into Hebrew. Cf. Kutscher (1961:41 ff.); and what he wrote in Kutscher 1937:136 ff., 1962:9–10, and 1970:5–19. Cf. also Rainey 1970, and Raphaël Kutscher 1970. There is no reason to avoid the assumption that the word entered Hebrew through an Aramaic conduit in late First Temple times. Even if it existed in Hebrew far earlier, though, Ps 107 still clearly reached its final form in late First Temple times or later.

וּמֵעֲוֹנֹתֵיהֶם (17).[14] The short form, on the other hand, is found only once: מִשְּׁחִיתוֹתָם[15] (20).[16]

It seems that the picture is quite clear: the short forms dominate in the early books of the Bible, and become less and less numerous in the later books, while the longer forms, which appear already in the early texts, become the dominant forms later on.

11.2.2 Mishnaic Hebrew

§ 7 The pattern sketched above continues into Mishnaic Hebrew. To be specific, the standard form in Mishnaic Hebrew is the long form, of which hundreds of examples are attested. I will mention just a few examples: וולדותיהן (Yeb̲amot 11:3; Temura 3:1; 6:3 [2×];[17] 6:5); חותמותיהם (Ta'anit 2:3);[18] נקיבותיהם (Yeb̲amot 8:3); קרקרותיהן (Kelim 2:2 [3×]);[19] תמורותיהן (Temura 3:1).

---

14 It should be noted that מְצוּקוֹת and מוֹסְרוֹת are not attested in earlier texts, as opposed to the nouns which appear in the earlier biblical books with the short forms of the suffix (e.g., אֲבוֹתָם, מִשְׁפְּחוֹתָם, גֻּלְגְּלֹתָם). The latter group may appear in later books with the short forms, as well, when later texts mimic their early counterparts, but our nouns, as expected, appear consistently throughout Ps 107 with the long forms. (The word מוֹסְרוֹתֵימוֹ [Ps 2:3] is of course not relevant to this issue.) The form עֲוֹנֹתֵיהֶם appears four times in the Bible: here in Ps 107, and in Jer 33:8; Ezek 43:10; and Ecc 5:7. On the other hand, the short form עֲוֹנוֹתָם is found only once, in Isa 53:11. In this case, too, then, there was no earlier precedent with the short forms to alter the natural state of events.

15 Some modern scholars doubt the masoretic text at this point; HALOT s.v. שְׁחִית cites the suggestion of BHS to emend to וימלט מִשַּׁחַת חַיָּתָם instead of וימלט מִשְּׁחִיתוֹתָם. Even if we reject this, it is clear that the MT is problematic.

It is possible that the text should read וימלטם משחיתותם (in which וימלטם would be similar to וירפאם in the parallel clause in the verse), and the final ם of וימלטם was assimilated into the initial מ of the following word, without leaving any record (the initial מ of משחיתותם has no *dagesh*). This seems to me to be preferable to the suggestion that the מ dropped due to haplography. It should also be noted that the word does appear elsewhere in the Bible: בִּשְׁחִיתוֹתָם in Lam 4:20.

16 To continue what was said above (§ 5), one may also add to the late First Temple books, in addition to Jeremiah and Kings, also Ezekiel, as was shown by Hurvitz (1982:24 ff.). I will add that Amoz Cohen published a short list of the masculine and feminine 3p pronominal suffix forms in BH (1975). Although there are some facts there, the analysis is very weak and not entirely cohesive, to say the least.

17 In the second attestation in m. Temura 6:3 is says וֵולְדֹּתֵיהֶן. The word is at the end of a line, and the scribe therefore did not write the ו after the *daleth* ד.

18 The printed editions have חוֹתְמֵיהֶן and MS Paris has it vocalized חוֹתַמֵיהֶן, but MS Kaufmann and Parma A (De Rossi 138) read חוֹתְמוֹתֵיהֶן. Without vocalization, the same reading is found in MS Cambridge (ed. Lowe) and the *editio princeps* (Napoli 1492), as well.

19 The first example is written and vocalized וְקוֹרְקְרוֹתֵיהֶן in MS Kaufmann (*a* > *o* before *resh*) but the vocalizer erased the ו and put a *pātaḥ* under the ק, yielding וְקַרְקְרוֹתֵיהֶן, like in the following two examples.

There are, however, more than a few attestations of the short forms in Mishnaic Hebrew, as well, such as אבותן (m. Nidda 4:2 [2×]);[20] שמותן (m. Rosh ha-Shana 2:9; t. Rosh ha-Shana 1:18);[21] אמותן (t. Sota 6:4).[22] We can also mention examples that are not as well known: רוחותן (Sifre Numbers § 83);[23] רוחותם (Mekhilta Bešallaḥ); פירותן (Sifre Deuteronomy § 42); ומעשרותן (m. Terumot 3:9);[24] מעשרותן (t. Terumot 1:6 [3×]);[25] במזונותן (m. Nedarim 4:3;[26] Sifra Behar 5:2); עיירותן/עיירותם (Mekhilta de-R. Ishmael Shira § 9; Mekhilta de-RŠBY 15:14);[27] גגותן (Sifra Deuteronomy § 42).[28]

§ 8 There is no reason not to think that at least in some cases this is due to dependence on biblical language. This is probably the case for the first three

20 This is the reading in the reliable MSS of the Mishna, such as MS Kaufmann (the second example is on a page of Nidda copied by the second scribe of the manuscript [K2]), Parma A, Parma B (De Rossi 497); MS Antonin (which both times has a final מ: אבותם). But the later printings show אבותיהן twice (so Kosowsky in אוצר לשון המשנה, and so reads Albeck in his edition). It should be noted that אבותן appears in Nidda in an embedded expression in biblical language: ללכת בדרכי אבותן (ללכת instead of MH לילך). For the biblical expression ללכת בדרכי, cf. Deut 8:6 and more, as was noted by Haneman 1980b: 239. My thanks to my friend Dr. H. A. Cohen, who reminded me of Haneman's comment and provided other helpful comments.

21 Although in Giṭṭin 3:1 MS Kaufmann reads ושמותיהן.

22 Thus MS Vienna ("שבמעי אמותן"), and so reads apparently also the *editio princeps* (judging from the silence of the critical apparatus in Lieberman's edition), but MS Erfurt reads אימן ("שבמעי אימן").

23 The data given here are taken from the databases of the Historical Dictionary project of the Academy of the Hebrew Language.

24 The printed editions have ומעשרותיהן.

25 The *editio princeps* reads the first two occurrences מעשרותיהן.

26 The printed editions read במזונותיהן.

27 The version עיירותם "their hatred, their vengeance" is found in the Mekhilta de-R. Ishmael in MS כ; MS א reads עירותם (cf. ed. Horovitz and Rabin, 147). The main text of the Mekhilta de-R. Šim'on b. Yohai reads עיוורותן, and Epstein (97) noted that "the correct text is עיירותן (a translation of 'revenge'; in the Pešiṭtā: עִיָרְתא ...)." In fact, this is the same text that Epstein himself cited (in his sigla, MS ק), עִיָירוֹתָן (the vocalization in the MS is Babylonian, which I have translated to Tiberian), and the unvocalized version עיירותן also in MS מ°; other witnesses read עירותן, with only one י. Epstein also cited the explanatory gloss found in MS מ²: "פיר' עדאוה ("hatred")." It should also be mentioned that this lexeme was discussed at length by Wartski 1970: 26–29 (I am indebted to my friend Dr. Mordechay Mishor, who drew my attention to this). It is true that we would perhaps expect the form עיירוּתָן (a singular form עיירוּת), with the abstract nominal ending וּת-, but the vocalization עִיָירוֹתָן cited is apparently based on the plural form עֲיָרוֹת (plural of עֲיָרָה or עֲיֶרֶת) "hatreds, vengeances" – plural! This ancient evidence is far more valuable than the logic of any modern scholar, but this is not the place to discuss this further.

28 There are also many examples of the short forms in Amoraic Hebrew, e.g., מזונותן (yKetubbot 4:11 [29b]; b. Šabbat 155b; etc.), and more.

examples – אֲבוֹתָן, שְׁמוֹתָן, and אִמּוֹתָן.[29] For these examples, it is fair to assume that the rabbinic texts are utilizing a biblical form for literary purposes. But what is to be done with the nominal forms that are not based on biblical precedents, but actually contrast with biblical usage?

Examples that are not dependent on biblical precedent include forms such as מזונותן, מעשרותן, רוחותם/רוחותן, and עיירותן. These are forms that do not appear in the Bible with 3mp pronominal suffixes, or nouns that are not at all attested in the Bible, such as עֲיָרוֹת.

Beyond this, there is even a case of a noun that appears in BH with the long form, but in MH with the short form of the suffix: גגותן (Sifre Deuteronomy § 42), which was mentioned above, contrasts with biblical גַּגֹּתֵיהֶם (Jer 19:13); גַּגּוֹתֵיהֶם (32:29).[30]

It is worth noting that later copyists and printers of rabbinic literature frequently "corrected" short forms, which make limited appearances within MH, to long forms (see nn. 20, 24, 25, 26); the forms אבותן, מעשרותן, and מזונותן, were all subjected to pseudo-corrections resulting in אבותיהן, מעשרותיהן, and מזונותיהן,[31] apparently because there was a sense among later students of rabbinic literature that the short forms were not used in MH. Reliable manuscripts, however, reveal the significant remnants of such use as just seen.

§ 9 One is forced to conclude, therefore, that although the diachronic scheme described above does extend into MH, and the long forms clearly are the standard forms there (as was correctly sensed by later copyists), the short forms were still alive and well in MH, and not merely a literary flourish with biblical overtones. Instead, it is evidence for morphological variation which remained strong within MH, and to some extent continues to bear fruit.[32]

11.3 A note on the Samaritan Pentateuch

§ 10 An echo of the process described (a transition from the short forms to the long forms) can be found in the Samaritan Pentateuch (SP). This is reflected in the differences between the SP and the Masoretic Text (MT). In a systematic examination of approximately 160 cases in which the MT has the short form, the SP shows the long form in three(!):

---

29 Comparable to אִמֹּתָם (Jer 16:4; Lam 2:12). For אֲבוֹתָן, see what I wrote above (n. 20).

30 Within MH וְגַגֹּתֵיהֶם ... וְגַגֹּתֵיהֶן is also attested (Ma'aser Šeni 3:8).

31 There are also changes of other types, such as אמותן > אימן (above, n. 22).

32 Cf. below, §§ 16–19.

MT	SP[33]
(Exod 34:13) מִזְבְּחוֹתָם	מזבחותיהם
(*ibid.*) מַצֵּבֹתָם	מצבותיהם
(Exod 36:34) טַבְּעֹתָם	טבעותיהם[34]

In the vast majority of cases I checked, though, the SP follows the MT in showing the short forms of the pronominal suffixes.[35] In their reading tradition, the Samaritans distinguish quite clearly between the short forms and the long forms.[36] For example, למשפחותם (Gen 36:40) is read *almašfūtimma*, but למשפחותיהם (8:19) is read *almašfūttīyyimma* (MT ־ָם corresponds to Samaritan *-imma*, and MT ־ֵיהֶם corresponds to Samaritan *-īyyima*).

11.4 QH and Ben Sira

§ 11 We now come to the period intermediate between BH and MH, that reflected in Ben Sira and the Dead Sea Scrolls. The data from Ben Sira has never been discussed in this regard. Qimron laid the groundwork for the analysis of the QH material in the Hebrew edition of his grammar (1976), but there is room to add, both in terms of the QH material itself, and from a comparative perspective. In other words, the findings need to be presented in a way that emphasizes their place in the sequence BH > QH > MH.

§ 12 The relevant examples in Ben Sira are not numerous – 12 words altogether – but the picture is quite clear: the short forms dominate.[37] Eleven out of the twelve examples show the short forms: מאבתם (7:9; read: מֵאֲבֹתָם); באשמרותם (43:10); בינותם (9:15); בדורותם (44:1); לדורותם (45:13); במחקרותם (44:4); ממטותם (48:6; read מִמְּטוֹתָם); במשמרותם (44:4);[38] עצמתם (49:10; read:

33 The data regarding the text is taken from Tal's edition (1994).

34 This was noted already by Sperber 1939:216, citing these three examples from the SP, but he could not have known about Tal's edition or about the Samaritan reading tradition described below. Hurvitz 1982:26 cites one of the examples from the SP (טבעותיהם), and one could get the impression from his presentation that this is a systematic change within the SP, but this is not the case.

35 There are cases among the 160 I checked in which the SP *reading* tradition shows a singular form in place of a plural in the MT, e.g., MT חַטֹּאתָם (Lev 16:16) → *ētåttima* (= חַטָּאתָם).

36 The data regarding the reading tradition is taken from Ben-Ḥayyim 1957–1977:4.295–296.

37 The Ben Sira material, too, is based on the databases of the Historical Dictionary, and the edition published by the Academy of the Hebrew Language (Jerusalem, 1973).

38 There have been suggestions to read here במשמחותם (or משמחתם; cf. the edition of the Academy of the Hebrew Language). My friend Prof. Menaḥem Kister does not think these suggestions are worth very much.

עַצְמֹתָם); בעקבותם (16:3); בְּפִיפִיֹּתָם (9:4).[39] On the other side stands a lone example with the long form: ובחידתיהם (8:8).[40]

The forms אבותם, בינותם, דורותם, משמרותם, and עצמותם are attested in the Bible, but אשמרותם, מחקרותם, מטותם, עקבותם, and פיפיותם are not, so dependence on biblical forms cannot be invoked as the explanation. Interestingly, a reverse pattern appears for the word חידותיהם: the short form חִידֹתָם is attested in Prov 1:6.

To me it is clear that this reflects an authentic phenomenon within the language of Ben Sira; in his language the short forms were apparently standard.

§ 13 The facts regarding QH were already described in the main by Qimron more than thirty-five years ago.[41] From Qimron's description two points emerge clearly:

A. In the non-biblical scrolls – in other words, the sect's own texts – the short forms are more popular. They are found 55 times, for example, למחנותם (War Scroll 7:3) and במחשבותם (Hodayot 4:14.19), both of which are without a ה to indicate a final *ā*; and צרותמה (War Scroll 1:12[42]) with a ה to indicate a final *ā*. The long forms, on the other hand, are exceedingly rare. Qimron mentions the words תועבותיהם (4Q169 3 III 1, and others), במושבותיהם (War Scroll 2:14, alongside במושבותם), ורוחותיהם (4Q176 21 3), without the final ה, and עוונותיהמה (Pešer Melchizedek – 11Q13 ii 6).

B. In the Great Isaiah Scroll (1QIsa^a), Qimron, following Kutscher, noted two examples of long forms in opposition to short forms in the MT:[43] במעגלותם (MT Isa 59:8) → במעגלותיהמה (1QIsa^a); וּמְגוּרֹתָם (MT 66:4) → ובמגורותיהםה (1QIsa^a).[44] There is a third example not cited by Kutscher or Qimron: במסלותם (MT 59:7) → במסלותיהמה (1QIsa^a).[45]

---

39 Thus vocalized in the Geniza fragment.

40 The form גויתהן (37:25) appears in a restoration, and not in Geniza fragment D itself (according to the sigla of the Academy's edition), so I have left it out.

41 In order to get the full picture from Qimron 1976, one must skip around within the work. One should begin on p. 243 (§ 322.18), then move to p. 245 (§§ (3) א–(3) ב), and finally to pp. 246–247 (§ 322.182).

42 Qimron noted another version – without the final ה – in another manuscript of the same text: צרותם.

43 Kutscher 1959:352.

44 It appears thus (with a final ם in medial position) in the edition of Qimron and Parry 1999:107.

45 Hurvitz 1982:126 does cite the example of 59:7 to exemplify the use of the long forms in 1QIsa^a, as opposed to the short forms in use in MT.

Qimron also pointed to וקשתותיהם in the Pešer on Psalms (37:15), as opposed to וקשתותם in the MT.

§ 14 I think it is very important to note that in the three examples within 1QIsa^{a}, the change from the short form to the long form may not be due to diachronic change, but rather analogy with nearby words in which the long forms are found. Isa 59:7 reads מַחְשְׁבֹתֵיהֶם מַחְשְׁבוֹת אָוֶן / שֹׁד וָשֶׁבֶר בִּמְסִלּוֹתָם. The MT shows stylistic variation within the sentence: one stich has a noun that ends with ־ֵיהֶם, and the other has a noun that ends with ־ָם. This variation was not sustained in 1QIsa^{a}: the form of the suffix on מחשבות influenced, by analogy, the form of the suffix on מסלות, and מחשבותיהמה created במסלותיהמה. The same is true in v. 8: MT has וְאֵין מִשְׁפָּט בְּמַעְגְּלוֹתָם / נְתִיבוֹתֵיהֶם עִקְּשׁוּ לָהֶם, and again the longer form spread in 1QIsa^{a}, yielding במעגלותיהמה alongside נתיבותיהמה. In the third example, as well; גַּם אֲנִי אֶבְחַר בְּתַעֲלֻלֵיהֶם / וּמְגוּרֹתָם אָבִיא לָהֶם (MT), and the form ובמגורותיהמה of 1QIsa^{a} may have risen by analogy to בתעלוליהמה; note that the preposition ב, too, seems to have spread from בתעלוליהמה to ובמגורותיהמה (< *ומגורותם).[46] If so, this is not a diachronic issue or early (MT) and late (1QIsa^{a}) versions, but textual issues introduced during the text's transmission because of the literary context.

§ 15 Since Qimron's work, new texts from Qumran have been published, but the majority of these texts are very fragmentary. Examination of all of the material from Qumran does not change the basic picture described by Qimron: the short form is the common one, and the long form is found less commonly.[47]

Qimron said nothing about the linguistic situation of Ben Sira in this connection, even though the Academy's edition of the book had already been

---

46 Two notes: (1) In two of the cases the second noun is altered to conform with the first noun, and in one of the verses it is the first noun that changed to bring it in line with the second noun. So it goes with analogies: they can go in either direction. (2) Throughout 1QIsa^{a} there is a marked tendency to smooth out variation through analogy, which strengthens the likelihood that this is what occurred here, as well. (Kutscher 1959 showed many examples of these phenomena.)

47 I should emphasize strongly that for the purposes of this study I relied on the texts in the databases of the Historical Dictionary project (which are incomplete with regard to Qumran; the many, mostly very fragmentary, texts published in the past 20 years have not been entered into the databases), and on the collection of data furnished to me by Dr. David Talshir. This collection is based on all the texts published to this point, but I know full well that the lists Dr. Talshir kindly shared with me are not entirely comprehensive, although they contain the vast majority of each type of pronominal suffix. In any event, on the basis of these findings it is possible to state that Qimron's findings are in no need of modification, although it seems that the use of the long forms is slightly more widespread than Qimron believed.

published. Instead, Qimron concludes his discussion with the statement that the short form is the standard one in QH, "and in Mishnaic Hebrew, too, the short form is not very rare. These dialects [i.e., QH and MH] prove that the short form was in use during Second Temple times and beyond, and was not forsaken entirely in favor of its competitor."[48]

11.5 Summary of the findings within Hebrew

§ 16 It seems to me a different summary should be offered, since the description of the data offered above leads to conclusions different from those reached by Qimron. It seems obvious that the data from Ben Sira and QH change the picture that otherwise emerges regarding ancient Hebrew. Alongside the trend discernible within BH, from the early books to the later books and then into MH, one must note a different trend, discernible in QH and Ben Sira. The presentation of the MH data, too, needs to be changed: it is not enough to note the extent of the short forms within it,[49] but the fact that this occurs even on nouns that are unattested in BH needs to mentioned, as well. I will suggest my own conclusions now.

1. The short form is the common one in the early books of the Bible; in later books it becomes increasingly uncommon but never disappears, and the long form gets correspondingly more common. This development becomes even clearer in MH: the short form is extremely restricted, and the standard pronominal suffix is the long form. However, the short form is in living use within MH, and it is found on nouns that are unattested with such forms within BH, such as רוחותן/רוחותם, מעשרותן, and so on.[50] There is also at least one example in which MH uses a short form on a noun attested in BH with the long form: גגותן, against BH גגותיהם.[51]
2. Ben Sira contains only one example of the long form; in its language the short form is standard. In QH, too, the short form is standard and the long form far less common. This is very striking, since Ben Sira and QH are both later than late biblical Hebrew, in which the short form is in very restricted use and the long form common.

48 Qimron 1976:247 (§ 322.182).

49 As did Qimron (in the quote above, in § 15): "and in Mishnaic Hebrew, too, the short form is not very rare."

50 At the hands of later copyists and printers, these rare forms tend to get "corrected" to long forms (cf. nn. 21, 25, 26, above).

51 I have already mentioned that the short form is used also in Amoraic Hebrew; it is also found there on nouns unattested in BH with such suffixes (this is hinted at briefly above, n. 28).

§ 17 I think it is possible to say that in this detail, in late Second Temple times we have two different language-types reflected in the textual evidence.[52] Within one type the trend toward the dominance of the long form over the short form is seen; as already discussed, this is found in the later strata of BH and in MH. It is likely that this reflects the spoken language in late Second Temple times (to some extent) and Tannaitic times (to a large extent). Within the second type there is stability in the use of the short form, as in the early books of the Bible; this is seen in Ben Sira and to a large extent in QH. It is possible that this is a more conservative usage, found in literature – the written language – which continued the practices of First Temple texts.

In any event it is clear that the two types of language existed alongside each other, and apparently influenced each other to some degree. It is thus possible to explain the appearance of the short form within MH on nouns unattested with this suffix in BH, and perhaps it is thus possible to explain the single instance of the long form in Ben Sira and the attestations of the long form within QH.[53]

11.6 Concluding comments

§ 18 It is possible, then, even in well-worn issues such as this one, to add new observations about the facts and their analysis, as well as the distribution of the data and what can be gleaned from them about the history of the Hebrew language. A more fundamental conclusion is that it is not possible to draw a line that runs through the strata of BH, through the Hebrew of Ben Sira and Qumran, and into MH; there are cases in which instead we must reconstruct parallel lines dividing between different dialects of one language,[54] each going in its own direction.

§ 19 In Chapter 13 below, I presented examples in which a single line could be drawn from early to late, showing diachronic change from BH through Qumran into MH. As opposed to that, in this case I have tried to examine a

---

52 But one should avoid talking about "dialects" on the basis of just this one detail.

53 At this stage, however, generalities should be avoided and conclusions should not be drawn regarding other aspects of the language. In other words, the possibilities just raised regarding the social locations of the two language types requires a wide-ranging and fundamental analysis involving many other linguistic features, which is beyond the scope of this study.

54 Note that although as a general rule I am comfortable speaking of "parallel lines dividing between different dialects of one language," in this particular case we are talking about language types, not dialects.

point of grammar in which two different lines are seen to run parallel, divided from each other within the history of the Hebrew language in these classical periods, when Hebrew was a spoken language and behind every Hebrew text lay living speech. Here one finds a literary language and a spoken language co-existing.

§ 20 In sum, it is impossible to evaluate all aspects of the history of language with the same tool set; every linguistic issue, lexical or grammatical, demands its own space and its own analysis. Occasionally such analysis gives rise to fundamental conclusions, and it is such an analysis that I have tried to demonstrate here.

12 Mistaken Repetitions or Double Readings?

12.1 The Data and the Interpretations Current in the Scholarly Literature

§ 1 In two places in Recension A of the Damascus Document from the Cairo Genizah we find the same phenomenon: the copyist wrote a word, and then wrote it again employing a different spelling; in the second instance he wrote a two-word phrase and then wrote it again such that the first word is spelled entirely differently. The editors of the text and other researchers have considered each one of the two examples, and Chaim Rabin has even correctly drawn a connection between the two.[1]

In my view, there still remains something to be said with regard to this phenomenon and its background. First, however, I will present the data and review the principal arguments that have been put forward by scholars.

§ 2 Here is the first example, according to the reading of the last editor (Qimron 1992, p. 19):[2]

ועל הנשיא כתוב לא ירבה לו סוסים[3] ודויד לא קרא בספר התורה החתום אשר היה בארון כי לא(נפ ○)[4] נפתח בישראל מיום מות אלעזר ויהושע ויוש'ע[5] והזקנים אשר עבדו את העשתרת (ה 1-4)

Of interest to us here are the words ויהושע ויוש'ע. As expected, Solomon Schechter's translation records one appearance of the name in his translation: "Eleazar and Joshua and the Elders," and in a note indicates that the combina-

---

1 See below, § 2.

2 I am citing the text in accordance with the edition of Qimron, who is the last to have edited the text, because of its superior accuracy with regard to its predecessors (Schechter 1910, Rabin 1958).

3 Qimron prints scriptural citations in small letters. This citation is taken, as is known, from Deut. 17:17. (In the Masoretic text the reading is slightly different: the first word is ולא, with conjunctive *waw*.)

4 Qimron indicates that in this place the copyist has written a word and then erased it. Of the erased word Qimron has identified the letters נפ, while another letter, written after them, is not readable in the manuscript. (This letter is indicated by him by means of a circle). Schechter 1910:5 does not refer to the correction in the manuscript. Rabin 1958 read the erased word as נפחת. In any case, it is clear that in this place one word was written for the first time, and since the copyist apparently thought that its spelling was corrupt, he erased it and re-wrote it correctly: נפתח (see also below, §§ 5, 7).

5 Qimron indicates in note 1 that ויוש'ע is a dittography. In his new edition (Qimron 2010:11), he accepts my view and writes, "double reading" (without mentioning that this was my proposal).

tion ויהושע ויוש'ע is simply a dittography.[6] Chaim Rabin, on the other hand, gives expression in his translation to the distinction between the two spellings, while preferring the first:[7] "Elazar and Jehoshua {and Joshua}."[8] In a note on the second orthographic variant he indicates that the copyist did not erase the word (ויוש'ע) on account of the fact that this is the form in which he found in his *Vorlage*, but rather added the correct spelling (i.e., the *waw* that the copyist suspended above the line). Rabin furthermore adds two brief notes: 1) he acknowledges that a similar case is found below, 7:17 (referring to the second case, given below in § 3); 2) he indicates that the spelling of the name without *he* is found in Palestinian sources.[9]

§ 3 The second example is also cited here according to the reading of the last editor (Qimron 1992, p. 23):

> כאשר אמר והגליתי את סכות מלככם ואת כיון צלמיכם מאהלי דמשק[10] ספרי התורה הם סוכת המלך
> כאשר אמר והקימותי את סוכת דוד הנפלת[11] המלך הוא הקהל וכיניי[12] הצלמים וכיון הצלמים[13]
> הם ספרי הנביאים[14] אשר בזה ישראל את דבריהם (ז 18-14)

The copyist first wrote וכיניי הצלמים and then (re-)wrote וכיון הצלמים. This double writing has also merited the notice of researchers. We will mention the

---

6 See Schechter 1910: XXXVI and note 9.

7 See Rabin 1958:18 and note 2 to line 4.

8 Rabin's preference for the first orthographic variant is expressed by means of the enclosure of the second variant between braces, which in his edition are used to indicate words that are to be deleted (see Rabin 1958:IX).

9 See the reference above in note 7, and especially the discussion of Talshir 1992:233–39, and see below, note 48.

10 The text indicated in small letters is an alternative version, including ellipses, of Amos 5:26–27: ונשאתם את סִכּוּת מלככם ואת כִּיּוּן צלמיכם כוכב אלהיכם אשר עשיתם לכם. והגליתי אתכם מהלאה לדמשק [...].

11 Here also is indicated a quote from Amos (9:11), differing slightly from the Masoretic text, which reads: אקים את סֻכַּת דויד הנפלת.

12 Schechter 1910:7 reads וכינוי, and from there is derived the reading of Ginzberg 1922:47–48 and 1970:34. Rabin, however, reads וכיניי, without a dot over the *yod* that follows the *nun* as in the edition of Qimron; i.e., he does not indicate any doubt with regard to the identification of the letter.

13 As opposed to the case above in note 5, here Qimron treats the entire string וכיניי הצלמים וכיון הצלמים as a dittography. But in Qimron 2010:16 he wrote, "double reading."

14 An interesting syntactical question pertains to the differing formulations of the two interpretations. In the first, ספרי התורה הם סוכת המלך, it is the *explicandum* סוכת המלך that comes after the copula הם. However in the second, וכיניי הצלמים וכיון הצלמים הם ספרי הנביאים, it is the *explicans* that comes after the copula הם. This is not the proper place for a thoroughly detailed discussion of this matter.

principal views that have been expressed.[15] Schechter (1910), who reads וכינוי הצלמים וכיון הצלמים, is of the opinion that that the copyist mistakenly wrote וכינוי and so re-wrote the entire correct phrase, including the word וכיון as in the verse in Amos.[16] As opposed to him, Ginzberg is of the opinion that the version (הצלמים) וכינוי is the originally intended one and that the purpose of the second writing (הצלמים) וכיון is to "override" the original version and to correct it in light of the verse in Amos. Rabin, too, who, as we have mentioned, reads וכיניי הצלמים, opines that this is the original version and that the repetition וכיון הצלמים is intended to suggest instead of it the "correct" version according to the verse in Amos. In this case as well Rabin expressed his view in the translation: "And the Pedestals (KENE) of the images {and the KIYYUN of the images}." The English "translation" of the phrase וכיון הצלמים, which in his view is secondary, is given in braces that indicate deletion.[17] Qimron, as we have indicated, refers to the entire sequence (וכיניי הצלמים וכיון הצלמים) as a "dittography" without indicating explicitly whether it is the first phrase or the second that is extraneous.[18]

§ 4 It should be noted that this section of the Damascus Document from the Cairo Genizah is apparently paralleled in a highly damaged scroll that was found at Qumran and published by the late Joseph Baumgarten: 4Q266, fragment 2, column 3. In line 18 Baumgarten reads:

הק]הל [וכיניי הצלמי]ם המה ספר[י] הנביא[ים][19]

In the English translation, however, Baumgarten compromises with this reading and writes "and the 'Kywn of the images',"[20] i.e., in the English translation he gives a transcription of the version וכיון. It is evident that this section of the Qumran scroll (which corresponds to the citation given above from recension A of the text from the Cairo Genizah) contains only one phrase, either וכיניי] הצלמי]ם or וכיון הצלמי]ם], since between הק]הל and [ם there is room for no more than 10–11 letters, together with a small space between the two words.

15 An overview of the different views is provided in a study that elucidates the background of the interpretation that is offered here (Chapter 15 below, §§ 5–7).

16 See Schechter 1910:XL, note 15.

17 As was done in the case of the string יהושע יושׁ'ע (see above § 2 and notes 7–8).

18 See above, note 13.

19 See Baumgarten 1996:44; see also Qimron 2010:16.

20 *Loc cit.*

12.2 A Proposal for a New Explanation of the Phenomenon

§ 5 I would like to indicate that it is not necessary to accept the above-mentioned proposals – either the one that prefers the first phrase, וכיניי הצלמים, over the second (thus Rabin),[21] or the one that prefers וכיון הצלמים (thus Schechter),[22] or the one that sees here a dittography without indicating which of the two phrases is to be preferred (thus Qimron),[23] or the one that reaches a tacit compromise between the variants וכיון/וכיניי without saying anything about either one (thus Baumgarten).[24]

I propose that another solution be considered. I do not accept the view that we are dealing with a dittography; if the copyist had thought that one of the two forms was corrupt, he would have deleted it as he did, e.g., in the case of נפחת (נפ) mentioned above[25] (i.e., seeing a corruption, he deleted the corrupt form and wrote the proper one in its place). There are other erasures in Recension A of the text from the Cairo Genizah. For example, in 1:8–9 (Qimron 1992:11) we read: ויבינו בעונם ויֵּדעו כי אנשים אשֻׁמִים הם. Dots have been placed above the letters of the word אנשים and inside them in order to indicate the deletion, as has been understood clearly by Qimron, in whose edition it is given in brackets. Indeed, he indicates in note 3–3 *ad loc.* that the three words אנשים אשימים הם that are found in Recension A the Qumran scroll 4QD[a] reads אשמים המה only. In 9:14–15 (Qimron 1992, p. 27) we read: וכל כן כל אבדה נמצאת ואין לה בעלים. It is plainly visible that the word וכל has been erased by means of scratching, and so Qimron gives it in round brackets. In 12:17 (Qimron 1992, p. 33) is written: וכל כלי מסמר מסמר או יתד בכותל. The copyist has deleted the first instance of מסמר by means of lines above its first three letters.[26]

---

21 As is known, this is also the opinion of Ginzberg, who accepts the reading וכינוי הצלמים that was proposed by Schechter. Indeed, Rabin cites Ginzberg 1922 as being in agreement with regard to preferring the first variant over the second.

22 See above, § 3.

23 See above, notes 5, 13.

24 See above, § 4.

25 See above, note 4. For our present purposes the precise form of the deleted word is irrelevant.

26 There are other erasures in the text. In one place, however, there is an error that seems to be a (partial) dittography that has not been corrected: ובפרוש שמו שמותיהם (2:13; Qimron 1992:13). It appears that שמו is an extraneous word, and that it is really the first three letters of the following word (שמותיהם). This explanation is supported by the reading of 4QD[a] from Qumran: [ ]בפרוש שמותי.

§ 6 The existence of Recensions A and B of the text in the Cairo Genizah points to the existence of various copies of various recensions. From the time of Schechter's original publication in 1910 until today discussion has continued with regard to the relationship between the two recensions, and the question has been addressed recently by two Israeli scholars: Menahem Kister[27] and Liora Goldman.[28] They and their predecessors have thoroughly elucidated, through the application of various arguments, the relationship between the two recensions as regards content. Kister bases his investigation on different understandings of verbal forms derived from the root מל"ט in the two recensions, in the sentence: וכל הנסוגים ה[ו]סגרו לחרב והמחזיקים נמלטו לארץ צפון (Recension A, 7:13–14; Qimron 1992, p. 23) as opposed to: אלה ימלטו בקץ הפקודה (Recension B, 19:10; Qimron 1992, p. 43).[29] Liora Goldman as well has contributed important considerations with regard to this matter.[30]

§ 7 The claim that we are dealing with a dittography is difficult to accept, since at issue here is the repetition of a word or a phrase using another spelling, *the repetition not being deleted*. It is, of course, possible to claim that the copyist corrected himself (as Schechter claims) or "corrected" himself (as Ginzberg and Rabin claim), but since he usually deletes errors it is difficult to see why he did not employ his usual method of correction in this case as well (i.e., by placing dots or lines above the letters or inside them in order to delete them, or by actually scratching them out).[31] Such corrections are desirable and even necessary in cases of dittography, as in וכל כלי מסמר מסמר.[32] In light of this consideration I am of the opinion that the copyist intentionally provided the two alternative versions, *juxtaposing them*.

§ 8 Let me explain my claim. In the first case יהושע is the biblical orthography, whereas the spelling יוש'ע reflects a later form, in which the *he* is dropped in pronunciation, as has already been noted by Rabin.[33] In the second case, the second instance of the phrase, וכיון הצלמים,[34] employs the biblical

27 See Kister 2005, and the literature reviewed by him.
28 See Goldman 2006.
29 See Kister 2005:213 ff.
30 See Goldman 2006.
31 See above § 5.
32 See *loc cit.*
33 See the discussion of his views above in § 2 (and see below §§ 11, 14).
34 The replacement of the form צלמיכם, found in the biblical verse, by the form הצלמים parallels the replacement of מלככם by המלך, as we find in the first portion of the *pesher* (see above § 3, and especially below § 13 [II]). This is a replacement that has almost no bearing on the word itself.

orthography in the first word, whereas the first instance, וכיניי הצלמים, the biblical word וכיון is explained. In another place I have suggested that וכיניי is a corrupt spelling of וכיני (וְכִנֵּי/וְכִינֵּי), the plural construct form of כֵּן, which denotes a scribal instrument (i.e., the reed pen or the ruler employed in the lineation of the parchment).[35]

It appears that two different copies of the text lay before the medieval copyist of Recension A, or that he was at least aware of two such copies. In one of these copies the words appeared in their biblical forms and in the other copy in alternative ones. These variants could represent pronunciation alternatives, as in the case of יושע instead of יהושע, or they could represent alternatives of another sort, such as an *explicans* (וכיניי [< וכיני] הצלמים) alternating with an *explicandum* (וכיון הצלמים).

§ 9 In order to bolster my claim I would like to examine the two Isaiah scrolls that were discovered at Qumran. Various researchers have already investigated the distinctions between the complete Isaiah scroll (1QIsa^{a})[36] and the incomplete Isaiah scroll (1QIsa^{b}).[37] The text copied in 1QIsa^{b} is generally close to the Masoretic text,[38] whereas the copyist of 1QIsa^{a} gives expression to his own linguistic habits, which are characteristic of Qumran Hebrew.[39] The following are only a few examples:

	MT	1QIsa^{b}	1QIsa^{a}
1. Isa. 52:11	מִשָּׁם	משם	משמה
2. Isa. 52:13	מאד	מאד	מואדה
3. Isa. 52:12	לִפְנֵיכֶם	לפניכם	לפניכמה
4. Isa. 52:12	וּמְאַסִּפְכֶם	ומאספכם	ומאספכמה
5. Isa. 52:15	פִּיהֶם	פיהם	פיהמה
6. Isa. 52:15	לָהֶם	להם	להמה
7. Isa. 58:4	בְּאֶגְרֹף	באגרף	בגורף
8. Isa. 59:5	בֵּיצֵי צִפְעוֹנִי	ביצי צפעוני	בצי[40] צפעונים

35 See Chapter 15 below, §§ 10–12.

36 The scroll was first published by Burrows *et al.* (1950) and most recently by Parry & Qimron 1999.

37 Published by Sukeinik 1954.

38 As pointed out already by Sukenik.

39 To this subject are dedicated most of the sections of Kutscher's book on the language of the Scroll and its linguistic background (Kutscher 1959).

40 Thus (with defective spelling: בצי) in 1QIsa^{a}! Kutscher has called attention to and investigated this matter (Kutscher 1959:114).

§ 10 In all of the above examples, the readings of 1QIsa^b are identical to those of the Masoretic text,[41] while the readings of 1QIsa^a differ from the Masoretic ones primarily in linguistic matters.[42]

Examples 1–2 reflect the use of adverbs with the ending ָה-, which is attested in Qumran Hebrew to a much greater extent than in Biblical Hebrew: שמה/משמה, מאודה/מואדה, ריקמה (an expanded form of רֵיקָם), etc.[43]

Examples 3–6 reflect the use of ָה- in the 2nd and 3rd person plural suffixed pronouns -כמה/-המה, so characteristic of Qumran Hebrew.[44]

In example 7 we find a noun for which MT (and 1QIsa^b) on the one hand and 1QIsa^a on the other employ different nominal patterns: אֶגְרֹף in MT and 1QIsa^b versus גורף (גֹּרֶף or a pronuciational variant thereof) in 1QIsa^a.[45]

In example 8 MT, together with 1QIsa^b, read ביצי צפעוני, the phrase being pluralized only in the construct form, while 1QIsa^a reads בצי צפעונים, with pluralization of both nouns , as we find in post-Biblical Hebrew (Second Temple literature, Qumran, and Mishnaic Hebrew),[46] e.g. בתי מדרשות, בתי כנסיות and so forth.

§ 11 The two Isaiah scrolls therefore reflect two parallel copies, the one transmitting the ancient version (the one close to MT) and the other a late version that gives expression to the language of the period.

I would like to claim that separate recensions of the Damascus Document, which were simultaneously current and distinct from one another with regard to content, are likely to have been distinct from one another in matters of language as well. Putting the matter explicitly: in the case of biblical words and phrases one version is likely to have hewn close to the biblical orthography or to the biblical formulation, while another version is likely to have contained

---

41 There are a few important differences between 1QIsa^b and the text of Isaiah found in MT (see Sukenik 1954:28–30). Particularly remarkable are the differences with regard to the addition or omission of conjunctive *waw*: e.g., אל תחשׂך (MT 58:1), ואל תחשך (1QIsa^b); ואותי (MT 58:2), אתי (1QIsa^b); ולא תדע (MT 58:3), לא תדע (1QIsa^b); ולהכות (MT 58:4), להכות (1QIsa^b); לא תצומו (MT 58:4), ולא תצומו (1QIsa^b), etc.

42 In addition to the many linguistic differences there are other distinctions of different sorts between MT and 1QIsa^a, such as the addition or omission of words, as well as significant textual divergences (see, e.g., Kutscher 1959, pp. 428–437, 437–445, together with other data that are gathered there in adjacent paragraphs).

43 See Kutscher 1959:316–317; Qimron 1976:284; above, Chapter 10, §§ 2–12.

44 See Kutscher 1959:351–359 and Qimron 1976:241–247.

45 See Kutscher 1959:152: "Because of the silencing of the *'aleph* (*'egrof* > *grof*) ..., the pattern of the word turned out to be nearly identical to the Aramaic *pu'l* pattern, the equivalent of Hebrew *p^e'ōl* ... The writer, in a sense, 'reconstructed' the 'Hebrew' form, creating the word *gorf* (a hypercorrection)."

46 See Kutscher 1959:488, and in greater detail in Qimron 1976:288.

spelling reflecting the speech form of the copyist and to have employed a phrase not in its biblical form but rather in the form of an *explanans* reflecting the sectarian interpretation.

Indeed, we find that recensions A and B of the Damascus Document that have been preserved in the Cairo Genizah differ from one another in their content.[47] And if this is the case with regard to content, there is nothing preventing us from supposing that there were versions in circulation the differences between which were like the differences between the two Isaiah scrolls. It therefore seems reasonable to me to suppose that this is the background that gave birth to the double writing: ויהושע, as in MT and ויוש'ע, as in the pronunciation of the name by the copyist of the text. It should be stressed that I do not mean to claim that the spelling יושוע in the Damascus Document reflects a pronunciational form current at the time when the Qumran scrolls were written, but rather that this is a form that significantly postdates the Qumran period.[48]

§ 12 As to the second example, we are quite familiar with the fact that biblical expressions are cited in later generations in accordance with their true meaning or their midrashic meaning or even in various corrupt forms, given to them by commentators or *darshanim* or people who altered them intentionally and unintentionally. The following are two known examples.

A. The prophet says (Isa. 40:3):

קול קורא
במדבר פנו דרך ה'
ישרו בערבה מְסִלה לאלהינו

Both the Masoretes as well as the *peshat* commentators understood clearly that after the phrase קול קורא "A voice calls," comes the direct speech: "Clear a path in the wilderness [for] the Lord!," as is confirmed by the parallel "Make straight in the steppe a highway for our God!" However, as a result of an alternative reading and punctuation of the verse, the expression/proverb קול קורא במדבר "a voice calling in the wilderness," expressive of calling out in

47 As indicated above, many researchers have devoted their efforts to elucidating the differences in content between the two recensions of this text (see Kister 2005, nn. 2–17 and his own investigation of this matter, as well as the investigation of Goldman 2006; see above notes 27–30).

48 Cf. the penetrating study of Talshir 1992:233–39. He shows there (pp. 233–35) that the form current at Qumran was ישוע, and that יושוע (referred to by him as the "Galilean spelling") postdates it. The latter is found in the Amoraic literature, in Tosefta Pe'ah 3:5, and here in the Damascus Document.

vain as one calls out in the wilderness without anyone listening or hearing, was born in later generations.

B. We find written in Proverbs (12:25): דאגה בלב איש יַשְׁחֶנָּה. The proverb recommends that one who is worried suppress/repress (יַשְׁחֶה) his worry. It is also possible that the saying simply describes a real-life situation: this is how people are wont to act, they suppress and repress their worries. The Talmud, however, says the following (TB *Yoma* 75a):

> "דאגה בלב איש ישחנה", רבי אמי ורבי אסי חד אמר ישחנה מדעתו וחד אמר ישיחנה לאחרים[49]

The second opinion took root in the course of the generations, and almost everyone who cites the verse reads דאגה בלב איש יְשִׂיחֶנָּה, as distinct from the Masoretic reading; the interpretation has therefore imposed itself on the text in Proverbs. This phenomenon is well known in later generations, but an early *payyetan* already writes: זכור דאגותיה לפניך משיחה ומכנסת (R. Meir ben Yitshaq, 11th century; תענית ציבור [*seliha* for Thursday]).[50]

In our case as well, the explanatory version, which interprets the first word in the phrase וכיון צלמיכם by means of the word וכיני (< וכיניי) employs the explanatory word in place of the explained word וכיון, whereas the alternative version retains the explained word in its original form.

§ 13 Recension A of the Damascus Document from the Cairo Genizah itself contains such cases, of biblical expressions quoted in accordance with their interpretation rather than in their original form. Let us restrict ourselves to citing two examples from the pericope under examination.

A. We read in Amos (5:27): והגליתי אתכם מהלאה לדמשק. This is the formulation reflected in the early Versions. The Septuagint translates ἐπέκεινα (= מהלאה), and thus also Targum Jonathan (מהלאה) and the Peshitta (להל מן), i.e., the *Vorlage* of these Versions was similar to the Masoretic text. However, as we have seen above, recension A of our text reads: והגליתי את [...] מאהלי דמשק.[51] We are not dealing here with a corrupt text, but rather with a *pesher* that interprets the biblical מהלאה as מאהלי, in accordance with the aims of the *darshan*, the interpretation being based on the shared letters *he*, *alef* and *lamed*: הלא (in the explained word מהלאה) and אהל (in the explanatory word

---

49 Thus also in b. Sota 42b and b. Sanhedrin 100b (here the printed editions read ישיחנה מדעתו, with a *yod* after the *shin*), as well as in Yalqut Shim'oni, vol. 2, § 950 (in § 755 we find another midrash to the verse).

50 The *seliḥa* תענית צבור קבעו תבוע צרכים is printed in אוצר התפלות (Ashkenaz), Vilna 1915, pp. 103–04 (among the *seliḥot*), and in *siddur* בית יעקב published by R. Ya'aqov Emden (Lemberg 1904), 557.

51 See above § 3.

(מאהלי). In the present case, the formulation of the *pesher* is employed in the text in place of the original formulation of the verse.

B. This phenomenon is even more remarkable in the phrase סכות מלככם, employed at the beginning of the pericope in accordance with the formulation of the quoted biblical verse (כאשר אמר): והגליתי את סכות מלככם.[52] However, in interpreting this phrase our text reads ספרי התורה הם סוכת המלך, i.e., סכות מלככם has turned into סוכת המלך as though before us were a different formulation of the verse and the explained formulation (מלככם) סכות is replaced by the formulation (המלך) סוכת. We can therefore clearly see that recension A of our pericope contains citations according to their original formulation as well as citations according to an interpretive formulation. This matter requires no further comment.[53]

§ 14 In my view, the innovation in recension A of the Damascus Document from the Genizah with regard to the two cases that we are investigating lies in the fact that it cites the two textual variants found by the copyist one next to the other, both in the first case as well as in the second. It seems to me that there is no importance to be attached to the fact that in the first case the word is first given in accordance with the biblical orthography (יהושע), and only afterwards in a form that accords with its pronunciation in the Amoraic period, which is the pronunciation that was employed by the copyist of the text hundreds of years after the Qumran period (יושוע). In the second example, on the other hand, the explanatory formulation (וכיניי הצלמים) is given first, and only afterwards is given the version that reflects the biblical orthography (וכיון הצלמים). For our purposes, it is the fact that the two variants are given one next to the other that is of importance. Someone, however, may wish to interpret the distinction between the two cases in the following way: in cases of orthographic and pronunciational variants the more ancient

52 See *loc. cit.*

53 The phenomenon of the replacement of one formulation by another is well known from rabbinic literature, as Prof. J. N. Epstein has taught us. The following is the series of replacements with which he opens the chapter entitled חילופי נוסחאות וחילופי לשונות in his magisterial work on the text of the Mishna. For example, the Mishna reads: שלוש נשים עוסקות בבצק, אחת לשה ואחת עורכת ואחת אופה (m. Pesahim 3:4) whereas the Tosefta replaces עורכת by מקטפת: שלוש נשים עסיקות בבצק, אחת לשה ואחת מקטפת ואחת אופה (t. Pesahim 2/3:8; Epstein [1948:1]). On occasion the distinction between the versions is such that that the source that cites interprets the cited source; for example: האשה שנתערב ולדה בוולד כלתה [...] מתו הכשרים התערובת לבני הזקנה חולצין ולא מייבמין [...] ובני הכלה אחד חולץ ואחד מיבם (m. Yebamot 11:4), whereas in the Yerushalmi we read: אמר רבי יוחנן כיני מתניתא לנשי בני הכלה לנשי בני הזקנה (y. Yebamot 11:4 [12a]). Epstein indicates (*loc. cit.*, 277–78): זהו פירוש, וכן פירש רש"י: לבני הכלה לאשת בן הכלה ודאי. There are, furthermore, many additional examples of the first and second types of replacement.

variant comes first, whereas in cases of explication and interpretation it seemed proper to first indicate the explanation, which contains an innovation *vis-à-vis* the formulation in the biblical verse.

§ 15 The existence of double readings, one beside the other, whether as a result of textual corruption or intentionally, as I claim has been done here in the Damascus Document, is well known from other sources, and has been examined in the literature. Different researchers have investigated the phenomenon of double readings both in the Bible as well as in other corpora. At present, we will restrict ourselves to a short exemplification based on the work of Shemaryahu Talmon.[54] Even if one does not accept all of the cases given by Talmon (and it is difficult to accept many of them), it is impossible to ignore the phenomenon and its relative frequency, whether as a result of scribal errors or glosses that have been incorporated into the text or intentional inclusion by a copyist before whom lay two versions that he copied one beside another. Let us give a few examples. In ויעלו כל בני ישראל וכל העם ויבאו בית אל (Judg. 20:26): the phrases כל בני ישראל וכל העם are clearly a double reading.[55] In ודוד בן איש אפרתי הזה מבית לחם יהודה ושמו ישי (I Sam. 17:12) David's origins are indicated by means of two formulations: בן איש אפרתי הזה and מבית לחם יהודה.[56] For practical purposes, both formulations convey the same information. The following is another example: וישלח מלך יריחו אל רחב לאמר הוציאי האנשים הבאים אליך אשר באו לביתך כי לחפר את כל הארץ באו (Josh. 2:3). It is clear that the sequence הבאים אליך אשר באו לביתך reflects a double reading.[57] Here is an example from the Isaiah Scroll (1QIsa[a]) *vis-à-vis* MT: ולקחום עמים והביאום אל מקומם (MT Isa. 14:2) as opposed to ולקחום עמים רבים והביאום אל אדמתם ואל מקומם (1QIsa[a]).[58] The phrases אל אדמתם and ואל מקומם are alternative readings. And there are many other such examples.[59]

In any case, it is clear that the existence of the phenomenon in the biblical literature as well as in the Qumran scrolls cannot be denied. In my opinion, the two examples from the Damascus Document are a part of this general picture.

---

54 Talmon 1956, 1960, 1961.

55 See Talmon 1960:169.

56 See Talmon 1960:166.

57 See Talmon 1960:176.

58 See Talmon 1960:155.

59 However, as I have indicated above, Talmon exaggerates on occasion, citing cases in which there is no need to see a double reading. For example, in the phrase תקות חוט השני (Josh. 2:18; Talmon 1960:165) there is no need to see in the construct phrase תִּקְוַת חוּט a double reading that has its origins in תִּקְוָה and חוּט. Thus also in the sentence ורבים מישני אדמת עפר יקיצו (Dan. 12:2; Talmon 1960:167): the phrase אדמת עפר is not necessarily the product of the two readings אֲדָמָה and עָפָר. But this is not the proper place to delve into the matter.

12.3 Conclusion

§ 16 To sum up, if I am correct in my proposal, neither in the first nor in the second case from recension A of the Damascus Document are we to see a dittography, and neither are we dealing with a preferred variant side by side with a less preferred, or even rejected, variant, but rather with two equally valid variants placed one next to another by the copyist of the manuscript. If the copyist had wanted to reject one variant in favor of another he would have deleted the latter, since he does not refrain from deleting words in those cases where considers this to be the correct procedure.[60]

§ 17 Does Rabin, who claims that the copyist gives the form יוש˺יע as he found it in the source from which he was copying,[61] intend the solution that I have proposed? Does Baumgarten too, who in his edition of the Qumran fragment reads וכיניי (הצלמים) in the Hebrew text while giving a transcription of the word וכיון in the English translation,[62] intend to indicate that the two variants are equivalent? If this is indeed the case, then I am happy to join them in their view, but I do not see them having said that which I have said here.

60 See above § 2 and note 4; §§ 5, 7.

61 See above § 2.

62 See above § 4.

13 Two Issues in Qumran Hebrew: Synchronic and Diachronic Perspectives

13.1 Introductory Comments

§ 1 The study undertaken here is designed to situate the Hebrew of the Dead Sea Scrolls[1] in the historical context of written Hebrew, which stretches more than 1300 years:[2] beginning with Biblical Hebrew, through the Qumran scrolls, and ending with the language of the Tannaim. Throughout this time, a spoken language stood behind this written heritage. The intent here is not to embark upon a general study, or to arrive at general conclusions regarding the relationships between these three strata of classical Hebrew. General conclusions require comprehensive examinations upon which to build, and what is necessary is this type of examinations of many grammatical and lexical issues. I would like to offer here studies of just two linguistic issues, which provide insights into the diachronic developments that encompassed these three strata. It is clear, however, that every linguistic fact that can be examined through diachronic lenses will add to the general picture of the language.[3]

Before turning to the data themselves, I would like to make two further introductory comments.

§ 2 First: it goes without saying that the Hebrew reflected in the Qumran texts should be described, on its own terms, as an independent entity. Scholar-

---

1 Obviously, I mean here the scrolls that were actually composed in the time of Qumran – roughly the beginning of the second century BCE through the second half of the first century CE. The scrolls from Qumran that were copied from earlier texts without any significant changes, such as the second Isaiah scroll from Cave 1, are not representative of Qumran Hebrew.

2 In other words, from archaic biblical poetry of the 11th or 10th century BCE through literature of the Tannaim, redacted in the third century CE.

3 There have been many studies of linguistic issues – whether grammatical or lexical – which have focused on the three major strata of classical Hebrew: biblical, Qumran (together with Ben Sira), and Mishnaic. I will mention only a few of these studies: first and foremost is Kutscher's book on the Great Isaiah Scroll (1959); also of particular note is Yalon 1967. Of course, the important works by M. Kister and E. Qimron belong here (see below, nn. 4–5). I, too, have tried my hand in this field (cf. Bar-Asher 2000 and 2002a = above, Chapter 9–10). Further literature is listed in Muraoka and Elwolde 2000:275–307; see also the list at the end of the book, pp. 309–310 (which are not paginated). I should also mention that whenever I speak of the Hebrew of Qumran or the Hebrew of the Dead Sea Scrolls, I mean what Shelomo Morag called "General Qumran Hebrew" (= GQH; Morag 1988a:11–12; 1988b:149).

ship should first establish its lexicon[4] and describe the grammar of the various texts within QH.[5] More than a few scholars have disputed the claim that QH is nothing more than a repository of Hebrew words and forms drawn from disparate sources, and that in this repository biblical Hebrew occupies pride of place, and Aramaic forms are found in abundance. Shelomo Morag and Elisha Qimron, each in his own way, see in QH an independent entity, i.e., an independent dialect and not merely artificial or literary forms.[6] But clearly this approach does not deny the necessity to study QH in its diachronic context, in a sequence beginning with biblical Hebrew and ending with Mishnaic Hebrew.

§ 3 Second: there is an important methodological difficulty in this type of study. On the one hand the dates of the Qumran texts are relatively well-known to us: they date from a period of roughly three hundred years, from the beginning of the second century BCE until the second half of the first century CE. Additionally, the texts come to us directly, without the intervention of scribes' tampering hands.

On the other hand, the Bible, which was completed – or, better, which crystallized – apparently around 200 BCE, and which includes texts written centuries earlier, reached us in copies dating only from the second half of the first millennium CE (the time of the Masoretes). In other words, a tremendous amount of time separates the dates of the biblical books' compositions from the dates of their earliest textual witnesses.[7] Additionally, Tannaitic literature, which was edited between the end of the second- and beginning of the third-century CE, was transmitted orally for many generations prior to being written, and the earliest manuscripts date no earlier than the eighth century; the best manuscripts we have are partly from the end of the first millennium and primarily from the beginning of the second millennium. So in some senses, QH is earlier not only than Mishnaic Hebrew, but than biblical Hebrew, as well.

Fortunately, however, we do not have to operate with only these texts in a vacuum. The historical study of Hebrew in the nineteenth- and especially the twentieth-centuries has shown that the Masoretes, in Tiberias, elsewhere in Palestine, and in Babylonia, transmitted a linguistic system whose basic fea-

4 In addition to the sources mentioned in the previous note, Kister's articles on the lexicon in QH and the Hebrew of Ben Sira belong here (Kister 2000 and his other studies listed in Muraoka and Elwolde 2000:289).

5 Here should be mentioned Qimron's books (1976 and 1986) and his many articles (Muraoka and Elwolde 2000:296–297). Qimron is currently working on an expanded and improved edition of his grammar of QH.

6 See Morag 1988b and Qimron 1992b and 2000; against this see Blau 2000.

7 Obviously this probably is less acute with regard to the biblical books that were copied at Qumran.

tures match the late biblical period, around 200 BCE, and that only very few later influences made their way into the masoretic text. The reliable manuscripts of rabbinic literature, too, reflect a Hebrew which preserves the basic nature it possessed centuries earlier when it was a spoken dialect. It should be emphasized that with regard to both the Bible and the Mishnah, the consonantal texts of the best witnesses – without the vocalizations – clearly reflect authentic representations of the original languages, or at least the languages spoken when these texts were finally edited.

It is therefore clear that we can trace phenomena diachronically, in the accepted chronological order: Bible, Dead Sea Scrolls, Mishnaic Hebrew. And it is understood that any phenomenon in the Hebrew of Qumran that is investigated in the context of this sequence needs to be checked carefully to ensure that the proper historical sequence is used.

I will now turn to the two phenomena to be discussed here, one nominal form and one verbal form.

13.2 (מָבוֹאִי) מָבוֹא/מָבוֹי

§ 4 The noun מָבוֹא occurs twenty-five times in the Bible. It can be said that it has two[8] basic meanings:[9]

A. A verbal noun of the Qal, which denotes the action done by one who is בָּא, in either of the two meanings of בָּא: one who arrives at a place, or one who enters a place. In other words, in this meaning מָבוֹא is the equivalent of the verbal noun – known from QH itself, and from MH – בִּיאָה.[10]

8 Here I follow Ben-Yehuda 1960:2767–2768, s. v., except that I am presenting the meanings in reverse order: what is given there as meaning 2 is cited here as meaning 1, and what is given there as meaning 1 is here meaning 2.

9 There are some who detect more than two meanings in the biblical attestations, since they divide the two meanings into various sub-areas (with no adequate justification). Such, for example, is the view of HALOT; there one will find four meanings.

10 In its only appearance in BH (וְהִנֵּה מִצָּפוֹן לְשַׁעַר הַמִּזְבֵּחַ סֵמֶל הַקִּנְאָה הַזֶּה בַּבִּאָה "and, behold, north of the gate of the altar was the infuriating image [סמל הקנאה] in the entrance" [Ezek 8:5]), the noun בִּיאָה has the second meaning of מָבוֹא: a noun meaning "opening, entranceway." In Qumran, on the other hand, the word functions as a verbal noun, as in לתחלת ביאתם לארץ "for the beginning of their entry into the Land" (4Q379 12:5; ed. Newsom in *DJD* 22 [1996], 270; although the editor read בואתם, the text should be read ביאתם). This verbal noun בִּיאָה also appears a few times in 4Q324, which was published by S. Talmon, J. Ben-Dov, and U. Glessmer in *DJD* 21 (2001). For example, in fragment 1, ll. 1, 4, 7 (pp. 104–105) we read: ביאת [אלישיב] "the coming of Eliashib," ביאת אמר "the coming of the *'mr*," ביאת ח[זיר] "the coming of *ḥ*[*zyr*]." The issue of the verbal noun in MH does not need to be discussed at length here. It is found in general use, such as ביאת המקדש (m. Nazir 7:4); הקיש ביאתן בימי עזרא לביאתן בימי יהושע (y. Qiddushin 51c), and in specialized usages: ביאת השמש "sunset" (found

This meaning is found in verses such as וְיָבוֹאוּ אֵלֶיךָ כִּמְבוֹא עָם וְיֵשְׁבוּ לְפָנֶיךָ "they will come to you as a people comes and sit before you" (Ezek 33:31), and בְּבֹאוֹ בִּשְׁעָרַיִךְ כִּמְבוֹאֵי עִיר מְבֻקָּעָה "when he enters your gates, as men enter a breached city" (Ezek 26:10).

B. A noun denoting the place[11] through which one enters into a different place. In other words, in this meaning מָבוֹא is an equivalent of the nouns פֶּתַח and שַׁעַר. This is the meaning in verses such as מָבוֹא הַשְּׁלִישִׁי אֲשֶׁר בְּבֵית ה' "the third entrance of the House of the Lord" (Jer 38:14) and עוֹמֵד עַל עַמּוּדוֹ בַּמָּבוֹא "standing by his pillar at the entrance" (2 Chron 23:13). This meaning should also be seen, in the derived meaning "port" < "place of entry into the sea," in הַיֹּשֶׁבֶת עַל מְבוֹאֹת יָם "who dwell at the gateway of the sea" (Ezek 27:3). Another sub-meaning apparently derived from this one is מָבוֹא in the sense of "the place of entry (= setting) of the sun" – i.e., the West[12] – in the expressions אַחֲרֵי דֶּרֶךְ מְבוֹא הַשֶּׁמֶשׁ "beyond the western road" (Deut 11:30), שֶׁמֶשׁ יָדַע מְבוֹאוֹ "the sun knows its setting" (Psalm 104:19), מִמִּזְרַח שֶׁמֶשׁ וְעַד מְבוֹאוֹ "from where the sun rises to where it sets" (Mal 1:11), and more.[13]

§ 5 By Mishnaic, or, more precisely, Tannaitic Hebrew changes had befallen the word מָבוֹא with in both morphology and meaning. There were two morphological changes:

A. מָבוֹא > מָבוֹי: Instead of forms containing a medial *waw* and a final *aleph* in Biblical Hebrew, in MH we find forms with medial *waw* and final *yod*. Although most forms, both nominal and verbal, from the root בו"א appear in manuscripts (and in printed editions) as derived from בו"א, rather than the secondary root בו"י – like הֵבִיא, לָבוֹא, יָבוֹא, בָּאתִי; תְּבוּאָה, הֲבָאָה, בִּיאָה, מֵבִיא, and more – a few forms do appear as derived from בו"י. Besides the noun מָבוֹי, the 3fs perfect in the Qal appears as בָּאת,[14] which is the form

in expressions like ביאת שמשו "his sunset" [bBerakhot 2a]), and sexual relations, such as ולא חלק בין ביאה לביאה (m. Yebamot 6:1).

11 This fits with the many other nouns of the pattern מקטָל which denote places, such as מִגְדָּל, מִקְדָּשׁ, מָדוֹר, and מוֹשָׁב.

12 A. Even-Shoshan, in הקונקורדנציה החדשה למקרא, was not correct when he defined מָבוֹא as sunset. In all the contexts in which מְבוֹא appears in the construct attached to the sun, it denotes the place, and not the act, of setting. Even if historically מְבוֹא השמש once meant sunset, its meaning changed to the *place* of sunset, as noted in *HALOT*: "descent, setting ... esp[ecially] of the sun > the west."

13 It is possible that the expression מבוא השמש is "the place into which the sun enters": not the entrance itself, but the entire area beyond the entrance. If this is true, we have two sub-meanings: מָבוֹא "entrance" and מָבוֹא "area into which one enters through the entrance."

14 For example, of the eighteen occurrences of the 3fs Qal perfect, 17 are vocalized in MS K as בָּאת (e.g., m. Yebamot 15:1[2]). The single exceptional occurrence of בָּאָה, as if from the

expected from a final *yod* root, and not the form בָּאָה,[15] as expected from a final *aleph* root.[16]

I want to emphasize that the form מָבוֹי, known to us from printed editions, is found already in reliable texts; this is the form in the "Eastern" sources of the Mishnah, such as Parma B,[17] MS Antonin (A),[18] and the Mishnah with Babylonian vocalization.[19] However, reliable "Western" texts show two other realizations: (a) מָבוֹיִ (māḇōyi) – in which the diphthong has been broken up, *oy* > *oyi*;[20] (b) מָבוֹאִי (*māḇōy* > *māḇōyi* > *māḇō'i*) – with an *aleph* in place of the *yod*.[21]

B. In biblical Hebrew two different plural forms appear: מְבוֹאִים as well as מְבוֹאוֹת. Both, however, appear only in the construct: כִּמְבוֹאֵי עִיר "at the entrances of the city" (Ezek 26:10); מְבוֹאֹת יָם "gateways of the sea" (Ezek 27:3). In rabbinic literature, on the other hand, only the plural ending ‑וֹת is attested, and the form is written מבואות in the absolute. It should be

---

root בו"א, is in m. Nega'im 5:1 (ספק שהיא היא, ספק שאחרת באה תחתיה). In MS Parma de Rossi 497 (Parma B), too, only בָּאת appears (e.g., m. Niddah 8:3; m. Yadaim 3:1[2]). But in the passage in m. Nega'im 5:1, Parma B also reads בָּאָה. Haneman (1980:396) already noted that Parma de Rossi 138 (Parma A) always reads באת, again excepting the passage in Nega'im, where Parma A, too, reads באה. According to Haneman, the *taw* with which the following word begins ("באה תחתיה") explains this exception as "nothing but a mistaken division of the continuous phonetic stringin which the *taws* were caught." In other words, באת תחתיה was analyzed as באה תחתיה mistakenly. See also Bar-Asher 2010b:26–33. Another possibility is that the form is not a perfect at all, but a participle; syntactically there is no obstacle to this interpretation.

15 On the other hand, it is worth emphasizing that the scribe who wrote the last pages of MS K (K2), in the single example within his corpus, reads בָּאָה and not בָּאת: מעשה באשה אחת שבאה לפני אבא (m. Yadaim 3:1).

16 In other verbs and nouns from roots which were originally final *aleph*, we also find III-*yod* forms alongside III-*aleph* forms. For example, we have נָשָׂאתִי, מַשָּׂא, and נִישּׂוּאִין on the one hand, but מַשּׂוּאִי/מַשּׂוּי, נָשׂוּי, and נִשֵּׂאת/נִשָּׂאת (Nip'al 3fs perfect forms) on the other hand. We even find suppletion within a single paradigm: מָצָאתִי alongside מָצִינוּ.

17 For example, בַּמָּבוֹי ... הַמָּבוֹי (m. Nidda 7:1, Parma B).

18 For example, במבוי ... המבוי (*ibid.*, A).

19 This is the form cited by Yeivin (1985:1023).

20 In MS K there are thirteen attestations of מָבוֹיִ (e.g., m. 'Eruvin 1:2) or מָבוֹיִי (e.g., m. 'Eruvin 1:1), but we also find מָבוֹי (m. 'Eruvin 1:2) and מָבוֹיי (m. Nidda 7:2) with the diphthong intact. In Parma A, too, the form מָבוֹיִ predominates (e.g., m. Šabbat 16:1). According to Haneman (1980b:20–21), the dot under the *yod* is not a *ḥiriq*, but a *mappiq*; in other words, the form in front of us is *māḇōy*, not *māḇōyi*. On the other hand, the existence of the form מָבוֹאִי in MS K, as we cite below, supports the understanding of מָבוֹיִ/מָבוֹיִי in this MS as a form with the diphthong broken up, *māḇōyi*; in מָבוֹאִי the glide [y] was replaced by the glottal stop [']. Further on this issue, cf. Bar-Asher 1980a:43–45.

21 There are eight example of מָבוֹאִי in MS K (e.g., m. 'Eruvin 5:2 [2×]; 6:8; 9:3).

noted that all the reliable witnesses vocalize the form מָבוֹאוֹת (with the קמץ preserved!): MS Kaufmann reads וּבְמָבוֹאוֹת אפילים (mTer 11:10) and וּבְמָבוֹאוֹת אֲפוּלִים[22] (mPes 4:4), and Parma A and MS Paris 328–329, too, read מָבוֹאוֹת (twice). This was also the reading of the Babylonian tradition – ובמָאבוֹאוֹת, with a plene spelling with *aleph*, or without it, ובמָבוֹאוֹת[23] – and so, too, in a Yemenite manuscript of Terumot (11:1).[24] The vocalization מְבוֹאוֹת (in the two *mishnayot* just mentioned) is found in the editions printed in Amsterdam in 1646, Venice in 1737, Mantoba in 1777, and Livorno in 1929. This was also the vocalization adopted by H. Yalon, as well as by H. N. Bialik (in Terumot).

§ 6 The (only?)[25] meaning of מָבוֹי (מָבוֹאִי ,מָבוֹי) in MH (and in the language of the Amoraim) is "a type of street ... between two rows of houses."[26] It is surprising that whoever wrote the entry for מָבוֹי in Ben-Yehudah's *Thesaurus* began the entry, "כמו מָבוֹא," intending, apparently, to equate MH מָבוֹי with BH מָבוֹא. They are clearly not the same, however: in MH there is something of an expansion of the meaning of the term, and also some specialization: מָבוֹי cannot denote the entranceway into a house or a city, but only a small street which serves as the conduit into courtyards and to a large street.[27] It should be emphasized that מָבוֹי, which means most basically "small street,"[28] is not only found in the rabbinic laws of *'ērūvīn*, but in other contexts as well. For

22 The letter between the פ and the ל in this word is certainly a *waw*, not a *yod*.

23 The vocalization of מָפוֹל-pattern nouns with the preservation of the קמץ in the plural is found also for the noun מָשׁוֹט: מָשׁוֹטוֹת (m. Makhshirin 5:7) – so in MSS K, Parma B, Antonin, and the Babylonian vocalization (Yeivin 1985:1025), as well as MS Paris.

24 The evidence from the Babylonian vocalization and the Yemenite tradition is cited by Yeivin 1985:1023; he also cited the form במָבוֹיֵי in a Yemenite manuscript of the *piyyutim* of R. S. Shabazi.

25 See below, n. 28.

26 Cf. Ben-Yehuda 1960:2678, s. v. ("כעין רחוב ... בין שתי שורות בתים"). A similar definition can be found in Kasovsky 1927: "רחוב צר שלפני שורות הצרות הפתוחות לו. והוא פתוח לרחובה של עיר – שהמבוי פתוח אליו."

27 Compare Kasovsky's definition, cited in the previous note.

28 It must be said that in one *mishnah*, at least, it is difficult to understand מבוי as a type of street: in the opening *mishnah* of 'Eruvin, the rule is given that מבוי שהוא גבוה מעשרים אמה ימעט "a *māḇōy* which is taller that twenty cubits, he shall reduce [it]." It is not, of course, possible that the rule is enjoining the reduction of the street itself by using a לחי and a קורה; instead, only the opening into the entranceway is being reduced. Perhaps מבוי here means the gate (opening) of the street, like the second meaning of the BH lexeme, as discussed above – in other words, an *opening* into the street whose top is more than 20 cubits (אמות) to drive needs to be made shorter. I wonder if this may not be an example of an early *mishnah* in which the word is used in its meaning as in BH, as we often find that early *mishnayot* utilized typically biblical elements (Epstein 1957:27; cf. Chapter 6 above, § 4).

example, it appears in the laws of ritual purity, as in the case השרץ שנמצא במבוי מטמא למפרע, עד שיאמר בדקתי את המבוי ולא היה בו שרץ "a [ritually impure] creeping animal which was found in a small street (מבוי) defiles retroactively, [as far back as] until one says, 'I checked the small street (מבוי) and there was no creeping animal there'" (mNid 7:2). In other words, this is a legitimate general feature of MH.

§ 7 I will turn now to the data in QH, and to the conclusions that can be drawn from them. There are now sixteen attestations of the noun in the texts from Qumran, and another three in restored passages in fragmentary texts.[29] I will first comment of the word's morphology at Qumran, and then move on to its meaning.

§ 8 a. The singular form appears 11 times, and it is almost always written מבוא, in its biblical form. In the absolute we find דלתי מגן לאין מבוא (Hodayot [1QH] 6:27–28),[30] and the rest of the attestations are in the construct. Two examples are, במבוא מועדים לימי חודש (Community Rule [1QS] 10:3)[31] and מבוא אור (Hodayot [1QH] 12:4).[32]

Once, however, we find the spelling מבואי: פתחי מבואי ושערי מוצא משמיעים כבוד המלך (Songs of the Sabbath Sacrifice [4Q405] 23 i 9).[33] It would appear that common spelling in the Scrolls – מבוא – is an imitation of the biblical form, but that the spelling מבואי[34] in the Songs of the Sabbath Sacrifice points towards the form known to us from rabbinic literature. This, then, provides us with evidence that the "rabbinic" form – מָבוֹי/מָבוֹאִי – was already in use in the living language in Palestine centuries earlier than its attestation in the Mishnah. To put it another way, the common writing with

---

29 There is one example in the War Scroll (1QM 14:13; cf. Yadin 1957:342), עם מ[בו]א יומם ולילה, and two examples in the Songs of the Sabbath Sacrifice:]אולמי מב[ואי] (11Q17 4:4; cf. García-Martinez and Tigchelaar in *DJD* 23 [1998], 275) and]°ם במב[וא (4Q402 1:1; cf. Newsom, *DJD* 11 [1998], 23).

30 See Licht 1957:117.

31 Licht 1965:209.

32 Licht 1957:172. One we find the word written defectively, מבא: "עם] מבא אור לממשל[תו" (Hodayot [4Q427] 8 ii 11; cf. Schuller, *DJD* 29 [1999], 110).

33 See Newsom, *DJD* 11 (1998), 335.

34 Prof. Elisha Qimron accepts the reading מבואי, but suggests considering also the reading מבואו, in which the final vowel of *mābō'*, following the quiescence of the *aleph*, is realized not as a long vowel /ō/, but as a doubly long vowel /ō:/! For a different explanation of מבואי proposed by the same scholar, see Qimron 1986b:353–354.

the biblical form reveals a literary stubbornness, whereas the single exception spelling provides us with crucial insight into the living language.[35]

b. It will be noted that the only plural form so far attested at Qumran is מבואים. Here, too, it appears in the construct, מבואי,[36] and with suffixed pronouns: הרחוקים מפתחיה הנדחים ממבואיה (Psalms Scroll [11QPs^a] 18:5–6),[37] and אולמי מבואיהם (Songs of the Sabbath Sacrifice, *ibid.*, 14–15:4).[38]

§ 9 The main uses of מבוא at Qumran are as follows:

A. A verbal noun with the meaning "coming" (arriving at a certain place or entrance into a certain place): for example, עם מבוא אור ממעו[נתו] (Hodayot [1QH^a] 12:4), meaning "with the coming (= arrival) of the light from its resting spot (i.e., the morning);[39] דלתי מגן לאין מבוא (Hodayot[40]), in which the word means "entrance" (the action of the enterer), meaning "דלתי מגן which does not allow entrance."

The word מבוא also means "arrival" in the sense of "beginning," as in במבוא מועדים לימי חודש (Community Rule[41]), meaning the beginning of the festivals ("תחילתם של המועדים," as indicated by Licht[42]). The same is true for the line מבוא יום ולילה (Community Rule [1QS] 10:10); as Licht insightfully noted, "מבוא ... the beginning of a period of time."[43] There are other examples of the same.

B. A noun meaning "gate, opening," as in אולמי מבואיהם (Songs of the Sabbath Sacrifice), which the editor, C. Newsom, perceptively translated, "the vestibules of their entryways,"[44] and פתחי מבואי ושערי מוצא משמיעים כבוד המלך (*ibid.*),[45] in which the first four words were translated by the editor, "the portals of entrance and the gates of exit."

---

35 In other places where the graphemic string מבואי is found, the plural construct form מְבוֹאֵי seems to be meant, e.g., מבואי מלך (Songs of the Sabbath Sacrifice [4Q405] 14–15:4; cf. Newsom, *DJD* 11 [1998], 330), and במבואי אלי דעת (*ibid.*, 23–1 l. 8).

36 See the examples cited in the previous note.

37 See J. A. Sanders, *DJD* 4 (1965), 39.

38 See Newsom, *ibid.*, 330.

39 Licht 1957:172.

40 Above, next to n. 30

41 Above, next to n. 31.

42 Licht 1965:209. Others, too, have translated correctly; cf., e.g., Wernberg-Möller 1957:36, who translates "At the entering of the times," which is approximately that of Carmignac and Guilbert 1961:66, as well: "A l'entrée des saisons."

43 Licht 1965:215. This is how it is translated by Wernberg-Möller 1957:37, as well: "the entering of day and night"; Carmignac and Guilbert 1961:70 translate, "l'arrivée du jour et de la nuit."

44 See above, n. 38. It might be noted that the expression אולמי מבואיהם can be well explained as an inverted construct phrase, equivalent to מבואי אולמיהם. This is a phenomenon well-known in QH, as was shown already years ago by Yalon 1967:85, but I cannot elaborate here.

45 Above, § 8a, next to n. 33.

§ 10 In essence, the two meanings of מָבוֹא in QH are the same as those in BH: a verbal noun, "coming," meaning both "arrival" and "entrance," and a noun meaning "gate, entryway." There are, however, two differences between BH and QH that should be stressed.

A. The first meaning, "coming," also serves with units of time to mean "the beginning." The expression מבוא מועדים is parallel to ראשי מועדים in the same text (Community Rule [1QS] 10:4–5), and equivalent to the biblical phrase ראש(י) חדשים; מָבוֹא and רֹאשׁ are, in other words, synonyms meaning "beginning."
B. The expression מבוא יום in QH means, therefore, "beginning of the day," as opposed to מבוא השמש in BH, which originally meant "the coming of the sun" into the west, and later on denoted "the west" itself.

Grammatically, however, מבוא is used in QH exactly as it is used in MH. The one exceptional form מבואי in the Songs of the Sabbath Sacrifice proves that this form, previously known only from later rabbinic literature, already existed at this early stage. In other words, this establishes that the transition to a form based on a final-*yod* root (מָבוֹא > מָבוֹי > מָבוֹאִי/מָבוֹיְ), known from Tannaitic literature, occurred in Second Temple times, long before the destruction in 70, and centuries prior to the redaction of the Mishnah.

§ 11 The following table summarizes the data in the three levels of the language:

Morphology

Biblical Hebrew	מָבוֹא	מְבוֹאִים/מְבוֹאוֹת[46]
Qumran Hebrew	מבוא/מבואי[47]	מבואים[48]
Mishnaic Hebrew	מָבוֹי > מָבוֹיְ > מָבוֹאִי	מָבוֹאוֹת[49]

46 These two forms are attested only in the construct, -מְבוֹאֵי and -מְבוֹאוֹת, as mentioned above (see also below, n. 48). The form מוֹבָאֶיךָ (2 Sam 3:25) seems to be a singular form, analogous to מוֹצָאֲךָ, and there is no reason to take it as a plural; the LXX, for example, translates these words with singular nouns of its own: τὴν ἔξοδόν σου καὶ τὴν εἴσοδόν σου "your exiting and entering."

47 As already discussed, מבוא is an imitation of the biblical form, whereas מבואי reflects the form known in the then-current living language.

48 The form is attested only in the construct (-מבואי) and with suffix pronouns (מבואיהם). The pl. construct alone is not enough, of course, to allow us to reconstruct the absolute form with certainty, since there are nouns with plurals ending in -וֹת whose construct form nevertheless shows the ending -ֵי . Cf. the excellent article by Sharvit 1990 on nouns with two plural endings.

49 The קמץ is preserved in all reliable witnesses, as detailed above (§ 5b).

Semantics

Biblical Hebrew	1. Verbal noun, "coming" ("arriving," "entering") 2. Noun meaning "opening, entryway"; the phrase מְבוֹא שֶׁמֶשׁ means "west"
Qumran Hebrew	1. Verbal noun, "coming" ("arriving," "entering"); with periods of time: "beginning" 2. Noun meaning "opening, entryway"
Mishnaic Hebrew	"Small street between two rows of houses" (the biblical meaning "opening" may be attested in one *mishnah*[50])

§ 12 To summarize, the morphological change (III-*aleph* > III-*yod*) took place already during Second Temple times, as the one attestation of מבואי in the Songs of the Sabbath Sacrifice shows, although scribes continue to write מבוא in its biblically-attested form. The semantics of the word remain constant through the Bible and Qumran, however, with two differences: (a) the phrase מבוא שמש is attested only in BH, and מבוא יום in QH means morning, not evening; (b) מְבוֹא in QH also means "beginning" (of a period of time). In MH, on the other hand, מָבוֹי is not used with the meanings it possesses in BH and QH, even in the tractates Middot and Tamid, which deal with the Temple. Its meaning was specialized, as described, to just a small narrow street between two rows of houses.

13.3 עָשָׂה and הֶעֱשָׂה (הֶעֱשִׂיא)

§ 13 As is known, the verbal root עש"י meaning "to do, to make," appears in the Bible only in the Qal[51] and Nip'al binyanim, and the contrast between them is active/passive,[52] as is the contrast between Qal and Nip'al for many verbs. Other forms in other binyanim differ either in meaning or etymology. For example, עִשּׂוּ (Ezek 23:3, 8) means "press, crush."[53] There are no attesta-

50 See n. 28, above.
51 In *HALOT*, עש"י "to do" is listed as עש"י I, and in the entry are given a number of examples of the verb in the Qal which are fact derived from other roots, such as בַּעֲשׂוֹת (Ezek 23:21), which is from עש"י II "to squeeze, crush." Actually, though, בַּעֲשׂוֹת may be explained as a development of an original בְּעַשּׂוֹת (Pi'el), as is indicated in *HALOT* later on (compare לַעְשֵׂר < לְעַשֵּׂר*). *HALOT* also lists עש"י III (cognate with Arabic غشي "to cover") and עש"י IV (cognate with غشو "to come, turn, outstretch"); see there.
52 No examples of the Nip'al with a reflexive meaning are found.
53 See n. 51 above. The form עֻשֵּׂיתִי (Ps 139:15), which looks like a Pu'al, is not necessarily related to the Pi'el form עִשּׂוּ cited in the text. Note that the Targum of Psalms there translates, אתעבדית ("I was made"), and it is possible that this is a Qal passive form – namely the passive of עָשָׂה "to do" – rather than a Pu'al, as mentioned by *HALOT*.

tions of the root, with the meaning "to do," in the causative, whether Hip'il or Pi'el. In other words, there is no verb comparable to Modern Hebrew הִפְעִיל "to cause one to do" (from Qal פָּעַל "to do")[54] or הֶעֱסִיק from Qal עָסַק.

§ 14 It is worth broadening the scope of this point. There are other words that have meanings similar to עָשָׂה, such as פָּעַל, עָבַד, יָצַר, בָּרָא, and יָגַע. It is true that some of these have more specific or limited meanings, such as the exertion implied by יָגַע and the intensive activity implied by many occurrences of עָבַד, but they are all squarely in the same semantic field as עָשָׂה.

The verbs פָּעַל and יָצַר also do not have causative forms attested, either Hip'il or Pi'el.[55] The verb בָּרָא, too, appears only in the Qal and the Nip'al, and the one example of the Hip'il (1 Sam 2:29) means "to feed, to fatten," and is irrelevant to this discussion.

§ 15 The words יָגַע and עָבַד, on the other hand, do have corresponding causative Hip'il forms. The two verbs appear together in two verses in Isaiah 43: לֹא הֶעֱבַדְתִּיךָ בְּמִנְחָה וְלֹא הוֹגַעְתִּיךָ בִּלְבוֹנָה "I have not burdened you with meal offerings, nor wearied you with incense" (v. 23) and הֶעֱבַדְתַּנִי בְּחַטֹּאותֶיךָ הוֹגַעְתַּנִי בַּעֲוֹנֹתֶיךָ "you have burdened me with your sins, you have wearied me with your iniquities" (v. 24).[56] It is easy to see that in these verses the verbs carry additional semantic baggage beyond simply "cause to work": in הוֹגִיעַ there is the additional sense of "to cause fatigue, exertion, and exhaustion,"[57] and the same is true for the other two attestations of הוֹגִיעַ in BH: הוֹגַעְתֶּם ה' בְּדִבְרֵיכֶם וַאֲמַרְתֶּם בַּמָּה הוֹגָעְנוּ "you have wearied the Lord with your talk, but you ask, 'With what have we wearied [Him]?" (Mal 2:17).[58]

§ 16 In the two verses from Isa 43 just cited, הֶעֱבִיד, too, carries additional semantic weight: it indicates forced labor, even actual servitude.[59] This is also seen in other biblical texts, such as Jer 17:4, וְהַעֲבַדְתִּיךָ אֶת-אֹיְבֶיךָ, which the Targum translates ותשתעבדון לבעלי דבביכון. In other verses, however, this semantic component seems to be absent from העביד, and all that remains is the causation; if the text does indicate that the labor is forced and difficult, this is weight not carried by the verb, but by other words in the sentence, as in וַיַּעֲבִדוּ מִצְרַיִם אֶת בְּנֵי יִשְׂרָאֵל בְּפָרֶךְ "the Egyptians forced the Israelites to work ruthlessly" (Exod 1:13). וַיַּעֲבִדוּ in this sentence means only "caused that

54 I mean the root פע"ל in the Qal and the Hip'il.

55 The form יוּצַּר (Isa 54:11) is best explained as a Qal passive form, rather than a Pu'al.

56 The Targum translates הוגעתיך with אתקיפית עלך "I overpowered you" and הוגעתני with אתקיפתא קדמי "you became strong in front of me."

57 Compare the Targum's translations (cited in the previous and following notes).

58 Here the Targum translates, (אלהיתון) אהליתון "you have tired (s.o. out)" and אהלינא (אלהינא) "we have tired (s.o. out)."

59 Again, compare the Targum: אסגיתי "I have multiplied" and אסגיתא "you have multiplied."

others might work (עב"ד)," and the servitude is indicated by the prepositional phrase בפרך. And in fact, here Onqelos does not translate with שַׁעְבֵּד, but with אַפְלַח: ואפלחו מצראי ית בני ישראל בקשיו. So, too, the Targum of Ezek 29:18, נְבוּכַדְרֶאצַּר מֶלֶךְ-בָּבֶל הֶעֱבִיד אֶת-חֵילוֹ עֲבֹדָה גְדוֹלָה אֶל-צֹר "King Nebuchadrezzar of Babylonia has made his army expend vast labor on Tyre": נבוכדרצר מלכא דבבל אפלח ית משרייתה פולחן רב על צור. The difficulty of the work is indicated by the internal direct object עבודה גדולה = פולחן רב.

§ 17 To sum up, in BH הוֹגִיעַ means "to cause to work with fatigue or exhaustion"; הֶעֱבִיד sometimes means simply "to cause to work," and on other occasions denotes "to enslave, to force (someone) to labor."

§ 18 I must stress, though, that nowhere in the Bible do we find any expression of causing another to perform the will of God, fulfill His teaching, or obey His commandments. We do find the opposite: alongside חָטָא we have the word הֶחֱטִיא, and the two even appear in tandem: אֲשֶׁר חָטָא וַאֲשֶׁר הֶחֱטִיא אֶת יִשְׂרָאֵל "(the sins) he committed and led others to committed" (1 Kgs 14:16; 15:30). The opposite, positive, expression, however, is almost not attested in the Bible. One may cite the verse mentioned above (§ 15), לֹא הֶעֱבַדְתִּיךָ בְּמִנְחָה (Isa 43:23), as an exception, but from the context it is clear that the meaning here is, "I did not weary you through the bringing of a meal offering," and not "I caused you to bring a meal offering to the Temple."

§ 19 In contrast, the use of the Hip'il and Pi'el of עש"י are attested in MH to denote "to cause to do." In some of the cases, there is nothing more than causation involved; in others, there is an element of force implied. Among the many examples are some in which the context reveals that the agent is causing another to do the will of God or fulfill His laws. Here are some examples:[60]

A. מעשה בחזקיה מלך יהודה שהעשה את הצבור לעשות פסח שני "Once Hezekiah, king of Judah, caused the community to do (העשה) the Second Paschal Lamb (*pesaḥ*)" (tPes 8:4).[61] Here the king is causing the people to perform a commandment, the paschal lamb, and it would appear that some element of force was involved, as well. Immediately thereafter the text continues, לא מפני שהעשי את הצבור לעשות פסח שני ... אף מפני

60 The texts quoted here (from rabbinic literature, *piyyut*, and other sources) are from the databases of the Historical Dictionary of the Hebrew Language Project of the Academy of the Hebrew Language. See also note 78 below.

61 Alongside the reading שהעשה of MS Vienna, we find also שעישה in MS Erfurt and שהעסיא (as if from a III-*aleph* root) in MS London. A confused form appears already in the *editio princeps*: שמעישה, which appears to be a mistaken development from Erfurt's שעישה with the addition of a מ, or of a plene spelling of MS Vienna's שהעישה, with the confusion of a ה with a מ. These data and those cited in the following note are quoted, of course, from Saul Lieberman's edition of תוספתא מועד.

שהעשי את הצבור לעשות פסח שני "not because he forced the community to do the second *pesaḥ* ... but because he forced the community to do the second *pesaḥ*" (tPes 8:5).[62] The same incident finds echoes in the Yerušalmi: חזקיה העשי לציבור לעשות פסח שני "Hezekiah forced the community to do the second *pesaḥ*" (yNed 9:6 [39d]) and עישה יחזקיהו לציבור לעשות פסח שיני "Hezekiah forced the community to do a second *pesaḥ*" (ySan 1:2 [18d]). It is mentioned in the Bavli, as well: מפני שהעשיא[63] את ישראל לעשות פסח שני (bSan 12a).

B. The expression גט מעושה/מעוסה is well known (mGiṭ 9:8).[64]

C. There are also contexts in which (הֶעֱשָׂה(הֶעֱשִׂיא is spoken of as a positive: כל המעשה[65] את חבירו לדבר מצוה מעלה עליו הכתוב כאילו עשאה "whoever causes his fellow to perform a commandment, Scripture counts it as if he performed it himself" (bSan 99b).

D. Also to be mentioned in this discussion is the well-known expression, גדול המעשה יותר מן העושה (bBB 9a),[66] and the meaning is clear: even more important than performing the commandments oneself is causing another to perform them.[67] Many similar examples can be cited in *piyyutim*.

§ 20 It has recently become clear that the idea of (הֶעֱשָׂה(הֶעֱשִׂיא with regard to Torah and religious obligations, which is found in Tannaitic literature and later, already held sway in the intellectual world, and in the language, of Qumran. Thus we find in 4Q470, in speaking of the righteousness of Zedekiah:

---

62 MS London has שהעשיא ... שהעסיא, and MS Erfurt has שעישה ... שהעשי.

63 The Vilna edition reads שהשיא, which is derived from שהעשיא with the loss of the *ʿayin*.

64 In later Hebrew, the same expression appears with forms of the binyan נתפעל: נתעשה (found a number of times in ספר הישר by Joshua b. Judah, in the translation by Jacob b. Šimʿon, in the eleventh century; this according to the databases [Ma'agarim] mentioned above, n. 60).

65 Of course, the orthographies מעשה and מעשין (participles), and יעשה and יעשו (futures) could be either Piʿel (מְעַשֶּׂה, מְעַשִּׂין, יְעַשֶּׂה, and יְעַשּׂוּ) or Hipʿil (מַעֲשֶׂה, מַעֲשִׂין, יַעֲשֶׂה, and יַעֲשׂוּ), but for good reasons, they are taken to be Piʿel forms by the reading traditions of the Sephardim and the Yemenites. It is possible that the Hipʿil forms – the participles מַעֲשֶׂה and מַעֲשִׂין/מַעֲשִׂין – were rejected because they were identical to the singular and plural forms of the noun מַעֲשֶׂה, and the future forms יַעֲשֶׂה and יַעֲשׂוּ were rejected because they were identical to the Qal forms. Only the participial and future forms with final *aleph*s (מעשיא/מעשי and יעשיא/יעשי) could be preserved; we in fact find the form למעשיאיהם in Yannai (קדושתות לשבתות השנה, Devarim 1, כי אתנן הם) and in Pesiqta Rabbati 33: שופט דן את הדין והשוטר' מעשי [מעשיא/מעשין] את הדין.

66 This phrase expresses clearly the opposite of the חָטָא/הֶחֱטִיא contrast found in the Bible and discussed above, although the syntax of this line differs from that one.

67 The forms העשיא/העסיא/העסי and מעשיאיהם (see n. 65 above) are not the only evidence for a shift from III-*yod* עש"י to III-*aleph* עש"א. For this, see below, Chapter 21, § 16.

לעשות ולהעשות את כל התורה "to do and to cause (others) to do[68] the entire Torah" (frg. 1 l. 4).[69] The orthography להעשות could represent the infinitive of the Nip'al or the Hip'il, but the context makes it certain that it is the Hip'il that was intended.[70]

It is true that syntactically the use of להעשות here in QH differs from its use in MH – here we find להעשות את התורה, and in MH we have העשיא את הציבור לעשות את הפסח – but the aspect of causation is common to both.

§ 21 Allow me now to summarize. When we speak of "doing" and its causation in biblical Hebrew, we find the pair יגע and הוגיע, which denote doing accompanied by fatigue or exhaustion, and we find the pair עָבַד and הֶעֱבִיד, the latter of which on occasion denotes simply "to cause to do" (as in הֶעֱבִיד אֶת-חֵילוֹ),[71] but on occasion denotes "to force to work hard, to enslave" (as in וְהַעֲבַדְתִּיךָ אֶת-אֹיְבֶיךָ).[72] If we focus specifically on doing, or causing another to do, God's commandments or Torah, we find that the concept is not attested in the Bible at all, although its negative counterpart – חָטָא and הֶחֱטִיא – is well attested: חָטָא is the basic word, and הֶחֱטִיא denotes the causation of a sin of one party by another. As opposed to the biblical state of affairs, in Qumran we find both the idea and the language of עָשָׂה and הֶעֱשָׂה; this is true also for Tannaitic literature and all later literature, as well, where we find עָשָׂה and הֶעֱשָׂה/עִישָּׂה.[73] Again, here are the results summarized in tabular form:

	Basic action	Causative
Biblical Hebrew	עָשָׂה	--[74]
Qumran Hebrew	עָשָׂה	הֶעֱשָׂה
Mishnaic Hebrew (and later)	עָשָׂה	הֶעֱשָׂה/הֶעֱשִׂיא/עִשָּׂה

68 The same combination of words, in reverse order, appears in a piyyuṭ of Yannai's: לשמוע ולעשות ולראות להעשות (קדושתות לשבתות השנה, Shemot, אשרי נאמן).

69 This fragment was published by E. Larson, L. Schiffman, and J. Strugnell in *DJD* 19 (1995), 237.

70 So, too, the editors (*DJD* 19:239). In 4Q440 3 i 21 (published by E. Schuller in *DJD* 29 [1999], 252), we find כולנו להעשותנו כיא[. This form of the verb could represent the Nip'al infinitive (לְהֵעָשׂוֹתֵנוּ) or the Hip'il infinitive (לְהַעֲשׂוֹתֵנוּ). The editor preferred the first (judging from her translation on p. 253), the fragmentary state of the text does not allow for certainty in either direction, and so no edifices can be constructed on this basis.

71 Cf. above, §§ 15–16. But see n. 78.

72 Cf. there.

73 Other examples from *piyyuṭ* of the pairing of עשה with העשה are found elsewhere in Yannai: ושכר עושה ומעשה שיויתה (קדושתות, Devarim, כל השומע, 4); [עושי]הם כמעשיאיהם (קדושתות, Vayyikra, אם לא חוקותי, 6); see also the citation above, n. 68.

74 Cf. what I wrote above (§§ 15, 18) regarding לא העבדתיך במנחה, as well as n. 78.

13.4 Concluding Comments

§ 22 As I indicated at the outset, I would not venture general conclusions at this point regarding the diachronic relationship between the three layers of Hebrew discussed here – biblical, Qumran,[75] and Mishnaic (specifically Tannaitic); I prefer to suffice with what arises from the two issues studied here. In conclusion, I would like to emphasize a number of aspects:

§ 23 (a) We have empirical evidence that the word מָבוֹא turned into מָבוֹי during Second Temple times already, and the only form attested in rabbinic literature (מָבוֹי > מָבוֹי֗ > מָבוֹאִי) is already glimpsed in the Dead Sea Scrolls, but only once. In the remainder of the cases, the scribes hewed closely to the biblical orthography.

Also with regard to עָשָׂה and הֶעֱשָׂה (or הֶעֱשִׂיא or עִשָּׂה), the Qumran text reveals that what was is seen in Tannaitic literature, and into the Amoraic period and piyyut, was in fact already a feature of the Hebrew in use in Hasmonean times. Furthermore, it is not only the linguistic fact, but the idea itself – that one who causes another to fulfill the Torah or commandments is listed alongside one who fulfills them him/herself – which was already formulated in the time of the Qumran sect. This idea has no expression in the Bible.

We see, then, that in both issues studied here, the data from Qumran show that aspects of Tannaitic Hebrew are actually far older than we would have otherwise known.

§ 24 (b) In contrast, when it comes to the semantics of מָבוֹא/מָבוֹי, we find that the dividing line is drawn sharply between biblical and Qumran Hebrew on the one hand, and Mishnaic Hebrew on the other. In the former, מָבוֹא (מבואי) is a verbal noun ("coming" and "onset [of time]") and a noun meaning "entrance, opening," whereas in MH the meaning of מָבוֹי (and מָבוֹי֗/ מָבוֹאִי) has become restricted to "a narrow street ... between two rows of houses." If there is even one attestation of the older meaning of מבוי in the Mishnah, it is a borrowing from the language of the Bible.[76]

§ 25 (c) This is how diachronic analysis must proceed: every lexeme and every grammatical feature has its own history. Sometimes important thematic developments underlie a word's development, as when the idea of causing another to fulfill a commandment comes to take its place alongside one's own fulfillment of the commandments, giving prominence to the term הֶעֱשָׂה (הֶעֱשִׂיא).

---

75 Clearly, when one wishes to speak of the Hebrew used in the period between the Bible and the Mishnah, one ought to include the Hebrew of Ben Sira alongside that of the Dead Sea Scrolls, and attention should also be paid to Hebraisms visible to us in translations, such as the LXX. But this is not the place to elaborate.

76 Cf. n. 28 above.

The real significance of this painstaking method, following each feature through all the stages of its history, is not only in the details thus uncovered, however; it also allows us to contextualize every stage within a diachronic framework stretching over many generations. It is especially important to realize that the transitions take place at different times for different features;[77] regarding one issue, Qumran may line up with biblical Hebrew and against later Mishnaic Hebrew, while in other cases Qumran and Mishnaic Hebrew are set off from biblical Hebrew.

§ 26 (d) Additionally, each of the two later layers of the language may go in one of two directions:

A. They may reveal the changes that have taken place in the language, by utilizing forms from the living language of the time. In our context, the uses of מבואי/מבוי and העשׂה in Qumran and Mishnaic Hebrew are examples of this.
B. They may utilize forms borrowed from the Bible: both the scribes of Qumran (to a great extent) and those of rabbinic literature (to a lesser extent) mimic biblical forms in their own texts. Here we have seen the examples of the biblicizing spelling מבוא at Qumran and, less certainly, the use of מבוי with the meaning "entryway" in the first *mishnah* of ʿEruvin.

Often distinguishing between these two is difficult work for the researcher, but accuracy in describing the language depends on success in puzzling out these details.[78]

---

77 For a penetrating study of the idea of a "transition language" in general, and in the history of Hebrew in particular, see Mishor 1988.

78 In addition to § 18, it should be observed that despite all that was said here, there is a single attestation of the *hif'il* of עב"ד in BH: ויסר יאשיהו את כל התועבות אשר לבני ישראל וַיַּעֲבֵד את כל הנמצא בישראל לַעֲבוֹד את ה' אלהיהם "Josiah removed all the detestable things form all the territory belonging to the Israelites, and he had all who were present in Israel serve the Lord their God" (2 Chronicles 34:33).

14 Grammatical and Lexicographic Notes on a Qumran Fragment (4Q374 ii)

14.1 Introductory Remarks

§ 1 Carol Newsom published sixteen fragments from scroll 4Q374: one important one which contains an extended passage of text, and another fifteen small fragments,[1] all of which were part of what has been titled "374: 4Q Discourse on Exodus/Conquest Tradition."[2] The passage that is significant is the second column of fragment 2. Newsom presented a good edition of the text (Newsom 1995:102) and it was accompanied, as is the norm, by an English translation (*ibid.*) and explanatory comments (*ibid.*, pp. 102–103), among them important data and reasonable explanations. Devorah Dimant, who reinvestigated all of the fragments of the scroll, discussed this fragment at length and proposed many important improvements in its reading and interpretation (Dimant 2006:28–41).

§ 2 Even so, with respect to linguistic issues these two scholars left plenty of room for later readers to make contributions. Not a few significant issues from all areas of linguistics – particularly in the details of morphology, syntax, and semantics – require additional clarification and exacting analysis. Here, I would like to concentrate on one grammatical detail and one lexical detail.

14.2 ארץ חמדות כל הארצות

§ 3 The following is the text of the fifth line in the second column of fragment 2, as published in DJD (Newsom 1995:102):

ויטע ל[נ]ו° בחירו בארץ חמדות כל הארצות ברין]

Dimant suggests that a slight change in the reading of the second word: לנ̊[ו]. While there is certainly a difference between the readings proposed by these two scholars, there is no linguistic difference between them. There is much to say about the syntactic structure of the sentence cited above and Dimant indeed wrote about it at length. Perhaps it is apposite here to mention some-

1 All that remains from many of them is a few letters – so few they can be counted – such as in fragments 5 and 8 (see Newsom 1995, pp. 106–107, and also Dimant 2006, pp. 44–45).

2 See the detailed review of Dimant 2006 regarding J. Strugnell's treatment of the manuscript before he transferred it to Newsom, as well as the comments she made regarding the first publication by Newsom.

thing which should be self-evident: when a text is fragmentary, it is difficult to be sure of the nature of many syntactic structures. Much relies upon the scholar's power of conjecture; it is impossible to reach definite conclusions, as there are barely any "facts" to speak of. Additionally, l. 5 of our fragment, discussed here, is cut off at the end. We therefore do not know what the concluding word, ברי], is; as a consequence, we cannot establish the sentence structure with precision or establish with any certainty what the syntactic relationship is between the verbal phrase ויטע לנו and the noun בחירו.[3] But this is not what I would like to deal with here: it will be enough for me to make a few comments about the word חמדות.

§ 4 I would like to begin with what Newsom says (p. 103) regarding the phrase בארץ חמדות. She appropriately cited the biblical expression אֶרֶץ חֶמְדָּה (Jer 3:19; Zech 7:14; Ps 106:24), but in the same context she suggests that the form חמדות is to be read חֲמֻדוֹת (sic, defectively!). According to her, ארץ חמדות is an expression parallel to the phrase איש חֲמֻדוֹת by which Daniel was called (Daniel 10:10, 19). Newsom even cites the RSV translation of that phrase, "man greatly beloved," as if to say that the expression אֶרֶץ חֲמֻדוֹת could be suitably translated, "land greatly beloved."[4]

§ 5 This argument surprises me: the text presents the interpreter with an actual biblical phrase, in only slightly different form, and yet Newsom opted to neglect the obvious allusion and instead compare the text to אִיש חֲמֻדוֹת. In my opinion, it is very difficult to not recognize here the author's use of a thrice-repeated biblical expression, ארץ חמדה. The writer of the phrase בארץ חמדות כל הארצות combined, in fact, two biblical expressions, ארץ חמדה and כל הארצות (this latter phrase appears nineteen times in the Bible, e.g., Gen 26:3,4; Isa 37:11,18).[5] The combination of the two expressions was likely inspired by what Ezekiel says twice in a single chapter: אֶל אֶרֶץ אֲשֶׁר תַּרְתִּי לָהֶם זָבַת חָלָב וּדְבַשׁ צְבִי הִיא לְכָל הָאֲרָצוֹת (20:6); אֶל הָאָרֶץ אֲשֶׁר נָתַתִּי זָבַת חָלָב וּדְבַשׁ צְבִי הִיא לְכָל הָאֲרָצוֹת (20:15). The expression אֶרֶץ (הָאָרֶץ) ... צְבִי was converted into the expression אֶרֶץ חֶמְדָּה in the Qumran scroll; the description in its entirety was converted as a result into אֶרֶץ חֶמְדַּת כָּל הָאֲרָצוֹת. Notice that in one of the appearances of the expression ארץ חמדה we find a parallel expres-

---

3 The written form בחירו can refer to בְּחִירוֹ (third-person singular) or בְּחִירָו (third-person plural). Both Newsom 1995:103 and Dimant 2006:33–34 decide in favor of the latter possibility.

4 Due to the syntactic structure, where three nouns in construct form are attached to one *somekh*, "בארץ חמדות כל הארצות," she adopts a different formulation in her translation: "in the land which is most desirable of all the lands," which reflects the same interpretation.

5 See the clear discussion of Dimant 2006:34–35.

sion that clearly identifies צְבִי with חֶמְדָּה: וְאֶתֶּן לָךְ אֶרֶץ חֶמְדָּה נַחֲלַת צְבִי (Jeremiah 3:19). From here it is but a short path to converting ארץ צבי into ארץ חמדה.

§ 6 Finally, an alteration in the construct ending occurred. The noun חמדה in the Qumran fragment is in the construct state, and the expected construct ending ־ַת- (in -חֶמְדַּת) changed into the ending ־וֹת- (i.e., -חמדות), yielding אֶרֶץ חֶמְדוֹת כָּל הָאֲרָצוֹת. This explains the Qumran text perfectly, so there is no reason to ignore the clear biblical expression ארץ חמדה and pursue a connection to the singular word חֲמֻדוֹת attested in the phrase אִישׁ חֲמֻדוֹת.

§ 7 The transition ־ַת- > ־וֹת- in the construct form is already attested once in Biblical Hebrew: בַּיּוֹם הַהוּא יָבוֹא הַפָּלִיט אֵלֶיךָ לְהַשְׁמָעוּת אָזְנָיִם (Ezekiel 24:26). It is clear that הַשְׁמָעוּת is the construct form of הַשְׁמָעָה, as many recent scholars[6] have seen correctly, like Bauer-Leander in their grammar[7] and Kutscher,[8] as well as Koehler-Baumgartner in their dictionary.[9]

This phenomenon is slightly more prevalent in the Qumran scrolls. Kutscher[10] already noted this in his remarks about the switch from הַכָּרַת פניהם (Masoretic text, Isaiah 3:9) to הכרות פניהם in the Isaiah Scroll.[11] Over time,

---

6 The medieval commentators did not view it in this way; for example, Ibn Janah 1964:182 cites הַשְׁמָעוּת as one form of the infinitive of the הפעיל conjugation: "and of the הפעיל it [the infinitive] will be either הַפְעִיל or הַפְעֵל ... and some will come as הפעלות, like להשמעות אזנים." In other words, this is one form of the infinitive of הפעיל – alongside הַפְעִיל and הַפְעֵל is הַפְעָלוּת – and it is not speaking about the construct of הַפְעָלָה. In the continuation Ibn Janah says: "and it will come as הפעלה" (namely, the infinitive of הפעיל comes in an additional pattern: the pattern הַפְעָלָה). As an example he brings הַרְבָּה (Genesis 3:16), which, in his opinion, evolved out of הַרְבָּיָה (in his words: "הרבה ... עקרו: הרבה"). Radak commenting on Ezekiel there (24:26) doubts the determination that it is discussing a noun. Perhaps Targum Yonatan got it right in using the infinitive of the Aramaic אַפְעֵל conjugation: "להשמעות אזנים – לְאַשְׁמָעוּתָךְ בְּסוֹרָא" (the vocalization follows Sperber's edition; I changed the vocalization from Babylonian to Tiberian). In the continuation, Radak cites Targum Yonatan in Aramaic; Rashi also cites the Targum, translated into Hebrew: לבשר בשורה (s.v. להשמעות אזנים, but s.v. ביום ההוא, Rashi simply says, להשמיע אזניך, without saying anything about the form of the word).

7 Bauer-Leander, p. 486, cites parallel forms to prove that it is a verbal noun (more precisely, an infinitive) of the *hif'il* הַכָּרָה*, הַצָּלָה, הֲנָחָה, and so forth. Prior to this, on pp. 361–362, toward the end of a section called "Abweichende Formen" (Irregular Forms), the noun הַשְׁמָעוּת is marked as an Aramaism, and on p. 505 it again notes that it is a construct form of the verbal noun in the manner of Aramaic.

8 Kutscher 1959:150 writes, "'השמעות', from the noun 'השמעה', appears here in construct, in the manner of Aramaic."

9 S. v. השמעות, HALOT (1.257), refers to Bauer-Leander pp. 486, 505.

10 See the citation of Kutscher in footnote 8 above.

11 Although the spelling הכרות can also be analyzed as הַכָּרוֹת (a plural form), it seems more plausible that the ־וּת- is comparable to the vocalization of the Biblical forms הַשְׁמָעוּת, the

additional examples[12] were uncovered, such as עורלות לבם (4Q434 1, line 4; Weinfeld and Seely 1999:270; Qimron 2006:191), which should be compared with the parallel expression עָרְלַת לבבכם (Deuteronomy 10:16) in the Masoretic text. Perhaps one can also translate the construct in the phrase להערי[בו]ת[13] השמש (MMT 2:15) in this way. It is possible[14] that this phenomenon in Qumranic Hebrew is not limited to the construct form (־ַת > -וֹת) alone but is also found in nouns attached to pronominal suffixes. Here are two examples:[15] קדמותה (1QIsa^{a} 23:7) compared with the Masoretic form קַדְמָתָהּ,[16] and, similarly, the word מסרותם in the sentence במבוא מועדים לימי חודש יחד תקופתם עם מסרותם זה לזה (Community Rule 10:3–4).[17] Licht already noted: "the intent is to the end of the holidays, to days in which one season hands over its dominion to another time ... from here [we see] that 'מסרותם' means מסירתם."[18] Let us be precise: we find here the noun מְסָרָה,[19] equivalent to מְסִירָה (through a well-known grammatical interchange), which appears here with a suffixed pronoun, thus מְסָרָתָם > מְסָרוּתָם.

At the end of Kutscher's discussion of the phrase הכרות פניהם in the Isaiah Scroll he says: "It appears to me that a reflex of this phenomenon can be found in Mishnaic Hebrew, but this is not the place to elaborate."[20] Kutscher did not explain what he meant, but I think it is likely that he was alluding to the many construct forms of the verbal noun in the *binyan* קל that have the pattern פְּעִילָה, which appear in the Mishna and in other corpora of Mishnaic He-

Mishnaic forms גְּמִילוּת חסדים and the like (as we will see below), and what we find in Biblical Aramaic הִתְנַדָּבוּת עַמָּא (Ezra 7:16), לְהוֹדָעוּתַנִי (Daniel 4:15), and so forth.

12 The four examples brought here from the Qumran scrolls were kindly provided by my friend Elisha Qimron from a draft of a new grammar on Qumranic Hebrew that he is currently writing. I thank him for this.

13 However, there is nothing stopping one from positing that the plural form העריבוֹת is intended here.

14 I have chosen to say "it is possible" and not use definitive language based upon Kutscher's opinion (see below, n. 16) regarding the form קדמותה brought below.

15 This is Qimron's view, since (as was mentioned above), he provided me with these examples.

16 Kutscher 1959:292 sees in the form קדמותה of the Isaiah Scroll an extended form of קדמות, founded upon the forms קדמות, קדמיות, קדימות of the Late Aramaic Dialects (see there), but Qimron's suggestion is not any less likely than Kutscher's.

17 See Licht 1965:209.

18 See Licht, *ibid.*, in his notes to line 4.

19 The form מְסָרָה need not be hypothetically reconstructed, for it is an attested grammatical and semantic alternative to מָסוֹרָה (see Ben-Ḥayyim 1992 at the bottom of p. 405 and n. 4 there, and Bar-Asher 1999a:329–332). Indeed, we encounter here a general grammatical interchange of the patterns פְּעָלָה/פְּעִילָה (verbal nouns of the *binyan* קל), reflected also in other pairs such as יְצָאָה/יְצִיאָה, דְּרָשָׁה/דְּרִישָׁה, and so forth.

20 See Kutscher 1959:150, but see Kutscher 1977a:131–133.

brew. They mainly follow the model -פְּעִילוּת in the singular construct form, such as גְּמִילוּת[21] חסדים, זריקות[22] דמים, נשיאות[23] כפים, סמיכות[24] זקנים,

21 It bears noting that in Mishnaic Hebrew we do not find the absolute form גְּמִילָה; the construct form of -גְּמִילוּת only appears in conjunction with the *somekh* חסדים (or חסד). It is vocalized this way in the Kaufmann manuscript (K) – though not only there – in all four of its appearances in the Mishna (Pe'a 1:1 [2×: in the first of its two appearances there is a correction in manuscript K: חסד < חסדים], BB 9:4, and Avot 1:2). Ben-Yehudah already remarked in his dictionary under the entry גְּמִילוּת that "the normal reading is גְּמִילוּת," and he rejected the possible reading of גְּמִילוּת based upon the Talmudic dictum 'את הדרך' – זו גמילות חסדים, 'ילכו' – זו ביקור חולים (bBQ 100a). *Prima facie*, there is at least one apparent attestation of the construct form with ־ַת: וגמילַת חסד (t. Pe'a 1:1 ed. Zuckermandel], and from there it made its way into Ben-Yehuda's dictionary). In the edition of R. Saul Lieberman, however, we find וגמילות חסדים. The one difference between the different attestations that Lieberman's edition points to is in MS Erfurt where the reading is חסד. We note that Ben-Yehuda's dictionary brings גְּמִילוּת as a separate entry from the noun גְּמִילָה and not as its construct form.

22 For this noun the absolute form זְרִיקָה is documented (m. Pesahim 5:6, 8; m. Zevahim 1:4 [2×]), both in reliable manuscripts and in printed versions. The normal construct form זְרִיקַת is attested in MS Kaufmann (m. Zevahim 12:1; m. Me'ila 1:2, 1:3, 1:4 [three out of four appearances because the second appearance in this mishna is missing due to a haplography]), and so the vocalizer of Kaufmann reads it at Pesahim 6:1 – וּזְ(י)רְ[י]קַת. (Did the scribe intend the form וְזִרְקַת, where in a word which has a second consonant *resh* we find בְּרִיָּה and בְּרִיַּת becoming בִּרְיָּה and בִּרְיַּת, or did he simply err in his placement of the *yod*? I am inclined to think the latter correct). The construct form זְרִיקַת is also attested in MS Parma A in Pesahim (ibid.), but in the other seven appearances of the construct form Parma A reads זריקות, in the recurrent expression זריקות דמים (Zevahim 12:1 [here there is a tear in the page and a scrap of paper (or parchment?) was attached to it, upon which there is text of something other than this *mishnah*, and this scrap divides זריקות from דמים; it is not difficult, however, to discern what is from the source and what is a later addition]; Me'ila 1:2, 1:3, 1:4 [4×]). It seems to me that it is possible to see the phrase זְרִיקוּת דמים here. However, nothing prevents one from saying that the intent here is for the plural of the construct and the סומך of זְרִיקַת דָּם (וּזְרִיקַת דמו [Pesahim 6:1]), in other words, זְרִיקוֹת דָּמִים.

23 The phrase נְשִׂיאוּת כפים occurs in the Tosefta (Pe'a 4:6, Demai 2:7 [ed. Lieberman]) without vocalization, as is known. Nevertheless, it appears that the singular construct form נשיאות is intended, which is parallel to נשיאות כפים (Ta'anit 26b). Indeed, that is how Jews from Yemen, Middle Eastern countries, and Sephardim read this phrase. We also find נשיאות עון (t. Shavu'ot 3:4 [ed. Zuckermandel]). Additional documentation can be found in Ben-Yehudah's dictionary. Parenthetically, his dictionary presents two entries here as well: נְשִׂיאָה (נשיאת in construct) and נְשִׂיאוּת (absolute and construct).

24 We do not have evidence that the *vav* is punctuated with a *shuruk* but it makes sense that the word should be read that way. It should be sufficient to bring the following *halakha*: סמיכה בשלשה וסמיכות זקנים בשלשה (t. Sanhedrin 1:1); in the absolute it is סמיכה and in the construct it is סמיכות. However, there is evidence that in the Amoraic language it functioned as an absolute: הסמיכות בשלשה. לא סמיכה היא סמיכות תמן קריי למנוייה סמיכותא (y. Sanhedrin 1:3 [19a]). Here, too, in Ben-Yehuda's dictionary there are two separate entries of סמיכה and סמיכות (see there) – citing the above Toseftan passage, he divided them, listing סמיכה in the first entry and סמיכות זקנים in the second entry.

שְׁפִיכוּת[25] דמים, etc. Aside from the פעילה pattern, we also find in Mishnaic Hebrew by an abstract noun: עגמות נפש.[26]

In conclusion, the phenomenon of ־ַת > ־וּת is not found often in Hebrew – in Biblical Hebrew, in the Qumran scrolls,[27] or in Mishnaic Hebrew – but there is no question that it exists.

§ 8 If we combine all of the words detailed above – השמעות אזנים in the Bible; להערי[בו]ת השמש, ערלות לבם, הכרות פניהם, and possibly קדמותה and מסרותם in the Qumran scrolls;[28] שפיכות דמים, סמיכות זקנים, גמילות חסדים, etc. in Mishnaic Hebrew – we see the transition ־ָת/־ַת[29] > ־וּת- occurring with verbal nouns (like הַשְׁמַעַת > הַשְׁמָעוּת, הַכָּרַת > הַכָּרוּת) and abstract nouns (in that manner one can understand עָרְלַת > עָרְלוּת in the phrase ערלות לבם and

25 We find הַשְּׁפִיכָה in the Mishna (Tevul Yom 4:7; it is read this way in the tradition of the second scribe-vocalizer of manuscript Kaufmann, namely, the scribe who copied the last pages of the manuscript. We also find it in MS Parma B as well as other witnesses). The form שְׁפִיכוּת occurs only in construct when it is part of the phrase שְׁפִיכוּת דמים (ʻAvoda Zara 2:1; Avot 5:9); this is the vocalization of the first two appearances in MS Kaufmann and other witnesses. Again, Ben-Yehuda's dictionary has two disparate entries, שפיכה and שפיכות, the latter functioning only in the construct. The dictionary made a mistake in providing the phrase מי שפיכות as an example of the use of שפיכות in the absolute. The reference is to the line מי שפיכות שירדו עליהן מי גשמים (m. Makhshirin 2:3), but it is simply not true! In the phrase מי שפיכות it is not שְׁפִיכוּת which appears, but the plural form שְׁפִיכוֹת: it is vocalized this way three times in Makhshirin in MS Parma B); in other words, this is the plural form of שְׁפִיכָה. There is also a reading שְׁפֵיכוֹת (thus vocalized 3× in MS K), which is the plural of שְׁפֵכָה (in the pattern פְּעֵלָה).

In conclusion, it can be said that MS K preserves a distinction between two semantically distinct words: (a) שְׁפִיכָה is the act of pouring; this is attested in the construct as שְׁפִיכוּת, in the passages from ʻAvoda Zara and Avot mentioned above, and (b) שְׁפֵכָה in the phrase מֵי שְׁפֵיכוֹת, which denotes poured water. I did not rely on the form שְׁפִיכָה in the Tevul Yom passage, as a contrast to שְׁפֵיכָה of Makhshirin, because the evidence for שְׁפִיכָה in Tevul Yom is based on the work of the second scribe-vocalizer of MS K. Further discussion would take us too far afield.

26 The more readily-recognizable עגמת נפש is intended here (m. Megillah 3:3), which we pronounce as עָגְמַת נפש. Indeed, it is this which the vocalizer of Parma A intended when he wrote עָגְמָת נפש. In contradistinction, in MS K we found that vocalizer corrected the scribe's version by erasing only the letter *mem*, reading עֲגָ)(מוּ]ת נפש.

27 As was noted above, it is possible that in Qumran Hebrew the transition ־ַת > ־וּת is attested not only for the construct form but also for the forms attached to a pronoun: קדמותה, מסרותם (brought above in this paragraph).

28 E. Qimron believes that there is a lot more evidence of the transition to ־וּת in the Dead Sea Scrolls, which will find their place in his new grammar (referred to above in note 12) when it comes out.

29 The punctuation of a *kamats* before the *tav*, ־ָת, is intended for forms attached to a pronoun like קַדְמָתָהּ.

עגמַת > עגמות in the phrase עגמות נפש). This also explains the transition חמדַת > חמדות nicely, namely, that the noun חֶמְדָּה in the phrase ארץ חמדה is a verbal noun that indicates the action of the desiring. Since it would occur in the construct, it was likely to be pronounced and written חֶמְדּוּת, as it in fact was.

§ 9 Scholars have established that the background for the ־ַת > ־וּת transition is the influence of Aramaic on Hebrew.[30] There is evidence of this transition in verbal nouns within various dialects of Aramaic. It is enough here to mention the dialects contemporary with the periods we are discussing (the period of composition or editing of the following works: Biblical Ezekiel, the Qumran scrolls, and Tannaitic literature). For example, the phenomenon is documented well in Egyptian Aramaic,[31] Biblical Aramaic,[32] Targum Onkelos, and Targum Yonatan to the Prophets.[33] In short, the close connection between Hebrew and Aramaic for hundreds of years left a little Aramaic behind in Hebrew in this phenomenon as well.[34]

14.3 מחיגה

§ 10 The following is the text of lines 6–9 in fragment 2 column 2, as presented in Newsom's edition:[35]

6 [ו]יתננו לאלוהים על אדירים ומחיג[ה] לפרעה עב.]
7 [י]תׄמוגגו ויתנועעו וימסו קרביׄ[ה]םׄ [ו]ירחם בכ °
8 ובהאירו פנו אליהם [ ]ל.מרפא <> ויגבירו לבׄ[ם] עוד. ודׄעת.]
9 וכׄל לא ידעוך ויתמוגגו ויתנׄ[ו]עׄעׄו חׄגׄוׄ לק[ול

Dimant's[36] suggested reading of these four lines is identical in most of its details with the formulation of Newsom. There is one salient detail that divides

30 See the references above in footnotes 7–9.

31 See Muraoka-Porten, p. 110: לזבנותה, לתרכותה, למנחתותה, מנחתותהם, [ל]החסנותה (see their explicit discussion on -ת/-ות on p. 109).

32 See the two examples brought above in footnote 11. Kutscher 1959:150, pointed out that in Biblical Hebrew that in the *binyan* אַפְעֵל/הַפְעֵל the transition ־ַת > ־וּת- is only attested in suffix forms, such as לְהוֹדָעוּתַנִי (Daniel 4:15), but not in construct forms (here we find forms with ־ַת, like וְאַחֲוָיַת אֲחִידָן [Daniel 5:12]), but we do find construct forms with וּת- in other *binyanim*, such as הִתְנַדָּבוּת עמא (Ezra 7:16).

33 See Dalman 1905:279.

34 I do not consider it necessary to weigh the possibility that it might be the singular form חמדות (absolute and constructe), as in הוֹלֵלוֹת: חכמה ודעת הוֹלֵלֹת ושכלות (Ecclesiastes 1:17 and so on) and חָכְמוֹת: חָכְמוֹת בנתה ביתה (Proverbs 9:1). In my opinion, the switch from חֶמְדַּת to חֶמְדּוּת in the phrase ארץ חֶמְדַּת (> ארץ חֶמְדּוּת) seems much more logical.

35 See Newsom 1995:102.

36 See Dimant 2006:28–29.

the two readings: Newsom reads the beginning of line 6 as [ו]יתננו, whereas Dimant reads it as יתננו,[37] for according to the latter "there is no lacuna at the beginning of the word; rather, the scribe began writing one letter away from the margin."

§ 11 It is easy to see that the entire fragment discusses Egypt; it is stated explicitly in the phrase "ומחיג[ה] לפרעה" in line 6. It is easy to see the relationship between the above fragment – in content and in language – to the two Biblical chapters, as Newsom and Dimant have shown. I will discuss this in detail, for doing so will serve to explain the use of several words in the Biblical chapters and our Qumran fragment.

A. In column 2 of fragment 2 of Scroll 4Q374, one can recognize a clear and strong connection specifically to Isaiah 19, which speaks about the plagues expected to afflict Egypt and the healing that would come at their end: וְסִכַּרְתִּי אֶת מִצְרַיִם בְּיַד אֲדֹנִים קָשֶׁה (v. 4), וְנָהָר יֶחֱרַב וְיָבֵשׁ (v. 5), עָרוֹת עַל יְאוֹר עַל פִּי יְאוֹר וְכֹל מִזְרַע יְאוֹר יִיבַשׁ נִדַּף וְאֵינֶנּוּ (v. 7), וְאָנוּ הַדַּיָּגִים וְאָבְלוּ כָּל מַשְׁלִיכֵי בַיְאוֹר חַכָּה (v. 8). Isaiah 19 speaks even more about the removal of wisdom from Egypt, on the loss of counsel of the wise and what occurred as a consequence of this: אַךְ אֱוִלִים שָׂרֵי צֹעַן חַכְמֵי יֹעֲצֵי פַרְעֹה עֵצָה נִבְעָרָה אֵיךְ תֹּאמְרוּ אֶל פַּרְעֹה בֶּן חֲכָמִים אֲנִי ... אַיָּם אֵפוֹא חֲכָמֶיךָ ... נוֹאֲלוּ שָׂרֵי צֹעַן ... הִתְעוּ אֶת מִצְרַיִם ... ה' מָסַךְ בְּקִרְבָּהּ רוּחַ עִוְעִים וְהִתְעוּ אֶת מִצְרַיִם ... כְּהִתָּעוֹת שִׁכּוֹר בְּקִיאוֹ ... בַּיּוֹם הַהוּא יִהְיֶה מִצְרַיִם כַּנָּשִׁים וְחָרַד וּפָחַד ... וְהָיְתָה אַדְמַת יְהוּדָה לְמִצְרַיִם לְחָגָּא[38] כֹּל אֲשֶׁר יַזְכִּיר אֹתָהּ אֵלָיו יִפְחָד (vv. 11–16), but after the afflictions the healing will come: וְנָגַף ה' אֶת מִצְרַיִם נָגֹף וְרָפוֹא ... וּרְפָאָם (v. 22).

B. There is a connection between the Qumran fragment to Psalms 107:26–27: יַעֲלוּ שָׁמַיִם יֵרְדוּ תְהוֹמוֹת, נַפְשָׁם בְּרָעָה תִתְמוֹגָג, יָחוֹגּוּ וְיָנוּעוּ כַּשִּׁכּוֹר וְכָל חָכְמָתָם תִּתְבַּלָּע.

§ 12 The two expressions מחיג[ה] לפרעה (line 6) and חגו לק[ול] (line 9) in the Qumran fragment have a sufficiently clear connection to the verses

37 This is not the place to appropriate place in which to discuss the question of whether the pronominal suffix is a third-person pronominal suffix (יתן אותו = יתננו) or a first-person plural pronominal suffix (יתן אותנו = יתננו).

38 Perhaps it is not superfluous to note that the word חָגָּא is the equivalent of the pattern פֻּעָּה, as in חֻקָּה, גֻּלָּה, and so on, except that the written form of the word changed: the *alef* replaced the *heh* (usually called Aramaic orthography), as in חגא instead of חגה, like כַּמַּטָּרָא (Lamentations 3:12). The vocalization of the word is also different: we find the letter *ḥet* with a *qamets qatan* instead of a *qubuts*. It appears that the guttural *ḥet* lowers the [u] vowel (קובוץ) to [o] (קמץ קטן). This change did not occur, however, in the noun חֻקָּה, despite that the vowel u is in between the guttural consonant *ḥet* and the emphatic consonant *quf*.

יָחוֹגּוּ וְיָנוּעוּ כַּשִּׁכּוֹר (Psalms 107:27); וְהָיְתָה אַדְמַת יְהוּדָה לְמִצְרַיִם לְחָגָּא (Isa 19:17) and the expressions [י]תמוגגו ויתנועעו (line 7 in the Qumran fragment) and ויתמוגגו ויתנ[ו]עעו (line 9 there) are connected to the expressions נַפְשָׁם בְּרָעָה תִתְמוֹגָג (Psalms 107:26) and יָחוֹגּוּ וְיָנוּעוּ (Psalms 107:27); the phrase וימסו וְהָיְתָה אַדְמַת יְהוּדָה לְמִצְרַיִם לְחָגָּא כֹּל אֲשֶׁר יַזְכִּיר קרביה[ם] (line 7) alludes to אֹתָהּ אֵלָיו יִפְחָד (Isaiah 19:16–17).

§ 13   As was mentioned, the two editors already made important points regarding the parallels between the Qumran fragment and the aforementioned Biblical chapters, and Dimant elaborated upon them. However, neither of the two discussed all of the aspects relevant to a comparative analysis. I would like to focus here upon the usage of verbs and nouns formed from the roots חג"ג and חו"ג – יָחוֹגּוּ (Psalms), לְחָגָּא (Isaiah), and חגו ... מחיגה (Qumran scroll) – and, most importantly, to explain the meaning of the word מחיגה.[39]

The editors have already noted that this word was unknown before its appearance here. Newsom translated מחיגה as "a cause of reeling"; in other words, she understood that מחיגה was "a cause for trembling or shaking". After saying a few words about its derivation, Dimant wrote: "it is possible that even at the very foundation of the word מחיגה stands an image of horror and trembling that seized Pharaoh until he 'shook like a drunkard'. This explanation is confirmed by verbs that express motions of fear and awe mentioned in the subsequent line[40] and from its return to them in line 9.[41] See the verb חגו in line 9."

§ 14   I contend that there is much merit to the analyses of Newsom (which explains the word מחיגה as meaning trembling and shaking) and Dimant (which explains it as horror and trembling), for indeed fear is expressed well in the sentence immediately following it: יתמוגגו[42] ויתנועעו וימסו קרבי[ה]ם. But in my view, this is not the primary meaning of the word מחיגה in the paragraph before us. Put more moderately: the concept of fear does not adequately exhaust everything that the noun מחיגה expresses in this context.

It may be worth mentioning something well-known: every word in a given text needs to be explained within both its narrow and wide contexts, obviously

---

39 Here is the full context: יתננו לאלוהים על אדירים ומחיגה לפרעה. A significant question is who the אדירים mentioned here are – the Egyptians? Pharaoh? the Israelites? It is possible that a clear contrast exists between the אלוהים על אדירים, that is to say the אלוהים over the Israelites, and the מחיגה לפרעה. There is a scriptural foundation for equating אדירים with the Israelites, but this is not the place to determine what אדירים in the fragment refers to.
40 See Dimant 2006:37. She is referring to the words יתמוגגו ויתנועעו וימסו קרבי[ה]ם.
41 She is referring to the words ויתמוגגו ויתנועעו.
42 The root מו"ג expresses, as is well known, the "melting" of the heart and fear, as is reflected in the verses נָמֹגוּ כֹּל יֹשְׁבֵי כְנָעַן (Exodus 15:15) and נָמֹגוּ כֹּל יֹשְׁבֵי הָאָרֶץ (Joshua 2:9).

without losing sight of its etymology. If we look carefully at the aforementioned passages in Isaiah and Psalms, concentrate on the words חָגָּא (Isaiah) and יָחוֹגּוּ (Psalms) from linguistic and contextual perspectives, and then look at the Qumran fragment that draws from them and uses their language – including the words מחיגה and חגו – it is possible to propose another meaning of מחיגה and of words similar to it.[43]

§ 15 Let us begin with the derivation of מחיגה. The plene spelling with a *yod* after the *ḥet* is most likely intended to be read מְחִיגָה and not מְחִגָּה (מְחִיגָּה), for the vowel *i* in a closed, unstressed syllable is *almost always* written in Qumran texts defectively (without the *yod*).[44] That is to say, מחיגה is derived from the root חו"ג and is patterned after the מְפִילָה pattern, as in מְדִיכָה (MS Parma B Teharot: Kelim 23:2; Tevul Yom 2:3,[45] and vocalized this way in the Babylonian vocalization[46]), מְדִינָה (Esther 1:1),[47]מְרִיבָה (Numbers 20:13),[48]מְשִׂימָה – attested in Mishnaic Hebrew in its plural form מְשִׂימוֹת (Yevamot 45b[49]).[50]

§ 16 Now, the hollow root חו"ג and the geminate root חג"ג have verbs and nouns which are similar in their meaning (just as other comparable pairs of roots produce nouns that are roughly synonymous). Both these two roots express the basic meaning of rotary, circular motion. With חו"ג it is given in the verb חג in חֹק חָג[51] על המים (Job 26:10), and with the nouns חוג and מְחוּגָה in וחוג שמים (Job 22:14), חוג הארץ (Isaiah 40:22), and וּבַמְּחוּגָה יתארהו (Isaiah 44:13). With חג"ג we find this meaning in the verb of the verse יָחוֹגּוּ[52] וינועו כשכור (Psalms 107:27).

---

43 I chose to use the phrase "words similar to it" and not "words identical to it" based upon what will be said later in §§ 15–16, for מחיגה seems to be derived from חו"ג (as "חגו" might be as well), whereas חָגָּא and יָחוֹגּוּ are derived from חג"ג.

44 See Qimron 1976:53–55.

45 However, MS K vocalizes it as מְדֵיכָה in m. Kel (on the pattern מְפֵלָה), and in m. Tevul Yom the vocalizer/second scribe of MS K read it as בִּמְדוּכָה (a form on the pattern מְפוּלָה).

46 So Yeivin 1985:1006. In the first of its two appearances the word is vocalized like מְדִיכָה (with Babylonian vocalization) and also like מְדֵיכָה in Tiberian vocalization.

47 It has this form as well in Bablyonian vocalization (see Yeivin, *ibid.*).

48 Yeivin, *ibid.*, brings this form from the Babylonian vocalization too.

49 R. Joseph Amer vocalized it this way in תלמוד בבלי מנוקד על פי מסורת יהודי תימן, and both Sephardim and Ashkenazim read it this way. From there the word, with this pronunciation, was transmitted to later periods and into Modern Hebrew.

50 The word appears in the middle of an exposition of the verse: ... שום תשים עליך מלך מקרב אחיך תשים עליך מלך (Deut 17:15): כל משימות שאתה משים לא יהיו אלא מקרב אחיך.

51 As was mentioned, חגו לק[ול] in line 9 of our Qumranic fragment is an ע"ו form.

52 It is superfluous to say that from the basic meaning the broader meaning developed: חגג came to mean "made a festival (חג)". This is not the appropriate place to speak about this more at length. On a different matter, is it possible that the *daghesh* in the verb יָחוֹגּוּ is from the type of *daghesh* that is used to mark words that have a negative meaning, and that the foundation of the word is the is the verbal form from the root חו"ג (יָחוּגוּ) as is reflected in its

§ 17 In my view, in the contexts where the noun חָגָּא (Isaiah 19:17) and the verb יָחוֹגּוּ (Psalms 107:27) appear there is an additional meaning, which may just be the most important one. The context in Psalms is discussing the wandering and spinning of a drunken person (יחוגו וינועו כשיכור), and in the eyes of the psalmist this situation expresses a temporary loss of reason during the state of inebriation, as is expressed in the parallelism that finishes the verse: וכל חכמתם תתבלע. It is detailed even further in the description of the Egypt's situation in Isaiah (19:11–22):[53] אוילים שרי צֹעַן חכמי יועצי פרעה עצה נבערה ... נואלו שרי צֹעַן, and someone whose wisdom has been taken is likely to go astray and lead astray, like the formulation התעו את מצרים that is stated twice (verses 13–14), and this straying is כְּהִתָּעוֹת שכור בקיאו (verse 14).

The image from both Biblical chapters is similar, save that it is presented in differing orders: in Psalms 107 יורדי הים באניות (verse 23) are described as drunk – יחוגו וינועו כשכור – and a consequence of this inebriation is the loss of wisdom – וכל חכמתם יתבלע. In Isaiah, those who lose their wisdom and counsel become ignorant counsel, those who became foolish, in whom a misguided spirit entered, became like drunks, like תועים (more precisely, נתעים, based upon כְּהִתָּעוֹת שכור בקיאו) and causing others to stray.

§ 18 The implication is that the drunk and his going in circles (his spinning and wandering) are an expression of confusion, a tangible expression of loss of counsel, wisdom, and reason, and perhaps it is speaking about a real madness. Put differently, חג"ג and חו"ג, which indicated originally as circular motion or walking in a spinning manner, shifted to express a wandering of the mind, confusion of mind and absence of counsel to the point of temporary confounding of their wisdom to the point of madness. It appears to me that when Isaiah says the land of Judah will be לְחָגָּא for Egypt, he is saying that the land of Judah will be a source of confusion and loss of reason for Egypt. That is also how I would like to explain מְתִיגָה: circular wandering and walking which shifted to indicate wandering and confusion of the mind and absence of wisdom, until the point of temporary madness, and this situation and image causes fear to anyone who sees it (וימסו קרביהם).

---

plene spelling, which is not found with ע"ע verbs (in a form from the root חג"ג we expect a defective writing without the *vav* like יָחֹגּוּ, similar to יָסֹבּוּ)? Yeivin (1985, p. 362) discusses this phenomenon: "in a few words the *daghesh* functions as a marker for a negative meaning". He refers to those who preceded him on this matter and adds his own material, such as בעבור הַרְּעִמָהּ (1 Samuel 1:6) compared with אל הכבוד הִרְעִים (Psalms 29:3). Can we argue that the noun חָגָּא was created from a similar process? I am not certain with respect to יָחוֹגּוּ nor חָגָּא that we have a secondary gemination (I would like to thank Dr. Mordechai Mishor for reminding me about Yeivin's analysis).

53 This is the reason for the focus upon detail in citing the passages from Isaiah 19 above in § 11 (above).

§ 19 In truth, Isaiah speaks about the fear as a consequence of the חָגָּא: והיתה אדמת יהודה למצרים לְחָגָּא, כל אשר יזכיר אותה אליו יפחד (verse 17). The behavior of the wandering drunk, who appears insane, arouses fear. Even prior to this it already says explicitly, ביום ההוא יהיה מצרים כנשים וחרד ופחד (verse 16). The fear is a consequence of the confused behavior of the sages and rulers of Egypt and of the loss of reason of Pharaoh's advisers. He whose reason has been taken from him looks like a bumbling drunk who lacks reason, who appears insane. He whose behavior is of a man without wisdom, whose confusion and lack of reason (חָגָּא) guide him and instill fear in all of those who see him and are dependent upon him.

In my view, this is the intent of the expression מחיגה לפרעה in the Qumran fragment. He who is lorded over by confusion and an absence of reason (מְחִיגָה) arouses fear in the midst of his citizens and those who depend upon him: יתמוגגו ויתנועעו וימסו קרביהם.

§ 20 If I am correct in explaining the word מחיגה – that its meaning expanded from a circular motion and movement and physical dizziness to confusion and lack of knowledge, as I am explaining חָגָּא in Isaiah and מְחִיגָה in Qumran – then we not only have a new word, but an expansion of meaning of two words derived from the roots חו"ג and חג"ג. This should not surprise us. We find in Hebrew, and outside of it, that verbs of motion that indicate wandering, confusion, and circular motion, shift to also indicate confusion and removal of reason.

§ 21 This is a known fact about the root בל"ל. The verb בלל indicates mixture, as in סלת ... בלולה בשמן (Numbers 28:5, and elsewhere) כי שם בָּלַל ה' שפת כל הארץ (Genesis 11:9). From this root the נפעל form נָבָל is derived,[54] which means is a boor: עם נָבָל ולא חָכָם (Deuteronomy 32:7). The root בלב"ל is, as is known, is a quadriliteral of בל"ל, and from it we have בִּלְבּוּל and מְבֻלְבָּל. In the words of Ben-Ḥayyim: "the Biblical נָבָל when intended to mean simpleton is someone whose mind is בלולה, טרופה. There are parallels to it in the later usages of מבולבל and מטורף."[55]

§ 22 This change in meaning is not restricted to roots that indicate mixture or a rotary, circular motion. We find that verbs of motion, meaning indicate swaying and shaking or grabbing, shift to indicate a loss of reason until the point of madness. For example, the verb טרף means grabbing or shaking,[56]

54 As was unambiguously demonstrated in Ben-Ḥayyim 1981:192–199. He distinguishes between נָבָל (from בל"ל), which means simpleton and fool, and נָבָל (from נב"ל), which means low and wicked.

55 See *ibid.*, p. 198.

56 Ben-Yehuda's dictionary cites this verb as טָרַף II. But מטורף (which means insane) and ניטרפה דעתו are cited under טָרַף I, which he defines as "snatched," and there he cites טרף האריה או הזאב את הכבש and other examples. It is clear that the presentation here is not precise.

from which developed the linguistic usage of נִיטָּרְפָה[57] דעתו and the participle that became nominalized as מְטוֹרָף. The basic meaning is found, for example, in the following places: טרף בקלפי (m. Yoma 4:1), שכל העם היו מְטָרְפִים את לולביהם והם לא נִיעְנִיעוּ (m. Suk 3:9 in MS Kaufmann),[58] but in the printed versions מטרפים was switched with מנענעין. From the verb טֵרֵף (the equivalent of נִיעֲנַע) developed the usages מְטוֹרָף, ניטרפה דעתו, and the like.

עִרְעֵר also originated indicated shaking and swaying, as in חמות בבל הרחבה עַרְעֵר תתערער (Jeremiah 51:58). Later, we find דברים שמערערין את הנפש (Maimonides, Mishneh Torah, Laws of Forbidden Foods 14:15), and from there evolved the adjective מעורער בנפשו > the shortened form מעורער.

§ 23 It is possible to posit that the usages that express distortion of mind arose by omission: one who is ניטרפה דעתו is מטורף דעת, in short מטורף; one who נתערערה נפשו is מעורער בנפשו, and, in short, מעורער. Alongside these forms the abstract nouns טירוף and ערעור formed, and in the same way, מבולבל דעת > מבולבל and the abstract noun בלבול. It is not improbable to posit that similar processes were at work that caused usages like נבל (simpleton) and abstract nouns like חָגָּא and מְחִיגָה to appear. It is possible that these usages began due to a different process, which is based upon the understanding the man's reason is seated in his head and sits there securely; as such, its movement is its distortion.[59]

§ 24 The image of the bridge from mixing and rotary, circular motion to "mixing" of the mind has a parallel in other languages.[60] I think it will be

---

57 As is well known, in later generations the *nif'al* replaced the *hitpa'el* in this expression.

58 The readings in MS Parma A MS Cambridge (ed. Lowe) are the same as those in MS K (with a minor difference: מְטָרְפִּין בלולביהן [in MS Cambridge there is of course no vocalization], and so it is in the Mishna of Yerushalmi (this example is cited in Ben-Yehudah's dictionary), and in the Yemenite manuscript of the Order of Mo'ed, and so on.

59 In truth, the opposite of מבולבל and מטורף is someone whose mind is מיושבת, and מיושב בדעתו > מיושב.

60 I made a list of many examples from different languages, such as usages that I found in Greek and English. I have in mind Greek πλανάω, whose basic meaning is "wander," "be lost," and so on, and which also developed the meanings "make a mistake," "be confused." What is even more interesting is that its English parallel, 'wander' also developed the meaning "made a mistake," "stray from the issue," and "be confused," as in the expression "his mind is wandering," whose meaning is "his mind is not remaining focused." An example from Moroccan Arabic (both Islamic and Jewish) is also forthcoming: the verb *txəlxəl*, whose basic meaning is "to be shaken" and from it developed the meaning "to be weak of mind," and from there the participle/adjective/noun *mxəlxəl*, whose meaning is "slightly insane" or "really insane." (Parenthetically, Colin's dictionary for Islamic Moroccan Arabic cites the verb *tḫălḫăl* and indicates the meaning "to become insane." But for the participle he cites *mḫălḫăl f-'ăqlo* (= out of his mind, crazy), but to the best of my knowledge the word *mxəlxəl* [= *mḫălḫăl*] alone is also used in this sense in the Jewish and Muslim dialects. Parenthetically, it should be noted that the transcriptions *xəlxəl* I used and *ḫălḫăl* used on Colin's dictionary, cited in

sufficient to cite one phrase and one word that seem to me to have evolved from Yiddish to modern Hebrew.[61]

A. It seems to me that the Yiddish adjective צומישט, whose meaning is mixed and someone's whose mind is confused,[62] which was translated by Judah Leib Gordon as מעורב בדעת, which is the title of his story: "המעורב בדעת".[63] The expression itself is used afterwards in the story itself: לא האריך ימים בלתי אם מוראי הגדול אשר יראתי מפני צבי המעורב בדעת[64],[65] and איש אשר רוח רעה תבעתהו, איש משוגע ומעורב בדעת.[66] Notice that the man who is insane is referred to as both משוגע and מעורב בדעת. Judah Leib Gordon, the great expert in the language of the primary sources, definitely knew the language of the Talmud "לעולם תהא דעתו של אדם מעורבת עם הבריות" (b. Berakhot 17a). Based upon this Talmudic passage the expression מעורב בדעת עם הבריות was formulated as one of the laudatory descriptions of the prayer leader in the prayer הנני העני ממעש, the prayer with which the prayer leader begins the *musaf* prayers according to the liturgy of Ashkenaz and Sepharad (Hassidic) on the High Holidays. It appears that from there Gordon borrowed the phrase מעורב בדעת and another meaning developed in order to translate the Yiddish's צומישט.

B. In modern Hebrew, the participle form מְסוֹבָב functions (pronounced by many as מְסוּבָב, the *vav* vocalized with a *shuruk*), which is clearly a translation of the Yiddish adjective צעדרייטער[67] (= confused, crazy, and so on).[68]

§ 25 We have already said above that it is possible to add to what I have brought, but what was brought until now should be sufficient to provide a basis for what I said regarding חָגָּא and מְחִיגָה as nouns derived from חג"ג and חו"ג, roots that indicate a circular motion. The meaning of confusion, loss of

---

this paragraph, represent a single pronunciation.) However, in the body of the text I bring only the two adjectives in modern Hebrew, for they appear to be loan translations from Yiddish.

61 For the meaning of the Yiddish words I received advice from my learned friends the late Samuel Werses and Chava Turniansky. I give my thanks to them for their help.

62 See Weinreich 198:339; the noun צומיש and the verb צומישן are brought there.

63 See Gordon 2000:126–140.

64 The last three words in the citation emphasized in the source.

65 *Ibid.*, p. 128.

66 *Ibid.*, p. 129.

67 See Weinreich 1968:351. There the verb צעדרייען is cited. The German parallel to צעדרייטער is, as is known, *verdrehter* (and its meaning is also "slightly crazy").

68 We note that Even-Shoshan's new dictionary cites מסובב without any example whatsoever.

reason and wisdom, and possibly even real madness (albeit temporary) appear to have developed in these nouns.

14.4 Conclusion

§ 24 Many Qumran scrolls have expanded our knowledge of Hebrew regarding all sorts of features, including revealing new words to us. Sometimes these texts shed new light on words that have long been known, however. The Qumran fragment discussed here allowed us to make each of these types of discoveries.

In the phrase ארץ חמדות כל הארצות, the word חמדות is a construct form of חמדה, to be read -חֶמְדּוֹת. This adds another example to a known phenomenon, one which existed in late First Temple Period Hebrew, throughout the Hebrew of the Second Temple Period, and into Mishnaic Hebrew.

מחיגה, on the other other hand, is a new word, as the publishers of the fragment said. The written form is apparently מְחִיגָה, from the root חו"ג. This root originally indicated a rotary, circular motion. Over time the meaning that indicated circularity of the mind developed into the sense "confusion of the mind and utter loss of counsel and wisdom." The same transition, it appears, took place within the related root חג"ג. It appears that this meaning, in the expression יחוגו וינועו כשכור, testifies that the wisdom of a drunk is swallowed up and forgotten. This is also the explanation of the noun חָגָּא (from חג"א). This meaning reflects the noun מחיגה. It is clear that any additional material from another source would assist in strengthening this suggestion.

15 כיון הצלמים / כיניי הצלמים

15.1 Introductory Remarks

§ 1 The texts from the Judean Desert have enriched our understanding of Israel's culture in every realm of Jewish studies: Halakha, history of beliefs, the text of Scripture and its interpretation, the Hebrew language and its development, and other areas as well. The renewed interest in the study of these texts in the wake of their complete publication has given renewed momentum to the study of all the texts, including those which were published soon after their original discovery sixty years ago. Continued interest is also generated by the Damascus Covenant, which was published more than 100 years ago in two versions[1] from the Cairo Geniza by Solomon Schechter. There are still, however, aspects of the text which remain to be discovered, and linguistic features and expressions which yet await elucidation.

§ 2 In my opinion, much work remains to be done in the area of the language used by the Judean Desert scrolls in light of the many connections – some apparent and some hidden – which exist between this language and the spoken language in use at the end of the Second Temple period, seen by us in the language of Rabbinic literature – Mishnaic Hebrew. This point was made already by the great Hebraists in the first generation of Qumran studies, especially Henoch Yalon,[2] Yechezkel Kutscher,[3] and Ze'ev Ben-Ḥayyim.[4] More recently, Elisha Qimron has also explored this subject in his research.[5]

---

1 Schechter devotes the first volume of his work to this subject (Schechter 1910).

2 See the collection of his articles in Yalon 1967. It should be noted here that many of the articles were first published in newspapers in the wake of the initial discovery of the Dead Sea Scrolls.

3 See Kutscher 1959. Since its first publication, this book has been a fundamental work on the language of the scrolls. Many of its conclusions remain valid, and will continue to remain valid for a long time.

4 I am referring first and foremost to his penetrating and comprehensive article (Ben-Ḥayyim 1958).

5 See his grammar in its two versions – in Hebrew (Qimron 1976) and in English (Qimron 1986) – as well as in many articles. Important contributions to scholarship regarding the language of the Scrolls and of Ben Sira are the two conferences that took place at University of Leiden in 1995 and 1997, which were organized by Professor Takamitsu Muraoka, the third conference which took place in Ben Gurion University in Beer Sheva, which was organized by Elisha Qimron (Muraoka and Elwolde 1997, 1999, 2000), and the fourth conference, organized by Jan Joosten, which took place at Strassburg in 2006 (Joosten and Rey 2008). The fifth conference, organized by S. Fassberg and myself, took place at the Hebrew University in 2009; the proceedings are in press. The sixth was organized by Pierre van Hecke and took place in Leuven in 2011. The Haifa Workshop for Qumran Studies (which hosted eight conferences

§ 3 In the texts of the Damascus Covenant, which have been continuously studied for a century already, there are also indications of the same Hebrew dialect known to us from most of the Qumran texts. This is a high literary language which contains many clear similarities to the language of Scripure, but also possesses characteristics unique to Qumran Hebrew. But within this text, as well, there are echoes – hidden and revealed – of the colloquial language from the time of the sect which produced these texts. It is this language which was destined to eventually crystallize into the written language of the Rabbis, first as the language of the Tannaim and then as the language of the Amoraim.

In this study I would like to suggest an interpretation relating to one of the *pesharim* within the Damascus Covenant which, I contend, is dependent upon Mishnaic Hebrew.[6]

15.2 A biblical expression in the Damascus Covenant and its pesher

§ 4 The verses וּנְשָׂאתֶם אֵת סִכּוּת מַלְכְּכֶם וְאֵת כִּיּוּן צַלְמֵיכֶם כּוֹכַב אֱלֹהֵיכֶם אֲשֶׁר עֲשִׂיתֶם לָכֶם. וְהִגְלֵיתִי אֶתְכֶם מֵהָלְאָה לְדַמָּשֶׂק "And you shall carry off your 'king', Sikkuth and Kiyyun, the images of your astral deity you made for yourselves, as I drive you into exile beyond Damascus" (Amos 5:26–27) are quoted, as is well known, in a version slightly different from what appears in the Masoretic text, and are interpreted in MS A of the Damascus Covenant from the Cairo Geniza. The following is the passage of interest to us, according to the texts most recent editor:

> כאשר אמר והגליתי[7] את סכות מלככם ואת כיון צלמיכם מאהלי דמשק[8] ספרי התורה הם סוכת המלך
> כאשר אמר והקימותי את סוכת דוד הנפלת המלך הוא הקהל וכיניי הצלמים וכיון הצלמים הם
> ספרי הנביאים אשר בזה ישראל את דבריהם (דף VII שורות 14–18).

When it says והגליתי את סכות מלככם ואת כיון צלמיכם מאהלי דמשק, the books of the Torah are the סוכת המלך "tabernacle of the king," as it is says, והקימותי את סוכת דוד הנפלת "I will raise the fallen tabernacle of David"[9] The king is the community, and וכיניי

---

between 2002 and 2009) also dealt with the language of the scrolls, as is well reflected in the volumes of *Meghillot* which have been published so far.

6 See also Chapter 12, above.

7 In Qimron's edition, biblical verses cited within the text are printed in a smaller font than the essential text.

8 This differs from the Masoretic text, which reads מהלאה לדמשק "beyond Damascus".

9 The portion of the verse that is quoted after the words "as it is stated" is from Amos 9:11, again in a slightly different version: the MT reads אקים את סֻכַּת דויד הנפלת.

הצלמים וכיון הצלמים refers to the books of the prophets whose words Israel has scorned (col. VII, lines 14–18 [Qimron 1992a, p. 23]).[10]

The text given by the first editor (Schechter 1910, p. 7) is identical in all practical aspects to Qimron's reading in the passage above, with one exception: where Qimron reads וכיניי, Schechter read וכינוי. The text given by Rabin (1958, p. 29, 31) is completely identical to Qimron's for this passage: he reads וכיניי (without indicating any doubt regarding the identification of the letter that follows the *nun*).

§ 5 Ever since the discovery and publication of the Damascus Document, the double language וכיניי (וכינוי) הצלמים וכיון הצלמים has attracted the attention of researchers. Schechter interpreted the first expression as a copyist's mistake, which was corrected by the insertion of the second one by the copyist[11] (who did not, however, erase the mistake itself). Louis Ginzberg, on the other hand, thinks that the original – and correct – version is וכינוי הצלמים, which was corrected, based on the verse in Amos, to וכיון הצלמים.[12] Chaim Rabin follows Ginzberg, and claims that the first expression (וכיניי הצלמים) is the original version which was corrected based on the "true" version found in עמוס.[13] Many years later Qimron reached the verdict that the two versions reflect dittography,[14] in other words, this is an example of a "mistaken redundancy."

§ 6 Many scholars have dealt with the Damascus Document. It will suffice to glance at the bibliography from the twenty-year-period 1970–1989 which was compiled by García-Martinez.[15] There[16] we find six items dedicated to the pericope from which the quotation above (§ 4) was taken. After the publication of Qimron's edition (1992a), scholarship on the text did not cease, especially

10 Qimron should be commended for including photographs of the Geniza fragments in his edition of the text. (In the edition of the text in the databases of the Historical Dictionary of the Hebrew Language at the Academy of the Hebrew language [Ma'agarim], only two corrections were made to Qimron's edition: in p. 11, col. I l. 4, ראשנים should be read without a *waw* after the *shin*, as can be seen clearly from the accompanying photo; and on p. 27, col. IX l. 14, the staff of the Historical Dictionary suggested reading הכל instead of וכל.) Special gratitude is also due to Magen Broshi, who initiated and edited the re-publication of the text (see Broshi, 1992:5–7).

11 Schechter 1910:XL, n. 15.

12 See Ginzberg 1970:34 = 1922:47–48. Ginzberg accepts Schechter's reading וכינוי without, apparently, any hesitations.

13 Rabin 1958:30, relying on Ginzberg 1922.

14 Qimron 1992a:23. See, however, above, Chap. 12 nn. 5 and 13.

15 See Garcia Martinez 1992:63–81.

16 *Ibid.*, p. 68.

with the publication of parallel sections of the text from Qumran,[17] and scholars also returned to our passage and offered new interpretations.[18]

Researchers have also struggled with the exact meaning of the double combination of the words כיניי (כינוי) הצלמים/כיון הצלמים. Schechter proposed the translation "Chiyun the images":[19] he was content to transliterate the word כיון (which in his opinion is the correct[20] version), without translating it. Ginzberg says that

> In view of the Midrashic character of this section it is not impossible that we have here an interpretation of כיון as "make straight" or "direct". The Prophetic writings (to use a Talmudic expression) "make their hearts directed (מכוונים לבם) to their father in heaven."[21]

Elsewhere he says

> The expression (Amos 5:26) כיון צלמיכם is taken as an illusion to the Prophetic books ... They read this word as כְּיָן, in the Aramaic connotation of "correct", "Orthodox".[22]

In short, in the first place Ginzberg thought that the *pašrān* connects the word כיון with the verb כִּוֵּן, which means to make straight; afterwards, however, he offers a different solution: he thinks that they read the word כיון as the Aramaic word כְּיָן, meaning something correct, accepted.

Rabin suggests a translation of both phrases, but he places the second one in parentheses. In this regard he follows Schechter and is satisfied with transliterating the words:

> and the Pedestals (KENE) of the Images {and the KIYYUN of the Images}.[23]

As we already noted, Rabin only translates the first part of the combination, "bases of (כַּנֵּי) the images."

Baumgarten and Schwartz were satisfied with translating the second version (i.e., they, too, follow Schechter, but they transliterate the word כיון itself):

---

17 See, for example, Baumgarten 1992, Baumgarten and Schwartz 1993, and Kister 1993.
18 See Baumgarten and Schwartz 1993, Kister 2005, and Goldman 2006. Kister 2005 reviews the research literature (see nn. 2–17 in his article), and offers a penetrating discussion and original solution regarding the relationship between MS B (which in his opinion reflects the older version) and MS A (which in his opinion reflects a later version).
19 Schechter 1910:XL.
20 See *ibid.*, n. 15.
21 See Ginzberg 1970:34; but see also what is cited from Ginzberg below in the next sentences. (See the reference in the following note.)
22 *Ibid.*, p. 365.
23 See Rabin 1958:30. In a similar fashion, Cothenet 1963:173 wrote: "Littéralement 'et les piédestals (*kynyy*) des images et kiyyoun (*kywn*) des images'" (cf. below, nn. 27 and 44).

and the "*kywn* of the Images" are the books of the prophets whose words Israel despised.[24]

§ 7 As is known, in a section of the 4Q266 scroll, a very fragmentary section survived which corresponds to the section in Copy A of the Geniza discussed above (= namely 4Q266 frg. 2 col. iii), which was edited and discussed by Joseph Baumgarten.[25] According to the reading he suggested, it is possible to identify, with great difficulty, the letters ה and ל of the word הקהל, and the final ם, apparently from the word הצלמים. If the arrangement of fragments which comprise this pericope is correct, the implication is that the repeated phrase (וכיניי [וכינוי] הצלמים / וכיון הצלמים) attested in Copy A from the Cairo Geniza was not attested in the space remaining; rather, only one or the other appeared: וכיניי or וכיון הצלמים. It is interesting that the modern editor (Baumgarten) restored the text in Hebrew with the word וכיניי, despite not a hint of the word in the text; in the English translation, however, he gives the transliteration "*kywn.*"

§ 8 Indeed, all the scholars who have dealt with the section have discussed its various versions and have worked on clarifying the meaning of the text and its intention; most recently, Menachem Kister and Liora Goldman[26] have delved into these issues. They have all dealt with the "what" – the content of the interpretation – but only a few have focused on the "how."[27] In other words, where does this interpretation, which identifies the words כיון צלמיכם with the Books of the Prophets, come from?

Of course, one may claim that what we have here is a logical extension with regard to the biblical verses. Since the *pašrān* already said that the "books of the Torah" are the tabernacle of the king, interpreting the words סכות מלכּכם (i.e. סוכת המלך) as the books of the Torah by associating the word סִכּוּת with סֻכַּת and the word מַלְכְּכֶם (= המלך) with King David, and thus established a connection with the verse והקימותי את סכת דויד הנפלת, he continued following the order in the verse in Amos 5:26 (את סכות[28] מלככם ואת כיון צלמיכם).

24 Baumgarten and Schwartz 1993:27. See, however, the solution offered by Baumgarten 1996, discussed below, § 7.

25 See Baumgarten 1996:44–45, who follows Milik.

26 See the references above in note 18.

27 The way this is understood by Ginzberg 1976 (cited above, § 6), Rabin 1958:30, and Cothenet 1963:173, should be mentioned here: from their translation of the word כיניי as pedestals (piédestals) – כיניי is the version preferred by both (Rabin and Cothenet) – it is clear that they connected the word with כֵּן or כַּנָּה (a base or support), as Dimant has already noted (2004:32 n. 49).

28 Note that when he turns to explain the phrase סִכּוּת מלככם, he represents it with the words סוכת המלך: in other words, the explanatory version סוכת is cited in place of the text to be explained, סכות (see Chapter 12, § 13b).

Thus, that which comes after the books of Torah, chronologically and in order of importance, namely the books of the Prophets, are identified with the phrase כיון צלמיכם, which follows in the order of the verse after the phrase סִכּוּת מלככם. This does not suffice, however: the first identification had textual support from the verse סֻכַּת דויד הנפלת, which can be rightly interpreted as describing the books of the Torah being in a state of retreat and collapse in the eyes of the interpreter (as סוכת דוד **הנפלת**), but upon what did he base his explanation that וכיניי/וכיון הצלמים are the books of the Prophets?

§ 9 I would like to consider a solution to this question based on the language which was in use during the time of the interpreter, namely, one of the dialects of Mishnaic Hebrew reflected in Rabbinic Literature.

I will first address the etymology of the nouns כיניי and כיון. Regarding the morphology of the noun כיניי, it appears to me that the basic form is וכיני,[29] to which an extra letter י was mistakenly added.[30] The word כיני can be interpreted as the plural construct form of a noun derived from the root כנ"ן, whose absolute form would presumably be כֵּן, declined as כִּנִּים, כִּנְּךָ, כִּנִּי, כִּנֵּי, etc. Alternatively, of course, the absolute form could be כַּן and the declension the same, similar to the forms of פַּת (פִּתִּי), גַּת (גִּתִּי), and the like.[31]

---

29 It would seem worthwhile to consider the possibility that כיניי is a writing of כְּנַיי (derived from כנ"י), with the *yod* reflecting a *shewa*. However, we do not find anything comparable in the text. There is, however, an example of a *shewa* being written with a *waw*: this is almost certainly attested in the two attestations of the word זונות in MS A of the text transcription of the word זונות in two instances in Version A of the scroll. I am referring to the words בדרכי זונות, which appear in MS A (Col. VIII, l. 15, Qimron 1992a:25), as opposed to בדרכי זנות in MS B (Col. XIX, l. 17, Qimron 199a:43, as Qimron himself comments [p. 25 n. 7]). Qimron also finds, apparently correctly, a second example of this spelling in the expression להסיר מן הזונות כמשפט (Col. VII ll. 1–2, ibid p. 23). The writing זונות reflects a pronunciation as z^{u}*nūt*/*zunūt*, which is parallel to the pronunciation z^{e}*nut* [זְנוּת] in the Masoretic tradition.

30 The shape of the first *yod* after the *nun* (in וכיניי) is different from all the other writings of this letter in the scroll: the head of the letter is not there at all, and the letter is faded. I think it is likely that the scribe went back and wrote another *yod* as a correction and then forgot to erase the first *yod*. Professor Qimron (in a conversation in February 2006) said: "this is not surprising, since the Scrolls in general, including this version of the Damascus Document included, are full of copying errors." One who checks Qimron's edition of the Damascus Document will find many notes that regarding copying errors, many of which relate to interchanges of the letters *waw* and *yod*; for example, on the very first page, nn. 7–8, he suggests reading ויעבורו instead of ויעבירו and לרוב instead of לריב (see Qimron 1992a:11).

31 This is as opposed to the scrolls at Qumran itself (which date from the times of the Second Temple), in which the letter *yod* is not used (almost never!) in a closed syllable. As Elisha Qimron (1976:53–55) established, MS A from the Geniza does contain such usages, such as לתיתו (Col. I, l. 6), וְכִימְגַשְּׁשִׁים (I, 9), וגיבוריהם (III, 9), ניתפשים (IV, 20), למילפנים (V, 15) and others. In these examples it can be seen that the *yod* is used whether the syllable is closed with germination or not, and therefore there is no obstacle to our reading the word כיני with a *dagesh* in the *nun*.

With regards to the alternative form, וכיון, it is clear that the noun כִּיּוּן, as it is vocalized by the Masoretes, is derived from the root כו"ן.

The nouns כיני (= כִּינֵּי) and כִּיּוּן, then, are derived from two related roots, and can be interpreted as alternatives whose meanings are the same. According to Ginzberg and Rabin, however, the first form, וכיני (וכינוי/וכיניי[32]) is primary and the second (וכיון) is a correction based on the language of the verse in Amos.[33]

I now arrive at my own suggestion regarding the background of the identification of כִּינֵּי (כיניי, written with an extra *yod*) and כיון as the books of the Prophets (ספרי הנביאים).

§ 10 In the Mishnah we find a list of various utensils, including four of the tools of the scribe: האולר הקולמוס ... והכן והכנה[34] (m. Kel 12:8).[35] The last two nouns are vocalized in the best manuscripts: וְהַכָּן וְהַכַּנָּה (MS Kaufmann); וְהַכָּן וְהַכַּנָּה (Parma B);[36] וְהַכַּן וְהַכַּנָּא (Parma A).[37] We have here a pair of nouns which are related to one another, and which share an etymology: both are derived from the root כנ"ן. In my view, in the tradition reflected in MSS Kaufmann and Parma B, the noun was built on the pattern *pa“* (פַּעּ), with the *patah* replaced by a *qames*.[38]

§ 11 And now to the main point: the meaning of the nouns כַּן and כַּנָּה. Medieval authorities already clarified the meaning of these two nouns already; here is what the author of the Geonic commentary on Teharot wrote:[39]

---

32 Recall that Ginzberg reads וכינוי, following Schechter, and that Rabin reads וכיניי (see above, § 5–6).

33 In my view, the copyist simply copied both versions of the text he found in front of him: the first quotes the texts which is being used to interpret (וכיניי הצלמים) and the second it the text being interpreted (וכיון הצלמים). Part of Chapter Twelve, above, is devoted to this double version.

34 This is the consonantal text of the four nouns in most of the original versions of the Mishnah (MSS Kaufmann, Parma B, Cambridge [ed. Loew], Parma A, the autograph of Maimonides' commentary on the Mishnah (ed. Qafiḥ), and others. In Parma A, the text first says האלר, and then someone wrote the word האולר within the elongated *resh*; it should be noted that this manuscript also writes והכנא with an *aleph*.

35 Additional scribal utensils (מוחק, מכתב) are mentioned in a following mishna: מכתב שניטל הכותב טמא מפני המוחק, ניטל המוחק טמא מפני הכותב.

36 MS Parma B includes cantillation signs, as well; see Bar-Asher 2009a:2.28–35 (§§ 1–14 in “Contextual and Pausal”).

37 The vocalization seen in Parma A here is very unclear, but after careful study it can be said that what is cited above faithfully reflects what is in the manuscript.

38 The punctuation of *qall* nouns with a *qames* is a regular occurrence in Parma B (see Bar-Asher 2009a p. 156–157). The exchanges of *patah* with *qames* in Kaufmann, while rare, are common enough that they cannot be ignored (see Bar-Asher 2009b:79 n. 39).

39 See Epstein 1982:27. In nn. 15–16 he comments on הפא < חפא (in the Babylonian dialect) and כמן (= כמין).

והכן פ' בסיס ...[40] והכנה פ' כמין אמת הבנין ששמו הפא (< חפא) בל[שון] חכ[מים], וכמן (= וכמין) זה שמסרגלין בו את הספרים.

The כן is the base ... and the כנה is a type of builder's tool, called a *hapa* (< *ḥapa*) in Mishnaic Hebrew, and like the kind used to score the lines in books.

The editor notes there that כנונתא in Syriac is a ruler,[41] and further cites what Maimonides wrote: "the כן is the ruler ... with which lines are scored, and the כנה is the board."[42] These interpretations were cited already by the Arukh s. v. כן II: "The כן and the כנה ... meaning, a ruler with which lines were scored, and the board under it."[43]

Might it be possible to assume that through metonymy, the *pašrān* in the Covenant of Damascus identified the word כיון in the term כיון צלמיכם in Amos with כן or כנה – two of the scribal tools used regularly in the preparation of scrolls[44] – and thereby with the scroll itself, and that this led him to use the plural construct form, כיניי = כִּינֵי (= כַּנֵּי)?[45]

§ 12 If there is substance to the linguistic relationships that I have suggested, we can say that the background of the interpretation has been uncovered. If we accept the suggestion that כיני (כיניי) is the primary reading, and כיון is a correction based on the scripture,[46] it can be seen that the connection between כנה/כן and כיני (which was mistakenly written כיניי) is quite close, and the background for the interpretation is very clear. But even if it is claimed that וכיון הצלמים is *not* a correction, but rather an authentic alternative read-

---

40 An alternative explanation is given here in parenthesis (see the reference in the next note).

41 See Epstein 1982:27 n. 17.

42 *Ibid.* Maimonides' words are translated by Qafih differently: והכן הוא הקנה אשר בו משרטטין השורות, וכנה הסרגל ("The כן is the reed with which lines are scored, and a כנה is a ruler").

43 The *Arukh* also adds that "some say that the כן is a scale."

44 This is against the opinion of Rabin 1958:30 and Cothenet 1963:173, who understood כיניי as being related to the nouns כן or כנה, which have to do with a base or support (as discussed above in n. 27).

45 It does not seem that one needs to go farther and claim that the interpretation of the word צלמים as related to the prophets has a scriptural basis. Indeed, צלם and דמות are often connected to each other: נעשה את האדם בצלמנו כדמותנו (Genesis 1:26), בדמותו כצלמו (Gen 5:3). And prophets, after all, often see in an "image" (דמות) in their visions: משא בבל אשר חזה ישעיהו בן אמוץ ... קול המון בהרים דמות עם רב (Isa 13:1–4); ... וארא והנה רוח סערה ומתוכה דמות ארבע חיות (Ezek 1:4–5); see also Ezekiel 10, 22, 26, and so on, as well as Daniel 10:16. Perhaps once the interpreter began, he not only connected כיון with scribal ruler and with books themselves, but also צלמים with those who see צלמים and דמויות, namely, the prophets; however, there is no need for this line of thought.

46 See above § 5.

ing,[47] it is still possible to connect a noun from a hollow (II-*w*) root (כיון) to a noun from a geminate root (כנה/כן).

We can say even more: it is possible that the interpreter [explainer] adopted the plural form כיני (which was written כיניי), and not the singular form כן, because he was [dragged after] [following] the plural form of the explanation, "ספרי" [books] (of the prophets].[48]

To sum up, I am not claiming that the solution that I suggested is the only solution that can be given to understand the background of the explanation, but it seems to me to be an eminently plausible suggestion.

15.3 Concluding Statements

§ 13 The crux of the discussion depends on the nature of the text and giving the proper weight to the linguistic dimension. But it should be clarified that even if the meanings of the words כֵּן and כַּנָּה are clear from Mishnaic Hebrew, the connection to כיני (= כיניי) / כיון in the Damascus Covenant should be seen only as a suggestion, which requires further substantiation.

We have seen that everything begins with clarifying what the facts are: the text itself and establishing its precise nature. The paucity of data and texts with even minor uncertainties require great caution, but do not prevent us from searching for possible interpretations of כיון הצלמים/כיניי הצלמים.[49]

---

47 See the details of my suggestion in Chapter Twelve above.

48 Or, in the words of Dimant 2004:32: "if the reading וכיניי הצלמים is to be upheld, [we can surmise that] the interpreter interpreted the word וכיון in the Masoretic text as a plural form in order to make it agree with the plural noun ספרי הנביאים "Books of the Prophets."

49 Chapter Twelve, above, also deals with the second example found in the Damascus Document that reflects a repetition – in my opinion this is not an erroneous repetition – of one given first name. In its first appearance it is written יהושע, in its Scriptural form, but the second time it is written יוש'ע, as it was in fact pronounced by the scribe of the text from the Geniza (see ibid, §§ 2, 11, 14 and others).

16 The Patterns *Peʿila* and *Piʿʿul* in Qumran Hebrew

16.1 Introductory Comments

§ 1 From the beginning of research into Qumran Hebrew, scholars have recognized the affinity between it and Classical Biblical Hebrew,[1] and especially to the late layer of Biblical Hebrew.[2] Similarly, scholars have examined the many linguistic features unique to this stratum of Hebrew.[3] Scholars have also written on the not-insignificant presence of Aramaic in Qumran Hebrew.[4] In addition to these three aspects,[5] scholars have pointed out a fourth feature of the Hebrew language of the Dead Sea Scrolls: evident within this dialect are linguistic features known from the manuscripts (and even the printed editions) of Mishnaic literature. These include lexical items as well as grammatical features. Anyone familiar with Mishnaic Hebrew can provide many examples of links between the Hebrew of Qumran and that of the Mishna.[6]

§ 2 Here are a few examples from the lexicon. The noun גודל appears in the War Scroll: והבטן ארבע גודלים "The belly (shall be) four thumbs" (1QM

1 Already at the early stage of research into Qumran Hebrew Hanokh Yalon pointed out this relationship in a series of publications (see for example Yalon 1967:9, 11, 30, etc.). Yalon's studies had been published between 1949–1952, over fifteen years before they were collected in his book.

2 See for example Kutscher 1959:23–34, and various issues dealt with on pp. 164–342.

3 One example is the use of the long independent personal pronouns הואה, היאה. See the material cited in Fassberg 2003.

4 Many have paid attention to the relationship between Qumran Hebrew and the Aramaic language. Important research into this aspect has been carried out by Kutscher in his study of the Isaiah Scroll (Kutscher 1959, especially pp. 19–22, 141–163) and Menahem Kister in a number of his articles (for example Kister 1999, Kister 2000).

5 Fassberg has recently written concise, important comments on the Hebrew language of the scrolls. See Fassberg 2003, especially in the introduction and the conclusions (pp. 227–229, 234–236).

6 Kutscher has brought many examples from the Isaiah Scroll, such as לרד (= לֵירֵד, Isaiah 30:2), which was corrected to לרד[ת]; להוכין (ibid. 40:20) conjugated as a I-*yod* verb, instead of להכין like a hollow verb; נודף (= נֻדָּף ibid. 41:2) in the verbal form נֻפְעַל (the alternative form for the נִפְעַל verbal stem, primarily used for I-*nun* and I-*yod* verbs) instead of נדף (= נִדָּף) the regular form of the stem נִפְעַל. (These three examples and others appear in Kutscher 1959:30). A condensed list of words and phrases in the Dead Sea Scrolls which appear in Mishnaic Hebrew can be found in Qimron 1976: 297–299. On pp. 299–300 he brings a list of words that appear in Amoraic Hebrew (as well as in the Piyyut and in Medieval Hebrew Literature). Since the publication of Qimron's book many items have been added and it is possible to enlarge these lists (See, for example what is cited in Kister 2000:138).

5.13).[7] This evidence antedates the use of the word גֶּדֶל/אֲגוּדָּל of Mishnaic Hebrew by hundreds of years. Similarly, גמר[8] appears in the Pesher Habakkuk (7.2): ואת גמר הקץ לא הודעו "but the fulfillment of the period he did not make known to him."[9] The noun כלל is found in a fragmentary scroll: לכלל חלליהם "the total of their slain" (4Q169 3ii3).[10] The noun ממון also appears several times in the scrolls; one example is in 1QS 6:2: וישמעו הקטן לגדול למלאכה ולממון "the lesser one shall obey the greater with respect to work and money." The scrolls also contain quite a few phrases known from Mishnaic Hebrew. One example is בני ברית: ואתם בני ברית התחזקו[11] "As for you, sons of his covenant, strengthen yourselves" (1QM 17.8–9). Another is the phrase לשון הקודש, found in a fragmentary scroll (4Q464 3i7), and one more is the expression חסדים טובים is brought in another fragment: כחסדיו הטבים[12] "according to his good mercies" (4Q185 1–2ii:1).[13] I will also mention here two verbs. גִּבֵּל is attested in the Thanksgiving Scroll (9 [1] 23), יצר החמר ומגבל המים[14] "he forms the substance and kneads the water," and in the Rule Scroll, והואה מעפר מגבלו "he whose kneading (is) from dust" (1QS 11.21).[15] Second, the verb יוֹפֵךְ – the future form of the root (הפ"ך >) אפ"ך in the Qal – is attested in ויופך [מימ]יהמה לדם "He turned their [water] to blood" (4Q422 iii 7); this form was previously known only from Mishnaic Hebrew. It is also worth mentioning the adverb עכשו "now." It only occurs once in Qumran in the scroll known as Pseudo-Jubilees: שמחים ואומרים עכשו יאבד "being happy and saying 'Now he will perish'" (4Q225 2 ii 7),[16] and is, of course, very common in MH.

§ 3 Here are a few examples from the area of grammar. The first person plural personal pronoun אנו is the most common pronoun in the scrolls.[17]

---

7 See Qimron 1976:297.

8 In Mishnaic Hebrew this noun has at least two traditional pronunciations: גְּמָר and גֶּמֶר.

9 See Qimron 1976:297.

10 *Ibid.*

11 *Ibid.*

12 This is the Hebrew word הטובים, spelled defectively; I do not think that the Aramaic form טָב is intended here.

13 The two phrases quoted above are mentioned in Kister 2000:138.

14 See Licht 1965:61. References to the Thanksgiving Scroll from Cave 1 (1QHᵃ) are quoted according to the edition by Stegemann and Schüller (2009) by column and line. Next to this reference the reference to columns in Sukenik's 1954 edition will appear in square brackets.

15 See Licht 1965:237; Yalon 1967:30, 43, 98; Yalon cited the example from the Thanksgiving Scroll and concentrated on its grammatical form. Kister (2000:138) brings the two examples and adds the noun גבול (= גְּבוּל, see below §§ 18, 20).

16 This example is mentioned by Kister (2000:138) among the various examples from Mishnaic Hebrew (he indicates that this is an Aramaic calque).

17 See Qimron 1976:224.

Already fifty years ago Kutscher pointed out the verb נודף in the Isaiah Scroll in the form נִפְעַל.[18] We can add to this example a form from the strong verb – נוכנעים "the lowly" (1QS 10.26).[19] Another grammatical feature is the double plural in construct phrases, that is the use of the plural form both in the *nomen regens* and in the *nomen rectum*, as is reflected in a number of expressions, such as the phrase ראשי שנים "the heads of years" in the Rule of the Community (1QS 10.6) and the phrase ובשני השמטים "but during the years of remission" in the War Scroll (1QM 2.8).[20] It is also found in the well-known expressions from the Isaiah Scroll, מאורות צפעונים "the cobra dens" and בצי צפעונים "cobra eggs," as opposed to Masoretic מאורת צפעוני "the cobra den" (Isaiah 11:8) and ביצי צפעוני "cobra eggs" (Isaiah 59:5).[21] In this use of the construct, Qumran Hebrew is similar to Mishnaic Hebrew in which the use of the double plural is quite common, as in the phrases ראשי שנים "New Years," בתי כנסיות "synagogues," בתי מדרשות "houses of study." Even so, it must be mentioned that this linguistic feature is already present in late Biblical Hebrew.[22] There is no reason not to assume that this structure entered into late Biblical Hebrew from the spoken dialect – that dialect which was consolidated, a few generations later, following the destruction of the Second Temple, into the literary language of Tannaitic literature – Mishnaic Hebrew.

§ 4 The authors of the Dead Sea Scrolls composed the texts in their own literary Hebrew, characterized by (1) a deep affinity to Biblical Hebrew, (2) unique linguistic features, and (3) the influence of Aramaic.[23] Despite this, we frequently encounter echoes of the spoken Hebrew dialect of their time, which was something like what is known to us as Mishnaic Hebrew. The scribes who composed the scrolls were taught to write in a certain type of Hebrew. This language type, which has quite a few unique linguistic features, is primarily a literary language, and perhaps even an artificial one.[24] In these dialects, or in

18 See note 6 above.

19 See Qimron 1976:177.

20 See Yadin 1957:268–269; Qimron 1976:288.

21 See Kutscher 1959:488. He only brings the second phrase (and note that the reference to Isaiah 49:5, instead of 59:5, is a mistake); see also Hurvitz 1972:38–39; Qimron 1976:288.

22 See the references to scholarly literature mentioned in the previous note.

23 See above the presentation of these points above in § 1.

24 In our discussion of the pronominal suffixes attached to third person forms such as שְׁמוֹתָם/שְׁמוֹתֵיהֶם (Chapter Eleven above) we have found that the pattern שְׁמוֹתָם is more prevalent in Qumran Hebrew than the pattern שְׁמוֹתֵיהֶם. This reveals a feature characteristic of a literary language. Even though I stressed that one should not formulate general conclusions from the data presented there, it is impossible to ignore the literary nature of the language of the scrolls. Not less important is Fassberg's comprehensive and thorough study (Fassberg 2003), which points out the literary-artificial nature of the use of lengthened forms in Qumran Hebrew (see the scholarly literature referred to there).

similar ones, were written the Bar Kokhba letters as well as the Rabbinic literature, especially Tannaitic literature. It is natural that these scribes would give expression to the customary modes of expression of themselves and the members of their community.

16.2 Specifics and Generalities in the relationship of Qumran Hebrew to Mishnaic Hebrew

§ 5 When clarifying the relationship between Qumran Hebrew and Mishnaic Hebrew, it is important to understand the nature of and the distribution of the particular linguistic features in Qumran Hebrew that are similar or identical to Mishnaic Hebrew which, as had been said, was the prime representative of the spoken Hebrew dialect in the Land of Israel in the period when the scrolls were composed.

Indeed, an examination of the linguistic features that penetrated the literature of Qumran from this dialect shows that these are specific features, but not general linguistic phenomena or whole grammatical categories. That is, the linguistic phenomena in Qumran Hebrew which are similar to Mishnaic Hebrew are limited to words and grammatical forms in one occurrence or in a small number of occurrences. That is how the situation seems according to the evidence before us today.

In this study I will examine two grammatical categories – the verbal nouns *peʿila* and *piʿʿul* – to see if the relationship to Mishnaic Hebrew in the scrolls is indeed limited to individual words appearing only once or twice.

§ 6 There is no doubt that these two patterns appear quite a bit in the scrolls. The first, *peʿila*, is the verbal noun pattern of the Qal and Nifʿal verbal stems; the second, *piʿʿul*, is the verbal noun pattern of the Piʿʿel and Hitpaʿʿel verbal stems (in the scrolls this verbal stem always appears with the consonant *he* and not *nun*).[25] The truth is these patterns already existed in Biblical Hebrew;[26] but in Mishnaic Hebrew they became much more extensively used and became a regular grammatical category.

---

25 In Mishnaic Hebrew the verbal noun of the active stem is also the verbal noun of its reflexive (and passive) stem (see Sharvit 2008:117); Sharvit presented the material well, in that he speaks of the verbal nouns of the "Qal system", that is the Qal and Nifʿal verbal stems in one category, and the "heavy, doubled system" meaning the Piʿʿel and Nitpaʿʿel stems in one category. See also Bar-Asher 2009b, chapter 1 p. 26 § 35.

26 For example, the forms אֲכִילָה and שְׁחִיטָה (see Kutscher 1977:110; Sharvit 2008:115); חִבּוּק, כִּפֻּרִים, גִּדּוּפִים (Sharvit ibid.).

In the Mishna alone Kutscher found approximately 130 *pᵉʻila* forms attested hundreds of times.[27] In all of Tannaitic literature Shimon Sharvit listed 190 nouns in the *pi"ul* pattern.[28] As mentioned, the examination of the material in the scrolls shows that many *pᵉʻila* and *pi"ul* forms are attested. However, the question that needs to be asked is whether the relationship between these forms and the verbs they are connected with is regular and automatic, as in Mishnaic Hebrew, or not.

I will now examine each of these patterns in Qumran Hebrew in a more detailed way. Following that I shall present the conclusions.

16.3 The Pattern *Pᵉʻila*

§ 7 First it should be said that based on a comparison of the nouns brought henceforth with vocalized forms in the Bible and the Mishna, I accept the generally held opinion of scholars that all of the nouns with the orthographic form פעילה belong to the *pᵉʻila* pattern and not to any other pattern.[29] I will present here a total of seventeen nouns whose total number of occurrences in the Qumran scrolls is more than one hundred fifty. Hereinafter will follow a comprehensive, annotated description of the examples.[30]

---

27 See Kutscher 1977:110–129. Actually, there is no verb that does not have a verbal noun. Segal is correct in saying that "the feminine form קְטִילָה is regularly used in Mishnaic Hebrew as the verbal noun of the Qal verbal stem ... it is possible to produce verbal nouns in this form from any verb" (Segal 1936:73; see also Sharvit's comments on "the degree of regularity between the pattern of the verbal noun and its stem" in Sharvit 2008:120). However, as is well known, the פְּעִילָה pattern is not the only pattern used as the verbal noun the Qal and Nifʻal stems. Kutscher (ibid pp. 110–130) described the verbal nouns of the Qal stem in the Mishna according to the Kaufmann manuscript; Sharvit (ibid p. 117) lists approximately 300 nouns in the patterns פְּעִילָה and פְּעֵלָה in all of Tannaitic literature.

28 See Sharvit ibid. Elitzur 1987:72–82 lists all of the nouns in the pattern derived from the Pi"el [stem] found in the Mishna according to the Kaufmann manuscript.

29 This view is reflected in all of the publications of the scrolls by various scholars, and no further comment on this matter is necessary.

30 I should add that over the years, I had collected only sixteen nouns with approximately one hundred forty five occurrences, but with the help of Elisha Qimron some material was added. I wish to thank him for his assistance. I will bring here a comprehensive exampling but not all of the appearences of the various nouns. Moreover there are another one or two nouns whose attestation is not certain. I have decided not to mention them since their presence or absence does not change the general picture that I am describing here (I will mention here that Qimron also provided me with a list of the nouns in the *pi"ul* pattern).

§ 8 Forms derived from strong roots:

בְּרִיאָה/בְּרִיָּה:[31] (Of course, we do not know if the form בְּרִיָּה, which is known from the most reliable manuscripts of Mishnaic Hebrew, also existed at Qumran.[32]) This noun occurs over ten times in the scrolls. For example in the Commentary on Genesis B, we read טהורים מן הבריאה "pure things from creation" (4Q253 2 3). In Pseudo-Jubilees[a] is found: עד יום הבריאה "until the day of the creation" (4Q225 1 7). The same, apparently, is intended in the Temple Scroll: עד יום הבריה "until the day of creation" (29 9). This is also in a clause in the Damascus Document: ויסוד הבריאה זכר ונקבה "while the foundation of creation" (CD MS A 4.21) and in a phrase from Jubilees[a] רוחות בריאתו "the spirits of his creatures" (4Q216 V, 9).

הֲלִיכָה: The reading in Jubilees[h] is עש]ה עמנו מיום [ה]ליכת אחיהו "he has don]e with us from the day his brother [Jacob w]ent" (4Q223–224 2 I 50).

חֲלִיפָה:[33] This form is attested a number of times in the scrolls. For example in the War Scroll, we read מערכה אחרת חליפה למלחמה "another line of the reserve in its turn to the battle" (1QM 16.12), and in the parallel text, we read חליפות למלחמה "in turns to the battle" (4Q491 1–3 12), מערכה אחרת חליפה למ]לחמה (4Q491 11 ii 1). This form also appears in the Community Rule (spelled with *ʿayin* instead of *het*): עליפות איש לרעהו "each man relieving another" (1QS 6.7).

יְדִיעָה: There is a correction in the Thanksgiving Scroll:[34] כי אל ה(י)ד(י)עות ואין אחר עמו "for the God of knowledge; none else is with him" (12, 13).[35] I assume that the scribe originally wrote אל הידיעות. The *nomen rectum* in this construct phrase is the definite plural form of the noun יְדִיעָה. Apparently, the scribe used this form which he borrowed from his own spoken dialect, but afterwards changed it (either he himself or someone who checked the text) to the biblical phrase אל (ה)דעות "God of knowledge." (1 Samuel 2:3).

---

31 Perhaps it is not unnecessary to note that the forms cited here are given with Tiberian vocalization, but this should not be taken a conjecture as to the pronunciation at Qumran.

32 See Kutscher 1977:272–273.

33 Because of the *plene* spelling (with *yod* after the *lamed*) there is no need to assume that the reading is חֲלִיפָּה according to the pattern *peʿilla* with double *lamed* (see Qimron 1976:53–57).

34 See Licht 1957:174. He pointed out the correction but in the edited text he brought the form הדעות; see also Qimron ibid p. 297. Qimron is still of the opinion that the text originally read הידיעות and was only corrected afterwards.

35 Stegemann and Schüller 2009:250 give the reading ה(ו)ד(י)עות; in their opinion the erased letter following the *he* is *vav* (but I accept Qimron's reading that the letter is *yod*). On page 256 they point out that in a parallel text from the fourth cave (4Q427 8 ii) the text reads א]ל הדעות הכ]ינה. They also refer to the phrase אל הדעות (Thanksgiving Scroll 22, 34; 25 [7], 22–32; and also in the Rule of the Community 3, 15). In all of these places the text reads הדעות like the emended text of the Thanksgiving Scroll from cave one as edited by Licht 1957.

מְשִׁיחָה: I have found only two occurrences of this noun. In the Apocryphon of Moses[a]: אשר יוצק על ר[ו]אשו שמן המשיחה "upon whose head will be poured the oil of anointing" (4Q375 1 i 9), and in the War Scroll שמן משיחת כהונתם "the oil of their priestly annointing" (1QM 9.8).

מְשִׁיכָה: This form appears in a halakhic text: ש המשיכה[36] "the drawing" (4Q251 1–2 4).

סְלִיחָה: This noun appears a number of times in the scrolls. For example in the Rule of the Community הצמאה עם הרווה לאין סליחה "thirst along with saturation, without forgiveness" (1QS 2. 14–15); in the Thanksgiving Scroll: רחמים ורוב סליחה "mercy and much forgiveness" (14[6] 12); and in the Damascus Document: ורוב סליחות לכפר בעד שבי "and manifold forgiveness, so as to atone for those who repent" (CD MS A 2.4–5), etc.

רְחִיצָה: This form appears in the Rule of the Community [בכל מי] רחיצה "[by any water] of ablution" (4Q262 1 3).

§ 8 Forms derived from hollow roots:

בִּיאָה: This noun is found eight times[37] in those sections of the scrolls that deal with the priestly divisions. For example, בעשרים ושמונא בוא ביאת מלכ[יה] "on the twenty-eighth in it (is) the entrance of Malki[ah]" (4Q324a fl ii 2); באחד עשר בשביעי ביאת [הפצץ] "on the eleventh of the seventh (month) the entrance [of Happiṣṣeṣ]" (4Q324 1 7). In these examples the word ביאה functions as a verbal noun – 'coming (entering)'.[38]

בִּינָה: There are over ninety occurrences of this noun in the scrolls. Here are a few examples. In the Damascus Document: אין בהם בינה "they have no discernment" (CD MS A 5.17); in the Rule of the Community: וטוב עולמים ושכל ובינה וחכמה וגבורה "and constant goodness, and of prudence, insight, and wisdom and might" (1QS 4.3); in 4QMysteries[b]: היש אתכם בינה "whether you have understanding" (4Q300 8 6).

גִּילָה: This noun appears in 4QShirot 'Olat HaShabbat[f]: קול גילות רנה השקיט "The sound of glad rejoicing falls silent." (4Q405 ii 20–22 13) and also in the War Scroll: יכתובו גילות אל במשוב שלום "they shall write 'Rejoicings of God in peaceful withdrawal'" (1QM 3.11).

---

36 The full context is lost, so we can not know the exact usage of the word.

37 I have not included the seven occurrences of the noun ביאה which appear in the Copper Scroll, such as בביאה מיריחו לסככא (3Q15 3 13), ביאתו תחת הסף הגדול (3Q15 2 12). In all of these cases the noun ביאה has the meaning 'opening' (as a variant of the noun מבוא/מבוי; see Chapter Thirteen above, n. 10). As is well known, the language of this scroll is very close to Mishnaic Hebrew and is not representative of Qumran Hebrew.

38 This is as opposed to its usage in the Copper Scroll as explained in note 37 above (see also below §§ 11, 14).

חִידָה: In Pesher Habakkuk (8.6): כולם משל עליו ישאו ומליצי חידות לו "all of them raise a taunt against him and interpreters of riddles about him", and in 4QMysteries[b]: אמרו המשל והגידו החידה "utter the parable and relate the riddle" (4Q300 1 ii 1) etc.

קִינָה: There are a few occurrences of this noun, like in the Thanksgiving Scroll: ואנחנו בכינור קינה "and we, on the lyre (sing) a dirge" (19[11] 22a), ערשי בקינה תשא "raise my bed on a dirge" (19[9] 4) etc.[39]

שִׁיבָה: In the Rule of the Community it states וגאולים בשו[י]בתו "and there are def[ilement]s where he returns" (4Q257 III, 4). This noun also appears in a narrative text: ויראה ה' את שיבתם (4Q461 1 10) "and God saw their returning."

שִׂיחָה: In the Psalms Scroll we find: שיחתם בתורת עליון "Their meditation is on the Law of the Most High" (11Q5 XVIII, 12).

שִׁירָה: In a text that refers to commandments it states: בלילה שירות שמונה "in the night: songs eight" (4Q334 4 4); there are two other occurrences in this scroll. A similar text in the Thanksgiving Scroll states: שירותיו קודש "his songs are sacred" (4Q433a 1 4).

§ 9 A form derived from a III-Yod root:[40]

רְמִיָּה: There are many occurrences of this noun in the scrolls. For example in the Rule of the Community: ורום לבב כחש ורמיה אכזרי "pride and hautiness, atrocious disguise and falsehood" (1QS 4.9). This noun comes in a number of expressions such as אנשי רמיה (Rule of the Community 9, 8), דורשי רמיה "those who study falsehood" (Thanksgiving Scroll 10[2] 18) and others.

§ 10 It is easy to see that not all of these forms function only as verbal nouns. Some of these nouns indicate the result of an action, such as בריאה/בריה, which indicates the action of the creator and also the result of this action, namely creation. This is similar to the noun מְצִיאָה in Mishnaic Hebrew which indicates both the action of the finder and the found object.[41] As is well

39 As is well known, this verb appears in the *binyan pi"el* (קוֹנֵן), as in, e.g., וְקוֹנְנוּ (Ezekiel 27:32). In MH only the nominalized feminine participle, מְקוֹנֶנֶת, is attested (M. Ketubbot 4:4; Mo‘ed Qaṭan 3:9), and this is a clear borrowing (or inheritance) from the Bible. It appears that the form קינון/קִנּוּן was blocked by the existence of the root קנ"ן, meaning "to build a nest (קֵן)," which is attested in both BH (e.g., Isaiah 34:15) and MH (e.g., M. Ḥullin 12:1). It would seem that this is the background for the existence of the noun קִינָה in a pattern associated with the *binyan Qal*, and not the *pi"el*.

40 I did not include the form בְּנִיָּה which the editors thought they had found at Qumran in the sentence חיץ יבחר לבניתה ותפל פח קירו (4Q424 1 3) because Qimron (2009:105) convinced me that it is not possible to rely on this reading. Other possible occurrences of בְּנִיָּה (in 4Q429 4 ii 9; 3Q14 3 2) depend on missing letters supplied by the editor and therefore I did not include them.

41 This is in opposition to Kutscher (1977:115), who brings a list of nouns that indicate the result of an action. He states there that "מציאה (apparently this does not exist as a verbal

known, there are forms which, over the course of time, no longer function as verbal nouns, but rather indicate only the result of an action. For example, the noun חֲתִיכָה which originally indicated the verbal noun[42] (cutting) indicates in later Hebrew the thing that is cut (a piece, a cut) and not the action of the one who cuts.[43]

§ 11 When considering the evidence presented above (in §§ 8–10), we must conclude that there is no direct relationship between the nouns in the *pᵉʿila* pattern in Qumran Hebrew and the grammar of Mishnaic Hebrew. Four out of the eight nouns derived from strong roots are already attested in Biblical Hebrew: בְּרִיאָה occurs once in the Pentateuch, as in ואם בְּרִיאָה יברא ה' "But if the Lord make a new thing" (Numbers 16:30). The form בריותיו is also attested in Ben Sira (16:16): רחמיו יראו לכל בריותיו "to all creation is his mercy manifest." The word הֲלִיכָה appears six times in the Bible. For example, רָאוּ הֲלִיכוֹתֶיךָ אלהים הֲלִיכוֹת אלי מלכי בקדש "They have seen thy goings, O God; even the goings of my God, my King, in the sanctuary" (Psalms 68:25). The noun חֲלִיפָה is attested four times, in, for example, אשר אין חֲלִיפוֹת למו "because they have no changes" (Psalms 55:20), as well as in Ben Sira (42:19): מחוה חליפות נהיות "relating the things that passed." The noun סְלִיחָה appears three times, in, for example, כי עמך הַסְּלִיחָה, "but there is forgiveness with thee" (Psalms 130:4); הרחמים וְהַסְּלִיחוֹת "mercies and forgivenesses" (Daniel 9:9); and also in Ben Sira (5:5): אל סליחה אל תבטח "Do not become fearless concerning atonement." On the other hand, the other four nouns – רְחִיצָה, מְשִׁיכָה, מְשִׁיחָה, יְדִיעָה – are not found in the Bible but are attested in Mishnaic Hebrew. The data regarding these nouns (in Mishnaic Hebrew) is as follows: אם היתה יְדִיעָה בנתים "If there was knowledge in the meantime" (m.

---

noun)." However, this noun does in fact function as a verbal noun: כל (שכל) הטמאות כשעת מציאתן "conditions of uncleanness are so accounted of as they appear at the time of their finding" (m. Teharot 3:5 [2×]; 4:12; 5:7; 9:9). Certainly, we can not hold anything against a scholar who brings hundreds of examples if, on rare occasions, he overlooks a few details.

42 This is its meaning in the phrase וַחֲתִיכַת יבלתו "cutting off its callus" (m. Pesahim 6:1) according to the text of the Kaufmann manuscript (see Kutscher 1977:110) and MS Parma A; this is also the form according to the Yemenite tradition (see Shivtiel 1971:220). An object that has been cut is called in the Mishna, according to the most reliable witnesses, חֲתִיכָה in the *pᵉʿilla* pattern (see Kutscher 1977:133. See also Shivtiel *ibid.*, who calls חֲתִיכָה "name of an action" and חֲתִכָּה "name of a thing").

43 Today we speak of the noun חִתּוּךְ as the verbal noun of the verbs חָתַךְ and נֶחְתַּךְ, and the noun חֲתִיכָה is the cut object. This is not the only verb in the Qal verbal stem whose verbal noun is in the *piʿʿul* pattern. In Modern Hebrew there is a clear distinction between the verbal noun [חִתּוּךְ] and the noun indicating the result of the action [חֲתִיכָה] (see additional examples in Sharvit 2008:120, towards the end).

Karetot 4:2);[44] יְדִיעוֹת הטומאה "Knowledge of uncleanness" (m. Shevu'ot 2:1); כל כלי וכלי טעון מְשִׁיחָה[45] "every vessel needs anointing" (Sifra Tzav Milu'im § 1); כל המיטלטלין נקנין בִּמְשִׁיכָה "All moveable goods are [legally] acquired [only] by the act of drawing [them into the purchaser's possession]" (m. Shevi'it 10:9);[46] יום הכיפורים אסור באכילה ... וּבִרְחִיצָה "On the Day of Atonement eating ... washing ... are forbidden" (m. Yoma 8:1).

I wish to stress that these four nouns are only sparsely attested in the scrolls. It is impossible to say whether the first of these nouns, the noun יְדִיעָה, is attested at all. As mentioned (above § 8), it was originally written as אל הידיעות but the scribe of the Thanksgiving Scroll, or someone who proofread the text, removed it from the text when he corrected it to אל ה(י)ד(י)עות (= הַדֵּעוֹת); the person who corrected the text replaced the original phrase with a phrase taken from the prayer of Hannah: אֵל דֵּעוֹת (1 Samuel 2:3). The other two nouns מְשִׁיכָה and רְחִיצָה each appear only once in the scrolls. מְשִׁיחָה occurs only twice in the scrolls. We can say that these four nouns are to be considered like all lexemes which appear only once in the scrolls, like the words ממון, עכשו and others.[47] That is to say, we can not consider these lexemes to be characteristic examples of the *peʿila* pattern of Mishnaic Hebrew in the scrolls. Rather, these are isolated words from it that were borrowed to be used in those specific places.

§ 12 What we have said about the verbal nouns of strong roots is also valid all the more so for nouns derived from hollow roots. All of the nouns that were found in the scrolls are already attested in the Bible: בִּיאָה (one occurrence in the Bible: בַּבִּיאָה, Ezekiel 8:5);[48] בִּינָה (37 occurrences, including, תתבוננו בה בִּינָה "you shall consider it perfectly," Jeremiah 23:20, as well as in Ben Sira 6:35, ומשל בינה אל יצאך "and do not let proverbs of understanding escape you." גִּילָה occurs twice in Isaiah: once in the absolute – הנני בורא את ירושלים גִּילָה "behold, I create Jerusalem a rejoicing" (65:18) and once with the feminine ending *-at* – אף גִּילַת ורנן "even with joy and singing" (35:2).

44 This mishna is missing from the Kaufmann manuscript. The (unvocalized) reading ידיעה is found in the Cambridge manuscript (Lowe edition) and in Maimonides' version (Kafih edition). This form is vocalized יְדִיעָה in MS Paris 328–329 as well as in the printed editions. MS Parma A (De Rossi 138) reads יְדוּעָה.

45 The vocalized form מְשִׁיחָה is found in the Vatican 66 manuscript of the Sifra (see Yeivin 1985:885).

46 The vocalizations יְדִיעוֹת, מְשִׁיכָה, and רְחִיצָה do not require any evidence; they are attested in the manuscripts and in the printed editions.

47 As we have said about most of the examples brought above in §§ 2–3 and many like them.

48 This word already here has the meaning of "opening," "entry" (see above § 9 and notes 37–38).

חִידָה occurs seventeen times, for example, in ולא יכלו להגיד הַחִידָה "and they could not ... expound the riddle" (Judges 14:14); again, the word is also attested in Ben Sira (47:17): בשיר מ[ש]ל חידה ומליצה "For songs and proverbs and ridles and illustrations." קִינָה has 18 occurrences, for example ושאי על שפיים קִינָה "and take up a lamentation on high places" (Jeremiah 7:29). שִׁיבָה occurs only once, in Psalm 126:1:[49] בשוב ה' את שִׁיבַת ציון "When the LORD turned again the captivity of Zion" (Psalms 126:1). שִׂיחָה is attested three times, for example, כי עדותיך שִׂיחָה לי "for thy testimonies are my meditation" (Psalms 119:99). שִׁירָה occurs thirteen times, as in, אז ישיר משה ... את הַשִּׁירָה הזאת "Then sang Moses ... this song" (Exodus 15:1).

§ 13 As has been stated, the only noun in this pattern derived from a III-Yod root is רְמִיָּה. This noun, which occurs many times in the scrolls, is very common in the Bible. It is attested 15 times, for example in the phrases מלשון רְמִיָּה, לשון רְמִיָּה "(from) a deceitful tongue" (Psalm 120:2–3). It would be difficult to claim that the use of רְמִיָּה in the scrolls is not dependant on the Biblical usage.

§ 14 We can summarize: only isolated nouns in the *pᵉʿila* pattern that are attested in the Dead Sea Scrolls and Mishnaic Hebrew, but not in the Bible, can legitimately be said to reflect a connection between Qumran Hebrew and Mishnaic Hebrew. There are four such nouns: יְדִיעָה, מְשִׁיחָה, מְשִׁיכָה and רְחִיצָה. These are sparsely attested in the scrolls (most occurring only once). The noun יְדִיעָה was rejected by the scribe or the corrector of the Thanksgiving Scroll. The two nouns מְשִׁיכָה and רְחִיצָה occur only one time each, and מְשִׁיחָה only twice. It can be said, therefore, that the *pᵉʿila* pattern was not adopted by the authors of the Scrolls from their spoken dialect (Mishnaic Hebrew), but rather reflects the literary influence of Biblical Hebrew on the language of Qumran.

16.4 The Pattern *Pi"ul*

§ 15 The *pi"ul* pattern is the common pattern of the verbal noun of the Pi"el and Hitpa"al/Nitpa"al verbal stems in Mishnaic Hebrew. As stated, the *pi"ul* pattern is already present in the Bible;[50] many of the nouns built according to this pattern are in the plural form, such as הִלּוּלִים (Leviticus 19:24;

49 I did not mention the second occurrence of this noun (והוא כלכל את המלך בְּשִׂיבָתוֹ במחניים "and he had provided the king of sustenance while he lay at Mahanaim" [2 Samuel 19:33]), since this can be derived from the noun יְשִׁיבָה (בְּשִׂיבָתוֹ במחניים > בִּישִׁיבָתוֹ במחניים).

50 See above § 6 and footnote 26.

Judges 9:27) and שִׁלּוּחִים (Micah 1:14). In Mishnaic Hebrew this pattern is a systematic grammatical category indicating the verbal noun and the result of the action for the Pi"el and Nitpa"al verbal stems. The use of this pattern is regular for any verb in these verbal stems.[51] In Mishnaic Hebrew the nouns in the *pi"ul* pattern occur mostly in the singular, although there are quite a few nouns which occur normally in the plural. For example, there is the well known group of nouns concerned with family status which use the plural form such as אֵרוּסִין, גֵּרוּשִׁין, קִדּוּשִׁין and שִׁבּוּקִין.[52] There are also other nouns which occur mostly in the plural, such as גִּדּוּלִים.[53] There is no reason to doubt the regularity of the use of this pattern as a verbal noun, and most of the verbs in the Pi"el and Nitpa"al verbal stems have verbal nouns attested in this pattern.[54] In the event that a verb in one of these verbal stems occurs in rabbinic literature but no verbal noun in the *pi"ul* pattern is attested for it, this is to be explained as a coincidence wherein the verbal noun was not attested.

Our examination has revealed that quite a few forms in the Dead Sea Scrolls are in the *pi"ul* pattern,[55] but here too a strong affinity with Biblical Hebrew is recognizable. It is not a coincidence that a number of these forms are in the plural, like in the Bible.

§ 16 Firstly I will present the findings from the scrolls and afterwards I will analyze them. I found that there are eleven certain forms of the *pi"ul* pattern,[56] with a total of close to one hundred occurrences.

Here are the examples:

גִּבּוּל: This is the very plausible reading of Menahem Kister in a sentence from the Rule of the Community: גבול סמוך לשמור אמונים (1QS 10:25). The word גבול is not *gevul* "border, boundary," but rather *gibbul*, derived from the verb *gibbel* "to knead, form (clay)," and hence "to create human beings)." The phrase גבול סמוך is an obvious synonym, then, of the biblical expression יצר סמוך, derived from Isa 26:2–3.[57]

---

51 See the demonstration and the excellent analysis of the Mishnaic material in Elitzur 1987: 72–82, 83. (Clearly, his distinction between these two verbal stems, Pi"el and Nitpa"el, is unnecessary, since in these stems only one verbal noun is used, as Sharvit has shown. See above in § 6 and in footnote 25).

52 See Segal 1936:77; he calls them "legal terms."

53 See Elitzur 1987:71–72.

54 As stated above in § 6, Sharvit counted 190 nouns in this pattern in Tannaitic literature.

55 Almost all of the forms in the Dead Sea Scrolls are written defectively, without *yod* (see Qimron 1976:53–57).

56 For this purpose I used a list that I had prepared together with the list prepared by Elisha Qimron (see above towards the end of footnote 30). Here too I ignored doubtful forms in the data presented here.

57 See the thorough and convincing discussion in Kister's important study: Kister 2000:157.

הִלּוּלִים: We read in the Temple Scroll יקדישו לו עם כול קוד[ש] הלוליהמה "they hallow me, with all their hol[y] (fruit) offering of praise" (60:4).

יִסּוּרִים: Apparently, all of the occurrences of this form in the scrolls are in the plural form יִסּוּרִים – as in Mishnaic Hebrew. Here are two examples out of the nine that I collected. First, in the Damascus Document: וכמשפט היסורים כסרך התורה "and the precept to instruct according to the rule of the Torah" (CD MS A 7.8); second, in the Rule of the Community: כי געלה נפשו ביסורי דעת "his soul detests instructions about knowledge" (1QS 3:1). Based on the fact that this word occurs eight times in the scrolls in the plural form, and that in Mishnaic Hebrew this word is also almost always plural,[58] it seems to me that we should read another occurrence as the nomen regens in the plural: בתמים קדש על פי כול יסורי[58a] [= יִסּוּרֵי] ברית אל "in perfect holiness (and) are governed according to all these instructions of God's covenant" (CD MS A 7:5).

כִּבּוּס: In the Damascus Document: אל יבא טמא כבוס "let him not come (when he is still) unclean after washing" (CD MS A 11.22); and also אל יבוא טמא כבוס "let him not come when he is unclean (due to un-)washed clothing" (4Q271 5i 15).

כִּיּוּר: This noun is attested in one certain occurrence in the Temple Scroll: ומקורה כיור ארז מצופה זהב טהור (26, 10–11). Yadin correctly vocalized this word כִּיּוּר and explained "this is a general noun for the adorned part of the roof which was visible from the outside."[59]

מִלּוּאִים: This noun occurs only once in the Temple Scroll: ולמלואים איל איל לכ[ו]ל "And for the consecration one ram for ea[ch" (11Q20 I, 12).

נִסּוּי: This noun appears as least five times in the scrolls, for example in the Paroles des Luminaires: ולא מאסנו בנסוייכה "we have not rejected your ordeals" (4Q504 1–2 vi 7); and in the Rule of the Community: ולא לשוב מאחרו מכול פחד ואימה ומצרף נסוים בממשלת בליעל "They must not turn back from following after him because of any terror, dread, affliction or agony during the reign of *Belial*" (1:17–18).

עִזּוּז: This noun occurs once in a liturgical text: ובמופתיכה ועזוז ימינכ[ה] "and your wonders and the might of your right hand" (4Q451 3).

פֵּרוּשׁ: There are at least seven occurrences of this noun in the scrolls: three in the Damascus Document and four in the War Scroll. For example: פרוש המשפטים "elaboration of the laws" (4Q266 11:18); פרוש שמותם "list of their names" (1QM 4:64, 6).

---

58 I have shown the possibility that the singular form may be attested in a Tannaitic work: יִסּוּר (see Bar-Asher 2009a:250 § 22; there is evidence that this singular form occurs in Ben Sira (see below § 17B).

58a Not יְסוֹדוֹ.

59 See Yadin 1977:110. Qimron agreed with his opinion (Qimron 1980:255).

שִׁלּוּם: This noun occurs at least five times in the scrolls. Here is one example from the Thanksgiving Scroll: ופקודת שלומם עם כול נגעיהם "and the order of their payment with all of their afflictions" (9[7]:19–20).

תִּכּוּן: This noun is very widespread in the scrolls, with approximately sixty occurrences. For example in the Rule of the Community: על פיהם יצא תכון הגורל לכל דבר "According to their order shall go forth the determination of the lot about everything" (1QS 5.3); in the War Scroll: מלומדי רכב ותכון ימיהם "drilled to mount, and the measure of their days" (1QM 6.13); and in the מוסר למבין = Instruction[d]: במוזני צדק שקל כול תכונם "For with righteous balances He has weighed out all their measurement" (4Q418 127 6).

§ 17 The collection of nouns detailed above is not uniform in so far as the relation of the various nouns to other layers of the Hebrew language. These nouns can be divided into two groups:

A. Six nouns were borrowed from the Bible in their exact form or they have a clear affinity to the Bible. It is clear that the use of the noun הִלּוּלִים – in the phrase קוד[ש] הלוליהמה – is based on the Biblical verse יהיה כל פריו קֹדֶשׁ הִלּוּלִים לה' "all the fruit thereof shall be holy to praise the Lord" (Leviticus 19:24). Also, the word מִלֻּאִים – in the phrase ולמלואים איל איל לכ]ול – was taken in its exact form from the Bible. This usage is clearly connected to the many verses that speak of איל המלואים "a ram of consecration" (such as in Exodus 29:22; Leviticus 8:22 and many others).[60] The nouns עִזּוּז and שִׁלּוּם are also borrowed from the Bible. The former appears in the verse רכב וסוס חיל ועִזּוּז "the chariot and horse, the army and the power" (Isaiah 43:17),[61] and the occurrence of this noun in Ben Sira (45:18) should be understood thus as well: ועדת קרח בעזוז אפם "and the gathering of Korah in the strength of their wrath." It is easy to see the connection between the quote cited earlier – ופקודת שלומם – and the verse באו ימי הַפְּקֻדָּה ימי הַשִּׁלֻּם "The days of visitation are come, the days of recompense are come" (Hosea 9:7).

We can add to this list the nouns נִסּוּי and תִּכּוּן. נִסּוּי is first attested in the Dead Sea Scrolls[62] and in Ben Sira. In Ben Sira we find: כי אם בנסוי ישוב ונמלט (36:1); ובניסוי נמצא נאמן (44:20).[63] The noun נִסּוּי can be

60 In the edition of Ben Sira of the Historical Dictionary Project of the Academy of the Hebrew Language the text reads פתוחי חותם במל[ואים] (45:11). In my opinion it would have been preferable to complete the word thus: במל[ואותם]. But I will not deal with this matter here.

61 However, the second occurrence of this word – ה' עִזּוּז וגבור "The Lord strong and mighty" (Psalms 24:8) – is a participle (functioning as an adjective) from the root עז"ז like לָמוּד from למ"ד. See what I wrote on this topic elsewhere (Bar-Asher 2008 § 32).

62 As was shown above in § 18.

63 The reference is to Abraham of whom the Bible states והאלהים נִסָּה את אברהם (Genesis 22:1).

clearly connected to the biblical verb נִסָּה in the verse והאלהים נִסָּה את אברהם “and God put Abraham to the test” (Genesis 22:1), and in other verses such as למען ענתך לְנַסֹּתְךָ “to humble you, to prove you” (Deuteronomy 8:2). Also תִּכּוּן, which is a noun characteristic of the Dead Sea Scrolls and which attested only in those texts within the entire corpus of Classical Hebrew,[64] is connected to the biblical verb תִּכֵּן (Isaiah 43:1, etc.).
§ 18

B. Five nouns – פֵּרוּשׁ, כִּיּוּר, כִּבּוּס, יִסּוּרִים, גִּבּוּל – were, until recently, thought to have been first attested within Mishnaic Hebrew (for the most part in Tannaitic Hebrew). Some of the examples are:

גִּבּוּל: עפר, דְּבר[65] גבול הוא “soil, which is kneadable” (b. Shabbat 18a)[66]

יִסּוּרִים: חביבין יסורין “suffering is desirable” (Sifre Deuteronomy § 32). Note that this word is also found in Ben Sira: יסור מעים “suffering of the intestines” (40:29) and also ויסרתיהו באסורים “will torment him with training” (4:17), with *aleph* instead of *yod*.

כִּבּוּס: אינו טעון כבוס “it does not require washing” (m. Zevahim 11:3)

כִּיּוּר: המוצא פלטרין בנכסי הגר וסד בהן סיוד אחד או כיור אחד קנאן “If a man finds a villa already erected on the estate of a [deceased] proselyte, and he adds one coat of whitewash or mural decoration,[67] he acquires ownership” (b. Baba Batra 53b)[68]

64 In using the term “Classical Hebrew,” I mean the Hebrew that had as its background as a living, spoken language (i.e. Biblical Hebrew, the language of Ben Sira, Qumran Hebrew and the language of the Tanna’im).

65 In this phrase only the word דְּבר (דְּ + בַר) is Aramaic, indicating that soil is kneadable.

66 The verb is attested in Tannaitic Hebrew (in the Qal and) Pi“el stem, for example נותנין מים לתוך קמח [...] שלא יגבל “One may put water into dough ... he should not knead it into a mass” (t. Shabbat 12:14).

67 The Ben Yehuda dictionary notes that there are witnesses that the text is faulty (they read כיוד with *dalet*), but the note states that the ‘Arukh also gives the spelling כיור with *resh*. See the quote from the Mishna in the following footnote (67) which brings the text סיידו וכיירו; the verb is כִּיֵּר in the Pi“el stem, and the verbal noun is כִּיּוּר. It is important to note that the word כִּיּוּר appears in Targum Yonatan: the phrase וספון בארז “paneled with cedar” (Jeremiah 22:14) is translated as מטלל בכיורי ארזיא (= covered with panels [= decorations] of cedar), and the phrase בבתיכם ספונים “your well-roofed houses” (Haggai 1:4) is translated as בבתיא דמטללין בכיורי ארזיא (= in houses roofed with decorations of cedar). The vocalization בְּכִיּוּרֵי with *vav* and *šuruq*, which is brought by Sperber in the texual variants,is to be preferred over בְּכִיּוֹרֵי with *holam* which appears in the text itself (Stadel 2008:70 n. 523 comments on these two verses in Targum Yonatan).

68 As stated, the verb כִּיֵּר is attested in Tannaitic Hebrew, for example בית שבניו מתחילה לשם עבודה זרה ... סיידו וְכִיְּירוֹ לשם עבודה זרה וחידש נוטל מה שחידש “if a house was built from the first for idolatry ... if it was plastered and bedecked for idolatry, or if aught was done to it anew, one only need remove what was done to it anew” (m. ‘Avoda Zara 3:7 according to MS Kaufmann).

פֵּרוּשׁ: פירושו של דבר "the meaning of the thing" (t. Taʿanit 2:10).

Thus, most of the forms in the *piʿʿul* pattern in the scrolls are attested in the Bible or are linked to biblical verbs. Only a minority (albeit a not insignificant minority) are known from Mishnaic Hebrew. However, all of these forms, with the exception of פֵּרוּשׁ, are sparsely attested in Qumran Hebrew.

§ 19 I wish to add two marginal comments to the above discussion concerning two nouns which were not included in paragraphs 16–18: יסוד and למודים.

A. The grapheme יסוד is ambiguous. It can represent the form יְסוֹד or the form יִסּוּד.[69] In the Temple Scroll we read וזרקו את דמו על יסוד מזבח העולה "… on the base of the altar of burnt offering" (52:21). Clearly this echoes the language of the verse in Leviticus אל יְסוֹד[70] המזבח "at the bottom of the altar" (for example 4:7; 4:18; 4:25). However, it is possible that some of the graphemes יסוד in the scrolls are to be vocalized יִסּוּד like the two examples below.[71] Here is an example from the Thanksgiving Scroll: תמיד בכול מולדי עת יסוד קץ "always in all beginnings of time, the foundation of the end" (20[12]:10–11). And an example from the Rule of the Community: והאיש אשר ילון על יסוד היחד "The man who grumbles against the authority of the Community" (1QS 7:17). Due to the uncertainty the grapheme יסוד was removed from the list in paragraph 16 above.

B. The noun לִמּוּדִים was also not included above in § 16. This noun appears at least seven times in the scrolls, four times with *plene* spelling (לימוד); four of the occurrences are in the Thanksgiving Scroll. For example, ולשוני כלמודיך "and my tongue as your teaching" (15[7]:13), אוזן בלמודיך "ear in your teaching" (1Q428 10:7), etc. Most, if not all, of these occurrences should be interpreted as passive participle forms of the *piʿʿul* pattern, לִמּוּד (a variant of תלמיד as in the Bible), and not as verbal nouns in the same pattern. There are two details that bear emphasizing. First, six out of seven

69 As is well known, the Tiberian tradition of the Bible provides a third form – יְסֻוד in the Peʿul pattern which is reflected in the phrase יְסֻד המעלה (Ezra 7:9). See what I wrote elsewhere: Bar-Asher 2009a 2:262 § 18 in the first footnote.

70 The Samaritan tradition also has the form יְסוֹד (yēsod), according to Ben-Ḥayyim 1957–1977:5.123. In fact, this is how it appears in the Babylonian vocalization, only that the *yod* with *shewa* is frequently replaced by *ḥiriq* as Yeivin (1985:906) pointed out.

71 This was apparently was Qimron had in mind when he included יסוד in the nouns in the *piʿʿul* pattern with which he was kind enough to provide me (see above the end of footnote 30).

occurrences are in the plural form – לימודים[72] – just like three of the four[73] occurrences of this noun in the Bible. Second, and even more important, is the connection between the usages of the word in the scrolls and the usages in the Bible. Obviously, this can only be said regarding the three occurrences in which the word appears in clear contexts. When the attestation is isolated, devoid of any context, it is impossible to say anything about the usage.[74] Here are the contexts of the three clear occurrences: the phrase למודי אל "taught by God" (CD MS B 20.4) is similar to the phrase לִמּוּדֵי ה' "taught of the LORD" (Isaiah 54:13); ולשוני כלמודיך "and my tongue as your teaching" (Thanksgiving Scroll 15[7]:13) is reminiscent of the scriptural expression לְשׁוֹן לִמּוּדִים "the tongue of the learned" (Isaiah 50:4); the phrase אוזן בלמודיך (1Q428 10:7) echoes the verse יעִיר לִי אֹזֶן לִשְׁמֹעַ כַּלִּמּוּדִים "he wakes my ear to hear like the learned" (Isaiah 50:4).

§ 20 In summation, most of the occurrences of the words in the *pi"ul* pattern in the Dead Sea Scrolls show a clear affinity to the Bible, with only *isolated* forms having an affinity to Mishnaic Hebrew. Examples of these are the use of the noun גודל, the verb יופך and the particle עכשו.[75] These examples indicate the penetration of isolated forms from the spoken language in this pattern, similar to the isolated forms in the scrolls from the *pe'ila* pattern, but do not reflect the consolidation of a systematic grammatical category in Qumran Hebrew.

16.5 Concluding Remarks

§ 21 Certainly, discovering elements common to Mishnaic Hebrew and Qumran Hebrew is an important task in and of itself. Every detail common to the two linguistic strata has importance for a number of reasons. Above all its importance lies in giving historical depth to the words or to the grammatical phenomena in Mishnaic Hebrew that already appear in the scrolls. I mean that

72 The sole occurrence in the singular form is in a portion of a scroll of blessings לשמוע למודו (4Q434 1 i4); perhaps this is also the plural form spelled defectively (למודו instead of למודיו, which is present in the scrolls; see Kutscher 1959:350; Qimron 1976:231–232. As is well known, others scholars also dealt with this issue). However, it should be noted that there is an alternative: the noun למוד may function as the verbal noun of the Pi"el verbal stem.

73 The sole singular form in the Bible is in the verse פרא לִמֻּד מדבר "a wild ass used to the wilderness" (Jeremiah 2:24).

74 For example we can not learn anything from the lack of context in this occurrence: [בלמודיכה] (Thanksgiving Scroll 12[2]:39).

75 See above § 2.

the discovery of these common elements adds an important chapter to their history. That is, we learn that they existed hundreds of years before Mishnaic Hebrew became consolidated as a literary medium following the destruction of the Second Temple. Therefore, the discovery and collection of these elements by scholars is a desideratum.

§ 22 It is very important to follow the development of words and isolated grammatical forms, but especially of complete grammatical categories. In this study I examined two grammatical categories, the verbal noun patterns *peʿila* and *piʿʿul*, in a comprehensive and detailed way. It turns out that the authors of the scrolls borrowed words in these patterns especially from Biblical Hebrew and to a much lesser extent from their spoken language. One of these language types is known to us as Mishnaic Hebrew which served as the written medium for Rabbinic literature. That is to say, the few words from these patterns that are common to both the language of the scrolls and to Mishnaic Hebrew do not indicate a common linguistic element shared by the scrolls and Mishnaic Hebrew. Rather, it indicates the few details in the two patterns which are common to the two periods. These details are to be considered as all of the many, isolated words in Mishnaic Hebrew which already appear in the Dead Sea Scrolls.

§ 23 In short, we can say that the most important element of the connection between Mishnaic Hebrew and most of the linguistic points in Qumran Hebrew are limited to details, namely, nouns, verbs, particles, and phrases from the spoken language, known to us from Rabbinic literature, which penetrated the writings of the authors of the scrolls. Among all of these details we find various forms of the verbal nouns in the *peʿila* and *piʿʿul* patterns, such as יְדִיעָה and גִּבּוּל. The appearance of these forms at Qumran should be considered in much the same fashion as the appearance of the words גֶּדֶל, מָמוֹן, and עַכְשָׁו. In other words, the authors of the scrolls utilized forms like יְדִיעָה and גִּבּוּל, drawn from their spoken language, in their writings in a sporadic fashion. These do not represent linguistic categories common to both Qumran Hebrew and Mishnaic Hebrew.

§ 24 I wish to strongly stress that any investigation into the connection between Qumran Hebrew and Mishnaic Hebrew needs to take into account various linguistic aspects, but firstly an effort must be made to uncover all of the details common to two literary collections from two different periods in time. Afterwards it will be possible to use this material in order to address other linguistic issues such as the historical dimension of the phenomena mentioned or the question of the different dialects of Hebrew during the Second Temple period and following that period. A collection of the data in this area and a discussion of these two important topics – the historical dimension of the phenomena mentioned and the importance of these phenomena for the description of different dialects of the spoken Hebrew during the Second Temple period and the tannaitic period – as well as others topics, can be found in a detailed study that I published a few years ago.[76] The goal of this study was to model the type of research needed by offering a refinement of the data regarding two grammatical categories, while also allowing us to discuss these basic issues as well as others.

76 See Bar-Asher 2010 = Bar-Asher 2012:196–212.

C. Mishnaic Hebrew and Aramaic

17 Mishnaic Hebrew: An Introductory Survey

17.1 Mishnaic Hebrew and Rabbinic literature

§ 1 Mishnaic Hebrew (MH) is the language of the Tannaim and Amoraim in Palestine and Babylonia. The Hebrew name for the language of these writings is *Ləšōn ḥăkhāmīn*, which means literally, "the language of the sages." Literature in MH covers a period of about 450 years, roughly between 70 CE and 500 CE. The literature of the Tannaim – which includes the Mishnah, the Tosefta, the halachic midrashim and Seder 'Olam Rabba – was redacted approximately between 70 CE and 250 CE. The literature of the Amoraim was formed over a period beginning at the end of the third century and continuing to about 500 CE. In Palestine, the work of the Amoraim includes the Jerusalem Talmud and the ancient aggadic midrashim, such as the Genesis Rabbah, Leviticus Rabba, and Pesiqta de Rab Kahana; in Babylonia, the works of the Amoraim is represented by the Babylonian Talmud.

§ 2 Most Tannaitic texts were redacted in roughly the period 200–250 CE, when Rabbi Judah the Patriarch completed his compilation of the Mishnah. However, research has shown that the Mishnah contains a great deal of material contemporary with the destruction of the Second Temple in 70 CE. Most of this material consists of texts describing the ceremonies performed while the temple still stood.[1] Thus, the offerings of first fruits (Bikkurim 3) is described almost wholly in the present tense, by one who had been present at this ceremony.

§ 3 Research has further shown that Hebrew was spoken in Palestine until roughly 200 CE. The view is generally accepted that the Hebrew preserved in Tannaitic literature reflects living speech current in various regions of Palestine.[2] The literature of the Amoraim, however, was formed in an environment where, in all probability, Aramaic rather than Hebrew was spoken. The dialect then current in Palestine is now termed Galilean Aramaic, or Jewish Palestinian Aramaic,[3] while the dialect current in Babylonia is termed Babylonian Aramaic. It is well known that certain portions of the literature of the Amoraim,

1 Epstein 1957: 21–58.

2 There is little doubt that Hebrew continued to be spoken here and there in Palestine at the time of the Amoraim, several generations after the close of the Mishnah. See Kutscher 1972:57–60, and the Oxford papyrus mentioned in § 4 below.

3 It is very likely that in Galilee, during the period of the Amoraim, the Jews spoke Aramaic only (except that Greek, too, was spoken in such cities as Tiberias and Beth-Shean). Some of their major literary works, however, continued to be produced in Hebrew (cf. Kutscher 1972:57–60).

both in Palestine and in Babylonia, are written in Aramaic, or on occasion in a mixture of Hebrew and Aramaic.

§ 4 The language reflected in the texts of rabbinic literature is also known to us from sources external to rabbinic literature itself, such as the Copper Scroll from Qumran,[4] the letters of Simon Bar-Koseba (Bar Kokhba) discovered in the Judean desert and dating to 132–135 CE,[5] synagogue inscriptions,[6] and also from slightly later letters, like that found in an Oxford papyrus dating from about 500 CE.[7] All these documents attest Hebrew as a spoken language used in daily life and not merely as a language of scholarship restricted to the learned.

---

4 The consensus of scholarly opinion would date it around the middle of the first century CE.

5 Kutscher 1977:66–67 surveys briefly the feature which MH shares with the Hebrew letters of Bar-Koseba. Examples are אַתֶּן (*'atten* as second person masculine plural pronoun) and אֵלּוּ (*'ellū*, plural demonstrative). Compare the important observations of Yalon in his chapter on spoken Hebrew (1964: 204–208).

6 This corpus is analysed in detail by Joseph Naveh (1978). See for example the inscription of Kfar-Bar'am (pp. 19–20): יהי שלום במקום הזה ובכל מקומות ישראל, יוסה הלוי בן לוי עשה השקוף הזה, תבא ברכה במע[ש]יו של[ו]ם "May there be peace in this place, and in every place in Israel. Yosé the Levite son of Levi made this lintel. May blessing come upon his works. Farewell." This text presents at least two features that point clearly to MH. The first is יוסה (*yōsē*), a name characteristic of the rabbinic period, and very probably an abbreviated form of יוסף (*yōsēph*). The spelling of the final vowel with *he* rather than the usual *yod* is unique to Palestine. The second feature is the word for "lintel." While biblical Hebrew (e.g., Exod 12:7, 22, 23) uses משקוף, the inscription has שקוף instead, which is typical of the Mishnah (e.g., Neg. XII 4, in both manuscripts and printed editions). It is true that H. J. Kosovsky's concordance to the Mishnah shows seven occurences of משקוף, but that concordance is based on printed editions, and in six of these passages the best manuscripts (Parma B, K) have שקוף. The six passages are as follows: (a) אין בינה לבין השקוף "between it and the lintel there was not …" (m. Ohalot 9:10); (b) והיא נוגעת בשקוף "it would … touch the lintel" (m. Ohalot 10:7); (c) and (d) מכנגד השקוף "opposite the lintel" (Ohalot 11:7); (e) and (f) מודבק לשקוף … הנוגע בשקוף "[if it] cleaved to the lintel … [if one] touched the lintel" (Ohalot 12:8[10]). The printed editions, however, systematically show the biblical form משקוף. There is only one place in the Mishnah where the true reading appears to be משקוף, namely, וטעון הזאה באגודת אזוב על המשקוף ועל המזוזות (m. Pesahaim 9:5: "this required sprinkling with a bunch of hyssop on the lintel and the side posts"). This is, however, a clear reference to the biblical prescription: ולקחו מן הדם ונתנו על שתי המזוזות ועל המשקוף "they shall take of the blood and put it on the two sideposts and on the lintel (ועל המשקוף)" (Exod 12:7). See, further §§ 13–15 and note 32 below.

7 Cf. Mishor 1989b. A few examples from the document are לעזר בן יוסה "Le'azar son of Yosé" (l. 4), מפני שבאת לכאן "since you came here" (l. 7), בערב השבת "on the eve of the Sabbath" (l. 16). This document tends to confirm the hypothesis that Hebrew continued to be used in daily life in some corner of Eretz Israel during and even beyond the period of the Amoraim (see n. 2 above).

17.2 The Origin of Mishnaic Hebrew

§ 5 Down to 200 BCE – in other words, prior to the Hasmonean period – the literary language of the Jews was Biblical Hebrew (BH), even in the late books of the Bible, such as Ezra–Nehemiah, Chronicles, and Esther. Literary works from before and after the exile, despite their grammatical and lexical differences, share an impressive array of common features. Most of the Qumran writings, composed (or copied) between 200 BCE and 100 CE, likewise exhibit a biblical style, despite the presence of certain special features, some of which re-appear in MH.[8] MH did not become a *literary language*, as stated above, until the end of the first century CE. What exactly is its origin?

§ 6 Most scholars agree that MH originates in the language spoken in various regions of Palestine throughout the period of the Second Temple. Some for further and believe that it reflects a Hebrew dialect of the era of the first Temple.[9] It is true that certain characteristics of the language of the Mishnah already appear sporadically in the Bible, proving that at least those features existed already then in some dialect, centuries before their appearance in MH. For example, the word בִּזָּיוֹן (*bizzāyōn*), meaning "outrage" or "contempt," is a typically mishnaic term, as in the following examples: רצה הכהן לנהוג ביזיון בעצמו אין שומעין לו "If a priest wished to behave contemptuously towards himself, one does not listen to him" (T. Sanh. 4:1), שלא לנהוג ביזיון בקדשים "so as not to treat holy things with contempt" (Y. Shab 11, 2; 13a). This word appears for the first time in Esth 1:18: וכדי ביזיון וקצף; "whence (will come) contempt and anger."

A second example: It is well known that MH uses the form *pā'ōl* as a *nomen agentis*, for example, *sārōq* "wool comber" (Kelim 26:5),[10] *ṭāḥōn* "miller" (Makhshirim 3:5).[11] This form is typical of MH, setting it apart from BH. Yet we find the first traces of this form in the book of Jeremiah, written more

8 See, e.g., Ben-Ḥayyim 1958 and Yalon 1967:29–30, 32–33, etc.

9 See Lifschitz 1917:40, and also Bar-Asher 1988:6, § 4 (and literature there cited) = below, chap. 18, § 4 nn. 12–18.

10 עוֹר הַסָּרוֹק (so MS K) "the hide of the comber," i.e., "the hide worn by the wool-comber."

11 The text in fact has המוליך חיטים לַטָּחוֹן "one who carries the wheat to the miller" (for grinding). The reading לַטָּחוֹן is found in two excellent manuscripts, Parma B and Antonin. In MS K and the editions, however, the word לטחון has been vocalized לִטְחוֹן "to grind," a *qal* infinitive. Likewise, in another passage of the Mishnah (Demai 3:4), the printed editions show three successive occurrence of the form לַטּוֹחֵן, i.e., the present participle being used as a noun: המוליך חיטים לטוחן כותי או לטוחן עם הארץ ... לטוחן נכרי "one who brings wheat to a Samaritan miller, or an ignorant miller ... or a gentile miller." The best manuscripts, however (MSS K and Parma A), as well as ten others, have instead three successive occurrences טָחוֹן, of the type *pā'lōn*. Cf. Segal 1936:75, 94.

than 700 years before the close of the Mishnah.[12] There we find the words *bāḥōn* (Jer 6:27) "watcher," *'āšōq* (Jer 22:3) "oppressor," *ṣārōph* (Jer 6:29) "metal-founder," *bāḡōḏā* (Jer 3:7, 10) "traitress." Likewise, it seems that the word *ḥ^{a}lōmōṯēḵem* (27:9; 29:8) should not be derived from *ḥ^{a}lōm* and rendered "your dreams," bur rather understood as "your dreamers," from *ḥālōm* "dreamer."[13]

Cases of this sort may be found in the biblical texts from the end of the First Temple period onwards, but especially in the post-exilic period. They attest the existence of a Hebrew dialect which was gaining currency towards the end of the biblical period but was to become a written language only after several centuries had passed. It was in fact to become the *written language* of the Tannaim, that is, Mishnaic Hebrew.

17.3 Biblical Hebrew and Mishnaic Hebrew

17.3.1 Common and Contrasting Features

§ 7 On comparing the grammar and vocabulary of MH with those of BH, one discovers numerous features common to the two eras (and literary corpuses) of the language. A few scholars go so far as to consider the grammar of BH and MH identical, particularly with regard to morphology.[14] However, there are undeniable differences between the two periods.[15] Here let us note the following phenomena:

A. Certain features of BH have disappeared in MH. For example, the modal forms of *yaf'ul*, such as the cohortative (*'āšīrāh* "I will sing," *'aqūmāh* "I

12 Cf. Segal 1939:154–156; Bar-Asher 1977:135–137 (= Bar-Asher 2009a 2:137–143), Bar-Asher 1985:93–94 (= Bar-Asher 2009a 1:123).

13 The vocalization חָלוֹמוֹתֵיכֶם (*ḥālōmōṯēḵem*) might have been expected. Indeed, the Masoretic vocalization חֲלֹמֹתֵיכֶם (*ḥ^{a}lōmōṯēḵem*) may well intend the plural of חֲלוֹם (*ḥ^{a}lōm*) rather than חָלוֹם (*ḥālōm*). However, the context shows that dreamers (and not their dreams) are meant, as the ancient versions recognized (cf. the excellent analysis in Segal 1939:154–155). Furthermore, the vocalization *ḥ^{a}lōmōṯēḵem* need not in fact indicate that *ḥālōm* was confused with *ḥ^{a}lōm* at all. This reading may rather reflect dissimilation of vowel quantity (*ḥālōmōṯēḵem* > *ḥ^{a}lōmōṯēḵem*), to avoid too many long vowels in succession. This phenomenon can be observed in the Bible in relation to other words. Thus, the feminine plural of צִידוֹנִי (*ṣīḏōnī*) is צֵדְנִיּוֹת (*ṣēḏniyyōṯ*) rather than *ṣēḏōnīyyōṯ*: the proximity of the other long vowels has caused syncope of the long vowel [ō] in the second syllable.

14 This question is the subject of Ben-Ḥayyim 1985.

15 This is the position of Bar-Asher 1985 (= Bar-Asher 2009a Vol. 1, chap. 5), as against that of Ben-Ḥayyim 1985.

will arise," *nāgīlāh* "let us rejoice!") are common in BH but completely absent in MH. Similarly, the shortened *yafʿul* (or jussive, e.g., *yāqōm* "may he fulfill," *ta'ᵃmēn* "have faith"), current in BH, has disappeared almost completely from MH.

B. Certain features typical of MH are almost wholly absent from BH. One example is the type *paʿlān/poʿlān*, used for nouns indicating occupation or quality, such as *gazlān/gozlān* ("thief"), *sarḇān/sorḇān* ("rebel").[16] Another feature of MH, never found in the Bible, is the type *niṯpa"el*, with nun (alongside *miṯpa"el*, with *mem*), for the present participle of the intensive-reflexive conjugation.[17]

C. Other features, too, are rare in BH but exceedingly frequent in MH. Thus there are hardly 30 occurences of *-īn* as the plural ending in the Bible; examples are *millīn* "words" (Job 12:11, and twelve further occurences, as against *millīm* in ten passages) and *ṣīḏōnīn* ("Sidonians," 1 Kings 11:33). Such cases are probably Aramaisms, limited to a few texts. However, the phenomenon becomes very common in MH. Its widening currency should be attributed not to Aramaic influence but rather to a phonological law connected to the treatment of the consonants *m/n* at the end of a word.[18]

The differences between BH and MH are particularly obvious in the realm of vocabulary. We need only cite one example, the word *ṣibbūr*. In the Bible, its meaning is "heap," as in שִׂימוּ אוֹתָם שְׁנֵי צִבֻּרִים פֶּתַח הַשַּׁעַר ("Put them in two heaps at the entrance of the gate," 2 Kgs 10:8). This sense is likewise found in MH, for example: שני צבורי זיתים וחרובים "two heaps of olives and carobs (Pe'ah 6:4). The principal and far more common meaning of the word, however, is "community," as in the following examples: אל תפרוש מן הציבור "do not separate from the community" ('Avot 2:4); העוסק בצרכי ציבור כעוסק בדברי תורה "he that occupies himself with the needs of the community has as much merit as he that occupies himself with Torah" (J. Berakhot 5, 1; 8d).

17.3.2 Diachronic Differences

§ 8 The differences between BH and MH can be seen on examination to be due in large measure to the chronological gap between them. The linguistic

16 Although the patterns *paʿlān/poʿlān* in fact occur in the Bible, they never designate followers of particular occupations or the like.

17 See Bar-Asher 1977:128–135.

18 See Bar-Asher 1985:84, n. 44, and references there cited. A fuller discussion of the examples mentioned in this paragraph will be found there on pp. 77–86.

situation of MH reflects a stage subsequent to that of MH. For example, the reflexive-passive form of the new intensive conjugation is expressed by *hiṯpa“al/hiṯpa“el* in the Bible, but by *niṯpa“al* in MH. Linguistic analysis shows that mishnaic form results from a development due to the analogy of the reflexive form of the simple action, *niph‘al*, whence initial *nun* has been borrowed.

§ 9 In the semantic domain, we may cite the word מְזוּזָה, *mᵉzūzā*. In the Bible, this indicates one of the two doorposts which stand to the left and right of the threshold and support the lintel. Examples are:

A. והגישו אדניו אל האלהים והגישו אל הדלת או אל המזוזה "his master shall bring him before the tribunal, and take him near the door or the doorpost" (Exod 21:6).

B. ולקחו מן הדם ונתנו על שתי המזוזות ועל המשקוף "they shall take from the blood and place it on the two doorposts and on the lintel" (Exod 12:7).

Mishnaic *mᵉzūzā*, however, indicates mostly the little parchment scroll upon which the two extracts of Deuteronomy (6:4–9 and 11:13–21) were copied, and which is fixed upon the right-hand doorpost in a Jewish house. For example: אין כותבין ספרים תפילין ומזוזות במועד "one does not copy scrolls (of the Torah) or (verses of) phylacteries or *mᵉzūzōt* on (the intermediate days of) a festival" (Mo‘ed Qaṭṭan 3:4).

In this case, too, it is clear that the sense of the word in MH results from diachronic change within the language: metonymy leads from a general sense to a specific sense connected with the Jewish way of life as determined by rabbinic law in the time of the Mishnah.

17.3.3 Dialectal differences

§ 10 Diachronic explanations, however, do not suffice to explain all the differences between the two strata of the language. In fact, on close scrutiny, one finds cases where MH actually shows a more ancient form than BH. Consider, for example, the proto-Semitic word **laylay* "night." This appears in the Bible in three forms: 1) *laylā*, 2) *layil*, 3) *lēl*. The first of these forms shows the reduction of the second diphthong *ay* > *ā*.[19] The two other forms, *layil* and *lēl*,

19 The diphthong *ay* is usually reduced in Hebrew to *ē*, e.g., בַּיִת (*bayiṯ/baiṯ*) > בֵּית (*bēṯ*). Sometimes, however, it is reduced to *ī*, as in דַּיִשׁ (*dayiš/dais*) > דִּישׁוֹ (*dīšō*, Deut 25:4). Occasionally it is reduced to *ā*, as in עֵינָם (*‘ēnām*, Josh 15:34), which is simply a reflex of עֵינַיִם (*‘ēnayim*, e.g., Gen 38:14). However, *laylā* can alternatively be explained as *layl* + adverbial *ā*, lit., then, "at night," which then became the simple noun "night."

are due to haplology. That is to say, one of the two diphthongs has dropped out: *laylay* > *layil*/*lēl*. Now, in MH we find a fourth form, *lēlē*, in the construct form of the singular. For example: לילה ויום כְּלֵילֵי שבת ויומו "a night and a day, like the night and the day of the Sabbath" (Nid 4:4). The context shows clearly that לֵילֵי is a singular, not a plural.[20] This form derives from *laylay* and has undergone in both syllables the normal monophthongization *ay* > *ē*. Remarkably, it is in MH, the later stage of the language, that we find the form which most resembles the primitive quadriconsonantal form *laylay* (root l.y.l.y).

Let us take a further example. In BH, the near demonstratives ("this") are the singular is זֶה (*ze*, masc.) and זֹאת (*zōṯ*, fem.). In MH, however, the two forms are זֶה (*ze*) and זוֹ (*zō*).[21] Comparative grammar shows that the form זוֹ, cognate with Aramaic דָּא,[22] is the older form, and זֹאת is a secondary form, derived from *zō* + *ṯ*: the *t* feminine ending has been added to mark the feminine more transparently.[23]

§ 11 How can one explain the fact that MH sometimes presents a more archaic form than BH for the same word? It is obviously not sufficient to imagine these two as two successive states of the language. We have to think, rather, of two simultaneous but distinct states, reflecting two different dialects. In other words, MH is the continuation not of BH itself, but of a related dialect. There is no other way to explain how the *later* form of Hebrew, that is, MH,

---

20 The mishnah is dealing with a period of 24 hours (לילה ויום "a night and a day"), and takes as an example לילי שבת ויומו, i.e., the duration of the night and day of the Sabbath.

21 The demonstrative *zō* is hardly ever found in the Bible, while *zōt* hardly ever appears in rabbinic literature. For further details, see Bar-Asher 1985:90–91, with notes 67–68.

22 The Arabic cognate, as is known, is *hāḏā*, which is, however, used for the masculine only.

23 One could not, of course, maintain that all forms which appear in a more archaic form in MH than in BH go back to different dialects. This caveat applies with particular force in the realm of vocabulary. For example, חתך "cut, slice," is found in the Bible only in the figurative sense "to decide, decree," as in שָׁבֻעִים שִׁבְעִים נֶחְתַּךְ עַל עַמְּךָ "seventy weeks are decreed upon your people" (Dan 9:24). The concrete sense, which must have been primary, appears first in MH, e.g., חתך את הראש ... חתך את הכרעים ... חתך את הידים "he cut off the head ... he cut off the shanks ... he cut off the forelegs" (m. Tamid 4:2); another occurrence is ואין חותכין את הפתילה לשנים "nor may one sever a wick into two" (Beṣah 4:4).

Another word whose primary sense appears in MH rather than BH is זֶרֶת. It BH it indicates a unit of measurement: זֶרֶת אָרְכּוֹ וְזֶרֶת רָחְבּוֹ "its length was one span, its breadth was one span" (Exod 28:16; 39:9). In MH, by contrast, זרת indicates the little finger (perhaps originally from זערת, as in b. Menaḥot 11a, which gives the terms for the five fingers: זו זרת, זו קמיצה, זו אמה, זו אצבע, זו גודל. In these two cases (cited already by Lifschitz 1917: 40 n. 27), the concrete sense first appears in MH, while BH has the figurative sense alone. From the semantic perspective, MH apparently reflects the more archaic state of the language. It is possible, however, that the usage attested in MH existed in biblical period and is only coincidentally not attested in the Bible.

which one would have expected to show in every area developments from earlier forms present in BH, instead exhibits at point a more archaic state.[24]

17.3.4 Difference of Tradition

§ 12 Quite apart from this question of historical and dialectal differences, there is one further point in which MH diverges from BH. This further difference is in the traditions by which BH and MH have come down to us. Let us recall that in Hebrew, as in other Semitic languages, not all the elements of the word are transcribed. Thus the grapheme דבר may be read *dāḇār* "word, thing," *deḇer* "pestilence," *dibbēr* "he spoke," *dabbēr* "speak!", *dubbar* "it was spoken of," etc. In itself, a certain written word or grapheme may be interpreted in various ways. Only a wholly vocalized text can give a complete picture of the word; without full vocalization, even the full context can sometimes leave some doubt as to the precise form of a word. An example is the vocalization of חרש at Gen 4:22, in the phrase (לֹטֵשׁ כָּל) חרש (נְחֹשֶׁת וּבַרְזֶל). The Tiberian vocalization has חֹרֵשׁ *ḥōrēš*, while the Babylonian tradition has חָרָשׁ *ḥārāš*. This is one of the cases where we have two divergent traditions, giving equally credible readings even though in purely historical terms one form alone could have been intended by the author.[25]

The fact that the script does not record every element in pronunciation has important implications in many areas of the history of Hebrew, not least with regard to the differences between BH and MH. For example, the name הלל occurs both in the Bible (Judg 12:13, 15) and in the Mishnah (e.g., Ševi'it 10:3). Today the name is read in both cases הִלֵּל (*hillēl*); however, certain manuscripts of the Mishnah read הֶלֵּל (*hellēl*). Some researchers have tried to explain this divergence in diachronic terms, claiming that in an unstressed closed syllable, the vowel [*i*] in MH changed to [*e*], and thus *hillēl* > *hellēl*.[26] A very different explanation, however, is possible. The difference between *hillēl* and *hellēl* is not diachronic, but reflects a difference in the traditions of the reading

24 Compare further Kutscher 1972:30 n. 5, and Bar-Asher 1985:89–93.

25 See Yeivin 1985:1163. Yeivin lists, at length, many differences between the Tiberian and Babylonian traditions of the biblical text. Most of these differences concern the vocalization, although a good number concern the consonantal text itself. Other examples are Tiberian שָׁבַר against Babylonian שִׁבֵּר at 1 Kings 13:28, or Tiberian לָקְקוּ against Babylonian לִקְקוּ at 1 Kings 21:19. Further discussion of the differences between the two traditions in individual passages would lie beyond the scope of the present work.

26 This is the thesis that Kutscher 1977:135–166***, sets out to prove.

of this name. One tradition, attached to a certain place (a dialect or school), read *hillēl*; the other, reflecting a different school or dialect, read *hellēl*; but those who pronounced *hillēl* would have read it this way consistently, both in the Bible and in the Mishnah, and those who pronounced it *hellēl* would have been equally consistent. We have reliable evidence for both readings, whether in the Bible[27] or in Mishnaic Hebrew.[28] We have no compelling evidence as to which is the older of the forms. The form for which we have the oldest evidence is, in fact, *hellēl*: the Septuagint gives Ελληλ,[29] a transcription of *hillēl*, as its rendering of the name in the passage from Judges just cited. However, we cannot therefore conclude that *hillēl* is the younger form, on the grounds that the attestations of it are later than the Septuagint;[30] we can only conclude that we have attested two traditions with different reading traditions for the same word. This example is far more unique.[31]

17.3.5 Literary Influence of Biblical Hebrew upon Mishnaic Hebrew

§ 13 The points raised above show how complex and delicate the distinction between BH and MH is. We now turn to another aspect of the problem, namely that MH is not only later than BH, but also less prestigious. The biblical text enjoyed such authority that its influence could not be escaped. That influence is apparent both in the redaction of rabbinic literature and in its transmis-

---

27 The reading *hillēl* is attested by both the Tiberian tradition (as in the examples from Judges cited above) and the Babylonian vocalization (Yeivin 1985:963); the reading *hellēl* is attested by the Septuagint, which reads Ελληλ.

28 Within MH, *hellēl* is the reading in MS K (as noted by Kutscher 1977:84–95, 150). The same form appears in MS Parma A (cf. Haneman 1980:2) and MS Paris, as well as other works of Italian origin (see Bar-Asher 1980:11, 64, 92). On the other hand, we find *hillēl* in MS Parma B (see Bar-Asher 1971:171, 183) and in the Babylonian vocalization of the Mishnah (cf. Yeivin 1985:963). One should perhaps emphasize that we have no case of a biblical manuscript and a mishnaic manuscript vocalized by a single scribe.

29 See n. 27.

30 The evidence for vocalization found in the Septuagint pre-dates all the vocalization systems for the Bible and the Mishnah. However, the vowels reflected in those systems represent the linguistic situation far earlier than the date of the invention of those systems. Thus, the Masoretic system of vocalizing the Bible is no earlier than the seventh century CE, and the corresponding system for the Mishnah is later still. The vowels that these systems present, however, reproduce the linguistic situation many centuries earlier; cf. Yalon 1967:16 ff.; Kutscher 1972:52–53; Kutscher 1977:73 ff.

31 See further n. 124 below.

sion, through the Middle Ages down to the present. We will consider two examples.

§ 14 To signify "further" or "onward" (of time), BH uses הלאה, while MH uses להלן or (מכאן ו)אילך. There is, however, one mishnaic passage where the word הלאה occurs twice:

> חטאות הציבור ועולותיהן ... כשרין מיום שלושים והלאה ... נדרים ונדבות הבכור והמעשר והפסח כשרים מיום שמיני והלאה, ואף ביום השמיני.
>
> The sin offerings and the burnt offerings of the community ... are acceptable from the thirtieth day onward ... Vows and freewill offering, the first-born, the tithe, and the Passover sacrifice ... are valid from the eighth day and onward ... (Parah 1:4).

Normal mishnaic usage would have been מיום שלושים ולהלן and מיום השמיני ולהלן (or ואילך), but instead the Biblical word והלאה is used. Evidently, the formulation of this mishnah was influence by the underlying biblical verse:

> וּמִיּוֹם הַשְּׁמִינִי וָהָלְאָה יֵרָצֶה לְקָרְבַּן אִשֶּׁה לַה'
>
> "From the eighth day onward, it shall be accepted as a fire-offering to the LORD" (Leviticus 22:27).

This borrowing is due to the literary influence of the biblical text on the language of the Mishnah. It seems authentic and in all probability goes back to the very author of the Mishnah in Parah.

§ 15 In contrast, there are changes which must be attributed to later scribes who substituted biblical forms for the original forms, which were in Mishnaic Hebrew. For example, the first person plural pronoun (when it is the subject of the sentence) was *'ānū*, as in הרי אָנוּ מטמאין את כולכם "we declare you all unclean" (Terumot 8:12). In two places, however, the biblical form אֲנַחְנוּ has crept into the printed editions of the Mishnah:

A. ... לפיכך אנחנו חייבים להודות "there we are obligated to praise ..." (Pesaḥim 10:4), and
B. אנחנו מעלין על נכסי אבינו "we add to the value of our father's property" (Ketubbot 10:2).

The biblical form אנחנו is the reading given by the Livorno edition, and by M. J. Kosovsky's concordance to the Mishnah. However, all the reliable manuscripts (Kaufmann, Parma A, Cambridge, Paris), as well as the *editio princeps* (Naples 1492) show, in both passage, the mishnaic form אנו. It was evidently later copyists who replaced MH אנו with BH אנחנו. Such modifications, due to the literary influence of the biblical text on rabbinic writings as transmitted by copyists, are certainly common[32] (although less so than has sometimes been thought).[33]

17.4 Unity and Diversity in Mishnaic Hebrew

17.4.1 The assumption of uniformity re-examined

§ 16 For a long time there was a widespread tendency to view MH as entirely homogenous. The grammar by M. H. Segal (1936) is an excellent representative of this conception: its many chapters offer examples culled from the language of the Tannaim, alongside the Palestinian and Babylonian Amoraim, without distinction, not to mention separation. Thus, when Segal discusses denominative verbs, he cites examples from the Mishnah – e.g., מתריעין "one plays the trumpet" (Ta'anit 3:1)," from the noun תרועה "trumpet blast" – and from the Babylonian Talmud – e.g., הנגיב "turn to the south" ('Eruvin 53a), from נגב "south, ידרים "turn to the south," from דרום, and יצפין "turn to the north," from צפון "north" (Bava Batra 25b). Similarly, in his chapter on I-y verbs, he cites לישן "to sleep," which is found in the Mishnah (Bava Batra 2:3), ליגע "to touch," which comes from the Palestinian Talmud (Berakhot 4:5; 14d), and לינק "to suck, to nuzzle," found in the Babylonian Talmud (Pesaḥim 112a). Likewise, H. Yalon studied different periods and different literary units as if they were one bloc. For example, in chapter 27 of Yalon 1964 (pp. 171–175) he speaks of "the present participle of the *qal* of II-w and geminate verbs with the vowel ō," and takes his examples from Tannaitic literature (Mishnah and Tosefta), Genesis Rabbah, Leviticus Rabbah, other midrashim, both Talmudim, etc.

---

32 The example of משקוף discussed above (n. 6) is relevant here, as well, since it illustrates the literary dependence of the Mishnah upon the Bible. That dependence affected both the author of the Mishnaic passage, at the moment of redaction, and the copyists in the Middle Ages. In this particular case, the use of the term משקוף in M. Pesaḥim is authentic, since the author of this mishnah had the text of Exodus 12 in mind; thus, the biblical text וראה את הדם על המשקוף ועל שתי המזוזות (Exod 12:23) has influenced the Mishnaic text, וטעון הזייה באגודת אזוב על המשקוף ועל שתי המזוזות (Pesaḥim 9:5). By contrast, the introduction of the word משקוף in place of שקוף in M. Oholot (6×) is probably due to a secondary change by a copyist. The older manuscripts prefer שקוף (and some have this form exclusively), but the printed editions replaced it on at least six occasions under the influence of the biblical text (see further in n. 6, above).

33 Kutscher 1977:73 ff. and also 1972:39–40 argues that cases where the Mishnah has been changed to agree with BH grammar are very numerous; against this, see the detailed analysis in Bar-Asher 1987:27–32.

The adherents of this approach, which treats the language of MH as uniform, attempt to show the cohesiveness of the different layers and texts within this dialect. More recent research, by contrast, takes pains to distinguish between the different elements in the language, and between the different traditions, and emphasizes the differences, in order to obtain a more exact and focused view of MH. Below, seven aspects that should be kept in mind are presented.

17.4.2 Contrasts between the language of the Tannaim and the language of the Amoraim

§ 17 Although MH does present a measure of unity, two main strata within the language can be distinguished: the language of the Tannaim (which may be designated MH1) and the language of the Amoraim (MH2). Within MH2 one must also distinguish between Palestine and Babylonia. This taxonomy was proposed and convincingly demonstrated by E. Y. Kutscher.[34] For example, אֵלּוּ/הָאֵלּוּ are the plurals of the near and far demonstrative pronouns, respectively, in Tannaitic Hebrew, while the Palestinian Amoraim use הַלָּלוּ or הַלֵּלוּ. The latter form is a combination of two demonstrative elements: *hāl* (*halla*) and *'ēllū*, as Segal (1936:50) already showed.

Another example is the first person singular of the future tense. In the language of the Tannaim and the Babylonian Amoraim, the form is אֶפְעֹל – with initial *'aleph*, as in BH. In the language of the Palestinian Amoraim, however, there is plenty of evidence to show that the form was נִפְעֹל, the result of influence from Galilean Aramaic. One example may be drawn from Genesis Rabbah, chap. 29:

> מעשה בחסיד אחד שיצא לכרמו וראה עוללה אחת וברך עליה, אמר: כדיי העוללה הזאת שנברך עליה.
>
> Once a pious man went out into his vineyard and saw one bunch of grapes. He made a blessing on it, saying, "This bunch is worthy that I should make a blessing on it."

The form שנברך, with *nun*, appears in the best manuscripts, though some correct to שאברך. Similarly, one may cite Pesiqta de-Rav Kahana, sec. 5 (החדש הזה; ed. Mandelbaum, p. 80):

> כל אותו היום היה אברהם יושב ותמה בליבו ואומר, לאיזו מהם נבור, לגיהנם או למלכיות זו קשה מזו?
>
> All that day Abraham sat and wondered in his heart, saying: Which of them shall I choose, hell or the heathen kingdoms, one stronger than the next?

34 See Kutscher 1972:30, § 4, and 40 ff., § 32 ff.

The verb "shall I choose" has the form נָבוֹר, not אָבוֹר.[35]

A third and final example is provided by the expression כל שהוא, literally, "whatever it be." In the language of the Tannaim, this is used to mean "a little," as in חגב חי כל שהוא "a grasshopper that is a little alive" (Shabbat 9:7), and the usage of the Palestinian Amoraim appears to be identical, as in נתן בתוכו מים כל שהוא "he put into it a little water" (Y. Berakhot 3:5; p. 6d). However, the Babylonian Amoraim express that sense with the word משהו, literally, "something," as in שתי שעות חסר משהו "two hours less a little" (B. Pesaḥim 12a).[36]

17.4.3 Mishnaic Hebrew and its different dialects

§ 18 In the Tannaitic period, when MH was a living language spoken in different regions, it was not, of course, uniform; it is only natural that different geographical regions should show differences within the language. Even though the texts in general show a reasonably homogenous written language, evidence for the existence of different dialects can still be traced, both in the literary sources and in other documents, outside the literary tradition.

For example, the word שֶׁל, indicating possession and equivalent to English "of," may be used in two different ways, both attested in various texts. In the letters of Bar Koseba, שֶׁל is written as an independent word, separate from the noun that it governs, as in שהיו של הגואין "that belonged to the gentiles" (Letter 2).[37] In the manuscripts of the Mishnah, however, it is always prefixed to the following word, and if that word begins with the definite article, syncope of the ה takes place (as after the בכ"ל prepositions), so that we find (systematically) שֶׁלַּגּוֹיִם rather than של הגוים. Here is but one example: ... שלתנור שלכירה "of the oven ... of the double stove" (Kelim 8:7).[38]

Another example involves the root אלמ"נ in the *binyan nitpa"al*, meaning "to be widowed" in MH. In reliable manuscripts, the form is נִתְאַלְמְנָה in the 3fs and נִתְאַלְמְנוּ in the plural (Yevamot 2:10; Nedarim 11:10; Makkot 1:1; and eight further cases).[39] In the printed editions of the Mishnah and the Bavli (as well as other texts), however, we find the reading נִתְאַרְמְלָה (Yevamot 6:3; 13:4 [2×]; Ketubbot 2:1; 4:2 [2×]; 6:1; Nedarim 11:9), derived from a different root,

35 Further details can be found in Sokoloff 1972:284–288.

36 See Breuer 1987:139–140. This article is devoted to the description and study of the linguistic features typical of the Hebrew of the Babylonian Amoraim.

37 See Kutscher 1977:57.

38 See Kutscher, *ibid.*, and also Yalom 1964:27–27, § 18, and 189–193.

39 See Bar-Asher 1980:33.

ארמ"ל. Some consider the latter a Babylonian form, since it is common in the Bavli and in manuscripts of the halakhic midrashim,[40] but it is also attested in a Palestinian dialect: in the Damascus Covenant from Qumran we find the form התארמלה, a *hitpa"al* form of the root ארמ"ל.[41]

Our third and final example in this category involves the word מַעְיָן "spring," which is very common in MH (e.g., Bikkurim 1:6). In Sifre Numbers § 22, however, in the story of a shepherd from the south who came to Simon the Just, we find a different pronunciation of this word: והלכתי למלאות מים מן הנעיים "I went to draw water from the spring" (reading with MS Rome 32), with metathesis of the מ and נ.[42]

These examples show clearly that there were regional dialects of Hebrew within Palestine. The literary language of the Mishnah (which belongs to a specific time and place in the country) may be contrasted with the language of neighboring regions: the letters of Bar Koseba in the south (של הגואין vs. שלגוים), Qumran in the region of the Dead Sea (התארמלה vs. נתאלמנה), and the shepherd from the south (נַעְיָם vs. מַעְיָן).

§ 19 With regard to this question of dialectal variants, there is a particular aspect of rabbinic literature which has to be considered. J. N. Epstein pointed out that some of the controversies within the Mishnah and the Tosefta are only apparent; the rabbis agree in these cases on the substance, but disagree on the wording, each following the linguistic usage of his region or school.[43] Thus we read in one mishnah (Kelim 8:9):

> בור שיש בו שפיתה טמא, ושל עושי זכוכית ... טמא.
> כבשן של סידין ושל זגגין ושל יוצרים טהורה.
>
> A pit in which a fire can be lit is susceptible to impurity; a pit o glassmakers ... is susceptible to impurity. The furnace of limeburners or of glaziers or potters is not susceptible to impurity.

In the first sentence, the artisans who work with glass are called עושי זכוכית "glassmakers," whereas in the second they are called זגגין "glaziers." Similarly, the artisans sometimes called חיטין "tailors" in the Mishnah (e.g., Shabbat 1:3; Pesaḥim 4:6; etc.) are elsewhere called תופרי כסות (Kil'ayim 9:6).

Another example may be found at Parah 2:5:

> היו בה שתי שערות שחורות או לבנות בתוך גומא אחת פסולה.
> רבי יהודה אומר, בתוך כוס אחד.

40 See Moreshet 1980:105.
41 Bar-Asher 1986a:185–186.
42 See Epstein 1933:192.
43 For further details, see Epstein 1957:234–240.

In one found [on a red cow] two black or white hairs within a single hole (גומא), it is invalid. R. Judah says: within a single hollow (כוס).

The Yerushalmi explains, הן כוסות הן גומות "holes and hollows are the same thing" (Avodah Zarah chap. 2, 42a). The "argument" between the first Tanna and R. Judah, then, rests on a simple problem of language. In such cases, however, we do not always have enough data to trace a particular dialectal form.

17.4.4 Linguistic differences within the Mishnah

§ 20 Even in a closed corpus such as the Mishnah, the language is not always uniform. Of course, generally speaking there is an evident homogeneity, but some sections are marked by peculiar features. As a rule, these textual sections depart from the norms of MH in the direction of agreement with BH.

A. The most ancient parts of the Mishnah, dating from around 70 CE (and therefore contemporary with the destruction of the Second Temple) exhibit grammatical or lexical usages proper to BH. One clear example is the verb "to begin." The usual word within MH is הִתְחִיל, a secondary form, found, e.g., in M. Pe'ah 7:2: התחיל בו "he began it." M. Tamid, however, uses the biblical form הֵחֵל, as in הֵחֵלּוּ מעלין "they began bringing up" and החלו עולין "they began going up" (Tamid 2:2–3).[44]

Another example is the form for "to take." In BH, this is the normal meaning of the verb לקח. In MH, however, the meaning of this root has shifted to "to buy." One may compare, for example:

לקח את ספר התורה הזה
Take (לקח) this book of instruction (Deuteronomy 31:26)[45]

with

לקח מן הנחתום ככר בפונדיון
He bought (לקח) from the baker a loaf for a *pondiyon* (M. Sevi'it 8:4).

To signify "to take," MH uses the root נט"ל, as in נטל ממנה מקל או שרביט "he took a branch or a twig from it" (Avodah Zarah 3:10). We do find,

44 See Epstein 1957:27, and Bar-Asher 1985:94–98.

45 One passage where BH לקח perhaps approaches the sense the word has in MH is Genesis 19:14, לוקחי בנותיו "those who took his daughters." Here the probable reference is to Lot's sons-in-law, who "took," i.e., "acquired," his daughters.

however, the biblical usage in an ancient mishnah from the period of the Second Temple, dealing with the sanctification of the New Moon:

ואם צודה להם, לוקחין בידן מקלות ... ואם היתה הדרך רחוקה, לוקחין בידן מזונות.
If any lie in wait for them, they take (לקח) staves in their hands ... and if the journey is long, they take (לקח) food in their hands.

Here it is the verb לוקחין (and not נוטלין)[46] which is used (twice) in the sense "to take."

B. In general, it is when discussing the cult that the language is most conservative and closest to BH. Examples include the phrases והשתחוה ויצא "he bowed down and went out" (Bikkurim 3:6) or התנדב "he made a freewill offering" (Menaḥot 12:6). These two passages deal with matters connected to the sanctuary, and the reliable witnesses show the use of the התפעל forms (השתחוה, התנדב), as in BH, rather than the usual MH forms on the pattern נתפעל, as in נתגייר "he converted" (Ḥullin 10:4), נתחייב "was liable" (Ḥallah 4:3), and נתמעט "it was reduced" ('Eruvin 7:5).[47]

C. The mishnaic texts which imitate the style of biblical poetry likewise show a particular affinity with BH. The best examples can be found among the exhortations in Avot, where we find, for example, the use of the jussive in אל תעש עצמך "do not make yourself" (Avot 1:8) and אל תאמן בעצמך עד יום מותך "do not believe in yourself until the day of your death" (Avot 2:4). The forms תעשה (rather than תעש) and תאמין (rather than תאמן) would have been expected in MH. Similarly, compare יהי כבוד חברך חביב עליך כשלך "let the honor of your friend be as dear to you as your own" (Avot 2:10),[48] with the BH jussive form יְהִי rather than indicative יִהְיֶה or the normal MH form יְהֵא.

17.4.5 Editions and manuscripts

§ 21 The works of the Tannaim were edited more than 1700 years ago, and those of the Amoraim go back more than 1400 years. We possess no manuscripts going back to those periods. Most of the extant manuscripts are from the second millenium; very few rabbinic texts survive that were copied before the year 1000.[49] Of these early manuscripts, few are complete. Nevertheless, several of them have been studied extensively in order to ascertain their relia-

46 See Kutscher 1961:55, and Bar-Asher 1985:96–97, § 27.
47 Compare the excellent analysis by Haneman 1980:208–211.
48 See Haneman 1980:31–33 and Sharvit 1976:12–14.
49 See Rosenthal 1981:96ff., and Kutscher 1972:52, § 53.

bility in linguistic matters. Most of the reliable manuscripts were copied between around 1100 and 1400.[50] The printed editions follow, from the end of the fifteenth century and on. The first edition of the Mishnah dates from 1492.

§ 22 Even after the final redaction, the Mishnah (and other Tannaitic texts) continued to be transmitted orally. Most scholars are agreed that few people possessed written copies. Many centuries were to pass before the Mishnah came to be copied in a large number of copies, probably around 700. In these circumstances, it was almost inevitable that modifications would be introduced into the text as it was transmitted. This is the reason that even the oldest manuscripts already reflect certain departures from the original language. Research has shown that, overall, most of the manuscripts from before 1250 (and even, to a large extent, those from before 1400) have faithfully preserved the original language. Divergence from that standard is to be found, however, in manuscripts copied from 1400 and on, and even more so in printed editions.[51] The reasons for this situation are beyond the scope of this paper. It is sufficient to note that many differences can be found between the manuscripts and the printed editions of the Mishnah.

§ 23 Some examples will illustrate this phenomenon. The words *qardōm* "ax" and *qarsōl* "peg" appears in those forms in the printed editions, while the manuscripts had קוֹרְדוֹם (M. Kelim 29:3 in MS Kaufmann) and קוּרְסֵל (M. Oholot 1:9 in MS Parma B and K). The reason that such forms were eliminated from the printed editions may be that they differ from BH.[52] Another example involves the *nitpa"al*. This could be used transitively when MH was a living language, as the manuscripts well attest, for example, גזל ועריות שנפשו של אדם מתאווה להם ומתחמדתן "robbery and incest, which a man's soul longs for and desires" (Makkot 3:5, MS Kaufmann). The verbal form of the last word here is accompanied by an accusative pronominal suffix: ומתחמדתן = ומתחמדת + אותן "she desires them." In the printed editions,[53] however, this

50 See Kutscher 1977:73–107, an outstanding study of the special value of MS Kaufmann. See also Haneman 1980 on MS Parma A, as well as Bar-Asher's evaluations of the importance of MS Parma B (1971) and MS Paris (1980). Compare further below, Chapter 19 §§ 8–14.

51 See Kutscher 1977:73 ff.; Bar-Asher 1980, esp. 34, 53–58; and below, Chapter 19.

52 See Bar-Asher 1971:171, 176, and references cited there. One possible explanation is that the process (which here led to the replacement, in certain editions, of *qursēl* by *qarsōl* and of *qōrdōm* by *qardōm*) is due to the biblical vocalization. However, one could equally well suppose that there were traditions of MH in which these (and other) words had always been read the way they are in the biblical tradition of vocalization. See § 12 above and § 46 (especially n. 124) below.

53 Even some good manuscripts have lost the reading ומתחמדתן: Parma A gives ומחמדתן.

form is replaced by the *pi"el* form, ומחמדתן, which would be the normal *binyan* for the active sense.[54] Examples of this sort could easily be multiplied.

17.4.6 Linguistic types in the manuscripts of the Mishnah

§ 24 Even the oldest manuscripts, which may have been expected to show the language in its original state, do not in fact give the impression of a uniform language. The totality of the manuscripts, complete and fragmentary, of Tannaitic literature and of the Mishnah in particular, may be classified from a linguistic perspective into three groups. A detailed study by the present writer sought to show that these three groups represented three different linguistic traditions (or types). The manuscripts may firstly be divided into a Babylonian branch and a Palestinian branch, and the latter may then be subdivided into a western and an eastern type. Each of these represents, to some extent, the different linguistic traditions current in Palestine when Hebrew was still spoken there, that is, before 200 CE.[55]

§ 25 The distinction between the Palestinian and Babylonian branches is marked by numerous linguistic differences, affecting various aspects of the language. For example, in the Palestinian branch we find the construction of relative ש + third person pronoun + present participle, as in, for example, שהוא שולח "who sends," שהיא עוֹשָׂה "who (fem.) does," שהן אוכלין "who eat." By contrast, the Babylonian branch uses a shorter construction, namely, relative ש + present participle: ששולח, שעוֹשָׂה, שאוכלין. It can be shown that both construction are as old as MH itself.[56]

§ 26 The Palestinian branch, as mentioned above, may be divided into two types: the western, represented for the most part by manuscripts of Italian origin, and the eastern, appearing in manuscripts copied in the Near East. The main differences between these two types are phonetic or morphological. In other word, we find the same graphemes, read differently.[57] For example, the word צפורן "nail" is read צִפֹּרֶן in the western type, but as צִפּוֹרֶן in the eastern.[58] Similarly, the plural of the noun אָחוֹת is אַחְיוֹת in the western and אֲחָיוֹת

54 Occasionally, even the printed editions preserve the special usage of the נתפעל with a direct object. In particular, the verb נתקבל provides a number of examples, such as ... אלמנה נתקבלה כתובתה "a widow ... received her *ketubba*" (Ketubbot 11:4), or התקבלתי ממך מנה "I have received one *mina* from you" (Ketubbot 5:1).

55 The various aspects of this question are examined in Chapter 19 below.

56 See Chapter 19, §§ 47,59.

57 See Chapter 19, § 38.

58 See Chapter 19, §§ 36,41.

in the eastern.[59] The present participle of the נפעל conjugation of III-y verbs is usually of the pattern נִפְעֶה in the western type, with the sole exception of the verb עשה "do, make," which shows the pattern נִפְעָה: נֶעֱשָׂה. By contrast, we find both נִפְעָה and נִפְעֶה in the eastern type, with a growing preference for the former.[60]

§ 27 In summary, it is clear that the two types (eastern and western) within the Palestinian branch differ in phonetic and morphological matters, while the differences between the Palestinian branch (as a whole) and the Babylonian branch extend not only to phonetic and morphological but also matters of syntax.

17.4.7 Special traditions

§ 28 There are a number of linguistic forms attested in one manuscript alone. Linguistic analysis of these features shows that there is no reason to suspect the authenticity of these uniquely attested forms. Of course, we cannot determine when these forms entered the language, and so it is impossible to know whether they reflect actual spoken Hebrew, or result from changes within the textual transmission of the texts during the Middle Ages. Given the complexity of this question, the most prudent course is simply to note carefully the linguistic facts offered by the manuscripts concerned, until new data or tools are available to assist. Here are three examples of such peculiarities.

A. The word צָפוֹן "north" appears in just that form in all manuscripts, except for one passage in Parma A, where instead we find לְצִפּוּנָה :צִפּוּן "northwards" (Rosh ha-Shana 2:6). This is identical with the Aramaic form, and also occurs in the Hebrew of the Samaritan Pentateuch (cf. Genesis 13:14: *ṣibbūnā*).[61]
B. All manuscripts and oral traditions give the plural form of אֵבֶר "limb" as אֵבָרִים, nearly always written *plene* (e.g., cf. M. Sheqalim 7:3). However, MS Parma B reads אֲבָרִים consistently (cf., e.g., M. Kelim 18:9). Yalon considered this to be a biblicizing form, but this is unjustified, since the plural of אבר never appears in the Bible.
C. The word עֶגְלָה "heifer" is extremely common in MH. When the Mishnah has the phrase עגלה ערופה "the heifer whose neck was broken" (cf. Deuteronomy 21:6), MS Kaufmann vocalized עֶגְלָה (e.g., M. Sotah 7:2; 9:1; etc.).

59 See Chapter 19 § 37.
60 See Chapter 21 §§ 5–20.
61 See Kutscher 1972:69.

However, when the definite article is prefixed to the word, this manuscript, and only this manuscript, reads הָעֲגָלָה (e.g., Sotah 9:7; Sanhedrin 1:3; Ḥullin 1:6; etc.),[62] although there is no obvious reason for such a distinction. The remaining manuscripts all agree is reading both עֶגְלָה and הָעֶגְלָה.

17.4.8 Written and Oral Traditions

§ 29 Those manuscripts which reflect ancient traditions faithful to the original form of MH were, as mentioned, written before 1400, and mainly before 1250. Despite the many centuries that elapsed before their writing, they stand far close to the spoken language than any of the printed editions. Apart from the manuscripts, however, research over the past eighty years has shown the need to to consider the oral traditions preserved by the sages of different countries and traditions. H. Yalon was the first to draw attention to the reading traditions of ancient Jewish texts, transmitted orally from master to pupil over the generations.[63] Following Yalon's lead, spcialists in MH began to examine closely the manner in which the Mishnah is read within the various Jewish communities by the oldest sages steeped in the tradition. It was found that often these sages, while perfectly well acquainted with the proper reading of the Bible, preserved in their reading of the Mishnah a number of linguistic forms which differed from those of the Bible. The oral traditions recorded in our day, while they can attest primarily to the situation only of recent centuries, can be shown, through careful scrutiny, to have preserved form that agree with those found in manuscripts a thousand years old. Such research has concentrated on the traditions of the Yemenite Jews and of other oriental Jewish communities such as those of Iraq, Syria, and North Africa.[64] There is also a growing interest in the Ashkenazi traditions of the Jews in Europe.[65]

§ 30 A few examples must suffice here. The Yemenites, like the Sephardim, read the form נתפעל with a *pataḥ* in the last syllable, i.e., as *nitpa“al*, not *nitpa“el* with a *ṣere*.[66] Again the Yemenites, Sepharadim, and Ashkenazim read the pronominal suffix of the second person masculine singular as ־ָךְ, not

62 This point is also discussed in Bar-Asher 1980:55 n. 262.

63 See for example Yalon 1965:11–23 and Bar-Asher 1990b:§ 3.

64 Compare Morag 1963 and Shivtiel 1972 (both dealing with the Yemenite tradition), Morag 1977 (on the traditions of the Jews of Baghdad), Katz (on the tradition of the Jews of Djerba, Tunisia), and Maman 1984 (on the tradition of the Jews in Tétouan, Morocco).

65 See Mishor 1989a on the traditions of Ashkenazi Jews.

66 Compare Yalon 1964:15–18.

ךְ-, thus בֵּיתָךְ "your house," סִפְרָךְ "your book," and so on.[67] Another phenomenon, preserved by both the Yemenite and Sepharadi traditions, is to double the ר as is done with other consonants, as in עֵרֵב "he mixed," אֵרֵס "he betrothed," לְעָרוֹת "to pour."[68] A recent study has shown that the same phenomenon is also attested in Ashkenazi tradition; the pronunciations מְעוּרָבִין (with *u* after the *'ayin*) and מְצְטַרְפִין (with *a* after the *ṭet*) have been rightly interpreted as evidence of the ancient pronunciations מְעוּרָּבִין and מִצְטַרְּפִין.[69]

17.5 Mishnaic Hebrew and Other Languages

17.5.1 The situation of multi-lingualism

§ 31 Throughout the Second Temple period, and for centuries later – for more than 700 years altogether – Hebrew was in direct contact with other languages. The biblical books from the Second Temple period reflect this multi-lingualism. Most importantly, we must consider contact with Aramaic, mainly Imperial Aramaic, which left its effects in the book of Ezra/Nehemiah, Daniel, Esther, and elsewhere; the Bible even includes whole passages in Aramaic.[70] In addition, Persian and Greek intrude to some extent in the later biblical books, as did Akkadian, doubtlessly through the medium of Aramaic.[71]

Contact with Aramaic continued into the Tannaitic period. The contact was, however, no longer with Imperial Aramaic, but with later forms of Aramaic, each with its own distinctive dialectal features. Again, Aramaic brought with it also the influence of other languages, notably Persian and Akkadian. Furthermore, the language of the Tannaim, and later that of the Amoraim, show clear signs of increasing contact with Greek and also Latin.[72] The question of the influence of these languages on MH will now be considered in detail.

---

67 See Yalon 1964:13–15, and Kutscher 1977:91–92.

68 See for example Shivtiel 1972:211, and Katz 1977:217.

69 See Mishor 1989a:102.

70 These are, of course, the phrase יגר שהדותא "heap of testimony" in Genesis 31:47, the verse in Jeremiah 10:11, and the Aramaic portions of Ezra and Daniel.

71 See Tur-Sinai 1937:261–264.

72 The basic materials can be found in the work of Krauss (1898–1899), although many points of detail have been corrected by later scholarship, notably in the works of J. N. Epstein (on the Mishnah and Talmudid) and Saul Lieberman (on the Tosefta and the Palestinian Talmud).

17.5.2 Mishnaic Hebrew and Aramaic

§ 32 Whether the Tannaim and other Jews at the time were truly bilingual is much debated. Some argue that true bilingualism existed throughout Palestine, so that speakers could express themselves equally well in either Hebrew or Aramaic. Others, however, believe that in certain regions only one of these languages was spoken, although it could well have been influenced by the other language.[73]

Contact between Hebrew and Aramaic is well attested in the written language. The extent of the influence of Aramaic on Hebrew is, however, the subject of intense debate. For example, some consider the usual MH form of the second person masculine singular independent pronoun, אַתְּ, to be a borrowing from Aramaic, overtaking original Hebrew אַתָּה.[74] Others, however, regard אַתְּ as a native Hebrew form.[75] The form אַתְּ is certainly attested occasionally in the Bible, for example, ואם ככה אַתְּ עושה לי, הרגני נא הרג "If you (אַתְּ) do this to me, kill me!" (Numbers 11:15), but it does not become established in the written language until MH.

Let us turn to another example. The best manuscripts of the Mishnah attest a peculiar verbal form, the פֵּעֵל, characterized by a long vowel after the first radical and the absence of gemination in the second, such as מְאָבְקִים "they cover with dust" (Shevi'it 2:2; MS Kaufmann).[76] One scholar saw here a conjugation borrowed from Aramaic and cognate with Arabic *fā'ala*.[77] Another view, however, regards this form as an internal development within Hebrew; according to this opinion, the form derives from the Hebrew *pi''ēl*, but with the expected gemination of the second radical replaced by lengthening of the preceding vowel;[78] thus מְאָבְקִין is a reflex of מְאַבְּקִין.[79]

Even those who argue a minimalistic position regarding Aramaic influence on MH agree, of course, that MH adopted certain grammatical, lexical, and semantic elements from Aramaic. One example is the *binyan* נִתַּפְעַל, used for I-y verbs, for example, נִתּוֹסְפוּ "they were increased" (M. 'Eruvin 7:7), מִתּוֹקֶדֶת

---

73 The theory was once proposed that MH had never been a living language, but was rather an artificial creation, and that the Jews in the Tannaitic period had spoken Aramaic exclusively. This view has now been universally abandoned. See Yalon 1964:204–208 and Kutscher 1977:68–69.

74 See Kutscher 1977:86 and Gluska 1987:186–187.

75 See Bar-Asher 1971:172 and Haneman 1980:460–465.

76 See Bar-Asher 1980:70 n. 361 and Chapter 20 § 19 below.

77 See Morag 1957:96.

78 See Ben-Ḥayyim 1957–1977:5.82–83.

79 See Bar-Asher 1980:125–126 and Chapter 20 § 19 below.

"[the fire] is consumed" (Leviticus Rabbah 7:8). This *binyan* is generally understood to be a late development, peculiar to Hebrew, from the Aramaic *binyan* הִתַּפְעַל, attested in several dialects.[80]

§ 33 Various Aramaic terms and expressions also entered the Hebrew language. One example is חצר הכבד (M. Tamid 4:3) "a lobe of the liver," which is a loan from Aramaic; thus, Onqelos translates היותרת על הכבד (Exodus 29:13, etc.) by חצרא דעל כבדא. The word שְׁבוּקִין, found in the expression אִגֶּרֶת שְׁבוּקִין "bill of divorce" (M. Gittin 9:3), is a Hebrew form – built on the native Hebrew pattern *pi"ūl*,[81] but with the Aramaic root שב"ק "to abandon, to leave." As a final example, the expression שכיב מרע "one who lay sick" (M. Pe'ah 3:7; Bava Batra 9:6) is borrowed from Aramaic, where we find not only the adjectival form, but also the verbal expression in the imperfect, ישכב מרע.[82]

§ 34 Aramaic influence is equally evident in calques, that is, words that are native to Hebrew but which develop a new usage or meaning under the influence of Aramaic; calques may be either lexical or grammatical.

One example is the verb אָחַז "to grasp, to hold," found already in BH, e.g., שלח ידך ואחוז בזנבו "put forth your hand and grasp its tail" (Exodus 4:4). The Aramaic cognate אֲחַד also had the meaning "to close," and the influence of the Aramaic verb caused the Hebrew אחז to develop the meaning "to close," as well. This occurs already in Nehemiah, from the period of the Second Temple: יגיפו הדלתות ואחזו "let them close and bolt the doors" (Nehemiah 7:3). The context makes it clear that closing, not grasping, is intended. The same meaning for אחז is attested in MH, in a midrashic explanation of the name Ahaz, the wicked king of Judah:

> ולמה נקראת שמו אחז? שאחז בתי כנסיות ובתי מדרשות.
>
> Why was he called Ahaz? Because he closed (אחז) the synagogues and the houses of study (Leviticus Rabbah 11:7).

In this case the Aramaic meaning has been transferred to the Hebrew cognate – a semantic calque.[83]

Let us now consider a grammatical calque. The words שָׂדֶה and כּוֹס occur both in the Bible and in the Mishnah, but change gender between the two. In the Bible, כּוֹס is feminine, as in תעבור כוס "the cup will pass" (Lamentations

---

80 See Yalon 1964:127–135.

81 Many terms related to family life are formed in MH on the *pi"ūl* pattern in the plural, such as קִידּוּשִׁין "betrothal," נִשּׂוּאִין "marriage," גֵּירוּשִׁין (< גִּירוּשִׁין*) "divorce," שִׁיבּוּקִין "release."

82 See Gluska 1987:1197–1198.

83 See Kutscher 1977:389, 404; Gluska 1987:139–140.

4:21), but in MH it is masculine, as in כוס ראשון "the first cup" (Pesaḥim 10:2). This change of gender no doubt derives from Aramaic כָּס, which is masculine.[84] Similarly, the word שָׂדֶה is masculine in the Bible, as in ויקם השדה "the field was assured" (Genesis 23:20), but almost always feminine in MH, as in שדה שקצרוה גוים "a field harvested by gentiles" (M. Pe'ah 2:7). In this case, too, it seems probable that the Aramaic חֲקַל, which is feminine, influenced the Hebrew.[85]

§ 35 Aramaic was sometimes the channel through which Akkadian and Persian words and form entered MH. Again, a few examples will suffice to demonstrate this.

The first occurrence in Hebrew of the word אסקופה "threshold," is in the Mishnah, e.g., היה קורא בספר על האסקופה "if one was reading a scroll on the threshold" (M. 'Eruvin 10:3). This evidently goes back to Akkadian *askuppātu*, which had been borrowed into Aramaic and had become current in many of its dialects, including those of Palestine.[86] Through the medium of Aramaic, which had long been in contact with Akkadian (and had in fact replaced Akkadian as the spoken language of Mestopotamia), this word penetrated Hebrew, as well.

Another example is the word אֶתְרוֹג "citron," whose first appearance in Hebrew is likewise in the Mishnah:

רבי ישמעאל אומר: שלושה הדסין, שתי ערבות, לולב אחד ואתרוג אחד.

R. Ishmael says: Three myrtle branches, two willow branches, one palm branch and one citron (M. Sukkah 3:4).

Research has shown that this term comes from Persian *turung*. It occurs in Aramaic texts of the Tannaitic period, such as Targum Onqelos:

פירי אילנא אתרוגין לולבין ...

fruits of the tree, citrons, palm branches ... (Lev 23:40).

Another Aramaic source is a letter of Bar Koseba:

וישלחן למחניה לותך לולבין ואתרוגין

and they shall send to you at the camp palm branches and citrons (letter 8, l. 3).

---

84 See Kutscher 1977:404; Gluska 1987:542–544.

85 See Kutscher 1977:404; Gluska 1987:1233–1235.

86 See Gluska 1987:170–171.

The word also occurs in the Palestinian Aramaic dialects of the period of the Amoraim.[87] It therefore seems certain that Aramaic was the channel through which this word reached MH.[88]

17.5.3 Borrowings from Greek and Latin

§ 36 Greek and Latin have also penetrated MH, but their influence is essentially limited to vocabulary.[89] Many terms borrowed from one or another of the languages have become naturalized in Hebrew; having appeared in MH, there remained in use throughout the Middle Ages and are preserved in Modern Hebrew. Such words as אִזְמֵל "chisel, scalpel" (σμίλη), פולמוס "polemic" (πόλεμος), פִּנְקָס "booklet" (πίναξ), and קתדרה "platform, pulpit" (χαθέδρα) have been current ever since the mishnaic period. The same applies to words of Latin origin, such as לִבְלָר/לַבְלָר "clerk" (*libellarius*) and ספסל "bench" (*subsellium*). It should be noted that in old manuscripts, these words appear in forms particularly close to the forms in their languages of origin. Thus, לבלר is vocalized לִבְלָר,[90] and ספסל is pointed סְפְסֵל.[91] The difference between Hebrew *pinqās* and Greek *pinaqs* arose because Hebrew avoids consonant clusters, and hence the consonants *qs* were separated by an *a* vowel. The original form is, however, preserved in the manuscripts in the plural, where we read פִּנַקְסִיּוֹת (Kelim 24:7).[92] The reason the original form is preserved here is that it is compatible with the rules of Hebrew phonology: the combination *qs* can stand, since it is not word final; the *q* ends one syllable and the *s* opens the following one.

§ 37 Lastly, it is important to note that nouns and adjectives borrowed from Greek and Latin have sometimes become so well naturalized in Hebrew that they have given rise to verbs of pure Hebrew pattern, which remain in use to this day. Thus, the term σπόγγος, which in Hebrew became סְפוֹג "sponge," itself gave rise to several verbal forms. The *qal* verb סָפַג means "sponge up, absorb," as in M. Zevaḥim 6:6, ולא סְפָגוֹ המלח "the salt did not absorb it." The *pi"el* verb סִפֵּג appears in M. Parah 12:2: יְסַפֵּג "it absorbs." We

87 See Gluska 1987:187–188.

88 For further material see Tur-Sinai 1927:265–278. Compare further Kutscher 1961, following the index on pp. 126–136.

89 This was the subject of Krauss 1898–1899; see also Albeck 1959:203–215.

90 See Bar-Asher 1980:56.

91 See Bar-Asher 2009a 2:147.

92 This vocalization is found in MS Parma A; MS K has the slightly different פִּנַקְסִיּוֹת, which also, however, preserves the stem *pinaqs* before the plural ending.

also find the נתפעל form, נִסְתַּפֵּג in M. Makhshirin 2:1, as well as the nouns סְפָג (in the expression מטפחות הַסְּפָג "bath-towels," Kil'ayim 9:3) and סִפּוּג "act of drying oneself" (M. Zavim 1:4).

The word χατήγωρ gave rise to the verb קִטְרֵג "to accuse," with metathesis of the last two consonants: אין השטן מקטרג אלא בשעת הסכנה "Satan accuses only at the time of danger" (Y. Shabbat 5:2; 5b).

From the adjective καλός "good, fine," came the verb קִלֵּס "praise," as in:

לפיכך אנחנו חייבין להודות להלל ולקלס

Therefore we are obligated to thank, praise, and extol (M. Pesaḥim 10:5).

אשרי המלך שמקלסין אותו בביתו

Happy is the king who is extolled in his own house (B. Berakhot 3a).

Lastly, Greek βάσις gave rise to the noun בָּסִיס and then to the verb בִּסֵּס, as in ומי בִּסֵּס העולם "and who laid the foundation of the world?" (Shir ha-Shirim Rabbah 1:9).

17.6 Mishnaic Hebrew from indirect sources

17.6.1 Direct and indirect sources

§ 38 In linguistics, the principle is taken for granted that a dialect or language can only be described on the basis of direct evidence, which may be in written or (preferably) oral form. This rule is easy enough to apply to the study of contemporary languages, given the advanced techniques of recording and preservation now available. It breaks down, however, when one is dealing with languages no longer spoken. Of course, the investigator of a language from the past, however ancient it may be, must go back to witnesses as close in time as possible to the linguistic information they transmit. Unfortunately, however, one does not always have access to documents containing all the linguistic data necessary for a complete description of the grammatical and lexical systems of a dead language. This is certainly the case for ancient Hebrew, both biblical and mishnaic.

§ 39 The study and description of MH, which ceased to be spoken 1800 years ago, encounters a number of difficulties. (Similar difficulties beset the study of biblical Hebrew, where are least 2200 years separate us from the spoken language.) Two problems are particularly acute:

A. The nearly complete lack of contemporary documents from the era when MH was actually spoken.

   As stated earlier, a few of our manuscripts date from the end of the first millennium CE, while the majority are from the beginning of the second millennium.[93] One of the most ancient rabbinic documents extant is the halakhic mosaic inscription discovered at Rehov, in the Beth-Shean valley. It probably dates to the seventh century CE,[94] some centuries after Hebrew ceased to be a spoken language.

B. The lack of information provided by the graphic system of Hebrew.

That system records the consonants, but even these are not recorded without ambiguity: it does not distinguish between שׁ /š/ and שׂ /s/(< /ś/), nor between allophones such as בּ /b/ and ב /v/. Vowels are only partially recorded: כפר, when it is to be read *kāfar*, bears no indication of the vowels, and in כיפר (to be read כִּפֵּר), only the first vowel is indicated. Hence, a single written sequence of letters may stand for a number of different forms. For example, מכתב could be read מִכְתָּב, מַכְתֵּב, מְכַתֵּב, מְכֻתָּב, and so on. This very word, in fact, gives rise to divergence among the manuscripts at M. Kelim 13:2:

מכתב שניטל הכותב טמא מפני המוחק

If a stylus has lost its writing point, it is still susceptible to impurity because of its eraser.

Manuscripts Parma A and Parma B read מַכְתֵּב, while K and Paris have מִכְתָּב.[95]

§ 40 The problem of lack of information in the written text of Tannaitic literature is partially solved by recourse to vocalized texts. Most of these, however, are (as already mentioned) later than 1000 CE, which prompts one to ask how early the vocalizations – more precisely, the reading traditions – are. This question is especially difficult since we know that these text were subject to conscious adjustments and involuntary errors in their transmission through the rest of the Middle Ages.

Of course, when a certain form is attested by several (if not all) of the extant witnesses, and these come from different geographical regions, it is very likely to be original. The form can then be attributed with some confidence to the era in which Hebrew was a living language. The word שעה "hour" provides an example. Many sources preserve the *qāmes* throughout the word's declension: שָׁעַת (not שְׁעַת), שָׁעָתִי (not שְׁעָתִי), שָׁעָתוֹ, שָׁעָתָם, and so on. As Yalon showed, the evidence of vocalized manuscripts and oral traditions converges here.[96] It is fair to conclude that this is an authentic form going back to prior

93 See §§ 21–23 above.
94 Compare Sussman 1974:88–158.
95 Further details can be found in Bar-Asher 1984:14–15.
96 See Yalon 1964:117–123.

to 200 CE. The sheer number of witnesses, and their mutual independence, point convincingly to this conclusion.

§ 41 There are a number of indirect sources which enable us to check the antiquity of the information given by the oral and written traditions whereby Tannaitic literature has been handed down. The witnesses, written and oral, that transmit those traditions are many centuries later than the spoken language of MH, but when the forms attested by those witnesses are supported by outside texts, this agreement forms a powerful argument in favor of the forms concerned.

There are a good number and variety of sources of indirect evidence: the writings discovered in the Judean Desert (including the Qumran manuscripts and the texts from the time of Bar Koseba), the Hebrew of the Samaritans, transcriptions of Hebrew words into Greek in the Septuagint, and other transcriptions into Greek and Latin by the church fathers. These sources have the advantage of being independent of the traditional transmission of Jewish literature.

The reason we need such outside checks on the information presented by the Jewish testimonies, written *and* oral, lies in the continuing tension between the different languages and dialects in which the various literary corpora handed down by the Jews have been edited. The language of the Bible, MH, and the language of prayer, each comprise a more or less separate linguistic system. Furthermore, the Aramaic portions of the Bible, the Targumim, the Palestinian Talmud, the aggadic midrashim, and the Babylonian Talmud, all reflect different Aramaic dialects. In such a vast array, some corpuses inevitably enjoy greater prestige than other. Hence, there is the suspicion that the language of one corpus may have been assimilated in transmission to the language of a more prestigious corpus.[97] Sources outside the Jewish tradition are not susceptible to this particular problem, and are therefore more objective, as a few brief examples will show.

17.6.2 Documents from the Judean Desert

§ 42 The suffixed preposition forms הֵימֶנּוּ "from him," הֵימֶנָּה "from her," are common in the Mishnah according to the Babylonian tradition. However, the reliable Palestinian texts of the Mishnah[98] prefer the form מִמֶּנּוּ "from him"

97 See Kutscher 1977:73, where, however, the formulation is too absolute. Contrast below, Chapter 19 §§ 48–60.

98 The question of different linguistic types was discussed in §§ 24–27 above.

and מִמֶּנָּה "from her."[99] At first glance, it may appear that the forms הימנו, הימנה were Babylonian innovations in the Talmudic period. But this pattern can now be shown to have existed already in second century CE Palestine, when Hebrew was still a living language: in the letters and documents discovered in the Judean Desert dating from the beginning of the second century, we find examples such as יותר הימנו עוד דינרים ששה עשר "more than 16 dinars more than that" (in a text from the Cave of the Letters).[100]

Similarly, the preposition -ב is realized in rabbinic literature in two forms, exemplified by בְּבֵית and אַבֵּית.[101] The latter pattern is rare in MH,[102] and for a long time its origin was unknown. The texts from the Judean Desert show that it already existed in the second century: in the phrase יעקב בן יהודה שיושב אבית משכו "Jacob b. Judah, who dwells in Beth Moshko" (Bar Koseba letter 8, ll. 3–4),[103] אבית appears instead of the more familiar בבית.

There are many more examples that fill out the record of the rabbinic sources.[104] Some of the forms attested in these indirect sources reflect a living Hebrew dialect spoken somewhere in Palestine at the time of, or shortly after, the existence of the Second Temple. The two examples given here seem to reflect dialects from the south of the country.[105]

17.6.3 The Samaritan tradition

§ 43 The tradition of the Samaritans is known to us primarily through the masterful work of Ze'ev Ben-Ḥayyim, who devoted a series of thorough studies to *Hebrew and Aramaic in the Samaritan Tradition*.[106] Although much of the information has been gathered from the Samaritans in modern times, Ben-Ḥayyim has used the linguistic texts of the Samaritans[107] to demonstrate that most of the features of the Samaritan tradition today go back to the period

---

99 The material is presented in detail below, Chapter 19 §§ 53–56.
100 See ibid., § 56.
101 This form developed from בְּבֵית, which became *bbēt* with loss of the initial *shewa*. This created a consonant cluster at the beginning of the word, and hence a prosthetic vowel was added at the beginning, producing *abbēt*. Compare Yalon 1967:69; Kutscher 1977:63; Ben-Ḥayyim 1957–1977:5.38.
102 See Epstein 1948:1258–1259.
103 See Kutscher 1977:62–63.
104 Compare the remarks above in § 18 about התארמלה in the Damascus Document.
105 Compare §§ 18–19 above.
106 See Ben-Ḥayyim 1957–1977.
107 The linguistic literature of the Samaritans is the subject of the first two volumes of Ben-Ḥayyim's work.

when Hebrew was a spoken language.[108] Hence, if any linguistic feature found in our witnesses of MH is also attested in the tradition of the Samaritans, that feature will be especially likely to represent an authentic survival from the era when Hebrew was a spoken language. Two examples will illustrate this.

§ 44 The pronunciation of צפורן as צְפוֹרֶן is representative of the eastern tradition of MH.[109] The western tradition uses instead the vocalization צִפּוֹרֶן,[110] found also in the Bible (in both the Tiberian[111] and Babylonian[112] vocalizations). It is tempting to view the eastern form as a secondary, medieval development that arose somewhere in the eastern Diaspora. However, the Samaritan tradition reads *sēfērən*,[113] and so tends to show that the spirant form of the פ is not late at all, but was already current in the spoken Hebrew language.[114]

Another example: the Mishnah attests two pronunciations for the place name אילת: either אֵילַת or אַיְלַת. The former appears in MS Kaufmann and Parma A in M. Ma'aser Sheni 5:2; the latter is supported by various other witnesses to the same passage,[115] and by the adjectival form אַיְלָתִית in MS Kaufmann (M. Makhshirin 6:3).[116] The Tiberian reading tradition gives the reading אֵילַת when the name occurs in the Bible (Deut 2:8; 2 Kgs 14:22; etc.). The Samaritan reading tradition, however, reads *mi'ayyålat* at Deut 2:8 (מאילת);[117]

---

108 Ben-Ḥayyim's works provide abundant evidence that the transmission of texts by the Samaritans preserves a language that goes back to the time when Hebrew and Aramaic were still spoken languages.

109 See § 26 above.

110 See ibid.

111 Compare צִפֹּרֶן in Jer 17:1, and צִפָּרְנֶיהָ in Deut 21:12.

112 See Yeivin 1985:1069.

113 Compare *sēferniyya* "her nails" (Deut 21:12), on which see Ben-Ḥayyim 1957–1977:3a.134. Ben-Ḥayyim reconstructed what he thought was a hypothetical Hebrew form צְפֹרֶן corresponding to the Samaritan reading. As it turns out, however, this form is actually attested: the form צְפֹרֶן is found in MSS Parma B and Antonin, in the Mishnayot vocalized according to the Babylonian system, and in the Yemenite tradition (see reference in n. 109 above).

114 This writer has elsewhere suggested that צְפֹרֶן could be a development from צִפֹּרֶן by haplology. On this view, the geminated *p* lost its gemination by haplology (*pp* > *p*), whereupon the *i* was reduced to *shewa* (Bar-Asher 1971:181). There is, however, an alternative possibility: both forms could be derived from an original form such as *ṣipōren*. As Ben-Ḥayyim 1957–1977:3a.134 has shown, the cognate word in other Semitic languages does not exhibit gemination of the *p*. The form may then have developed in two alternative directions: (a) *ṣippōren*, where the first syllable became closed in order to protect the short *i* vowel, and (b) *ṣəfōren*, where the first syllable remains open and the vowel *i* is indeed reduced to *shewa*. The same double process seems to underlie the doublet אִסָּר and אֱסָר "vow," both of which likely evolved from אִסָר* (compare Num 30:3 and 30:6).

115 See Bar-Asher 1980:127.

116 See Kutscher 1977:444–445, but Parma B reads אֵילָתִית in the Makhshirin text.

117 See Ben-Ḥayyim 1957–1977:4.317.

in other words, it has a diphthong *ay* in the first syllable. The Greek transcriptions, likewise, have Αιλα and Αιλαθ, as already observed by Kutscher.[118]

17.6.4 Greek and Latin Transcriptions

§ 45 Transcriptions into Greek and Latin are a rich additional source for establishing the authenticity of mishnaic forms. Some of the forms shown in these transcriptions differ from those of the Tiberian vocalization of the Bible, and yet agree perfectly with the readings of the manuscripts (vocalized or unvocalized) of rabbinic literature. Two instances from the Septuagint have already been cited: Ελληλ, corresponding to הֵלֵּל,[119] and Αιλα, Αιλαθ, corresponding to אֵילַת.[120] Space allows us to cite just one more example, out of many possible ones.

§ 46 The word קרסל "ankle" appears in two parallel passages in the Bible – 2 Sam 22:37 and Ps 18:37 – in a suffixed form vocalized קַרְסֻלָּי "my ankles" in the Tiberian tradition. The singular, according to this tradition, would presumably have been *qarsōl* (< *qarsul*). This angrees with the reading קַרְסוּלָיו "his ankles" found in M. Bekhorot 7:6,[121] according to MS Kaufmann, as well as in the Babylonian vocalization of the Mishnah.[122] However, we also find the form קורסל in M. Oholot 1:8, in MS Kaufmann,[123] and Parma B vocalizes קוּרְסֵל. This agrees with Origen's transcription in the second column of the Hexapla at Psalm 18:37, χορσελαι (compare Kutscher 1959:359). Thus, Origen's form is identical with the form *qursēl*/*qorsēl* attested in MSS Parma B and K (the first hand). Origen lived at the time of the redaction of the Mishnah, and his evidence is, essentially, contemporary with the era when Hebrew was spoken, many centuries earlier than the Mishnah manuscripts available to us today.[124]

---

118 See Kutscher 1977:444–445. At Deut 2:8, the inseparable preposition -מ "from" precedes the name; the Tiberian vocalization reads -מֵ while the Samaritan reading is -מִ.

119 See § 12 above.

120 See § 44 above.

121 The last two letters of this word are written over an erasure: קרסול[יו].

122 See Yeivin 1985:987.

123 This is the consonantal text written by the scribe, but the vocalizer erased the *waw* and pointed קַרְסֵל.

124 It is worth emphasizing once more that alternations of the type ממנה/הימנה, צִפּורן/צְפּורן, אילת/אֵילַת, קרסל/קַרְסֵל, need not represent two diachronic stages of a single form, even those Kutscher tended to regard them as such. Instead one could see two alternative form that were in simultaneous use, perhaps in different dialects.

17.6.5 The language of Liturgy and the Piyyut

§ 47 The importance of indirect sources for knowledge of the grammar and lexicon of MH should now be clear. Other types of Jewish sources may be added, such as the language of the liturgy and *piyyuṭ*, which both contain forms parallel to those found in the Mishnah. It was shown by Yalon[125] and Kutscher,[126] and more recently by Eldar[127] and Yahalom,[128] that many of the the forms characteristic of the Mishnah's language are also attested in the language of the prayers and in numerous *piyyuṭim*. An example is the binyan נֻפְעַל. This is found in the manuscripts of the Mishnah in, e.g., Soṭah 9:12: נוּטַל טעם הפירות "the taste of fruits has been taken away."[129] The same form נוּטַל is found in the liturgy; one example occurs in the phrase וְנֻטַּל כבוד מבית חיינו "and glory has been removed from the house of our life," from the prayer אתה יצרת recited when the New Moon occurs on the Sabbath. Many *piyyuṭim* offer further examples of this *binyan*.[130] Another example is the *po'lān/pu'lān* pattern, which is very common in the manuscripts of the Mishnah and also found in the *piyyuṭim* and other prayers, as Edar has shown:[131] in the Mishnah it appears in, for instance, בּוֹיְשָׁן (= בַּיְשָׁן "shy") in M. Avot 2:5, and תּוּרְגְּמָן/תּוֹרְגְּמָן "translator," found twice in M. Megillah 4:4. Such examples are easily multiplied.[132]

17.7 Conclusion

§ 48 This survey has attempted to outline the basic issues in research into MH. First, having defined the literature written in this language, we examined its origin and its character in relation to Biblical Hebrew (five different aspects of that topic were examined). Second, we considered the homogeneity of MH, under seven different headings. Third, we examined the relationship between MH and other languages. We indicated what light could be shed by indirect sources, and in particular by three of those sources, upon our knowl-

125 See Yalon 1964, *passim*, and n. 129 below.
126 See Kutscher 1972:53–54.
127 See notes 130 and 131 below.
128 See Yahalom 1985:162–176.
129 See Yalon 1964:152–159.
130 See Eldar 1979:381–383, and the references cited there.
131 Eldar 1979:180, 184, etc.
132 The question of the relationship between MH and the language of the rabbinic liturgy and the *piyyuṭim* has been the subject of a number of important observations (see the references in notes 125–131, above), but room remains for a full in-depth analysis.

edge of MH, and we also pointed out the kinship between MH and the Hebrew of the liturgy and *piyyuṭ*.

§ 49 Each topic discussed above offers ample material for decades of scholarly research. The purpose of the present work is not, of course, to exhaust the field, but rather to open up perspectives for those interested in an area of Jewish Studies which has entered a new phase of expansion, and is attracting a new generation of investigators – especially in Israel.[133] Careful examination of numerous manuscripts and research into oral traditions[134] are constantly modifying our understanding of this discipline. In this way, research and analysis of problems old and new, both of grammar and lexicon, have become more rigorous than ever before.

133 The number of doctorates devoted to MH and presented over the last forty years at Israeli universities (especially the Hebrew University in Jerusalem) is well into the double digits.
134 See Bar-Asher 1990b:§§ 8–21.

18 The Study of Mishnaic Hebrew Grammar Based on Written Sources: Achievements, Problems, and Tasks

18.1 Introductory Remarks

§ 1 Three remarks must be made at the outset, to define the parameters of the current paper.

A. The present survey will concentrate primarily on the written sources of MH, in particular, manuscripts of the Mishna, and to a lesser extent the printed editions. (The oral traditions require a separate discussion).

B. This paper will be divided into two parts. First a description of the research that has been conducted and its achievements will be presented, and then we will turn to the problems and tasks that remain. Because of the nature of the subject, however, it is impossible to separate completely the two aspects of the present study. I do provide here an outline of the study of Mishnaic Hebrew grammar, and take up some major points in detail, to summarize what has already been accomplished. I will also try to deal with several linguistic features, some more general in nature, some more specific, that have not been treated at all or have not been treated satisfactorily.[1]

C. I shall focus on the modern scientific study of Mishnaic Hebrew, which began about 90 years ago. I am aware, of course, that in doing so I am ignoring the contributions of earlier scholars such as A. H. Weiss, author of *Studien über die Sprache der Mischna*.[2] I feel that it is justified, however, not only because of the limitations of space, but also because modern research is distinct from that which preceded it both in its scope and achievements. An important landmark in the terrain is Segal's *Grammar of Mishnaic Hebrew* from 1927, which was presaged by his 1908 article in the *Jewish Quarterly Review*. More importantly, during the same period, H. Yalon, the distinguished Hebrew scholar, began his research into Mishnaic Hebrew.

---

1 See, e.g., the use of the definite article on the noun and its modifier (§ 9), the orthography of the plural ־וֹת (§ 10), the 3 pl. pronominal suffixes ־וֹתֵיהֶם/ן, ־וֹתָם/ן (§ 11), the verbal noun קִבֵּל and the plural ־ִיינִין (§ 16), שׂוֹנְאִים/מְשַׂנְּאִים (§ 31 n. 148), and agreement in the construct chain (§ 43). Additional points presented in a new manner can be found throughout this study.

2 See Segal 1936:XXII for literature on earlier works.

18.2 Research and Achievements

18.2.1 Description of Mishnaic Hebrew Studies

§ 2 It is possible to describe the history of research into Mishnaic Hebrew chronologically, dividing the field into by stages, and in doing so to emphasize the central role played by different scholars during the various stages. This is the method followed by E. Y. Kutscher[3] and adopted by several of his students:[4] one begins with A. Geiger, moves on to M. H. Segal, H. Yalon and contemporaries, and concludes with Kutscher and his contemporaries and students. In this manner one notes the important stages of the research and the scholarly views concerning the research. The first stage is represented by Geiger, who claimed that Mishnaic Hebrew was an artificial language that was never spoken. The next is marked by the contribution of Segal. It in turn is followed by the assessment and criticism of Segal's work by Yalon[5] and Kutscher.[6] Yalon's contribution lies in his focusing on the language of Mishnaic manuscripts and in noting the importance of oral traditions of the Mishna.[7] Kutscher[8] perfected Yalon's methodology and differentiated between reliable manuscripts and those less reliable. The final stage is made up of the works of Kutscher's contemporaries and students, who, today, continue the research into the grammar of Mishnaic Hebrew.[9]

This commonly accepted method of presenting the history of Mishnaic Hebrew research has its obvious benefits; however, I doubt if it is the best way to examine the field. Part of what Segal presented in his grammar is still valid and not all of what Kutscher proposed has been completely accepted. For this reason, I believe that the study of Mishnaic Hebrew should be viewed somewhat differently: both by its stages, and, in a more general way, by the whole period.

18.2.2 Some Central Questions in the Study of Mishnaic Hebrew

§ 3 Modern research into Mishnaic Hebrew makes use of the same two primary methods that characterize all modern linguistic research into the study

3 See Kutscher 1977b:73 ff.
4 See, e.g., Bar-Asher 1971:168–169 (= Bar-Asher 2009a Vol. 1 §§ 10–12); Sharvit 1981:221–224.
5 See Yalon 1971:104–112. This article first appeared in *KirSef* 1936–1937
6 Kutscher wrote about Segal's work on several different occasions. See, e.g., Kutscher 1977b:73.
7 Yalon's main publications on Mishnaic Hebrew have been collected (Yalon 1963; Yalon 1971).
8 See the bibliography at the end of this volume for his publications.
9 Many of these works are detailed in the references in this chapter and throughout this book.

of ancient languages – the synchronic and diachronic. These complementary approaches are applied to Mishnaic Hebrew in the discussion of central questions, the examination of specific grammatical topics, and the investigation of hundreds of isolated phenomena.

The following are some of the central questions that have been discussed and re-discussed in the scientific literature.

§ 4 What are the origins of Mishnaic Hebrew and when was it first written down? Figuring prominently in the literature is the opinion championed by Ben Yehuda,[10] Segal,[11] Sznejder,[12] and others, who have turned to the end of the First Temple period for the roots of Mishnaic Hebrew. They believed that Mishnaic Hebrew was a colloquial language spoken in one area of Palestine at that time, or at the latest, during the beginning of the Second Temple period.[13] Much has also been said about the date when Mishnaic Hebrew was written down. This question has been addressed by the scholars just listed, as well as those who have dealt with the language of the Second Temple Biblical books, including, in our generation, C. Rabin,[14] A. Bendavid,[15] and A. Hurvitz.[16] Recent studies on the history of the Hebrew language, including the period of Mishnaic Hebrew, have re-examined and the processes which gave rise to Mishnaic Hebrew. It was apparently a gradual process that lasted hundreds of years, from the end of the First Temple period until the Tannaitic period, i.e., from around the time of the destruction of the Temple until the end of the period in which Hebrew was a living, spoken language.[17]

§ 5 Another way of looking at Mishnaic Hebrew research is by asking: what is the relationship between Biblical Hebrew and Mishnaic Hebrew? Almost all who have dealt with Mishnaic Hebrew have grappled with the question and have contributed, to varying degrees, to its elucidation. Two differing points of view emerge from many nuanced opinions that have been advanced. The first limits the extent of the differences between the two periods of Hebrew. The two most outstanding proponents of this view are Segal,[18] first in articles,

---

10 See Ben Yehuda1948:83 ff.

11 See Segal 1926:30–44, and before him, Lipschütz 1923:39–42

12 See Sznejder 1934–1935:305–308 and *passim*.

13 See, e.g., Rabin 1965:152, and the extensive bibliography in Steiner 1992.

14 Rabin 1965:152.

15 See Bendavid 1967:60–94.

16 See Hurvitz 1972:13 ff.

17 See Bar-Asher 1985:93–99 (= below, Chapter 19 §§ 23–30). Recently Talshir 1993 has proposed a bold theory as to the origin of Mishnaic Hebrew.

18 See Segal 1908; idem 1926. He says explicitly (Segal 1908:734): "Our survey of some of the chief features of MH grammar has revealed the fact that as far as strict grammar is concerned, MH is absolutely independent of Aramaic; that it is identical in the main with BH ..."

and later in his *Grammar of Mishnaic Hebrew*, and Z. Ben-Ḥayyim, in his many books, articles,[19] and seminars. In the case of Segal, this may be because his description of Mishnaic Hebrew was based on printed editions in which the differences between Mishnaic Hebrew and Biblical Hebrew are not all that great. This contrasts significantly, however, with the differences between the two strata of the language as reflected in Mishnaic manuscripts, particularly those which Kutscher has labeled as "reliable."[20] Ben-Ḥayyim presented explicitly his view of the unity of the two dialects in his profound article, "The Historical Unity of the Hebrew Language and Its Division into Periods."[21] It should be stressed that in that study, Ben-Ḥayyim deals exclusively with the written language, and he believes that the grammar of Biblical Hebrew and Mishnaic Hebrew are the same in morphology and syntax:[22] "There are no decisive differences between these two, not in the entire realm of morphology, nor in syntax."[23]

§ 6 Proponents of the second view maintain that Biblical Hebrew and Mishnaic Hebrew differ. Both Yalon, who immersed himself in the study of manuscripts and the oral traditions, and Kutscher, who concentrated primarily on manuscripts (and of those, primarily MS Kaufmann),[24] as well as other scholars, pointed out both details and more general phenomena in which Biblical Hebrew and Mishnaic Hebrew differ. For example, one finds the distinction between Biblical *hitpa"el* and Mishnaic *nitpa"al* (Yalon often dealt with this point);[25] the 2ms pronominal suffix בֵּיתְךָ vs. בֵּיתָךְ;[26] the plural of nouns ending in *-ut*: מַלְכֻיּוֹת vs. מַלְכִיּוֹת;[27] הִלֵּל vs. הֶלֵּל.[28] Some of the features reflect temporal differences between Biblical Hebrew and Mishnaic Hebrew: diachronic changes affected Hebrew between the periods of the Bible and the Mishna, accounting for some of the differences. For example, one should view the difference between *hitpa"el* and *nitpa"al* as a chronological development; the newer form was created in a late period by analogy with *nif'al*.[29] It is clear, however, that not all of the differences between Biblical Hebrew (primarily

19 See particularly Ben-Ḥayyim 1985.
20 Yalon, Kutscher, and others, whose studies are based on manuscripts, have revealed and highlighted the many differences between Biblical grammar and Mishnaic grammar
21 See Ben-Ḥayyim 1985.
22 Ben-Ḥayyim 1985:53
23 Sznejder 1930:18, 21 thought (naively, as is characteristic of his writing) that only the vocalic systems of Biblical Hebrew and Mishnaic Hebrew were identical.
24 See the bibliography for their different works on Mishnaic Hebrew. See also the references in nn. 25–28 below.
25 See, e.g., Yalon 1964:15 ff.
26 See Yalon 1964:13 ff; Kutscher 1977b:261 ff.; Steiner 1979.
27 See, e.g., Kutscher 1969:1–3.
28 See, e.g., Kutscher 1977b:257–258; idem 1968:233–236; Bar-Asher 1980:11, 64, 92.
29 See, e.g., Segal 1936:118.

according to the Tiberian tradition) and Mishnaic Hebrew (primarily according to MS Kaufman and similar manuscripts) are to be attributed to chronology, since it is entirely possible that the difference between הִלֵּל and הֶלֵּל and חֲנֻיוֹת and חֲנִיּוֹת reflect differences of tradition and not of time.[30]

§ 7 The works of the late G. Haneman, particularly his comprehensive and enlightening investigations of the tradition of MS Parma A, deal in part with tracking the development of linguistic features from the early books of the bible up through Mishnaic Hebrew. Thus, for example, he studied the distributions of רַב and חַי,[31] on the one hand, and רָבָּה and חָיָה, on the other.[32] Other scholars have also dealt with similar issues. Bendavid's book *Biblical Hebrew and Mishnaic Hebrew*, is comprised of, as its name indicates, a series of similar investigations. S. Morag has also adopted this approach in several of his important discussions on the grammar of Mishnaic Hebrew in the Yemenite tradition as well as in other traditions, e.g., the relationship between the two pointings of the relative pronoun *šin*: שֶׁ vs. שְׁ.[33] The pointing with *šewa* appears in certain traditions of Mishnaic Hebrew in different forms: שְׁאִם, שְׁאֵין, שְׁהוּא, שְׁהִיא, etc.,[34] and it reflects a later development than that of the pointing with the *segol* (or with *pataḥ*).[35] Sarfatti's discussions should be mentioned here, particularly, his treatment of the syntagm ערב פסחים.[36] Especial attention should also be paid to the discussion of the tradition of MS Parma B.[37]

§ 8 A question which reappears occasionally in the literature concerns the background of the differences between Biblical Hebrew and Mishnaic

---

30 See §§ 30–32 below.

31 See Haneman 1974b:8–14

32 Haneman presented tables of the distribution of roots, forms, and words, which prevent certain false conclusions. It suffices to mention his thorough investigation into אַתְּ/אַתָּה (Haneman 1980b:460–465), in which he, too, determines that אַתָּה existed in Mishnaic Hebrew (see my remarks concerning the pronouns in Bar-Asher 1971:172). He believes, as do others, that both אַתְּ and אַתָּה occurred in at least the written language.

33 See Morag 1953:184–185

34 See Bar-Asher 1971:180

35 The pointing of the relative pronoun *šin* with *pataḥ*, which is known from a few examples in the Tiberian tradition of Biblical Hebrew (e.g., שַׁקַּמְתִּי Judg. 5:7), is known also in tradition of Mishnaic Hebrew. It is not only limited to those traditions in which *pataḥ* and *segol* have merged, as in the tradition which is reflected in the mishnayot containing Babylonian pointing and the Yemenite tradition (in these there is no difference between the realization of the *pataḥ* and the *segol* in the Bible and the Mishna, but also in the consistent tradition of MS Antonin of the Order Teharot (e.g., שַׁשֵּׂעָר in m. Nega'im 4:3; שַׁיִּטַּמְּאֶנּוּ in m. Nega'im 7:4 – since it is an eastern manuscript). It is also known, however, in all of the traditions according to the indirect evidence of עַכְשָׁו, which is the result of the contraction of עַד כְּשֶׁהוּא (*šin* with a *pataḥ*!), as Ben-Ḥayyim has shown (Ben-Ḥayyim 1954:81–82). See also below, Chapter 24 § 18.

36 See Sarfatti 1977.

37 See Bar-Asher 1971:183 and *passim*.

Hebrew: are the differences essentially chronological or are they dialectical? Mishnaic Hebrew is obviously later than Biblical Hebrew, but is it a direct descendant of the language of the First Temple period that is reflected in the Bible – if we assume, for the moment, that Biblical Hebrew is a uniform language – or is it a descendant of a dialect only related to Biblical Hebrew?[38]

§ 9 The following example exemplifies this problem well both because of what is certain and what is uncertain. The standard grammar of Biblical Hebrew claims that in a definite noun phrase consisting of a noun and an adjective, *both* have to have the definite article. Thus, המזבח הפנימי and הלילה הראשון reflect the expected construction. However, the syntagms מזבח הפנימי and לילה הראשון are found in both Biblical Hebrew and Mishnaic Hebrew.[39] Yet, as is now well known,[40] this construction is very rare in Biblical Hebrew, and relatively more common in Mishnaic Hebrew. Moreover, of the two constructions, the second, with the definite article only on the adjective, appears to be older than the first: at first the definite article was added only to the adjective, and only later was it added to the noun, as well, by attraction, thus producing המזבח הפנימי and הלילה הראשון. The different distribution in the Bible and Mishna is curious. If the earlier syntagm is more common in the later literature, is this a stylistic trait only – i.e., Mishnaic Hebrew extended the use of a rare Biblical syntagm – or does this detail taken together with other details show that Mishnaic Hebrew is descended from a dialect in which attraction of the definite article to the noun preceding the determined adjective was more limited? If the latter is true, this feature together with others[41] might be interpreted as pointing to two different dialects and not two levels of the same dialect.

Moreover, whoever speaks of the dependence of Mishnaic Hebrew on Biblical Hebrew – and no one will deny that there was such dependence, in all fields of the language (orthography, phonology, morphology, and syntax) – should keep in mind that it is possible that any given feature was more common in Mishnaic Hebrew than is reflected in its witnesses (i.e. in manuscripts and printed editions). Often, under the influence of Biblical Hebrew, features which distinguished MH from BH were “corrected” by copyists and printers,

---

38 Scholars have frequently dealt with the question whether or not Mishnaic Hebrew is a descendant of a Biblical dialect (see recently Kutscher 1972b:30; above, Chapter 17 §§ 10–11).

39 See Sznejder 1930:26; Segal 1936:55–56; Berggrün 1973:225 ff. A recent and penetrating investigation of this question can be found in Ben-Ḥayyim 1987:99–103.

40 The data in manuscripts, as against the data in printed editions, have not been properly investigated. Segal 1936:55–56 hints at differences between MS Kaufmann and the printed editions. See now Sarfatti 1989.

41 See n. 38 above.

in an effort to make the Mishna accord with expectations of Hebrew grammar.[42] One must emphasize, however, that one should not exaggerate the dialectal differences between Mishnaic Hebrew and Biblical Hebrew. Comments like those of Sznejder[43] and others, who claim to know exactly where the dialect of Mishnaic Hebrew comes from, are exaggerated and naïve.[44]

§ 10 The literary relationship of Mishnaic Hebrew to Biblical Hebrew is also a topic that has occupied scholars. For example, Haneman took up this question in a brief but instructive lecture "Biblical Borrowings in the Mishna."[45] There he discussed, for example, the use of the form נערה מאורשה/מאורסה (m. Nedarim 10:1 and elsewhere) as opposed to מאורסת, or the form ככה and not כך in m. Soṭa 9:6. All aspects of the language show the relationship of Mishnaic Hebrew to Biblical Hebrew. The boundaries, however, are not always clear, and have often been confused. Two different types of examples shall suffice. The first is orthographic: it is known that *scriptio defectiva* is still found in Biblical books, especially the earlier ones, even when the vowels are long. Thus, for example, the plural ending -ות is written frequently defective, e.g., אָבֹת (Exod. 12:3; 20:4); אבעבעֹת (Exod. 9:9, 10). This orthographic practice changed considerably in Mishnaic Hebrew. The ending was written regularly -ות: שָׁעוֹת (m. Berakhot 1:2), בַּלֵּילוֹת (m. Berakhot 1:5), בְּאוֹתוֹתֶיהָ/בְּאוֹתִיּוֹתֶיהָ[46] (m. Berakhot 2:3), etc. Sometimes, however, *scriptio defectiva* is found, e.g., שוֹאֲבֹת (m. Terumot 10:3 and m. Makšhirin 3:3[47] in MS Kaufmann) without a *waw* in the final syllable. It is possible that the Biblical הַשֹּׁאֲבֹת[48] (Gen. 24:11) served as a model for the scribe of MS Kaufmann, or for the scribe of the manuscript from which he copied the Mishna. Also relevant here are the observations made by H. Cohen about the use of אתו, rather than אותו, in MS Kaufmann.[49] Until when was the orthography of Mishnaic Hebrew dependent on the orthography of Biblical Hebrew? It is more likely that this reflects the habits of copyists many generations after the close of the Tannaitic literature than to a practice which was common when the language was alive. Nonetheless, one cannot ignore the defective spellings found, for example, in Bar

42 I do not necessarily intend that it was restricted as a result of later copyists (see Sarfatti 1983). Rather, it is possible that the original scribes of Mishnaic Hebrew continued the writing habits of Biblical Hebrew.

43 See Sznejder 1934–1935:305–308.

44 See § 23 below and Talshir 1993.

45 See Haneman 1980:6.

46 See Epstein 1948:1257–1258; Bar-Asher 1980a:28.

47 The vocalizer adder a *waw* after the *bet* and pointed a *ḥolem*.

48 The *waw* after the *šin* is also absent in this occurrence in Genesis.

49 See Cohen 1983:210 n. 5.

Koseba's letters, e.g., אכלין, דאגין[50] (Letter 1), לישע (= לישוע, Letter 7), שידע (= שידוע), עלתי (= עליתי), שהגיים (= שהגויים, Letter 8), alongside cases of plene spellings, which are the rule.

§ 11 In order to show just how complicated the dependence of Mishnaic Hebrew on Biblical Hebrew is, I shall cite another example that is germane for several reasons: the 3mp and 3fp suffixes on plural nouns ending in -וֹת: שֵׁמוֹת, דּוֹרוֹת, אָבוֹת. In early Hebrew (from the Bible up to Mishnaic Hebrew) one finds אֲבוֹתָם, שְׁמוֹתָם/שְׁמוֹתָן, but also אֲבוֹתֵיהֶם, שְׁמוֹתֵיהֶם. Almost all who have dealt with this question have erred, some more and some less, in presenting and analyzing the data.[51] I shall only briefly touch on it here. It is clear that the older form in Hebrew was -וֹתָם/וֹתָן, but already in an early period the form -וֹתֵיהֶם/-וֹתֵיהֶן appeared, as evidenced, e.g., by מְכֵרוֹתֵיהֶם in the blessing of Jacob (Gen. 49:5) which by all accounts is an early text. In the course of time, however, the order became reversed and the use of -וֹתֵיהֶם/-וֹתֵיהֶן became prevalent, and the use of וֹתָם/וֹתָן restricted, as is apparent from the later books of the Bible and from the Mishnaic corpus. The distribution of אבותם/אבותיהם exemplifies this. In Chronicles one finds אֲבוֹתָם 13× and אֲבוֹתֵיהֶם 26×; in Tannaitic literature אֲבוֹתָם/ן occurs 6× as against אֲבוֹתֵיהֶם/ן, which is found 16×.[52] Similarly, אִמּוֹתָם occurs 3× in the Bible, but in Tannaitic literature אִמּוֹתָן 1× and אִמּוֹתֵיהֶן 4×.[53] One receives the impression that the source of the spellings of אֲבוֹתָן (e.g., m. Abot 2:2; m. Nidda 4:2 [2×]),[54] אִמּוֹתָן (t. Soṭa 6:4 in MS Vienna; in MS Erfurt אימן [sing.]) lies in the literary influence of the Bible, i.e., "borrowing", to quote Haneman. One should not attribute these forms to later copyists under any circumstance, since the occurrence of the examples in different manuscripts demonstrates that it is early. Thus, this feature belongs to the Tannaim, the authors of the texts. It seems reasonable that this is the explanation for the form זכות אבותן in Avot, a tractate, which has a clear literary connection to the Bible.[55] It is not to be attributed to the corrections that copyists introduced into the text under the influence of the Biblical language. And what of the form רוחותן, which occurs twice in Tannaitic litera-

---

50 See Kutscher 1977a:55 ff.

51 In addition to the standard grammars, see, e.g., Bendavid 1971:452 (he devotes one line), Cohen 1975:303–305; Hurvitz 1982:24–27. Qimron 1976:243 ff. is an exception. Even though he does not take up the subject in all periods of the language, the material is presented properly.

52 See Chapter Eleven, above.

53 *Idem.*

54 These Mishnaic readings are found in MS Kaufmann and other manuscripts (cf., e.g., MS Parma B for the examples in m. Nidda).

55 As pointed out by many scholars. See recently Sharvit 1976, *passim*; Haneman 1980a, *passim* (e.g., "shortened imperfect," 31–33).

ture: מארבע רוחותן (Sifre be-Midbar, § 83, ed. Horovitz, p. 79; also MS Vatican 32 and other MSS) and in the Mekhilta de-R. Šimʿon ben Yoḥai (ויהי, ed. Horovitz and Rabin, p. 81, in MS Oxford and three additional witnesses)?[56] Here, too, should one say that the Bible is responsible, although neither רוחותם nor רוחותיהם is attested in BH: the suffix has been transferred from the forms אבותם and שמותם to רוחות, and displaced the expected רוחותיהן. It should be noted that this is the common suffix in the non-Biblical scrolls from Qumran; it is not limited to the biblical forms אבותם and דורותם but also occurs in the non-Biblical מסורותם and מצודותם.[57] Indeed, it seems that the use of -ותן never ceased to exist in Hebrew, and survived through the Mishnaic period. It is possible that in literary Hebrew this form was preserved even at a late period.

To sum up, the extent of dependence on the Bible and the extent of Biblical borrowing are important questions in Mishnaic Hebrew research. Each feature analyzed must be examined separately and carefully.

§ 12 Another question concerning the relationship of Biblical Hebrew to Mishnaic Hebrew is the extent of Aramaic influence (and of other languages) on Mishnaic Hebrew. The literature is replete with discussions and remarks attributing many of the differences between Biblical Hebrew and Mishnaic Hebrew to the influence of Aramaic on Hebrew in the Second Temple period and later. This belief, expressed already in preceding centuries by S. Levisohn[58] and A. Geiger,[59] and many years ago by Ben Yehuda,[60] Schneider,[61] and others, still exists today. One of Kutscher's criticisms of Segal was that "in trying to prove the uniqueness and independence of Mishnaic Hebrew, he exaggerated and tried by all means to limit the role of Aramaic in shaping its image."[62] Segal is not the only scholar who believed that Aramaic influence on Mishnaic Hebrew was limited. Ben-Ḥayyim, too, is of the opinion that much of what is commonly attributed to Aramaic influence in Mishnaic Hebrew is really a different form of Hebrew (similar to Aramaic), which was marginal in the Biblical period and became dominant only in the later period.[63] Claims

---

56 The editors cite only רוחותיהם.

57 Qimron has published some of the data (see n. 51 above). I thank him for making available to me unpublished data.

58 See S. Levisohn, "On the Mishnaic Hebrew Grammar" (Hebrew), which was published in many editions of the Mishna before the Order Zeraim, e.g., in the Warsaw edition.

59 As is well known, Geiger claimed that Mishnaic Hebrew was an artificial *Mischsprache* composed of Biblical and Aramaic elements (see Kutscher 1977b:73 ff.).

60 See Ben Yehuda 1948:83 ff.

61 See his comments on קבע and other forms (Sznejder 1930:15).

62 See Kutscher 1977b:74.

63 See especially his remarks at the end of vol. 5 (Ben-Ḥayyim 1957–1977:5.251–259).

of Aramaic influence are widespread in the literature; it suffices to mention Kutscher's remarks on the 2ms and 2fs pronominal suffixes ךְָ- and ךְִי- in forms like בֵּיתָ-ךְ, בֵּיתִיךְ,[64] or Morag's detailed discussion of the rise of the conjugations *pa'el* and *nitpā'al*.[65] Bendavid also attributes many features in Mishnaic Hebrew to Aramaic;[66] he even hints on occasion of a relationship of Mishnaic Hebrew to Greek grammar.[67] The relationship of Mishnaic Hebrew to other languages has come up in the literature, primarily with regard to vocabulary.[68]

18.2.3 Results of Mishnaic Hebrew Research

§ 13 I shall now turn to the results of research into Mishnaic Hebrew, including the description of printed editions and manuscripts,[69] as well as the methodology of the description. Here, too, I limit myself to general remarks since it is impossible to summarize adequately the result of 70 years of research, which consists of dozens of books and hundreds of articles.

Grammars such as those of Segal,[70] Porath,[71] and Haneman,[72] the monumental work of I. Yeivin,[73] and comprehensive treatments such as Yalon's two books,[74] Bendavid's two volumes,[75] and the study of MS Paris,[76] have drastically changed our knowledge of Mishnaic Hebrew. These works have not only contributed to specific topics in all fields of grammar, but they have also presented us with a new overall view of Mishnaic Hebrew. The many articles on the subject have also significantly changed our understanding of the field. One must mention in chronological order the works of Segal and Sznejder,[77]

---

64 See Kutscher 1977b:89 ff., and the more nuanced view of Steiner 1979.

65 See Morag 1971a:93.

66 Bendavid 1971 is full of examples. See, e.g., p. 479.

67 See Bendavid 1971. For example, in notes on pp. 653 and 660 he says, "perhaps Greek aided it."

68 See, e.g., Kutscher's remarks on the Akkadian origin of אֲפַר (Kutscher 1977:444–454) and on Persian influence (idem 1972:24 ff.). See also above, Chapter 17 §§ 31–37.

69 For details on Mishnaic Hebrew manuscripts and other works that have been investigated, see above, Chapter 17 §§ 1–14. One should now add MS Erfurt of the Tosefta, which was examined by H. Nathan (1984).

70 See Segal 1927 and Segal 1936.

71 See Porath 1938.

72 See Haneman 1980.

73 See Yeivin 1985.

74 See Yalon 1964; idem 1971.

75 See Bendavid 1971.

76 See Bar-Asher 1980a.

77 See the bibliography at the end of this volume.

Yalon,[78] Kutscher,[79] and Ben-Ḥayyim and their colleagues, students, and students' students. Some of the studies have dealt with more theoretical questions such as similarity between Mishnaic Hebrew and the Samaritan traditions of the Pentateuch and the similarity between the two of them and the Qumran tradition.[80] Also theoretical in nature are the brilliant articles of Kutscher[81] dealing with the nature and essence of Mishnaic Hebrew. Other works have examined thoroughly and comprehensively one manuscript[82] or one grammatical topic in a manuscript, while some have taken up a general topic in a literary unit or period. Example of the latter are the important work of B. Gross on nouns ending with the suffixes *-on, -an,*[83] M. Mishor on the tense system of Tannaitic Hebrew,[84] and S. Sharvit's monograph on the Tractate Abot.[85] Most of these works are characterized by philological investigations and linguistic descriptions, some of which are diachronic, and others descriptive-synchronic (to the extent that the term is relevant when dealing with a non-living language).

§ 14 The study of manuscripts has yielded many results affecting all aspects of Mishnaic Hebrew. The following are just a few features from the verbal system:[86]

A. The conjugations *nuf'al, nittaf'al*[87], *pē'ēl, nitpa''ēl,* and *nippə'al* are virtually unattested in printed editions;[88] the examination of manuscripts revealed them.
B. The investigation of the relationship between *hiṯpa'ēl* and *niṯpa'al,* which Yalon initiated, was furthered by Haneman and others, based solely on examination of the manuscripts.[89]
C. Uncommon forms in the verbal system such as the *hif'īl* of II-*waw* on the analogy of I-*waw*;[90] the *qal* participial II-*waw* with *ḥolem,* e.g., זונים,

78 These have been collected in Yalon 1963 and Yalon 1971.
79 Most of them have been collected in Kutscher 1977a.
80 See Ben-Ḥayyim 1971.
81 Especially Kutscher 1977b.
82 E.g., Bentolila 1989, which is a systematic grammar of one manuscript.
83 See Gross 1971; idem 1993.
84 See Mishor 1983.
85 See Sharvit 1976 and Sharvit 2004.
86 Haneman 1980a is full of examples, many of which, however, have been previously described in the literature.
87 On the *nuf'al* and *nittaf'al,* see, e.g., Yalon 1964:152 ff. See also Moreshet 1980b on *nuf'al.*
88 On *pē'el* and *nitpā'al* see Morag 1971a and 1971c, and Chap. 20 §§ 17–21 (see the literature cited there). On *nippə'al* see especially Chapter 20 below, which deals extensively with all the *binyanim* of Mishnaic Hebrew.
89 See Segal 1936:118–119; Yalon 1964:15 ff.; Haneman 1980:208–211 ff.; Bar-Asher 1980:20–21.
90 See Yalon 1964:165 ff.; Bar-Asher 1983b:152.

מולים;[91] the alternation of participial forms *pōʿēl* and *pāʿēl*;[92] the use of the participle *nitpaʿēl* alongside *mitpaʿēl*;[93] forms of *hitpaʿēl* with assimilated *taw*.[94]

D. The use of verbal forms, including participial forms such as נידון and נָדוֹן, חַי and חָיָה, רַב and רָבָה,[95] נִרְאָה and נִרְאֶה,[96] the use of *pāʿēl* for legal terms.[97]

§ 15 The investigation of manuscripts continues to uncover scores of previously unknown details and entire grammatical categories. I should especially like to point out the role of the present generation of scholars, such as G. Birnbaum[98] on the pointing of the definite article in the tradition of the vocalizer of MS Kaufmann; C. Cohen[99] on pronominal suffixes; and S. Naeh[100] in his comprehensive and thorough work on the linguistic traditions in MS Vatican 66.

§ 16 As already noted, scholars at times focus on general questions and at other times concentrate on only one specific point. I shall mention just two details in the tradition of the scribe of MS Kaufmann. The form קיבול (apart from the syntagm בית קיבול) occurs six times in the Mishna in tractate Zevaḥim: in three of the occurrences the scribe of MS Kaufmann writes קיבול (m. Zevahim 1:4[6];1:5;3:5);[101] however, in the three other occurrences he writes קיבל and the vocalizer adds a *waw* above the *bet* (m. Zevahim 5:1,2,4). Probably the scribe of MS Kaufmann knew both קִבֵּל and קִבּוּל to be verbal nouns of *piʿēl*, as is true for דִּבֵּר and דִּבּוּר.[102]

---

91 See Yalon 1964:171 ff.; Haneman 1980:276 ff.; Bar-Asher 1983b:21–22.

92 See Haneman's discussion (1980a:92 ff.), and most recently the excellent study of Nathan 1984:279 ff, and Naeh 1989:89 ff.

93 See Qimron 1977:144 ff.; Bar-Asher 1977b:128 ff.; idem 1980a:106 ff.

94 See recently Bar-Asher 1983b:145–148.

95 See Haneman 1980a:283 ff.

96 See below, Chapter 21.

97 See Nathan 1984, and especially Mishor 1983.

98 See Birnbaum 1983. Even though questions arise as a result of this study, they do not detract in any way from the basic, well-grounded investigation.

99 See Cohen 1983; idem 1992.

100 See Naeh 1989.

101 I do not attach any importance to the fact that קיבול occurs alongside הילוך in m. Zebahim 1:4. The other occurrences of קיבול are not found in the vicinity of *piʿul* forms, which could conceivably serve as the source of analogy.

102 See Berggrün 1971:254.

A second example is the plural of יין. Dictionaries and grammars cite only יינות (e.g., *Šeq.* 4:3). MS Vatican 32 of the Sifre (it is not alone) evidences the form יינין: ... מיין ושכר יזיר בשאר היינין חוץ מיין מצוה (par. 23, ed. Horovitz, p. 27).[103]

18.2.4 Unity of Mishnaic Hebrew

§ 17 Several fundamental aspects of the unity of Mishnaic Hebrew have been examined and re-examined in different grammatical investigations. I shall mention only the most important.

§ 18 On the one hand, Segal treated all the divisions of Mishnaic Hebrew as one unit, i.e. Tannaitic Hebrew and Amoraic Hebrew, in Palestine and in Babylonia. Yalon did the same.[104] On the other hand, it has been argued that one should separate Tannaitic Hebrew from Amoraic Hebrew, or to use Kutscher's terms: Mishnaic Hebrew 1 (MH1) and Mishnaic Hebrew 2 (MH2), the first reflecting Mishnaic Hebrew when it was still a living language, and the second when it was a literary language alone – and within this to distinguish between the language of the Palestinian Amoraim and that of the Babylonian Amoraim.[105]

§ 19 Additional distinctions within the divisions themselves can be found in the literature, e.g., the separation between "early Mishnayot" and the essential part of the Mishna suggested by past (e.g., Sznejder,[106] L. Ginzberg,[107] J. N. Epstein[108]) and present[109] scholars.

Some scholars have attempted to use other criteria in distinguishing different units in the language of the Mishna, e.g., the difference between ritual, which is inclined towards conservatism and a close connection to Biblical Hebrew, and most of the Mishna. Haneman employed this distinction in analyzing the use of *hitpaʿʿal* forms (השתחוה, התנדב, התפלל), which he found in ritual descriptions, as opposed to *nitpaʿʿal* in non-ritual contexts in the Mishna.[110]

---

103 Horovitz incorrectly cites in the apparatus היינות as occurring in MS Vatican 32.

104 Sharvit points this out, but one wonders about his criticism of Yalon.

105 On this subject, see Kutscher 1972b:40 ff.; Moreshet 1972; idem 1974a; idem 1974b; and recently Breuer 1985; idem 1993.

106 See Sznejder 1934–1936:307.

107 See Ginzberg 1919:41–65.

108 Epstein 1957:21 ff.

109 See Bar-Asher 1985:§§ 26–28 (pp. 95 ff.).

110 See Haneman 1980a:208 ff.

Distinctions have also been made on the basis of different literary divisions, e.g., distinguishing between the parts of the Mishna that deal with halachic decisions and e.g., Abot, which has a different literary structure – aphorisms that continue to a great extent the writing norms of Biblical poetry, as shown by Haneman and especially Sharvit.[111] Another distinction attested in the literature is between the main part of the Mishna as against Aggadic portions of the Mishna, e.g., the aggada found at the conclusion of many tractates.

To sum up, all the studies referred to above have shown that the Mishna on the whole reflects a pristine Mishnaic Hebrew, whereas its other divisions (the oldest division of the Mishna, mishnayot which deal with ritual, the language of the aphorisms in the Tractate Abot, and selections of aggada) reveal a close connection to the Bible.

§ 20 A different type of distinction within Tannaitic Hebrew was made by J. N. Epstein, primarily in the Mishna and Tosefta. He pointed out many imaginary disagreements that are nothing more than linguistic alternations between Tanna'im, each Tanna using different language. For example, the three versions in m. Kelim 8:9 and the parallel in t. Kelim Baba Qamma 6:17 speak of an oven (פורנה) that has ליזביז or אסטגיות or סָפִּיוֹת (שָׁפִּיוֹת).[112] The Tosefta already remarks that they are three different words for the same object: כולן שם אחד הן. Epstein cites many examples, all from the realm of the lexicon. He viewed them as "variant synonyms"[113] and not different words. Perhaps he was hinting that they reflect different dialects.

§ 21 The demand that one distinguish between the language of the Tosefta and that of the Mishna, and that one differentiate the two from the language of Halakhic midrashim (if they reflect one language type), and all of these as opposed to Seder 'Olam,[114] have undergone a process of refinement. This approach has proven itself on the basis of an examination of texts. The distinction pointed out by Nathan is relevant here: she was able to show an opposition between נלקח in the Mishna and ניקח, with assimilated *lamed*, in the Tosefta. Her investigation reveals additional examples, as well.[115] The general question concerning the distinction between the different divisions of Tannaitic literature, however, still awaits a thorough and comprehensive examination.

111 See n. 55 above.

112 See Epstein 1957:234–240. (See also Albeck 1959:100–101, who cites this example indicating "a division in the language").

113 See Epstein 1957:240.

114 An interesting preliminary attempt can be found in the MA thesis of the late Z. Pashḥur (Pashḥur 1986).

115 See Nathan 1984: חוצה לארץ/חוץ לארץ (p. 19), נלקח/נקח (p. 165). See also pp. 364 ff.

§ 22 Progress has recently been made in further dividing and classifying the reading traditions, at least within the general framework of the Hebrew of the Mishnah. One can claim that every manuscript stands by itself. My sense, however, is that it is possible to be more general and say that there are different traditions – at least three broad ones. Since this has been treated elsewhere,[116] I shall limit myself to a few short remarks. First, one must divide the traditions into two primary branches: a Palestinian branch and a Babylonian branch. They are distinguished grammatically (including syntactically) and lexically, e.g., the distinction between the syntagm שהוא קורא and שקורא.[117] Within the Palestinian branch there is a further distinction between an eastern and a western tradition. The two are similar in the consonantal text, but preserve distinctions in phonology and morphophonology, e.g., the limited use or absence of *dageš* with *reš* in the western tradition,[118] as against its relatively regular occurrence in the eastern tradition.[119]

---

116 See below, Chapter 19.

117 See ibid., § 47.

118 See Chapter 19 § 24, where it is noted explicitly that in MS Kaufmann there is a *dageš* with the *reš* after the relative *šin*, like the isolated Biblical Tiberian example שֶׁרֹּאשִׁי (Shir ha-Shirim 5:2). T. Zurawel has pointed out that there is a *dageš* with *reš* in the manuscript also after the interrogative מה, e.g., מַה רָּאַת (m. Nedarim 9:9), מַה רָּאִיתָה (m. ʿEduyot 6:3 [4×]), מַה רָּאִיתָ (ibid.), but וּמַה רְאָיָה (m. Pesahim 6:2) without *dageš*. MS Kaufmann however, does not contain all the traits that characterize the eastern tradition: *dāgēš* in *rēš* in the derived conjugations that have gemination (e.g., *piʿēl*) or the noun classes that have gemination. This is true, too, for the relative ש, which is found to a limited extent in some of the western manuscripts: שְׁהִיא, שְׁהוּא, שְׁהֵן, וּשְׁאֵינוֹ, in MS Parma A (see Yeivin 1985:1162). שְׁאֵינוֹ is also attested in MS Deinard (see Bentolila 1989:112–113), however, the extent of the phenomenon is limited as I have indicated, in Italy, where the *šewa* was realized as *e* (like *segol/ṣere*), with the exception of the forms וּשְׁאֵינוֹ, וּשְׁאֵין, n which the *šewa* is quiescent, it is not a morphophonological trait (see below, Chapter 19 § 25). In general, the attempt to classify all Mishnaic manuscripts, and, to a certain extent, also the oral traditions into groups and present them in three primary language traditions has not been an easy task. I emphasized this in Chapter 19 § 19–20. ("Consistency of the Proposed Divisions"): "No division of manuscripts or of traditions is without flaw. There will always be some exceptions or deviations ... This is not surprising. The peregrinations of the Rabbis, of entire communities, and of manuscripts in the Middle Ages, with the concomitant mingling of communities with different backgrounds brought different traditions into contact. As a result, differences between traditions were blurred ... These occasional deviations do not, however, undermine the general picture." I concluded (§ 68): "In a work of a general nature such as this, much caution is required and much of that has been said requires further examination and support. What today is considered doubtful, tomorrow may be show to be certain and what is certain today may turn out to be doubtful tomorrow." My conclusion was provisional. Further investigation is necessary.

119 An additional example that differentiates the two traditions is חֲדָרִים as opposed to חֲרָרִים (see Bar-Asher 1986:187–188).

It appears that even if different language varieties are uncovered in the Babylonian tradition, they cannot blur the dichotomy between the Babylonian and Palestinian traditions.[120]

§ 23 One issue that needs to be addressed, and is directly related to several of the previous topics, is the subject of dialects within Mishnaic Hebrew. What is the source of the distinctions that have to be noted – the different branches and traditions within Mishnaic Hebrew, the different sections of Tannaitic literature (e.g. the Mishna vs. Tosefta: נלקח vs. נקח), linguistic differences among the Rabbis (ליזבז vs. אסטגיות vs. ספיות)? Do these data evidence different dialects within Mishnaic Hebrew?

This question has engaged scholars (e.g., Segal, Yalon, Kutscher)[121] for many years. Even though there is no decisive evidence with regard to the place or time of the different divisions or traditions, the answer is an unqualified yes. This is supported by material that is embedded in literary sources and by material that has been discovered in our generation in non-literary documents. In this context I should mention what was said about the language of the "men of the south."[122] Epstein pointed out that the "man from the south" who came to Simon the Righteous (שמעון הצדיק) is said to have used the word נַעְיָם "spring," and not the regular מַעְיָן.[123] Linguistic features that seem to differentiate different dialects in Mishnaic Hebrew can be found in material from the Judean Desert, e.g., in the Bar-Koseba letters: אַבֵית vs. בְּבֵית, הימנו and הימנה vs. ממנו and ממנה, non-proclitic של;[124] and התארמלה in the Damascus Document[125] from Qumran vs. נתאלמנה in MS Kaufman and similar manuscripts (these forms and others are also attested in the Babylonian branch of Mishnaic Hebrew).

There can be no doubt that a language that was spoken in many areas of Palestine must have had different dialects; however, the relative paucity of written material and the slight epigraphic evidence[126] does not allow one to

120 See Chap. 19 §§ 47–60

121 See, e.g., Segal 1936:18–19.

122 Cf. Epstein 1933:192; Lieberman 1968:75–91 (such as the use of להקל ולהחמיר – "to expound an inference from minor to major" and many other examples).

123 See Epstein 1933:192.

124 See Kutscher 1977a:57; Bar-Asher 1980a:100, 104; Nathan 1984:321–323.

125 See above, Chap. 17, § 18.

126 M. Mishor has discussed the epigraphic material. It must be remembered, however, that the epigraphic material is too scant to allow us to construct far-reaching conclusions.

An example of lacunae in the epigraphic material can be found in the verbal system. The Reḥov inscription, for example, which has approximately 350 words, has only 17 verbal forms (29 occurrences in all), most of which are participles (including participles functioning as nouns). These are the examples (the readings are those of the Databases of the Historical Dictionary of the Academy of the Hebrew Language): perfect: four forms (five occurrences):

reconstruct the geographic boundaries of those dialects. All one can say with certainty is that we know of dialectal features.

§ 24 A related subject is the distinction that ought to be made between Tannaitic Hebrew and Amoraic Hebrew. The studies of Sokoloff on the Hebrew of Bereshit Rabbah, Moreshet on the *bārāytōt* in the Babylonian Talmud, and Kutscher's insights have advanced research in this field.[127] The distinction between the language of the Tanna'im, which was crystallized while Mishnaic Hebrew was fully alive, and the language of the Amora'im – in Palestine and Babylonia – which was crystallized in the shadow of other spoken languages (in the west with Palestinian Aramaic and Greek, in the east with Babylonian Aramaic and Persian) has been accepted by scholars. One cannot, of course, ignore the problems related to the texts themselves.[128]

היתיר, קנו (2×), נאסר (participle?), שה[חזיקו]. All other forms are participles: *qal* active: אוסרין, אומרין, הבאין, ההולכת, חוששין; *qal* passive [including *pa'el*]: אסור, אסורין (2×), אסורות, האסורות, היבישין; *nif'al*: הנאגד, הנאגדת, הנימכרין (2×); *nitpa''al*: מתאסרין, מתעסרין (3×), מתקנין; *hif'il*: המודות; *huf'al*: מותר, מותרין, המותרין. Sussmann 1973–1974 presents the data slightly differently (e.g., the distribution of the verbal forms on p. 48).

The data are impressive. But what morphology of the verb can be deduced from it, or, for that matter, from the Copper Scroll, which has more than double the number of words (yet how many of them are verbs)? For grammatical descriptions, manuscripts or other material with as much as 2000 verbal forms are not sufficient for even a partial description of the verbal paradigm.

Although it is clear that the epigraphic material deserves to be investigated and described fully, it should be realized that the results will be limited. The essential part of the grammar of Mishnaic Hebrew depends on the traditions found in manuscripts, which also have their limitations, but of a different kind.

Moreover, one must remember that the epigraphic material is not monolithic. These are different kinds of literary crystallizations from different geographical provenances. The letters of Bar Koseba differ from the Reḥov inscription. The latter is primarily a composition from a Rabbinical school of the Galilee. In this respect, no text could be better for comparison with Rabbinic Hebrew. It is the most reliable of the reliable texts (אבי אבות הטקסטים, Sussmann 1974:148). The Bar Koseba letters, on the other hand, have a different background. They are letters from army camps in southern Palestine. The mention of לולבין ואתרגין ... הדסין וערבין in Aramaic letter 8 (Kutscher 1977a:129) does not make them halakhic compositions. These inscriptions and letters differ also from the Copper Scroll from Qumran. The epigraphic evidence belongs to different periods, deals with different types of subjects, and comes from different places.

127 See Sokoloff 1971; Moreshet 1972; idem 1974a; idem 1974b; Kutscher 1972b:40 ff. See now also the important and excellent work of Breuer 1985; idem 1993.

128 Ben-Ḥayyim 1963:7 concludes that many problems are related to the age of the linguistic phenomena and the date of the witnesses that transmit the linguistic phenomena.

18.3 Problems and Tasks

§ 25 I now turn to some of the problems involved in researching Mishnaic Hebrew as well as some of the tasks that remain. Even though some have been touched on already, this subject merits a separate treatment that will include the problems and tasks that have not yet been mentioned.

18.3.1 Investigations of Reliable Manuscripts and other Manuscripts

§ 26 One of the most salient signs of the Jerusalem school of Rabbinic studies has been the search for and use of reliable manuscripts of Rabbinic literature, upon which such outstanding scholars as Epstein, Lieberman, and Yalon insisted.[129] Research into Mishnaic Hebrew that is based on excellent manuscripts differs fundamentally from that based on printed editions. A comparison between the Mishnaic material in the Concordance of the Historical Dictionary of the Academy of Hebrew Language, which is drawn from MS Kaufmann, and the *Thesaurus Mishnae* of Kasovsky is sufficient to show how different the two are.

§ 27 In this regard the unique work of Kutscher stands out. His contributions to the study of Mishnaic Hebrew are numerous, comprising those found in his own works as well as those inspired by him and found in the works of his students. There is no doubt that his insistence on investigating "reliable manuscripts" (אבות טקסטים), i.e., manuscripts which faithfully reflect the language, revolutionized the study of Mishnaic Hebrew and of Galilean Aramaic. The concentration on reliable manuscripts, a term that has come to be closely connected with his name and work on Galilean Aramaic, Babylonian Aramaic, and Mishnaic Hebrew, has produced immeasurable benefits.[130] The search for manuscripts that preserve completely or at least significantly the original form of Mishnaic Hebrew has greatly proved itself. As noted, Kutscher was not the first to take up the study of reliable manuscripts; however, he gave impetus to its use and refined its applications. Many hitherto unknown features and details, as well as entire grammatical subjects, have been uncovered thanks to the perusal of reliable manuscripts, e.g., כָּרָתָן, רַבּוֹן,[131] the distinction between

129 For references to the publications of Epstein and Yalon, see the bibliography at the end of this volume. As for Lieberman, all his studies were based on manuscripts of the works which he investigated (see, e.g., Lieberman 1983, one of his last articles).

130 See Kutscher 1977a:73 idem 1977a:169 ff., 227 ff.

131 See Kutscher 1977a:95–99.

חֲתִיכָה (verbal noun) and חֲתִיכָּה ("piece, cut"),[132] the participial form *nitpa'ēl* alongside *mitpa'ēl*.[133] The results have more than justified Kutscher's approach as against that of Segal and his followers.[134]

§ 28 Research into reliable manuscripts has proven that Mishnaic Hebrew grammar differs from the grammar known to us in the past. This method of research, however, has distracted us from other manuscripts, or at least diminished their value in our eyes and the value of the traditions they contain. The view that anything that deviates from MS Kaufmann (Kutscher was not always careful to distinguish between the consonantal tradition and the pointed tradition of this manuscript, nor have we, his students, always done so either)[135] or only most of that which deviates from MS Kaufmann is due to copyists who were influenced by the Tiberian tradition of Biblical Hebrew or the language of the Babylonian Talmud,[136] appears to be a bit exaggerated, to say the least. Not everything that agrees with the Tiberian tradition of Biblical Hebrew need be a correction, nor is whatever follows the Babylonian Talmud deliberate or accidental interference on the part of copyists. I shall again touch on only two details:[137] the forms הימנו and הימנה[138] and נתארמלה and נתארמלו,[139] which are most common in the Mishnayot of the Babylonian Talmud, existed in Palestine in the Bar Koseba documents or in the documents from Qumran. Therefore, why should they not be considered early representatives of an old tradition that moved from Palestine to Babylonia – and not only to Babylonia? There is no reason to view them as late features that originated in Babylonia. The investigation of manuscripts and of the oral traditions that have already been studied demonstrates, as noted above,[140] that there were different traditions within Mishnaic Hebrew – as mentioned, at least three. Moreover, the branch of the Mishna which is designated Babylonian, is, as is known, related

---

132 See Kutscher 1977a:133; Bar-Asher 1980a:62 (and the bibliography cited there).
133 See Qimron 1977; Bar-Asher 1977b:128–135; idem 1980:106–121.
134 On this point, see also Yalon's criticism in Yalon 1971:104–112.
135 It is true that Yalon 1971:28 ff., Kutscher 1977b:78 ff., and many of those who have followed them (see, e.g., Bar-Asher 1971:169 ff.) have distinguished between the two main traditions of MS Kaufmann; however, recently the distinction between the two has been sharpened and each tradition has been subjected to increased analysis (see Bar-Asher 1983a; idem 1984).
136 See Kutscher 1977b:247 ff.
137 See Chapter 19 § 47–60.
138 See ibid. §§ 53–57.
139 See ibid., § 50. In Bar-Asher 1986:185–186 this example is discussed further and its existence in Qumran is demonstrated.
140 See § 22 above.

to the language reflected in manuscripts of the Tosefta. This branch has recently benefited from investigation.[141]

§ 29 Nonetheless, I feel the need to stress what to me appears to be an important point. The manuscripts belonging to the Babylonian branch of Mishnaic Hebrew have not yet been sufficiently examined. There is a need for a thorough study of many manuscripts, similar to D. Rosenthal's work on the Tractate 'Aboda Zara.[142] Certainly much remains to be done. It is entirely possible that, as a result of additional studies, some of the results we now have will need to be modified. I do not say this merely because the manuscripts are from the 13th or 14th centuries CE,[143] as compared with Mishnaic manuscripts of the Palestinian variety, such as MS Kaufmann and MS Parma A, which survive from the 11th century CE.[144] Caution is required not because of the lateness of the Babylonian Talmud manuscripts, but rather because of our limited knowledge of the manuscripts.

18.3.1 Strata versus Traditions

§ 30 One problem that is evident in Mishnaic Hebrew research of the last generation (but also previously) is the confusing of chronological and dialectical features. Not every phenomenon that is found in a Mishnaic manuscript, even in a manuscript that is considered the most reliable of manuscripts, and which diverges from the Tiberian tradition of Biblical Hebrew, necessarily reflects a chronological development that originated between the Biblical and Mishnaic periods. One must keep in mind that many of these differences depend on the pointing tradition, which crystallized generations after Hebrew ceased being a living language in Palestine during the Tannaitic period.

§ 31 I shall explain with several examples. A number of years ago Ben-Ḥayyim demonstrated that many verbs that occur in *qal* in the Bible, turn up in Mishnaic Hebrew and other sources in *pi'ēl*.[145] This is reflected also in the Biblical pointing. A paradigm such as דִּבֵּר-דּוֹבֵר-יְדַבֵּר is explained fully only if we assume that at some point in the Biblical period one also said דָּבַר-דּוֹבֵר-יִדְבֹּר. When *pi'ēl* replaced the *qal*, there was no difficulty in reading the perfect and imperfect forms as *pi'ēl*; however, the participle remained in *qal* because

141 See Nathan 1984, especially the closing chapters, pp. 359 ff.

142 See Rosenthal 1981, especially pp. 57–95.

143 E.g., MS Munich was written in 1343 (see Rosenthal 1981L 135); MS New York of *'Avoda Zara* was written in Spain in 1290 (Rosenthal 1981:140).

144 See Rosenthal 1981:123 ff, 140.

145 See Ben-Ḥayyim 1958:236–242 and previously Ginsberg 1934.

reading מְדַבֵּר instead of דּוֹבֵר involved changing the consonantal text. In Mishnaic Hebrew only דִּבֵּר-מְדַבֵּר-יְדַבֵּר exists.[146] This phenomenon,[147] no doubt, is part of a process that reflects a developing and evolving language. It is first attested in the late books of the Bible and, thus, the use of different conjugations in Biblical Hebrew and Mishnaic Hebrew is to be attributed to different layers of the language.

§ 32 On the other hand, if one finds in the Tiberian tradition of Biblical Hebrew הִלֵּל, and in MS Kaufmann and related manuscripts הֶלֵּל,[148] כֶּפֶל as against כָּפֵל,[149] or Tiberian Biblical חֲנִיּוֹת vs. חֲנֻיוֹת in Mishnaic manuscripts,[150] one is not obligated to take the Tiberian Biblical forms as early and the Mishnaic forms as late. Both turn up in pointing traditions, and it is possible that these are merely different reading traditions that were common at the same time in different locales.[151] It is also possible that those who read הִלֵּל, כֶּפֶל, and חֲנֻיוֹת in the Bible also read these same forms in the Mishna, and therefore one should not talk of Biblical forms as opposed to Mishnaic forms. And it is no less possible that those who read הֶלֵּל, כָּפֵל, and חֲנִיּוֹת in the Mishna read them the same way in the Bible. The readings αενιωθ, ανιωθ are found in the Greek transliteration of Jeremiah (37:16), as shown by Kutscher several years ago.[152] One might say that these forms are Mishnaic, or "substandard" to use Kutscher's term, which were transplanted into Biblical Hebrew; however, one might also argue that there were those who read חֲנִיּוֹת and not חֲנֻיוֹת in the Mishna and in the Bible too. Similarly, הִלֵּל, which occurs in different mishnayot, need not be viewed as a transplanted Biblical form, but rather was read in that way in the Bible and in the Mishna. These are all possibilities that require caution, and can only be resolved through the accumulation or discovery of more data.

---

146 Zurawel 1984 has added important details to the description of this phenomenon.

147 As an aside, it should be noted that this process was not complete; sometimes the opposite is found, as is reflected in the homiletical interpretation in Sifre Be-Midbar: וינוסו משנאיך – וכי יש שונאים לפני מי שאמר והיה העולם (par. 84 ed. Horovitz, p. 81). In this case it is Mishnaic Hebrew that uses *qal* as against the Biblical *piʿel*. משנא occurs 15 times in the Bible. שנ"א is not attested in *piʿel* in Tannaitic literature.

148 See Kutscher 1963:257–258; idem 1968:233–236; Bar-Asher 1980:11, 64, 92.

149 See Kutscher 1969:15–16; Bar-Asher 1980a:55 (where it is noted that these two forms sometimes occur in the same manuscript).

150 See Kutscher 1969:51–53.

151 Cf. Ben-Ḥayyim's remarks on this subject: "One can forgive the scholars of those days [1910–1930s – M. B.-A.] who erred in viewing the pronunciation of אוֹגְנִין as a phenomenon of Mishnaic Hebrew and did not take it as one of several different reading traditions of the Mishna, if today [1980s M. B.-A.] there are Hebrew scholars who do not differentiate between these two" (Ben-Ḥayyim 1985:14).

152 See Kutscher 1969:52.

18.3.3 Reliable Traditions and Scribal Corrections

§ 33 In concluding the subjects just discussed, I feel obliged to emphasize that I do not deny that there were scribal corrections in Mishnaic Hebrew in accordance with Biblical Hebrew, as claimed by Yalon and others.[153] There is no doubt that during the past few centuries the amount of scribal corrections under the influence of Tiberian Hebrew has increased, especially in the printed mishnayot (and in *siddurim*). See, for example, what R. David Altaras did to the mishnayot that he published in Mantua and Livorno,[154] as well as what Solomon Zalman did to the liturgy in שערי תפילה, not to mention others. Details can be found in Yalon's works.[155] Tiberian Biblical grammar, which crystallized in the beginning of the second millennium CE and spread over hundreds of years, influenced rabbis and other learned members of the Jewish community and led them to "Tiberianize" Mishnaic texts. Was this, however, also true 1000 years ago? Is the consistent pointing אֲבָרִים in MS Parma B to be attributed to a Biblically influenced vocalizer, as claimed by Yalon?[156] Note that the plural form of אבר does not occur in the Bible. Must we prefer אֵיבָרִים, since the reading אֲבָרִים is limited to one manuscript?[157] Why should we not assume that two reading froms existed – one with a *ḥaṭef pataḥ* and the other with a *ṣere*, which in this environment reflects a *ḥaṭef segol*?[158]

§ 34 It seems probable that the different traditions intermingled over the centuries as a result of the migration of communities and scholars from place to place.[159] The manuscripts themselves often evidence this historical reality. MS Kaufmann has more than two witnesses embedded in it, and this itself testifies to a meeting of traditions. At times one hand reflects a combination of two separate traditions. This is true of MS Kaufmann (e.g., the orthography

153 For numerous examples, see Yalon 1964 and also n. 157 below.
154 See Bar-Asher 1980:93.
155 See e.g., Yalon 1964:12–13 (for additional examples, see the index on p. 232).
156 See Yalon 1964:30 n. 73.
157 The reading tradition אֲבָרִים in MS Parma B was known to R. Samuel ha-Nagid, as I learned from Professor Ben-Ḥayyim in a seminar he conducted in 1965. The reading אֲבָרִים (אֱבָרִים?) with *ḥaṭef pataḥ* or *ḥaṭef segol* is supported by an analysis of the meter: ועפנו לשמע חנותם אליהם, וטשנו עליהם כבעל אֲבָרִים (see Jarden 1966:113). The form אברים parallels the upcoming words עֳפָרִים, גְמוּרִים, סְדוּרִים, יְעָרִים, etc., all of which begin with a reduced vowel (= *šewa*). This evidences the reduced vowel of the *alef*. The fact that אברים of R. Samuel ha-Nagid refers to wings, similar to the use of אבר in the Bible and against the Mishnaic Hebrew use of אבר indicating parts of the body, is not relevant.
158 See Yalon 1964:40. *ṣere* also occurs in place of a *ḥaṭef* vowel in the Tiberian Biblical tradition, e.g., אֵפוֹ (= אֱפוֹ Exod. 16:23).
159 On this subject, see Chapter 19 § 20, and n. 119 above.

שה of the relative pronoun *šin*, which is found only in a few places, primarily in the Order Neziqin and most frequently in the Tractate 'Eduyyot, as against the common orthography -שֶׁ),[160] and the vocalizer, who preserves two different reading traditions for many words, e.g., לִידְתָן alongside לֵידָתָה.[161] Migration is reflected clearly in MS Parma B, whose primary tradition crystallized in the East where it was copied, pointed, and accent signs (*ṭeʻāmim*) were added to it. When it reached Italy, however, marginal notes reflecting a different tradition were added to many pages, e.g., פְּלוֹנִית in the text of the manuscript as against פְּלָנִית[162] in the margin.[163]

§ 35 Nonetheless, it is reasonable to assume that most linguistic features of many old traditions were preserved for centuries because of the devotion of those who transmitted the text. Not everything found in a manuscript of a tradition that corresponds to Tiberian Biblical grammar is necessarily a deliberate or accidental scribal correction. Although Tiberian grammar spread in the East, many linguistic traits which differ from it have been preserved to the present day. This is true for all the living eastern traditions, though there are differences in the number and distribution of features that distinguish them from the Tiberian tradition of Mishnaic Hebrew. S. Morag[164] has dealt with this at some length and I will mention only one detail, the preservation of the *dageš forte* in *reš* in eastern traditions in forms of the derived conjugations, e.g., עֵרֵּב and related forms,[165] as against the lack of gemination of *reš* in Tiberian Hebrew.

18.3.4 Expanding the Fields of Research

§ 36 There is a basic need to expand the fields of research in Mishnaic Hebrew. Research should include:

18.3.4.1 Investigation of the Different Periods of Mishnaic Hebrew

§ 37 Research has concentrated to a large extent on the language of the Mishna. It is only proper that it should also extend to the other divisions of

160 See Bar-Asher 1984:9 n. 45.
161 See Yalon 1964:56.
162 See Bar-Asher 1980a:63 n. 307.
163 The differences in linguistic traditions between the text of the manuscript and the margins are discussed in Bar-Asher 1990a.
164 See Morag 1985.
165 See Morag 1971b:190 ff.; idem 1980:236–237; and Chapter 19 § 24.

the Tannaitic language, and it need hardly be said that this is especially true for the Amoraic language. In grammar, Sokoloff's work on the Hebrew of Bereshit Rabbah according to MS Vatican 30, which was carried out 30 years ago, has not been pursued. Only recently has more work been done in this field – that of Y. Breuer on the Hebrew of the Babylonian Talmud Tractates Sukka and Pesahim.[166]

18.3.4.2 Investigation of Traditions and Other Manuscripts

§ 38 In principle I believe that every manuscript and tradition deserves to be studied. The manuscripts of different Rabbinic compositions ought to be studied comprehensively. I do not, of course, think that every study needs to deal with every detail. It would suffice to deal with selections that demonstrate the salient features of the different aspects of Mishnaic Hebrew.[167] Many manuscripts have yet to be investigated. For example, MS Cambridge, which was published by W. H. Lowe over a hundred years ago and which is mentioned in most scholarly works, has not yet been properly studied. The same is true for the Genizah fragments (individually or in groups).[168] Even the first printed edition still awaits proper study. Similarly, the manuscripts of non-Mishnaic composition such as MS Wien and MS London of the Tosefta need re-examination.[169] The source book of the Academy of Hebrew Language lists many manuscripts that have not yet been systematically investigated, including many manuscripts of the Babylonian Talmud.

§ 39 Here, too, one must be careful not to confuse different levels of study by identifying the language of a manuscript with the language of the composition. The language of Sifre Devarim is not the same as the language of MS Vatican 32 or the language of MS Oxford 151.5 As a rule, all manuscripts and oral traditions testify primarily to their locale and period. In Zurawel's recent study of MS Sasson of the Mishna, i.e., the autograph of Maimonides,[170] she showed that the vowel *a* before a geminated consonant was reduced in the tradition of the manuscript; she also demonstrated that the *šewa* was usually pronounced as *ă*. By enlarging the scope of her study, Zurawel was able to determine that this was the reading tradition of Cordoba in the 12th century. Concerning the reduction of the vowel before a doubled consonant, there is

166 See Breuer 1985, 1993, and 2002.
167 See Bar-Asher 1986:50.
168 Now we have the important book of Birnbaum 2008.
169 Nathan 1984 contains important information on these two manuscripts.
170 See Zurawel 1987.

no evidence earlier than that of Maimonides' autograph. One must look for additional evidence in order to demonstrate how far back the 12th century tradition of Cordoba goes.

§ 40 In sum, only a comprehensive and comparative investigation of manuscripts and traditions will enable us to date adequately early features. That is not to say, of course, that the results of previous research should be ignored. The position of reliable manuscripts which have been investigated and whose traditions have been evaluated properly – especially MSS Parma A, Parma B of the Mishna, MS Vatican 66 of the *Sifre*, MS Vatican 32 of the *Sifre* and others – cannot be undermined. These manuscripts are the foundation on which to base the grammar of Mishnaic Hebrew.

§ 41 Nevertheless, general and common features differ in nature from specific features that have been preserved in a single manuscript. The latter deserve special and separate investigation and consideration. It is possible that some of them reflect local features or personal traits of the transmitter, e.g., the unique phenomenon in the tradition of the vocalizer of MS Kaufmann, who reads עֶגְלָה without the definite article, but הָעֲגָלָה with the definite article.[171] It is possible, however, that some of these features are early.[172] As a first step, each feature must be recorded; only later can it be investigated and evaluated in light of the history of the language.

18.3.4.3 Investigation of Traditions and Examination of General Grammatical Topics

§ 42 Research should not proceed in one direction alone. There is a need both to examine individual traditions by themselves be they written (manuscripts) or oral, and to continue to investigate more general topics in grammar. Research must not be limited to the study of separate traditions. The main and final goal should be a descriptive grammar comprising all aspects of the language. The description of a morphological phenomenon in Tannaitic Hebrew should take into account the distribution of the feature throughout Tannaitic literature for what it may reveal in a more general nature about the different division of the period. The same is true for all aspects of Mishnaic Hebrew.[173]

§ 43 I shall now turn to one syntactic point. In the Mishna Kelim we read: מחצלת מאימתי מקבלת טומאה משתתקנב היא גמר מלאכתה (20:7). MS Kauf-

171 See Bar-Asher 1980a:55.

172 For a wide-ranging discussion, see Bar-Asher 1986, especially the second half, pp. 189–208.

173 Note the individual preference of scholars: some prefer to describe manuscripts, some prefer to investigate general topics, and others deal with both.

mann reads והיא גמר מלאכתה (also in MS Cambridge and MS Parma A).[174] The pronoun, היא, agrees with the *nomen rectum*, מלאכה, and not with the *nomen regens*, גמר, as expected. An investigation of the Mishna, however, shows that this is not a rare exception, at least as concerns the syntagm גמר-מלאכה. It is found in other passages, too, e.g., היא גמר מלאכתן (m. Kelim 4:4; MS Cambridge, MS Paris, MS Parma B, and the hand that corrected MS Kaufmann); the first hand in MS Kaufmann and MS Parma A read והוא גמר מלאכתן.[175] A third example is איזו היא גמר מלאכתו (m. Kelim 5:1 in MS Kaufmann,[176] MS Parma A, MS Parma B, MS Cambridge[177]) and also איזו היא גמר מלאכתה (m. Kelim 5:2 in MS Kaufmann, MS Parma A, MS Cambridge, MS Parma B, MS Paris), and in Sifre be-Midbar § 110, אי זו היא גמר מלאכתה (this is also the reading in MS Vatican 32).[178] This limited material shows that this is not an isolated feature of one tradition or one manuscript alone, or even a feature attested only in the Mishna. This is only one small example of a larger grammatical topic, i.e., the agreement between *nomen regens* and *nomen rectum*, which requires a comprehensive study.

18.3.4.5 Proportions between Research Fields

§ 44 The last example hints of the lack of proper proportion in the study of the different aspects of Mishnaic Hebrew grammar. The extent to which phonological and morphological features have been studied is far greater than the extent of syntactic ones. One of the few who have dealt extensively with syntax is Bendavid in his important book *Biblical Hebrew and Mishnaic Hebrew*. Mishor's work on the tenses system is an important milestone in the study of morphosyntax. Other scholars have also investigated the syntax of Mishnaic Hebrew to varying degrees.[179] Nonetheless, much remains to be done both in the study of individual manuscripts and in the investigation of more general syntactic topics. In reality, the research into Mishnaic Hebrew syntax

---

174 MS Parma B and MS Paris read והוא גמר מלאכתה.

175 The first hand in MS Kaufmann wrote הוא without the conjunctive *waw*, and a second hand changed it to והיא.

176 Originally איזה, and not איזו, was written.

177 MS Paris reads ואיזו גמר מלאכתו.

178 In the Sifra (Nega'im 8:1), however, one finds ואיזה הוא גמר מלאכתן; in the Tosefta (t. Kelim Baba Meṣi'a 5:1,2) ואי-זהו גמר מלאכתו (these data are culled from the databases of the Historical Dictionary Project of the Academy of Hebrew Language).

179 See, e.g., Blau 1980; Sarfatti 1980; idem 1989; Sharvit 1987; idem 1993; Moreshet 1983a; Friedman 1980; Kaddari 1974. See also Azar 1995.

is no different from the research into syntax in other periods of Hebrew. The whole field lags behind the study of orthography, phonology, morphology, and the lexicon.[180]

18.3.5 Preparing a New Grammar of Mishnaic Hebrew

§ 45 A major desideratum is a new grammar of Mishnaic Hebrew. Segal's grammar, which was written some 70 years ago,[181] is still the most recent comprehensive grammar on Mishnaic Hebrew that exists. A question that must be first asked is: should our goal be one grammar, or several grammars since the language is distinguished by different traditions? I believe that our efforts should be directed towards one grammar. Although the groundwork for such a grammar must consist of a separate examination and description of each tradition, it is to be hoped that such an undertaking will ultimately bring together all the different traditions and synthesize all the disparate data. In ferreting out the distinct linguistic traits that characterize the traditions, the general picture should not be neglected. I am convinced that what is common to the different traditions is greater than what is distinct, and this fact should not be forgotten. G. Bergsträsser's *Hebräische Grammatik* could serve as an example in this regard: in describing the Tiberian tradition of Biblical Hebrew he managed to include material on the other traditions of Biblical Hebrew at that time. He presented Biblical Hebrew as one language with many different traditions.

§ 46 It is no secret that the task of writing a new grammar of Mishnaic Hebrew is not within easy reach at the moment. It is doubtful whether one researcher alone can accomplish such a goal. Perhaps it would be best if we content ourselves in this generation with writing an introduction which would summarize what has been done to date. Such an introduction would greatly simplify the search for information and would prevent a rehashing of subjects already discussed in the literature. It would also provide an overview of the field and allow scholars to compare and contrast both details and general features of the different traditions. This is a desideratum not only for Hebrew linguists, but also for those interested in Jewish Studies.[182]

---

180 There are other specialized fields that have not yet been investigated properly, e.g., the grammar of personal names in Mishnaic Hebrew.

181 I.e., the English version.

182 This project has already been undertaken.

18.4 Concluding Remarks

I shall conclude with the following remarks.

§ 47 The synchronic description should precede other investigations in all studies since this provides us with the basis of the language. Only one a manuscript or tradition has been subjected to synchronic analysis, can diachronic studies be fruitfully conducted. The treatment of theoretical problems such as those with which we began this paper, e.g., the relationship between Mishnaic Hebrew and Biblical Hebrew, or between Mishnaic Hebrew and Aramaic, ought not to be neglected. We would make more progress, too, if we admitted more often that there are still many basic questions concerning Mishnaic Hebrew for which we do not at this time have the answer.

§ 48 We must remember that we still face many obstacles in investigating the Mishnaic Hebrew (at least the traditions of Tannaitic Hebrew) that was in use at the end of the second century or beginning of the third century CE. For example, Mishnaic Hebrew became a written language through a slow and protracted process that commenced a few generations before Hebrew ceased to be spoken in Palestine. Moreover, we must keep in mind that the written sources that have been preserved were apparently initially preserved orally for centuries, including throughout the Amoraic period followed by the Geonic period. Similarly, we should not forget that most of the manuscripts we possess were written more than 800 years after the close of the Tannaitic period.[183] These obstacles as well as others demand of us the utmost caution in dealing with anything regarding the history of Mishnaic Hebrew. It is wrong to look at the history of the language from just one angle and to conduct research in only one direction, e.g., the view that many of its features are the result of Aramaic influence, or the influence of Biblical Hebrew on one (pointing) tradition or another.

§ 49 I have concentrated on the direct sources of Mishnaic Hebrew. Much can be said about the indirect sources, their contribution to the study of the language, and their importance in research. By indirect sources I refer to, e.g., the material in the few Hebrew and Aramaic epigraphic documents that have survived,[184] the Samaritan traditions of Hebrew and Aramaic,[185] the Dead Sea

---

183 The earliest manuscript of the Oral Law, i.e., a Mishnaic manuscript, which is mentioned in the literature, may be from the beginning of the 8th century CE (see Rosenthal 1981:96 and the literature cited there).

184 Kutscher, more so than others, frequently used this material in his studies on Mishnaic Hebrew and Aramaic.

185 There is scarcely a work of Ben-Ḥayyim on the Hebrew or Aramaic of the Samaritans that does not contain an investigation of either a general linguistic problem or specific feature in the grammar of Mishnaic Hebrew.

Scrolls, and other documents from the Judean desert,[186] the Greek and Latin transcriptions of Hebrew,[187] not to mention the language of early liturgy,[188] early *piyyūṭ* and medieval *piyyūṭ*,[189] which also contain material that shed light on Mishnaic Hebrew, as M. Beit-Arié and especially I. Eldar, among others,[190] have shown.[191]

186 See Yalon 1967; Kutscher 1974; Qimron 1986.
187 See, e.g., Kutscher 1968.
188 I have gathered the material on this subject and hope to present it in written form in the future.
189 See, e.g., Yahalom 1981; idem 1985.
190 See Beit-Arié 1971; Eldar 1978.
191 There is a detailed discussion of the indirect sources for Mishnaic Hebrew in Chapter 17, §§ 38–47. Bar-Asher 1990b contains a discussion of the contribution of the Samaritan tradition to Mishnaic grammar.

19 The Different Traditions of Mishnaic Hebrew

19.1 Introduction

§ 1 Research into Mishnaic Hebrew, which has made great strides in the past seventy years, has concentrated primarily on the language of the *Tannaim*. Only a few studies have been devoted to works or manuscripts belonging to later periods of rabbinic literature;[1] and even within the language of the *Tannaim*, scholars have mainly dealt with the language of the Mishna.[2] The revered status of the Mishna within *tannaitic* literature is well-reflected in the following two points: (1) several complete manuscripts of Mishna are extant as well as hundreds of poorly preserved, fragmented manuscripts of Mishna. There are, on the other hand, very few manuscripts of other *tannaitic* works; and (2) it is the only corpus of *tannaitic* literature for which a regular reading tradition has been preserved in the many different dispersed Jewish communities. This situation has led scholars to concentrate their efforts on the study of the language of the Mishna, neglecting other *tannaitic* corpora. As a result, there are scores of studies dealing with the grammar of the language of the Mishna.

§ 2 In many of these studies, especially those dealing with early manuscripts, one clearly discerns the desire of the researchers to recover the earliest features of mishnaic Hebrew. All studies attempt to lay bare changes and corrections which have entered the language during the long course of its transmission. J. N. Epstein and H. Yalon paved the way for such research with their exemplary studies; these scholars were followed by E. Y. Kutscher who gave added momentum to this method of research (Kutscher 1963). Kutscher sought, as he had done with Galilean Aramaic, to base the linguistic description of the Mishna on reliable manuscripts, i.e., manuscripts which either preserved or partially preserved the original language and text of the Mishna.[3] According to Kutscher, MS Kaufmann (K) was the most reliable manuscript of the language of the *Tannaim* in general, and the language of the Mishna in particular. He

---

1 For example, see Sokoloff 1971 and especially Breuer 2002.

2 The works of the late M. Moreshet on the Hebrew *baraitot* of the Babylonian Talmud (Moreshet 1974a and 1974b) constitute noteworthy exceptions. See also Haneman, 1974, Bar-Asher 1983b, and Yeivin 1965.

3 Kutscher's main criticism of M. H. Segal's *A Grammar of Mishnaic Hebrew* (1936) focused on the fact that Segal based his grammar on printed editions of rabbinic literature and ignored the evidence found in manuscripts. The existence of manuscripts was already known at the time he wrote his earlier edition of the grammar in English (1927). See Kutscher 1968:1.

also, however, recognized the need and importance of taking into account the data preserved in other manuscripts as well as from oral traditions.[4]

§ 3 Since the publication of Kutscher's important article, "Mishnaic Hebrew," in the H. Yalon Jubilee Volume, four additional manuscripts of Mishna have been studied in a comprehensive manner.[5] Some fragmentary manuscripts have also merited scholarly treatment,[6] as have some of the oral traditions of the Mishna.[7] All of these studies have succeeded in recovering much of the grammar of mishnaic Hebrew and in enriching our knowledge of the language in hundreds of details.[8]

19.2 The Division of Mishnaic Hebrew into Different Traditions

§ 4 One of the salient results of research into mishnaic Hebrew has been the uncovering of different traditions within the grammar of the language.[9] Unfortunately, there has been a considerable amount of confusion in describing and categorizing these traditions. The terms "early" and "late," "original" and "secondary," "reliable" and "suspect," are frequently yet inconsistently used. One often reads of an Eastern tradition standing in contrast with a Western tradition, or a Palestinian tradition standing in contrast with a Babylonian

---

4 This can be seen in his works on mishnaic Hebrew which are replete with references to other manuscripts (not only that of MS Kaufmann) and oral traditions. It is also evidenced by the investigation of manuscripts which his students have undertaken.

5 Haneman 1980 deals with MS Parma A; Bar-Asher 1971 deals with MS Parma B; Bar-Asher 1980 deals primarily with MSS Paris and Florence. Other works of Kutscher as well as of the author also deal with MS Kaufmann.

6 See Netanel 1972 dealing with MS Antonin and Ben-Tolila 1973, dealing with MS Deinard, and especially Birnbaum 2008.

7 Such as the Yemenite tradition treated by Shivtiel 1971, Morag 1963, and Kara 1980. See also Morag 1977 on Baghdad, Katz 1978 on Djerba, Katz 1981 on Aleppo, and Maman 1984 on Tetuoan, Morocco.

8 In my opinion, research into mishnaic Hebrew should follow two directions, as, indeed, is the case: (a) a general, exhaustive description of one manuscript or one tradition, and (b) an investigation of a general problem based on several manuscripts or selected traditions. See, e.g., Mishor 1983; Morag 1957; and Bar-Asher 1977 and 1983a.

9 I am excluding from this discussion the question of the different dialects of *tannaitic* Hebrew (when Hebrew was still a spoken language – see Bar-Asher 1985, § 16. I am not dealing here with the linguistic differences which distinguish the early Mishnayot from most Mishnayot (ibid, §§ 26–28), nor am I dealing with the distinctions which should be made between the different within *tannaitic* literature, e.g., the difference between the Mishna and the Tosephta.

tradition, as well as a Palestinian branch of the language standing in contrast to a Babylonian branch. It is not always clear to which category a particular manuscript belongs. MS Parma B, for example, is sometimes assigned to the same linguistic tradition as MS Kaufmann and at other times to the same linguistic tradition as the Mishnayot with Babylonian pointing, both of which are, on occasion, classified together with the Mishnayot of the Babylonian Talmud. Yet all are contrasted with Manuscript Kaufmann. There are those who seem to forget that the language tradition of MS Parma B is fundamentally closer to that of MS Kaufmann than to the Mishnayot of the Babylonian Talmud and to those Mishnayot which have been deliberately made similar to it. Thus one linguistic feature is explained as an original feature and another is considered to be an implanted trait in the tradition, the result of foreign influence.[10] The determining criteria are not always ascertainable.

§ 5 The purpose of this study is to present an up-to-date description of the different traditions of mishnaic Hebrew in the light of all the studies which have been devoted to the language of the *Tannaim*, and especially to the language of the Mishna. I seek to investigate both the details and the more general features of these different traditions.[11] A re-analysis of the division of traditions of mishnaic Hebrew is especially important since the question of the division has recently been raised in two studies – Morag 1980[12] and Rosenthal 1981.

§ 6 In my judgment, mishnaic Hebrew can be divided into two main divisions:[13]

Early manuscripts of the Mishna which do not contain the Babylonian Talmud (manuscripts referred to as *Seder Hamishna*[14]) and which do not show a direct link to it, on the whole, all reflect one early language tradition. This tradition stands in contrast with the tradition reflected in the Mishnayot of the Babylonian Talmud – both Mishnayot originally similar to the Babylonian Talmud, and Mishnayot which were deliberately made similar to them.[15] Following previous studies, I shall call the first the Palestinian branch and the second the Babylonian branch.

---

10 This is especially the case since Kutscher 1963. Most studies follow this approach.

11 This is a desideratum to which I have indirectly alluded elsewhere. See Bar-Asher 1971, especially 180–82; Bar-Asher 1983a, § 30, especially n 102; and *apud* Rosenthal 1981:67.

12 Morag deals mainly with the transmission of the traditions since the Middle Ages, with particular attention paid to the crystallization and transmission of the Sephardi traditions of today. We, on the other hand, are interested in the different linguistic types prevalent at the end of the first millennium, seeking the roots of these traditions in the first few centuries after the redaction of the Mishna.

13 Other divisions are less important and have not yet been fully investigated. See n. 9 above.

14 See Rosenthal 1981:20.

15 See §§ 10–14 below.

The Palestinian branch can be further subdivided into two traditions: a Western tradition and an Eastern tradition. This conclusion is based on the evidence supplied by early manuscripts and oral traditions of the *Tannaim*, primarily as reflected in the Mishna itself.[16] The subdivision appears to have taken place around the time when Hebrew ceased to be spoken in Palestine.

§ 7 This study seeks to answer the following questions which arise from the division proposed above: (a) What are the representatives of each of the two branches and what are the representatives of each of the two traditions of the Palestinian branch? (b) What are the linguistic features on which our suggested division is based? (c) What are the roots and the historical background of each of the proposed traditions? In other words, where and when did the divisions take place? What is original and what is secondary (which developed as a result of changes which occurred in the process of transmission of mishnaic Hebrew)?

We shall begin with a discussion of the representatives of the different traditions within the Palestinian branch. The discussion will then turn to the different representatives of the Palestinian branch vis-à-vis those of the Babylonian branch. The rest of the study will be devoted to an analysis of the nature of the different traditions and the criteria on which the suggested divisions are based.

19.3 The Western tradition vis-à-vis the Eastern tradition within the Palestinian branch

§ 8 There are many representatives of the Western tradition.[17] We shall mention only the most prominent: the consonantal text of MS Kaufmann (K)[18] and the vocalized text of MS Kaufmann,[19] MS Parma A and MS Cambridge.[20]

---

16 For the purpose of this study, the Mishna is treated as one unit. Both the early Mishnayot and the Mishna of Rabbi are included in this term.

17 This is especially the case if one includes the many Geniza fragments which have been published and if one includes manuscripts belonging to other divisions of *tannaitic* literature such as MS Vatican 32 of *Siphre beMidbar*, and particularly reliable manuscripts such as MS Vatican 66 of *Siphra* (see below § 53).

18 Although most of the features to be discussed in below (§§ 24–37) arise from the vocalization tradition, quite a few phenomena are revealed by the *plene* orthography of the consonantal text (see § 38, on the orthography of ציפורן and the noun pattern פועלן).

19 For a discussion of why one must differentiate between the consonantal text and the vocalized text, see Bar-Asher 1983a, especially §§ 28–36.

20 Our remarks in n. 18 above concerning the consonantal text of MS Kaufmann also apply to MS Cambridge.

The most recent representatives of this linguistic tradition are MS Paris, MS Florence,[21] and related manuscripts[22] of the end of the 14th century CE from Italy. In terms of the reliability of the tradition they preserve, I would rank these manuscripts in the following order: (1) the consonantal text of MS Kaufmann is by far the most reliable representative;[23] (2) the vocalized text of MS Kaufmann, MS Parma A, and MS Cambridge to a lesser extent; (3) MS Paris and MS Florence are far less reliable representatives.

§ 9 The representatives of the Eastern tradition of the Palestinian branch are also numerous. The most important among them are fragments of Mishna with Babylonian pointing, MS Parma B of *Seder Teharot*, and MS Antonin 262[24] which also contains *Seder Teharot* (from the beginning of *Nega'im* to the end of *Zabim*).[25] The primary representatives of this tradition are MS Parma B and MS Antonin by virtue of their length, and especially MS Parma B because of its uniformity, complete vocalization, and system of accents.[26] The fragments of Mishna with Babylonian vocalization are very important, particularly the oldest fragments. As indicated by their name, however, their fragmentary nature undermines their value. Only a corpus of many such fragments would yield a worthwhile grammatical investigation.[27] Other representatives of this tradition are the oral oriental traditions. Foremost is the Yemenite tradition, followed by that of Djerba, and finally the other oriental traditions such as that of Babylonia-Iraq (Baghdad tradition), Syriac (mainly known from the tradition of Aleppo, i.e., Aram Zobah), and North Africa (such as the communities of Marrakech, Meknes, Fes, Sefrou, Tetouan, and Tafilalt).[28] It should be

---

21 As has been shown, MS Paris and MS Florence belong to the same tradition. See Bar-Asher 1980, especially pp. 7–15.

22 For details, see Bar-Asher 1980:91–93.

23 For many well-known phenomena which are preserved only in the consonantal text of this manuscript, see Kutscher 1963, Bar-Asher 1977 and 1983a.

24 This evaluation is based on the examination by Netanel 1972 and further examination by the author.

25 The manuscript (or manuscripts) used by the author of the gaonic commentary to *Seder Teharot*, edited by J. N. Epstein reveal(s) an undeniably close relationship to MS Parma B and MS Antonin. This relationship merits a full investigation.

26 There is no manuscript belonging to this tradition which contains the entire Mishna or even those *Sedarim* which were most studied – *Mo'ed*, *Nashim*, and *Neziqim*. The two principle manuscripts, MS Parma B and MS Antonin, contain *Seder* (order) *Teharot* (all or in part), which suffered a fate different from that of other *Sedarim (orders)*. The fact that it contains no *gemara* probably saved it from those influences which affected the other *Sedarim* (See Bar-Asher 1984, § 40 and n. 79).

27 Nonetheless, much important work has been done by Porath 1938 and Yeivin 1985.

28 See the bibliography in n 7 above. These traditions sometimes differ considerably from one another and I refer only to their common features which all come from one tradition.

noted, however, that the importance and value of later traditions, such as those of 14th century Italy mentioned above (MSS Paris and Florence) and the still extant oral traditions merit a separate treatment and will be dealt with.[29]

19.4 The Palestinian branch vis-à-vis the Babylonian branch

§ 10 We now turn to the other division within mishnaic Hebrew, i.e., the Palestinian branch as opposed to the Babylonian branch. I hasten to emphasize that the discussion centers on language, and language alone. All of the manuscripts which are classified as belonging to either the Western tradition or the Eastern tradition of the Palestinian branch stand in contrast with the Mishnayot of the Babylonian branch. Research into rabbinic literature[30] has demonstrated that one must distinguish between codices of early Mishnayot which reflect a tradition of Mishna study alone (known as *Seder Ha-mishna*), and which are not dependent on the Babylonian Talmud, and between the Mishnayot of the Babylonian Talmud. Those manuscripts containing uninterrupted portions of the Mishna without gemara have preserved the old tradition of mishnaic study (without the *gemara*) and differ linguistically from those Mishnayot which are related to the Babylonian Talmud and to compositions dependent on the *Talmud* such as the gaonic responsa (and in later generations also Mishnayot with Maimonides' Commentary), etc.[31] Since the gaonic period, Mishnayot of this sort have increased in number and already before the invention of the printing press became the most common version of the Mishna. The language reflected in the early manuscripts of Mishna represents the Palestinian branch, whereas the language reflected in the Mishnayot of the Babylonian Talmud and in related Mishnayot reflects the Babylonian branch.[32]

§ 11 In other words, we place most of the early manuscripts – be they of the Western tradition, i.e., the consonantal text of MS Kaufmann as well as the vocalized text, MS Parma A, MS Cambridge and related Geniza fragments, or of the Eastern tradition, i.e., MS Parma B, MS Antonin, and Mishnayot with

29 The Ashkenazi traditions have not yet been properly investigated. Consequently, nothing definitive can be said about them at this time, but Mishor 1989 is an excellent start.

30 The principle points made in this and other sections on rabbinic literature were discussed with Prof. Y. Sussman and Dr. D. Rosenthal, for which I am most grateful. The formulation is, of course, mine.

31 The collection of Mishnayot with Maimonides' Commentary is itself a worthy subject of study. See Rosenthal 1981:158–59.

32 The distinction between the Palestinian (Jerusalem) branch and the Babylonian branch is, of course, not based solely on language. See Epstein 1927:7.

Babylonian pointing – together in one category in contrast with the Mishnayot which were related to the Babylonian Talmud, such as, for example, both the Sephardi and Ashkenazi manuscripts included by D. Rosenthal in his edition of Aboda Zara (e.g., MS NY 44830, edited by S. Abramson in 1957[33] and MS Munich[34]).

§ 12 All studies dealing with early and late, original and secondary features in mishnaic Hebrew lay a foundation for this division. This is especially the case with Rosenthal's lucid and insightful investigation into the Mishna of Aboda Zara. Although the corpus he deals with is limited, it is varied enough to conclude that most, if not all, linguistic features he mentions – distinguishing between manuscripts of the Palestinian branch and those of the Babylonian branch – are found in manuscripts of both the Eastern tradition and the Western tradition, and stand in contrast with the manuscripts of the Babylonian branch. This general picture is not disturbed by occasional, slight variations.

§ 13 I shall give a number of examples. Note, for instance, the contrast between חָנִיּוֹת of the Palestinian branch and חָנוּיוֹת of the Babylonian branch,[35] i.e., the plurals of nouns ending with -ūt, חנות, מלכות, פורענות. In MS Kaufmann and similar manuscripts of the Western tradition, the plural *-iyyōt* is attested: פּוּרְעָנִיּוֹת, חָנִיּוֹת, and מַלְכִיּוֹת. Manuscripts from the Babylonian branch, on the other hand, form the plural *-ūyōt*[36] which is already known from the Tiberian tradition of the Bible, חֲנֻיוֹת, מלכֻיות.[37] One also finds evidence in manuscripts of the Eastern tradition, e.g., חנִיות and חָרִיוֹת in MS Parma B[38] and MS Antonin,[39] and the pointings גָּלְיוֹת, נְזִירִיוֹת, and מָלְכִיוֹת, which occur in the Babylonian pointed Mishnayot.[40] Similarly, the plural form תרנוגלים of the sg. תרנגול/תרנגולת, pointed out by Rosenthal (1981:74, following Abramson and others), is characteristic of the Palestinian branch, as

33 See most recently Rosenthal 1981:140–42.

34 Rosenthal 1981: 135–38. See also Rosenthal in *Researches in Talmudic Literature: A Study Conference in Honor of the Eightieth Birthday of Shaul Lieberman* (Jerusalem, 1983) 92 (in Hebrew).

35 Rosenthal 1981:73 gives only this example from *Aboda Zara*. Much material may be found in other studies mentioned in nn. 37–40 below.

36 Despite what is often stated in grammars, the plural form *-uyot* has no *dageš* in the *yod* in the Tiberian Bible. Thus, the form is *-ūyot* and not *-uyyot*.

37 Kutscher 1969a:102–104. On the origin of this form in the Babylonian branch, see § 58 below.

38 See Bar-Asher 1971:173.

39 Netanel 1972 (chap. 7, § 16, p. 55) mentions only חָנִיוֹת (Tehar. 6:3), but חָרִיוֹת is also found there (Para 3:11). One finds חריות unpointed in the geonic commentary to *Seder Teharot* (Epstein 1924: 104).

40 Porath 1938:137.

against תרנגולים of the Babylonian branch.[41] Here, too, MS Parma B, MS Antonin, and the Babylonian pointed Mishnayot preserve תרנוגלים/תרנוגלין.[42] The differences between the two branches can be seen in many different types of examples.

§ 14 In conclusion, Mishnaic Hebrew can be divided into a Palestinian branch which stands in contrast with a Babylonian branch. The Palestinian branch may further be subdivided into an Eastern tradition and into a Western tradition.

19.5 Comments on the Proposed Divisions

§ 15 Before dealing with the delineating features on which the proposed divisions are based and the historical background of each of the linguistic traditions, I should like to clarify some preliminary remarks.

§ 16 The later traditions, namely, the 14th century Italian tradition reflected in MS Paris and MS Florence as well as the oral oriental traditions, raise some difficulties. These traditions reveal features of both the earlier Eastern and Western traditions of the Palestinian branch. In some respects, the language of the Italian manuscripts may be classified together with the manuscripts of the Western tradition while the oral oriental traditions preserve features of the Eastern tradition. At the same time, salient features of the Babylonian branch are attested both in Italy[43] and the oral traditions. It is clear that the later traditions are heavily dependent upon the Babylonian Talmud. They are all connected to printed editions. Even the most reliable informants who know the entire Mishna by heart, or a good part of it, are tied to the printed Mishnayot.[44] It is rare to find an informant who deviates from the version in the printed editions.[45] Thus, it is no wonder that many of those features which characterize the editions of the Mishnayot from the Babylonian branch also

---

41 Epstein 1924:104; Kutscher 1969:157; and Morag *CPMH*, 1:204.

42 In MS Parma B we find תַּרְנוּגְלִין (Tehar. 3:8). This is probably also the reading in MS Antonin, תרנגלין (*ibid.*). For the Babylonian pointed Mishnayot, see Porath 1938:135 (the form also appears there with *o* following the *gimel*). In Yeivin 1985:1070 we find תַּרְנָגְלִים and תרנגולים.

43 For details see the description of the transmission of the tradition of MS Paris (Bar-Asher 1980: 1–94). It must be remembered that even within Italy there were significant linguistic differences.

44 See, for example, Shavtiel, 1971:217, 1:217: "I primarily used a printed edition of the Mishna ..."

45 An exception is the Yemenite tradition which preserves של prefixed to the following word, as distinct from what is found in the printed Mishnayot. But, today, even the Yemenite tradition depends almost exclusively on the printed editions.

characterize the oral traditions, since these features are fundamental data of the later traditions. Consequently, when we say that MS Paris and MS Florence belong to the Western tradition while the oral oriental traditions belong to the Eastern tradition, we must be extremely cautious.

§ 17 Nor are the earlier manuscripts free from Babylonian influences. No early manuscript from either the Western or the Eastern tradition is free from forms borrowed from the Babylonian branch. Even the most reliable of the Palestinian manuscripts, MS Kaufmann (the consonantal text), which often is the only manuscript to preserve some original linguistic features of the Palestinian branch, also contains linguistic features of the Babylonian branch. An outstanding example is הימנו/הימנה of the Babylonian branch as against ממנו/ממנה of the Palestinian branch. These forms are attested 22 times.[46] Compare also the 3 ms. pl. pronominal suffix *-on* (as in רֹאשׁוֹן, הֶסֵּיטוֹן, in place of רֹאשָׁן, הֶסֵּיטָן),[47] which is attested only a few times in MS Kaufmann and only in neglected Mishnayot of *Seder Teharoth*. The vocalizer of MS Kaufmann either removed these forms when he recognized them or corrupted them when he no longer understood them.[48]

Nonetheless, the earlier manuscripts preserve most of the characteristic features of the Palestinian branch, while the later manuscripts and the later oral traditions have lost many of these features. The later the manuscript, the more it is influenced by the Babylonian branch. This difference is not only one of quantity, but also of quality.

§ 18 I should like to explain why I have chosen the terms "Eastern" and "Western" traditions rather than "Palestinian" and "Babylonian" traditions in describing the linguistic categories reflected in early Mishnayot. As will be demonstrated, it is impossible to separate wholly the Eastern tradition from Palestine and place it in Babylonia. The Eastern tradition has its origin in Palestine and, therefore, it is not appropriate to call it Babylonian. Further, in the transmission of mishnaic Hebrew, most of the manuscripts which represent the Eastern tradition come from a number of different places in the East, as, for example, MS Parma B, which probably originates in Persia.[49] Similarly, those descendants of this tradition (even if only partially continuing the tradi-

46 See §§ 53–57 below.

47 See Bar-Asher 1984:5–8.

48 Bar-Asher 1984:8.

49 Both the Eastern-Persian cursive script and the contents of the page preceding the first-Mishnayot of Kelim, Chapter 1, indicate a Persian origin. This is further suggested by the linguistic tradition reflected in the manuscript which preserves the distinction in pronunciation between *pataḥ* and *qameṣ* which was not preserved in any of the Eastern Sephardi communities except Persia (and Yemen, but MS Parma B is not a Yemenite manuscript!).

tion) are also from different Eastern communities (e.g., Yemen, Syria, etc.) or areas such as the Maghreb which are designated "Eastern." In contrast, most of the manuscripts which represent the Western tradition come from areas to the west of Palestine, mainly Italy and her surroundings, and not from Palestine itself[50] (although we do know of similar fragments which are not from the West[51]). Thus, it is more appropriate to use the terms "Palestinian" and "Babylonian" to designate what I have called the branches of the language, distinguishing them from the Western and Eastern traditions of the Palestinian branch.[52]

§ 19 **Consistency of the Proposed Divisions**. No division of manuscripts or of traditions is without flaw. There will always be some exceptions or deviations. For example, if one takes ten manuscripts, the first five manuscripts may be distinguished from the remaining five in a number of features, however, with regard to some other feature, the third manuscript may be closer to manuscripts 6–10, while, with regard to yet another feature, the eighth manuscript may be closer to the first five manuscripts (1–5) etc. Two examples will suffice. All early manuscripts preserve the fm. participial forms with object pronominal suffixes פּוֹעְלַתּוֹ, מְפַעְלַתּוֹ, פּוֹעֲלַתָּה, מְפַעְלַתָּה, פּוֹעְלַתָּן, מְפַעְלַתָּן, which resemble the 3 feminine singular perfect with 3rd person pronominal suffixes פְּעָלַתּוֹ, פְּעָלַתָּה. In contrast, the Babylonian vocalization has פּוֹעַלְתּוֹ, פּוֹעַלְתָּה, פּוֹעַלְתָּן, with no distinction between these fm. participial forms and participial forms with possessive pronominal suffixes. This is not the case in related manuscripts such as MS Parma B, MS Antonin, and the Yemenite tradition.[53] Another example is the form רָקַק, a geminate verb inflected like a strong verb, as against the form רַק, in which the biconsonantal form of the geminate is preserved. These readings distinguish between the Palestinian and Babylonian branches of Mishna *Aboda Zara*. MS Paris 1337 (National Library, Paris, Babylonian) and MS NY 44830 (Jewish Theological Seminary, New York,

50 The important manuscripts — MS Kaufmann, MS Parma A — of the Western tradition have their provenance in different locations in 11th century Italy. See Rosenthal 1981:123–24.

51 I refer principally to mishnaic fragments from the Geniza which come from different parts of Palestine and neighboring areas.

52 The divisions under discussion do not encompass the phonological differences which are reflected in the Tiberian and Babylonian pointing of rabbinic literature, such as those distinguishing the tradition of the consonantal text and the tradition of the vocalized text in MS Vatican 66 of the *Sifra* (Haneman 1974:14 ff.), e.g., Tiberian *segol* as against the Babylonian *patah* in nouns of the class *pᵊli*, כילי and שיחי, against כַּלי and שַׁחי, and the form היסגירו as against הַסגירו in the verbal noun of *hip'il*, etc. These features are not unique to the Mishna.

53 See, for example, Yalon 1964 in *Tarbiz* 33: 107 (in Hebrew) and Bar-Asher 1971:171.

Babylonian, Abramson's edition) which generally belong to the Babylonian branch, in this detail, however, correspond to the Palestinian branch.[54]

§ 20 This is not surprising. The peregrinations of the Rabbis, of entire communities, and of manuscripts in the Middle Ages, with the concomitant mingling of communities with different backgrounds brought different traditions into contact. As a result, differences between the traditions were blurred.[55] Only when the Babylonian Talmud occupied the central position in the study of the Oral Law did the influences move in only one direction, namely, from the Babylonian Talmud outward. These occasional deviations do not, however, undermine the general picture.

§ 21 **Distinctive Features of Manuscripts and Traditions.** Another important point which must be noted is that there is scarcely an early manuscript or oral tradition without its own unique or almost unique features. A few examples are the loss of gemination of the *yod* in MS Parma B;[56] indefinite עֶגְלָה (עֲרוּפָה)[57] but definite הָעֲגָלָה[58] (noun class *pəʿālāh* instead of *piʿlāh*) in MS Kaufmann; the distinction preserved only in MS Deinard in the form אותה[59] where, when functioning as an object pronoun, the *he* appears with *mappiq* – אוֹתָהּ, but when functioning as a demonstrative pronoun, the *he* is not phonetically realized[60] – אוֹתָה.[61] Similar examples are plentiful in the pointing and orthography of MS Paris and MS Florence.[62]

§ 22 These distinctive features, be they early or be they individual scribal peculiarities, are an integral part of any linguistic description.[63] They must be

---

54 See Rosenthal 1971: 77. On the inflection of geminated verbs in the *qal* perfect, see Haneman 1980: 304 ff.

55 MS Parma B is an example of an Eastern manuscript which reached Italy. (On the change from פלונית to פלנית in the margin of the manuscript, see Bar-Asher 1980:63, n 307).

56 However , see Yeivin 1983, particularly Radak's comments cited there (p. 301).

57 This phenomenon requires separate investigation.

58 See Bar-Asher 1980:55 n. 262.

59 See Ben-Tolila 1973:68.

60 The quiescent *he* in the 3rd personal pronoun is documented in other sources (Bar-Asher 1980:127–28; 1981:85–88), but the existence of two conditioned variants as in MS Deinard appears to be unique.

61 When אותה serves as an object pronoun, e.g., ומחללין אוֹתָהּ ... ונותנין אוֹתָהּ ... ולוקחין אוֹתָהּ ... לוקחין אוֹתָהּ (*Šeqal.* 4:5, and another 9×, see Ben-Tolila 1973:68), it plays an independent syntactical role, but when it serves as a demonstrative pronoun, it is proclitic to the following word, e.g., אוֹתָה העיר (*Ned.* 5:4–5), אוֹתָה שעה (*Ned.* 9:10). Its proclitic status may cause a weakening of the *he* especially when the following word has initial *he* (e.g., אוֹתָה העיר).

62 See מגילות instead of מְגָלּוֹת, Bar-Asher 1980:24, where one can see that some of the features which were formerly thought to be distinctive are no longer so since the discovery of other material. See especially pp. 69–77.

63 There are many unique features in the consonantal text of MS Kaufmann, but in most cases they can be seen as early features preserved only in MS Kaufmann. See, for example,

noted, investigated, and clarified. They must not, however, distract the student of mishnaic Hebrew from the main task at hand, namely, finding and collecting features common to all manuscripts and describing the language according to all its branches and traditions.

§ 23 These preliminary remarks (on §§ 15–22) underline the caution necessary in dealing with mishnaic Hebrew and seek to eliminate some of the confusion found in this discipline.

I shall enumerate six general features and two details which serve to differentiate these two language types:[64]

19.6 The Western and Eastern traditions of the Palestinian branch

19.6.1 Gemination of *rēš*

§ 24 An outstanding feature of Western manuscripts is the lack of gemination of the *rēš*. As in Tiberian Hebrew, the *rēš* is not geminated. It is generally preceded by compensatory lengthening, e.g., אֵירַם (Yebam. 6:4, in MS Kaufmann and MS Paris, and אֵירָם in MS Parma A),[65] גֵּירֵשׁ (Yebam. 3:7, in MS

the 3 m.pl. pronominal suffixes discussed in § 17 above and the forms בדילה (instead of פתילה) and הגביה (instead of הגיה) (Bar-Asher 1983: especially 69–77).

64 The following may be added to the features described below (§§ 24–37): (a) realization of the vowel [i] in a closed unstressed syllable as the low vowel [e] (*segol/sere*). This feature is still apparent in a number of words in the vocalized text of MS Kaufmann and in individual words in other manuscripts, e.g., הֶלֵּל. In the Eastern tradition, the *segol* is found (in manuscripts in which the *segol* is not replaced by the *patah*) mainly in words beginning with *aleph* such as אֶלָּא (Kutscher 1969b, particularly 144 ff., where he discusses mishnaic Hebrew. He does not mention MS Parma B); (b) spirantized *bgdkpt* in the Babylonian vocalized tradition and in the traditions of the Jews of Baghdad, Yemen, and Djerba, as in מִטְפַּחַת and הַקְּפָּדָה (Morag 1980:237). This is a characteristic of some of the Eastern traditions (the phenomenon occurs in MS Parma B following *rēš*, e.g., מַרְפֵּק, מַרְכּוֹף – and it is not limited to *pē*), but the data from the different traditions are not completely consistent (see Morag 1980: 237); (c) the existence of forms such as גָּזְרוּ (*gazru*) and נוֹפְלִין (*noflin*), in which the *šewa mobile* has become a *šewa quiescens* and the accent is penultimate. The existence of these forms has been shown only for the living traditions (See Morag 1980:240, and the sources cited there). I believe that the details in §§ 24–37 are sufficient to support a distinction between the traditions under discussion.

65 One must remember that MS Parma A, MS Paris, MS Antonin to a large extent, and MS Kaufmann to a limited extent, are pointed with the so-called Palestinian-Tiberian pointing system which reflects a pronunciation commonly called Sephardi. This is reflected in the fluctuation of *patah* and *qameṣ* (both representing [a]), the fluctuation of *segol* and *sere* (both reflecting [e]), and the fluctuation of *hatep qameṣ* (sometimes *qameṣ*) and *holem* (reflecting [o]).

Kaufmann, and גֵּירָשׁ in MS Parma A and MS Paris), הַמְּאָרֵס (Ketub. 4:2, in MS Kaufmann and MS Parma A, and הַמְּאַרֵשׁ in MS Paris), נִיתְעָרֵב (Halla 1:2, in MS Kaufmann, and נִתְעָרַב in MS Parma A and MS Paris), הָרֹאשׁ (Yoma 1:2, in MS Kaufmann and MS Paris, and הָראשׁ in MS Parma A), מאוֹרֶסֶת (Yebam. 9:4, in MS Kaufmann, MS Parma A,[66] and MS Paris). As Yeivin pointed out some years ago,[67] rarely does a *dageš* appear in the *rēš* in MS Kaufmann, and then usually after the relative particle *šin*, e.g., שֶׁרָּאוּ (Roš Haš. 1:7), שֶׁרָּאָה (Roš Haš. 1:9).

In Eastern manuscripts and oral oriental traditions, by way of contrast, the *rēš* may be geminated like other consonants. The following are some examples from MS Parma B: סִירְּגָן (Kelim 22:9), מְסוּרָּס (Nid. 3:5), גַּרָּע (Kelim 12:4), סַרָּגִין (Kelim 24:8), שֶׁרָּאָה (Zabim 1:5), שֶׁרַּגְלַיִם (Ohol. 16:3), etc.[68] I know of only a few examples in MS Antonin[69] in which the *rēš* is treated as an ordinary consonant but where there is no graphic representation of the *dageš*: מְסוּרָס (Nid. 3:5) and not מְסוֹרָס, מְעוּרָבִין (Miq. 6:5) and not מְעוֹרָבִין. This phenomenon is widespread in the oral traditions of Yemen,[70] Djerba,[71] and in all other oriental traditions which have been examined (Morocco,[72] Aleppo,[73] and Baghdad[74]) and has been shown by several scholars, particularly, S. Morag.[75] The extent of this phenomenon in eastern traditions was probably far greater than is reflected in the manuscripts and oral traditions. The influence of the Tiberian vocalization of the Bible, however, appears to have displaced this feature even in early manuscripts.[76] This seems to be the reason for the complete absence of *dageš* following the definite article.[77]

In this connection it is important to note the deviation of the Babylonian vocalization. Yeivin (1968:959) cited a small number of words with Babylonian pointing such as בְּסִירוּס, בְּפִירוּשׁ (there is no *dageš*, but the *hireq* suggests gemination of the *rēš*).

66 In the first occurrence in MS Parma A the word is written with a *sin*, מְאוֹרֶשֶׂת.
67 Yeivin 1968:216.
68 Bar-Asher 1971:180–81.
69 The number of pointed words in this manuscript is very small (See Netanel 1972: 20).
70 See Shivtiel 1971:211; Morag 1963:32 ff.
71 Katz 1978:52 ff.
72 In addition to the material cited in n. 75 below, see Maman 1984 on the tradition of Tetouan; the same tradition existed in Tafilalt and Marrakesh.
73 Katz 1981:32–36.
74 Morag 1977:41–44.
75 Morag 1957: 190 ff.; 1980:236–37.
76 See § 43 below.
77 Bar-Asher 1971:181.

At first glance, this difference between the two traditions appears to be limited to a single phonological feature. A second glance, however, demonstrates that this feature is related to morphological patterns (the derived verbal conjugations, noun patterns with geminated consonants, etc.). Therefore, this is a salient feature which clearly distinguishes between the two traditions.

19.6.2 The relative *šîn* with *šəwa*

§ 25 In the Western tradition, as in the Tiberian pointing of the Bible, the relative ש is always pointed with a *segol* and followed by a geminated consonant, unless that consonant is *alep*, *he*, *ḥet*, *'ayin*, and *rēš*, in which case there is no gemination. The Eastern tradition differs in two respects. First, *rēš* following the relative *šin* is geminated. Second, the *šin* occurs with *šewa* when it precedes certain words, namely, the 3rd person independent personal pronouns: הוּא, הִיא, הֵם/הֵן → שְׁהוּא, שְׁהִיא, and שְׁהֵם/שְׁהֵן; the 1st person independent sg. pronoun: אֲנִי → שְׁנִי (< שאני); the negative particle, אֵין → שְׁאֵינִי, שְׁאֵינָה, שְׁאֵינוּ; and the conditional particles אִם and אִילוּ → שְׁאִם and שְׁאִילוּ. This phenomenon is documented in Babylonian pointed Mishnayot, MS Parma B, and the Yemenite oral tradition.[78] It is not attested, however, in MS Antonin.

19.6.3 The realization of the short vowel [u]

§ 26 The original short vowel [u] was preserved in the different traditions of Hebrew only in closed unstressed syllables. Its distribution in this phonological environment is highly regular in the Tiberian pointing of the Bible.[79] On the whole, the realization [u] (graphically represented by *qibbūṣ/šūreq*) is preferred before a geminated consonant, e.g., לֻמַּד and דֻּבִּים.[80] In other environments, the realization [o] (graphically represented by *qameṣ qatan*) is preferred, e.g., הָשְׁלַכְתָּ, שָׁרְשׁוֹ.[81] In contrast, in the Babylonian vocalization of the

---

78 This has been extensively discussed by Morag 1963:184–85 (and previously in Leshonenu 21 [1957] 110 ff.). See also Bar-Asher 1971:180. The pointing שְׁאִילוֹ is known to me only from MS Parma B; the pronunciation שְׁ is, however, well known in Italy in medieval times.

79 Bergstrasser, Hebräische Grammatik (Leipzig, 1918) 1. § 26n.

80 There are some exceptions. A *qameṣ* is occasionally found preceding *dalet*, e.g., מְאָדָּם (Nahum 2:4), מְאָדָּמִים (Exod 25:5 and 5×), יְשָׁדֵּם (Prov 11:3), שָׁדְּדָה (Nahum 3:7), but see also שֻׁדְּדָה (Jer 4:20 and elsewhere).

81 There are some exceptions, especially in the *hup'al* participle: הַמֻּפְקָדִים (2 Kgs 22:5 and elsewhere), מֻשְׁלָךְ (2 Sam 20:21), where מָ is sometimes found, e.g. מָפְנֶה (Ezek 9:2), מָרְאֶה (Exod 25:40), and מָשְׁחָת (Prov 25:26).

Bible, there is an almost complete preference for [u], before both geminated and nongeminated consonants, e.g., חֻקִּים, הֻגַּד, מְאֻדָּם (one exception Yeivin cites is כֹּרַת).[82] Some examples before non-geminated consonants are לְשֻׁמְרָה, לְקֻרְבָה, קֻדְשִׁי, אֻרְכּוֹ (only a few examples show a realization of *o* represented graphically by ḥolem, הֹפְדָה, יִשְׁמֹרְךָ, קָדְקֹד).[83]

§ 27 The situation in the pointed manuscripts of the Mishna has, until now, been studied only in MS Kaufmann and MS Paris. For the purposes of this study, a third manuscript has been examined, MS Parma B. Here, too, the different linguistic traditions are clearly distinguishable. In MS Kaufmann, Kutscher systematically showed that the realization [o] (*qameṣ qatan*, *ḥolem*)[84] was preferred before geminated and non-geminated consonants, e.g., אֻגְרוֹפּוֹ, קוֹרְקוֹרְתָה, קוֹמְקוֹם, גּוֹדְלָן, זוֹגִּין, אֶתְרוֹגֵיהֶן, אוֹמָּן, including many *hup'al* forms such as הוֹכְשְׁרוּ (Hul 2:5), הוֹזְכְּרוּ (Kelim 17:5), etc. Exceptions are given by Kutscher.[85] My study of MS Paris reveals a similar situation: קוֹמְצוֹ, מוֹרְאָה, לוֹגִּין, חוֹלְדָה, חוֹלְיָה, גּוֹלְגֹּלֶת (although many forms have a realization of [u] – e.g., the consistent pointing of *hup'al* הוּסְבַּךְ, הוּכְשְׁרוּ[86]). Kutscher's work demonstrated that the evidence in MS Kaufmann (and MS Paris) was in agreement with that found in Greek and Latin transcriptions.[87]

§ 28 A completely different tendency is apparent in MS Parma B. My study of a number of categories of words shows a clear preference for [u] (*qibbūṣ*/*šūreq*). Before geminated consonants, one almost always finds [u], e.g., זוּגִּין (Kelim 9:6), חוּלִּים-חוּלִּין (Tehar. 2:7), כּוּכִּין (Ohol 6:6), לוּגִּין (Kelim 2:2) (this is always the case in the noun pattern *pol*/*pull*); similarly in the feminine גּוּמָּה (Para 2:5), קוּפָּה (Ohol 6:2), etc., אֻגְרוּפּוֹ (Kelim 17:12, in MS Kaufmann אֻגְרוֹפּוֹ[88]), נַחְתּוּמִין (Makš. 2:9), קוּלַּר (Kelim 12:1, in MS Kaufmann קוֹלַר), and in the *hop'al* of I-n verbs, e.g., הוּתְּזוּ (Ohol. 1:6), הוּסַּק (Kelim 5:9), הוּנַּח (Tehar. 8:3). Exceptions are rare. In addition to אוּמָּן (Kelim 26:1, 3×), אוּמָּנִין (Kelim 17:9, Tehar. 7:3), there are two occurrences of אָוּמָּן (Kelim 5:4, 9).

Before non-geminated consonants. [u] appears consistently in *hup'al* and is not limited to the participle,[89] e.g., הוּזְכָּרוּ (Kelim 17:5, 2×), הוּחְלָטָה (Kelim

82 Yeivin 1985:374–376.

83 *Ibid.*

84 *Qameṣ qatan* and *ḥolem* are interchangeable, as is usually the case in manuscripts whose pointing reflects a Sephardic pronunciation. See n. 65.

85 Kutscher 1969b:153 ff.

86 Bar-Asher 1980:58–59.

87 Kutscher 1969b:137–44.

88 The material in this paragraph from MS Paris and MS Kaufmann is cited for comparative purposes and is taken from the sources in nn. 86–87 above.

89 See n 81 above.

6:3, 2×), הוּטְבָּלוּ (Miqw. 5:6). Examples of participles are, e.g., מוּדְבֶּקֶת (Ohol 10:7), מוּחְלָט, מוּסְגָּר (Kelim 1:5 and elsewhere), מוּכְשָׁר (Para 11:6), מוּסְאָבוֹת (Kelim 8:10), מוּשְׁלָךְ (Makš. 2:7), מוּתְקָן (Para 3:3). The same phenomenon occurs in a large number of words, including loan words, e.g., חוּלְיָה (Kelim 5:10, 2×; Ohol 2:3; in MS Paris it usually appears as חוֹלְיָה), גּוּלְגֹּלֶת (Ohol 2:1 and another 4× with [u]; in MS Paris the forms גּוֹלְגֹּלֶת, גֻּלְגֹּלֶת, appear alongside גֻּלְגֹּלֶת), נְחוּשְׁתּוּ (Kelim 8:3, 9:1, 3, 2×, in all these cases MS Paris has נְחוֹשְׁתּוֹ),[90] בּוּרְיָה (Kelim 24:17, 2×), תּוּרְוָוד (Kelim 17:12, 2×), תּוּרְבָּד (Ohol 2:2), תֻּרְבָּד (Ohol. 2:1),[91] טוּמְטוּם (Para 12:10; Nid. 3:5, 3×; Zabim 2:1; in MS Kaufmann טוֹמטום), לוּכְסָן (Kelim 18:5, MS Kaufmann לוֹכְסָן), קוּרְדוּם (Para 12:5, this is its only occurrence; elsewhere MS Parma B has קֻרְדוּם, in MS Kaufmann קוֹרדום), קוּרְסֵל (Ohol 1:8), קוּלְמוֹס (Kelim 12:8, MS Kaufmann קוֹלמוס), קלוּסְטֵר (Kelim 20:1, MS Kaufmann קלוֹסטר), קוּמְקֻומוֹס (Kelim 3:7; 14:1; 25:8; Miqw. 9:2; MS Kaufmann קוֹמְקוּם in Miqw. 9:2 alongside קוּמְקוּם 3× in Kelim), קוּרְקוּרְתָה (Kelim 28:10, 2×; Ohol 9:16, MS Kaufmann has קוֹרְקוֹרְתָה in these three cases), תּוּרְמָל (Kelim 16:4; 19:8; 20:1 [in this occurrence תּוּרְמַל]; Neg. 11:11; Miqw. 10:3), תֻּרְמָלִין (Kelim 24:11, in MS Kaufmann תּוֹרְמֵל/תּוֹרָמָלִים), תּוּרְפָּה (Nid. 8:1, 3×; MS Kaufmann תּוֹרְפָּה), תֻּרְנוּגְלִין (Tehar. 3:8; MS Kaufmann תַּרְנָגְלִים/ן and תַּרְנוֹגְלִים).

It should be pointed out that even in the noun pattern *po'el* which in MS Parma B consistently has *o* in closed syllables, many forms with [u] can be found, e.g., אָזְנוֹ (Kelim 4:1), אֻורכּוֹ (Neg. 12:3), גָּרְנוֹ (Makš. 3:5), חָפְנָיו (Para 5:5), כּוּתְלֵי, כָּתְלֵי (Ohol 11:8), צָרְכוֹ/צָרְכָהּ (Kelim 19:1; Makš 4:1), רָחְבּוֹ (Neg. 12:3 and elsewhere), שׁוּרְשֵׁי/שָׁרְשֵׁי ('Uq. 1:2), etc. as opposed to גּוּלְמֵי (Kelim 12:6, alongside גָּוּלְמֵי in Kelim 12:8), חוּמְרוֹ (Kelim 8:2, and 5×, alongside the one occurrence of חָומְרוֹ in Kelim 3:1), לוּגְמָיו (Kelim 17:11), עֻקְצָה, עוּקְצָה (Kelim 13:5), and עֻקְצֵי, עוּקְצֵי ('Uq. 1:6), עוּשְׁפּוֹ (Kelim 13:3, 2×), שׁוּגְמִין (Kelim 10:6).

§ 29 In the main, there seem to be three traditions: (1) the Tiberian tradition of the Bible which prefers [u] before geminated consonants and [o] before non-geminated consonants; (2) the tradition reflected in the Western tradition of the Mishna – MS Kaufmann and MS Paris – which reveals a clear tendency towards [o] before geminated and nongeminated consonants; (3) the tradition reflected in manuscripts of the Eastern tradition – MS Parma B – which demonstrates a clear preference for [u] in all cases, sharing in common a feature of the Babylonian pointing of the Bible (and of the Mishna[92]). Although this is not a consistently delineating feature between MS Kaufmann and MS Paris, on

---

90 In MS Kaufmann it is always pointed נחוּשתן, נחוּשתו. See Bar-Asher 1980:58–59.

91 The form is also found with *taw* with *patah*: תַּרְבָּד. See Bar-Asher 1971:171.

92 See Yeivin 1985:374.

the one hand, and MS Parma B, on the other, in general, this feature can be said to distinguish the Western tradition from the Eastern tradition.

19.6.4 The Final Vowel in the *Qatt* and Related Noun Patterns

§ 30 Nouns and adjectives (and participles) of geminate roots of the *qatt* noun pattern, such as the nouns בַּד, כַּד, צַד, שַׂק, and adjectives קַל, עַז, etc. are pointed with *pataḥ* in the absolute form; the expected shift of *pataḥ* > *qameṣ* does not take place. As I have shown elsewhere,[93] there is clear evidence in the Eastern tradition as demonstrated in MS Parma B and the Babylonian pointing system that these forms were pointed with a *qameṣ* even in the absolute case, e.g., קָל, צָד, כָּד, בָּד, שָׂק, עָז.

This is also true for nouns whose final consonant is *ʿayin*, e.g., קַרְקַע, אֶצְבַּע, אֶמְצַע. MS Parma B, the Babylonian pointed Mishnayot, and the Yemenite tradition vocalize such words with a *qameṣ*, e.g., קַרְקָע, אֶצְבָּע, אֶמְצָע.[94]

§ 31 It is difficult to examine this phenomenon in most of the manuscripts of the Western tradition, such as MS Parma A and MS Paris, since these manuscripts regularly confuse the *pataḥ* and the *qameṣ*, as is the case in the so-called Palestinian-Tiberian system. The same applies to MS Antonin of the Eastern tradition.[95] Similarly, although the vocalizer of MS Kaufmann does not confuse the *pataḥ* and *qameṣ* quite so much as his predecessors, the frequency with which he does confuse them suggests that they were both realized as a.[96] This is a salient feature of the Eastern tradition, because it maintained the distinct realization of the two vowels and distinguished between the absolute forms (with *qameṣ*) and the construct forms (with *pataḥ*) in the noun patterns mentioned above, e.g., בָּד as against בַּד-, צָד as against צַד-. In contrast, the Tiberian pointing of the Bible does distinguish between *qameṣ* and *pataḥ*. Nonetheless, it has *pataḥ* in both the absolute and constructforms (בַּד/-בַּד).

19.6.5 The Definite Article with *segol* before *'aleph* with *qameṣ*

§ 32 In the Eastern tradition, there is evidence that the rule according to which the definite article takes segol before עָ, חָ, הָ is extended to cases where

93 Bar-Asher 1971:181–82.

94 *Ibid.*

95 Netanel 1972:21.

96 In a random examination of the word אצבע in MS Kaufmann, I found the form אֶצְבַּע seven times (Yoma 1:7; Hul. 3:6; Bekh. 6:7; Kelim 10:3; Ohol 1:8, 2×, 7:2), and the form אֶצְבָּע three times (Kelim 17:9; in ᶜEd. 3:5 the pointing was not clear in the photograph I used).

it precedes אָ. In MS Parma B, we find the word הֶאָרִיג (Neg 11:10[11]), בֶאָרִיג (*Neg* 11:10[11]; 11:11[12]); this word appears once in MS Antonin as הֶאָרִיג[97] (Neg. 11:11[12]) as well as the word הֶאָפֵל[98] (Neg. 2:3). This phenomenon is paralleled also in Babylonian pointing – הַאָח, הַאָמוּר, בַאָרִיג, לַאָנוּס (in Babylonian pointing the vocalization of the definite article with *pataḥ* = Tiberian *segol* is not limited to *'aleph* with *qameṣ*, e.g., הַאֲמוּרָה; הַאִיוָה[99]). The well-known reading of כדבר הֶאמור על יד נביאך in the *qəduša* prayer of the *musaf* service in different communities is more easily understood in the light of this phenomenon.

§ 33 In sum, the pointing of the definite article with *segol* preceding אָ is rare; the definite article is usually pointed with a *qameṣ*. It is difficult to tell whether this is the beginning of a phenomenon encompassing all gutturals or the remains of a more general phenomenon. Whatever the case may be, this feature characterizes only the Eastern tradition, and is not found in the Western tradition at all.

19.6.6 Noun Pattern *po'lān/pa'lān*

§ 34 One noun pattern characteristic of mishnaic Hebrew is that of the *nomen agentis* (nouns denoting profession or permanent attribute) with the ending *-ān*. In the Western tradition, this ending appears in the form *po'lān*:[100] בּוֹישן, קוֹפדן, גָוזלן/גוֹזלן, etc. Details are given by B. Gross.[101] In the Eastern tradition, on the other hand, one finds *pa'lān*. As can be seen in Yeivin's work,[102] one regularly finds *pataḥ* in the first syllable: בַּטְלָנִים, בַּיְשָׁן, גַּזְלָן, רַצְעָנִין, רַחְמָן, רַבְצָנִית, קַפְדָן, קַבְלָן, נַשְׁכָנִית, נַגְחָן, כַּפְרָן, חַמְסָנִין, גַּרְגְּרָן, etc. Only in the word סָרְבָן does a *qameṣ* appear in the first syllable. In two other nouns, one finds *waw* following the first consonant, reflecting *u*: עוּבְדָן (alongside עַבְדָן with *pataḥ*) and תוּרְגְמָן.

In MS Parma B one finds *pa'lān*: גַּזְלָן (Kelim 26:8[9] 2×), גַּרְגְּרָן (Nid. 10:8), גַּרְגְּרָנִיוֹת (Tehar. 7:9[11]), עַסְקָנִיוֹת (Tehar. 7:8[9]). The only exception is עוּבְדָן

97 MS Antonin preserves the alternation of *ṣere/segol* (see Netanel 1972: 22). These examples may be found in Netanel 1972:41.

98 *Ibid.*

99 These details are taken from Yeivin 1985:1147.

100 Regardless of whether they are related to the *qal* conjugation, e.g., גוֹזְלָן from גָּזַל, or from a different conjugation, e.g., קוֹפְדָן from הִקְפִּיד. See Gross 1993:57–103.

101 *Ibid.* The mishnaic material can be found on pp. 57–75, and the linguistic discussion on pp. 195–265.

102 See Yeivin 1985:1044–1046.

(Kelim 26:8[9]). In MS Antonin there is even less evidence: גַּרְגְּרָן is pointed with *pataḥ* (Nid. 10:8) alongside גורגרניות (Nid. 10:8) and עוסקניות (Nid. 10:8).[103]

§ 35 These data may be explained in different ways. It might simply be said that the dominant pattern in the East is *pa'lān*. In the forms עובדן (in Babylonian pointing and MS Parma B), גורגרן (in MS Antonin), סָרבן, תורגמן (in Babylonian pointing), [a] > [o]/[u], under the influence of the following labial (*bet*) or *rēš*.[104] This is a phonetic phenomenon which is well-documented in early manuscripts from both the West and East. But how should one explain the form עוסקניות in MS Antonin? It may be either a foreign loan from the Western tradition or else the remains of an early reading prevalent in Palestine (which was wholly preserved in the most reliable of the Western manuscripts). The *pa'lān* forms which are characteristic of the Eastern tradition are thus, as shown by Gross,[105] an innovation.

The following two words give evidence of two additional differences between the Western and Eastern traditions.

19.6.6.1 צִפּוֹרֶן/צְפֹרֶן

§ 36 The noun צפורן is treated in the Western tradition as in the Tiberian tradition of Biblical Hebrew: צִפּוֹרֶן. The *ṣade* is pointed with *ḥireq* and the *pe* with *dageš*. This is known from the consonantal text of MS Kaufmann (e.g., והציפורן in Ohol 3:3)[106] and from the vocalized text (e.g., הַצִּפּוֹרֶן in Miqw. 9:4). It is also found in MS Parma A, where the word is generally written with a *yod* following the *ṣade*, e.g., והציפורן (Hul. 1:2; Ohol 3:3, and elsewhere).[107] This word occurs once with *yod* in MS Cambridge, ציפורניו (B. Qamma 8:1).[108] This is the form throughout MS Paris.[109] In contrast, this noun is realized in the Eastern tradition as צְפֹרֶן, with a *šewa* with the *ṣade* and *rāfē* with the *pe*. The

103 Netanel 1972:57.

104 Ben-Ḥayyim, "Introduction to the Historical Dictionary of the Hebrew Language of the Academy of Hebrew Language," *Source Book*, Part 1: *From the Bible to the end of the Gaonic Period* (Jerusalem, 1963) 10, n. 9, and the refernces cited there (in Hebrew). See also Bar-Asher 1971:171; 1979:189; and 1983b:149–50, §§ 24–26.

105 See Gross (n. 100 above).

106 The writing of *yod* after *sade* can be found in MS Kaufmann in Ohol. 3:3 and Neg. 6:8 ציפורין (the second *yod* was erased by the vocalizer).

107 There is one attestation of the pointing צִיפּוֹרְנָיו (Shabb. 10:6). MS Parma has in one verse צפורתה מדולדלת and not צפורן (Miqw. 9:4).

108 Elsewhere one finds צפרן without *yod*.

109 This is reflected only in the vocalized text: צִפּוֹרֶן (Hul. 1:2), צִפֳּרְנַיִם (Tehar. 1:2, 3). There is one example of *šureq* after *pe*, צִפּוּרְנָיו (Shabb. 10:6).

evidence from MS Parma B and from the Babylonian pointing has been discussed elsewhere,[110] and applies to the situation in MS Antonin where some of the occurrences of this form are וְהַצִּפּוֹרֶן (Neg. 6:8), צִפּוֹרֶן (Nid. 6:2, first occurrence in this Mishna),[111] as against הַצִּיפּוֹרֶן (Miqw. 9:2), הַצִּיפּוֹרֶן (Miqw. 9:4[5], first occurrence in this Mishna[112]) and in the plural וְהַצִּפָּרְנַיִם[113] (Tehar. 1:2, 3 [= MS Parma B]).[114]

19.6.6.2 The plural אֲחָיוֹת/אַחְיוֹת

§ 37 The plural of the noun אָחוֹת appears differently in each of the traditions. The Western tradition preserves the form אַחְיוֹת/אַחֲיוֹת,[115] the *'aleph* with a *pataḥ* and the *ḥet* with a *šəwa* or *ḥataph pataḥ*.[116] The Eastern tradition, on the other hand, has אֲחָיוֹת, the *'aleph* with a *ḥataph pataḥ* and the *ḥet* with a *qameṣ* as evidenced by two Babylonian manuscripts and as in the Yemenite tradition.[117] This word does not occur in *Seder Teharoth*, and therefore, MS Parma B and MS Antonin provide no evidence.

19.7 The Nature of the Differences between the Western and Eastern Traditions

§ 38 Most of the features which distinguish the Western tradition from the Eastern tradition of the Palestinian branch relate to the reading tradition, rather than to the consonantal text. For example, the difference in pronunciation between עָרֵב and עֵרֵב, between מְסוּרָּס and מְסוֹרָס, between אֲחָיוֹת and אַחְיוֹת, between צִפּוֹרֶן and צִפֹּרֶן, and הֶאָרִיג and הָאָרִיג. Even the differences between *po'lān* and *pa'lān*, and ציפורן and צִפּוֹרֶן, which occur in the consonantal text and not only in the pointing indicate a shift in the initial vowel of those forms. In fact, we find two by-forms of the same pattern, e.g., in *po'lān*/*pa'lān*.[118] These differences indicate two different reading traditions of the

110 Bar-Asher 1971:181 (where it is noted that the attested plural in MS Parma B is צִפָּרְנַיִם).
111 See Netanel 1972:57.
112 The form צִפֹּרֶן is more revealing of the tradition of MS Antonin than the cases with expected Tiberian pointing.
113 See n. 110 above.
114 Elsewhere the form is not vocalized in MS Antonin, צפורן (e.g., Nid. 6:2, the second occurrence in the Mishna).
115 For details see I. Ben-David, *Leshonenu* 41 (1977) 237–240, and Bar-Asher 1980:121 f.
116 Note also the unique pointing אַחִיּוֹת. See Bar-Asher 1980:125, especially n. 25.
117 See Bar-Asher 1980:122.
118 Or, at most, two different noun patterns distinguished from one another by their first vowel.

same consonantal text,[119] unlike the differences we find between the Palestinian and Babylonian branches (as will be seen). There, the differences occur in the text itself: differences of formation, which are occasionally derived from a different consonantal text (e.g., מועט/ממועט or מסואבות/מוסאבות), differences in syntax, and differences in vocabulary (see below § 47 f.).

19.8 The Historical Background of the Different Traditions of the Western Branch

§ 39 What is the background and what are the roots of the linguistic features which distinguish each of the two traditions? This is an important question in the history of the Hebrew language on the whole, and in the history of mishnaic Hebrew in particular. The relationship of the Western tradition, in its principal manifestations, to Palestine is well known and has been proved. Forms, such as *po'lān*, have been found in manuscripts of the Jerusalem Talmud and in early Palestinian *piyyutim*. The relationship of the short vowel [o] in closed unstressed syllables to Palestine in Greek and Latin transcriptions (and in fragments of the Palestinian Targum published by Kahle) has been shown by Kutscher.[120] The loss of the *dageš* in the *rēš* and other phenomena are Palestinian features, as evidenced by their occurring in the Tiberian pointing of the Bible. Indeed, those features which are common to both traditions and which can be found in manuscripts from both the West and the East, and which, as well, are not found in the Tiberian Bible, have, in the main, been shown to have their origins in Palestine. For example, the plural ending *-iyyot* of nouns such as חָנוּוֹת and מַלְכֻיּוֹת is known to be related to Palestine from Greek transcriptions of Jer 37:16 in which one finds ανιωθ, αενιωθ.[121]

§ 40 What is the origin of the characteristic features of the Eastern tradition? Did these features originate in the East? Do they represent a change which took place during the process of transmission or are these early features which were passed on from Palestine itself? In other words, is an early Palestinian linguistic tradition preserved in the Eastern tradition? As noted above, Gross thought that the noun class *pa'lān* was an innovation of the East under the influence of phonological rules of Babylonian Aramaic.[122] Recently, the

119 This also applies to the linguistic phenomena hinted at in n. 64 above. In those examples, there is only one consonantal text with different reading traditions.

120 Kutscher 1969b, passim.

121 Kutscher 1969a: 109.

122 See Gross, n. 100 above.

gemination of the *rēš* in the Eastern tradition has been interpreted as Babylonian influence, or in the words of Morag:

> It seems reasonable to assume that the gemination of the *rēš* in the oral traditions of Mishnaic Hebrew in the different communities has its source in Babylonia. This is indicated by the fact that all those communities which preserve the gemination of the *rēš* in Mishnaic Hebrew also preserve it in Babylonian Aramaic.[123]

Yeivin argues that the realization of the short back vowel as [u] in closed unstressed syllables before geminated and non-geminated consonants is also a feature whose roots are in Babylonia.[124] Is this true of all features which characterize the Eastern tradition?[125] In my opinion, this is not so. Most of the characteristic features of the Eastern tradition appear to be quite original and the fact that they have their origins in Palestine is beyond doubt. We begin with a few details.

§ 41 צְפֹרֶן as against צִפֹּרֶן. It can be said with certainty that both forms existed side by side in Palestine, regardless of whether the first is a reflex of the second[126] or both are reflexes of a third original form.[127] צִפֹּרֶן is well documented as a Palestinian form in Tiberian Biblical Hebrew and in Western manuscripts of the Mishna. In contrast, a form similar to צְפֹרֶן is attested in the Samaritan Pentateuch. The reading *ṣēferniyya* as against צִפָּרְנֶיהָ (Deut 21:12) in the Tiberian reading shows that the spirantized form was in use in Palestine. If this is the case, there is surely no reason to regard this form as an Eastern innovation when it corresponds with what was familiar to the Samaritans.

§ 42 The Eastern אֲחָיוֹת has been discussed by J. Blau.[128] He believes that comparative Semitics proves that this form is earlier than אַחֲיוֹת/אֲחָיוֹת. It is clear that this form is not a scholarly innovation in the Eastern tradition, but rather simply adhered to an earlier tradition. It is the Western form which is

---

123 Morag 1980: 144, n. 16.

124 Oral communication from Yeivin.

125 In general, there is a widespread tendency to view many features which deviate from known or expected features as innovations in Babylonia. See, for example, Yalon (1964:189) and Bendavid 1971:1.129; 2.630 on the weakening of definition (definite article) in MH (see also Bar-Asher 1980:97 ff., and especially 102 ff.). See also Kutscher (§ 48 ff.) on the disfiguring of the language reflected in the printed editions.

126 See Bar-Asher 1971:181 where צְפֹרֶן was interpreted as a reflex of צִפֹּרֶן. By a process of haplology the gemination was lost, followed by a change of *hireq* to *šewa* mobile.

127 One could reconstruct a form **ṣiporen* which had two possible reflexes: (a) *sipporen* in which secondary gemination preserved the short vowel [i]; or (b) *ṣəporen* in which [i] > [ə] in an open unstressed syllable. Similar processes were at work in many words in Hebrew and one can find both in the same word, cf. אִסָּר as opposed to אֱסָרֶיהָ (Num 30:4, 6).

128 J. Blau, *Leshonenu* 41 (1977) 304.

an innovation, apparently by way of analogy to the construct form and to the inflected plural forms. One cannot be certain if this innovation occurred while mishnaic Hebrew was still a living language or emerged in the process of its transmission.[129]

§ 43 Now to a more general feature: the gemination of the *rēš*. Because of the almost complete absence of gemination of *rēš* in the Tiberian tradition of the Bible and in Western manuscripts of the Mishna, it is tempting to attribute its existence in the Eastern tradition to the influence of Babylonian Aramaic. This view, however, is not free of problems. The gemination of *rēš* in the Eastern tradition is absent in many words and forms in which we expect to find it. This absence is usually interpreted as a very early influence of the Tiberian biblical tradition. For example, עִרֵּב with geminated *rēš* in *pi'el* vis-à-vis נִתְעָרַב with non-geminated *rēš* which is found in many written documents and oral traditions of the Eastern tradition.[130] This latter form is attributed to the Tiberian pointing of the Bible where *hitpa'el* (without gemination) is attested, e.g., וְהִתְעָרְבוּ (Ezra 9:2), יִתְעָרַב (Prov 14:10), וַיִּתְעָרְבוּ (Ps 106:35). There is, however, no *pi'el* form עֵרֵב which could have displaced the form עִרֵּב in the Eastern traditions.[131] Some of the forms in which there is gemination in the Eastern tradition are difficult to explain. Why is the *rēš* geminated in classes (and words) in which there are no parallel forms in Aramaic, as, for example, after the relative particle *šin*? Should we argue in this case that this gemination came from Babylonian Aramaic via transmitters of the Eastern tradition of mishnaic Hebrew who transferred it to non-Aramaic forms? Why did the Tiberian biblical tradition not prevent this? There is no need to resort to this type of hypothesis since we do possess explicit evidence concerning gemination. The gemination of *rēš* is well attested in Palestinian reading traditions, particularly in the Samaritan tradition, as well as being documented in Greek transcriptions of personal names from different periods. As Morag has shown previously,[132] the Eastern tradition agrees with the Samaritan tradition on this point. It is in this light that the existence of more than ten words containing geminated *rēš* in Tiberian Hebrew should be explained, e.g., שֶׁרֹּאשִׁי נמלא טל

---

129 See Bar-Asher 1980:121–25. See also Sarfatti 1983 (n. 154 below) on changes which have occurred in the transmission of mishnaic Hebrew.

130 Bar-Asher 1971:180.

131 *Ibid.*

132 Morag 1957:191–92: "in these dialects [i.e., the tradition of Babylonia, Aleppo, Maghreb, and Yemen – M. Bar-Asher] the reš could be geminated, as in Samaritan Hebrew ... with regard to the conclusions which have a more fundamental significance, we raise the possibility that, in certain features, the dialect of Tiberian Biblical Hebrew is not identical to other Hebrew dialects *which existed at the time when our language was spoken*" [emphasis, M. Bar-Asher].

(Shir ha-Shirim 5:2), כָּרַּת שָׁרֵּךְ (Ezek 16:4). From where could the Tiberian biblical vocalization which crystallized in the 7th century CE (if not already in the 6th century CE) come, if not from a tradition prevalent in Palestine?[133]

§ 44 Furthermore, the pointing of the relative ש with *šəwa* appears in the Tiberian Bible in two words: שְׁהוּא (Qoh 2:22), and שְׁהֵם (Qoh 3:18). This is several hundred years earlier than the evidence provided by MS Parma B and the Babylonian pointed Mishnayot, the ancestors of the Yemenite pronunciation, which regularly points ש with *šəwa* before 3rd person pronouns and other words. What is found only occasionally in Tiberias became a rule in the Eastern tradition, which drew it from the same source as did the Tiberians.[134]

§ 45 It might reasonably be argued that there is one feature distinguishing between the Eastern and Western traditions which has its source outside of Palestine, in the East. That is the difference between *po'lān/pa'lān*. Recently we have learned that the form *pa'lān* is not an innovation that was created in the orient outside Eretz Yisrael. Beside the form attested in the Bible רַחֲמָנִיּוֹת (Lamentations 4:10) and we do have it in Qumran: גדפן.[135]

§ 46 On the whole, the Eastern and Western traditions are two faces of mishnaic Hebrew in Palestine. They are two different reading traditions of one text, both of which became crystallized in Palestine, even if, here and there, slight changes occurred in them in the process of their transmission in the Diaspora. It may also be said that these are two dialects[136] within Palestine itself, although it is not clear exactly where either of them originated. In the course of the dispersion of the Jews, one tradition spread westwards, perhaps

133 In this way one should interpret the few pointings of geminated *reš* following the relative *šin* which occur in MS Kaufmann (mentioned above in § 24).

134 There is nothing to prevent us from presenting a similar argument with other phenomena reflected in the pointings בֶּאָרִ״ג and הֶאָפֵל (see § 32 above), where there is an extension of the rule of vocalization concerning the definite article with *segol* before עָ, חָ, הָ. (There is, of course, a difference in the conditioning of this pointing before חָ as opposed to הֶ before הָ, עָ in Tiberian pointing) and before אָ. Similarly, with the pointings קָל, עָז, צָד, בָּד in the absolute case and אֶמְצָע, אֶצְבָּע, קַרְקָע, here there is also an extension of the rule that the *pataḥ* is replaced by *qameṣ* in a stressed syllable in the noun of all noun patterns (including nouns whose final consonant is geminated when declined or whose final consonant is '*ayin*). The realization of the short back vowel [u] in any closed syllable may be an extension of a phonetic rule which was prevalent in Palestine (the Tiberian pointing from Palestine always preserves it before geminated consonants and occasionally when it does not precede a geminated consonant). There is no reason why these features of the Eastern tradition should be attributed to eastern transmitters who changed their pronunciation rather than be attributed to an extension of phonetic rules known from the Tiberian vocalization in Palestine.

135 See above Chapter 9 at n. 12.

136 See Morag 1957, n. 132 above. He refers to dialects which existed while the language was still spoken.

through a particular academy, while the other tradition moved eastwards, perhaps through a different academy. Local influences must have surely affected each tradition, and such influences must have accumulated over time, particularly in the centuries just preceding the invention of printing. At the end of the first millennium CE and soon thereafter,[137] the two traditions can still be seen preserving their distinctive features. Both those features which distinguish between them, as well as the many more features which they share in common (and which constitute the bulk of the grammar), can be characterized as very early. Most of them have grown out of the different varieties of mishnaic Hebrew spoken in Palestine.

19.9 The Palestinian Branch and the Babylonian Branch

§ 47 The division into a Palestinian and a Babylonian branch is a separate matter. Many of the features which differentiate the two branches are known to scholars of mishnaic Hebrew. These differences relate to all categories of the language.

1. Different orthographies,[138] such as the graphic representation of the final diphthong *-ay* as י- or יי- in the Palestinian branch as against אי- in the Babylonian branch, e.g., שמיי, שמי, vs. שמאי; פני, פניי; vs. פנאי.[139]
2. Graphic representation of final [a] by ה in the Palestinian branch as against א in the Babylonian branch, e.g., עקיבה/עקיבא, בתירה/בתירא, דיגמה/דוגמא; the marking of medial [a] by א in the Babylonian branch and the almost complete absence of any representation in the Palestinian branch, e.g., כאן as against כן.[140]
3. Similarly, individual words are spelled differently, e.g., in the Palestinian branch יוסה as opposed to יוסי in the Babylonian branch.
4. One also finds differences in phonology, e.g., מִיגְמָר, סִיפְּגָן, מִשֵּׁם in the Palestinian branch as against מוּגְמָר, סוּפְּגָן, מֵשׁוּם in the Babylonian

137 Most of the manuscripts extant are from the beginning of the 2nd millennium. Some of them were, of course, copied from manuscripts of earlier periods, from the end of the 1st millennium.

138 Most of the details mentioned here are well known and, consequently, few references will be given.

139 Manuscripts from the Eastern tradition correspond to features of the Babylonian branch on certain points, e.g., the use of אי in MS Parma B (Bar-Asher 1971:169–170), although the forms with י- and יי- also occur.

140 In a number of words, medial *'alep* is used as a mater lectionis to mark the vowel [a] even in manuscripts of the Western tradition, e.g., שיארא, גאָפן (Epstein 1948:1234; Bar-Asher 1971:170 ff.).

branch;[141] the pattern דְחָיוֹ, קְנָיָה, הַזָּיָה, הוֹרָיָה, with *yod* in Palestine as against דְחָאוֹ, קְנָאָה, הַזָּאָה, הוֹרָאָה in Babylonia; or the plurals פנקסיות and מרחציות against פנקסאות and מרחצאות; or שזרה, קורסל, and קורדום as against שדרה, קַרסול, and קַרְדום, and many other words.

5. There are also many differences in morphology, e.g., the plural of nouns ending in *-ut* mentioned above, פורעָנִיּוֹת, מַלְכִיּוֹת as against פורענויות, מלכויות or the forms ממועט/ממועטין as against מועט/מועטין and ידיים מוּסְאָבוֹת as against ידים מסוֹאָבוֹת.
6. Furthermore, the two branches are distinguished from one another in matters of syntax and vocabulary, such as subordinate clauses beginning with relative שֶׁ. In the Palestinian branch the 3rd person pronoun follows the שׁ, e.g., שהוא קורא, כשהוא עושה, שהן אוכלין, whereas in the Babylonian branch there is no pronoun, e.g. שקורא, כשעושה and שאוכלין; or בין הקברות as against בית הקברות; אסור מלפעול as against אסור לפעול;[142] ממנו/ממנה as against הימנו/הימנה; נתאלמנה as against נתארמלה;[143] על אתר as against לאלתר,[144] and many other examples. Studies on mishnaic Hebrew are filled with similar examples and discussions.

19.10 Background of the Linguistic Differences between the Two Branches

§ 48 What is the background of the differences between the two linguistic traditions reflected in these two branches? Some scholars, particularly Kutscher, attributed the differences to two principle factors. In his words:

> There was a change, a conscious and unconscious editing, whose purpose was to bring Mishnaic Hebrew closer to Biblical Hebrew ... and the language and orthography of the Babylonian Talmud also had influence.[145]

§ 49 It is clear that there are some linguistic features in the Babylonian branch which are the result of foreign influences on early transmitters and

---

141 A widespread phenomenon in both traditions is the backing of the front vowels [i], [e], [a] to [u], [o] in the presence of neighboring labials. Some words or forms, however, exist in one branch and not the other, e.g., *pi'el* forms קוּבַּלְתִּי, טוּמֵּא in MS Kaufmann do not appear in the Babylonian branch, whereas סוּפְגָן, מְשׁוּם of the Babylonian branch do not occur in the Palestinian branch and when we find them in Palestinian branch they are probably the result of foreign influence (this is the case with מְשׁוּם in MS Kaufmann and similar manuscripts).

142 For a recent discussion, see Rosenthal 1981:82–83 and Sarfatti 1983:454.

143 Bar-Asher 1980:33, and Moreshet 1981:102, 105.

144 See Z. Frankel, *Mevo HaYerushalmi* (Breslau, 1870, reprint Jerusalem, 1967) 12, and S. Lieberman in the *Ben-Ḥayyim Jubilee Volume*, 331 n. 15.

145 Kutscher 1963:2–3; Yalon and Bendavid in sources cited in n. 125 above.

copyists. These influences may have come from Tiberian Biblical Hebrew of the language of the Babylonian Talmud. Many of the forms which characterize the Babylonian branch correspond with those in the Tiberian tradition of the Bible, and it is reasonable to suppose, as did Kutscher, that the prestige of Biblical Hebrew displaced original mishnaic forms.[146] For example, it is quite possible that the interrogative particle of mishnaic Hebrew לְאַיִן became לְאָן under the influence of Biblical Hebrew: לְאַיִן (Ter. 4:11; Rosh ha-Shana 2:4; Aboth 3:1, 2×).[147] לאן was analogized from אן and אנה of Biblical Hebrew.

This would also seem to explain the displacement of many rare forms from the language of the Babylonian Mishna. The disappearance of the *nitpa'el* participle (with initial nun), e.g., נִיטַּמִּין, נִתְכַּפֵּר, נִתְמַלֵּא provides us with a few examples. It seems that the loss of the nun may be attributed to biblical influence. These forms were replaced by their biblical parallels, מִיטַּמִּין, מִתְכַּפֵּר, מִתְמַלֵּא, etc. This phenomenon (disappearance) is also apparent in manuscripts of the Palestinian branch, as I have discussed elsewhere.[148]

§ 50 There are, of course, a number of forms which penetrated as a result of the influence of the Babylonian Talmud. I shall mention just a few of the many examples which have been cited in previous studies. על-אתר used as an adverb in two passages in *m. Git.* (3:3; 8:8) in the Palestinian branch (MS Kaufmann, MS Parma A, MS Cambridge, even in MS Paris and the first printed edition in Naples 1492) was replaced in editions of the Mishnah under the influence of Baylonian Talmud by לאלתר, which in turn is clearly influenced by Babylonian Aramaic.[149] The verbal forms נתאלמנה, נתאלמנו occur eleven times in all of the early manuscripts (MS Kaufmann, MS Parma and MS Paris in Yebam. 2:10, 6:3, 13:4, 2×; Ketub. 2:1, 4:2, 2×; 5:1; Ned. 11:10; Mak. 1:1). These editions which were influenced by the Babylonian Talmud replaced this form with the Aramaic-like forms נתארמלה, נתארמלו in most cases (there are three exceptions – Yebam. 2:10; Ned. 11:10; Mak. 1:1).[150] The form משחילין (Beṣah 5:1, משחילין פירות דרך הארובה ביום־טוב) preserved in manuscripts of the Palestinian branch (MS Kaufmann, MS Parma A) became מְשִׁילִין in the Babylonian branch (found already in MS Cambridge משלין and in MS Paris משילין). This may be a substitution of the mishnaic verb שחל by the biblical verb נשל, under the influence of כי ישל זיתך (Deut 28:40). Alternatively, משחילין may

146 This phenomenon increased during the Middle Ages as the scholarly study of biblical Hebrew increased. The grammar of biblical Hebrew was the only grammar of Hebrew known at that time (Yalon 1964:12).

147 Kutscher 1972:68; Bar-Asher 1980:22, 92.

148 Bar-Asher 1977:128–35.

149 See the references in n. 144 above.

150 See the references in n. 143 above.

have become משילין by the loss of *ḥet* as in the Babylonian pronunciation.[151] The noun חדות, which usually appears as הדות and occurs only in *Seder Teharoth*[152] as חדות, also seems to be the result of Babylonian influence. ה (< ח) was later wrongly interpreted[153] as the definite article.

§ 51 In contrast, some of the characteristics of the Babylonian branch are extremely early.[154] Some of them display a clear link to Palestine, to the period of the 2nd century CE These are forms about which it cannot be said that they are the result of Babylonian influence, biblical influence, or mistakes by copyists. I shall give two examples.

§ 52 Consider the expression ידיים מסואבות/ ידיים מוסאבות. In the early manuscripts, the form מוסאבות is dominant. (It is almost always this form which appears in MS Kaufmann, MS Cambridge and occasionally in MS Parma. It always takes this form in MS Parma B and in its one occurrence in MS Antonin.)[155]

---

151 Epstein 1948:318–20.

152 *Ibid.*, 1233.

153 It is difficult to assume that the shift חדות > הדות was due to the graphic similarity of the letters het and he. (Could such a graphic error have been so systematically carried through?) Another difficulty is that not only was the *ḥet* replaced by *he*, but also, an indefinite noun became replaced by a definite noun. In reality, however, the form חדות was החדות (Rosh ha-Shana 3:4: התוקע לתוך הבור או לתוך החדות as in MS Kaufmann), but the tendency to drop the definite article before a guttural (Yalon 1964:46; Bar-Asher 1980:103–4 and sources cited there) turned החדות to חדות so that externally it no longer appeared to be definite. The Babylonian pronunciation of הדות for חדות restored the original definite article.

154 Sarfatti has recently suggested (1983:457) that many of the changes which characterize the grammar of mishnaic Hebrew are the result of a natural development: "We see that the tradition of Mishnaic Hebrew in its transmission from copyist to copyist has a life of its own and that apart from changes introduced into the texts with the intention of bringing them closer to the ideal of Biblical Hebrew, other changes reflect natural development similar to that occurring in a living language. Mishnaic Hebrew after the final redaction of the Mishna was not a living, but rather a literary language ... as a *literary language* artificial corrections were made in order to make it correspond more closely to the language of the Bible, but as a *living literary language*, natural changes took place as in a living language." Whether or not one agrees with all of the details of Sarfatti's analysis of twelve phenomena in Mishna Berakoth, his general conclusion is convincing.

155 In MS Kaufmann, the scribe reads מוסאבות four times (Hal. 2:2; Hul. 2:5; Kelim 8:10; Tehar. 2:1). Only in Hag. 3:3 do we find מסואבות. The vocalizer points them all as מסואבות belonging to *pu'al* (sometimes the *'aleph* is pointed with a *hatep pataḥ*, e.g., מְסוּאֲבוֹת – Kelim 8:10; Tehar. 2:1). The second scribal hand in MS Kaufmann also reads מְסוּאָבוֹת (Tebul Yom 2:2, 4:1); MS Cambridge (according to Epstein 1948:1255) reads מוסאבות five times and only in Hal. and Hag. do we find מסואבות. MS Parma A (according to Haneman 1980:197) has מוסאבות in Hal. and Hag. and vocalizes it the same way (as opposed to the consonantal text) in Kelim. 8:10. Elsewhere the word appears as מסואבות (Hul. 8:10; Tehar. 2:1; Tebul Yom 2:2; and the consonantal text of Kelim 8:10) and in one place סאובות (Tebul Yom 4:1). MS Parma B has a *hup'al* form four times in *Seder Teharot* מֻסְאָבוֹת, מוּסְאָבוֹת (Tebul Yom 4:1) as does MS Antonin

The form ידים מסואבות of the Babylonian Talmud is prevalent in the printed Mishnayot.[156]

An examination of this phenomenon reveals that the pu'al form is the original form. This verb is attested in mishnaic Hebrew predominantly in the derived conjugations,[157] e.g., נסתאב, נסתאבו (Menah. 13:9), יסתאבו (Pesah. 9:8). The expected passive participle is the pu'al form מסואב (and therefore ידיים מסואבות), and not the hup'al form. This is the case in the Babylonian branch and occasionally in the Palestinian branch.[158] The *hup'al* form, or apparent *hup'al* form, מוסאבות (and only as a participle), is found mainly in manuscripts from the Palestinian branch. It is clearly a secondary form.[159] This example is just one of the many *pu'al* participles which developed into *hup'al* forms as the result of a phonetic process by which מפועל > מופעל.[160] This is the case with מפונה > מופנה, מתוקן > מותקן, מפורש > מופרש, מאוחר > מואחר, etc.[161] The Babylonian branch reflects a linguistic situation in which the earlier form was preserved; in the Palestinian branch, the younger form was more prevalent.[162] It appears, however, that both forms emerged in the period when mishnaic Hebrew was a living language.

§ 53 A more certain example of an early feature is ממנו-ממנה as opposed to הימנו-הימנה. An examination of the literature reveals that the most common forms in the Palestinian branch are those known from the Bible, i.e., ממנו-ממנה, whereas הימנו-הימנה are more frequent in the Babylonian branch. For

---

in the one passage where it is attested, מוּסָאָבוֹת (Tehar. 2:1). MS Paris, on the other hand (Bar-Asher 1980:31) has only the *pu'al* form מסואבות (Hal. 2:2; Hag. 3:3; Hul. 2:5; Kelim 8:10; Tebul Yom 2:2), or the *qal* form סאובות (Tehar. 2:1; Tebul Yom 4:1).

156 Cf., e.g., in the Babylonian Talmud, *Hag.* 24b and *Hul.* 33b.

157 This verb is only found in mishnaic Hebrew in the *nitpa'al* and *pu'al* (participles). A *pi'el* is not attested. In Aramaic, however, it generally appears in conjugations with a geminated second radical. (See Moreshet, n. 143, above, for a survey of the Aramaic expression in which it is found.) Occasionally we also find forms in the *qal* (see, e.g., n. 155 above and the form תסאב – *qal* or *nip'al*? in t. Pesah 9:2; and וסאובות in t. Para 12:10). Apart from the form מוסאבות, this root is not attested in *hip̄'il/hup̄'al.*

158 See n. 155 above.

159 See n. 157 above.

160 Epstein 1948:1254–55; Hanemen 1980:197 ff.; Bar-Asher 1983b: par. 37.

161 Haneman 1980:197 ff. discusses this phenomenon and suggests an interesting explanation for מופעל in place of מפועל (and also מפעיל for מְפַעֵּל). One wonders whether this is not related to the pronunciation of the *šəwa* in Palestine: מְסֹאָב was realized as *m°so'āb*, and the *o* following the *mem* (i.e., the *šəwa*) was realized as a full vowel, and the [u], [o] following the first radical was then elided by haplology. This requires further investigation.

162 The form מסואבות which occurs in MS Kaufmann and other manuscripts alongside מוסאבות is not necessarily the result of Babylonian influence, but might be an older, peripheral, Palestinian feature.

example, D. Rosenthal finds in m. Aboda Zara 3:9, נטל ממנה כרכר as against נטל הימנה כרכר.[163] Previously G. Haneman demonstrated that one finds the forms הימנו-הימנה in the Sifra MS Vatican 66[164] in the language of the Mekhilta deMillu'im, which is directly related to the language of the Babylonian Talmud. On the other hand, in the basic part of the Sifra in this manuscript – whose language is related to that of the Palestinian branch[165] – one consistently finds ממנו-ממנה.[166]

§ 54 Some words of clarification are in order. H. Y. Kosovsky's Concordance of Mishnaic Literature contains about 85 examples of the forms הימנו-הימנה, as against only 22 occurrences of these forms in MS Kaufmann. It is likely that these 22 examples are a foreign addition in MS Kaufmann (and related manuscripts).[167] Not only the frequency of the forms, but where they occur must also be taken into account. *Seder Teharoth*, which was studied less than other *sedarim*, testifies to this: there is not a single occurrence of הימנו-הימנה in MS Kaufmann in Teharoth; only ממנו-ממנה is attested.

§ 55 A similar picture emerges from most other manuscripts containing *tannaitic* compositions which have been selected as the basis of the edition of the Historical Dictionary of the Hebrew Language Academy. On the whole, one finds ממנו-ממנה; infrequently one finds הימנו-הימנה.[168] Only in the Tosefta, according to MS Vienna, is הימנו-הימנה frequent (300 of the 386 occurrences of all examples in all manuscripts containing *tannaitic* literature occur in this manuscript). This is only one of many examples which demonstrate the linguistic affinity between the Tosefta and the Babylonian Talmud (at least according to its known sources).

§ 56 הימנו-הימנה, which is characteristic of the language of the Babylonian Talmud and compositions related to it – where are its roots if not in

163 Rosenthal 1981:65.

164 Haneman 1974:19.

165 Haneman 1974:18–24 does not use the terms Palestinian branch and Babylonian branch, but this distinction is clearly his principle conclusion.

166 There are 91 occurrences of ממנו-ממנה and only one occurrence of הימנו in the essential part of the Sipra, as against four occurrences of הימנו-הימנה in the Mek. deMilluim (the fifth occurrence was probably הימנו which was changed to ממנו [see Haneman 1974:19, 23]).

167 The distribution of הימנו-הימנה was not examined in other manuscripts. I limited myself to MS Kaufmann.

168 The forms הימנו-הימנה (and הימך twice [Sifre Bemidbar § 42 and t. Kelim 6:4]) are found in rabbinic literature 386 times (this number is taken from the Concordance of the Academy of the Hebrew Language): 22 times in the Mishnah (according to MS Kaufmann), 300 times in the Tosefta (MS Vienna), 13 times in the Sifra, 12 times in Sifre Bemidbar, 9 times in Sifre Devarim, 22 times in Mekhilta de-Rabbi Ishmael, 4 times in Mekhilta de-R. Shimon b. Yohai, 3 times in *Baraita de-Melekhet ha-Mishkan*, and once in Seder Olam.

Palestine? Its existence in the Bar Koseba documents from Wadi Murabba‘at and from the Cave of Letters has been known for a generation: הכול חכרתי המך (Murabba‘at 24, Document 2, line 13), תשטר הלז חכרתי המך מן היום עד סוף ערב (Murabba‘at 24, Document 5, line 8), ותחנה בן שמצון ואלמא בן יהודה שוקלים תחצי הכסף הלז ויתר <ה>ימנו עוד דינרין ששה עשר שהם סלעים ארבעין (P. Yadin, Cave of Letters 44, line 7).[169]

§ 57 It appears that these forms, which were current in southern Palestine at the beginning of the 2nd century, found their way to the Mishna which was transported to Babylonia at the beginning of the 3rd century where they were preserved in the Babylonian language tradition. Thus, these forms have come down to us also via the Babylonian branch of the Mishna. Must one claim that all of the occurrences of these forms in reliable manuscripts containing *tannaitic* works are the result of influence from the Babylonian branch? What prevents us from assuming that the examples found in MS Vatican 32 of Sifre beMidbar[170] (a linguistically reliable manuscript) are not originally peripheral Palestinian forms.[171]

§ 58 Our remarks concerning מסואבות and especially concerning הימנו-הימנה force us to pose the following question: Do the linguistic features of the Babylonian branch which are completely identical in form to those of Tiberian Biblical Hebrew, belong (at least in part) to an original Palestinian reading tradition of the Mishna which was transported to Babylonia at the time when Rab moved there at the beginning of the 3rd century? Why must one assume

---

169 This is taken from the Data bases of the Historical Dictionary of the Academy of Hebrew Language.

170 See n. 168 above.

171 A related example is the forms of the participle ממועט, ממועטות, ממועטין found in reliable Mishnayot, principally MS Kaufmann, MS Parma A, MS Cambridge, MS Parma B, etc., as against the Babylonian branch in which one finds the forms מועט, מועטת, מועטין. The forms with only one mem may be the result of haplology (Sharvit, Ben-Ḥayyim Jubilee Volume, 559); alternatively, it may be an old passive qal form similar to אֻכַּל, יֻלַּד, לֻקַּח (Bar-Asher 1981: 91). We have early evidence that this form was prevalent in Palestine: it may be attested in the Dead Sea Scrolls. (It should not be confused with the form מועט in MMT, since there it is only a variant of the noun מְעַט). מועט, however, in the Damascus Rule probably is the participial form, and it is this form which occurs in the Babylonian branch of the Mishna (Bar-Asher, *ibid.*). Once again we see a form which was prevalent in southern Palestine find its way to the Mishna and become prevalent in Babylonia. As the prestige of the Babylonian Talmud increased, this form became more common in the Mishnayot and displaced the form with two *mems*. However, in view of the sparse evidence, the one example in the Damascus Rule must remain a conjecture and be treated with great care.

that forms like מְדוּכָה, טַבּוּר, קַרְדֹּם, קַרְסֹל, מלכויות, חנויות,[172] and the particle of grief אוי[173] of the Babylonian branch, as against the Palestinian forms מדיכה, טיבור, קוֹרְדּוֹם, קוֹרְסל, מלכִיּוֹת, חנִיּוֹת, אִי, and related forms are the result of Tiberian biblical influence and not original Palestinian forms belonging to another reading tradition of the Mishna which was transferred to Babylonia at an early period?

Returning to ממנו-ממנה as against הימנו-הימנה: if the influence of the Tiberian Bible is responsible, why did it not completely displace the forms הימנו-הימנה and replace them with ממנו-ממנה, as noted by D. Rosenthal?[174] There is no doubt that the Tiberian Bible influenced the language of the Mishna; however, need its influence be as great as thought by Kutscher?

§ 59 Similarly, as regards the construction שהוא מכנים (Aboda Zara 1:9) and שהן חשודין (Aboda Zara 2:1) of the Palestinian branch as against שמכנים or שחשודין of the Babylonian branch[175] – it is tempting to think that the Babylonian construction is a product of Babylonian Aramaic which has the construction ד + participle, e.g., דבעי, דקרא, דאמרי (and not דאינהו אמרי, דהו בעי, קרי). In late Biblical Hebrew, however, one finds the construction שֶׁ + participle without the independent personal pronoun, as, for example, in שנאחזים (Qoh 9:12), שֶׁיֹּצָא (Qoh 10:5), שֶׁיֹּרֵד (Ps 133:2, 3). There is no reason to assume that the Babylonian branch was influenced by Babylonian Aramaic rather than assuming it preserved the original Hebrew tradition which was known in the later books of the Bible.

§ 60 In summary, the Babylonian branch of the Mishna is distinguished from the Palestinian branch by a large number of linguistic features. We must not forget, however, the large number of features the two branches share in common. While many of these distinctive features have been interpreted as the result of changes which occurred in the Babylonian branch – the product of conscious or unconscious editing and mistakes by copyists and transmitters – some of the features may be original Palestinian forms. It is possible that not only forms such as מסואבות, הימנו-הימנה (and מועט)[176] are of Palestinian origin, but also a significant number of forms which have been viewed as corrections made in the process of transmission according to Tiberian Biblical Hebrew or Babylonian Aramaic (e.g., שקורא for שהוא קורא) are, in part, origi-

172 Bar-Asher 1971:183; 1980:29, 78.
173 Kutscher 1963:21–22, 35; Bar-Asher 1971:178; 1980:22.
174 Rosenthal 1981:13.
175 Rosenthal 1981:180. See also § 47 above.
176 See n. 171 above.

nal readings of the Mishna which were prevalent in Palestine, and which also occur in Tiberian Biblical Hebrew.[177]

19.11 Conclusion

§ 61 It is important to remember that it is quite reasonable to assume that there were a number of traditions in the reading of the Mishna. As long as the Mishna was transmitted orally, it was only to be expected that linguistic variations determined by time and place would shape the tradition of the transmitter. The linguistic differences between the Western and Eastern traditions of the Palestinian branch and some of the differences between the Palestinian and Babylonian branches (those which were not imposed on the text by the transmitters)[178] reflect different readings of one text.

§ 62 Research into mishnaic Hebrew has shown that there are different linguistic traditions within this language. It is most apparent in the reading of the Mishna itself. Examination of those readings which are known today, both from early sources and from oral traditions which preserve early linguistic features, reveals three main traditions:

§ 63 The Palestinian branch vis-à-vis the Babylonian branch. The Babylonian branch is reflected in the Mishnayot of the Babylonian Talmud which are distinguished from the Palestinian branch in orthography, phonology, morphology, syntax, and lexicon. It is clear that in a number of instances the two branches preserve different consonantal texts. Some of these distinctive features are the result of biblical influences and some are the result of Babylonian Talmud influences (and there are forms which are the result of faulty transmission). I believe most of these distinctive features, however, originated in Palestine and were preserved in Babylonia during the period of the Amoraim and thereafter.

§ 64 The Palestinian branch was preserved in the early Mishnayot which reflected the tradition of Mishna study alone (without *Gemara*). This branch

---

177 It is not possible to argue that every case or that every example is an original Palestinian form which was transplanted in the Babylonian branch rather than a form introduced by scribal correction (bringing it in line with the Bible). Every case must be examined individually. Our discussion here is meant to refer to the general principle rather than to individual details.

178 It is hardly necessary to repeat that in the past few hundred years the number of conscious corrections made in order to bring mishnaic Hebrew closer to Biblical Hebrew has increased. Yalon shows this to be true of European grammarians (Yalon 1964:12–13, and throughout this book). R. David Alataras, who vocalized the Mantova and Livorno Mishnayot according to the biblical grammar did the same (Bar-Asher 1980:93).

can be subdivided into two traditions, a Western tradition and an Eastern tradition which are distinguished from one another primarily in matters of phonology and morphophonology. In other words, the same text was read in different ways. One tradition was transmitted in the West and has been preserved mainly in Italian manuscripts, while the other was transmitted in different communities in the East.

§ 65 Some of the oral traditions from the 14th century onwards are closer to the Western tradition, principally the Italian tradition; some are closer to the Eastern traditions, namely, the oral traditions of Jewish communities in Islamic countries stretching from Persia to North Africa. These latter oral traditions reveal a clear link to the linguistic features of the Babylonian branch. Many of their links with the Palestinian branch have disappeared.

§ 66 One might say that there are three varieties of mishnaic Hebrew (in the Mishna alone), or three reading traditions originating in Palestine.[179] The distinctive features of the Palestinian branch clearly demonstrate their link to Palestine, and even in the Babylonian branch there are original independent features which can be traced back to Palestine. Despite the relationship between certain phenomena of the Babylonian branch and the area of southern Palestine in the period of Bar Koseba, it is impossible to identify the specific area within Palestine in which these features took shape. The meeting of, and interaction between different dialects in one area may have taken place while mishnaic Hebrew was flourishing. The meeting of scholars from different areas is already reflected in the language of the Mishna.[180]

§ 67 Our study has sought to demonstrate: (i) the existence of three different linguistic varieties; (ii) the identification of some of their distinctive features; (iii) the identification of manuscripts and oral traditions associated with these different linguistic varieties; (iv) that not all the distinctive features of the Babylonian branch are late corrections, but rather some may be early features; (v) the clear relationship of the three language varieties – three reading traditions – to Palestine.

§ 68 Our study relies, in large part, on the investigations and results of a large number of scholars who have worked on rabbinic Hebrew, and particularly on the language of the Mishna. In a work of a general nature like this, much caution is required and much of what has been said requires further examination and support. What today is considered doubtful may tomorrow

---

179 The question of different dialects in mishnaic Hebrew (or more precisely the language of the *Tannaim*) is a question unto itself. See n. 9 above.

180 Epstein, *Introduction to the Literature of the Tannaim* (Jerusalem, 1957, in Hebrew) 234–40.

be shown to be certain, and what is certain today may turn out to be doubtful tomorrow. I hope that I have presented some of the questions and problems facing researchers of mishnaic Hebrew.

20 The System of *binyanim* in Mishnaic Hebrew (A Morphological Study)

20.1 The *binyanim* in general

§ 1 The grammatical system of Mishnaic Hebrew recognizes a long list of *binyanim* in the verb. Some of these *binyanim* are complete, meaning that they include a full set of forms for all tenses; others are incomplete, and have a more limited use. Among the latter, there are forms which are clearly authentic, for they are attested in many, reliable sources; there are also forms which appear only in a few traditions, or only in one tradition, and their claim to authenticity needs further support, in order to convince us that these were actually living forms in Mishnaic Hebrew. These forms have been discussed in various disparate studies, and sometimes the various scholars have been of different minds regarding the interpretation of certain phenomena associated with the *binyanim*. I feel that the time has come to examine the larger picture, and then to go back and consider many of the specific phenomena, and explain them.[1] Our study here will focus mainly on the language of the Tannaim. We shall begin by presenting the system of *binyanim* in general, and then proceed to comment about the specific *binyanim*, as needed.

Let us present the *binyanim* in two groups: the common ones, and the less common ones.

§ 2 A. The common *binyanim*:

1–2	*pā'al (qal) – nif'al*
3–4	*pi''el – nitpa''al* (or *hitpa''al*)[2]
5–6	*hif'il – huf'al*

B. The uncommon *binyanim*:

7	*pu''al*
8–9	*nuf'al, nippə'al*
10–11	*pē'ēl (pā'ēl) – nitpā'al*
12–13	*pō'ēl – nitpō'al*
14	*nittaf'al*

1 Naturally, a scholar who is interested in the broader picture will try to draw connections between the various details, to come up with a general approach. On the other hand, one who is studying a specific phenomenon, or a specific reading-tradition, will have a very detail-oriented approach.

2 *Binyanim* 3–4 include the geminated, the quadrilateral, and (in hollow and geminate roots) the extensive heavy *binyan*. Apparently, they also include the קל העין and המוארך השלם. (See §§ 3, 30, below.)

20.2 Comments on the common *binyanim*

Not much needs to be noted about the group of common *binyanim*, but a few clarifying notes are in order.

§ 3 Within the group of "heavy *binyanim*" (numbers 3–4 in paragraph 2), there are five sub-groups:[3]

A. the **geminated** heavy *binyan*: *pi"ēl* (קִדֵּשׁ) – *nitpa"al* (נִתְקַדֵּשׁ)
B. the **quadriliteral** heavy *binyan*:[4] *pilpēl* (תִּרְגֵּם, שִׁחְרֵר, and the like) – *nitpalpal* (נִתַּרְגֵּם, נִשְׁתַּחְרֵר, and the like)
C. the **extensive** heavy *binyan* (in hollow and double roots): *pōlēl* (עוֹרֵר, רוֹעֵעַ*[5]) – *nitpōlal* (נִתְעוֹרֵר*, נִתְרוֹעַע).

The first two of these sub-groups, the geminated and the quadrilateral, are regular paradigms in Tannaitic Hebrew; the extensive form, on the other hand, is not actively used in this dialect. Most of the extensive forms in Tannaitic literature are simply inherited from Biblical Hebrew,[6] such as: מְקוֹנְנוֹת (Mo'ed Qatan 3:9), לְרוֹמֵם (Pesaḥim 10:5). We must note also נִתְרוֹעֲעָה (Kelim 3:4; 4:2 2x); this form appears in MS K,[7] Paris, and the first printed edition, as well as today's printed editions, although a different form appears in MSS Parma B, Parma A, and Cambridge, namely נתרעעה, using the paradigm of the strong verbs.[8]

We can add two others included among the uncommon *binyanim*:
A. The "simple *ayin*" pattern: *pē'ēl* – *nitpā'al* (see below, §§ 17–24, 30).
B. The elongated form: *pō'ēl* – *nitpō'al* (see below, §§ 25–30).

§ 4 The forms *nitpa"al* and *hitpa"al* are alternative forms of the same *binyan*. The older form, התפעל, used in Biblical Hebrew, underwent a change of form in Mishnaic Hebrew. The ה was replaced with a נ, apparently on anal-

3 See Segal 1936:144–146 (§§ 262–263). See also Haneman 1980:29–30; although he distinguishes between the three paradigms (geminated, doubled, and extended), he sees them all as embodiments of essentially the same phenomenon.

4 I prefer the term **quadriliteral** over the term *pilpēl/nitpalpal*, for the former term is more general, whereas the latter term refers only to roots in which the last two letters are identical to the first two, in the form ABAB.

5 The asterisked forms are reconstructed; they are not actually attested in Tannaitic Hebrew. (See immediately below.)

6 See Haneman 1980, pp. 302–303. Segal (1936) distinguishes between *pōlēl/nitpōlēl*, in hollow verbs (p. 145), and *pō'ēl/nitpō'ēl*, in geminate verbs (p. 148).

7 In MS K the word is written plene, ניתרועעה.

8 Haneman 1980:208 n. 804 believes that נִתרועעה is a form of נִתְרָעֲעָה with the shift ā > ō; according to him this form does not belong to the binyan *nitpōlēl*.

ogy to the *nif'al*.[9] Because of the parallel functions of these two *binyanim*,[10] the forms of the two were brought closer to each other, as well: *hitpā'al* > *nitpā'al* like *nif'al*.

The newer form *nitpā'al*, which was not used in the Bible, was still grafted into Biblical Hebrew in scattered examples of verbs which were almost certainly originally forms of the *nif'al*. This is the best way to explain forms like וְנִוַּסְּרוּ (Ezek 23:48),[11] וְנִכַּפֵּר (Deut 21:8).[12] So, too, וְנִלָּחֵם (< וְנִתְלָחֵם, Dan 11:11) in the Palestinian vocalization, as Kahle showed well,[13] as opposed to וְנִלְחַם in the Tiberian vocalization. The Samaritan reading tradition of the Pentateuch has many such examples, such as nibbårrådu (Gen 10:5, 32), corresponding to נִפְרְדוּ in the Tiberian tradition.[14]

The form *nitpā''al*, which is the dominant form in MH, did not entirely displace the form *hitpā''ēl*. There are still certain frozen forms, such as התודה, התנדב, השתחווה, התפלל, and התקבל. These forms (with the exception of התקבל) were explained by Haneman[15] as literary imitations of Biblical language, or the result of pseudo-corrections made by later copyists.[16]

§ 5 The *huf'al* is a regular *binyan* in Mishnaic Hebrew. In the Mishnah alone it is attested often, with examples such as הוכשר (Ma'asrot 1:8), הוכשרה (Me'ilah 2:1), and others; הוזכרו (Gittin 1:5 and 6 other attestations), הוחמו (Shabbat 3:4 2×), הותזו (Ohalot 1:6), הותר (Shevi'it 6:4 and dozens of more times), and many other similar examples. H. Yalon's claim that there was "an attempt to impose the *nittaf'al* in place of the *huf'al*" appears to be exagger-

---

9 See Segal 1936:118.

10 Both were originally reflexive in their meanings, and later became passive (*nif'al* – reflexive-passive of the *pā'al*; *hitpā'al*/*nitpā'al* – reflexive-passive of the *pī'ēl*).

11 Indeed, the root יס"ר is unambiguously used in the *nif'al*, as in יסרתני ואִוָּסֵר (Jer 31:17), יִוָּסֵר (Prov 29:19).

12 For the active meaning, this root appears in the *pī'ēl*, as in וְכִפֶּר ... יְכַפֵּר (Exod 30:10); in the passive, both *pū'āl* (כֻּפַּר, Exod 29:33) and *hitpa'ēl* (יִתְכַּפֵּר, 1 Sam 3:14) are attested, and apparently *nif'al* as well, as in the example cited from Deut 21:8. Ben-Ḥayyim 1955–1975:5.85 with n. 35 assumes that at some point the *pā'al* was also used, כָּפַר in the meaning כִּפֶּר, and that this is the source of the use of the *nif'al*, which is used in the Samaritan tradition (cf. Ben-Ḥayyim (*ibid.*), p. 86: wnikkåfər נִפְעַל [> נִפְּעַל]).

13 See Kahle 1967 [1930]:23*; Yalon 1971:385.

14 For details see Ben-Ḥayyim 1955–1975:5.85–86; this is the *binyan* he calls "*nif'al* with geminated middle letter."

15 Haneman 1980:208–211; Breuer 2002:175–178. See also what Nathan 1981:148–149 wrote about התקבל (in formal legal formulae) as opposed to נתקבל (in regular usage).

16 Related issues such as the thematic vowel in the forms נתקדֵּש/נתקדַּש, יתקדְּשו/יתקדָּשו and so on, deserve to be discussed in a study of the internal morphology of the *binyanim* (this will be elsewhere).

ated.[17] So, too, when Kutscher writes about the "rare *huf'al*,"[18] his words must be understood correctly: the *binyan* is rare relative to the *pā'al* and other *binyanim*, but it is used regularly and often.[19]

20.3 Comments on the uncommon *binyanim*

The *binyanim* which are not common require comment both regard to the data and to more analytical issues they raise.

20.3.1 *Pu'al*

§ 6 The six common *binyanim* in Mishnaic Hebrew continue a regularity that existed already in the Bible. An additional *binyan* which serves regularly in the Bible but which disappeared nearly entirely from MH is the *pu'al* (the internal passive of the *pi'el*).[20] In the primary verbal tenses – the past and the future[21] – very few examples of the *pu'al* survive, and, furthermore, some of these alleged survivals are doubtful. The process of the disappearance of the internal passives, which began within the Bible with the Qal passive, gained strength and nearly went to completion in MH, with the internal passive of the *pi'el*. Even the printed editions of the Mishnah and of the rest of Rabbinic literature show that this *binyan* (the *pu'al*)[22] had retreated from the language,[23]

17 Yalon 1964:129.

18 Kutscher 1977:106.

19 What was just said does not, of course, include direct borrowings or quotations from the Bible, such as כי יותן (Makhshirin 1:1 and dozens of more times), a phrase taken from Lev 11:38, or כי יֻתַּץ (Avordah Zarah 3:9), taken from Lev 11:35. The forms יֻתַּן and יֻתַּץ are internal Qal passives (cf. Haneman 1980:257), but synchronically speaking they are *huf'al* forms within MH.

20 Segal 1936:116–117; Yalon 1964:136–151; Haneman 1980:29 with n. 110 and esp. 189–197; see also Naeh 1989:157–158.

21 But see § 8 below.

22 Cf. Segal 1936, *ibid.*

23 In paytanic Hebrew, on the other hand, there are many examples of the *pu'al*, as scholars have shown (cf. Yalon 1931:354; Kutscher 1977:104; Yahalom 1985:51 ff.; see also Eldar 1979:2. 362–267, who lists about 60 examples just in the past tense). There is interesting data regarding Maimonides: in his copy of the Mishnah, there are essentially no examples of the *pu'al* in the past or future (see n. 26 below), but in his Mishneh Torah – which, he says, he wrote in the language of the Mishnah – the *pu'al* makes many appearances in both the past and the future forms. For example: משה רבינו לא האמינו בו ישראל מפני האותות שעשה ... נמצאו אלו **שׁשולח** להם הם העדים על נבואותו (Laws of the Foundations of the Torah 8:1–2); עד **שירוחמו** מן השמים (Laws of Fasts 1:4).

and when one studies the data in the manuscripts, the picture becomes even starker.

This issue was studied already by H. Yalon.[24] He was able to show that some of the forms which had been interpreted as *pu'al* forms were not, in fact, correctly analyzed. Only a few forms are certain examples of the *pu'al* (and generally speaking, it is only the vocalization that shows this, whereas the consonantal text could be interpreted otherwise), such as גדיש שלא לוּקַּט (Pe'ah 5:1, as vocalized in Kaufmann,[25] and similarly in Parma A and in the Mishnah used by Maimonides[26]); חוּתַּךְ מן העובר שבמיעיה (Hullin 4:1 in Kaufmann[27]); ותעוּבּר צורתו (Pesahim 7:9 in Parma A; Kaufmann reads תְּעֻבַּר, spelled defectively. Kaufmann reads תְּעֻבַּר, spelled defectively, in Zevahim 5:4, as well, where Parma A reads תעובר, unvocalized. But in Sheqalim 7:3, Kaufmann as well as Parma A reads תְּעַבֵּר צורתו.)[28]

There is room to doubt, as indicated, whether the scribes in fact intended *pu'al* forms in these cases. The spelling תעובר, for instance, could well be for the form תְּעוּבֵּר, a *pi'el* form (denoting a change of state[29]), with a shift of a > u before a labial consonant.[30] The spelling חותך, too, was not understood by Yalon as a *pu'al* form, but rather a Qal participle, חוֹתֵךְ.[31] I will mention two further examples. First, careful study showed that זוּקָּקָה (Nega'im 4:5 in Kaufmann) is a mistake: the reading of all the other versions – זוֹקְקָה – is the original one (Bar-Asher 2009:1.225–227), and the vocalizer of Kaufmann made the mistake. Second, as opposed to שֻׁוָּתָה (1737 Venice ed., Karetot 2:4) and שׁוּוָּתָה (1646 Amsterdam ed., ibid.), all the reliable witnesses read a Qal form, שָׁוַות (Kaufmann, unvocalized in Parma A and Cambridge). There are other similar examples, as well.[32] It appears that most of the *pu'al* forms, if not all, exist only due to the vocalizers.

---

24 Yalon 1964:136–151.

25 Yalon 1964:137, where further data are presented.

26 Zurawel 2004:116 (§ 12.6.1.1). This is, apparently, the only *pu'al* form attested in this manuscript.

27 See Yalon 1964:144–145.

28 Haneman 1980:196.

29 Yalon 1964:160 ff.

30 The spelling תעבר, which was vocalized תְּעֻבַּר in Kaufmann, is almost certainly not correctly interpreted, since [u] is generally indicated with a ו. Clearly, the scribe intended the form תְּעַבֵּר, as the vocalizer correctly wrote in Sheqalim 7:3. Indeed, it is even possible that the form תְּעוּבַּר is a *pi'el* form: [a] > [u] before the labial [b], and *pataḥ* in place of *ṣere* before the ר (as in אֵחַר). The vocalizer, however, did apparently have a *pu'al* form in mind.

31 Yalon 1964:144–145.

32 Many of them are surveyed by Yalon 1964:136–149.

§ 7 **False *pu'al* forms:** It is worth saying a bit more about false *pu'al* forms, which occur with some frequency in Tannaitic literature, but which are actually certain *pi'ēl* forms. They appear like *pu'al* forms because of scribal errors which changed a *yod* to a *waw*, or because of phonetic changes which turned an [a] or [i] into an [o] or a [u]. A few examples will suffice here. One is קוּבַּלְנוּ (Eduyot 8:3, Kaufmann), and אם טוּמֵּאתָה ... שכן טִימֵּאתָה ... תְּטַמֵּא (Eduyot 6:3, Kaufmann). Compare, too, וכי מטומאה שהכתוב מטהרה (Sifre Numbers MS Rome 32 § 19, ed. Horovitz, p. 23). In this context, מטומאה should be interpreted as מִי טוּמְאָה (< מִי טְמְאָה),[33] and similarly with regard to the forms פורשנו (= פֵּרַשְׁנוּ),[34] מורחה (= מֵרְחָה),[35] and גולח (= גילח)[36] in other places in this same manuscript. In some of these, this is a simple scribal error: a *yod* was elongated into a *waw*. This would appear to be the correct interpretation of טומאתה – alongside טימאתה – in MS Kaufmann in Eduyot 6:3. But in some of the cases, the *waw* shows that the vowel had shifted to *o/u* (instead of *a* or *i*) before a labial consonant or before a ל or ר. Ben-Ḥayyim demonstrated this phenomenon with regard to the verb נומיתי (from the root נמ"י) < נִמֵּיתִי, and the active participle מרובה (< מְרַבֶּה);[37] Yalon utilized this principle to explain יַפִּי as the *pi'ēl* of יפ"י.[38] It is also possible to explain some of the forms just mentioned in MS Rome 32 this way: מטומאה, פורשנו, מורחה, and גולח. However, the validity of these forms, based as they are on a single manuscript, with no tradition of vocalization, is not beyond doubt; it is entirely possible that some (or even all?) of these are mere copyist's errors, and a *waw* was written in place of a *yod*. Either way, these are false *pu'al* forms, and actually belong to the *pi'ēl*.[39]

§ 8 In the participle, however, forms on the pattern *pu'al* were retained as part of the *binyan* of the *pi'ēl* verbs. In other words, the *pi'ēl* has complete and regular paradigms in the past and future forms, imperatives, infinitives,

33 See Bar-Asher 1979:186–190.
34 See Bar-Asher 2009:1.252.
35 See *ibid.*
36 See *ibid.*, §§ 27–28.
37 Ben-Ḥayyim 1963:10 n. 9.
38 Yalon 1964:137–140.
39 Phonetic changes "spoil" grammatical regularity, of course: a form which in fact belongs to a certain pattern is disguised as a different pattern. This is the case with a number of "false *huf'al* forms" within MH, such as הורע כחו (Ketubbot 8:4 [2×]), which, as Yalon 1964:138–140 (see also Haneman 1980:326) showed, is actually a *hif'il* verb (הֵרַע), as can be seen by the semantics of the word: the point is that the biblical text "weakened" (or strengthened) one side's claim (see below, n. 189, regarding the form הוֹקְרָא < הִקרא). Similarly, the form מוֹעֲלִין instead of מַעֲלִין (Miqva'ot 7:1, 7:2 [a number of times in Parma A]) is disguised as a Qal participle from מע"ל rather than a *hif'il* participle from על"י. This is well known.

and active and passive participles (מְפַעֵל and מְפֻעָל). The relationship between מְקַדֵּשׁ and מְקֻדָּשׁ, or between מְקַבֵּל and מְקֻבָּל, is like the relationship between כּוֹתֵב and כתוּב or שׁוֹמֵר and שָׁמוּר and so on. The active participle is dynamic, and normally refers to actions in the present and the future; the passive participle is static and perfective, and refers to actions which were completed in the past and to statuses in the present.

§ 9 A note: Yalon drew attention to a number of examples of verbs on the מְפֻעָל pattern that are written defectively, without the *waw*.[40] When these are found in vocalized manuscripts, they are sometimes vocalized מְפֻעָל, but other times are vocalized מְפַעַל. It is worth mentioning some of the examples attested in the manuscripts: מְפֻגֶּלֶת (m. Menahot 2:3), מְפֻגלין (m. Menahot 2:4), מְבֻקר (m. Tamid 3:4), מְחֻלחלת (m. Ohalot 9:3) – these are all the forms found in MS Kaufmann. In the expression "וכן הוא מפורש על יד יחזקאל" (m. Tamid 3:7; m. Middot 4:2), MS K reads מְפָרֵשׁ (or מְפַרֵשׁ) in both occurrences, and MS Cambridge reads מפרש (without vocalization). The spelling מעכב appears, alongside מעוכב, a number of times in the witnesses to the Tosefta (t. Soṭa 4:7), as well as elsewhere. Yalon concluded that this form, is "none other than the [passive] participle, מְפַעַל, on the Aramaic pattern."[41] It is true that the absence of the *waw* is surprising, since it is characteristic of the manuscripts of rabbinic literature that they write *u* vowels *plene* (including *u* vowels in closed unstressed syllables). It should be emphasized, however, that we have no evidence[42] for a form מְפַעַל (or מְפַעָל) within Hebrew.[43] It seems that we must see some of these defectively written forms as originally reflected מְפַעֵל forms, as in the expression, וכן הוא מְפָרֵשׁ על יד יחזקאל "thus is it interpreted (מְפָרֵשׁ) by Ezekiel."[44]

20.3.2 *Nuf'al*

§ 10 The *nuf'al* pattern is used primarily for verbs of two types: I-*nun* (including hollow verbs which are conjugated on the pattern of I-*nun*), and

40 Yalon 1964:176–180.

41 Yalon 1964:176.

42 The vocalizer of the Kaufmann manuscript reveals his confusion regarding such spellings at times. This would appear to be the only way to interpret the puzzling form הַמְסֻכַּן (m. Giṭṭin 6:5).

43 The Samaritan evidence adduced by Yalon (1964:178), which reads מְפַעַל, against Tiberian מְפֻעָל, is no evidence at all, since the shift of [u] to [a] or [i] is widespread within the Samaritan tradition (see, for instance, Ben-Ḥayyim 1957–1977:5.148).

44 See, e.g., Shemot Rabbah 1:35.

I-*yod*, in the past and participle; a few examples are also found with strong verbs. The pattern is well-known in the manuscripts of Tannaitic literature (and the rest of rabbinic literature), but primarily from the scribal tradition: some of these *nuf'al* forms (with a *waw* after the *nun*) with misunderstood, as we will see below. The vocalized examples come mostly from old *maḥăzorim* and *siddurim*, as well as from the reading traditions of some Jewish communities.[45]

Some examples: קנה שלזיתים ... נוטל בשבת (m. Shabbat 17:3 in MS Kaufmann; the vocalizer changed the *waw* into a *yod* and pointed it נִיטַּל), שנוטל נוטל מזה צומת הגידים (m. Hullin 4:6 in Parma A;[46] Kaufmann reads שֶׁנִּיטַּל), ומזה רביעית נוֹטֵל (m. Ohalot 3:5 in Parma B, where it is mistakenly pointed נוֹטֵל; all other witnesses read שֶׁנִּיטַּל),[47] נוטלת מן הטהור על הטמא (= נוּטֶּלֶת, m. Halla 2:8 in MS Kaufmann, although the vocalizer wrote נוֹטֶלֶת and other witnesses read ניטלת).[48] Explicit evidence for this form is found in MS Vatican 66 of the Sifra, which points נוּטְלוּ twice.[49] Many similar forms are found in the prayers and *piyyuṭim*,[50] such as ונוצל מידו (t. Berakhot 3× in MS Erfurt, but MS Vienna reads וניצל in all three).[51] There is also evidence for the reading נֻצַּל in *piyyut*.[52] Similarly, הנושא על גבי הזב (= הַנּוּשָּׂא in Parma A, m. Zabim 5:2, alongside הנישא),[53] and forms of נֻתַּן: נוּתְנוּ (MS Vatican 66 of the Sifra),[54] נותנים לכהנים (m. Bikkurim 3:5, 8, in some MSS),[55] and נותנים/נותנין (in some MSS of Sifre

45 The important work on this *binyan* was doen by Yalon 1964:152–159 and Moreshet 1980, who included many of the attested examples. See also Qimron 1988. Other (limited) pieces of data are scattered throughout the literature: see Shivitel 1972:212 (first published in 1937), Morah 1970:204; Haneman 1980a:260–261; Bar-Asher 1983:153; Nathan 1984:146; Naeh 1989:193; and see also Kara 1980:34. Many examples from *piyyut*, as well as a synthetic discussion and references to the literature, can be found in Eldar 1979:381–383.

46 Haneman 1980a:260.

47 Goldberg 1955:28.

48 Zachs 1975.

49 Yeivin 1985:594; Naeh 1989:193.

50 For example, ונֻטַל כבוד מבית חיינו (from the prayer אתה יצרת said on Shabbat Rosh Ḥodesh, according to the old *siddurim* and the traditions of some communities). There are also many examples in early Ashkenazic *piyyuṭ*, such as נוּטַל, נוּטְּלוּ, and נוּטְּלָה, as established by Eldar 1979:381.

51 Moreshet 1980:137; Nathan 1984:146.

52 Eldar 1979:381.

53 Haneman 1980a:260.

54 See the sources cited in n. 49 above.

55 Zachs 1975 *ad loc.*

Numbers).[56] In all these sources, the form is apparently meant to represent נֶתָּנִים/נֶתָּנִין; there is also evidence for this reading of this verbal form in *piyyuṭ*.[57]

In hollow verbs, medial *waw*: הנוער בלילה (m. Abot 3:4 in Geniza MSS)[58] = נֶעָר, a biform of נֵעוֹר;[59] לחם שנוטה באיברים (Mekhilta Va-yissa‘ § 3, ed. Horovitz, p. 167, according to the reading in the Constantinople edition)[60] – in other words, נֶטָּה, a biform of ניטוה.[61] The reliability of these forms for II-*waw* verbs is increased by the reading tradition of forms such as נֶידָּן and נוּצָד in the Ashenazic *piyyuṭ* tradition.[62]

In II-*yod* verbs, the *nif‘al* pattern is known, for Tannaitic Hebrew,[63] primarily from the Yemenite tradition: נוּצַרְתָּ[64] (m. Abot 4:3); נוּלְדָה (m. Nega‘im 4:10), and the participles נוּלָד and נוּצָר (m. Abot 4:22).[65]

§ 11 Besides the forms just discussed, scholars have also noted scattered occurrences with strong verbs: שנוגאלו בלילה[66] (Sifre Deuteronomy § 128, MS Vatican 32),[67] ולא נוחלק ר׳ (א)ליעזר ור׳ יהושע (Geniza fragment of t. Pesahim 1:5, but MSS Vienna and Erfurt read נחלקו), והיו נוהגין זה עם זה (m. Shabbat 12:4–5) in place of נֶהֱגִין (the vocalizer of MS Kaufmann read נֶוּהְגִין [he erased the *waw*] in mishna 4, and נֶהְגִים in mishnah 5; Parma A read נוֹהֲגִין[68] [a Qal active participle from נהג]), נוהנין לו (MS Vienna to t. Nedarim 2:4, but MS

56 Bar-Asher 1983:153.

57 Compare נֶתְּנֵנוּ, cited by Yalon 1964:156 from an Italian *maḥazor*, and other examples cited by Eldar 1979:382. The form נותזין (m. Makhshirin 5:2), quoted by Haneman 1980a:260 as an example of a *nuf‘al* verb, is in fact a Qal active participle (נוֹתְזִין), as pointed by Parma B and Kaufmann.

58 Sharvit 1976:56–57; Moreshet 1980:134.

59 See also Nathan 1984:146.

60 Moreshet 1980:135 with n. 53.

61 This is found in two manuscripts.

62 Eldar 1979:382.

63 It is found also in the Tiberian, and Babylonian vocalizations of the Bible, in the form נוּלְדוּ (1 Chron 3:5; 20:8), as scholars established earlier (e.g., Morag 1971b:187;. Yeivin 1985:608, and the literature cited by both).

64 Shivtiel 1971:212; Morag 1970:204; Yeivin 1985:609 with n. 5; Kara, cited above, n. 45.

65 In the Ashkenazic *piyyuṭ* Eldar (1979:381) found, besides נוּצָר, נוּסְדוּ/נוּסָדוּ and נוּשָׁרוּ (see his note on this verb, *ibid.*).

66 Moreshet 1980:130–134 distinguishes between the strong verbs and the III-*yod* verbs, but we have found no justification for this division.

67 Moreshet 1980:131.

68 See Yalon 1964:159; Haneman 1980a:261. The reading נוהגין is supported by other witnesses, as well; see Goldberg 1976:245–246.

Erfurt: נהנין[69]).[70] The credibility of at least one of the examples cited here has been brought into question by S. Naeh's comprehensive study.[71] In his view, נוהגין in m. Shabbat (12:4,5) does not reflect a form of הג"ה, but of נה"ג in the Qal (in agreement with the reading in MS Parma A).[72]

§ 12 It is possible to argue that some of the examples just cited (in §§ 10–11) are simply scribal errors, in which a *yod* was replaced by a *waw*. The fact that the reading traditions and vocalizations agree, however, strongly supports the existence of a *nuf'al* pattern. It is found in MS Vatican 66, in the oral tradition and the manuscripts of the Yemenites (in I-*yod* verbs), in *piyyutim* in old *maḥazorim* from Ashkenaz and from other regions, and in both the Tiberian and Babylonian vocalizations of the Bible (although in strong verbs this is only true in relatively recent Babylonian manuscripts). There is, therefore, no reason not to assign forms such as נוטל, נותנים, and נושא to this pattern.

§ 13 Scholarly views are divided regarding the rise of the *nuf'al* pattern. It is impossible to deny that it is most often used for verbs with an initial weak consonant.[73] According to Yalon,[74] the form originated in I-*nun* verbs. In order to distinguish between נִטַּלְתִּי (Pi'el) and נִטַּלְתִּי (Nif'al), the language fell back on the *nuf'al* form, with the *u* vowel characteristic of passive verbs[75] (such as the passive participle *muf'al* and the *huf'al* stem). Indeed, in the verb נטל itself, alongside נִטַּל in the *nif'al* (> נֻטַּל in the *nuf'al*), the *pu'al* is also attested: מה כוכבים רבים ומנוטלים (Sifre Devarim § 47, ed. Finklestein, p. 106). The form מנוטלים testifies also to the existence of a form נִטֵּל in the *pi'ēl*, which must have existed in the language although it is not documented. The meanings of the Qal and *nif'al* verbs נָטַל and נִיטַּל (which have to do with leaving and distancing) are different from the meanings of the *pi'ēl*/*pu'al* verbs נִטֵּל and מְנֻטָּל, which have to do with lifting.[76] Moreshet saw in the transition from *nif'al*

69 Moreshet (1980:130,132) mentioned the word נוכנעים in a Qumran text, and noted, following Yalon (1964:157) also the phrase חמץ נוקשה from the Bavli, as opposed to Biblical נִקְשֶׁה (Isaiah 8:21). I learned from Yochanan Breuer, however, that there is no basis for the participle נוקשה.

70 Yeivin (1985:504) cited a few *nuf'al* forms in strong verbs, found in relatively recent Babylonian manuscripts: נֻרְדַּפְנוּ (Lam 5:5), etc.

71 See Naeh 1992:278–290.

72 Even one who does not accept Naeh's conclusions will be convinced, I think, that the posited development of נֶהגין > נוהגין has been weakened (see Naeh, *ibid.*).

73 Even Moreshet, after all of his challenging questions, could not refute the fact that "its center of gravity occurs in I-*nun* roots" (Moreshet 1980:130).

74 Yalon 1964:157 (and earlier in *Lešonenu* 3 [1931], 307), and Ginsberg 1934:208 n. 2.

75 The suggestion of N. Berggrün, that the original form was *nof'al* (with an /o/), has no real justification (see Eldar 1979:382).

76 See Yalon 1964:152–153.

to *nuf'al* clear signs of passiveness.[77] According to Qimron, the *nuf'al* verbs may be relics of an ancient pattern that was the passive counterpart of the *nif'al*: just like *pi'ēl* and *pu'al*, *hif'īl* and *huf'al*, and *hitpa'ēl* and *hutpa'ēl*, so too is *nuf'al* the passive of *nif'al*, which itself was originally a reflexive, rather than a passive, stem.[78]

Qimron's speculation remains only a theory (and an implausible one, at that), with no facts to buttress it. To my mind, the most likely explanation is a combination of the views of Yalon and Moreshet: the development of *nif'al* into *nuf'al* within I-*nun* verbs was motivated by a desire to keep separate the *pi'ēl* form (נִטַּלְתִּי) from the *nif'al* form (נִטַּלְתִּי). The shift may have been aided by the fact that the *nif'al* in MH was so commonly a passive form;[79] on analogy to the *huf'al* and the participle *muf'al*, then, the [u] vowel became associated with passiveness. From I-*nun* verbs, the pattern spread to other similar classes of verbs: the hollow verbs which are conjugated like I-*nun* verbs and the I-*yod* verbs. Eventually, the pattern began spreading to strong verbs, as well.[80] No matter how we interpret the origins of the *nuf'al*, it is clear that it is an allomorph of the *nif'al* form.

20.3.3 *Nippə'al*

§ 14 The *nippə'al* pattern (with a *dagesh* and a *shewa* in the first radical) occurs (outside of hollow verbs) only in the tradition reflected in MS Parma B, and there only in one verb, in the past tense: נִיטְּמֵאתִי (m. Teharot 5:9, 2×), נִיטְּמֵאתָה (ibid., 2×). This issue has been explored elsewhere.[81] In the II-*waw* verbs, however (including geminates and I-*nun* verbs which are conjugated like II-*waw* verbs), this is the dominant form in the various traditions of MH, in the past and the participle. A few examples in the past tense: שֶׁנִּילּוֹשׁ (m. Kelim 10:2), שֶׁנִּילּוֹשָׁה (m. Halla 2:2), נֵעוֹרָה (m. Gittin 5:2), שֶׁנִּיצּוֹדוּ (m. Beṣah 3:2). And participles: נִידּוֹן ... נִידּוֹנִים (m. Rosh ha-Shana 1:2), נִיזּוֹנֶת (m. Ketub-

77 Moreshet 1980:129–130.

78 Qimron 1988.

79 Although Moreshet did not formulate his theory in quite this way, I take this to be the gist of his theory.

80 There is nothing surprising about this; the spread of a pattern from one class of verbs to another is a common phenomenon. For example, the [ī] vowel in the *hif'il* forms (e.g., הִפְקִיד, מַפְקִיד, etc.) originated in II-*waw* verbs (e.g., הֵקִים, מֵקִים, יָקִים) and then spread to the rest of the verbs.

81 Bar-Asher 1986:190–192; 1991:56–60.

bot 11:1), נִידּוֹכִין (m. Beṣah 1:8), נֵיאוֹתִין (m. Shabbat 3:5),[82] as well as נִימּוֹקִים (m. Rosh ha-Shana 3:8), from the root מק"ק, and, from I-*nun* verbs, נִיצּוֹלֶת and נִיצּוֹלִין (m. Para 11:1),[83] and נִיזּוֹקִים (m. Bava Qamma 3:13). In Biblical Hebrew, the *naf'al* (a form of *nif'al*) is attested.[84] In the past tense, for example, we find נָבוֹכָה (Esther 3:15), נָכֹנוּ (Ezekiel 16:7), נָסֹגוּ (Isaiah 42:17), and more. In the participle, we find נָכוֹן (2 Samuel 7:16), נָלוֹז (Proverbs 3:32), and more. Also attested, however, is the form *nippᵉ'al* itself: נִמּוֹל (Genesis 17:26), נֵעוֹר (Zechariah 2:17), נִמּוֹלִים (Genesis 34:22).[85] The form *naf'al* (נָבוֹךְ and the others like it) disappeared from Mishnaic Hebrew in the past tense. In the participle, it remained, but in restricted use: נָדוֹן is attested, alongside נִידּוֹן, but the two have different meanings, and while the latter is a normal verb, the former is only used nominally, as Haneman showed in his excellent study.[86]

The *nippe'al* form is also the usual one in the Samaritan tradition for the strong verb: *niffåqådti*,[87] etc., which reflects a form like *nippə'alti* within the Tiberian tradition.[88] (Regular *nif'al* forms are also attested there, such as *nis-tårå* = נסתרה).[89]

§ 15 Z. Ben-Ḥayyim, following Nöldeke,[90] explained nicely the forms נִמּוֹל, נֵעוֹר, and the like, in the past and participle, as built on an analogy with the future forms. נִמּוֹל is like יִמּוֹל, נֵעוֹרָה is like תֵּעוֹר. One might think that the forms נִיטְמֵאתִי and נִיטְמֵאתָה in the tradition of MS Parma B might be explained along similar lines, as being built on analogy to אֶטָּמֵא. It must be admitted, however, that there is a difficulty in this explanation, because the passive of טמ"א in MH is always in the *nitpa''al* form, not the *nif'al*: נִטַּמָּא, מִטַּמֵּא, יִטַּמֵּא.[91] Do we have to assume that the forms נִיטְמֵאתִי and נִיטְמֵאתָה

82 These examples are cited according to the good mauscripts, but are also found in the printed editions.

83 In MS Parma B, a scribe wrote נִיצָּלִין in the margin.

84 Of course, the canonical form *nif'al* is a reflex of **naf'al*, with attenuation of [a] to [i] in the closed unstressed syllable. The original *naf'al* form, with the shift of [a] to [ā], was preserved when the first syllable was open – נָלוֹז, נָקֹל – and a reflex of it is found when the initial consonant is *waw*, and [aw] contracted to [ō] – **nawda'* > *nōda'* (נוֹדַע).

85 With regard to the fundamentals, the Tiberian and Babylonian vocalizations agree on these issues (see Yeivin 1985:642–644).

86 Haneman 1980a:283–287.

87 See the table in Ben-Ḥayyim 1957–1977:5.84.

88 As is known, Tiberian *shewa* surfaces in the Samaritan tradition as a full vowel.

89 Ben-Ḥayyim *ibid.* interprets most *nif'al* forms as participles, and a reading like *niksafta* (Genesis 31:30) is seen by him as if derived from נכס"ף.

90 See Ben-Ḥayyim, *ibid*.

91 See Haneman 1980a:432–434; Bar-Asher 1991:59 and the literature cited in there.

were created at a time when *nif'al* forms were still common with this root?[92] This seems very doubtful to me. The alternative is to not exaggerate the chronology, and to assume that alongside the *nitpa''al* (נִטַּמָּא/יִטַּמֵּא), the *nif'al* forms (נִטְמָא/יִטָּמֵא) continued in use, and that נִיטְמֵאתִי is the product of an analogy (נִטְמֵאתִי > נִטַּמֵּאתִי on analogy to אֶטָּמֵא). It is worth observing that in the tradition of MS Kaufmann, in the mishna in Teharot under discussion, the reading is נִטְמֵאתִי and נִטְמֵאתָה,[93] in the *nif'al*. In truth, no matter what the origin of the *dagesh* in the first radical of טמ"א in the forms in MS Parma B, there morphology is clear: they are on the *nippe'al* pattern.[94] The pattern that is the norm for the past and participle forms of hollow verbs and other, similar roots, is attested at least occasionally with the verb טמ"א.

§ 16 In sum, *nif'al*, *nuf'al*, and *nippə'al* are all related forms; alongside the expected and usual form are two alternatives. The two are connected, originally, to weak verbs: the pattern *nuf'al* arose among I-*nun* verbs, spread to similar types of roots and then eventually to strong verbs; the pattern *nippə'al* arose at first among II-*waw* verbs and then spread to similar roots, reaching the verb טמ"א alone, in just one tradition. (The existence of this pattern in just one manuscript raises questions regarding the antiquity of the forms נִיטְמֵאתִי and נִיטְמֵאתָה.)

20.3.4 *Pē'ēl (pā'ēl), pō'al (məfō'āl), niṯpā'al*

§ 17 In studying all of the various traditions of Mishnaic Hebrew,[95] three *binyanim* emerge which have in common that they are derived from the D-stem ("heavy") *binyan* – which has gemination of the middle radical – but these do *not* have that gemination, and instead have a long (unchangeable?) vowel before that consonant. These are the *binyanim*: *pē'ēl* (*pā'ēl*),[96] *po'al* (*məfo'al*),

---

92 In the Tiberian and Babylonian traditions of Biblical Hebrew, the *nif'al* of טמ"א is productive in the past and the participle. In the future, the forms are pointed as if from the *nitpa''al* stem. Compare נִטְמֵאתִי (Jeremiah 2:23) and נִטְמְאִים (Ezekiel 20:30) with יִטַּמָּא (Leviticus 21:1). It appears that these future forms reflect a tradition of vocalization according to the norms of MH, rather than BH, and that within BH the form was *nif'al* in the future, as well (see Haneman 1980a:432 n. 820).

93 See Bar-Asher 1991:59–60 and n. 20 there.

94 Elsewhere (Bar-Asher 1986:191–192) I have rejected the possibility that these forms are artificial hybrids of *nif'al* together with *nitpa''al*, or echoes of an Aramaic form, *'eppe'ēl* < *'etpe'ēl*.

95 With a finer-grained analysis of the various traditions, it may be possible to present the date discussed in these sections (§§ 17–24) in a slightly different way. Our goal, however, is to present as global a perspective as possible (see n. 1, above).

96 See below, § 18.

and *nitpā'al.*[97] In terms of their appearance, these are nearly always like *pi"ēl* and *pu"al* forms of roots in which the middle radical is a guttural (especially an *aleph*): *bē'ēr*, *pērēš* (*pēraš*), alongside *mi'ēṭ* and *niḥēm*; *məšo'ār*, *məṭorāf*, *məḇo'ār*, *məroḥāq*, alongside *məyuḥād*; *nistā'aḇ*, *niṯ'ārəsā*, *mištā'ereṯ* (m. Uqṣin 2:8 in MS Parma B) alongside *mišta'ărīn* (in the same MS), *tiṯyaḥēd*. In other words, these are all "heavy" roots lacking the *dagesh*.[98] In the following paragraphs, first the data will be presented, and afterwards I will offer some comments about the data.

20.3.5 *Pē'ēl*

§ 18 Let us begin with an introductory remark. It is accepted in the scholarly literature that this pattern as *pā'ēl*, but in fact there are no examples of verbs in the past tense with the form *pā'ēl*.[99] All the forms which are attested with a *qameṣ* under the first root letter are participles (or future forms?). In the past, only forms with a *ṣere* (or *ḥiriq*)[100] under the first root letter are attested:

rēqēn: שֵׁרֵיקְנָה (m. Uqṣin 1:3,[101] 5; this is the reading in MS Kaufmann [second scribe], as well as in a Geniza fragment with Babylonian vocalization),[102] שֶׁרֶיקְנוּ, [103]שֵׁרֵיקְנוּ (K2 in Uqṣin there, as well as in the same Geniza fragment[104]).[105]

97 Morag (1957, 1992) vocalizes *nitpā'ēl*, and Yeivin vocalizes *hitpā'ēl*. See n. 135 below.

98 These were termed by Ben-Ḥayyim "*pi"el* without the *dagesh* in the *'ayin*," and "*nitpa"al* without the *dagesh* in the *'ayin*" (Ben-Ḥayyim 1957–1977:5.82,87).

99 See, for example, Shivtiel 1972:209, and Morag 1971a and 1992; all others have followed this practice. See also Yeivin 1985:582, who already noted the pattern *pē'ēl* in parentheses. Morag made an excellent point: past-tense forms on the pattern *pā'ēl* could be understood as *binyan Qal* verbs. One must search, therefore, for participles of the pattern *məfā'ēl*, whose past tense is *pā'ēl*/*pā'al*.

100 In the Samaritan tradition, the *pi"el* verbs with simple *'ayin* appear with an [a] vowel after the first root letter (e.g., såfər, kåfər), but in regular *pi'el* verbs with geminated medial consonants, the [a] is also attested (e.g., faqqəd, not fiqqəd), as we learn from Ben-Ḥayyim 1957–1977:5.81–82. In Tiberian Hebrew only one verb with this feature has been preserved: נַשַּׁנִי (Genesis 41:51, and not נִשַּׁנִי, with the expected [a] > [i] shift). This is presumably the result of the force of analogy with the associated name מְנַשֶּׁה.

101 In mishna 3, the *mappiq* in the *heh* is not visible.

102 Yeivin 1985:582.

103 The second scribe of MS Kaufmann – like other Italian manuscripts of "Sephardic" tradition – interchange *ṣere* with *segol*.

104 Yeivin, *ibid.* In the fragment with Babylonian vocalization, רֵיקְנוּ is attested twice with *ṣere* under the *resh*.

105 In MS Parma B, the verb is vocalized שרִיקְנָה (2×) and שרִיקְנוּ (2×), in normal *pi'el* forms.

qēfā: היין משיקפה אף על פי שֶׁקֵּיפָּה (m. Ma'asrot 1:7,[106] in a fragment with Babylonian vocalization[107]).[108]

It is possible that the forms כִּיפֵר and כִּיפְרוּ (attested a number of times in MS Vatican 66 of the Sifra) – with a simple *peh* but a *ḥiriq* under the *kaph* – also belong here.[109] In other words, just like רֵקֵן and קֵיפָּה (and גֵּזֵר?) correspond to בֵּאֵר and אֵרֵשׁ, כִּיפֵר would correspond to נִאֵץ and נִחֵם.

§ 19 In the participles, one finds, as expected, a *qameṣ* following the first radical of the root: מְאָבְקִים (m. Shevi'it 2:2, MS K),[110] מְזָמְמִין (m. Makkot 1:7 according to the vocalizer of MS K[111]),[112] מְזָמְנִין (m. Berakot 7:1; m. Halla 1:8, in the Babylonian vocalization and the Yemeni tradition),[113] מְשָׁיֵר (m. Shevi'it 3:4, in Babylonian vocalization), מְשָׁלֵק (m. Ma'asrot 1:5 in Babylonian vocalization),[114] מְזָלְפִין (m. Shabbat 19:3). Similar forms are found in the Yemeni reading tradition:[115] מְחָטְפִין (m. Sukka 4:5), מְעָקְדִין (m. Tamid 4:1), מְתָלְשִׁין (m. Yoma 6:4).[116]

Possibly also relevant are the form with non-geminated middle radical, but with a *pataḥ* rather than a *qameṣ* before it, as is attested in the Babylonian

106 The first form, משיקפה, is vocalized in the fragment as a Qal future form, יִקְפָּה (Yeivin *ibid.*).

107 Kaufmann and Parma A read קֵיפָּה ... יְקַפֶּה – regular *pi"el* forms.

108 Yeivin (*ibid.*) cited Ayala Loewenstamm, as observing that also relevant may be the forms גזרה/גֵיזרה (= גֵּזֵר אותה), in a Karaite commentary to Genesis; Yeivin himself leaves this with a question mark.

109 Yeivin 1985:515. Compare also the form פִּיַּיסְתָּ (in an Ashkenazic *piyyut* – Eldar 1979:384, and his comments there).

110 Bar-Asher 1980:125.

111 The original scribe, who wrote מזמין, presumably intended the *hif'il* verb מְזִמִּין.

112 Bar-Asher, *ibid.* Morag 1971a, 1992 distinguishes between *pā'ēl* and *nitpā'al* forms of strong verbs and *pā'ēl* and *nitpā'al* forms from hollow and geminate roots (including זמ"ן, which is similar to זמ"ם in light of the merging of [m] and [n] in word-final position. He interprets the latter as biforms of *polel* and *nitpolel*, with an [ā] in place of [ō] (in Aramaic fashion). Against this, Yeivin (1985:582) treats all these forms as examples of a single phenomenon. In practice, there is no disagreement here: Morag adopts a diachronic perspective and is searching for the origins of the various forms, while Yeivin is describing patterns synchronically. Our purpose, too, is primarily synchronic, and we are therefore discussing these different forms together.

113 Shivtiel 1972:209; Morag 1992:§ 2.2.

114 All the data regarding Babylonian readings is drawn from Yeivin 1985:582.

115 See Morag 1992, *ibid.*, and compare also Shivtiel 1972:209 and Gamliel 1989:42.

116 This pattern is attested in the Yemeni tradition in other sources, as well – in the Talmud, Midrash ha-Gadol, and their spoken Hebrew (see Morag 1992:§ 2.2).

vocalization: מְכַפְּרִין/מְכַפְּרִים,[117] מְקַפֵּיחַ.[118] In other words, מְאָבֵק and מְשָׁלֵק are like מְסָאֵב and מְבָרֵךְ, and מְכַפֵּר and מְקַפֵּיחַ are like מְנַחֵם and מְנַאֵץ.

20.3.6 *Pōʻal*

§ 20 Forms on the pattern *pōʻal* are expected, according to our understanding of the various patterns, only in the participle form: *məfoʻāl*.[119] Indeed, one certain form of this type is attested in the tradition of the vocalizer of MS Kaufmann:[120] ופינה את הגחלים הֲלָךְ הַלָּךְ וחתה מן הַמְאוֹכָלוֹת הפנימיות וירדו ועירן לתוך של זהב "he cleared away the live coals, to this side and that side, and swept away some of the consumed, inner [coals],[121] and then went down and emptied them into a gold [pan]" (m. Tamid 5:5[122]).[123] Clearly we are dealing here with a passive perfect – the coals שֶׁנִּתְאָכְלוּ (= שֶׁנִּתְאַכְּלוּ)[124] and are now מְאוֹכָלוֹת "consumed." The forms מְהוֹגָן and מְרוֹגָזִין, cited by Morag from the Yemeni tradition, are to be interpreted along similar lines.[125]

20.3.7 *Nitַpāʻal*

§ 21 The number of attestations of verbs on the *nitpāʻal* pattern in the language of the Tannaim is not large. In MS K there are two such words:[126] נִיתְאַכַּל הבשר (m. Sanhedrin 6:6 [12])[127] and האיברים והפרדים שלא נִיתְאָכְלוּ

117 Yeivin 1985:520, although the future form is יְכַפְּרוּ, with the *dagesh* (ibid. 527).

118 Yeivin 1985:522.

119 Just as there is no *pu"al* in the past or future tenses (see §§ 6, 8 above), so is there no *pōʻal* in the past or future; and just as there is a *məfu"āl* (מְקֻדָּשׁ, מְקֻבָּל), so do we expect to find *məfōʻāl* (מְאֹכָל).

120 See Bar-Asher 1980:126. Unfortunately, due to a typographical error there, פּוּעַל was printed instead of פּוֹעַל (= *pōʻal*).

121 As Albeck explains (*ad* m. Tamid 1:4), this refers to the coals which were closest to the fire, which were thoroughly burned.

122 The words מן המאוכלות הפנימיות are missing in the printed editions.

123 In the parallel passage, however (m. Tamid 1:4), the vocalizer in MS K pointed, וחתה מן הַמְּאֻוכלוֹת הפנימיות (see Bar-Asher 1980:126 with n. 2).

124 See below, § 21 and n. 128.

125 See Morag 1992:§ 2.4 (they are cited there among the forms of the *pōʻel*; see above, n. 120).

126 See Bar-Asher 1980:126; further details regarding the forms cited are given there.

127 The *pataḥ* under the *aleph* reflects the Sephardic merger of *pataḥ* with *qameṣ*, as is often found in MS K (see Bar-Asher 1993:§ 17 n. 39).

מבערב (m. Tamid 2:1).[128] In the Babylonian vocalization, at least two more forms are attested:[129] נִסְתָּפָג and מִיתְכָּוֵין.[130] In the Deinard manuscript from the Geniza, published by Bentolila,[131] we find נִשְׁתַּפָה (m. Gittin 2:6, 2×[132]).[133] In the Yemeni tradition, too, that word is read נִשְׁתָּפָה (m. Gittin *ibid.*),[134] and there is evidence for a *nitpāʿal* form[135] outside the Mishna, as well, such as נִתְפָּגְמָה (b. ʿArakhin 10b), מִתְאָנֵח (b. Berakhot 59b), and also in the spoken language.[136]

20.4 Comments on these three *binyanim*

§ 22 Similar forms are also attested in some of the reading traditions of the Bible. In the Tiberian tradition, perhaps, is attested מְאַסְפָיו/[137]מְאָסְפָיו (Isaiah 62:9).[138] These forms are especially common within the Samaritan tradition, such as *kåfər* (= Tiberian *kipper*), *såfər* (= *sippēr*), *ēkåbēdåk* (= *ʾakabbedka*), and so on,[139] all of which are examples of the "*piʿēl* with simple *ʿayin*" or "*piʿēl* without the *dagesh*."[140]

---

128 In the parallel passage in m. Tamid 2:5, the word is vocalized נִיתְאַכְּלוֹ, in the *nitpa"al* pattern, and similarly in m. Berakhot 8:7, עד כדי שֶׁיִּתְאַכֵּל המזון (ש)במעיו. M. Mishor reminded me of the form תְּאָכְלֵהוּ אש (Job 20:26), which looks like a תְּפָעֵל form (from the *pēʿēl* pattern), which would tally with נִתְאָכֵל and מְאוֹכָלוֹת in MS K (in all of these occurrences, אכל means "burn"). The reading tradition with a *qameṣ qatan* – *təʾoxlehu* – however, militates for taking it as a form of תֹּאכְלֵהוּ, in the Qal. Further discussion would take us too far afield.

129 Yeivin 1985:583.

130 Yeivin cites another possible example: נִיטַּמּוּ.

131 Bentolila 1989:52.

132 This manuscript, too, interchanges *pataḥ* with *qameṣ* regularly.

133 Bentolila sees the fricative *feh* as the result of contamination from שָׁפוּי.

134 Morag 1992:§ 2.2.

135 For the forms נתאכַל and נסתפַג cited above, which have [a] after the second radical rather than [ē], there is evidence for the reading *nitpāʿal* (rather than *nitpāʿēl*) in the past tense.

136 Morag 1992:§ 2.2.

137 The reading מְאַסְפָיו is supported by the Aleppo Codex, the Leningrad Codex, and other MSS. There are other, less certain witnesses to the reading מְאָסְפָיו (see M. Breuer, "הנוסח והמקורות," *apud* Amos Hakham's commentary on Isaiah in the *Daʿat Miqra* series [Jerusalem, 1984], p. 74). Compare also לְמְנַאֲצַי (Jer 23:17), as opposed to יְנָאֵץ (Ps 74:10).

138 This form was discussed by Morag 1969:124–125. Both Morag (at length) and Ben-Ḥayyim (1957–1977:5.83) also relate to the form תְּרָצְּחוּ (Ps 62:4); they saw the *dagesh* as secondary, but the reading traditions that distinguish between *qameṣ gadol* and *qameṣ qatan* do in fact read *təroṣṣəḥū*.

139 See Ben-Ḥayyim 1957–1977:5.82–83.

140 The forms of התפעל without *dagesh* were interpreted by Ben-Ḥayyim (*ibid.*, p. 87) as parallel to Aramaic *etpəʿel* forms, and the נפעל without *dagesh* were taken by him to be related

§ 23 These patterns have been previously discussed in the literature. The most important discussions were those of Morag's, first in his article in *Tarbiz* (reprinted as Morag 1971a) and then in his study in the Yeivin Festschrift (1992). In this last study, he summarized all the data in the various traditions of Hebrew and Aramaic, and then went back to deal with the origin of the different forms.

These were his major conclusions: he distinguished two groups within the verbs of the forms פָּעֵל and נִתְפָּעַל, the strong verbs (such as מְאָבְקִים and נִסְתָּפָג), and the hollow and geminate verbs (such as מְחָיֵךְ and מְזָמֵם). These last examples are the Aramaic counterparts of Hebrew פּוֹלֵל and נִתְפּוֹלֵל forms (הִתְגּוֹלֵל, הִתְבּוֹנֵן, סוֹבֵב, קוֹמֵם), whereas the former type is the counterpart of Arabic *fā'ala* and *tafā'ala* forms. These are known in the Bible as פּוֹעֵל and הִתְפּוֹעֵל (see below, §§ 25–29). At first, Morag believed that these were Aramaic cognates (with /ā/ after the first radical) to the Hebrew הִתְפּוֹעֵל/פּוֹעֵל forms, which had then been borrowed into Hebrew,[141] but later[142] he saw them – because of their relative rarity in Jewish Aramaic,[143] and their relative frequency in Samaritan Hebrew and the Yemeni tradition[144] – as ancient Hebrew forms, cognate to *fā'ala* and *tafā'ala*, in which the Canaanite shift ([ā] > [o] under stress) did not take place).[145]

Ben-Ḥayyim, on the other hand, argued that there are simply non-geminated equivalents of the *pi"ēl* and *hitpa"al/nitpa"al* forms; where there is gemination, the previous vowel is short, and where the gemination is lost (as in the present cases), the previous vowel is long.[146]

In Morag's last discussion (1992, § 2.8.2, end), he claimed that the loss of gemination is not a common phenomenon in the Samaritan tradition of Hebrew.[147] This is why he reached the conclusion just summarized, based on

---

to words such as נִמּוֹל, in other words, *nippᵉ'al* forms (see §§ 14–15 above). Some may actually be MH נתפָּעֵל forms, but this is not the place to pursue this further.

141 Morag 1971a:96, 100.

142 Morag 1992.

143 It is possible that they were particularly frequent in Christian Palestinian Aramaic, if I was correct in the way I interpreted the forms with fricative second radicals, in the later texts of that dialect, such as *יִפָּתַח, *יִתְיָתַר, מִשְׁתָּתַק, *אִשְׁתָּתַף, *חָתֵם, *אֶתְבָּדרו, *אֶצְטָדַק (see Bar-Asher 1987a:117–124).

144 See Morag 1992:§§ 2.2, 2.8.5.

145 See there, §§ 2.8.2–2.8.4. Morag argues that the great Samaritan grammarian Avi-Yitzḥaq already said as much (see there).

146 See Ben-Ḥayyim 1957–1977:5.83. Ben-Ḥayyim speculates that perhaps "the loss of gemination first occurred in forms with a *shewa*, such as מְבַקְשִׁים, and it then spread to other forms"; one could interpret מְאַסְפָיו along these lines (see § 22 above).

147 One should not ignore, however, the numerous oppositions between the Samaritan pronunciation and the Tiberian tradition, in which one form, but not the other, shows gemination,

weighty considerations: he sees these forms as cognate with *fā'ala* and *tafā'la*, with the preservation of the original /a/ in the Samaritan and Yemeni traditions.

§ 24 Whatever the origins and developments of the forms פֵּעֵל (מְפָעֵל),[148] פִּעֵל with no gemination, פֹּעַל (מְפֹעָל),[149] and נִתְפָּעֵל, they should be associated, synchronically, with the geminated forms. A number of points of data lead to this conclusion:

1. The attested past tense forms in our traditions[150] of the active פָּעִיל stem are all reflexes of פִּעֵל (and not of פָּעֵל). Thus, רֵקֵן, שֵׁיפָּה (perhaps also גֵּזֵר in Karaite Hebrew), and כִּיפֵּר all appear to be פִּעֵל forms which have lost their gemination, and have no connection to פָּעֵל (derived from *fā'ala*).
2. The forms (participles and future) that have [ā] after the first radical have their counterpart in the Tiberian tradition (which does not freely interchange *pataḥ* with *qameṣ*) in the form מְאַסְפָיו (Isaiah 62:9; see n. 146 above). This form stands relative to מְאָבְקִים in the same relationship that מְנַאֲצַי stands to יְנָאֵץ (or מְבָאֵר stands to מְנַחֵם). The same is true within the Babylonian tradition of Mishnaic Hebrew, regarding the relationship between מְשָׁלֵק and מְכַפְּרִין and מְקַפֵּיחַ.
3. The non-geminated counterparts of the geminated forms, within one tradition or between different traditions, support the proposition that on a synchronic level, the geminated forms (פִּעֵל, נִתְפַּעַל) and the non-geminated forms (פֵּעֵל, נִתְפָּעַל) are reflexes of the same original forms. Compare, for instance, biforms such as נִתְאַכַּל and נִתְאַכַל in MS K (see § 21 and n. 128, above), מְתָלְשִׁין and מְתַלְּשִׁין in the Yemeni tradition,[151] or רִיקֵּן in MS Parma B as opposed to רֵקֵן in MS K2 and a vocalized Babylonian fragment (see § 18 above, and n. 105 there). Just as עֵרֵב, סֵרְקָן, מְסֹרָס, and מְעָרְבִין are biforms of עִירֵּב (m. Ohalot 10:1, MS Parma B), סִרְקָן (m. Kelim 15:2, MS Parma B), מסוּרָס (m. Nidda 3:5), and מְעָרְבִין (m. Miqva'ot 6:2, MS

such as יָמִין (Num 20:17) vs. *yammən* on the one hand, or אַדִּירִים (Exod 15:10) vs. *ådirəm* (reflecting a singular אָדִיר) on the other hand. This is not the place to pursue this further.

148 This should not be called the *binyan* פָּעֵל, because in the past tense it is not a *qameṣ* under the second radical, but a *ṣere* or a *ḥiriq*.

149 We actually have attested only the passive participle, and so this should be combined with the פֵּעֵל and פִּעֵל (with no *dagesh*); see above, § 8, and below, § 34.

150 See what I wrote above, in n. 99, regarding the vowel of the second root radical in Samaritan Hebrew.

151 See Morag 1992, nn. 83 and 107.

Parma B)[152] – so to one should see רֵקֵן, קֵיפָה,[153] נִסְתָּפַג,[154] מְאוֹכלוֹת, as biforms רִקֵּן, קִיפָּה, נִסְתַּפַּג, and מְאוּכָּלוֹת. Both sets are attested in the various traditions of Hebrew.[155]

20.4.1 *Po'ēl, Nitpo'ēl*

§ 25 In the grammar of Biblical Hebrew, there are a number of forms in the *pō'ēl* and *nitpō'ēl* patterns, the cognates of the Arabic III and VI forms, *fā'ala* and *tafā'la*. Some examples: יוֹדַעְתִּי (1 Samuel 21:3), מְשׁוֹפְטִי (Job 9:15), מְלָוֹשְׁנִי (Ps 101:5 – the *ketiv* intends מְלוֹשֵׁן),[156] וִיסֹעֲרֵהוּ/וִישַׁעֲרֵהוּ (Babylonian tradition of Job 27:21),[157] יְסֹעֵר (Hosea 13:3), וְהִתְגֹּעֲשׁוּ (Jeremiah 25:16), יִתְגֹּעֲשׁוּ (Jeremiah 46:8), מִנֹּאָץ (Isaiah 52:5 – the vocalization apparently intends the form מִתְנֹאָץ, with assimilation of the *taw*).[158] The small number of such examples in the Bible shows that these patterns were in the process of disappearing from the language. Indeed, of all the verbs just mentioned, only one is perhaps (perhaps!) attested in Mishnaic Hebrew: וְסוֹעֲרָתוֹ (m. Kil'ayim 1:7. in MS Parma A).[159]

The certain examples of the *pō'ēl* and *nitpō'al* patterns in the various traditions of Mishnaic Hebrew are exceedingly rare. These are they:

---

152 The geminated forms are also attested in other traditions (see, e.g., Shivtiel 1972:211, and Katz 1978:53–57).

153 See above, n. 107.

154 See, for instance, the beginning of m. Makhshrin 2:1, in MSS Kaufmann and Parma B.

155 One should not reject the possibility that some of these forms with non-geminated middle radicals are the results of analogies with other forms, or of other types on influence. Thus, מְאָבְקִים may be influenced by אָבָק (Bar-Asher 1980:70 n. 361) and נִשְׁתָּפָה as the result of influence from שָׁפוּי, as was argued by Bentolila (1989:52), like להשתָבֵץ from שִׁבֵּץ and התחָבֵר from חָבֵר in Israeli Hebrew. In this way, it is clear that we cannot talk about original פֵּעֵל and נתפָּעַל in Hebrew. From a synchronic perspective, however, these are enmeshed among the *binyanim* without gemination.

156 See Ibn Janaḥ 1964:163.

157 See Yeivin 1985:583; the Tiberian tradition has וִישָׁעֲרֵהוּ.

158 Some of these examples are preserved in the scribal tradition of the Bible (the *ketiv*), as can be seen from the inclusion of the *waw* in יודעתי, משופטי, and מלושן, and others are found in the reading tradition (the *qere*), such as ויסערהו, יסֹער, והתגֹעשו, יתגֹעשו, מנֹאץ.

159 See Morag 1992:§ 2.4. This piece of data was cited already by Haneman 1980a:157, but he did not believe that it was a *po'ēl* form (see below, § 26).

20.4.2 *Pōʿēl*

§ 26 סוֹעֵר (?): היה עובר בכרם ונפלו ממנו זרעים ... הזורע וסיערתו הרוח לאחריו מותר (m. Kil'ayim 5:7).[160] The reading וסיערתו is found in the printed editions, and finds support in many witnesses, including MS K (סיערתו) and MS Cambridge (וסיערתו).[161] MS Parma A, however, reads וְסוֹעֲרַתּוּ, and this is the reading (without the vocalization) in the *editio princeps* and three later witnesses, as well.[162] A similar reading is found in MS Erfurt of the Tosefta: והסעורתו (which should probably be emended to והסוערתו).

Haneman (1980a:157), who discovered the reading in MS Parma A, interpreted it as a past tense form of a *piʿēl* verb. On his view, סיערתו became סוערתו through a shift of i > o/u. Morag (1992:§ 2.4, and see n. 57 there) interpreted it as a *pōʿēl* form, and connected it to ויסֹערהו in the Babylonian tradition of vocalization in Job.[163] It is also possible the וסוערתו is merely a scribal error for וסיערתו, with a *waw* for a *yod*,[164] and the vocalizer of the manuscript may simply have been misled by the consonantal text.[165] Still, one cannot reject Morag's speculation that this is a *poʿēl* form, since this very verbal root has the forms יסֹעֵר and יסֹערהו (in the Babylonian tradition). If this is correct, there is a single, unique verb which is, in one tradition of Mishnaic Hebrew, identical to one tradition of Biblical Hebrew.[166]

20.4.3 *Niṯpōʿal*

§ 27 There are two or three certain attestations of *nitpōʿal*-pattern verbs.

נִתְיוֹאֵשׁ – This is the reading of MS K in every occurrence in the Mishna: נתיואשו (m. Baba Qamma 10:2, 2×; Kelim 26:8), מתיואשין (m. Baba Qamma

160 In the continuation of this mishna, the printed editions have: סיערתו הרוח לפניו, ר' עקיבא אומר אם עשרים יופך ..." The original reading, however, was סיעתו/סייעתו, as is found in the reliable manuscripts of the Mishna and the Tosefta (see Lieberman, תוספתא כפשוטה זרעים, 629).

161 Zachs 1972:264 (where other witnesses are listed, as well).

162 See Zachs, *ibid.*

163 See § 25 above.

164 See Haneman 1980a:157.

165 Furthermore, is it not possible to imagine that this is a Qal feminine participle, with a masculine singular pronominal suffix, such that וסוערתו = וסוערת אותו? The vocalization would then be appropriate, as well. See also the reading in MS Erfurt of the Tosefta given above; this demands further investigation.

166 Another example from a later text is found in the Maḥăzor of Saadia Gaon (see Yalon 1971:143–144); in place of יאשתי ציצית מטלית ("I removed the *tsitsit* from the *tallit*"), one manuscript has יואשתי (see further below, § 27).

10:2), תתיואש (m. Abot 1:7). In three out of these four cases, the vocalizer erased the *waw*, and pointed them נִתְיַאֲשׁוּ/נִתְיָאֲשׁוּ and מִתְיַאֲשִׁין. In Abot, however, he read תִּתְיוֹאֵשׁ. The Geniza fragments of Abot, too, know the form תתיואש; other fragments read נתיואשו in Baba Qamma, as well.[167] Yalon already showed[168] that the form is also attested in early *piyyuṭ*.[169]

נִתְרוֹקֵן – נִתְרוֹקְנָה רשות (m. Nedarim 10:2, 2×, in MSS K,[170] Parma A, and Paris;[171] the same is found in the Babylonian vocalization).[172] The form is known, unvocalized, in many witnesses. It is also attested outside the Mishna in this spelling: נתרוקנה (t. Nedarim 6:2, 2×); מתרוקנת (Sifre Bemidbar §§ 153, 155, ed. Horovitz pp. 202, 203, 207; in all, 5 times in MS Vatican 32 and in other witnesses).

נִתְקוֹץ – In m. Shevi'it 4:2 we read: שדה שנתקוצה תזרע במוצאי שביעית, in which ניתקוצה means "whose thorns [קוץ] have been removed."[173] It has already been observed that MS K reads שֶׁנִּתְקַוְּוצָה, in the *nitpa"al*,[174] and the same is true in MS Parma A, which reads שֶׁנִּיקַּוְּוצָה (with assimilation of the *taw* before the *qof*),[175] and in other witnesses.[176] Katz found, however, the reading נִתְקוֹצָה in the tradition in Djerba.[177] Indeed, this reading is attested in a number of vocalized printed editions, as well: Amsterdam 1646; Venice 1704; Mantua 1777; Livorno 1929. I also heard this reading from Moroccan scholars (the editions just mentioned circulated in the communities of North Africa, including Djerba and the Moroccan cities). נִתְקוֹצָה appears to have been influenced by the noun קוֹץ.[178] There is no way of knowing the antiquity of this form, and whether it was, as it appears, created in the process of transmission or whether (though this is very doubtful) it reflects a relic of the language from when it was a spoken dialect.

---

167 Sharvit 1976:45–46.

168 Yalon 1963:35.

169 In other manuscripts of the Mishna (Parma A, Cambridge, Parma B [for m. Kelim], and more), the form used is נִתְיַאֵשׁ (נִתְיָאֵשׁ): נתיאשו, מתיאשין, תתיאש (see Bar-Asher 1980:30). Yeivin (1985:552) hints to one possible occurrence of נתיואש (with an erased *waw*), but normally the Babylonian form is also נתיאש.

170 In MS K the word was divided (twice), for some reason, into two: ניתרו קנה.

171 In MS Paris the word is vocalized נִתְרוֹקָנָה.

172 Yeivin 1985:583.

173 See Albeck's commentary, *ad loc.*

174 Katz 1977:292.

175 Haneman 1980a:207.

176 See Zachs 1975 *ad loc.*

177 Katz, *ibid.*

178 See above, n. 155.

§ 28 We have, then, three certain forms of the *nitpō'al* verbs in Mishnaic Hebrew.[179] There is no need to emphasize that the reliability of נתיואש and נתרוקן, which are attested in ancient witnesses, far exceeds that of נתקוצה, found only in late printings and oral tradents in North Africa. In all cases, however, these are not forms inherited from the Bible: יא"ש appears only once in the geminated forms in the Bible, in the *pi"ēl*, לְיַאֵשׁ (Qohelet 2:20).[180] The verb ריקן/נתרוקן is entirely an innovation within MH; it is a verbal root derived secondarily from רֵיקָן (= רֵיקָם).[181] It is difficult to argue that patterns which were on the wane in Biblical Hebrew were productive in Mishnaic Hebrew.[182]

§ 29 It is possible to explain the rise of the forms נתיואש and נתרוקן in a different way.[183] Sharvit already raised the possibility that these forms show the shift of [ā] > [ō],[184] and Haneman explicitly espoused this view, as well.[185] In other words [ā] > [ō] is part of the larger shift of [a] and [i] to [o] and [u] in Mishnaic Hebrew.[186] It is true that a general shift of this sort is still not proven to have occurred, although it undoubtedly did take place in certain phonetic environments, such as before a labial (מְסַבִּין > מְסֻבִּין) and before a *resh* (קַרדום > קוֹרדום) or a *lamed* (קַלגס > קוֹלגס), especially in a closed unstressed syllable.[187] Here, too, it may be that we are dealing with a phonetic change of /ā/ to /ō/ in specific a phonetic environment: perhaps נתיָאש shifted

---

179 Yeivin 1985:583 also mentions נִתְאוֹנָה from the Halakhot Pesuqot and the Halakhot Gedolot, as well as others (he refers to Ben-Yehuda 1910–1960 s. v.). Morag 1992 (§ 2.4, end) wrote: "We do not include here the form נִתְאוֹנָה ... meaning 'he was cheated', because this is derived from the noun אוֹנָאָה" (see n. 155 above). Morag's perspective was a diachronic one, and therefore appropriately omitted this form. We are omitting it here, despite our synchronic orientation, because of its lateness, being attested only in Geonic literature.

180 It is also attested a number of times in the *nif'al*, e.g., וְנוֹאַשׁ (1 Samuel 27:1).

181 See Ben-Yehuda 1910–1960:14.6736א. It is, perhaps, because of the derivation from רֵיקָן that the verb preserved the *ṣere* following the first radical and the non-geminated second radical (and see again n. 155 above).

182 If סוערתו (above, § 26) is indeed a *pō'ēl* form, it would appear to be an innovation under biblical influence, and not a direct inheritance from the Bible.

183 I am setting aside the North African form נתקוֹצה here, which was, as mentioned, created on analogy to the noun קוֹץ (above, § 27).

184 Sharvit 2004:185.

185 Haneman 1980a:208. נתרוקנה is mentioned there twice, and נתיואש, which is not attested in MS Parma A, is cited in n. 804. (The form נתרועעה in MS K is also interpreted by Haneman as a shift of נתפָּעל > נתפוֹעל, and not as an originally נתפועל form.)

186 Haneman 1980a:208 speaks about a shift of the short vowels to o/u. Might he have believed that the *ḥolem* in נתרוקנה is a short vowel (= *qameṣ qatan*)?

187 See Ben-Ḥayyim 1963:10 and n. 9 (and the literature cited there); Kutscher 1959:391–392; Bar-Asher 1983:149–151; and n. 185 below.

to נתיואש because of the proximate guttural consonant?[188] The same is true with regard to נתרוקן. It should be mentioned that we have explicit evidence for the verb רֵקֵן without gemination in the ק (above, § 8). The expected passive form is נתרָקַן/נתרָקְנָה, with a simple (non-geminated) ק and a *qameṣ* before it. Might we assume that the emphatic *qof* encouraged the shift of [ā] to [ō] (a more back vowel), thus shifting נתרָקנה to נתרוֹקנה?[189]

The bottom line is that we have only very few *nitpo'al* forms. One of them (נִתְקוֹצָה) may well not be ancient, and the other two also do not appear to be original forms, but rather late innovations in rabbinic times. The most likely explanation is that they represent phonetic reflexes of נִתְפָּעַל, with a shift of [ā] to [ō], but this still awaits decisive proof.

§ 30 In sum, we can say that the heavy *binyanim* in Mishnaic Hebrew have four or five different forms:

1. The heavy form: *pi"el – nitpa"al*
2. The quadriliteral heavy form: *pilpal – nitpalpal*[190]
3. The lengthened heavy form: *pōlel – nitpōlal*
4. The ungeminated heavy form: *pē'ēl (pi'ēl) – nitpā'al (nitpa'al)*[191]
5. The lengthened heavy form (strong verbs): *pō'ēl – nitpō'al*

The last two (if there is any justification for the theory that *nitpo'ēl* is a reflex of *nitpā'al*) can be seen as biforms of the normal *pi"el* form (but it is clear that *pō'ēl* – such as סוֹערתו – is not a phonetic alternative of *pi"el*, but further discussion would take us too far afield).

20.4.4 *Niṯṯap̄ 'al*

§ 31 In all of Tannaitic literature, there are no certain attestations of this pattern, with the exception of one verb alone: נִתּוֹסַף, found only once in the

188 Such a hypothesis would need to be supported by other cases. There is at least one other example of a *qameṣ* shifting to *ḥolem* in the environment of *aleph*: in Sifre Bemidbar we read, ואת האיל יעשה זבח שלמים ... מה איל מיוחד שהוא בא כנדר ונדבה וטעון נסכים (§ 32, ed. Horovitz p. 39). In MS Vatican 32 the reading is מה הואיל מיוחד שהוא בנדבה וטעון נסכים – i.e., הָאַיִל > הוֹאַיִל.

189 I do not know of any other examples of this process. There is a similar example, in which [i] (a front vowel) shifted to [o] before *qof*: the form הִקְרָא (a *hif'il* form of קר"א, conjugated like a III-*yod* verb), attested as הוֹקְרָא in m. Yebamot 12:6 in MSS K and Parma A, and (unvocalized) also in MS Cambridge (Haneman 1980a:395).

190 See above in the discussion at n. 4.

191 Note the lack of gemination in the second consonant in all these forms.

Mishna: נִתּוֹסְפוּ (m. ʿErubin 7:7). This is the reading in MS Parma A,[192] MS Paris,[193] and many of the vocalized printed editions;[194] this is also how the form is read in Yemen,[195] Djerba,[196] and Ashkenaz.[197] It is also found outside the Mishna – unvocalized – such as: נתוסף (Mekhilta Pisḥa § 16, ed. Horovitz-Rabin, p. 59); שנתוספו (t. ʿErubin 6:1; t. Soṭa 7:5); נתוספו (t. ʿErubin *ibid.*), וניתוספו (Sifre Bemidbar § 6, ed. Horovitz, p. 10).

Yalon already provided a full explanation of this phenomenon,[198] and he was able to provide further examples, as well, nearly all from I-*yod* verbs outside of Tannaitic literature (נִתּוֹקַד, נִתּוֹכַח, נִתּוֹתַר, and also מִתּוֹצֵאת, reflected in a *derasha* in b. Soṭa).[199] Clearly this is an Aramaic *ʾettafʿal* borrowed into Hebrew and converted, by analogy to *nifʿal* and *nitpaʿal*, to *nittafʿal*. The Aramaic pattern is found in the Targumim and the late Aramaic dialects, such as Syriac and Jewish Babylonian Aramaic in the east, as well as Jewish Palestinian Aramaic, Samaritan Aramaic, and Christian Palestinian Aramaic in the west.[200] It is not clear why the usage of this pattern was restricted to I-*yod* verbs alone, and, within Tannaitic Hebrew, to one verb alone.[201] (H. Yalon pointed out the *nittafʿal* pattern, for strong verbs, in Geonic Hebrew.[202]) It would appear that the pattern only began to take root in the language near the end of its existence as a living language, and therefore never became widespread.

---

192 See Haneman 1980a:250. In MS K, the *nun* was omitted, and we find תּוֹסְפוּ.

193 Here it is vocalized נִתּוֹסָפוּ.

194 I found this form in the editions from Amsterdam 1646, Venice 1707, Matua 1777, and Livorno 1929.

195 Gamliel 1989:58.

196 Katz 1977:263.

197 According to the testimony of A. H. Weiss, משפט לשון המשנה (Vienna, 1867), 93. (He suggested a change to נִתְוַסַּף; see in detail, Yalon 1964:127–128.) The same reading is found in the vocalized Mishna with accompanying "Taytsh" (ed. Levin and Epstein), and this is also how the word is pointed by Kasovsky, presumably on the basis of Ashkenazic tradition.

198 Yalon 1964:127–135.

199 See b. Soṭa 10b: היא מוצאת היא מיתוצאת מיבעי ליה. The basis of the *derasha* is the assumption of the Aramaic-speaking *darshan* that the Biblical verb (מוּצֵאת) should be replaced by an *ʾettafʿal*/*nittafʿal* verb (see Yalon 1964:134–135).

200 In Biblical Aramaic the pattern is attested with hollow verbs: יִתְּזִין (Daniel 4:9), יִתְּשָׂם (Ezra 4:21) – both in place of *ʾetpəʿēl*.

201 There are no known forms on the *nitpaʿal* that go back to *hifʿil* verbs, in which case we could presume an ancient vocalization *nittafʿal* (see Mishor 1983:205 n. 173).

202 He suggests reading נִתַּחֲזַק, like איתַּחזק (as the Yemenis read it) in Aramaic.

20.5 Other *binyanim*?

§ 32 *Šif'el/ništaf'al*? Segal devoted a separate paragraph to these *binyanim*,[203] and enumerated a few forms, such as: שִׁחְרֵר, שִׁעְבֵּד, נשתחרר, נשתעבד – these are from Mishnaic Hebrew, and others are found in Amoraic Hebrew. Comparative grammar has taught us that the *šaf'ēl* forms in various Semitic languages (such as Akkadian) correspond to the *hif'īl* and *haf'ēl* of Hebrew and Aramaic. Segal already observed, however, that this was not synchronically perceived as a *binyan*: "In truth, the causative aspect of these forms had been lost to the native speakers, and they were used simply as quadriliteral verbs." They should be seen, therefore, as quadriliteral roots borrowed, through Aramaic, from Akkadian.

Haf'ēl: In one verb for which a *hif'īl* form is usually found in MH, הִלְקִיט, a parallel *haf'ēl* form is also attested – הַלְקֵט: ומהלקטים לתרנגולין (m. Shabbat 24:3).[204] Although in its origins this is an Aramaic *haf'ēl* form, synchronically one should classify this, following Segal, as a quadriliteral verbs הלק"ט. This would then be similar to מְהֻקְצָעוֹת (Ezekiel 46:22), which should be analyzed as a *pu'al* form of הקצ"ע (rather than a *huf'al* participle from קצ"ע).

Nitpi'al: In his article on the grammar of Mishnaic Hebrew current in Yemen, Shivtiel (1972:209) writes: "In the Yemeni tradition there are *binyanim* that do not exist in Tiberian Hebrew, and these are: (1) פָּעֵל ... (2) נִתְפָּעֵל ... (3) נִתְפַּעַל." From the material he presents, however, it seems clear that this form is only current in the spoken language of some of the groups within Yemen (as a biform of נִתְפַּעַל), and not actually in MH.[205]

The general conclusion is that there is no place for the *binyanim* שפעל/ נשתפעל or הפעל in a grammar of Mishnaic Hebrew; the forms alleged to belong to these groups are to be classified as quadriliteral verbs. The נִתְפַּעַל form of the Yemeni tradition also does not belong to the grammar of MH.

20.6 Conclusion

§ 33 The verbal *binyanim* of Mishnaic Hebrew can be divided into two groups: the common ones, of which there are six, and the uncommon ones, of

203 Segal 1936:122, § 212.

204 מְהַלְקֵט means "feeding chickens by hand," while מַלְקִיט means "throwing food on the ground and causing the chickens to gather it up" (see Segal 1936:123).

205 This was confirmed by Morag and Gluska, and now see what Morag said in his eulogy for Yitzḥak Shivtiel, in ספר שבטיאל – מחקרים בלשון העברית ובמסורות העדות (Ramat Gan, 1992), 17.

which there are eight. They are enumerated above (§ 2). All of the relevant details have been discussed above, in the appropriate sections of our discussion. We have argued that among the eight uncommon *binyanim* are two which stand on their own: פֻּעַל, which is on its way out of the language (in the scribal tradition, it is not clear that there are more than two or three certain forms, and the vocalization traditions add a few more examples), and נִתַּפְעַל, which is apparently on its way into the language but did not become widespread prior to the cessation of Hebrew as a spoken language.

The other six uncommon *binyanim* should be seen as alternative forms of the regular *binyanim* (and this is one of the primary theses of this chapter):

- The regular *binyan* נִפְעַל supports two less common forms, נֶפְעַל and נִפְּעַל, both of which are related to specific classes of verbs. The former began with I-*nun* verbs and then spread to similar verbs and some others; the latter exists primarily with II-*waw* roots and other similar verbs, as well as one other verb, ניטמאתה, ניטמאתי.[206]
- פִּעֵל and נִתְפַּעַל (with gemination of the second radical and a short vowel immediately preceding) support uncommon series of forms. Alongside the heavy quadriliteral and the heavy lengthened forms (for II-*waw* and geminate roots), there are two other secondary sets of forms: the heavy non-geminated, פֵּעֵל and נִתְפָּעַל (with a non-geminated middle radical and a long vowel immediately preceding), and perhaps also פּוֹעֵל and נִתְפּוֹעֵל (the heavy lengthened forms with strong verbs) are reflexes of the classic heavy geminated verbs. Some of these secondary forms in the last sets are the products of analogy or other influences from nouns, such as מְאָבְקִים from אָבָק, נִשְׁתָּפָה from שָׁפוּי, נִתְקוֹצָה from קוֹץ, and רֵקֵן under the influence of רֵיקָן. Synchronically, however, these verbs have all been absorbed into the *binyanim* mentioned.

This presentation has not focused on the diachronic development of these forms (although when necessary, we have dealt with that aspect as well), but attempts to present everything from a synchronic perspective.

§ 34 When looking at the participles, the regular verbs can be divided into eight *binyanim*:

A. 1-2-3 ("light") נִפְעָל – פָּעוּל – פּוֹעֵל
B. 4-5-6 ("heavy") מִתְפַּעֵּל – מְפֻעָּל – מְפַעֵּל
C. 7-8 (causative) מֻפְעָל – מַפְעִיל

206 It should be reiterated that the antiquity of this reading is not known.

Notes:

A. In the participle of the *pi'ēl* verbs, Yalon argued for the possibility that there were passive forms on the pattern מְפַעָּל (or מְפֻעָּל), borrowed from Aramaic. His conclusion was based on defective spellings, without the *waw* after the first root radical, but there is no evidence for this from the reading traditions. In some of the cases, in fact, these may actually be מְפַעֵּל forms.

B. In the heavy *binyanim* – in all their secondary series – there are, in practice, three types of participles:
1. מתגלגל – מגולגל – מגלגֵל
2. משתעבד – משועבד – משעבד

In the heavy *binyan* without gemination in the *'ayin*, the three are מְפָעֵל (e.g., מְשָׁלֵק) – מְפֹעָל (e.g., מְאוֹכָלִין) – מִתְפָּעֵל (e.g., מִתְאָנֵחַ).

§ 35 The system of verbal nouns depends on just three foundation:
נִפְעַל – קַל
נִתְפַּעֵּל – פִּעֵּל
הֻפְעַל – הִפְעִיל

In the verbal nouns, the nominal abstractions of the verbs, the language operates with a far more limited and restricted system. The verbal noun of the *binyan* קַל is the same as that of the נִפְעַל; the very common pattern פְּעִילָה,[207] for example, is productive for every verb in the *Qal* (including the passive participle) and the *nif'al*. This is the case, for instance, with the noun אֲכִילָה – it is the noun of אָכַל, אָכוּל, and נֶאֱכַל; the word שְׁמִירָה is the noun of שָׁמַר, שְׁמוּרָה, and נִשְׁמַר. The same is true for every pattern of verbal noun, such as *pə'ālā*; the noun זְעָקָה is the verbal noun of זָעַק and נִזְעַק, and the noun תְּקָלָה is the verbal noun of נִתְקַל (this verb has no *qal* form).[208] The same is true for the patterns פִּעּוּל and פַּעָּלָה,[209] the verbal nouns of verbs in the פִּעֵּל, of מְפֻעָּל,

207 Kutscher (1977:110–133) has an excellent presentation of the patterns of the *qal* verbal nouns (he counts 16 different patterns, and a few more uncertain ones). For the present purposes we have sufficed with two of them.

208 It is nearly certain that the original forms of this noun were תְּקָלָה, which is the reading found in many communities and in old *siddurim*, or תַּקָלָה, as it is read by the Yemenis. The vocalization תַּקָּלָה (MS K, m. Berakhot 4:2; m. Sanhedrin 7:4; m. Para 9:5) reflects analogy to תַּקָּנָה, a close semantic and literary partner, as noted by Kutscher (1977:120). There are other transitions within nouns from pattern to pattern, including transitions of nouns from the verbal noun pattern of one *binyan* to that of another. Thus, for the verb נָשָׂא אישה, the verbal noun is נִישּׂוּאִין, the *pi''ūl* pattern (in the plural), because of the close connection to other words in the semantic field of familial relations (אֵירוּסִין, קִידּוּשִׁין, גֵּירוּשִׁין, and more).

209 Sharvit (2005:181) established that פִּעּוּל is more common than פַּעָּלָה.

and of נִתְפַּעֵל; thus שִׁיבּוּשׁ is used alongside שִׁיבֵּשׁ, alongside מְשַׁבֵּשׁ, and alongside נִשְׁתַּבֵּשׁ. Similarly, the הֶפְעֵל and הַפְעָלָה patterns[210] are used for הִפְעִיל and הֻפְעַל verbs, so הֶקְטֵר and הַקְטָרָה are used for the verbs הִקְטִיר and הֻקְטַר.

I have been teaching the description just presented in my classroom lectures for many years, on the basis of my own study of the data in the Mishna.[211] The excellent and comprehensive investigation of this topic carried out by Sharvit regarding all of Tannaitic literature confirms this presentation very clearly with regard to the issues of verbal nouns.[212]

§ 36 To conclude: we have established that there are fourteen *binyanim* within Mishnaic Hebrew, which essentially are reflexes of eight different patterns. There are six common *binyanim* (קַל-נִפְעַל, פִּעֵל-נִתְפַּעַל, and הִפְעִיל-הֻפְעַל), and six uncommon *binyanim* which are derived from the common ones and are alternative forms of theirs (נֻפְעַל and נִפְעַל, פֻּעַל and פִּעֵל, נִתְפָּעַל and פּוֹעֵל and נִתְפּוֹעַל), and finally, two more uncommon patterns (פֻּעַל, which was on its way out of the language, and נִתַּפְעַל, which was on its way in).[213]

If we arrange the *binyanim* according to the participial forms, there are eight common *binyanim*; if we arrange them according to their verbal nouns, there are only three common ones.

---

210 Again, Sharvit (*ibid.*) pointed out that הַפְעָלָה is more common than הֶפְעֵל.

211 At least since the early 1990s, this has been how I taught the material.

212 See Sharvit 2005:181 ff.

213 An overly-detailed presentation of this issue, including many irrelevant details, can be found in the study by Har-Zahav (1930:155–175); no fewer than 86 *binyanim* are enumerated, counted, examined, and included in his lists. There is no need to say more. On the other hand, it is well worth considering the perspectives reflected in the medieval grammatical treatises presented very lucidly by Eldar (1980).

21 The Formation of the *Nif'al* III-*yod* Participle in Mishnaic Hebrew

§ 1 The present study is devoted to the masc. sing. form of the *nif'al* participle of III-*yod* verbs. The investigation of this grammatical phenomenon sheds new light on the grammar of Mishnaic Hebrew as reflected in manuscripts and printed editions of the Mishna. The results of our study are interesting and unexpected and clearly demonstrate differences between the various traditions of the manuscripts and the oral traditions.

21.1 The Reading Traditions in the Bible

§ 2 In the two main traditions of the Bible, viz., the Tiberian and Babylonian vocalization traditions,[1] the dominant form of the *nif'al* masc. sing. participle of verbs III-*yod* in both the Tiberian and Babylonian systems is vocalized with *segol*, on the pattern נִפְעֶה: נִבְזֶה (Ps 15:4), וְנִקְלֶה (1 Sam 18:23).[2] There are occasional forms in both traditions, however, vocalized with *qameṣ*, on the pattern נִפְעָה, e.g. Tiberian הַנִּלְוָה (Isa 56:3), הַנִּרְאָה (1 Kgs 11:9; Dan 8:1), נִרְאָה אתה ה' (Num 14:14), and Babylonian ונקלָה (Ps 38:8), נספָּה, etc.[3] The original form is with *segol* (as are all forms of the masc. sing. participle in all conjugations); the *qameṣ* is the result of analogy with the form of the perfect. Rather than reflecting the replacement of the masculine form by the feminine, as one might understand from I. Yeivin's discussion,[4] this is actually part of a general process of the identification of the participle with the perfect, and a subsequent merger of the two in non-transitive verbs and passive conjugations, as Z. Ben-Ḥayyim has shown.[5] (Sometimes the form of the perfect is the result of analogy with the participle, which also leads to the identification and merger of the two tenses. For example, such an analogy is regularly at work in the *nif'al* of strong verbs in the Babylonian vocalization tradition,[6] in the Yemenite

1 See § 23a below.

2 See Yeivin 1985:717.

3 See Yeivin 1985:717, including material from the Tiberian Bible (in n. 39).

4 *Ibid.*

5 See Ben-Ḥayyim 1957–1977, 5:139; see also Bar-Asher 1977b:94.

6 See Yeivin 1985:498 and especially Naeh 1989:126.

tradition,[7] and to a certain extent also in the tradition of MS Parma B of the Order Ṭeharot.[8])

§ 3 It should be noted that modern Biblical grammarians have doubted the originality of the participial forms with *qameṣ*, as can be seen in the discussions of Gesenius[9] and Joüon[10] regarding the forms הַנִּלְוָה and הַנִּרְאָה. In their opinion, the forms have been mistakenly vocalized as perfect verbs in place of the regular participial forms הַנִּלְוֶה and הַנִּרְאֶה. Indeed, the view of modern grammarians, that the *nir'āh* form is always the perfect and the *nir'eh* form is always the participle, has been anticipated by earlier grammarians such as Ibn Ezra. He did not claim they were mistakes, but rather argued that the forms with *qameṣ* were indeed perfect verbs and not participles. Cf, e.g., Ibn Ezra on the verse אחרי הַנִּרְאָה אלי בתחלה (Dan 8:1): אחרי הנראה – אשר נראה, כמו העיר ההוללה,[11] ההלכוא אתו[12]. In other words, he understood הַנִּרְאָה as a regular form of the perfect preceded by the relative *hē*.[13] We do not, however, necessarily have to accept this explanation if we assess the extent of the phenomenon in the traditions of Mishnaic Hebrew[14] and if we realize that this is a linguistic phenomenon which is part of a general process in which the form of the participle was analogized with the form of the perfect.

21.2 The Mishnaic Hebrew Traditions that have been Studied

§ 4 Yeivin has shown[15] that the Babylonian vocalization tradition of Mishnaic Hebrew contains two different forms, נראֶה and נראָה. This is especially true in younger Babylonian sources. The tradition of MS Parma A pre-

7 See Shivtiel 1971:225.
8 See Bar-Asher 1990c:§ 96 (pp. 85–86).
9 GKC § 138k (p. 447).
10 Joüon and Muraoka 1991:§ 145e.
11 איך אבדת נושבת מימים העיר הַהֻלָּלָה (Ezek 26:17).
12 אנשי המלחמה הֶהָלְכוּא אתו (Josh 10:24).
13 See also Ibn Ezra on other passages אשר עין בעין נִרְאָה אתה ה' – (Num 14:14): נראה פעל עבר וטעמו נראת אתה ה' וכו'. Similarly, אשר אין נַעֲשָׂה פתגם מעשה הרעה מהרה (Eccl 8:11): בעבור שלא נעשה דבר נקמה ותשלום ותגמול על מעשה הרעה מהרה. He replaces אשר אין נעשה by שלא נעשה.
14 See §§ 4, 6, 7 below.
15 See Yeivin 1985:717. In the light of Naeh's work (Naeh 1989:60, 243), one should qualify Yeivin's remarks since there is free fluctuation in MS Vatican 66 to the Sifra between *qameṣ/pataḥ (segol)* in the different categories of III-*yod* verbs, and, therefore, the fluctuation of the two forms in the manuscript has no relevance for our inquiry. Consequently, only in younger Babylonian sources is there clear evidence of the exchange of נפעֶה/נפעָה.

serves only the first type, i.e. the second root letter with a *segol*,[16] נִפְעֶה:[17] הַנֶּעֱשֶׂה, נֶהְנֶה, נתלֶה, נִרְאֶה, נִיפְדֶּה, נכסֶה.[18] A similar picture emerges from the tradition of the autograph of Rambam's Mishna with commentary, as demonstrated by T. Zurawel:[19] נִתְלֶה, נִרְאֶה, נִפְדֶה, וְנִכְפֶה, נֶהְנֶה. She noted that there is one form with a *qameṣ* in the commentary to the Mishna: הַנֶּהְנָה.[20]

The Yemenite tradition apparently is only familiar with the form with *qameṣ*, as Y. Shivtiel has determined:[21] נהנָה, נפדָה, נתלָה, נראָה. In systematically examining MS Jerusalem (from Yemen), I found about 40 examples from the three Orders that the manuscript contains, all of which are vocalized with *qameṣ*: נִפְדָה, נַעְשָׂה, נִכְפָּה, נִכסָה, נִהנָה, נִגְלָה, נַאְפָה, נִתְלָה, נִרְאָה.[22] The same is true for the tradition of Djerba, which was described by K. Katz:[23] נִהְנָה, נִתְלָה, נִרְאָה, נִפְדָה.

21.3 Other Traditions of Mishnaic Hebrew

§ 5 So far research into this aspect of Mishnaic Hebrew has ignored the findings in the most important Mishnaic manuscripts: MSS Kaufmann, Parma B, and Antonin, to which MS Paris should be added. An investigation of these manuscripts and the Livorno edition[24] again reveals the diversity of Mishnaic

16 As is well known, MS Parma A and the autograph of Rambam's Mishna with commentary show a free interchange of *segol/ṣērē* as well as *pataḥ/qameṣ*.

17 See Haneman 1980a:§ 213 (p. 358). The only example he cites with *paṭaḥ* (= *qāmeṣ*) – נהיַה – is in the blessing שהכל נהיה בדברו. He explains this as a perfect form (see p. 357 n. 210).

18 On the pointing of the form הַנֶּעֱשֶׂה, see § 17 below.

19 See Zurawel 2004:161.

20 See the important remarks in Zurawel 2004:11–12.

21 See Shivtiel 1971:213.

22 I found the following forms in MS Jerusalem: נַאְפָה (m. Menahot 11:1,9), נִכסָה ... נִגְלָה (m. Sanhedrin 2:1), נִהנָה (m. Baba Qamma 9:10; m. Baba Meṣi'a 4:8; m. Karetot 3:9; m. Me'ila 5:1,2), נִכפָּה (m. Bekhorot 7:5), נַעְשָׂה (m. Sanhedrin 8:1,2,3,4 [3×]; m. Avoda Zara 3:3;4:4), הַנַּעְשָׂה (m. Shevu'ot 1:3,6,7 [m. Shavu'ot 1:2 is written שנעשָׂה in place of הנעשה, which occurs in other versions, and it is possible that it should be explained as the 3 masc. sing. perfect]; m. Ohalot 18:1); וְנעשָׂה (in "Qinyan Tora" – Avot 6:1); נִפדָּה (m. Menahot 10:4; m. 'Arakhin 8:1; m. Me'ila 6:2), נִרְאָה (m. Bekhorot 3: 4[2×]; m. 'Arakhin 2:2; m. Nega'im 2:4 [3×]; m. Miqva'ot 10:8 [2×]), הַנִּרְאֶה (m. Nega'im 11:4; m. Para 2:5); the manuscript reads הַמַּרְאַה in m. Miqva'ot 7:5, as against הַנִּרְאֶה in older manuscripts (see § 7 below); נִתלָה (m. Sanhedrin 6:4 [2x]; m. Zavim 2:4). The only example that I found in MS Nahum to the Order Mo'ed is vocalized הַנַּעְשָׂה (m. Yoma 7:3).

23 Katz 1977:312–313.

24 Add now also the Amsterdam edition (see § 22 in the Appendix).

Hebrew traditions. I believe that the findings reflect, to a great extent, an authentic linguistic reality, and are not the result of innovations that took place in the process of transmission during the Middle Ages.

21.4 MS Antonin

§ 6 MS Antonin (to the Order Ṭeharot) has only 10 examples of the 3 masc. sing. *nif'al* of III-*yod* verbs, of which seven are vocalized. The data show an almost even relationship between the forms נִפְעֶה and נִפְעָה. There are four examples of נִפְעֶה:[25] הנראֵה (m. Para 2:5[7]) and נראֵה (m. Nega'im 2:4 [3×]); as against three of נִפְעָה: הַנִּרְאָה (m. Nega'im 11:4), נִתְלַה ... וְנִתְלָה (m. Zavim 2:4[5].) הנראה (m. Miqva'ot 7:5[7]) and נראה ... נראה (m. Miqva'ot 10:8) are unvocalized.

The distribution of the two forms is not conditioned.[26] It would appear that they are free variants; this is shown by the two different vocalizations in the expression הכל הולך אחרי הנראה: הַנִּרְאָה (m. Nega'im 11:4), הנראֵה (m. Para 2:5[7].)

21.5 MS Parma B

§ 7 There are 11 occurrences of the masc. sing. *nif'al* participle in verbs III-*yod* in the Order Ṭeharot of MS Parma B. This manuscript, too, preserves two different forms, נִפְעֶה, which is found only three times, as against נִפְעָה, which is attested eight times. The difference is not only one of quantity.

נִפְעֶה is found in הכל הולך אחר הַנִּרְאֶה (m. Nega'im 11:4; m. Para 2:5[7]; m. Miqva'ot 7:5[7]). We should add that at least in Miqva'ot there is late evidence of another reading: הכל הולך אחרי הַמַּרְאֶה (for הנראה); this is the reading in MS Jerusalem, the Livorno edition, and modern editions.[27] The older manuscripts, however, read in all three passages הנראה (MSS Kaufmann, Parma A, Antonin, Paris, and also MS Cambridge).[28]

נִפְעָה is attested in:

A. כיצד בוצרין בית-הפרס, מזין על האדם ועל הכלים ושונין ובוצרין ומוציאין חוץ לבית פרס ... אמר ר' יוסי במה דבר' אמו', בכרם הַנַּעֲשָׂה בית פרס, אבל הנוטע בית פרס ימכר לשוק (m. Ohalot 18:1);

25 *Ṣērē/segol* and *qameṣ/pataḥ* also fluctuate freely in MS Antonin.

26 Unlike in the traditions of MSS Parma B, Kaufmann, Paris, and the Livorno edition (as described in § 7 ff.).

27 Thus in all the modern editions I examined.

28 As cited by Lowe in his edition of MS Cambridge.

B. כיצד ראיית הנגע האיש נִרְאָה כעודר וכמוסק זתים ... כשם שהוא נִרְאָה לנגעו כך הוא נִרְאָה לתגלחתו (m. Nega‘im 2:4);
C. חץ שהוא תחוב באדם בזמן שהוא נִרְאָה חוצץ אם אינו נִרְאָה טובל ואוכל בתרומתו (m. Miqva’ot 10:8);
D. הזב מטמא את המשכב בחמישה דרכים ... עומד יושב שוכב נִתְלָה ונשען ... עומד יושב שוכב ונִתְלָה ונשען במגע ובמשא (m. Zavim 2:4[5]).

§ 8 If one looks at the contexts in which the forms of the masc. sing. *nif‘al* participle of verbs III-*yod* occur in MS Parma B (described above), one discovers that the distribution of the two forms is conditioned. When the participle functions nominally one finds the old form with *segol* (נִפְעֶה), and when the participle functions verbally the form with *qameṣ* (נִפְעָה) appears. In the sentence הכל הולך אחרי הַנִּרְאֶה, the participle functions nominally. הַנִּרְאֶה is a passive form, i.e., a static form that has in fact become a noun, and, consequently, one can understand how it was exchanged with the noun מַּרְאֶה[29] in some of the witnesses.[30]

In the other examples in MS Parma B the forms of the participle clearly function as verbs. This is true for נִרְאָה (m. Nega‘im 2:4 [3×]; m. Miqva’ot 10:8 [2×]); נִתְלָה (m. Zavim 2:4[5] 2×). In בכרם הַנַּעֲשָׂה בית פרס (m. Ohalot 18:1), נַעֲשָׂה is a dynamic and not static participle, i.e., it functions verbally.[31]

§ 9 The situation described in MS Parma B is unique in two respects: a) the most common participial form occurs with *qameṣ* (נִפְעָה; over 72 %); b) more importantly, it reflects a conditioned distribution; the older form of the participle נִרְאֶה acts as a noun, whereas the younger form נִרְאָה and its congeners function as verbs.

These data correspond to what we know about participial biforms in Mishnaic Hebrew. This is true for the relationship between רַב, חַי, and נָדוֹן (the

---

29 See the beginning of § 7 above.

30 It is possible, of course, to argue that the reading הַמַּרְאֶה for הנראה has resulted from the graphic exchange of the letters ני (*nun* and *yod*) and מ (*mem*), a phenomenon that is found in old manuscripts (cf., e.g., Epstein 1948:1255, 1308). If, indeed, graphic confusion is responsible, one must admit that the version הַמַּרְאֶה was tolerated (in several witnesses) since it did not entail replacing an actual verb (active participle) by a noun, but rather a noun by a noun. Such a replacement would not have been tolerated when the participle functioned verbally, e.g., in a sentence like האיש ניראה כעודר וכמוסק זתים (m. Nega‘im 2:4), where even if a graphic confusion of ני led to מ, such a mistake would not have survived in different witnesses and would surely have been corrected.

31 There is no need to add that the prefixed *hē* (הנעשה) in this case functions as the relative pronoun and not the definite article.

older forms of these participles) as against רָבָה, חָיָה,[32] and נָדוֹן[33] (younger forms of the participle), as demonstrated by G. Haneman. Similar is the relationship between נִזָּק and נִזּוֹק, as discussed by M. Mishor.[34] נָדוֹן, חַי, רַב, and נִזָּק no longer functioned as verbs, but rather served as nominal forms (nouns or adjectives), whereas רָבָה, חָיָה, נִדּוֹן, and נִזּוֹק functioned verbally. One must stress, however, that the distribution and functions of נִפְעֶה (נִרְאֶה) and נִפְעָה (נִרְאָה) are preserved, at this point, only in the tradition of MS Parma B. Although this is a reliable manuscript, whose antiquity is not doubted, the certainty of this (and all) linguistic feature(s) increases with the number of sources that preserve it.

21.6 MS Kaufmann, MS Paris, and the Livorno Edition

§ 10 It is clear from an investigation of MS Kaufmann, which yielded approximately 70 examples,[35] that the prevalent form is נִפְעֶה: נֶאֱפֶה (m. Menahot 11:1,9), נִיגְלֶה[36]... נִיגְלֶה[37] (m. Sanhedrin 2:1), נֶהְנֵה (m. Terumot 3:8), נֶהְנֶה (m. Nedarim 3:11 [5×][38] and another 11 occurrences elsewhere in the Mishna), נִיכְפֶּה (m. Bekhorot 7:5[6]), נִיפְדֶּה (m. Ma'aser Sheni 3:6,10 [2×];[39]m. 'Arakhin 8:1; m. Me'ila 6:2), נִפְדֶּה (m. Menahot 10:4), נִקְנֶה (m. Qiddushin 1:2,3), נִיקְנֶה (m. Qiddushin 1:2), נִרְאֶה (m. Kil'ayim 5:1,3; m. Nega'im 2:4 [3×]; 1:4 + 8×), נִירְאֶה (m. Kil'ayim 2:7;3:3), נִתְלֶה (m. Soṭa 3:8), נִיתְלֶה (m. Sanhedrin 6:4 [2×]).[40] Altogether נִפְעֶה is attested 50 times.

---

32 See Haneman 1980a:332–334 and for more details Haneman 1980c. We have examined MS Parma B and found that the distribution of forms corresponds to that described by Haneman. Our results will be presented in a study of the tradition of MS Parma B.

33 See Haneman 1980a:283–287.

34 See Mishor 1983:164–177 and especially pp. 172 ff.

35 Although the data was not collected in an exhaustive reading of the entire manuscript, I have reason to believe that most of the forms of the masc. sing. participle of III-*yod nif'al* are included here.

36 The *lamed* may be pointed with a *ṣērē*. (Fluctuation of *segol*/*ṣērē* and *pataḥ*/*qameṣ* is also attested at times in MS Kaufmann.)

37 The version attested in modern editions and in reliable manuscripts (such as MS Parma A) is הן נכסין והוא נגלה הן נגלין והוא נכסה (m. Sanhedrin 2:1). There is an error in MS Kaufmann: הן נכסים והוא ניגלה הן ניכ(נ)סין והוא ניגלה.

38 נהנה in the last occurrence in this mishna is added in the margin by a second hand.

39 ניפדה is unpointed in the third occurrence in this mishna.

40 The scribe who wrote and pointed the last pages of MS Kaufmann (his tradition differs from the tradition of the main vocalizer of MS Kaufmann) reads נִיתְלָה (m. Zavim 2:4 [2×]). See § 24.b below.

§ 11 Only the verb עשה, however, is attested in MS Kaufmann, with *qameṣ* in all 16 of the examples:[41] שהוא נֶעֱשָׂה (m. Nedarim 9:2 [2×]), כל הנֶעֱשַׂה (m. Qiddushin 1:6), הוא נֶעֱשָׂה (m. Sanhedrin 8:1; m. 'Avoda Zara 3:3), אינו נֶעֱשָׂה (m. Sanhedrin 8:2,3,4 [2×]; m. 'Avoda Zara 4:8), שעיר הנֶעֱשָׂה (m. Shevu'ot 1:2,3,6,7), ושער הנֶעֱשָׂה (m. Yoma 7:3), בכרם הנֶעֱשָׂה (m. Ohalot 18:1).

§ 12 The data in MS Paris correspond almost completely to what we found in MS Kaufmann (as described above). All in all, there are 46 examples of נִפְעֶה (נִפְעֵה):[42] ונאפֵה (m. Menahot 11:1), נגלֶה (m. Sanhedrin 2:1),[43] נהנֶה (m. Terumot 3:8), נהנֵה (m. Nedarim 3:11[9] and another 15×[44]), נִפְדֶּה (m. Ma'aser Sheni 3:10 [3×]), נפדֶה (m. 'Arakhin 8:1 [3×]),[45] נקנֶה (m. Qiddushin 1:2 [2×],3), נראֶה (m. Kil'ayim 2:7; m. Nega'im 2:4 [2×][46] and another 12×), נתלֶה (m. Soṭa 3:8; m. Sanhedrin 6:4 [2×]).

In only three passages do we find a *qameṣ* in a verb other than עשה: נֶאֱפָה (m. Menahot 11:9[11]), הַנֶּהֱנָה (m. Me'ila 5:1),[47] נִתְלָה (m. Zavim 2:4[48]).[49]

In the verb עשה, the forms of the participle are always vocalized with *qameṣ* (*paṯaḥ*), e.g. נַעֲשָׂה ... נַעֲשֵׂה (m. Nedarim 9:2), הנֶעֱשָׂה (m. Yoma 7:3), הנֶעֱשָׂה (m. Shevu'ot 1:3), and another 13 occurrences.[50]

§ 13 The data in the Livorno edition correspond to a considerable extent to our findings in MSS Kaufmann and Paris:[51] נִגְלֶה (1×), נֶהֱנֶה (18×), נִכְסֶה (1×),

41 Katz 1977:313: "In MS Kaufmann there are forms with *qameṣ*, e.g. הנֶעֱשָׂה ... (m. Qiddushin 1:6), הנֶעֱשָׂה ... (m. Yoma 7:3) alongside forms with *segol*, e.g. נִקְנֶה (m. Qiddushin 1:2), ... נֶהְנֶה ... (m. Nedarim 3:11), וְנִיפְדֶּה ... (m. Ma'aser Sheni 3:4)." She did not conclude from the few examples that she cited that the participle נֶעֱשָׂה should be treated differently from the participles of other verbs.

42 Because of the many fluctuations in MS Paris between *segol* and *ṣērē*, and between these two vowel signs and the *ḥaṭef-segol*, we shall only mark the final vowel of the participle. Almost all the forms cited here are fully pointed in the manuscript.

43 There is also a copyist error in this mishna. MS Paris reads הם נכנסים והוא נגלה (see n. 37 above). The copyist made a mistake with the verb נכסין and omitted the second sentence הן נגלין והוא נכסה.

44 It is pointed כנְהֱנֶה in m. Karetot 3:9 (11) [note the *nun* with *shewa* in place of the *segol*].

45 There is a mistake in m. Me'ilah 6:2 in MS Paris where one finds נפדית in place of נפדה: שההקדש נפדית בכסף ובשוה כסף.

46 The first occurrence of נראה in this mishna was deleted by mistake leaving האיש כעודר וכמוסק instead of האיש נראה כעודר וכמוסק.

47 Was the first hand the one that pointed the *qameṣ* beneath the *nun*?

48 This sentence, including the second occurrence in this mishna, was omitted in MS Paris.

49 The form נכפה (m. Bekhorot 7:5) is unpointed in MS Paris. It is well known that rare forms are often unpointed in this manuscript. (This is evidence of the laxness of the vocalizer's tradition.) See Bar-Asher 1980:53 ff.

50 For the passages see § 10 above. One should also note that in the additional occurrence of נעשה in this manuscript, the participle is pointed with *qameṣ*: וְנֶעְשָׂה כמעין המתגבר (Abot 6:2).

51 For the passages see § 10 above on MS Kaufmann. We shall comment on the special forms.

נִכְפֶּה (1×), נִקְנֶה (3×), נִפְדֶּה (4×),[52] נִפְדֵּה (1×), נִרְאֶה (14×),[53] נִתְלֶה (m. Sanhedrin 6:4 [2×]; m. Zavim 2:4 [2×]).[54] There are a total of 47 examples with *segol* occurring in eight different roots.

There is a *qameṣ* in two attestations of two of the verbs: הַנִּרְאָה (m. Nega'im 11:4),[55] נִתְלָה (m. Soṭa 3:8). Two additional verbs are regularly pointed with *qameṣ*: וְנֶאֱפָה, (m. Menahot 11:1) נֶאֱפָה (m. Menahot 11:9),[56] נַעֲשָׂה (m. Yoma 7:3; m. Abot 6:2,[57] and another 17×).

§ 14 In fact, the participial form with *segol* prevails in MS Kaufmann in nine verbs (about 50 occurrences), but the verb עשה is regularly vocalized with *qameṣ*: נֶעֱשָׂה. The two additional witnesses are almost identical to it with regard to the vocalization of most verbs as well as the vocalization of נעשׂה. In MS Paris there are three exceptional forms: נֶאֱפָה (1× out of 2×), נֶהֱנָה (1× out of 18×), נִתְלָה (1× out of 4×). In the Livorno edition there are four exceptional forms: נֶאֱפָה (2× out of 2×), נִרְאָה (1× out of 15×), נִתְלָה (1x out of 4×).[58] It would seem that these are late deviations from the crystallized tradition reflected in MS Kaufmann; apparently, the two relatively late witnesses (MS Paris and the Livorno edition) show a mixing of different traditions[59] in which נִפְעָה occurred with the verb נַעֲשָׂה as well as with other verbs.

The regular vocalization of MS Kaufmann (and to a great extent also in MS Paris and the Livorno edition) is נִפְעֶה, and only in the verb עשה does one consistently find נֶעֱשָׂה (נַעֲשָׂה). What is the reason for this?

§ 15 It is clear that one should not assume that analogy with the 3 masc. sing. perfect form took place only in the verb עשה. If analogy is responsible, it is difficult to understand why the analogy should work only with this verb (one should keep in mind that there are no other verbs in MS Kaufmann in which the participle has *qameṣ*). In my opinion, the reason lies in the special nature of this verb (עשה). I believe that this is additional evidence that עשה was inflected as a III-*'aleph* verb, i.e., נֶעֱשָׂה[60] like נִקְרָא, נִמְצָא, נִבְרָא.

---

52 In m. Me'ila 6:2 the participle is pointed with *ṣērē*.

53 נִרְאָה occurs, however, once (see below).

54 נִתְלָה is attested once (see below).

55 The tradition of the Livorno edition differs in the three passages in which the expression הכל הולך אחר הנראה occurs: הַנִּרְאָה (m. Nega'im 11:4), הַנִּרְאֶה (m. Para 2:5), הַמַּרְאָה (m. Miqva'ot 7:5).

56 It is certain from the context that we are dealing with forms of the participle and not the perfect (cf., e.g., Menahot 11:1: שתי הלחם נלושות אחת אחת ונאפות אחת אחת, לחם הפנים נלוש אחד אחד ונאפה שנים שנים).

57 See n. 50 above.

58 Note that in two of the verbs נֶאֱפָה, נִתְלָה in MS Paris and in the Livorno edition agree in vocalization (and yet they occur in different passages).

59 It is no wonder that in the late witnesses the mixing of traditions increases.

60 See n. 74 below.

§ 16 Indeed, there is evidence from several Mishnaic Hebrew sources that this verb was partially inflected as a III-' verb:[61] העשי (t. Pesahim 8:5 [2×], MS Vienna; MS Erfurt only in the second occurrence), העשיא ... העסיא (ibid., MS London), and שהעסיא (ibid., 8:4, MS London).[62] Note also כְּמַעֲשִׂיאֵיהֶם in the Babylonian tradition.[63]

It is significant that this is the only III-*yod* verb in all manuscripts of Mishnaic literature in which the inflection of the third person of *qal* in the perfect with object pronominal suffixes is that of III-': עֲשָׂאוֹ, עֲשָׂאָהּ, עֲשָׂאָן, עֲשָׂאוּהוּ, עֲשָׂאוּהָ like מְצָאוֹ, נְשָׂאוֹ, מְצָאָהּ, etc.[64] We have not found any evidence of the type עֲשָׂיוֹ, עֲשָׂיָהּ, עֲשָׂיָן.[65] It should also be noted that all other III-*yod* verbs in the best manuscripts are inflected as III-*yod* verbs:[66] דְּחָיוֹ (m. Makhshirin 5:1), טְלָיָיהּ (m. Kelim 27:6[8]), כְּפָיָיהּ (m. Para 7:8), קְנָיָיהּ (m. Nidda 5:4).[67]

Hence, נעשׂה is a III-*'aleph* verb in the tradition of MSS Kaufmann, Paris, and the Livorno edition. The orthography with *hē* should not prevent us from taking נעשה as a III-*'aleph* verb.[68] One must say, then, that in MS Kaufmann and to a slightly lesser extent in MS Paris and the Livorno edition the *nif'al*

61 The III-*'aleph* verbal class was not completely absorbed into III-*yod* in Mishnaic Hebrew. A considerable portion of the inflection of III-*'aleph* was preserved as shown by Haneman (1980a:431–442). This has become even clearer to me from my examination of the tradition of MS Parma B.

62 But שהעשה in MS Vienna (like שהעשו t. San. 2:11) and שעישה in MS Erfurt.

63 See Yeivin 1985:683.

64 It is possible that שהעשיא, מעשיאיהם were preserved because there are no similar forms in the Bible (the *hif'il* of עשה does not exist) and because forms like עֲשָׂאוֹ / עֲשָׂאָן are very frequent in Mishnaic Hebrew. The Biblical forms in the III-*yod* verbal class are of the type עֲשָׂהוּ, עָשָׂם (see n. 75 below).

65 One who argues that the *'aleph* in עֲשָׂאוֹ, עֲשָׂאָהּ is a transition sound and *yōd* > *'aleph* (see, e.g., Sharvit 1988:57–58) is dealing with etymology or a phonetic process, whereas we are concerned with the result, i.e., the phonetic reality. The consonant of the third root letter is *'aleph*, it is found in עֲשָׂאוֹ like מְצָאוֹ, עֲשָׂאָהּ like נְשָׂאָהּ, and the verb acts in these forms like a III-' verb.

66 The data are taken from MS Parma B. The *yod* functions as a consonant in all III-*yod* verbs.

67 There are a few exceptions with *'aleph* in III-*yod* verbs in MS Kaufmann, e.g., בנאו (m. Eduyot 7:9). For details see Bar-Asher 1985:82.

68 I do not think that this is the explanation for the exceptional form נִתְלָה, which occurs in MS Paris and in the Livorno edition (see §§ 12–13 above); it is also the form found in the tradition of the second scribe of MS Kaufmann (see n. 40 above). Even though there is evidence in the Bible for תלה in III-*'aleph* – תְּלָאוּם (the *qerē* in 2 Sam 21:12), תְּלוּאִים (Deut 28:66, Hos 11:7) – one should not assume the same for the reading traditions of Mishnaic Hebrew without additional proof for the existence of the root תלא in Mishnaic Hebrew. It is more reasonable that נִתְלָה in some traditions of Mishnaic Hebrew, like other forms, is the consequence of a mixing of traditions in which *qāmeṣ* occurs in all verbs (see § 4 above and also § 24 below).

participle of III-*yod* verbs is inflected נִפְעֶה, with the exception of עשה, which is inflected like נִפְעָה, a III-*'aleph* participle.

§ 17 The tradition of MS Parma A differs somewhat with regard to the participle נעשה. (MS Parma A is also of Italian provenance like MSS Kaufman and Paris, and the Livorno edition.) The participle of all verbs in MS Parma A is vocalized with *segol* – נִפְעֶה.[69] One learns from Haneman[70] that the inflection of the participle of עשה is נעשָׂה alone. A more precise formulation, however, is needed: of the 17 occurrences of the participle נעשה, 14 are found in the unvocalized portions of the manuscript and only three are vocalized. In his discussion of the participle of *nif'al* III-*yod*, Haneman cited only one of the vocalized examples: הַנֶּעֱשֶׂה (m. Yoma 7:3). The other two are שהוא נַעֲשֶׂה סופר ... שהוא נַעֲשָׂה בית כנסת (m. Nedarim 9:2), and can be found in his treatment of verbs I-guttural.[71] He notes that the *segol* in the first occurrence is corrected from *qameṣ/pataḥ* and in the second was vocalized נעשָׂה. Consequently, we learn that in two of the three vocalized examples the participle was נעשָׂה/ נעשָׂה, as in the tradition of MS Kaufmann,[72] MS Paris, and the Livorno edition. It is not clear to me why Haneman was content to cite only the example of הַנֶּעֱשֶׂה in his treatment of the *nif'al* participle of III-*yod*.[73] In sum, the first hand in the manuscript vocalized נעשָׂה (2×) and נעשֶׂה (1×), whereas the reverse is true for the second hand: נעשָׂה (1×) and נעשֶׂה (2×).

21.7 Summary

§ 18 An examination of Mishnaic Hebrew traditions reveals that there were four principal ways of inflecting the masc. sing. *nif'al* participle of verbs III-*yod* in Mishnaic Hebrew.

a) The participle was consistently vocalized נִפְעָה in all verbs. This is the case in MSS Kaufmann, Parma A, and the autograph of Rambam's Mishna (there is one attestation of נִפְעֶה in the commentary, which may reflect another tradition), MS Paris, and the Livorno edition (in the latter two there are a few exceptional forms נִפְעֶה). Three of the witnesses – MS Kaufmann, MS Paris,

69 See § 4 above.

70 Haneman 1980a:358.

71 Haneman 1980a:125.

72 We have ignored MS Cambridge (ed. Lowe) in our description since it is not pointed. The consonantal text consistently shows forms with *hē* – נאפה, נהנה – from which one cannot learn anything. In one passage the final vowel is marked by *'āleph*: נהנא (m. Terumot 3:5). Does the orthography hint at *qameṣ* (= נהנָא) or perhaps [e] (= נהנֶא)?

73 Haneman 1980a:358.

and the Livorno edition – clearly distinguish between the forms of עש"ה: נעשָׂה (with a *qameṣ*), and the participle of other verbs. It appears that עש"ה was inflected as a III-*'aleph* verb נַעֲשָׂה[74] = נַעֲשָׂא like נִמְצָא, נִקְרָא;[75] there is also evidence in MS Parma A (two out of three attestations in the vocalization of

---

74 There is one participle with *segol* in the Tiberian Bible: ואשר היה נַעֲשָׂה ליום אחד (Neh 5:18). In addition there are quite a few attestations of נַעֲשָׂה as the 3 masc. sing. perfect, e.g., מה שהיה הוא שיהיה ומה שֶׁנַּעֲשָׂה הוא כי לא נַעֲשָׂה כפסח הזה (2 Kgs 23:22; see also v. 23) and שיעשה (Eccl 1:9). נַעֲשָׂה also appears as the fem. sing. participle: וכל מנחה אשר תאפה בתנור וכל נַעֲשָׂה במרחשת ... לכהן המקריב אותה לו תהיה (Lev 7:9), as explained by Ibn Ezra: וכל נעשה שם התאר לשון נקבה כמו 'אין אבן נראה' (מל"א ו,יח) כי לשון זכר, 'אשר היה נעשה ליום אחד'. Onqelos already understood it this way (דתתאפי ... דתתעביד) as did Sa'adia Ga'on.

In addition to these examples, there are 10 occurrences of נַעֲשָׂה in Ecclesiastes that merit a short discussion. Examine the following verses: 1:13;2:17;4:3;8:9,11,14,16,17;9:3,6. One of them is apparently the form of the participle: אשר אין נַעֲשָׂה פתגם מעשה הרעה (8:11). Despite Ibn Ezra's comments (see n. 13 above), it seems clear that this is a form of the participle. Translators and commentators have understood it this way, e.g., Tg. Qohelet (דלא מתעביד), the Peshiṭta (דלא מתעבדא), but not Rav Sa'adia Ga'on (ולמא לם ינפד – see the explanation of Y. Qafiḥ on the *Tafsir* of Sa'adia). In his commentary, A. Kahana was troubled by the syntax of נעשה as a feminine form, and as a result had to treat the noun פתגם as feminine. And what about the other occurrences, e.g., כי רע עלי המעשה שֶׁנַּעֲשָׂה תחת השמש (2:17)? Tg. Qohelet and the Peshiṭta took it as the perfect – (דאתעבד) דאתעביד; Sa'adia, on the other hand, translated it אלד'י יעמל, probably intending the participle. Similarly, what of וחלק אין להם עוד לעולם בכל אשר נעשה תחת השמש (9:6)? The Peshiṭta (דמתעבד), Sa'adia (מא יעמל), and Tg. Qohelet (ed. Sperber, דמתעביד; but cf. ed. Qafiḥ, דאתעביד) in their translations take נַעֲשָׂה as a participle. (There are several places, however, in which these targumim understand נַעֲשָׂה as a perfect form.)

The form is unequivocal in the plural. The perfect is attested once in Ecclesiastes, המעשים שֶׁנַּעֲשׂוּ תחת השמש (1:14), as is the participle, וראה את כל העשוקים אשר נַעֲשִׂים תחת השמש (4:1). Thus, there is a support for interpreting נַעֲשָׂה as a perfect as well as a participle.

Is the frequency of נַעֲשָׂה in the Tiberian Bible (those forms which can be understood as participles) the source of the regular pointing of נעשָׂה in different Mishnaic manuscripts? (Actually, it is only in MS Parma A that נֶעֱשֶׂה occurs with *segol* [once or twice].) An affirmative answer to this question would be based on the assumption that the vocalizer of MS Kaufman was completely dependent on the pointing of the Bible and had no independent tradition of his own. Such an assumption is no longer viable in the light of modern research into Mishnaic Hebrew. We must bear in mind that we have here a *possible* exegesis of the Tiberian pointing tradition, which consistently points the participle with *qameṣ* נַעֲשָׂה (and let us not forget that נַעֲשֶׂה does occur in Nehemiah as noted by Ibn Ezra) alongside the certain independence of the pointing tradition of MS Kaufmann, which has the participial forms pointed with *qameṣ* (נֶעֱשָׂה). It is possible to go even further and ask if all the forms of נַעֲשָׂה in Ecclesiastes are indeed participles; if so, does the Tiberian Biblical tradition also (as in MS Kaufmann and in related manuscripts) treat עשה as a III-ʾ verb? After all, both are late reading traditions (of Ecclesiastes and the Mishna) that are not far apart in time. Nonetheless, it must be remembered that נַעֲשָׂה in Ecclesiastes is still generally assumed to be a perfect.

75 One should view the forms נֶעֱשָׂה, עֲשָׂאוֹ/עֲשָׂאָן, מַעֲשִׂיאֵיהֶם, העשי/העשיא (= נֶעֱשָׂא) as isolated examples of the more widespread phenomenon of the transition from עשה (III-*yod*) to

the first hand) of a reading נִעְשָׂה. We do not know how the participle of נעשה was read in the autograph of Rambam's Mishna since there is no vocalized example.[76]

b) The consistent use of נִפְעָה in all verbs is attested only in the Yemenite tradition[77] and in the tradition of Djerba.

c) The mixed use of the two forms נִפְעֶה and נִפְעָה comes down to us in MS Antonin and is also known from the Babylonian tradition of Mishnaic Hebrew, primarily in the younger sources.[78] In the Babylonian tradition נפעֶה is more common than נפעָה;[79] in MS Antonin, however, the distribution is almost equal: נִפְעֶה 4×, נִפְעָה 3×. (Of course, one must exercise caution when dealing with so few examples.[80])

d) MS Parma B also has both נִפְעָה and נִפְעֶה; here, however, the distribution is conditioned: נִפְעֶה functions nominally and נִפְעָה verbally, similar to the doublets of other participles (רַב, חַי, נָדוֹן, נִזָּק function as nouns whereas רָבֶה, חָיֶה, נִדּוֹן, נִזּוֹק function as verbs).

§ 19 A final summary is now required. Manuscripts of the western type[81] – MSS Kaufmann, Parma A, Paris, and the Livorno edition – represent a linguistic situation in which only the old form, נִפְעֶה, is preserved. The participle נַעֲשָׂה is a special case that is related to a specific linguistic process, viz., the transition from III-*yod* to III-*'aleph*. (In MS Paris and the Livorno edition, which are younger, at times one finds נִפְעָה also in other verbs, apparently the result of a mixing of different traditions, which is reflected in other linguistic phenomena, too; there is some hesitancy in MS Parma A with regard to the verb עשה; however, in the vocalization of the first hand נעשָׂה 2× and נעשֶׂה 1×.)

עשא (III-*'aleph*); it is possible that the frequency of עשה in the Bible (more than 2600 occurrences) and the literary tradition of Hebrew, which never freed itself from the Biblical Hebrew norm, overwhelmed the existence of additional categories in Mishnaic Hebrew in which there was a transition from III-*yod* to III-*'aleph* in this verb (see n. 64 above).

76 See Zurawel 2004:161, who cited only vocalized forms of other verbs

77 In this study we have supplemented Shivtiel's description with the consistent evidence from MS Jerusalem. See the details in n. 22 above.

78 We have already noted that the fluctuation of the forms נפעֶה/נפעָה in MS Vatican 66 of the Sifra is insignificant, as determined by Naeh (n. 15 above). We refer here to the younger sources of Babylonian pointing, including Mishnaic manuscripts, which possess both forms.

79 So we understand from Yeivin 1985:717.

80 There is also a mixing of forms in both the Tiberian and Babylonian Biblical traditions; although נִפְעֶה is most frequent, there are also a few examples of נִפְעָה (see §§ 2–3 above). This fluctuation also occurs to a certain extent in those witnesses of the Mishna where נִפְעֶה is more common than נִפְעָה (as we found to be true in MS Paris, the Livorno edition, and the Amsterdam edition; see § 22 below).

81 See above, Chapter 19, § 8–9, 24–46.

Manuscripts of the eastern type[82] reflect a linguistic state in which the two forms נִפְעֶה and נִפְעָה existed side by side. This is the situation in MS Antonin and in Babylonian vocalized manuscripts, including the vocalized mishnayot.[83] MS Parma B reflects a further development in language: exploitation of the two forms in order to express semantic differentiation. The Yemenite tradition and the tradition of Djerba reflect a stage in which the younger form, נִפְעֶה, entirely displaced the older form, נִפְעָה.

§ 20 We have no reason to doubt the antiquity of these traditions, especially those that reveal a surprising consistency – MS Kaufmann, on the one hand, and MS Parma B, on the other. May we assume that originally there were two traditions of inflecting the *nif'al* participle in verbs III-*yod* in the living language, and that in one of the traditions נִפְעֶה was the rule (with the exception of the participle נֶעֱשָׂה, which was treated as a different verbal class), and in the other both forms coexisted at first without distinction? Is it possible that the latter tradition further developed a semantic differentiation between the two forms (as reflected in MS Parma B)? Moreover, did the complete dominance of נִפְעֶה (according to the testimony of the traditions of Yemen and Djerba) take place in the process of transmission in the Middle Ages during the Geonic period (before or after it), or does it go back to the period of spoken Mishnaic Hebrew?

At any rate, the existence of נִפְעָה as a variant of נִפְעֶה (Babylonian vocalization, MS Antonin and MS Parma B) in the eastern traditions or as a unique form (Yemen and Djerba) can be seen in later related traditions, e.g., the tradition of the mishnayot commentary in the Rambam's autograph, MS Paris, and the Livorno edition.[84]

§ 21 In conclusion, the grammatical feature discussed in this study, like many other linguistic features, teaches us that Mishnaic Hebrew, as is true for any living language, was not uniform. The consistency and regularity in frequency and distribution testify to the living nature of the language, which displays variation over time (different levels or strata). Copyists and transmit-

82 *Ibid.*

83 See our comments in nn. 15, 78 above concerning MS Vatican 66 of the Sifra.

84 Does the autograph of Rambam's Mishna follow the first type, and is it mere coincidence that there is no vocalization נֶעֱשֶׂה in addition to the five vocalized examples (נִפְעֶה)? Here, too, one must be careful because of the paucity of examples and the limited knowledge that can be drawn from them. At any rate, the pointing נֶהֱנֶה found in the commentary of the mishnayoth (see § 4 above) may provide some testimony about the relationship of the linguistic tradition reflected in the commentary of the mishnayoth to the language type that has features which spread in the east (see especially Zurawel 1986:21–27) and which read נִפְעֶה/נִפְעָה or only נִפְעָה.

ters (no matter how sophisticated) were not capable of creating such linguistic variety. Even if the stages of development we outlined above[85] remain a hypothesis, the data reflect an ordered mosaic and not a random collection.

21.8 Appendix

§ 22 I examined the Amsterdam edition of the Mishna (printed 1646) and found the following: נִגְלֶה (1×), נֶהֱנֶה (18×), נִכְסֶה (1×), נִכְפֶּ' (= נִכְפֶּה 1×), נִפְדֶּה (6×), נִקְנֶה (3×), נִרְאֶה (13×) including הכל הולך אחר הַנִּרְאֶה (m. Nega'im 11:4; m. Para 2:5; but in m. Miqva'ot 7:5: אחר הַמַּרְאֶה[86]); נִתְלֶה (m. Sanhedrin 6:2 [2×]; m. Zavim 2:4 [2×]) as against נֶאֱפָה (m. Menahot 11:9 [2×]), נִתְלָה (m. Soṭa 3:8: האיש נִתְלָה ואין האשה נתלית), and consistently נֶעֱשָׂה (17×, including the *beraita* in m. Abot 6:2[87]).

The picture is almost identical in all of its details to the data in MS Paris and the Livorno edition.[88] All verbs have the form נִפְעֶה, and the *nif'al* participle of עשה has *qameṣ*: נֶעֱשָׂה. נֶאֱפָה also occurs with *qameṣ* (twice as in the Livorno edition; in MS Paris only once) as does נִתְלָה (once in the same mishna in which it also occurs in the Livorno edition). The vocalization נִתְלָה is also found in MS Paris (m. Zavim 2:4 [1×][89]), and that is the version of the second scribe of MS Kaufmann, who wrote and vocalized the Tractate Zavim.[90] We have already said everything there is to say about the exceptional forms above. In general the data from MS Kaufmann are found with slight variations in MS Paris (1400 CE), the Amsterdam edition (1646 CE), and the Livorno edition (20th century).

§ 23 I wish to add two comments concerning what I did not find in my investigation:

A. I did not come across any evidence of a *nif'al* participle III-*yod* in Greek and Latin transcriptions of Hebrew.
B. The readings of the early manuscripts and of the old printed editions show up only in the vocalization tradition. The orthography of נפעה could reflect נִפְעֶה or נִפְעָה. An investigation into the spelling reveals that as far as we know, there were not any forms of the participle of *nif'al* III-*yod* with *yōd* in Tannaitic literature. In other words, we have not found spellings like

85 See § 20 above.
86 See § 7 above.
87 See n. 50 above.
88 See §§ 12–13 above.
89 See n. 48 above.
90 See n. 40 above.

נגלי (= נִגְלֶה), נקני (= נִקְנֶה), etc., which testify unequivocally to נִפְעֶה forms. A survey of the attestations of the participles נכפה, נכסה, נהנה, נגלה, נאפה, נפדה, נקנה, נראה, נתלה, and נעשה in the Databases of the Historical Dictionary of the Hebrew Language of the Academy of the Hebrew Language – in Tannaitic literature and other sources, including, e.g., the Dead Sea Scrolls – showed that these participles are consistently written with *hē* (there are scores of examples). It should be emphasized that the forms of the participles in other conjugations are almost always written with *hē* (עושה, מראה, etc.). On the whole, in the forms we know of that are written with *yōd*, the *yōd* marks the vowel *ṣērē*, e.g., מוכי שחין (= מוּכֵּה) (m. Ketubbot 7:10, MSS Kaufmann and Parma A and others)[91] and הרבי (= הַרְבֵּה MS Vatican 32 to Sifre be-Midbar);[92] however, infrequently there are forms where *yōd* marks a *segol*, e.g. יבני (= יִבְנֶה)[93] and האשה לא תְשָׁרֵי את המורסן (= תְּשָׁרֶה; m. Pesahim 2:7, MS Kaufmann),[94] including forms of the participle in other conjugations: המדלי (m. Kil'ayim 6:3 [2×],4, MS Kaufmann;[95] in all other witnesses we find הַמַּדְלֶה[96]), and also הוֹוֵי (m. Nedarim 5:3), שָׁוֶוי (m. Rosh ha-Shana 3:5), both in MS Kaufmann.[97]

§ 24 Two final remarks about the uniqueness of the forms we have discussed in this study are called for:

A. It is possible to argue that the participle נֶעֱשָׂה (vocalized as such in MSS Kaufmann, Paris, and in the Amsterdam edition, but in the Livorno edition – נַעֲשָׂה[98]) is the result of dissimilation of vowels, i.e., נֶעֱשֶׂה with identical vowel [e] three times in a row – *ne'ᵉese* > *ne'ᵉesa*. If so, why didn't this process also occur in the forms נֶהֱנֶה (*nehᵉene*), נֶאֱפֶה (*ne'ᵉefe*) as in the consistent tradition of MS Kaufmann, in which there is not even one form נֶהֱנָה, נֶאֱפָה?[99] In other Mishnaic witnesses there are isolated forms like this: נֶהֱנָה occurs once in MS Paris (as against 17× נהנֶה – נהנֶה)[100]

91 See Yalon 1967:33.
92 Bar-Asher 1983b:143.
93 Ibid.
94 Yalon 1967:33.
95 I thank Mordechai Mishor, who reminded me of this example.
96 See Sacks 1972 and before him Epstein 1948:1251.
97 Epstein 1948:1251 also cited the last two examples.
98 נַעֲשָׂה, as in the tradition of MS Parma B, is the only occurrence of this participle: הַנַּעֲשָׂה (see § 7 above), and it is possible that there is a similar form in the Tiberian Bible (see n. 74 above). Traditions that do not distinguish between *segol* and *pataḥ* are not of concern here.
99 See § 10 above.
100 See § 12 above.

as does נֶאֱפָה (but נֶאֱפָה 1×).[101] נֶאֱפָה is attested twice in the Amsterdam and Livorno editions, but not נֶאֱפָה;[102] נֶהֱנָה alone occurs 18×.[103] These deviations are not a continuation of an old tradition (in Italy), and MS Kaufmann proves that it knows also נֶאֱפָה, נֶהֱנָה. Therefore, the explanation offered above seems to me the best, viz., that נֶעֱשָׂה stands by itself as a special case,[104] and the slight deviations נֶאֱפָה, נֶהֱנָה, are the consequence of the mixing of traditions that occur at times in late witnesses. נֶהֱנֶה, נֶאֱפֶה (like נִגְלֶה, נִפְדֶּה, etc.) are the basic forms in the original tradition of MS Paris and the Amsterdam and Livorno editions; however, isolated forms from the eastern variety such as נֶאֱפָה, נֶהֱנָה, נִרְאָה (Livorno edition),[105] נִתְלָה (m. Soṭa 3:8 in both editions)[106] penetrated the original tradition at a later date.

B. Nathan Braverman has drawn my attention to the fact that the *qameṣ* of נִתְלָה in m. Zavim 2:4 is the tradition of the second scribe of MS Kaufmann,[107] and that the tradition of MS Paris[108] may be the result of attraction: the position of the participle נִתְלֶה in one mishna followed by the participle נִשְׁעָן (נתלה ונשען) could have led to נִתְלָה וּנִשְׁעָן. If this is the reason, it would be similar to the attraction of מְרוּבָּה (for מְרוּבֶּה) to neighboring ממועָט[109] in MS Parma A. This explanation may indeed be correct for the occurrence in Tractate Zavim, but only in this specific passage.

---

101 *Ibid.*

102 See §§ 13, 22 above.

103 *Ibid.*

104 The solution is presented in §§ 15–16 above.

105 See § 13 above.

106 See §§ 13, 22 above.

107 See n. 40 above.

108 See § 12 and n. 48 above.

109 See Haneman 1980a:357; he viewed the vocalization of מרובָה as a mistake, rather than seeing מרובָּה as the result of attraction to ממועָט.

22 Comments on the Morphology of Nouns in Mishnaic Hebrew: Nouns Attested and Unattested in Biblical Hebrew

22.1 Introduction

§ 1 The scientific investigation of the morphology of Mishnaic Hebrew (= MH) has focused primarily on the verb and the pronouns, and very little on the noun. Only in the past few years have scholars begun to deal with nominal morphology as well.[1] I myself have recently been occupied with a systematic description of the nominal patterns based on the best of the manuscripts of the Mishnah: first and foremost MS Kaufmann and MS Parma B (De Rossi 497). In my work the data from these two manuscripts are described fully, both on the level of details and the level of synthesis. The findings that arise from these two MSS are compared with data from a series of other witnesses, such as MS Parma A (De Rossi 138), MS Cambridge, ed. Lowe, and MS Antonin of Seder Ṭeharot.[2]

§ 2 By its nature, the study of the morphology of nominal patterns focuses on details and sub-details; each and every noun that appears in the Mishnah is checked, at every occurrence, in the two primary witnesses and in many other witnesses, in order to establish which nouns are to be classified under each pattern, and thus to enable a complete and accurate description of the sum of the patterns. A comprehensive inspection of many witnesses reveals that there are more than a few nouns found as one pattern in one MS, a different pattern in another MS, and sometimes even a third pattern in yet another MS. The study of the details is exhausting, but often thrilling as well; in any event without it no worthy description of nominal morphology can be completed.

§ 3 It is not even necessary to mention that while working on the detailed analysis, and in its aftermath, our investigation has extended to a number of

1 We will mention here only one example: Yeivin 1985. It should be noted that Yeivin's description of the morphology of nouns in biblical Hebrew in the Babylonian vocalization is accompanied in every chapter and every paragraph by a description of the data from rabbinic Hebrew in its Babylonian form. A complete and detailed bibliography of what has been done on the morphology of nouns in rabbinic Hebrew is found in my article, Bar-Asher 2004a, nn. 1–10.

2 In addition to my articles mentioned in n. 10 of the aforementioned article, I will also mention here my articles, Bar-Asher 2004b, and Bar-Asher 2009c. See also Bar-Asher 2009a, Vol. 2, Chapters 7–16.

broader questions and issues. Here I would like to make a few short comments on one such broader issue relating to the MH nouns: the morphology of nouns attested in biblical Hebrew (= BH) as opposed to those unattested there.[3]

§ 4 There is no doubt that the analysis of all the nouns in the Mishnah reveals a clear picture: the nouns found in BH are found, generally, in their BH forms. But in nouns unattested in BH appear many morphological differences, even among the best witnesses, and sometimes even one witness, may preserve two or three variants of the same noun. For example, MS Parma B preserves two forms of the noun פסול "flaw": פְּסוּל *pəsūl* is the absolute form, and פִּסּוּל *pissūl* is the form found with pronominal suffixes, as in פְּסוּל *pəsūl* (Kelim 10:4) as opposed to פִּיסּוּלָהּ *pissūlāh* (Parah 4:4), בפִּיסּוּלּוֹ *be-pissūllō* (Miqva'ot 3:1). Another example is the noun שפוד "spit," for which MS K preserves two distinct vocalizations, reflecting two different nominal patterns: שְׁפוּד *šəpūḏ* (Pes 7:1) as well as שְׁפוֹד *šəpōḏ* (Kelim 5:5).

22.2 Nouns Attested in BH

§ 5 From the totality of biblical nouns attested in the Mishnah, two groups must be distinguished: (a) nouns whose mention is an implicit citation of a word or a phrase from BH, or an intentional insertion of biblical language, and whose use then does not prove that they were in living use in MH; (b) nouns found both in BH and in MH which we can assume were in use in the living languages of both biblical and tannaitic periods.

§ 6 **In the first type** we find, as expected, a faithfulness to the form as found in BH according to the Tiberian or the Babylonian vocalizations. For example, the nominal pattern פְּעֹלֶת *pəʿōleṯ* includes the noun כתובת, which is attested only once, and only in the phrase כְּתֹבֶת קעקע *kəṯōḇeṯ qaʿᵃqaʿ* (Mak 3:6). It is mentioned there adjacent to the verse cited: הכותב כְּתוֹבֶת קַעֲקָע, כתב ולא קיעקע, קיעקע ולא כתב ... ר' שמעון בן יודה או' משם ר' שמעון אינו חייב עד שיכתוב שֵׁם הַשֵּׁם, שנ' 'וּכְתֹבֶת קַעֲקַע[4] לא תתנו בכם אני ה"[5] (Lev 19:28) "One who writes a כתובת קעקע, if he wrote but did not engrave, or engraved

3 The issue of the morphology of BH nouns found in MH is discussed from different vantage points in other articles of mine (cf. Bar-Asher 2004c:§ 7 and Bar-Asher 2004b:§§ 7–10). Here I will deal with this on a different level.

4 In the biblical citation, MS K vocalizes the second ק in the noun קעקע with a *pataḥ*, like the Tiberian vocalization in the Bible, but in the occurrence in the text of the Mishnah, which is here cited at the beginning of the excerpt, this ק is vocalized with a *qameṣ*.

5 This citation is taken directly from MS K with only one change: in the MS the name of God is written as three *yods*.

but did not write ... R. Šimʿon b. Yudah says in the name of R. Šimʿon, he is not liable unless he writes the name of God, as it says, 'You shall not incise any writings (כתובת קעקע) on yourselves, I am God.'" This is in effect a type of citation. The same is true regarding a few nouns of the פְּעוּל *pəʿūl* pattern, which includes, for example, תְּנוּךְ *tənūḵ* and כְּרוּב *kərūḇ* ("angel"). But both of these nouns appear in the Mishnah in contexts which reveal that they are being used as cited lemmata or are being woven into a phrase derived intentionally from BH. In other words: (a) we find the expression תְּנוּךְ אזנו *tənūḵ ʾoznō* in a Mishnah (Negaʿim 14:9) which discusses the verse from Leviticus (14:4), על תְּנוּךְ אזן המִטהר הימנית "on the ridge of the right ear (תנוך אזן) of him who is being cleansed," which seems to be a type of citation; (b) in m. Berakhot we read in the text of Birkat ha-Zimmun, נברך אלוהינו ... יושב הַכְּרוּבִים ... "Let us bless our God ... Enthroned on the Cherubim" (Ber 7:3). It is well known that liturgical texts from the tannaitic and amoraic periods contain woven within them biblical phrases, and this is the case here as well: the only attestation of כְּרוּב *kərūḇ* "angel" in the Mishnah[6] is nothing other than an insertion of a phrase found a few times in BH, יושב הַכְּרֻבִים *yōšēḇ ha-kərūḇîm* (e.g., 1 Sam 4:4).

§ 7 **In the second type** there are many nouns which were used in the living language both in biblical and tannaitic times; among such nouns are גַּנָּב *gannāḇ* "thief," חָרָשׁ *ḥārāš* "smith," חֶרֶשׂ *ḥereś* "clay," כְּלוּב *kəlūḇ* "cage," נְעֹרֶת *nəʿōreṯ* "chaff," סֵפֶר *sēfer* "book," and many others. Some have the same meaning or similar in the two periods, and others have meanings in MH different from those they had in BH, but generally their forms are identical in the two periods. More precisely I can say, as their biblical morphology in either the Tiberian or Babylonian traditions, so their form in the Mishnah, or in other words, the nominal pattern found in MH is that found in BH. Such is the case, for example, for everything related to the six nouns just mentioned: there is no morphological difference between the words as they appear in BH and in MH.

§ 8 Even so, we have found nouns which appear in different patterns in BH and MH, such as the noun כתונת "shirt." In both the Tiberian and the Babylonian traditions of BH its form is always כֻּתֹּנֶת *kuttōneṯ*,[7] such as הַכֻּתֹּנֶת *ha-kuttōneṯ* (Gen 37:31), כֻּתָּנְתִּי *kuttontī* (Song 5:3). It is perhaps not beside the

6 In printed editions the phrase יושב הכרובים is found twice in m. Berakhot 7:3, but the MSS support only one occurrence (for details, see Zaksh *ad loc.*).

7 There is, though, one time where the absolute appears vocalized like the Mishnaic vocalization: ושבצת הכְּתֹנֶת שש (Exod 28:39), as is mentioned below. There is more to add and to be said on this detail, but this is not the place to deal with it.

point to mention here that the gemination of the *taw* is known also from the Samaritan tradition to the Pentateuch, which reads *kittånət*.[8] But in MH the noun is always found in the pattern פְּעֹלֶת *pə'ōlet̠*, as in כְּתוֹנֶת *kət̠ōnet̠* (absolute singular form: m. Yoma 7:5) in all the reliable witnesses.[9]

§ 9 An example of a different type is the noun גבול "border." This noun is found often in the Bible, and its pattern is always גְּבוּל *gəb̠ūl*, of the pattern פְּעוּל *pə'ūl*. It is plausible that this is the form of the noun in MH when suffixes are attached to it, whether pronominal or pluralizing: בִּגְבוּלָהּ *bigb̠ūlāh*, בִּגְבוּלִי *bigb̠ūlī* (AZ 3:4), וּבַגְּבוּלִין *u-b̠aggəb̠ūlīn* (m. Shabbat 1:11). However, in the singular absolute the best MSS show the form גּוֹבָל *gōb̠āl* (m. Kil'ayim 3:1 [4×]; 3:2); this is how it appears in MS K, MS Parma A, and also (with or without vocalization) in other witnesses, including a number of Genizah fragments.[10] But in less reliable MSS and in printed editions the form is גְּבוּל *gəb̠ūl*, even in the aforementioned examples from Kil'ayim. It is very probable that the version in the less reliable MSS and the printed editions is a correction made based on BH, a correction which serves to obliterate a rare and unrecognized form of MH.

Even so it can be said that most of the BH nouns attested also in the Mishnah appear in the majority of reliable witnesses in the same forms as they appear in the Bible, and only for a minority of nouns do the [reliable] witnesses of the Mishnah preserve forms other than those preserved by the vocalization traditions of the Bible, as we saw for כתונת and גבול.

§ 10 But sometimes the differences between the traditions reflect two forms of the word which reflect two authentic linguistic variants, and can thus inform us about the parallel existence of two dialects or language-types.[11] Here is an explicit example:

The noun גֹּמֶד *gōmed̠* "small cubit, half-cubit" is found in the Bible only once, and only in the Tiberian vocalization: ויעש לו אהוד חרב ... גֹּמֶד ארכה "Ehud made for himself a dagger ... a *gomed* in length" (Judg 3:16). In the Mishnah, too, it is attested only once, in the plural: והגומדין של ערביים (m. Kelim 29:1). This form is found vocalized גּוּמְדִין *gumd̠īn* (K, and also LIV and YEM) and also גּוֹמְדִין *gomd̠īn* (thus in MS Paris); these two vocalization both reflect a singular גֹּמֶד *gōmed̠*, as above, known to us from BH and similar to כֹּתֶל *kōt̠el* (singular) ~ כּוּתְלִין/כּוֹתְלִין *kut̠līn*/*kot̠līn* (plural), according to the

8 Ben-Ḥayyim 1957–1977:4.146.

9 This is found in the Babylonian vocalization of Mishnaic Hebrew, and it is vocalized thus in MSS K, Parma A, PARIS, LIV.

10 See Zaksh *ad loc.*

11 For an analysis of the language-types of MH see above, Chapter 19.

pattern known as the "Aramaic plural." As opposed to these, Parma B shows גּוּמְּדִין *gummədin* (with geminated *mem*!); this is the plural form of גּוּמֵּד *gummēḏ*. It is totally clear that there is no error here; גּוּמֵּד *gummēḏ* is the equivalent of Aramaic גרמידא/גורמידא.[12] These Aramaic forms appear to be developments of גּוּמֵּד via dissimilation (*mm* > *rm* : *gummeḏ* > *gurmeḏ*), although it is possible that גּוּמֵּד developed from גורמידא via assimilation (*gurmēḏa* > *gummēḏa*).[13] In any case, it would be very difficult to deny the connection between these two forms, the Hebrew and the Aramaic.

For our purposes the two forms attested in the Mishnah – the one a segolate shared by the Bible and some of the MH traditions (גֹּמֶד) and the other geminated and found in Parma B (גּוּמֵּד), which shows a relationship to the Aramaic[14] – reflect, to my mind, two authentic forms from two language-types or two dialects.[15]

§ 11 It is important to comment that occasionally we find nouns common to both BH and MH, but the data in BH are not complete and the precise patterns are not known to us. This is exemplified by the noun זכור "male"; we find זְכוּרְךָ *zəḵūrḵā* (Exod 23:17 and more), זְכוּרָהּ *zəḵūrāh* (Deut 20:13). These vocalizations could reflect either of two different absolute forms, which represent two different nominal patterns: (a) a פְּעוּל *pəʿūl* nominal form, זְכוּר *zəḵūr*; this is in fact found in MS K at San 6:4 (2×) and also in YEM there; Yeivin found this vocalization in the Babylonian tradition as well; (b) a פָּעוּל *pāʿūl* nominal form, זָכוּר *zāḵūr*; this is how MS K vocalizes at San 4:7, and thus also in Paris in all the word's occurrences in the Mishnah, and Yeivin found Babylonian traditions along these lines, as well.[16] In a case such as this there is no avoiding the assumption that we have preserved two reliable traditions, which record two authentic variants that were used in the language when it was spoken (and even in BH?).

§ 12 We can summarize and say that the BH nouns found also in the Mishnah usually appear in Mishnaic Hebrew in the same forms they had in BH, but there are not a few forms that show findings worthy of note; the examples above – כְּתֹנֶת as opposed to כֻּתֹּנֶת, גְּבוּל alongside גּוֹבָל – give some expression to the features separating two layers of the language. The last exam-

12 See the dictionaries of Jastrow (for the Talmudim and Midrashim), Sokoloff (for Babylonian Aramaic), Brockelmann (for Syriac), and Macuch (for Mandaic).

13 The distinction between Hebrew *gummēd* with *ē* and Aramaic *gurmīda* with *ī* is a secondary development that does not need to be addressed here.

14 It should be clear that I am not implying that this form is borrowed from Aramaic.

15 I will point out that the pair גּוּמֵּד/גֹּמֶד is parallel to another pair familiar to all: שַׁרְבִיט/שֵׁבֶט (< *šabbitu*) "scepter," one form a segolate and the other consisting of two closed syllables.

16 For the details of this issue, see Bar-Asher 2004b:§ 9.4.

ple – זְכוּר as well as זָכוּר – exemplifies the lacunae in our data about the Hebrew of the Bible.

22.3 Nouns Not in BH

§ 13 The question of the morphology of non-BH nouns in the Mishnah is a complex one, and on this topic a few brief comments will have to suffice here. First we will point out that one must distinguish between very common nouns, such as פטור "exemption" and פסול "flaw," and rare nouns which appear in the Mishnah once or, maximum, twice, like some of the פַּעָל *pa“āl* nouns: בַּקָּר *baqqār* "cattle owner,"[17] סַכָּרִין *sakkārīn* "makers of dams (סְכָרִים)," כַּתָּן *kattān* "cotton merchant," סַקַּיי/סַקָּאי *saqqay/saqqāʾy* "sack maker,"[18] and more.[19] The same is true for a number of the nouns of the pattern פְּעֹלֶת *pəʿōleṯ*, such as גְּרֹדֶת *gərōdeṯ* "the material scraped [נגרד] from vessels while they are being made," קְצֹצֶת *qəṣōṣeṯ* "the material cut [נקצץ] from vessels while they are being made," שְׁחֹלֶת *šəḥōleṯ* "the waste material that falls from vessels while they are being made."[20]

§ 14 In the decisive majority of the rare nouns there is disagreement among the witnesses (MSS and printed editions) as to the consonantal structures, and not just regarding the vocalization (i.e., the vocalic structures), and therefore the disagreement finds expression in, among other questions, the classification of the nouns by nominal pattern. Thus, for example, regarding the noun גרודת (Kel 11:3); only some of the best witnesses have the correct form, גְּרוֹדֶת *gərōdeṯ*, in the פְּעֹלֶת *pəʿōleṯ* pattern. Others read גְּרוֹרֶת *gərōreṯ* or גְּרוּרוֹת *gərūrōṯ* with a *reš*, and some have גְּרוּדוֹת *gərūḏōṯ* – the plural of גְּרוּדָה *gərūḏā(h)*.[21] Even for a noun as common as פטור, although there is no disagreement regarding its consonants, the MSS are divided about its vocalization: פְּטוּר *pəṭūr*, פְּטוֹר *pəṭōr*, or פִּיטּוּר/פִּטּוּר[22] *piṭṭūr*.[23]

§ 15 Many of the rare nouns which are not attested in BH and were checked in the best MSS of the Mishnah show situations similar to that

---

17 The details of this noun were discussed in Bar-Asher 1999b:52–55 (§§ 7–10).

18 סַקַּיי is what is found in MS K, while סַקָּאי is the version in Parma B.

19 These nouns and others of the pattern פַּעָל are discussed in Bar-Asher 2004c:§§ 20, 22–23, 27.

20 Various aspects of nouns of the פְּעֹלֶת pattern are discussed in Bar-Asher 2009c.

21 For details, see Bar-Asher 2009c:§ 4.1.

22 The addition of a *yod* (פִּיטּוּר) or a lack thereof (פִּטּוּר) is not a question of the consonantal structure, but only of vocalic orthography.

23 The details of this noun are discussed in Bar-Asher 2004b:§§ 9.16, 17, and more.

described for גְּרֹדֶת *gərōdet*. The transmission reflected within each and every witness depends on the nature of the tradition and the degree of faithfulness of the copyist/vocalizer (or printer). There are times when authentic variants have reached us, and times when a MS (or a printed edition) transmits a corrupt form. Generally, the best MSS – especially K, Parma A, Parma B, Antonin – preserve authentic versions.

§ 16 It is worth emphasizing that the issue of the non-BH nouns is exceptionally broad. Many nouns – and especially the rare ones – require, as mentioned, philological clarification prior to morphological discussions. In the decisive majority one finds that the good MSS transmit variant forms that give expression to the different authentic forms.

It must be said that the investigation of the non-BH nouns is an area upon which many fundamental issues of the nominal morphology within MH depend, and we cannot elaborate here.

22.4 Summary

§ 17 By way of summary, we can say that the detailed description of the nominal patterns in the Mishnah allows wide-ranging investigation of linguistic phenomena into the morphology of the noun; one of these phenomena is the relationship of MH as seen in MSS to BH in its two main traditions – the Tiberian and the Babylonian. Nouns from the Bible, in which the text of the Mishnah shows a relationship to the biblical texts – i.e., when we encounter an explicit citation of, or an allusion to, the biblical text, or we can clearly recognize the integration of a biblical word or phrase – they are always found in their BH forms. Of the nouns in living usage in both periods, a decisive majority show an identical form in the Bible's main traditions (Tiberian and Babylonian) and the main traditions of MH. However, there are more than a few exceptions, of different types, as exemplified above in §§ 7–11.

§ 18 The research into MH has to deal primarily with the nouns that do not appear in the Bible. In their investigation, many nouns require first philological study, in order to ascertain what precisely the consonantal structure of the noun is and what its precise meaning is. Only subsequent to that can the questions of its vocalic structure be raised and the noun assigned to a nominal pattern. We have already seen that in a few cases a noun can belong to one pattern in a certain reliable tradition, but another pattern according to another reliable tradition, such as פְּטוּר in one tradition as opposed to פִּטּוּר in a second.

§ 19 A different issue is the degree of authenticity of two (or, sometimes, more than two) given parallel traditions regarding the vocalization of a certain noun such as פְּטוֹר/פִּטּוֹר: do we have two (or more) authentic forms that derive from the living language, thus showing the linguistic variety or different dialects within rabbinic Hebrew, or do we simply have one authentic form and one form that arose at a late date in the course of transmission of Mishnaic Hebrew as only a literary language? This issue, like many other broader issues, will be dealt with in the course of time in the context of a complete description of the morphology of the noun in the language of the Mishnah.

23 Mishnaic Hebrew and Biblical Hebrew

23.1 Introductory Remarks

§ 1 The fact that the two major layers of classical Hebrew – biblical and Mishnaic Hebrew – differ in many respects needs no proof. Even Ze'ev Ben-Ḥayyim, who argued for the unity of the Hebrew language in both sections on the basis of the morphology, was well aware of the many differences that distinguished the two in the realms of lexicon, semantics, phonology, and syntax.[1] And indeed, one cannot ignore the many differences between the languages of the two periods in the realm of morphology, either, as I have shown elsewhere.[2]

§ 2 On the other hand, it must not be ignored that the *transmission histories* of the literary blocs composed in biblical Hebrew and in Mishnaic Hebrew are intermingled. The transmitters of the biblical text after its canonization spoke Mishnaic Hebrew, prior to its exit from the world of living languages; on the other side, the transmitters of rabbinic texts were entrenched in the Bible and its language. Each stratum left its imprint on the other in the *transmission processes* of the Bible and of rabbinic literature over the generations.

§ 3 I will explain what I mean through two examples, chosen from among many.

The form of the infinitive construct of the Nif'al verbs with a prefixed preposition לְ/כְּ/בְּ in biblical Hebrew is בְּהִפָּעֵל, כְּהִפָּעֵל, לְהִפָּעֵל, with the retention of the intervocalic ה: examples are בְּהִשָּׁמַע (Est 2:8); כְּהִדּוֹשׁ (Isa 25:10); לְהִנָּצֵל (*ibid.* 20:6). In Mishnaic Hebrew, however, only the form with prefixed ל is used, as is the case for all infinitive constructs of all binyanim, and in these forms the ה is often elided (לִפָּעֵל[3]), apparently due to the well-known analogy constructed between the infinitive and the prefixed conjugation (the

---

1 See Ben-Ḥayyim 1985b, reprinted slightly expanded in Ben-Ḥayyim 1992:3–35. For the point about the historical unity reflected in the verbal morphology, see esp. pp. 19–21 in the original publication.

2 See Bar-Asher 1985. See esp. pp. 77–86 (§§ 4–13) there.

3 One who studies this issue thoroughly, in all the best manuscripts of the Mishnah, will find that alongside the לִפָּעֵל forms there are forms of the type לְהִפָּעֵל with retention of the ה, such as לִיכָּנֵס alongside וּלְהִכָּנֵס in MS Kaufmann at m. Makkot 2:2, or לִיכָּנֵס in m. Ohalot 18:7 alongside לְהִכָּנֵס in 3:7 in Parma B. It would appear that the form without the ה (לִיפָּעֵל) was the one in use in the living language, and that the form with the ה (לְהִיפָּעֵל) betrays the influence of the biblical language on the copyists of the Mishnah. A clear statement of a similar position can be found already in Haneman 1980a:38 (the data is enumerated there on pp. 132–133).

"future"), creating לִיכָּנֵס (m. Makkot 2:2 [first occurrence] in MS Kaufmann; Ohal 18:7 in Parma B), on the model of יִכָּנֵס, תִּכָּנֵס, etc.

In the course of transmission of the Bible, this form was occasionally grafted onto verbs in the Qal. One famous example[4] appears in Exod 10:3, עַד-מָתַי מֵאַנְתָּ לֵעָנֹת מִפָּנָי. The full explanation is as follows. The verb עָנָה with the meaning "to subjugate, to weaken,"[5] is found in the earliest strata of the Bible in the Qal, such as וְעָנָה גְאוֹן יִשְׂרָאֵל בְּפָנָיו וְיִשְׂרָאֵל וְאֶפְרַיִם יִכָּשְׁלוּ בַּעֲוֹנָם (Hos 5:5; cf. also 7:10). It is found also in Psalm 116:10: אֲנִי עָנִיתִי מְאֹד. But already in the late books of the Bible we find that the Nif'al has replaced the Qal, as often occurred within intransitive verbs (such as כָּשַׁל > נִכְשַׁל). In fact, in later texts we find נַעֲנֵיתִי עַד-מְאֹד (Psalm 119:107) and נִגַּשׂ וְהוּא נַעֲנֶה (Isa 53:7).

After the canonization of the Bible, one who was aware of the replacement of עָנָה by נַעֲנָה but found in a text the consonantal string ענה, could not simply replace it with נענה without altering the texts. If, however, he found the form לענות, which was originally written to represent the Qal – as in עַד מָתַי מֵאַנְתָּ לַעֲנוֹת מִפָּנָי (i.e., *to submit to me*), he would have been prone to reading it as a Nif'al, לֵעָנוֹת, as was accepted in late biblical Hebrew. This form would have been well-known to the copyist, after all, from rabbinic literature. It seems that this is what occurred in Exod 10:3; the examples of this type number in the hundreds, as scholars have shown.[6]

§ 4 The next example shows the opposite process, in which biblical language left its mark on rabbinic literature over the course of the latter's transmission. A dividing line between the grammars of biblical and Mishnaic Hebrews is the form of the 3fs perfect ("past") of the III-*y* verbs. In the Bible the attested form is -תָה: גָּלְתָה, נִפְדְּתָה, גִּלְּתָה, and so on, whereas in the Mishnah one finds גָּלַת (גָּלָת), נִפְדַּת (נִפְדָּת), גִּלַּת (גִּלָּת), and the like. This topic has been analyzed in detail recently and the differences detailed and explained.[7] We know, however, that in later manuscripts, in printed editions of the Mishnah, and in printed editions of other works of rabbinic literature, many attestations were "corrected" based on the biblical paradigm: עשת > עשתה; נפדת > נפדתה; הגלת > הגלתה.[8]

4 Besides the example discussed here (לֵעָנוֹת), there are a number of others. Two of the better-known examples are בְּכָּשְׁלוֹ (Prov 27:17) in the Nif'al instead of בְּכָשְׁלוֹ in the Qal, and בֵּעָטֵף in Lam 2:11 instead of בַּעֲטֹף.

5 Avraham Even-Shoshan, in his *Concordance*, saw fit to distinguish three roots ענ"ה; the one we are dealing with is his ענ"ה3. This root ענ"ה in the Qal is an instransitive verb, and עִנָּה in the Pi"el serves to denote causation, as in אִם-עַנֵּה תְעַנֶּה אֹתוֹ (Exod 22:22).

6 Many have dealt with this; a substantial contribution was made by H. L. Ginsberg 1934.

7 See Bar-Asher 1993 (= Bar-Asher 2009a, Vol. 2 Chapter 3).

8 See Bar-Asher 1993: 52 n. 70 and 72–73 n. 182.

§ 5 The two changes just discussed, along with many others like them, occurred, as I mentioned, in the process of transmission of the biblical and rabbinic texts long after the languages of those texts ceased to be spoken languages. The degree of preservation depended, therefore, on the reliability of the transmission and that of the transmitter. It seems that the influence of Mishnaic Hebrew on biblical texts took place at an early date, and occurred in the times when Mishnaic Hebrew was a spoken language, in the days of the Tanna'im and somewhat later, as well. The influence of biblical Hebrew on rabbinic texts, on the other hand, took root and grew along with the belief that the only real grammar of Hebrew was the biblical variety, and familiarity with the Bible exceeded familiarity with rabbinic texts. This began in the late first millennium CE, and increased throughout the second, from beginning until practically the end.

One could say that a significant portion of the scholarship regarding the grammars of biblical and Mishnaic Hebrew, especially the latter, has been devoted to untangling the original rabbinic forms from later forms that were borrowed from the grammar of the Bible and grafted onto rabbinic texts by those who transmitted them.[9]

§ 6 The study of the relationship between the two strata is not solely focused on their respective transmission histories, but also deals with them as independent entities, which existed both side by side and in competition in all aspects of linguistic life, when each was a living language, as the modern study of Mishnaic Hebrew has shown throughout the 20th century. This was recognized already by M. Z. Segal and his disputant Henoch Yalon with regard to grammar, and Eliezer Ben-Yehuda with regard to the lexicon, and the recognition has persisted and been amplified until our own day. Modern scholarship aims to describe each of the strata of language after the features secondarily imposed on them have been stripped away. This is especially true for Mishnaic Hebrew.

§ 7 My purpose, too, on this occasion is a precise description of the grammar of Mishnaic Hebrew. It is true that one cannot offer a precise description of the grammar (or lexicon) without fully analyzing every detail and every issue to discover to what extent it is similar and to what extent it differs from the biblical grammar. In other words, it seems to me that there are three necessary aspects of the study of Mishnaic Hebrew grammar:

1. The dependence of the rabbinic grammar on biblical grammar.
2. The elements both grammars have in common.
3. The differences between the two grammars.

---

9 It suffices to refer to the seminal studies of Yehezkel Kutscher; a prime example would be his article, 1963.

Only by rigorously maintaining these three categories and scrupulously investigating each within every point of grammar will a precise description of rabbinic grammar be guaranteed.

23.2 Rabbinic Hebrew vis-à-vis Biblical Hebrew in Nominal Morphology

On this occasion I intend to exemplify these three aspects by attending to a segment of the grammar of Mishnaic Hebrew that has been little studied: the morphology of the noun, and above all, the nominal patterns.

The study of the noun patterns within the language of the Mishnah, yielding expansive but detailed descriptions of the data, quickly highlights the need to distinguish between nouns attested in the Bible and those unattested there. I have already shown some of the distinctions that exist between these two groups.[10] The nouns that are unattested in the Bible have many distinguishing characteristics, and they will be dealt with here only in passing.[11]

§ 9 Here we will focus on the picture that emerges from studying the nouns that are attested in both the Bible and rabbinic literature. Within most nominal patterns, one can identify two major groups, one of which can be subdivided:

1. Clear borrowings from the Bible, quasi-quotations within rabbinic literature from biblical literature. These nouns do not belong to the living Mishnaic Hebrew, and rather formed part of the academic language of the study hall.[12]
2. Nouns that were in use in both the biblical and rabbinic periods and are found in living usage in both bodies of literature. These can be divided into two sub-groups:
   2a. Those whose forms are identical in the two periods;
   2b. Those whose forms in Mishnaic Hebrew differ from their forms in biblical Hebrew.

§ 10 Before I detail these claims, I would like to stress that my focus here is on the Mishnah and not other literary works. The Mishnah has many textual witnesses, and some are complete witnesses since they are vocalized. Additionally, the Mishnah has oral traditions that preserve many of its ancient forms.

---

10 Cf. Chapter 22; Bar-Asher 2004b and 2004c., esp. § 7.

11 See below, § 23, and the sources cited in the previous note.

12 Cf. the important article by Haneman 1969.

23.2.1 Nouns borrowed from the Bible

§ 11 The first group consists of nouns that exist in rabbinic literature only as literary borrowings from, or allusions to, the Bible. These forms did not exist in the living language, but only in the language of the *beit midrash*. Some examples will make this clear.

§ 12 One example is from the nominal pattern פֶּע (pa“). The organ of smell, known in English as the nose, is known in the Bible as the אַף, and in rabbinic literature as the חֹטֶם. This is true in all thirteen instances in which the Mishnah needs to discuss the nose in a natural and not literary context. For example, m. Yeḇamot 16:3: אין מעידין אלא על פרצוף פנים עם החוטם. However, the Mishnah utilizes three expressions in which the form אַף appears: חֲרוֹן אַף, ארך אַפַּיִם, and נִזְמֵי הָאַף.

The Mishnah in Sanhedrin (10:5–6) discusses the case of an idolatrous city (עיר הנידחת) and expounds parts of Deut 13:14–18. Mishnah 6 ends with a discussion of the verse, וְלֹא יִדְבַּק בְּיָדְךָ מְאוּמָה מִן הַחֵרֶם לְמַעַן יָשׁוּב ה' מֵחֲרוֹן אַפּוֹ (13:18), and comments, שכל זמן שהרשעים בעולם, חרון אף בעולם; אבדו רשעים מן העולם נסתלק חרון אף מן העולם “for whenever (שכל זמן[13]) wicked people exist in the world, divine anger (חרון אף) exists in the world; should the wicked perish from the world, divine anger (חרון אף) would leave the world.” The biblical expression מֵחֲרוֹן אַפּוֹ was adapted for use by the rabbinic commentator twice. And note well: חרון אף, not כעס.

In the Mishnah in Shevu‘ot 4:12 is woven the language of the oath, משביע אני עליכם ... בחנון וברחום בארך אפים ורב חסד וכל הכינויים “I adjure you ... by the Compassionate, the Merciful, the Long of Anger (ארך אפים) and Great of Kindness – or any of the names of God.” It is obvious that whoever formulated this sentence borrowed the sequence of names, including ארך אפים, from the verse enumerating the “thirteen attributes”: ה' ה' אֵל רַחוּם וְחַנּוּן אֶרֶךְ אַפַּיִם וְרַב חֶסֶד וֶאֱמֶת (Exod 34:6).[14]

Similarly, the Mishnah in Aḇot, written in poetic language deeply influenced by the Bible, teaches: עשרה דורות מאדם ועד נוח להודיע כמה אֶרֶךְ אַפַּיִם לפניו שכל הדורות היו מכעיסים לפניו ... עשרה דורות מנוח ועד אברהם להודיע כמה אֶרֶךְ אַפַּיִם לפניו שכל הדורות היו מכעיסים לפניו עד שבא אברהם אבינו “There were ten generations from Adam to Noah, to teach about the forbearance (אֶרֶךְ אַפַּיִם) He possesses, as all the generations were infuriating to Him ... there were ten generations from Noah to Abraham, to teach about the forbearance (אֶרֶךְ אַפַּיִם) He possesses, as all the generations were infuriating to Him until our forefather Abraham arrived” (5:2).

---

13 MS Kaufmann reads “כל זמן.”

14 Another verse to be mentioned in this context is Num 14:18: ... ה' ארך אפים ורב חסד.

The same is true for the expression נזמי האף, except that in this case the connection to the biblical text is less obvious – but it is clear to one familiar with the texts. Mishnah Kelim 11:8 enumerates some jewelry of women: עיר שלזהב, קטליות, נזמים וטבעות ונזמי האף "a [crown in the shape of a] city of gold, necklaces, rings, signet rings, and nose rings (נזמי האף). There is no doubt but that the author of the Mishnah borrowed the list from the description of women's jewelry in Isa 3; a short verse there reads, הַטַּבָּעוֹת וְנִזְמֵי הָאָף (3:21). The Tanna' of the Mishnah in Kelim, too, used the phrase וטבעות ונזמי האף, following the lead of the biblical text, except that he or a later glossator added a parenthesis to make further details clear: וטבעות – טבעת בין שיש עליה חותם ובין שאין עליה חותם – ונזמי האף "and rings (וטבעות) – whether or not they have a seal attached to them – and nose rings."

From all this it is clear that the Mishnah uses the word חֹטֶם when freely discussing the nose, but if a biblical verse is echoing in the immediate or more distant literary context, the Mishnah utilizes expressions containing the biblical word אַף. One may conclude that אַף in the Mishnah serves a literary purpose only.

§ 13 As a second example, we may single out a noun of the pattern פְּעֹלֶת (*pᵉʿōlet*): כְּתֹבֶת, which appears only once. Mishnah Makkot 3:6 reads, הכותב כתובת קעקע כתב ולא קעקע, קעקע ולא כתב אינו חייב עד שיכתוב ויקעקע בדיו ובכוחל ובכל דבר שהוא רושם "One who writes a tattoo, if he wrote but did not etch, or etched but did not write, is not liable, until he writes and etches – with ink, paint (ובכוחל),[15] or anything with which one writes."

In formulating this law, the author of the Mishnah uses the phrase כתובת קעקע, but later on in the Mishnah we read, רבי שמעון בן יודה משום רבי שמעון אומר, אינו חייב עד שיכתוב את השם, שנאמר 'וכתובת קעקע לא תתנו בכם אני ה' "R. Shimʿon b. Yuda said in the name of R. Shimʿon, one is not liable until he writes the [divine] name, as it says, 'do not tattoo yourselves, I am the LORD' (Lev 19:21)." Here we have a quotation from the Bible. It is clear, then, that the first occurrence of the expression כתובת קעקע in the Mishnah, too, is not an example of living usage, but is a literary allusion made by the author to the biblical verse from which his own formulation draws.

It is true that the scribe of MS Kaufmann wrote כתובת קעקע in the line in Mishnaic Hebrew, as opposed to כְּתֹבֶת קעקע, without the ו, in the citation from the biblical text, and the vocalizer of the manuscript wrote קַעֲקַע in the Mishnaic sentence, as opposed to קַעֲקַע in the Tiberian tradition of the biblical text, but these are secondary details, and the fact remains that the expression was borrowed from the Bible.

---

15 The word used (as vocalized in MS Kaufmann) is וּבַכּוֹחַל; printed editions have ובכחול (and Yalon vocalized וּבַכְּחוֹל).

§ 14 A third example: one who studies the pattern פְּעוּל in the traditions of the various MSS will find two different nouns כְּרוּב: (a) כְּרוּב "angel"; (b) the vegetable כְּרוּב, which is the Hebrew form derived from Greek κράμβη. The former noun is well-known from the Bible, but its use in rabbinic texts is limited to liturgical formulae, and it is never used in describing realities in rabbinic times. Liturgical formulae are almost always based upon biblical expressions and language. The Mishnah (m. Berakhot 7:3) gives the formulation of one blessing, for example: ברוך ה' אלוהינו אלוהי ישראל אלהי הצבאות יושב הכרובים "Blessed is the Lord our God, God of Israel, master of the hosts, seated on the כרובים." This is essentially a borrowing, a quasi-quotation, of the common biblical expression יושב הכרובים (e.g., 1 Sam 4:4).[16]

§ 15 It is true, as may be gathered from the foregoing examples, that borrowings from biblical language are particularly common in multi-word expressions: חרון אף, ארך אפים, ניזמי האף, כתובת קעקע, and יושב הכרובים. This is not, however, always the case, and there are many examples of borrowings from the language of the Bible which consist of a single word alone; the noun מַשְׁקוֹף is a good example. Mishnah Pesahim 9:5 reads, פסח מצרים מקחו מבעשור, וטעון הזאה באגודת אזוב על המשקוף ועל שתי המזוזות "For the Egyptian *pesah*, the paschal lamb was to be taken beginning on the tenth [of Nisan], and it required sprinkling with a bundle of hyssop, on the lintel (משקוף) and the two doorposts." All the textual witnesses read משקוף here, but in every other mishnaic discussion of a lintel, the best manuscripts (e.g., Kaufmann and Parma B) read שקוף (vocalized שָׁקוּף or שָׁקוֹף). This was the form of the noun in use in the living language, as is proven not only by its occurrences in the Mishnah, but in its epigraphic attestation in the Bar'am synagogue inscription:

יהי שלום במקום הזה ובכל מקומות ישראל
יוסה הלוי בן לוי עשה השקוף הזה
תבא ברכה במע<ש>יו של[ום]

Let there be peace in this place and in all the places of Israel.
Yose the Levite, son of Levi, built this lintel.
May a blessing come to all he does. Peace!

In the Mishnah Pesahim, on the other hand, all the reliable witnesses read משקוף, since the entire formulation is based on the biblical text (Exod 12:22): וּלְקַחְתֶּם אֲגֻדַּת אֵזוֹב ... וְהִגַּעְתֶּם אֶל הַמַּשְׁקוֹף וְאֶל שְׁתֵּי הַמְּזוּזֹת "Take a bunch of hyssop ... and touch the lintel (משקוף) and the two doorposts."

The author of the Mishnah here relied on the verse, and made use of words and expressions directly borrowed from the Bible: אגודת אזוב, משקוף, שתי

16 See Bar-Asher 2004b:§ 9.10 (p. 64).

המזוזות. But in the other mishnaic texts, as mentioned, all the best textual witnesses read שָׁקוּף/שָׁקוֹף. For example, הייתה (הכוורת) עומדת בתוך הפתח אין בינה לבין השקוף פותח טפח "If [the hive] was standing in the doorway, such that there was not between it and the lintel an opening of a handbreadth" (m. Ohalot 9:10); והיא נוגעת בשקוף "it was touching the lintel" (10:7). Some of the manuscripts, however (including some good ones, such as Parma A), as well as the printed editions, substituted the biblical form משקוף for the original mishnaic שקוף.

Within this single example can be seen both aspects of the mutual influence I mentioned above: (1) the influence of the Bible within the process of transmission (the substitution of שקוף by משקוף as a pseudo-correction, which actually erased the original version, in the example from Ohalot); (2) the literary influence of the Bible on the authors of the Mishnah, seen in the use of the biblical lexeme משקוף in the Mishnah Pesahim, based on the language of the verse in Exodus.[17]

23.2.2 Nouns Common to the Languages of the Bible and the Mishnah

§ 16 Many nouns found in the Mishnah and also in the Bible, however, are in fact common to the spoken languages reflected in each. Within this group of words, there are two subgroups.

The first subgroup includes nouns that appear in both bodies of literature in the same form. This is the case with regard to nouns such as גָּמָל, חָצֵר, גַּנָּב, שָׁקֵד, נַעֲרָה, כְּלוּב, and many similar ones. Within almost every nominal pattern, one finds that approximately a third – and sometimes more – of the nouns are shared by biblical and rabbinic languages. One finds occasionally semantic differences between the two eras, such as אֵבֶר, which in the Bible denotes the wing of a bird and the Mishnah usually denotes a body-part.

There is no doubt that most nouns in use during the two eras appear in the same form in both bodies of literature.

§ 17 The second subgroup is those nouns that appear in different forms in the two literatures. We should not make the mistake of thinking that nouns that appear in the Bible were mechanically read by those involved in transmitting the Mishnah (the transmitters of the Mishnah in oral form, the scribes of the manuscripts, and the printers of the later editions) in their biblical forms, and that we do not in fact know with any reliability what the original mishnaic forms were. We have much evidence that this was not the case.

17 I discussed the issue of שקוף and משקוף in Chapter 17, nn. 6, 32, above.

There are not a few nouns that appear in the Bible, and are read differently in the Mishnah than in the Bible. I will suffice with a few examples.

§ 18 The noun כֻּתֹּנֶת appears in the Tiberian and Babylonian vocalizations in this form (*kuttóneṯ*). A form with a geminated ת is attested also in Samaritan Hebrew: *kittå̊nət*; it appears this way constantly, without any exceptions. But in the Mishnah, all the vocalized witnesses show the form as כְּתֹנֶת (*kᵉṯóneṯ*), with a reduced vowel in the first syllable and (therefore) a non-geminated ת. For example, כהן גדול משמש בשמונה כלים וההדיוט בארבעה בִכְתֹנֶת ומכנסים ומצנפת ואבנט "The High Priest serves in eight pieces of clothing and the simple priest in four: in the undercoat (בִכְתֹנֶת[18]), the pants, the turban, and the belt" (m. Yoma 7:5). H. Y. Kasovsky, who vocalized the word as בְּכֻתֹּנֶת in his אוצר לשון המשנה, was in fact following the biblical form.

§ 19 In the Bible, a plural form בְּצָלִים is attested (Num 1:5), which indicates the existence of an unattested singular form בָּצָל, which is found in the Mishnah (e.g., בָּצָל [m. Terumot 2:5 in Kaufmann and Parma A]). On the other hand, another form is attested: בָּצֵל, a פָּעֵל-pattern noun. It appears thus in Kaufmann and Parma A in a number of places: וּבָצֵל (m. Shabbat 10:1; K); בָּצֵל (m. Nedarim 9:8 [2×]; Parma A). One need not go to the extreme of claiming that בָּצֵל was the only form in use in the living language of the Mishnah and that בָּצָל was merely a literary relic of the Bible; it is sufficient to establish that בָּצֵל was *also* in use.

§ 20 The form כְּרֵשׂוֹ (Jer 51:34) is based on a singular form כָּרֵשׂ, which in fact appears in rabbinic literature in the form כָּרֵס (with a shift of שׂ > ס), but there is evidence for a segolate form כֶּרֶס. The vocalizer of MS Kaufmann, for example, reads הַכֶּרֶ(י)ס in m. Hullin 3:1 and Tamid 4:2,[19] and MS Paris 328–329 reads thus in these two mishnayot, as well.

§ 21 Another example with interesting unique aspects is found with regard to a noun of the פֹּעֶל pattern: the biblical *hapax legomena* noun גֹּמֶד, found in וַיַּעַשׂ לוֹ אֵהוּד חֶרֶב וְלָהּ שְׁנֵי פֵיוֹת גֹּמֶד אָרְכָּהּ "Ehud made for himself a sword with two edges, its length was a *gomed*" (Jud 3:16). All the ancients, including the Greek translators and the ancient exegetes, understood that גֹּמֶד meant "half a cubit" or "a small cubit." This noun also appears in the Mishnah, once and only once: נומי כפח של זקנה והגומדין שלערביין "the strings of

---

18 Note that although this Mishnah is based on the biblical verses describing the priestly garments, the form used is still not כֻּתֹּנֶת but כְּתֹנֶת. It seems clear that the one responsible for the formulation has in mind a living reality from the priestly existence of his own day.

19 It seems likely that the form כריס is intended to represent the form כָּרֵיס, rather than כֶּרֶיס, but it also seems likely that the vocalizer of Kaufmann and Paris 328–329 are preserving an authentic form they received.

the head-covering of an old woman, and the half-cubit-long head coverings[20] of the Arabs" (m. Kelim 29:1). Many witnesses, including MS Kaufmann, read גּוֹמְדִין or גּוּמְדִין, i.e., an "Aramaic plural form" of the word גֹּמֶד, akin to כּוּתְלִין/כּוֹתְלִין. Others read גְּמָדִין (like גְּרָנוֹת) or גְּמָדִין,[21] i.e., the textbook plural form of a Hebrew פֶּעֶל noun.

The Parma B MS, however, reads וְהַגּוּמְּדִין, a form which seems to indicate a singular form גּוּמֵּד. One could, of course, simply claim that this form is a mistake made by the scribe of Parma B, but it seems to me more plausible that in fact the form הַגּוּמְּדִין is authentic. This tradition knew a singular form גּוּמֵּד, and it is possible that this was derived from גַּמֵּד under the influence of the bilabial מ. A pair such as גַּמֵּד/גּוּמֵּד would have a clear parallel in the Aramaic pair גַּרְמִידָא/גּוּרְמִידָא, the definite forms of גַּרְמִיד/גּוּרְמִיד.[22] The pair גַּמֵּד/גּוּמֵּד could have developed into גַּרְמֵד/גּוּרְמֵד through dissimilation (*mm > rm), or the reverse development (*rm > mm) could have taken place due to assimilation. The parallel between the two pairs (Hebrew and Aramaic) is so clear that the difference in vowel (*i* vs. *e*) seems to be a secondary issue.

If this is all true, it turns out that Hebrew recognized two different forms: a segolate noun גֹּמֶד and a different form גּוּמֵּד, which was known to at least one tradition (or one dialect) of the Hebrew of the Mishnah.

To conclude it seems appropriate to point to another case in which Hebrew knew two alternative forms of a noun, one segolate and the other quadriliteral: שֵׁבֶט and שַׁרְבִיט. In this case, the latter is a descendant of Akkadian *šabbītu*.[23]

23.3 Conclusion

§ 22 In general, the languages of the Bible and the Mishnah had much in common with regard to nominal morphology, but the need for precision in our descriptions necessitates the division of the common forms into three categories:

A. Nouns borrowed from the Bible, for which a literary dependence of the Mishnah upon the Bible is evident;
B. Nouns shared by the Bible and the Mishnah, whose form is the same in both;

20 This is an example of metonymy (specifically, synecdoche), since the word גֹּמֶד stands in for "head-covering a גֹּמֶד in length."

21 See Yeivin 1985:851.

22 Cf. the lexicons of Brockelmann for Syriac, Drauer-Macuch for Mandaic, and Sokoloff for Jewish Babylonian Aramaic.

23 Cf. KB³ s. v. שַׁרְבִיט.

C. Nouns shared by the Bible and the Mishnah whose form differs between the two. Of these, some show the different form in all traditions and witnesses of Mishnaic Hebrew, as was the case regarding the different forms כֻּתֹּנֶת and כְּתֹנֶת, and others are attested only in a single tradition, which stands opposed to the consensus of the other witnesses, as in the pair גֹּמֶד/גּוּמֵּד. This detail and others like it may be able to demonstrate dialectal differences, or at least differences between various traditions of Mishnaic Hebrew.

§ 23 Another significant issue, in which the most basic differences between biblical and Mishnaic Hebrews is to be seen, is that of the mishnaic nouns that do not appear at all in the Bible. It is here that the primary differences between the language of the Bible and that of the Mishnah are seen. Within practically every nominal pattern found in Mishnaic Hebrew, close to 50 % of the nouns are not found in the Bible.

These nouns, unattested in the Bible, display their own behavioral tendencies. Those among them that are rare, and appear only once or twice in the entire Mishnah, often show differences in form among the various witnesses, extending not only to the vocalization, but even to the consonantal structures. Those that appear frequently, on the other hand, remained very stable through the process of transmission. Here, too, however, the various traditions often show differences.[24]

These nouns are the heart of a full discussion of Mishnaic nominal morphology, and I have already discussed it in a number of places recently,[25] and this is not the place to discuss it again. Although there are both details and general and fundamental points that I could add to what was previously said, constraints of space prohibit discussing them here.

§ 24 I am not able to conclude this discussion without a few additional comments:

A. Everything said here about the morphology of the noun applies also to the morphology of other parts of speech as well – the pronouns, verbs, and particles. In other words, within every category one finds the groups we have distinguished: borrowings from biblical language, shared elements – some of which are identical in all respects, and others which differ in form – and elements not found at all in the Bible.
B. I did not discuss here the question of when to view a borrowing from biblical language as work of the author of the Mishnah, and when to view

24 See Bar-Asher 2004b:§§ 10–17 (73–76); Bar-Asher 2004c:§§ 8–12 (25–27).
25 See the sources cited in the previous note.

such a borrowing as work of a later scribe. Every detail and every case must be investigated independently. To oversimplify the matter, though, it can be said that if an element is attested in all the textual witnesses, and especially the best of them, its originality within the text is virtually beyond question. On the other hand, an element not found in all or some of the most reliable witnesses, and whose presence is only attested in copies which have been shown to be fundamentally unreliable in their preservation of Mishnaic Hebrew forms, has probably been introduced, consciously or unconsciously, by a later copyist. For our present purposes, this will have to suffice.

24 On the Language of the Beit 'Amar Papyrus

§ 1   An interesting papyrus was recently published by Esther and Chanan Eshel and Ada Yardeni.[1] The papyrus, dated to "year four of the destruction of the house of Israel," is a receipt for a *ketubba*, and is written in a mixture of Hebrew and Aramaic (see below). According to the *editio princeps*, the text reads:

1. בתרין עשר לכסילו שנת ארבע לחרבן בית ישראל
2. בית עמר מרים ברת יעקוב מסעלב ארמלת
3. שאול בר שמעון שועל מענב העלינה אמרת
4. לאבשלום בר שמעון שועל מן ארשתובול מודה
5. אני לך הימה הזה בכֹולמֹא שאהיה לך על יד שאול
6. אחיך שאהיה בעלי קודם כך כתבה וביה וקנין
7. ומהר תיכול התקבלת ודין ודברים אין בכֹל
8. מה שאהיה לבֹּעילי קודם כך תיכל התקבלת
9. וכל אדם שאיוהב רשתי לידך על חשבן מאשא
10. כתבא חזה פוטר רכושי לותך אלא דין ותשלמתא
11. לך מנכסי ואפֹר<ע>ך מה לעמת כך וקים לי עליך
12. לעמת כך מרים ברת יעקוב על נ[פש]ה̇ כתבת מן ממרה
13.   יהוסף בר שמעון שהד
14.   יהורם בר זכריה [שהד]
15.   יהוסף בר יעק[ו]ב ספרא[

24.1 Preliminary Notes

§ 2   **Filling gaps.** The edition and commentary published by Esther and Chanan Eshel and Ada Yardeni deals with the text and many of the issues it raises, including some of the important linguistic issues. I will therefore discuss only topics which they did not deal with, or which they mentioned only in passing.[2]

§ 3   **Doubts.** In this text, as in many written epigraphic finds, there are many words whose real form is unknown. There are also unique forms in this text which may reflect interesting linguistic features, but it also possible that these forms are only scribal errors. I will discuss these issues with regard to the issues I discuss here, but of course only limited weight will be accorded to these uncertain phenomena.

---

1 Esther Eshel, Hanan Eshel, and Ada Yardeni, ":"שטר מ"שנת ארבע לחרבן בית ישראל "עדות נדירה לגזרות הדת אחרי מרד בר כוכבא? *Cathedra* 132 (2009), 5–24; "A Document from 'Year 4 of the Destruction of the House of Israel'," *Dead Sea Discoveries* 18 (2011), 1–28.
2 My work, too, does not exhaust all there is to say about the language of this text.

§ 4 I will begin with a general note on the nature of the language in the text, after which I will discuss some other issues in greater detail.

24.2 On the General Nature of the Language in the Document

§ 5 Out of document's 106[3] words over twenty are proper names of people and places. Although the majority of the remaining 80 words are written in Hebrew, the text can actually be said to be in Aramaic. What is in Hebrew is a rather long text of a Hebrew acknowledgment formula, into which Aramaic elements have been mixed in a variety of ways. Obviously, the language of a text should be established not based on the quantity of words in one language or another. The following will clarify what I mean.

§ 6 Lines 1–4: The opening 28-word[4] sentence is written in Aramaic: בתרי עשר [...] מרים ברת יעקוב [...] ארמלת שאול בר שמעון [...] אמרת [...] “in the twelfth ... Miriam daughter of Jacob ... widow of Saul son of Simeon ... said ...”

Lines 12–14 (and also the end of line 15 according to the suggested restorations of the editors): this passage, which presents the names of the writer of the document, the witnesses on the document and the scribe, is also written in Aramaic: מרים ברת יעקב על [נפש]ה; כתבת מן ממרה, יהוסף בר שמעון שהד, יהורם בר זכריה [שהד], יהוסף בר יעק[וב ספרא] “Miriam daughter of Jacob, for herself, wrote from her words. Joseph son of Simeon – witness; Jehoram son of Zechariah – [witness]; Joseph son of Jaco[b, scribe].”

On the other hand, the acknowledgement in lines 4–12, which is written in the name of Miriam daughter of Yaakov, is written, in essence, in Hebrew. This is recognizable from the grammar of the written text, and in many of the words and expressions that make up the style of the text: מודה אני and not אנא מודיא[5]; בכולמא שאהיה and not בכל מא דהוה; שאהיה [= שֶׁהָיָה] בעלי and שאהיה לבעילי, and not דהוה בעלי and דהוה לבעילי; אחיך and not אחוך; אין and not לית. The direct object marker preserved as a prefix reflects Hebrew את: תיכול, תיכל (< את הכל, with the loss of the aleph at the beginning of the word את).[6] There are also further words and expressions in Hebrew within this

3 This enumeration of words in the document does not include the last word on line 14 or on line 15, which are restorations (however plausible) by the editors.

4 Fourteen of these words are personal names.

5 This form is familiar to us from the Targum Yonatan to the Book of Prophets. In the Targum, the verse אנכי אשירה אזמר לה' אלהי ישראל “I will sing, I will make music to the Lord, God of Israel” (Judges 5:3), is rendered, אנא משבחא מוֹדְיָא ומברכא קדם ה' אלהא דישראל (I thank Uri Melamed for pointing this text out to me).

6 See below, § 9.

section of the text: לעמת, פוטר, כל אדם, דין ודברים, מהר, קנין, כתבה (כְּתֻבָּה) כך (2×), and more. But interspersed here in the wording of the document are also some Aramaic elements: וביה "and the house,"[7] לותך (לְוָתָךְ), חשבן (חֻשְׁבָּן),[8] התקבלת (הִתְקַבְּלֵת),[9] תשלמתא (תַּשְׁלֻמְתָּא [תַּשְׁלֻמָה + אָ] = the payment[10]); there is also another definite noun which appears with the Aramaic definite article: כתבא (כְּתָבָא = הַכְּתָב "the text"). In one place, the Aramaic definite article is added on top of the Hebrew definite article: the noun הים (= הַיּוֹם), to which has been added the Aramaic definite article: הימה = היום + ־ָה. If the reading שאיוהב(?) is correct, then we have an Aramaic verb (יהב [= Hebrew נתן]) whose form is a hybrid: שאיוֹהֵב[11] is an active participle of binyan qal.[12]

24.3 Orthography

§ 7 Even though there are many words written plene, the tendency to write defectively is evident. In writing the back vowels, however, there is a mixture

---

7 This form is explained below, in § 16.

8 It is, however, possible this is the Hebrew word חשבון written defectively, much like the word העלינה (rather than העליונה), written without a *waw*.

9 I vocalized the word as the 1st person form of the Aramaic binyan *hitpa"al* in accord with the very reasonable understanding of the Eshels and A. Yardeni. One should note that this word, quite characteristic of the document's wording, retains its ancient form — *hitpa"al* with a *heh* and not *'etpa'al* with an aleph. This is also the case in the Hebrew found in the documents of the Mishnah and other rabbinic compositions: the verb appears in binyan *hitpa"al* form with a *heh* and not in the *nitpa"al* with a nun. In fact, the reflexive is used here, as in other places, with an active sense, and it takes a direct object (תיכול התקבלת/תיכל התקבלת "I received it all").

10 See below, n. 14.

11 In many Aramaic dialects the root יה"ב serves in the qal conjugation only in the past, participle, and imperative, and it is found in complementary distribution with נת"ן, which serves in the future and the infinitive. (Tal also shows the infinitive form from יה"ב in the kal conjugation, see Tal [2000:335]). Here in the text the form of יה"ב is a hybrid and is modeled on the Hebrew active participle. It is true that the reading is questionable, but since the verb appears in the known expression יה"ב רשות, as the editors note, this reading is eminently reasonable, and is preferable to the alternative suggestion שאירהב.

12 It is also possible that this text has an Aramaic structure on which was grafted a Hebrew structure: if indeed the words בתרין עשר לכסילו appear in the date formula, as the editors noted, and not בתרי עשר לכסילו, it is possible that the Hebrew structure בשנים עשר (with the pronunciation of the final מ as a נ) was grafted on top of Aramaic בתרי עשר (and note the spelling of עשר with a ש); it should be noted that the orthography שנין (= שְׁנַיִם), with a נ, is attested elsewhere. See, for example, Bar-Asher 2009b:200. Nevertheless, it should be emphasized that in our text there is not even a single example of the interchange of a final *mem* with *nun* or vice versa, and this is therefore only a (remote) possibility.

of plene and defective spellings. I should first note that I have found no reason to distinguish between words inherited from the Bible and words that are not, for an inherited word, such as יעקב, is written once plene (יעקוב), and a new word, such as רשות, is written once defectively (רְשֻׁתִי). The details are as follows.

§ 8 The vowel [u] in a closed, unstressed syllable – which is an originally short vowel – is written defectively every time it appears: לחרבן (לְחֻרְבָּן), כתבה (כְּתֻבָּה), חשבן (חֻשְׁבָּן),[13] לעמת (לְעֻמַּת) (2×); ותשלמתא (ותשלֻמְתא) may also belong on this list.[14] On the other hand, the originally long vowel [ū], in either an open or closed stressed syllable is nearly always written plene with a *waw*: שועל (2×), רכושי, שאול (2×) – but we find also רשתי (רְשֻׁתי) with no *waw*.

§ 9 The long vowel [ō] – whether it reflects an originally long vowel,[15] or a vowel lengthened under the stress (ā > ō), or the result of a monopthongized diphthong (aw > ō) – is usually written plene: מודה, ארישתובול, שמעון (3×), יהוסף, יהורם, (l. 2), יעקוב, פוטר, שאיוהב,[16] תיכול (< את הכול), קודם (2×: קוֹדם) (2×) – altogether 14 occurrences of plene spelling. There are also six defective spellings of long /ō/: העלינה (= העלֹינה), הימה (= הימֹה), ומהר (= ומֹהר), תיכל (< את הכֹל), יעקב (l. 12), אבשלם (= אבשלֹם).[17] The vowel [o] in a closed unstressed syllable, which is an originally short vowel, is found in the word כל (= כָּל), and this is written twice defectively – בכל (l. 7) and וכל (l. 9) – and once plene – בכולמא (l. 5).[18]

§ 10 The vowel [i] in a closed unstressed syllable is always written defectively: לכסילו (= לִכְסִילו), מרים (= מִרים [2×]), מסעלב (= מִסַּעלב), שמעון (3×), ארשתובול (= אִרְשְׁתובול), וקנין, התקבלת (= הִתְקבלת [2×]), מנכסי (= מִנְּכסי).[19]

---

13 See above, note 8.

14 In Ben-Sira, the singular form תשלומת appears twice (12:2; 14:6). As opposed to the [o] vowel known from Hebrew, I have cited the form from our text with an [u]. It should also be noted that the evidence of our text antedates the form תשלמה attested in Samaritan Aramaic, in the *piyyut* of Marqa: תשלמתה דאנון לקין, which Ben-Ḥayyim translated, "the punishments which they suffered" (Ben-Ḥayyim [1957–1977:3/2.142, l. 90). The word is pronounced tåšlēmātå, which is a *taf'ēlā* pattern, תַּשְׁלֵמָה. (Tal cited this singular form ת[ו]שלמה without vocalization; cf. Tal [2000:904].) The meaning of the word is identical in our text and in Samaritan Aramaic (where it means "punishment"); payment is, of course, one type of punishment.

15 That which is known in traditional biblical grammar as a חולם חסר.

16 See above, § 6, end.

17 Since this is a well-known name, I do not consider it a serious possibility that the intended vocalization was אַבְשָׁלֵם.

18 If this reading is correct, of course.

19 I did not cite the 1cs Aramaic form כתבת "I wrote" in this context, since as is known, the Palestinian Aramaic form was כַּתְבֵת, with an [a] vowel in the first syllable, and not כִּתְבֵת with an [i] vowel, as in Biblical Aramaic.

The scribe only wrote the [i] vowel in a syllable closed by a geminated consonant, in the compound word תיכול, תיכל, with a *yod* ('et hakkol > tikkol). The form תיכ(ו)ל shows that the initial *aleph* had been elided along with its vowel, and the *heh* of the definite article disappeared as well; the [a] vowel was attenuated in the closed unstressed syllable to [i]. On the other hand, the originally long [ī] is always written plene, with a *yod*, not only in word-final position (אני, בעלי, בעילי, רשתי), but also in medial position (אחיך, דין, ודברים).

§ 11 The vowel [ē], which reflects a lengthened vowel,[20] is written defectively: מענב (= מעֶנב; under the מ, as well, if we assume there would have been compensatory lengthening there, yielding מֵעֶנב), פוטר (= פוטֵר), וקים (= וקיֵּם). On the other hand, the [ē] which is the result of the contraction of the [ay] diphthong is always spelled with a *yod*: בית, אין, עליך. The originally long [ē] in the Aramaic word מאמרה* from which the *aleph* has been lost, however, is written defectively: ממרה. This is the result of a chain of processes: מֶאְמרה > מֵאמרה > מֵימרהּ > מֵמרה.

§ 12 In general, there is no marking of any [a] vowel in the orthography.[21]

§ 13 All the consonantal *yod*s are written with a single *yod*, as in העליונה, וקנין, וקים. Consonantal *waws* are also written with only one *waw*: לותך.

§ 14 Note: this text teaches that the use of the *waw* as a vowel letter was more widespread than that of *yod*, like the spelling practices known to us from the Dead Sea Scrolls and reliable manuscripts of rabbinic literature. It should also be noted that the use of *waw* as a vowel letter is much more common for long vowels, but very rare for short vowels. Nevertheless, not a few words with originally long vowels are written defectively (העלינה, הימה, רשתי). It should be emphasized that this tendency toward defective spelling is characteristic of epigraphic texts.

24.4 Orthography and phonology

§ 15 **The realization of the *šin*.** It seems quite likely that the spelling of two place names in the text reveal how the *šin* was pronounced by the scribe.

20 This is the vowel known in Biblical grammar as צירי חסר.

21 See, however, what I say below in § 18, on the spelling -אש of the relative particle.

It is true that in most of the words in the text, the consonants *šin*, *śin*, and *samekh* are used in the normal ways, as in שנת, שאול, שמעון, לאבשלם; עשר;[22] מנכסי, יהוסף. But two place names show something exceptional in their spelling. The GN ארישתובול is Greek;[23] the Greek consonant σ could be expected to be transcribed with a ס (as אריסתובול), but here it is transcribed with a ש.[24] The place name שעלב[ים] appears here סעלב. The preservation of the ע shows that we are dealing with the original Semitic name (without the plural ending), and not the Greek form Saalab, but the appearance of a ס in place of the original ש is surprising. It appears that the two transliterations ארישתובול and סעלב show that the scribe's pronunciation was influenced by Greek pronunciation, namely, both the ש and the ס were pronounced [s] by him (always?). This is the only way to explain why he wrote סעלב with a ס, meant to reflect an original שׂ, and ארישתובול with a ש, as a hypercorrection. Despite this, the scribe managed to write the rest of the words with historical spellings, including the word עשר with a שׂ.

§ 16 **The noun ביה.** In the middle of a series of four indefinite nouns, the noun ביה (= בַּיִת) is included: כתבה וביה וקנין ומהר. As is known, the final ת was lost from the absolute form of the Aramaic noun בית in Qumran Aramaic and the other Palestinian Aramaic dialects. Its form therefore was *bay*, is written בי/ביי/באי.[25] It seems that the spelling in our text with a ה, ביה, reveals that diphthong [ay] contracted to [e], which aligns with the evidence from Papyrus Nahal Ṣe‘elim 13: וקים עלה אנה שלמצין (ll. 9–10).[26] There the spelling עלה with a ה in place of עלי (עליי = עֲלַי) clearly shows that the diphthong [ay] had contracted to [e], as Elisha Qimron well argued.[27] To be more precise, one ought to say that the spelling in the text, ביה, appears to be the grafting of the post-contraction spelling בה [bē] on top of the pre-contraction spelling בי [bay].[28]

---

22 This word is Aramaic.

23 The name Ἀριστόβουλος is a very popular name.

24 The spelling with ת rather than ט is also surprising. In Rabbinic literature it appears, as expected, אריסטובולוס/אריסטובלוס, with a ט (cf., e.g., bBQ 82b, bMen 64b), but in Yosippon it is very common with a ת, as אריסתובולוס/אריסתובלוס (the data are culled from the Ma'agarim of the Historical Dictionary of the Hebrew Language of the Academy of the Hebrew Language).

25 See the data collected in Tal 2000:87.

26 Yardeni (2000:134), and see the literature cited in Bar-Asher 2009b:206 n. 70.

27 H. M. Cotton and E. Qimron, “XḤev/Se ar 13 of 134 or 135 CE: A Wife's Renunciation of Claims,” *JSS* 49 (1998), p. 110.

28 This is also how I interpreted the spelling מלאכה (מַלְאָכֵי < מַלְאָכַי [mal'akay]) – a morphological alternative to מלאכים which is attested in the Vision of Gabriel. Cf. Bar-Asher (2009b:205–208).

§ 17 **בית עמר.** Line 2 opens by noting the dwelling place of Miriam daughter of Yaakov – Bet ʻAmar. The Eshels and Yardeni translated this nicely as "[in] Bet ʻAmar," since it is clear that the spelling בית represents the form בבית (= בְּבֵית). This is most likely not an example of scribal haplography, but rather phonological haplology, *bəḇēt* > *bēṯ*; in other words, in the first syllable, which is pronounced similarly to the beginning of the following syllable, was elided in pronunciation, as we find frequently in the Bible and in rabbinic literature.[29]

§ 18 **The particle שא.** The relative particle is found five times in the text. In four of these attestations it is written attached to the word that follows it, and in one appearance it is attached to the one which precedes it; in all five of its appearances it is written שא: שאהיה (3×), שאיוהב, מאשא. This spelling is also known from elsewhere. For example, it is attested in MMT: שא א[נ]ח[נו], שא יהיה, שא יאכל, and more.[30]

Even when the particle is spelled -שא, it has been common practice[31] to vocalize it according to its pronunciation in the Tiberian tradition of biblical Hebrew and in reliable manuscripts of rabbinic literature: שֶׁ (*šin* with a *segol* and a *dagesh* in the following consonant when it is not a guttural: שֶׁמֶּלֶךְ).[32] One may ask: is it true that the spelling with an א refers to the vowel [ɛ] and not to the vowel [a] – שַׁא (שָׁא[33])? The motivation for this suggestion is that the primary use of *aleph* as a vowel letter in both medial and final positions is to represent the vowel [a].[34] The vocalization of the relative -שׁ with an [a]

29 See Sharvit (2008:65–66) (numerous examples are cited there from the Bible and from rabbinic literature). It does not seem appropriate to me to go so far as to assume that the *shewa mobile* in the first syllable was dropped entirely and the word was pronounced [bbēt] > [abbēt] – in other words, that the resulting initial consonant cluster was resolved by the addition of a prosthetic vowel – as we find in the Bar Koseba letters (אבית משכו), in the Dead Sea Scrolls (אבית גלותו), and in rabbinic literature (אבית/אבבית נפש) – except that here the א indicating the prosthetic vowel was not written. See Epstein (1948:1258–1259), and Bar-Asher (2010:§§ 13–14), and the literature cited there. As was said, one should not go so far as to reconstruct a pronunciation not evidenced in the written text we have; it should be noted, however, that Sharvit already raised the possibility that the spelling בית in place of בבית reflects the pronunciation אבית (Sharvit, *ibid.*, 66).

30 Qimron and Strugnell (1994:48, 50, 68).

31 Qimron writes: "*aleph* for the phoneme /ɛ/ is found primarily after the relative -ש" (Qimron [1980b:344]).

32 I am ignoring here the vocalization of the particle with a *shewa* before small words (שְׁהוּא, שְׁאֵין) which come in close proximity to the following word. See Morag (1964:184–186), and above, Chapter 19 § 25.

33 Before a guttural, the *šin* would be vocalized with a *qamets*, similar to the vocalization שָׁאַתָּה (Judg 6:17).

34 With regard to the use of the *aleph* as a vowel letter to represent an [a] vowel in medial position, see the presentation of the data in Qimron (above, n. 31), p. 335–348. For its use for

vowel is also known as a very rare alternative even within the Tiberian tradition: שַׁקַּמְתִּי (Judg 5:7), בְּשַׁגַּם (Gen 6:3), שָׁאַתָּה (Judg 6:17). Furthermore, one ought to bring into the discussion the fact that we have clear evidence of the vowel [a] in the relative particle -שׁ in a very common word in Mishnaic Hebrew, עַכְשָׁיו/עַכְשָׁו. This is a reflex of עַד + כְּשַׁהוּא, the Hebrew parallel to Aramaic עַד כַּד הוּא (= עַד כַּדּוּן).[35] The word עַכְשָׁיו ends in the diphthong [aw] after עד כשהוא contracted into a single word, which involved loss of the ה of הוא between the vowels [a] and [u]: ‘ad kəšahu > ‘akkəšahu > ‘ak̠šaw.[36] In light of all that has been said, I believe there is no reason not to assume that the writing שא – whether written independently or attached to the following word – is intended to represent [ša].[37]

Of course, one should not disregard the existence of the very widespread Hebrew tradition in which the vowel of the relative particle was an [e], not only in the reliable testimony of the Tiberian Masoretes regarding biblical Hebrew, but also in the evidence available regarding the pronunciation in Second Temple times and the oral tradition of Mishnaic Hebrew. The writings of the relative particle with a *yod* (-שי) in reliable manuscripts of Mishnaic Hebrew, such as שיעלעילה and משיביחלו, show clearly that there was a tradition of pronouncing the particle with an [e] vowel.[38] The spelling with *heh* which is found in the Kefar Devora inscription (שהלרבי),[39] in Qohelet (שהתקיף [6:10], שהסכל [10:3]), and in manuscripts of rabbinic literature (שֶׁהשִּׂמְחָה [mMQ 1:7], שֶׁהַדַּרְכָּן [mBQ 1:1]], שֶׁהִבְּתוֹכוֹ [m‘Eduy 1:14] in MS Kaufmann)[40] could represent either of the two vowels, [e] or [a].[41]

---

this purpose in word-final position, it should suffice to point out the tendency in reliable manuscripts of rabbinic literature to use an *aleph* to represent the feminine ending on non-biblical words, e.g., גּוּמָא (mKil 3:5 etc. [4×]), הַקּוּפָּא (mNaz 1:5 etc.) in MS Kaufmann (and there are other, similar, examples in other witnesses), and לָעוּקָא (mMa‘as 1:7) in a Mishnah with Babylonian vocalization; see Bar-Asher 2009a Vol. 2:279, 284, 286.

35 See: Ben-Ḥayyim (1954:81–82), and Bar-Asher (2009a:1.35).

36 As is known, this is not the only series of words which contracted into a single new word. Compare משהו < מה + ש + הוא, מנדעם/מדעם < מן + ידע + מה (> מידי in Babylonian Aramaic).

37 The two orthographies of שא – independent and attached to the following word – match the data cited above, n. 34.

38 See Epstein 1948:1243.

39 See Orman (1971:406).

40 See Bar-Asher 2009a Vol. 1:231.

41 I have consistently used the transcription [e], as opposed to [ɛ], as the particle is realized today. It should be noted that Steven Fassberg suggested another explanation of the spelling with a *heh*: according to him, it represents the gemination of the following consonant. See Fassberg (1996).

§ 19 **The pronunciation of gutturals.** It should be noted that all the velar and uvular consonants (ה, א, ח, ע) are written in their proper etymological places in our text. For example: for א, see לאבשלם, אני, שאול; for ה, see מהר, התקבלת, שאהיה; for ח, see חשבן, אחיך, לחרבן; for ע, see ארבע, עשר, לעמת, שועל. This certainly indicates that the guttural consonants had stable pronunciations. On the other hand, there are a couple of details which may point to some instability. It should be said at the outset, though, that these details appear in words whose reading is doubtful, so what is said here is speculative. I think it fitting to list the examples, however, in case the hope of the editors – that other documents related to this one will be discovered – is fulfilled, in which case it will be possible to resolve the doubts. The words I have in mind are the following.

A. ואפר<ע>ך: since this is a very plausible interpretation, this would be clear evidence for the loss of the ע.
B. לבעילי: if the reading is correct, it seems that this is evidence for a form such as לְבֶעְלִי. Perhaps the writing with the י is connected to the loss of the ע, showing a development to a pronunciation such as לְבֵילִי = לְבֵ(ע)ילִי = lə-ḇēlī (?).
C. See also the discussion of the combination כתבא חזה below, in § 24.

§ 20 **The writing כסילו.** It should be noted that the month name Kislev is written in epigraphic texts as כסלו;[42] in rabbinic literature it is attested plene, כסליו (e.g., mRH 1:3 in MS Kaufmann and in other witnesses). Is the spelling כסילו in our text, with a *yod* after the *samekh*, a mistaken reflex of כסליו, in which the *yod* was accidentally written before the *lamed* rather than after it, or is it simply a scribal error, and the *yod* does not belong at all?[43] But perhaps the spelling כסילו is evidence for a syllable formerly closed by a sibilant which was opened: *kislew* > *kisəlew.* Such a process is known to us from a few words in BH, such as עִשְּׂבוֹת (Prov 27:25); קַשְּׁתוֹתָם (Jer 51:56); הַצְּפִינוֹ (Exod 2:3), and so on; in all these cases, a syllable closed by a sibilant was opened secondarily.[44] I am not inclined to render a decision in this issue, in as much as one ought not to build on an isolated example that is possibly the result of a mistaken spelling produced by a scribe.

---

42 In her concordance of the texts from the Judean Desert, Yardeni listed three attestations of the spelling כסלו, and a fourth which is plausibly restored [כס]לו. Cf. Yardeni (above, n. 26), *Vol. 2: Paleography and Concordance.*

43 The spelling כסליו does not accord with the orthographic practices of our text, since [e] vowels are not written plene; compare קַיָּם, פּוֹטֵר, עֵנָב, and see the discussion above § 11.

44 The *dagesh* in the sibilant testifies with the force of a hundred witnesses that the *shewa* is *mobile* and the syllable is open!

24.5 Minor items in Configuration and Syntax

§ 21 I have already discussed in earlier paragraphs some matters of morphology, such as the form שאיוהב (above at the end of § 6), I will suffice here with a short note on one morphological detail and add two syntactic notes (one regarding the use of different forms and one regarding sentence structures). In all three of these issues, the language of our text differs somehow from the norm. In this context it is worth pointing out that although in most respects the language of our text is clear, the mixture of languages does reveal some signs of confusion. The details are as follows.

§ 22 **התקבלת.** As discussed above, it seemed best to accept the interpretation of the form התקבלת (ll. 7, 8) as a 1st person common singular Aramaic form, put in the mouth of the writer of the text: הִתְקַבְּלֵת. That being the case, it is very surprising that all the verbs in the declaration Miriam bat Yaakov makes to her husband's brother are in Hebrew (מודה אני, שאהיה [3×], שאיוהב [?],[45] פוטר), and the forms of the verbs ואפר<ע>ך and קים are also well explained as Hebrew forms, but the single word התקבלת is in Aramaic. Nevertheless it should be noted that this is the verb which expresses the essential point of Miriam's declaration, and this is written in the language understood by her.

§ 23 **The absence of the definite article.** The absence of the definite article on the series of four nouns in ll. 6–7, כתבה וביה וקנין ומהר, is most surprising. All of these items, or nearly all of them, are objects identifiable at the time the writer of the document refers to them, so the definite article is expected. Even if the words are all Aramaic, the rules of Palestinian Aramaic grammar obligate marking such nouns with the definite article.

§ 24 **Strange syntax.** In one place there is a syntactic structure which is strange and not easily understood: in ll. 9–10 we read, על חשבן מאשא כתבא חזה פוטר רכושי לותך. (A different reading was proposed by Qimron, but his proposal – to read כתב שהיה שטר in place of כתבא חזה פוטר – does not produce an intelligible text.[46]) The editors translated this as, על חשבון מה שהשטר ראוי – פוטר רכושי אצלך "on account of what the document is fit for – it exempts my property which is under your control." I do not understand the phrase which is translated, "what the document is fit for." If this is what the text meant, the scribe would have written, על חשבן מאשא כתבא אמר "on

45 If indeed this is the correct reading of the text, although the root is borrowed from Aramaic, the form is Hebrew.

46 See Esther Eshel, Hanan Eshel, and Ada Yardeni, "A Document from 'Year 4 of the Destruction of the House of Israel'," *DSD* 18 (2011), 5 n. 14 and 16.

account of what the text *says*." Therefore I would like to suggest a slightly different reading, with one additional word and a different interpretation of another word; I suggest a different sentence structure: על חשבן מאשא <היה> כתבא חזה [= הזה] פוטר רכושי לותך. I assume that the word היה was omitted (מא שא היה), as in the expression which is repeated a number of times, מא שאהיה (= מה) (ll. 5, 8). Likewise, I propose that the word חזה may be a reflex of הזה "this one" with replacement of the ה with a ח.[47] If my suggestion is accepted, a sentence with perfectly clear structure would emerge. It should then be translated, "anyone who gives my property to you, on account of what was, this document absolves my property under your control." It should be acknowledged, however, that the suggestion which yields such a clear sentence relies on a correction and an orthographic interpretation which each require support in order to be convincing.

24.6 Concluding note

§ 25 Not all that needs to be said about the language of this text has been said, not only regarding the details which were discussed here in brief, but even regarding the issues which were accorded more detailed discussions. With regard to the larger questions of the admixture of Hebrew within Aramaic and of Aramaic within Hebrew, there is much that needs to be added and clarified. Most crucially, what I said at the outset should be stressed: the presence of quite a few uncertain readings requires repeated and careful study. It is clear that what is presented here is just the beginning of the linguistic analysis of this text. If some of the uncertain readings become certain, and if other similar or related texts are discovered, we will be able to reach a better understanding of the nature of this text, in terms of both content and language.

---

47 If this is correct, this is an additional detail testifying to the loss of the gutturals in our text. The definite article (הַ) before the pronoun זה was written as ח, yielding חזה. I should note that when I discussed the loss of the ה above, I refrained from also discussing the ה written by the second witness, in the names יהורם and זכריה in l. 14, both of which look like ח (as already noted by the editors!), because my focus was on the text written by the scribe. Additionally, it appears that the signature shows that this witness was not expert in writing.

25 From Oral Transmission to Written Transmission (Concerning the meaning of some orthographic forms in the manuscripts of the Mishnah and of Rabbinic Literature)

25.1 Introductory Comments

§ 1 The manuscripts of rabbinic literature – first and foremost the manuscripts of the Mishnah – often transmit orthographic forms and morphological formations that are unusual and strange. As is well known, in the process of copying texts, various types of errors can and do occur.[1] Any unusual and strange spelling can be easily interpreted as such an error from ancient times. However, the comprehensive and thorough study of rabbinic manuscripts shows that many of these anomalies are not errors, but rather special linguistic features that reflect an authentic linguistic reality. I intend in this study to deal with a few of these orthographic forms, which are only a small sample of a much wider phenomenon.

§ 2 I maintain that most of the unusual orthographic forms dealt with in this study share a common background: the transition of an orally-transmitted text to writing. Sometimes the example in question is evidence of what happened as an individual scribe at some point in time wrote down what he heard when a text was read to him. There is sometimes even a sound reason to believe that the example in question dates from an early stage in the transmission of the text: perhaps the seventh or eighth centuries when rabbinic texts, chiefly the Mishnah, orally transmitted for hundreds of years, were written down for the first time. While errors do occur in the transition from the oral to the written, these are often pseudo-errors. These orthographic forms reflect unique scribal practices already forgotten in ancient times. Those early scribes who copied the texts written by their predecessors did not understand the forms in question and thus passed on forms with no bearing in the given context.[2] The examples that I shall present and discuss will clarify my intention. Most of these examples are from the Mishnah, while a few are from the manuscripts of other Tannaitic works.

---

1 Cf. chapter 9 in Bar-Asher (2009a:1.223–239).

2 See what happened to the scribes of the Parma A and the Cambridge manuscripts of the Mishnah to Bekhorot 6:2 (see § 9 below).

25.2 Unusual orthographic forms and their meanings

25.2.1 רובע עצמות/רוב עצמות – a quarter-*qab* of bones

§ 3 Prof. J. N. Epstein long ago showed that in one place in the Mishnah (m. Nazir 7:3) the scribe of the Kaufmann (K) manuscript, the most reliable of the Mishnaic manuscripts, wrote ורוב עצמות instead of ורובע עצמות.[3] The vocalizer of the manuscript corrected this by adding the letter *'ayin* to the first word in the phrase: וְרוֹבַ[ע] עצמות. Clearly the noun *roba'* and the noun *rob* are two nouns that signify different amounts: *roba'* signifies an exact quantity – a quarter-*qab* (as well as the measuring tool of that quantity), while *rob* signifies an unspecified but large amount. The context of this mishnah confirms that *roba'* is the original version.

§ 4 It is easy to explain how the version ורוב עצמות came into being. In the expression ורובע עצמות the consonant *'ayin* appears twice consecutively, and these two coalesced in oral recitation into one geminated consonant (*roba''ătsamot*). The text was apparently recited orally to the scribe, who heard the geminated *'ayin*, but transcribed it as a single *'ayin*, since in Hebrew, whether biblical, rabbinic or other, a geminated consonant is always written with one letter.[4] Thus the spelling ורוב עצמות was formed instead of ורובע עצמות. The wrong noun is thus attested here: the noun רוב (instead of רובע), which does not fit the context.

25.2.2 בָּאָת/בָּאָה – has arisen

§ 5 The mishnah in Nega'im (5:1), according to all reliable manuscripts, reads as follows: ... כל ספק נגעים טהור ... מי שהיתה בו בהרת כגריס והסגירה ספק שהיא היא ספק שאחרת בָּאָה תחתיה טמא = "Any condition of doubt in what concerns leprosy-signs is deemed clean ... If a man had a bright spot the size of a split bean and it was shut up, ... and it is in doubt whether it is the same or whether another has arisen in its place, he is nevertheless unclean." Thus it appears in all of the reliable manuscripts of this mishnah – Kaufmann, Parma B, Antonin[5] – and it appears thus unvocalized in the manuscripts

3 See Epstein 1948:1212.

4 Only rarely is a geminated consonant represented by a double letter in Hebrew literature, including rabbinic literature (as Epstein has shown, for example: מדדה for מְדָּה see Epstein [1948:1258–1259]; see also Bar-Asher [1985] for the spelling שטטוואתו instead of שטוואתו [examples from Aramaic were also cited]).

5 The *dagesh* is not visible in the letter *bet* in manuscript Antonin.

Parma A, Cambridge, Maimonides. All these manuscripts have the form בָּאָה and not בָּאָת, which is the regular form in Mishnaic Hebrew according to all of the reliable manuscripts of the Mishnah.[6] Gideon Haneman already recognized this form and explained it:[7] In the sequence בָּאָת תחתיה the two consecutive *taws* coalesced in oral recitation into one geminated consonant (*ba'aṯ taḥteha* > *ba'attaḥteha*), and the geminated consonant was written with one letter. Since the phrase in question is composed of two words, the second vowel of the first word was represented by the letter *he* at the end of the word, and thus the version בָּאָה תחתיה was formed, concealing the original construction בָּאָת תחתיה.

§ 6 As stated, it is clear that the omission of the letters *'ayin* and *taw* in the two words above occured when the orally-transmitted text was first transcribed. There is, however, a difference between the two examples. The first example from Tractate m. Nazir (7:3) – ורוב עצמות instead of ורובע עצמות – attested in only one manuscript (K) seems to be an isolated occurrence resulting from a single scribe's work when copying the oral recitation into writing. On the other hand, the second example – בָּאָה instead of בָּאָת – is attested in many sources, in fact, in all of the ancient and reliable manuscripts of the Mishnah. It can thus be assumed that this latter spelling dates from an early stage in the history of the transmission of the text, perhaps when the Mishnah was written down for the first time at the end of the seventh century or the beginning of the eighth. We can therefore understand why this change is attested in all of the reliable manuscripts of the Mishnah.

25.2.3 עֵינָב/עֵינָיו[8]

§ 7 Another most interesting example, clearly a result of a similar development, occurs in Tractate Bekhorot of the Mishnah (6:2), where various defects of the eye are specified: הרי בעיניו דק תבלול חלזון נחש וענב.[9] I will focus on the sequence חִלָּזוֹן נָחָשׁ וְעֵנָב.[10] Hanokh Albeck explains these three words as follows: "diseases of the eye which are similar in their form or in their nature to a snail or a snake or a berry." It is the third defect listed here

6 See Haneman (1980a:396) and Bar-Asher (2009:2.89).

7 See Haneman (1980a), *ibid*. He explains it as follows: "This is an erroneous separation of the phonetic sequence."

8 In this example transliteration of the words is provided rather than transcription.

9 This mishnah is quoted according to the printed text.

10 This excerpt is quoted according to H. Albeck's edition of the Mishnah with vocalization by H. Yalon (Albeck 1952).

which is of interest to me: ענב/עינב (the plene spelling is attested in the Maimonides manuscript and in the first printed edition; the form עֵינָב is also attested in the Mishnah with Babylonian vocalization [m. Nedarim 11:6]).[11] This form is also indicated in the Tosefta (Bekhorot 4:2) with a slight variation in spelling (*aleph* instead of *'ayin*): חלזון כמשמעו נחש כמשמעו אינב כמשמעו (חלזון: according to its meaning, נחש according to its meaning, אינב according to its meaning").[12]

§ 8 The K manuscript, in contrast, reads הרי בעינו דק חלזון נחש עֵינָיו. A similar reading is found in the Vatican manuscript of the Sifra (Emor 3:1) חֲלַזוֹן לַחַשׁ עֵינָיו.[13] It is clear to me that the form עֵינָיו (in the K and Vat manuscripts) is a variant spelling of the form עֲנָב/עֵינָב. Assumingly, in the transition from oral to written transmission the "unusual and popular" form עיניו came into being.[14] One may presume that two factors brought about the appearance of the form עֵינָיו instead of עֵינָב (עֲנָב): 1. the identical pronunciation of the *waw* and the spirant *bet* in Mishnaic Hebrew; both were probably pronounced [v]. 2. The fact that the defect in question is of the **eye** and the present context echoes the Biblical verse או תבלֻל בְּעֵינוֹ "or that hath a blemish in his eye" (Leviticus 21:20).[15]

§ 9 Examining the findings in two of the most reliable manuscripts of the Mishnah – Cambridge and Parma A – shows that already in ancient times the scribes misunderstood the spelling עיניו (= עינב) in the above text in Tractate Bekhorot. In the Cambridge manuscript the word in question is written with the addition of the particle בְּ: בעיניו (in his eyes). It also appears thus in the Parma A manuscript except that in this manuscript the word is split into two: ב עֵינָיו (the letter ב appears at the end of the line and the word עֵינָיו at the beginning of the following line). The letter ב, however, has a dot above it to indicate that it is to be erased. Thus, following this correction, the evidence from the Parma A manuscript joins the evidence of MS Kaufmann and the Vatican manuscript of the Sifra. The whole phrase in MS Cambridge (and in MS Parma A manuscript before the correction) reads הרי בעינו דק תבלול חלזון נחש בעיניו. It seems that in the original text that lay before the two scribes or in the original text of the manuscripts that they used as their sources, the

---

11 See Yeivin (1985:931).

12 This version is quoted according to the Databases of the Historical Dictionary Project of the Academy of the Hebrew Language.

13 There is a marginal note in the Vatican manuscript that brings the alternative forms נָחָשׁ עֵינָב for the two nouns לַחַשׁ עֵינָיו (sic!) that are in the body of the text.

14 The spelling עיניו for עינב is not only "unusual and popular," but also an expected spelling in reliable manuscripts, similar to the spelling יוונה for יַבְנֶה.

15 See the continuation of the homiletic interpretation in *Sifra* to this verse.

reading was עֵינָיו, as in the Kaufmann manuscript and the Vatican manuscript of the Sifra. However, the scribes of the Cambridge and Parma A manuscripts did not correctly understand the spelling עֵינָיו as a variant for עֵינָב, but rather as the noun עֵינַיִם ("eyes") to which the pronominal suffix has been added. That is to say, they understood עֵינָיו to mean "his eyes"; therefore the particle בְּ ("in") was added to yield the form בעיניו ("in his eyes"). This unique reading – עֵינָיו instead of עֵינָב – was preserved in the Italian Mishnah until the twentieth century, as evidenced in the 1929 edition of the Mishnah printed in Livorno. The text reads וְעֵינָיו but the form בעיניו is brought as a variant reading.

25.2.4 היות/להיות

§ 10 I will now bring an example from outside of the Mishnah. Liora Grilak recently wrote a doctoral dissertation on the language of the Mekhilta de-Rabbi Ishmael (Grilak 2008), based on the findings in the Oxford 151.2 manuscript of this text.[16] Grilak's work provides a comprehensive and detailed analysis of verbal and nominal morphological formations in comparison with other Mishnaic Hebrew texts, primarily the language of the Mishnah as analyzed by recent generations of scholars. There are quite a few unusual forms of interest in the comprehensive description of the grammatical issues analyzed by Grilak. Many of these require additional interpretation and complementary remarks; I will touch on only one point here.

§ 11 In her discussion of the tense system (p. 64) Grilak points out the unusual tense "היות אומרים" instead of "להיות אומרים". Grilak brings two citations of what is essentially the same sentence:

1. ר' אלע' המודעי או':[17] למידין היו ישר'[18] היות או'[19] דברי תרעומת על משה (Massekhta de-Vayyassa‘ I, p. 155).[20]

16 Grilak brings the findings from the Oxford 151.2 manuscript according to the text that appears in the Ancient Literature Database of the Historical Dictionary Project of the Academy of the Hebrew Language.

17 = אומר

18 = ישראל

19 = אומרים

20 Unfortunately Grilak did not realize that only the first quote is taken from the Oxford manuscript. The second quote is a completion in the aforementioned database from the Munich 117 manuscript.

2. ר' אלעזר המיודעי או'[21]: למידים היו ישר'[22] היות' אומ'[23] דברי תרעומת על משה
(Massekhta de-Vayyassa' I, p. 159)[24] "The Israelites were in the habit of speaking words of complaint against Moses".

Indeed, the form in the manuscript is היות instead of להיות (the infinitive construct with *lamed*). להיות is the usual form used in the verbal system of mishnaic Hebrew, where the infinitive construct without *lamed* does not exist. Grilak apparently concludes from these lines that there are examples in the Mekhilta of the form היות, the infinitive construct without *lamed* as in Biblical Hebrew. I disagree with this conclusion and intend to offer an alternative explanation.

§ 12 It seems to me that the unusual form can be explained in a simpler fashion, thus negating Grilak's conclusion. It will be noted that in the two excerpts the word היות follows the word ישראל, which is written twice in an abbreviated form – ישר'. Had the word been written in its full form, it would have been easy to discern the exact construction of the phrase: למידין (למידים) היו ישראל היות אומרים. The word ישראל ends with the consonant *lamed*, and the phrase in its original form almost certainly accorded with the regular construction in rabbinic Hebrew: ישראל להיות (*Yisra'el lihyot*). In this sequence the two *lameds* coalesced into one geminated *lamed*, which was transcribed only once as with any geminated consonant. We can only assume that someone recited the text orally before the scribe, who heard a geminated *lamed* but transcribed it with only one letter as is the rule.[25] Over the course of time this entire picture disappeared as the scribal practice of writing common words in an abbreviated form became accepted. Thus appeared the spelling ישר' היות, concealing the pronunciation of the sequence ישראל היות wherein two *lameds* coalesced into one.[26] The acceptance of my proposed explanation then negates

21 see note 17.
22 see note 18.
23 = אומרים
24 The form המיודעי (in the second quote) is attested five times and only in the Munich manuscript. The remainder of the appearances of the word in the Munich manuscript are in its usual form המודעי.
25 The fact that the first *lamed* and not the second one was transcribed has no bearing. To a Hebrew scribe the phrase ישראל היות appears more appropriate than ישרא להיות wherein the first word appears to be defective.
26 By the way, it should be pointed out that Grilak brings an additional example from Midrash Tehillim with a construction identical to the examples she brings from the Mekhilta: מיד התחיל היות שואל "He immediately began to ask". Here too the word היות comes after the word התחיל that ends in *lamed*. It seems that here too התחיל להיות was transcribed as התחיל היות – a construction written with one *lamed* instead of two.

Grilak's finding that in the *Mekhilta* the infinitive construct היות instead of להיות is used.

§ 13 All four examples cited in this study contain unique or strange spellings that appear to deviate from orthographic and grammatical rules: רוֹב עצמות instead of רוֹבַע עצמות, בָּאָה instead of בָּאַת, עֵינָיו instead of עֵינָב, היות instead of להיות. On observing these and examining their meanings, they seem unfamiliar because of their unusual orthographies. I have sought to explain their appearance as connected to the transcription of texts from an oral transmission.

§ 14 In two of the examples the change in question is attested in only one manuscript (ורובע עצמות < רוב עצמות in the Kaufmann manuscript of the Mishnah, להיות אומרים < היות אומרים in the Oxford manuscript of the Mekhilta), while the other two examples were attested in all the reliable manuscripts (באת תחתיה > באה תחתיה in all of the reliable manuscripts of the Mishnah, עֵינָיו instead of עֵינָב in two reliable manuscripts: K and Vat and in Pa after the correction as well as in other manuscripts in a mistaken manner). We can surmise about the first examples that the change occurred through the pen of one scribe. In the other places the change apparently came about at an early stage when the texts of rabbinic literature, transmitted orally for many generations, first made the transition to written transmission in the second half of the first millennium.

25.3 Additions

§ 15 The four examples above are only a few of many. This appears to me to be the correct way to interpret some of the special orthographic forms that scholars recognized in the past, but did not offer a proper and complete explanation of their appearance in the Mishnah or in other rabbinic texts. I am referring to changes in the word לָה to לַ and the word לֹא to לֹ or לַ in a few Mishnayot and to the fusion of other particles with the following words into one orthographic word. I explain these as I explained the four spellings above. This should be explained in somewhat more detail:

25.3.1 לָה > לַ, as in וקוצה לחלה < וקוצה לה חלה

§ 16 The verb קָצָה, which means cut, slice, etc., takes a direct object as its complement. For example תאינים של שביעית אין קוצין אותן = "Seventh Year figs may not be cut off" (m. Shevi'it 8:6); האשה יושבת וקוצה חלתה ערומה = "A woman may cut off her Dough-offering while sitting and naked"

(m. Halla 2:3). Twice in the Mishnah we see that, according to the K manuscript, the verb seems to take an indirect object, and the verb קָצָה is governed by the particle לְ:

A. ומודים שהיא אוכלת במעשר וְ(ב)קוֹצָה לַחַלָּה = "But they agree that she may eat of [Second] Tithe and set apart the *ḥalla*" (m. Nidda 10:7). However, other manuscripts read "וְקוֹצָה לָהּ חַלָּה ...". This is the text in MS Parma B, and it appears thus, unvocalized, in Parma A, Cambridge, Antonin,[27] and Maimonides, as well.[28] This is also the text in all of the current printed editions.

B. אי זו היא דת משה ... ולא קוצה לחלה = "What [conduct is such that transgresses] the Law of Moses ... or does not set apart *ḥalla*" (m. Ketubbot 7:6). This, as has been stated, is the text of the Kaufmann manuscript scribe, but the vocalizer corrected the text to read: "ולא קוצה (ל)[לָהּ] חַלָּה ...". The reading of the Kaufmann manuscript vocalizer agrees, again, with MSS Parma A, Cambridge, and Maimonides, all of which read, אי זו היא דת משה ... ולא קוצה לה חלה.

§ 17 As previously stated, the reading וקוצה לחלה (= לה חלה) is preserved only in the K manuscript in m. Ketubbot (7:6) and m. Nidda (10:6). In Ketubbot the text was corrected, while in Nidda the vocalizer apparently did not understand that the orthography לחלה meant לָהּ חַלָּה, and therefore did not correct it. It seems therefore that the K manuscript indicates that the verb קוֹצָה is governed by the complement that begins with the invariable particle לְ.

§ 18 In order to explain the reading in K, it is important to note the clear evidence that the consonant *he* of the third person feminine singular pronoun was not pronounced in many reading traditions of rabbinic Hebrew, including that of the K manuscript. This is clearly attested by spellings such as שֶׁבָּא (m. Shevi'it 9:3, MS Kaufmann), reflecting שֶׁבָּהּ*, and **אוירא** של חצר (m. Baba Batra 4:4, MS Cambridge), as opposed to **אוירה** in other manuscripts. There are additional such examples in many manuscripts.[29] In light of this it is clear that the form לָהּ was pronounced *la*, rather than *lah*. It is clear then how the sequence וקוצה לה חלה was pronounced וקוצה לַחַלָּה. One who vocalizes לַחַלָּה (the *lamed* is vocalized with a *patah* as if to be vocalized as the definite article), as the K manuscript vocalizer does in Nidda, shows that he did not understand the reading. Also in this case it stands to reason that in the transition from

27 Here the *lamed* of the word לה is vocalized with a *pataḥ* (לַה).
28 The data from these manuscripts relate only to the words וְקוֹצָה לָהּ חַלָּה.
29 See Bar-Asher (1985:85–88) and also Bar-Asher (1980a:25).

the oral form to the written text the two words לָה חֲלָה (< לָהּ) coalesced into one orthographic word – לחלה.[30] Thus, the complement of the verb קָצָה is a direct object even according to the Kaufmann manuscript.

25.3.2 לֹא > לְ

§ 19 The development described above of the sequence לה חלה becoming coalesced into לחלה is reflected in the fusion of the negative word לֹא with the following word. I will explain by analyzing a few examples brought by Epstein: לחולין (< לא חולין), לאוכל (< לא אוֹכֶל), לקרבן (< לא קרבן), לנתן (< לא נתן).

Here are the explicit examples: האומר לא חולין לא אוכל לך ... אסור = "If he said, 'May what I eat of yours be "not *hullin*" ...' it is forbidden to him" (m. Nedarim 1:3). In other words, one who vows and says to his fellow "I shall not eat anything of yours that is non-consecrated but only from a sacrifice" is like one who vows regarding a sacrifice, and he is forbidden to eat from his fellow's food.[31] There is some textual evidence for the writing of לא חולין as לחולין, including a Genizah fragment which reads לחולין לא אוכל לך or לאוכל לך.[32] A similar case is in the following mishnah: – לקרבן לא אוכל לך רבי מאיר אוסר (m. Nedarim 1:4).[33] Here too, the meaning of the text is לא קרבן "not for a sacrifice," written as לקרבן. The orthography with two words (לא קרבן) is attested in MSS Kaufmann, Parma A and Cambridge, but the one who reads לקרבן[34] as לַקָּרְבָּן (< להקרבן = "for the sacrifice") did not understand that the *lamed* represents the negative particle לֹא.

An additional example from the Kaufmann manuscript of the Mishnah exists: מת הבן בתוך שלשים יום אף על פי שנתן לכהן יחזיר לו ... לאחר שלשים

30 The word should have been vocalized לָחֲלָה with the *lamed* vocalized by a *kamats* (which reflects the *kamats* of the word לָהּ) and not לַחֲלָה with the *lamed* vocalized by a *pataḥ*. It seems that the vocalizer of K did not properly understand the word. However, it is also possible that the vocalizer correctly understood the word but nevertheless transcribed the *lamed* with *pataḥ* since the two vowel signs, *pataḥ* and *kamats*, were pronounced identically by him – [a]. The two vowel signs are frequently interchanged; in other words, in the vocalizer's reading tradition לָחֲלָה = לַחֲלָה.

31 See Albeck's (1952) commentary to this mishnah.

32 For the details see Epstein (1948:1213). Albeck (1952) *loc. cit.* also notes a similar reading: בנוסח אחר: לחולין (= לא חולין) שאוכל לך. All of the examples brought by Epstein appear under the heading "Haplography", namely that is "spelling mistakes".

33 See Epstein loc cit.

34 This is the vocalization in the Livorno edition of the Mishnah and that found in. Albeck (1952), with the vocalization by Yalon.

יום אפעלפי שֶׁלֹּנָתן [< שֶׁלֹּא נָתן][35] יתן = “If the son died within thirty days, although he had paid [the five *selas*] to the priest, the priest must give them back ... after thirty days, even if he had not paid, he must pay the priest” (M. Bekhorot 8:6).[36] In this case the vocalizer correctly understood the orthography without *aleph*.

§ 20 It is clear that in all of the examples cited above, the sequences לא חולין, לא קרבן, etc. were pronounced, and therefore written, as one word: לחולין, לקרבן. Sometimes the readers of the texts understood the unusual spellings, as is evident in the vocalization of the word שֶׁלֹּנָתן in the Kaufmann manuscript. The addition of the letter *aleph* comes to clarify the form, but sometimes scribes did not understand the abbreviated orthographies as reflected in the faulty vocalization of the word לְקָרְבָּן.

25.3.3 The spelling of short words

§ 21 Anyone familiar with the study of rabbinic Hebrew knows of the tendency of its scribes to write other short proclitic words connected to the word that follows them, for example, האם (< הָא אִם), משנגמר (< מִי שֶׁנִּגְמַר). In my opinion, it is the proximity of the short words to the following words that caused them to become fused into one word in oral pronunciation. Therefore, when the texts were transcribed, these words were written as one orthographic word. This is how we can explain all of the phrases mentioned in the research such as באצלן (< בא אצלן), והנוגעות (< וְהֵן נוֹגְעוֹת), משהן (< מַה שֶּׁהֵן), משנגמר (< מִי שֶׁנִּגְמַר), האם (< הָא אִם), האין (< הָא אֵין) etc.[37]

25.4 Summary

§ 22 The forms that deviate from the orthography and grammar of rabbinic Hebrew discussed here were not understood by scribes and sometimes not by scholars, or were interpreted differently by scholars. Sometimes these forms were removed from the text and more common, relevant forms were written in their stead; sometimes these forms were exchanged for forms that disrupt the context. Only careful study of the forms reveals their correct mean-

35 In this example: A. after the *lamed* was vocalized with a *ḥolam*, a small *aleph* was added (by whom?) between the lines with a *ḥolam* placed above it. B. The *tav* was not vocalized.

36 See Epstein *ibid*. However, he did not comment on the correction.

37 See details in Epstein (1948:1216–1220).

ing. As I have already reiterated: all the examples cited here are forms that came into being as a result of the transcription of orally transmitted texts.

§ 23 I have already stated that when there is much textual evidence and the form is substantiated many times, especially in primarily reliable texts, we can say that these forms originate in an early stage of the text's transmission. Indeed it is quite possible that the appearance of these unusual forms can be traced to the earliest stage of the transmission, when the orally transmitted texts were transcribed for the first time. However, when dealing with isolated evidence, when the phenomenon is attested in only one manuscript, we can assume that the text was recited orally to the scribe while transcribing. Certainly there are intermediary examples where we don't know the time of written transmission – whether these forms appeared in the earliest stages, when the Mishnah was written down for the first time, or whether they appeared at a relatively late stage when written manuscripts of the Mishnah already existed, but the scribe wrote down the text recited to him orally. In this case we can say: we have no intention of determining the exact timeline of when **orthographic** changes took place, but can rather indicate the possible process in which the unusual orthographic forms came into being.

Bibliography

Albeck, Chanoch. 1952. *Shishah Sidre Mishnah (The Six Orders of the Mishnah)*, 6 Vols. Jerusalem: Bialik Institute.

– 1966. *Mavo la-Mishnah (Introduction to the Mishnah)*, Jerusalem: Bialik Institute.

Allegro, J. M. 1968. "158. Biblical Paraphrase: Genesis, Exodus" in *Qumrân Cave 4: I (4Q158–4Q186)*, Edited by J. M. Allegro and A. A. Anderson, Discoveries in the Judaean Desert V, Oxford: Clarendon Press: 1–6.

Allen, W. S. 1974. *Vox Graeca: A Guide to the Pronunciation of Classical Greek*, Cambridge: Cambridge University Press.

Amar, J. 1979–1980. *Talmud Bavli Menuqqad al-pi Massoret Yehude Teman (Babylonian Talmud Vocalized According to the Yemenite Jewish Tradition)*, 20 Vols, Jerusalem: Menaqqed Press.

Avinery, I. 1964. *Yad ha-Lashon: Otzar Leshoni be-Seder Alef-Bet shel ha-Nosa'im* (Hebrew) Tel-Aviv: Izreel.

– 1976. *Heikhal ha-Mishqalim: Otzar kol Shemot ha-Shorashim ba-Lashon ha-'Ivrit m-ime ha-Miqra ve-'ad ha-Yom*, Tel-Aviv: Jzre'el Press.

Avishur, Y. 1974. *Pairs of Words in Biblical Literature and their Parallels in Semitic Literature of the Ancient Near East* (Hebrew), PhD dissertation, The Hebrew University of Jerusalem.

– 1984, *Stylistic Studies of Word-Pairs in Biblical and Ancient Semitic Literatures*. Alter Orient und Altes Testament 210, Kevelaer: Verlag Butzon & Bercker.

Avniyyon, E. et al. 1998. *Millon Sappir: Millon 'Ivri-'Ivri Entsiqlopedia be-Shittat ha-Hoveh, be-Hishtattefut Anshe Lashon, Hinnukh u-Madda'*, Tel-Aviv: Ita'av.

Azar, M. 1995. *Taḥbir Leshon ha-Mishnah*, Jerusalem: Academy of the Hebrew Language and University of Haifa Press.

Bahat, S. and Mishor, M. 1995. *Millon ha-Hoveh: Millon Shimmushi la-'Ivrit ha-Tiqnit, [Dictionary of Contemporary Hebrew]*, Jerusalem: Sifriyat Ma'ariv.

Baillet, M. 1982. *Qumran Grotte 4: III (4Q482–4Q520)*, Discoveries in the Judaean Desert VII, Oxford: Clarendon Press.

Bar-Asher, E. A. 2008. "The Imperative Forms of Proto-Semitic and a New Perspective on Barth's Law", *Journal of the American Oriental Society* 128: 233–255.

Bar-Asher, M. (ed.). 1971. Qovets Ma'amarim bi-Lshon Ḥazal: *A Collection of Articles on the Language of the Sages*, Vol. 1, Jerusalem: Academon Press.

– 1977a. "The Mishnah in Ms. Parma B of Seder Teharot – Introduction" (Hebrew), in Bar-Asher 1971:166–185 (= Bar-Asher 2009a, Vol. I: 131–161).

– 1977b. *Palestinian Syriac Studies: Source-Texts, Traditions, and Grammatical Problems Grammar* (Hebrew), Hebrew University.

– 1979. "Two unrecognized compound words" (Hebrew), *Lĕššonénu* 43: 185–193 (= Bar-Asher 2012a: 346–354).

– 1980a. *The Traditions of Mishnaic Hebrew in the Communities of Italy* (Hebrew), *Edah ve-Lashon* VI, Jerusalem: Magnes.

– 1980b. "Rare Forms in Mishnaic Hebrew" (Hebrew), *Lĕšonénu* 41 ([1977): 83–102 (= Bar-Asher 2009a, Vol.II: 126–144).

– (ed.) 1980. Qovets Ma'amarim bi-Lshon Ḥazal: *A Collection of Articles on the Language of the Sages*, Vol. II, Jerusalem: Academon Press.

- 1983a. "Forgotten Forms in Mishnaic Hebrew, Between the Scribe and the Vocalizer of MS Kaufmann of the Mishnah" (Hebrew), in Bar-Asher et al. (eds.) 1983: 110–183 (= Bar-Asher 2009a, Vol. I: 195–222).
- 1983b. "First Studies in the Mishnaic Hebrew Reflected in MS Rome of Sifre Numbers" (Hebrew), *Te'udah* 3: 139–165 (= Bar-Asher 2009a, Vol. I: 240–268).
- 1984a. "The Different Traditions of Mishnaic Hebrew" (Hebrew), *Tarbiẓ* 53:187–220 (= Bar-Asher 2009a, Vol. I: 76–108) .
- 1984b. "On Vocalization Errors in the Kaufmann Manuscript of the Mishnah" (Hebrew), *Massorot* 1: 1–17 (= Bar-Asher 2009a, Vol. I: 223–239).
- 1985. "The Historical Unity of Hebrew and Mishnaic Hebrew Research" (Hebrew), *Language Studies* 1: 75–99 (= Bar-Asher 2009a, Vol. I: 109–127).
- 1986. "Linguistic Investigations in Mishnaic Manuscripts – Language Types and Salient Features" (Hebrew), *Proceedings of the Israel Academy of Sciences and Humanities* 7: 183–210 (= Bar-Asher 2009a, Vol. I: 271–300).
- 1987. "The Different Traditions of Mishnaic Hebrew", in *Working with No Data: Semitic and Egyptian Studies Presented to Thomas O. Lamdin*, Edited by David Golomb, Winona Lake, Ind.: Eisenbrauns: 1–38.
- 1987a. "Two Phenomena in the Grammar of the Verb in Syro-Palestinian" (Hebrew) *Language Studies* 2–3: 111–126 (= Bar-Asher 2012a: 289–304) .
- 1990a. "L'hébreu mishnique: esquisse d'une description", *Comptes rendus de l'Académie des Inscriptions et Belles-Lettres*, Paris, pp. 199–237 (= Bar-Asher 1999b: 3–45).
- 1990b. "L'hebreu mishnique et la tradition samaritaine de l'hébreu", *Comptes rendus du premier congrès mondial des études samaritaines*, Tel-Aviv, pp. 315–330 (= Bar-Asher 1999b: 47–60).
- 1990c. "Contextual Forms and Pausal Forms in Mishnaic Hebrew According to MS Parma B." (Hebrew), *Language Studies* 4: 51–100 (= Bar-Asher 2009a, Vol. II: 28–70).
- 1991. "Details in the Grammar of III-*aleph* and III-*yod* verbs in Mishnaic Hebrew" (Hebrew), *Shay le-Chaim Rabin: Asuppat Mehqerei Lashon*, Jerusalem, pp. 55–66 (= Bar-Asher 2009a, Vol. II: 145–154) .
- 1992. "The Verbal Conjugations (= *The Binyanim*) of Tannaitic Hebrew: A Morphological Study" (Hebrew), *Language Studies* 5–6: 123–151 (= Bar-Asher 2009a, Vol. II: 3–27).
- (ed.) 1992. *Israel Yeivin Festschrift* (Hebrew) = *Language Studies* 5–6, Jerusalem: Magnes.
- 1993. "The Third Person Feminine Singular Past Tense of III-*yod* and III-*aleph* Verbs in Mishnaic Hebrew" (Hebrew), *Mehqerei Talmud* 2: 39–84 (= Bar-Asher 2009a, Vol. II: 71–111).
- 1998. "Additional Aspects on the Hebrew Component in the Vernaculars of the Jews in Southwestern France" (Hebrew), *Pe'amim* 74: 60–86 (= Bar-Asher 2007c, Vol. I: 144–172).
- 1999a. *Traditions linguistiques des Juifs d'Afriques du Nord* (Hebrew), 2d ed., Jerusalem: Bialik Institute.
- 1999b. *L'hébreu mishnique: études linguistiques*, Leuven-Paris: Peeters.
- 1999c. "Mishnaic Hebrew: An Introductory Survey", *Hebrew Studies* 40: 115–151.
- 2000. "A few Remarks on Mishnaic Hebrew and Aramaic in Qumran Hebrew", *Diggers at the well: Proceedings of a Third International Symposium on the Hebrew of the Dead Sea Scrolls Ben Sira*, Ed. T. Muraoka & J. E. Elwolde, Leiden-Boston-Köln: Brill, pp. 12–19.
- 2002. "On Several Linguistic Features of Qumran Hebrew" (Hebrew), *Lĕšonénu* 64: 7–31 (= Bar-Asher 2012a: 100–121).
- 2002b. "Modern Hebrew and Its Classical Background" (Hebrew), *Te'udah* 18: 203–215 (= Bar-Asher 2012b: 56–79).

- 2003. "Two Phenomena in Qumran Hebrew: Synchronic and Diachronic Aspects" (Hebrew), *Meghillot* 1: 167–183 (= Bar-Asher 2012a: 122–136).
- 2004a. "Comments on the Morphology of Nouns in Mishnaic Hebrew: Nouns Attested and Unattested in Biblical Hebrew", *Studia Orientalia* 99: 23–30.
- 2004b. "The *Pəʿul* Pattern and Its Implications" (Hebrew), *Lĕšonénu* 66: 59–85 (= Bar-Asher 2009a Vol II: 245–268).
- 2004c. "On Nominal Morphology in Mishnaic Hebrew" (Hebrew), *Studies in Samaritanism, Hebrew, and Aramaic, Presented to Avraham Tal* (Hebrew), Ed. M. Bar-Asher and M. Florentin, Jerusalem: Bialik Institute, pp. 189–212 (= Bar-Asher 2009a Vol. II: 157–177).
- 2006a. "Grammatical and Lexical Phenomena in the Dead Sea Scrolls (4Q374)" (Hebrew), *Meghillot* 4: 153–167 (= Bar-Asher 2012a: 163–176).
- 2006b. "The Modern Study of Mishnaic Hebrew: Achievements and Challenges" (Hebrew), *Lĕšonénu* 68: 11–29 (= Bar-Asher 2009a Vol. I: 58–75).
- 2007a. "*Kynyy hṣlmym / kywn hṣlmym*" (Hebrew), *Meghillot* 5–6: 279–288 (= Bar-Asher 2012a: 177–184).
- 2007b. "Mishnaic Hebrew and Biblical Hebrew", *Materia giudaica* 12/1–2: 63–71.
- 2007c. *Les traditions de l'Hebreu des communautes juives du Sud-Ouest de la France* (Hebrew), 2 Vols, Jerusalem: Bialik Institute.
- 2008. "On the Language of 'The Vision of Gabriel'", *Revue de Qumran* 23[92]: 491–524.
- 2009a. *Mehqarim bi-Lshon Hakhamim* (*Studies in Mishnaic Hebrew*), 2 vols., Jerusalem: Bialik Institute.
- 2009b. "On the Language in the 'Vision of Gabriel'" (Hebrew), *Meghillot* 7: 193–226 (= Bar-Asher 2012a: 232 – 261).
- 2009c. "The *pəʿolet* Pattern in Mishnaic Hebrew" (Hebrew), *Maśʾat Aharon: Linguistic Studies Presented to Aron Dotan* (Hebrew), Ed. M. Bar-Asher and C. E. Cohen. Jerusalem: Bialik Institute, pp. 92–101 (= Bar-Asher 2009a Vol. II: 269–277) .
- 2010a. "Qumran Hebrew and Mishnaic Hebrew" (Hebrew), *Meghillot* 8–9: 287–317 (= Bar-Asher 2012a: 196–222).
- 2010b. "Phenomena in the Morphology of Mishnaic Hebrew" (Hebrew), *Mishnaic Hebrew and Related Fields: Studies in Honor of Shimon Sharvit*, Ed. E. Hazan and Z. Livnat, Ramat-Gan – Ashkelon: Bar-Ilan University, pp. 17–33 (= Bar-Asher 2009a Vol. II: 178–194).
- 2012a. *Leshonot Rishonim: Studies in the Language of the Bible, the Dead Sea Scrolls, and Aramaic* (Hebrew), Jerusalem: Magnes Press.
- 2012b. *Studies in Modern Hebrew* (Hebrew), Jerusalem: The Academy of Hebrew Language.
- et al. (eds.). 1983. *Linguistic Studies Presented to Ze'ev Ben-Hayyim on his Seventieth Birthday* (Hebrew). Jerusalem: Magnes Press.
- et al. (eds.) 1993. *'Iyyunei Miqra u-Farshanut 3: Moshe Goshen-Gottstein Memorial Volume* (Hebrew), Ramat-Gan: Bar-Ilan University Press.
- et al. (ed.). 2007a. *Teshurah Le-'Amos – Collected Studies in Biblical Exegesis Presented to 'Amos Hakham*, Alon-Shevut: Tevunot.
- et al. (ed.). 2007b. *Shai le-Sara Japhet: Studies in Bible, its Interpretation, and its Language*. Jerusalem: Bialik Institute.

Barth, J. 1913. *Die Pronominalbildung in den semitischen Sprachen*, Leipzig: Hinrichs.

Bauer, H. and Leander, P. 1922. *Historische Grammatik der hebräischen Sprache*, Halle: M. Niemeyer.

Baumgarten, J. M. 1992. "The Laws of the Damascus Document in Current Research", in Broshi (ed.) 1992: 51–62.
– 1996. *Qumran Cave 4. XIII: The Damascus Document (4Q266–273)*, Discoveries in the Judaean Desert XVIII, Oxford: Clarendon Press.
– and Daniel Schwartz. 1993. "Damascus Document (CD", *The Dead Sea Scrolls: Hebrew, Aramaic, and Greek Texts with English Translations: Volume 2: Damascus Document, War Scroll and Related Documents*, Ed. J. H. Charlesworth, Tübingen: J. C. B. Mohr (Paul Siebeck), pp. 4–9.
Beit-Arié, M. 1971. "The Vocalization of the Mahzor of the Congregation of Worms" (Hebrew), in Bar-Asher (ed.) 1971: 302–347.
– 1980. "The Kaufmann Manuscript of the Mishnah – Its Place and Date of Origin" (Hebrew), in Bar-Asher (ed.) 1980: 84–99.
Bendavid, A. 1971. *Leshon Miqra u-Lshon Hakhamim* (*Biblical Hebrew and Mishnaic Hebrew*), 2 vols. 2nd ed., Tel-Aviv: Devir.
Ben-Ḥayyim, Z. 1954. *Studies in the Traditions of the Hebrew Language*, Madrid: Instituto Arias Montano.
– 1957–1977. *Literary and Oral Tradition of Hebrew and Aramaic Amongst the Samaritans* (Hebrew), 5 Vols., Jerusalem: Bialik Institute.
– 1971. "The Samaritan Tradition and its Ties with the Linguistic Tradition of the Dead Sea Scrolls and with Mishnaic Hebrew" (Hebrew), *Lĕšonénu* 22 (1958): 223–245 (republished in Bar-Asher [ed.] 1971: 36–58).
– 1963. *Sefer ha-Meqorot* (*The Book of Source-Texts*), Jerusalem: Academy of the Hebrew Language.
– 1971. "Comments on the Inscriptions of Sfire" (Hebrew), *Lĕšonénu* 35: 243–253.
– 1971. "The Form of the Pronominal Suffixes *-ka*, *-ta*, and *-ha* in the Traditions of Hebrew" (Hebrew), in Bar-Asher (ed.) 1971: 59–92.
– 1981. "Word-Studies III" (Hebrew), *Tarbiẓ* 50: 192–208.
– 1982. "Further Study of the Evaluation of Chronology in Language" (Hebrew), in *Isaac Seeligman Volume*, vol. 1. Eds. Y. Zacovitch and A. Rofe, Jerusalem: A. Rubenstein, pp. 25–41.
– 1985. *Tibat Marqe: A Collection of Samaritan Midrashim: Edited, Translated and Annotated,* (Hebrew), Jerusalem: The Israel Academy of Sciences and Humanities.
– 1985. "The Historical Unity of the Hebrew Language and its Division into Periods" (Hebrew), *Language Studies* 1: 3–25.
– 1987. "Notes on Grammar and Lexicology" (Hebrew), *Language Studies* 2–3: 99–109.
– 1992. *Be-milḥamtah shel Lashon* (*Struggle for Language*), Jerusalem: Academy for the Hebrew Language Press.
Ben Sira. 1973. *Sefer Ben Sira: The Text, Concordance, and Grammatical Analysis of the Lexicon*, Jerusalem: Academy of the Hebrew Language and the Shrine of the Book.
Bentolila, Y. 1972. "The Language of MS Deinard of the Mishnah (Selections of Sedarim *Mo'ed* and *Nashim* = MS 138 of the Jewish Theological Seminary)" (Hebrew), M. A. thesis, Hebrew University.
– 1989. *A French-Italian Tradition of Mishnaic Hebrew* (Hebrew), Eda ve-Lashon XIV, Jerusalem and Beer Sheva, Ben Gurion University Press.
Ben-Yehuda, E. 1948. "Introduction", in Ben-Yehuda 1948–1960.
– 1948–1960. *Complete Dictionary of Ancient and Modern Hebrew* (Hebrew), 17 vols., Jerusalem.
Ben Ze'ev, J. L. 1807. *Otzar ha-Shorashim*, Wein.

Berggrün, N. 1932. "The Participle with the Personal Pronouns" (Hebrew), *Lĕšonénu* 4: 173–177 (= Berggrün 1995: 108–112).
– 1971. "Forms of Mishnaic Hebrew in the Passover Haggada" (Hebrew) in Bar-Asher (ed.) 1980: 252–256 (= Berggrün 1995: 73–76).
– 1973. "*'Leshon ha-ra', 'ayin ha-ra'* ", *Lĕšonénu La-'Am* 24: 224-233 (= Berggrün 1995: 177–180).
– 1980. Lexicological Studies in Mishnaic Hebrew (Paying Attention to Dialectology)" (Hebrew), in Bar-Asher, ed. 1980: 143–171 (= Berggrün 1995: 24–35, 62–63, 96, 100–107, 160–167, 251).
– 1995. *'Iyyunim ba-Lashon ha-'Ivrit* (*Studies in the Hebrew Language*), Jerusalem: Academy for the Hebrew Language.
Berlin, A. 1985. *The Dynamics of Biblical Parallelism*, Bloomington: Indiana University Press.
Bialik, C. N. 2001. *Shirim be-Yiddish, Shirei Yeladim, Shirei Haqdasha* (*Yiddish Songs, Children's Songs, Dedicatory Songs*), Tel-Aviv: Devir.
Birnbaum, G. 1983. "The Definiteness of the Noun in Mishnaic Hebrew, According to Ms Kaufmann" (Hebrew), M. A. Thesis, Witwatersrand University.
– 2008. *The Language of the Mishna in the Cairo Genuza: Phonology and Morphology*, Jerusalem: The Academy of the Hebrew Language.
Black, M. 1954. *A Christian Palestinian Syriac Horologion*, Cambridge: Cambridge University Press.
Blau, J. 1980. "The Passive Participle with an Active Meaning" (Hebrew), in Bar-Asher (ed.) 1980: 100–114 (originally published in *Lĕšonénu* 18 [1953]: 67–81).
– "'Or that' (-אוֹ שׁ) in Mishnaic Hebrew" (Hebrew), in Bar-Asher, ed. 1980: 115–122 (originally published in *Lĕšonénu* 21 [1957]: 7–14).
– 1996. "On the Border between Mishnaic Hebrew and Aramaic (A Possible Abstract Grammatical Borrowing)" (Hebrew) in *Studies in Hebrew and Jewish Languages Presented to Shelomo Morag*. ed. M. Bar-Aher. Jerusalem: Bialik Institute, pp. 73–78.
– 2000. "A conservative view of the language of the Dead Sea Scrolls," in Muraoka and Elwolde (eds.), pp. 20–25.
Bolle, M. 1986. *Sefer Yirmiyah 'im Perush Da'at Miqra* (*The Book of Jeremiah with the Da'at Miqra Commentary*), Jerusalem: Mosad ha-Rav Kook.
Borg, A. 2000. "Some Observations on the יום השׁשׁי Syndrome in the Hebrew of the Dead Sea Scrolls", in Muraoka and Elwolde (eds.), pp. 26–39.
Braverman, N. 1977. "Synonyms in the Mishnah and in the Tosefta" (Hebrew) in *World Congress of Jewish Studies* 11 (1994): Division D: Volume I, pp. 17–24.
Breuer, M. (ed.). *Torah, Nevi'im, Ketuvim*, Jerusalem: Mosad ha-Rav Kook.
Breuer, Y. 1985. "Features of the Amoraic Language in the Bavli, Based on Massekhet Sukkah (MS Oxford A-51-2667)" (Hebrew), M. A. thesis, Hebrew University.
– 1987. "On the Hebrew Language of the Amoraim in the Babylonian Talmud" (Hebrew), *Language Studies* 2–3: 127–153.
– 2002. *The Hebrew in the Babylonian Talmud according to the Manuscripts of Tractate Pesaḥim* (Hebrew), Jerusalem: Magnes Press.
Brockelmann, C. 1928. *Lexicon syriacum*, Halle: Sumptibus M. Niemeyer.
Brody, H. 1935. *Diwan: The Poems of R. El'azar b. R. Ya'akov ha-Bavli* (Hebrew), Jerusalem: Mekitzei Nirdamim.
Brønno, E. 1943. *Studien über hebräische Morphologie und Vokalismus*, Abhandlungen für die Kunde des Morgenlandes 28, Leipzig: Harrassowitz.

Broshi, M. (ed.). 1992. *The Damascus Document Reconsidered*. Jerusalem: The Israel Exploration Society.

– et al. 1995 (eds.). *Qumran Cave 4 XIV: Parabiblical Texts, Part 2*. Discoveries in the Judaean Desert XIX, Oxford: Clarendon Press.

B.D.B = Brown, F. S. R. Driver, C. A. Briggs. 1953, *A Hebrew and English Lexicon of the Old Testament with an Appendix Containing the Biblical Aramaic: Based on the Lexicon of William Gesenius*, Oxford: Clarendon Press.

Burrows, M. et al. 1950. *The Dead Sea Scrolls of St. Mark's Monastery* 1, New Haven: American Schools of Oriental Research.

Buxtorf, J. 1639. *Lexicon Chaldaicum Talmudicum et Rabbinicum*, Basel: Sumptibus & typis Ludovici König.

Choueka, Y. 1997. *Millon Rav-Milim le-Bet Sefer*, Tel-Aviv: Steimatsky and Merkaz le-Technologyah Ḥinnukhit.

Cohen, A. 1975. "*Limshofti* (Job 9:15)", *Beit Mikra* 20/61: 303–305.

Cohen, C. 1983. "The Use of the Pronominal Suffixes as Direct Objects, as Opposed to the Use of '*'et* + Suffix' in Mishnaic Hebrew" (Hebrew), *Lĕšonénu* 47: 208–218.

Colin see Sinaceur.

Cothenet, E. 1963. "Le Document de Damas." ed. J. Carmignac and E. Cothenet, *Les Textes de Qumran*, Paris: Letousey et Ané, pp.131 – 204.

Cotton, H. M. and E. Qimron. 1998. "XḤev/Se ar 13 of 134 or 135 C. E.: A Wife's Renunciation of Claims", *Journal of Jewish Studies* 49: 108–118.

Dalman, G. 1905. Grammatik des jüdisch-palästinischen Aramäisch: nach den Idiomen des palästinischen Talmud, des Onkelostargum und Prophetentargum und der jerusalemischen Targume, 2nd ed.; Leipzig: J. C. Hinrichs.

De Balmes, A. 1523. *Miqneh Avraham* (Hebrew) Venice: Daniel Bomberg.

Dimant, D. 1994. "A Quotation from Nahum 3: 8–10 in 4Q 385–6" in ed. S. J APHET, *The Bible in Light of its Interpreters: Sarah Kamin Memorial Volume*, (Hebrew), Jerusalem: Magnes, pp. 31–37.

– 1998. "4Q 386 II–III: A Prophecy in Hellenistic Kingdoms." *Revue de Qumran* 18:5: 511–529.

– 2001. *Qumran Cave 4: XXI: Parabiblical Texts Part 4: Pseudo-Prophetic Texts*, Discoveries in the Judaean Desert XXX, Oxford: Clarendon Press.

– 2004. "Not Exile in the Desert but Exile in Spirit: The Pesher of Isa. 40: 3 in the *Rule of the Community*" (Hebrew), *Megillot* 2: 21–36 .

– 2006. "A Prayer for the People of Israel: On the Nature of Manuscript 4Q374" (Hebrew), *Meghillot* 4: 25–54.

Dotan, A. 1973. *Torah Nevi'im, Ketuvim: Prepared According to the Vocalization, Accents, and Masorah of Aaron ben Moses ben Asher in the Leningrad Codex*, (Hebrew), Tel-Aviv: Adi Press.

Drower, E. S. and R. Macuch. 1963. *A Mandaic Dictionary*, Oxford: Clarendon Press.

Ehrlich, A. 1899–1901. *Miqra Ki-fshuto*, Berlin: M. Poppeloyer's Bukhhandlung.

Eisenman, R. and M. O. Wise. 1992. *The Dead Sea Scrolls Uncovered*, Shaftesbury: Dorset.

Eldar, I. 1978. *The Pre-Ashkenazic Reading Tradition: Its Nature and the Shared Elements with the Spanish Tradition* (Hebrew), *Edah ve-Lashon* IV–V, Jerusalem: Magnes Press.

– 1980. "'Primary and Secondary' in the System of *Binyanim*" (Hebrew), *Lĕšonénu* 44: 157–160.

Elitzur, Y. 1987. "The Pattern *Qittul* in Mishnaic Hebrew According to Codex Kaufman", *Language Studies* 2–3: 67–93.

Encyclopdia Talmudit. 1951–2004, 26 Vols. Jerusalem: Encyclopedia Talmudit Press.

Epstein, J. N. 1927. "The Science of the Talmud and its Needs" (Hebrew), *Bulletin of the Institute for Jewish Studies* 2: 7.

– 1933. "The Commentaries of R. Jehuda ben Nathan and the Commentaries of Worms (Conclusions)" (Hebrew), *Tarbiẓ* 4: 153–192.

– 1955. *Mekhilta de-Rabbi Shim'on bar Yohai*, Jerusalem: Mekize Nirdamim.

– 1957. *Mevo'ot le-Sifrut ha-Tanna'im (Introductions to Tannaitic Literature),* Jerusalem: Magnes Press.

– 1960. A *Grammar of Babylonian Aramaic*, Ed. E. Z. Melammed (Hebrew), Jerusalem – Tel-Aviv: Magnes Press & Devir.

– 1982. *Perush ha-Ge'onim le-Seder Teharot* (*The Geonic Commentary on the Order Teharot*, Tel-Aviv: Devir & Magnes Press.

– 2000. *Mavo le-Nusah ha-Mishnah* (*Introduction to the Text of the Mishnah*), 3rd Edition (1st edition 1948), Jerusalem: Magnes Press.

Even-Shoshan, A. 1988. *A New Concordance for the Tanakh* (Hebrew), Corrected edition, Jerusalem: Kiryat-Sefer.

– 2003. *The Even-Shoshan Dictionary, A new edition* (Hebrew), 6 vols., Israel: ha-Millon he-Ḥadash Press.

Fassberg, S. E. 1996. "The spelling -שה for the Relative Pronoun: Did ה serve as a Mater Lectionis for /ɛ/ in Second Temple Times?" (Hebrew), *Language Studies* 9: 109–118.

– 2003. "The Preference for Lengthened Forms in Qumran Hebrew", *Meghillot* 1: 227–240.

– and Hurvitz A. (eds.). 2006. *Biblical Hebrew in its Northwest Semitic Setting*, Jerusalem: Magnes Press.

Fisch, S. 1973. *Midrash ha-Gadol*: *Sefer Devarim* (Hebrew) Jerusalem: Mosad ha-Rav Kook.

Fishbane, M. 1985. *Biblical Interpretation in Ancient Israel*, Oxford: Clarendon Press.

Florentin, M. 2001. "*kly ḥms mkrtyhm* (Gen 49:5) as Reflected in Samaritan Traditions" (Hebrew), *Lĕšonénu* 63: 189–202.

Friedman, S. Y. 1980. "The Short Comes First" (Hebrew) in Bar-Asher (ed.) 1980: 299–326 (originally published in *Lĕšonénu* 35: 117–129, 192–206).

Fuenn, S. J. and S. P. Rabbinowitz. 1912. *Ha-'Otzar: 'Otzar leshon ha-Miqra ve-ha-Mishnah*, Warsaw: Aḥi'asaf.

Garcia, Martinez F. 1992. "Damascus Document: A Bibliography of Studies 1970–1989", in Broshi (ed.) 1992: 63–83.

– Tigchelaar, E. J. C. and A. S. Van der Woude 1998. *Qumran Cave 11: II: 11Q2–18, 11 Q20–3,* Discoveries in the Judaean Desert XXIII, Oxford: Clarendon Press.

Gesenius, W. 1812. *Hebräisch-deutsches Handwörterbuch über die Schriften des Alten Testaments etc.*, Zweiter Theil, Leipzig: F. C. W. Vogel (Erster Theil 1810).

– 1815. *Geschichte der hebräischen Sprache und Schrift*, Leipzig: F. C. W. Vogel.

– 1817. *Ausführliches Grammatisch-kritisches Lehrgebäude der hebräishen Sprache mit Vergleichung der verwandten Dialekte,* Leipzig: F. C. W. Vogel.

– 1823. *Hebräisches und chaldaisches Handwörterbuch über das Alte Testament,* Leipzig: F. C. W. Vogel.

– 1835–1858. *Thesavrvs philologicvs criticvs lingvae hebraeae et chaldaeae Veteris Testamenti*, Leipzig: F. C. W. Vogel.
– 1960. *Gesenius' Hebrew Grammar*, Ed. and enlarged by E. Kautzch and A. E. Cowley, Second edition, Oxford: Clarendon Press.
Ginsberg, H. L. 1934. "From behind the Massorah" (Hebrew), *Tarbiẓ* 5: 208–223.
Ginzberg, L. (Levi). 1919. "Tamid: The Oldest Treatise of the Mishnah", *Journal of Jewish Lore and Philosophy* 1: 33–44, 197–209, 265–295.
– 1922. *Eine unbekannte jüdische Sekte*, New York: Georg Olms Verlag.
– 1970. *An Unknown Jewish Sect*, New York: Jewish Theological Seminary of America Press.
Gluska, I. 1983. "On the grammatical gender of *śadeh* in Mishnaic Hebrew" (Hebrew), *Bar-Ilan* 20–21: 43–66.
– 1988. *Influences of Aramaic on Mishnaic Hebrew* (Hebrew), Ph. D. diss., Bar-Ilan University.
Goldman, L. 2006. "A Comparison of the Genizah Manuscripts A and B of the *Damascus Document* in Light of Their *Pesher* Units" (Hebrew), *Meghillot* 4: 169–189.
Gordon, J. L. 1960. *The Writings of Judah Leib Gordon: Prose* (Hebrew), Tel-Aviv: Devir.
Greenberg, M. 1995. "The Etymology of *Niddah* (Menstrual Impurity)" in Z. Zevit et al. (eds.) *Solving Riddles and Untying Knots*, Winona Lake, Ind.: Eisenbrauns: 67–77.
Greenfield, J. C. 2001. *'Al Kanfei Yonah: Collected Studies of Jonas C. Greenfield on Semitic Philology*, 2 Vols., S. Paul et al (eds.), Leiden: Brill.
Grilak, L. 2009. Morphology of Mishnaic Hebrew according to Mekhilta of Rabbi Ishmael. PhD Thesis, Tel-Aviv University.
Gross, B.-Z. 1971. "The Patterns with the Endings *-ōn* and *-ān*, including only Nouns with Semitic Origins, and their meanings in the Bible and in Mishnaic Hebrew" (Hebrew). Ph.D. diss., Hebrew University.
– 1993. *The Nominal Patterns פעלון and פעלן in Biblical and Mishnaic Hebrew* (Hebrew), Jerusalem: The Academy of the Hebrew Language Press.
Grazovsky, (Goor) J. and D. Yellin 1919. *Ha-millon ha-'Ivri*, Tel-Aviv: Etan & Shoshana.

Hakham, A. 1970. *Sefer Iyyov 'im Perush Da'at Miqra*, Jerusalem: Mosad ha-Rav Kook.
– 1979–1981. *Sefer Tehillim 'im Perush Da'at Miqra*, Jerusalem: Mosad ha-Rav Kook.
– 1984. *Sefer Yesha'yahu 'im Perush Da'at Miqra*, Jerusalem: Mosad ha-Rav Kook.
Halevy, Y. 1946. *Shirei Ḥol shel rabbi Yehuda Ha-Levi*, Tel-Aviv: Y. Zemuri.
Halper, B. 1910. "The Participial Formations of the Geminate Verbs", *ZAW* 30: 42–57, 99–126.
Haneman, G. 1976. "On the Preposition בֵּין in the Mishna and in the Bible" (Hebrew), *Lĕšonénu* 40: 33–53 (= Bar-Asher [ed.] 1980: 30–50).
– 1980a. "Biblical Borrowings in the Mishna" (Hebrew). Pages 95–96 in *Fourth World Congress of Jewish Studies*, volume 2. Jerusalem: World Union of Jewish Studies, 1969: 95–96 (= Bar-Asher [ed.] 1980: 6–7).
– 1980b. *A Morphology of Mishnaic Hebrew, Based on the Tradition of MS Parma (De Rossi 138)* (Hebrew), Tel-Aviv: Tel-Aviv University.
– 1980c. "Standardization and Differentiation in the Histories of Two Hebrew Verbs" (Hebrew) in Bar-Asher (ed.) 1980: 8–14.
– 1980d. "On the Spelling Tradition of the Vocalized Manuscript of the Sifra" (Hebrew) in Bar-Asher (ed.) 1980: 15–29.
Har-Zahav, Tz. 1930. "The *binyanim* of the Hebrew Verb" (Hebrew), *Lĕšonénu* 2: 155–175.

Ḥarīrī, 1950. *Maḥberot Itiel be-Targum Yehudah b. Shelomo al-Ḥarizi*, Translated by Yitsḥak Perets, Tel-Aviv: Mahbarot le-Sifrut.
Hasid, Y. 1964. *"The Crown of the Torah": The Tāj of the Five Books of the Torah* (Hebrew) Jerusalem.
Havazelet, M. and Melammed, U. 2002. "Commentaries on the Alphabetic Acrostics in Psalms" (Hebrew), *Pe'amim* 88: 4–20.
Heltzer, M. and Malul, M. (eds.). 2004. *T^e^shûrôt La-Avishur – Studies in the Bible and Ancient Near East in Hebrew and Semitic Languages* (Hebrew), Tel-Aviv: Archeological Center Publications.
Hirschler, P. 1930. *Torah, Prohets and Writings: With a Critical Commentary: Five Megillot* (Hebrew), Ed. A. Kahana, Tel-Aviv: Zitomir.
Holy Scriptures, The 1917, Philadelphia: Jewish Publication Society.
Horovitz, H. S. (ed.). 1966. *Sifré on the Book of Numbers and Sifré Zuta* (Hebrew), Jerusalem: Wahrmann Books.
– and I. A. Rabin 1960. *Mekhilta de-Rabbi Ishmael*, Jerusalem: Bamberger & Wahrman, 1960.
Hurvitz, A. 1972. *Ben Lashon le-Lashon: le-Toldot leshon ha-'Ivrit bi-Ymei Bayit Sheni*. Jerusalem: Bialik Institute.
– 1982. *A Linguistic Study of the Relationship Between the Priestly Source and the Book of Ezekiel: A New Approach to an Old Problem*, Cahiers de la Revue Biblique 20, Paris: J. Gabalda.

Ibn Ezra, Abraham. 1827. *Sefer Tsaḥut ba-Lashon*, Ferarra.
– 1868. *Sefer Tsaḥut ba-Diqduq* (Hebrew), Berlin.
Ibn Ezra, Moshe. 1934. *Shirei ha-Ḥol* Ed. H. Brody, Berlin: Shoken.
Ibn Janaḥ, Abu al-Walid Marwan. 1964. *Sefer ha-Riqmah*, Translated to Hebrew by Judah ibn Tibbon, 2 Vols, Ed. M. Wilensky, Second edition, Jerusalem: Academy of the Hebrew Language Press.

Jarden, D. (ed.). 1966. *Diwan Shemuel Hanagid: Ben Tehillim*, Jerusalem: Hebrew Union College Press.
Jastrow, M. 1903. *A Dictionary of the Targumim, the Talmud Babli and Yerushalmi, and the MIdrashic Literature*, 2 vols., New York: G. P. Putnam's Sons.
Joosten, J. and J. S. Rey (eds.). 2008. *Conservatism and Innovation in the Hebrew Language of the Hellenistic Period: Proceedings of a Fourth International Symposium on the Hebrew of the Dead Sea Scrolls & Ben Sira*, Studies on the texts of the desert of Judah 73, Leiden: Brill.
Joüon, P. 1923. *Grammaire de l'hébreu biblique*, Rome: Pontifical Biblical Institute.
– and T. Muraoka 1991. *A Grammar of Biblical Hebrew*, Rome: Pontifical Biblical Institute.

Kaddari, M. Z. 1974. "*Mah le-*: a nominal construction Prior to the Sentence in Mishnaic Hebrew" (Hebrew), in Kaddari (ed.) 1974: 85–95.
– 1974 (ed.). *Erkhey ha-Millon he-Ḥadash le-Sifrut Ḥazal*, Ramat-Gan: Bar-Ilan University.
– 1984. "On the Independent Personal Pronoun in the non-verbal Clause in Mishnaic Hebrew" (Hebrew), *Millet* 2: 351–55.
– 2006. *Millon ha-'Ivrit ha-Miqra'it*, Ramat-Gan: Bar-Ilan University Press.
Kahana, M. 1999. *The Two Mekhiltot on the Amalek Portion* (Hebrew), Jerusalem: Magnes Press.

Kahana, M. 2009. *Language and Interpretation in Targum Jonathan to the Prophets from Naḥum to Malachi* (Hebrew), Ph. D. diss., Hebrew University.
Kaplan, H. 1978. "A Samaritan Church on the Premises of 'Museum Haaretz'" (Hebrew), *Qadmoniot* 11 [42–43]: 78–80.
Kare, Y. 1980. "Yemenite Traditions of Mishnaic Hebrew, Based on a Sixteenth-Century Manuscript" (Hebrew). *Lĕšonénu* 44: 24–42.
Kare, Y. and S. Morag. 1983. *Babylonian Aramaic in the Yemenite Manuscripts of the Talmud* Eda ve-Lashon XXIV (Hebrew), Jerusalem: Magnes Press .
Kariv, A. 1970. *The Seven Pillars of the Bible* (Hebrew), Tel-Aviv: Am Oved.
Kasovksy, C. Y. 1927. *Otzar Leshon ha-Mishnah*, 2nd edition, Jerusalem: Massada.
Katz, K. 1977. *Hebrew Language Tradition in the Community of Djerba* (Hebrew), 'Eda ve-Lashon II, Jerusalem: Hebrew University Institute of Jewish Studies.
Kil, Y. 1981. *Sefer Shemu'el 'im Perush Da'at Miqra*, Jerusalem: Mosad ha-Rav Kook.
Kimchi, David. 1948. *The Book of Hebrew Roots* (Hebrew), New York, 1948 (originally Berlin, 1847).
Kister, M. 1983. "On the Margins of the Book of Ben Sira" (Hebrew), *Lĕšonénu* 47: 125–126.
– 1989. "Additions to the article 'On the Margins of the Book of Ben Sira'" (Hebrew), *Lĕšonénu* 53: 36–39.
– 1989–1990. "A Contribution to the Interpretation of Ben-Sira" (Hebrew), *Tarbiẓ* 59: 303–378.
– 1993. "On a New Fragment of the Damascus Covenant", *Jewish Quarterly Review* 84: 249–251.
– 1999. "Studies in 4QMiqsat Maase HaTorah and Related Texts: Law, Theology, Language and Calendar" (Hebrew), *Tarbiẓ* 68: 317–371.
– 2000. "Some Observations on Vocabulary and Style in the Dead Sea Scrolls", in Muraoka and Elwolde (eds.): 137–165.
– 2005. "Toward the Origin of the Two Recensions of the Damascus Document" (Hebrew), in Z. Talshir and D. Amara (eds.), *On the Border Line: Textual meets Literary Criticism* (Hebrew), *Beer-Sheva* XVIII, Beer-Sheva: Ben-Gurion University of the Negev Press: 209–223.
Klein, M. 1980. *The Fragment-Targums of the Pentateuch according to their extant sources. Analecta Biblical* 76, Rome: Biblical Institute Press.
Knohl, I. 2007. "Studies in the 'Vision of Gabriel'" (Hebrew), *Tarbiẓ* 76: 303–328.
– 2008. "'By Three Days, live: Messiahs Resurrection, and Ascent to Heaven in *Hazon Gabriel*", *The Journal of Religion* 88: 147–158.
Koehler, L. and W. Baumgartner. 1953. *Lexicon in Veteris Testamenti libros: Wörterbuck zum hebräischen Alten Testament in deutscher und englischer Sprache*, Leiden: Brill.
– 1983. *Hebräisches und aramäisches Lexikon zum Alten Testament*, 2nd edition. Leiden: Brill.
– 1994–2000. *The Hebrew and Aramaic Lexicon of the Old Testament*, 3rd edition, Rev. by W. Baumgartner and J. J. Stamm, Trans. by M. E. J. Richardson, Leiden: Brill.
Kohen, Y. 1992. *My Friend Had a Vineyard: Investigations in Halakhah* (Hebrew), Israel: Quiboutz Sa'ad.
Kosovsky, M. 1979–2004. *Otzar Leshon Talmud Yerushalmi* (Hebrew), 10 Vols. Jerusalem: The Israel Academy of Sciences and Humanities.
Kugel, J. 1981. *The Idea of Biblical Poetry: Parallelism and its History*, New Haven: Yale University Press.

Kutscher, E. Y. 1937. "Lexicographical Questions" (Hebrew), *Lĕšonénu* 8: 136–145 (= Kutscher 1977a: 367–376).
– 1959. *The Language and the Background of the Complete Isaiah Scroll from the Dead Sea* (Hebrew), Jerusalem: Magnes Press.
– 1961–1962. "The Language of the Hebrew and Aramaic Letters of Bar Koseba and His Generation" (Hebrew), *Lĕšonénu* 25: 117–133; 26: 7–23 (= Kutscher 1977a: 36–70).
– 1963. "Mishnaic Hebrew" in Eds. S. Lieberman et al., *Henoch Yalon Jubilees Volume on the Occasion of his Seventy-Fifth Birthday* (Hebrew), Jerusalem: Qiryat Sefer: 246–280 (= Kutscher 1977a: 73–107).
– 1965. *Words and Their Histories* (Hebrew), Jerusalem: Qiryat Sefer.
– 1968. "Z. Ben Ḥayyim's *The Literary and Oral Tradition of Hebrew and Aramaic Amongst the Samaritans*", *Tarbiẓ* 37: 397–419.
– 1969. "Studies in the Grammar of Mishnaic Hebrew" (Hebrew), *Bar-Ilan* 10: 51–77 (= Kutscher 1977a: 108–134).
– 1970. "In the Wake of Ugaritica V" (Hebrew), *Lĕšonénu* 34: 5–19 (= Kutscher 1977a: 377–393.
– 1972a. "Some Problems of the Lexicography of Mishnaic Hebrew and Its Comparison with Biblical Hebrew" (Hebrew), in Kutscher (ed.) 1972, pp. 29–104.
– 1972b. "The Status of the Study of Mishnaic Hebrew (Especially Lexicography) and Its Tasks" (Hebrew), in Kutscher (ed.) 1972, pp. 3–28.
– 1972 (ed.). *'Erkhei ha-Millon he-Ḥadash le-Sifrut Ḥazal*, Vol. 1, Ramat-Gan: Bar-Ilan University.
– 1974. *The Language of Linguistic Background of the Isaiah Scroll (1Q Isa^a)*, Studies in the Texts of the Desert of Judah VI, Leiden: Brill.
– 1977a. *Hebrew and Aramaic Studies* (Hebrew), Jerusalem: Magnes Press.
– 1977b. = Kutscher 1963.
– 1977c. "The Realization of the Vowels *i* and *u* in Transcriptions of Biblical Hebrew, in Galilean Aramaic, and in Mishnaic Hebrew" (Hebrew), Binyamin De-Friz Festschrift, Jerusalem 1968: 218–251 (= Kutscher 1977a: 135–168***) .
Kutscher, R. 1970. "The Sumerian Parallels to *maḫāzu*" (Hebrew), *Lĕšonénu* 34: 267–269.

Lambert, M. 1900. "L'emploi du *Nifal* en hébreu", *Revue des Études Juives* 41: 196–214.
Lange, A. and H. Taeuber. 2008. "Ein jüdisches Amulett", in J. Tiefenbach and E. Fertl (eds.), *Die Bernsteinstraße: Evolution einer Handelsroute*, Wissenschaftliche Arbeiten aus dem Burgenland 123; Eisenstadt: Burgenländische Landesregierung: 177–179.
Lemaire, A. and A. Yardeni. 2006, "New Hebrew Ostraca from the Shephelah", in Fassberg and Hurvitz 2006 (eds.), pp. 197–223.
Leslau, W. 1989. *Comparative Dictionary of Ge'ez (Classical Ethiopic)*, Wiesbaden: Harrassowitz.
Levine, B. 1989. *Leviticus*. Jewish Publication Society Torah Commentary, Philadelphia: Jewish Publication Society.
– 1993. *Numbers 1–20*, Anchor Bible Commentary, New York: Doubleday.
Levita, E. 1541. *Sefer ha-Tishbi*, Izna.
Licht, J. 1957. *The Thanksgiving Scroll from the Wildernes of Judaea – Text, Introduction, Commentary, and Glossary* (Hebrew), Jerusalem: Bialik Institute.
– 1965. *The Manual of Discipline of the Dead Sea Scrolls* (Hebrew), Jerusalem: Bialik Institute.

Liddell, H. G. and R. Scott. 1966. *A Greek-English Lexicon* Revised by H. S. Jones, et al. Reprinted ninth edition, Oxford: Clarendon Press.
Lieberman, S. 1955–1983. *Tosefta Ki-fshutah*, Second edition, New York: Jewish Theological Seminary of America Press.
– et al. (eds.). 1963. *Sefer Hanoch Yalon: Collected Essays* (Hebrew), Jerusalem: Kiryat-Sefer.
– 1983. "Counting Letters" (Hebrew), in Bar-Asher (ed.) 1983: 329–335.
– 1984. *Greeks and Hellenism in Jewish Palestine* (Hebrew), Jerusalem: Bialik Institute.
Lipschütz, E. M. 1949. *Ketavim* Vol 2, Jerusalem, Mosad ha-Rav Kook.
Lowe, W. H (ed.). 1883. *The Mishnah on which the Palestinian Talmud Rests* (Hebrew), Cambridge: Cambridge University Press.
Luzzatto, S. D. 1965. *Perush Shada"l 'al Ḥamishah Ḥumshei Torah* (Hebrew), Tel-Aviv: Devir.

Maman, A. 1984. "The Reading Tradition of the Jews of Tétouan in the Bible and the Mishnah: Aspects of Phonology" (Hebrew), *Massorot* 1: 51–120.
Mandelkern, S. 1955. *Concordance on the Bible* (Hebrew), New York: Schulsinger Brothers.
Margoliouth, J. P. S. 1967. *A Compendious Syriac Dictionary: Founded upon the Thesaurus Syriacus of R. Payne Smith*, Oxford: Clarendon Press.
Milgrom, J. 1991. *Leviticus 1–16*, Anchor Bible Commentary, New York: Doubleday.
Mirsky, A. 2002. *Sefer Devarim 'im Perush Da'at Miqra*, Jerusalem: Mosad ha-Rav Kook.
Mishnah. 1954. *The Six Orders of the Mishnah with the Commentaries of the Rishonim and Aḥaronim* (Hebrew), Jerusalem: El ha-Meqorot.
– 1971, 1975. *Mishnah 'im Shinuyei Nusḥa'ot: Zera'im* (Hebrew), 2 vols., Jerusalem: Mekhon ha-Talmud ha-Yisraeli ha-Shalem.
Mishor, M. 1983. *The Tense System in Tannaitic Hebrew* (Hebrew), Ph. D. diss., Hebrew University.
– 1988. "From the Work on the History of Words" (Hebrew), *Lĕšonénu la-'Am* 39: 186–199.
– 1989. "The Study of the Ashkenazic Traditions: On the Way to a Method" (Hebrew), *Massorot* 3–4: 87–127.
– 2000–2001. "Some Linguistic Peculiarities of First Revolt Period Documents" (Hebrew), *Lĕšonénu* 63: 327–332.
Morag, S. 1964. *Ha-'ivrit she-be-fi Yehudei Teman*, Jerusalem: Hebrew Language Press.
– 1969. "The Tiberian Tradition of Biblical Hebrew: Homogeny and Heterogeny" (Hebrew), in E. S. Rosenthal (ed.) *Peraqim* 2: 105–144, Jerusalem Schoken.
– 1971a. "The *binyanim pā'ēl* and *nitpā'ēl* (Towards the Analysis of Some Forms within Mishnaic Hebrew)" (Hebrew), Pages 93–101 in Bar-Asher 1971 (ed.): 93–101 (Originally published in *Tarbiẓ* 26 (1957) 349–356).
– 1971b. "On the Study of Mishnaic Hebrew according to the Traditions of the Jewish Communities in the Diaspora" (Hebrew), in Bar-Asher 1971 (ed.): 186–198 (Originally published in *Tarbiẓ* 26 (1957) 4–16).
– 1971c. "More on the Topic of *pā'ēl* and *nitpā'ēl*" (Hebrew), in Bar-Asher 1971 (ed.): 101 (Originally published in *Tarbiẓ* 27 (1958) 356).
– 1980. "Between East and West" (Hebrew), in Bar-Asher, 1980 (ed.): 234–249.
– 1985. "The Study of Mishnaic Hebrew – the Oral Witnesses: Nature and Appraisal" (Hebrew), pp. 39–53 in *Proceedings of the Ninth World Congress of Jewish Studies*. Jerusalem: World Union of Jewish Studies. Reprinted in Morag, *Massorot ha-Lashon ha-'Ivrit ve-ha-Lashon ha-Aramit she-be-fi Yehudei Teman*, in Yosef Tobi (ed.), Tel-Aviv: Afikim, 2002 (English translation published in *Scripta Hierosolymitana* 37 (1998) 43–57).

– 1988a. "The Language of the Dead Sea Scrolls: Structural Features and their Nature" (Hebrew), in *Ha-Brit Ha-'Ivrit ha-'Olamit: The Sixth Scholarly Hebrew Conference in Europe (London 1984)*, (Hebrew). Jerusalem: 11–19.
– 1988b. "Qumran Hebrew: Some Typological Observations", *Vetus Testamentum* 38: 148–164.
– 2002. *Babylonian Aramaic in the Yemeni Tradition* (Hebrew), Jerusalem: Magnes Press.
Moreshet, M. 1972. "New and Renewed Verbs in the Baraitot of the Bavli (With Comparison to the Yerushalmi") (Hebrew), in Kutscher 1972 (ed.): 117–162.
– 1974a. "Additions to the Language of the Hebrew Baraitot in the Bavli and Yerushalmi" (Hebrew), in Kaddari (ed.) 1974: 31–73.
– 1974b. "The Hebrew Baraitot in the Bavli are not Mishnaic Hebrew 1" (Hebrew), in Lieberman et al. (eds.) 1963: 277–316.
– 1980. "On nuf'al conjugation in Post-Biblical Hebrew" in Sarfatti 1980 (ed.): 126–139.
– 1981. *A Lexicon of Verbs that Are Innovated in Tannaitic Hebrew* (Hebrew), Ramat-Gan: Bar-Ilan University Press.
– 1983a. "The Object Preceding Two Subjects in Mishnaic Hebrew, with Notes Regarding Modern Hebrew" (Hebrew) in Bar-Asher (ed.) 1983: 359–378.
Morgenstern, M. 2002. "Jewish Babylonian Aramaic in Geonic Responsa" (Hebrew), Ph. D. diss., Hebrew University.
Muraoka, T. and Elwolde, J. F. (eds.). 1997. *The Hebrew of the Dead Sea scrolls and Ben Sira: Proceedings of a Symposium held at Leiden University, 11–14 December 1995*. Studies on the texts of the desert of Judah 26. Leiden: Brill.
– (eds.). 1999. *Sirach, Scrolls, and Sages: Proceedings of a Second International Symposium on the Hebrew of the Dead Sea Scrolls, Ben Sira, and the Mishnah, held at Leiden University, 15–17 December 1997.* Studies on the Texts of the Desert of Judah 33. Leiden: Brill.
– (eds.). 2000. *Diggers at the Well: Proceedings of a Third International Symposium on the Hebrew of the Dead Sea Scrolls and Ben Sira*, Leiden: Brill.
Muraoka, T. and Porten, B. 1998. *A Grammar of Egyptian Aramaic,* Leiden: Brill.

Naeh, S. 1986. "Variant Traditions in MS Vatican 66 of the Sifra" (Hebrew), M. A. thesis, Hebrew University.
– 1989. "Tannaitic Hebrew in the Sifra According to MS Vatican 66" (Hebrew), Ph. D diss., Hebrew University.
Nathan, H. 1981. "The Linguistic Tradition of MS Erfurt of the Tosefta" (Hebrew), Ph. D. diss., Hebrew University.
– 1984. "Was the Opposition of 3fs and 3mp/3fp Nullified in the Pronominal Suffixes in Mishnaic Hebrew?" (Hebrew), *Massorot* 1: 121–134.
Nathan ben Jehiel of Rome. 1878–1937. *Aruch completum* (Hebrew), Ed. by A. Kohut et al. 9 vols., Vienna: Georg Borg.
Newsom, C. A. 1995. "4QDiscourse on the Exodus/Conquest Tradition", in Broshi 1995 (ed.): 99–110.

Orman, D. 1971. "Hebrew Inscriptions from Kefar Devorah in the Golan" (Hebrew), *Tarbiẓ* 40: 406.

Perles, F. 1902–1903. "Five Megillot" (Hebrew), In *Torah, Nevi'im, Ketuvim with a Scholarly Commentary*, Ed. by A. Cahana, Z'itomir: A. Kahana.

Parry, D. W. and Qimron, E. 1999. *The Great Isaiah Scroll (1QIsa^{a}): A New Edition*. Studies on the Texts of the Desert of Judah 32, Leiden: Brill.

Pashḥur, Z. 1986. Biblical Expressions in Seder ʻOlam Rabbah (Hebrew), M. A. thesis, Hebrew University.

Pomis, D. de. 1587. *Tzemaḥ David*, Venice: Apud Ioannem de Gara.

Porath, E. 1938. *Leshon Ḥakhamim le-fi Massorot Bavliyyot she-bi-kitvei Yad Yeshanim*, Jerusalem: Bialik Institute.

Qafiḥ, J. 1966. *Tehillim – Tirgum u-Pherush Rabbenu Seʻadia ben Yoseph Phayumi*, Jerusalem: American Academy of Jewish Knowledge.

– (ed.). 2001. *Siddur Tefilla Nusaḥ Baladi, Siaḥ Yerushalayim*, Kiryat-Ono: Mechon Mishnat ha-Rambam.

Qimron, E. 1975. "Medial *aleph* as a Mater Lectionis in the Hebrew and Aramaic Documents from Qumran with Comparison to Other Hebrew and Aramaic Texts" (Hebrew), *Lĕšonénu* 39: 133–146 (Reprinted in Bar-Asher [ed.] 1980: 335–348).

– 1976. A *Grammar of the Hebrew Language of the Dead Sea Scrolls* (Hebrew), Ph. D. diss., Hebrew University.

– 1977. "The *nitpa"el* Participle", *Lĕšonénu* 41: 144–157.

– 1980a. "The Vocabulary of the Temple Scroll", *Shenaton (An Annual for Biblical and Ancient Near Eastern Studies)* 4: 239–262.

– 1986. *The Hebrew of the Dead Sea Scrolls*, Harvard Semitic Studies 29, Atlanta: Scholars Press.

– 1986. "C. Newsom, Songs of the Sabbath Sacrifices: A Critical Edition" – A Review, *HTR*79: 349–371.

– 1992a. "The Text of the CDC", in Broshi (ed.) 1992: 9–49.

– 1992b. "Observations on the History of Early Hebrew (1000 B.C.E. – 200 C.E.) in the Light of the Dead Sea Documents", in D. Dimant and U. Rappaport (eds.), *The Dead Sea Scrolls: Forty Years of Research*. Leiden: Brill: 349–361.

– 1996. *The Temple Scroll: A Critical Edition with Extensive Reconstructions*, Beer-Sheba: Ben-Gurion University of the Negev Press.

– 2000. "The Nature of DSS [= Dead Sea Scrolls] Hebrew and its Relation to BH and MH", in Muraoka and Elwolde (eds.) 2000: 232–244 .

– 2003. "גְּדֹל הזרוע, גְּבֹהַּ הקומה וקֹדֶש ההיכל" in *Qol le-Yaʻakov: Collected Essays in Honor of Yaakov ben Tolilah* (Hebrew), Beer-Sheba: Ben-Gurion University of the Negev Press: 327–339.

– 2006. "Improving the Editions of the Dead Sea Scrolls (4): Benedictions" (Hebrew), *Meghillot* 4: 191–200.

– 2009. "Problems in Reading and Editing the Qumran Scrolls", in M. Kister (ed.), *The Qumran Scrolls and Their World* Ed. By M. Kister, Jerusalem: Yad Ben-Zvi Press: 91–106.

– and J. Strugnell. 1994. *Qumran Cave 4: V: Miqṣat Maʻaśe ha-Torah*, Discoveries in the Judaean Desert X, Oxford: Clarendon Press.

Rabin, C. 1958. *The Zadokite Documents: I. The Admonition, II: The Laws*, 2nd revised edition Oxford: Clarendon Press.

– 1965. "The Historical Background of Qumran Hebrew", *Scripta Hierosolymitana* 4: 144–161.

– 1970. "La correspondance *d* hébreu – *ḏ* arabe", *Mélanges Marcel Cohen* (ed. D. Cohen), The Hague: Mouton: 290–297.

– 1971. "The Historical Background of Qumran Hebrew" (Hebrew translation of Rabin 1965), in Bar-Asher (ed.) 1971: 355–382.
Rainey, A. 1970. "Notes on the Syllabic Vocabularies from Ugarit" (Hebrew), *Lĕšonénu* 34: 180–184.
Ratsaby, Y. 1965. *Sefer ha-Musar: Maḥberet R. Zekharya al-Ẓahari*, Jerusalem: Makhon Ben-Zvi of the Hebrew University.
Rin, Z. 1961. "The ending *-ē* for the Absolute Plural" (Hebrew), *Lĕšonénu* 25: 17–19.
Rosenthal, D. 1981. Mishnah 'Avodah Zarah: Critical Edition and Introduction (Hebrew), Ph. D. diss., Hebrew University.
– 1999. "Eretz Yisrael Traditions, and Their Paths to Babylonia" (Hebrew) *Cathedra* 92: 7–48.
Ryzhik, M. 1998. "A Neglected Witness? The First Edition of the *Otzar Leshon ha-Mishnah* of Rabbi C. Y. Kosovsky" (Hebrew), *Lĕšonénu* 61: 73–86.

Saadia ben Joseph. 1963. *The Commentaries of Rabbenu Sa'adia Gaon on the Torah* (Hebrew). Edited by Joseph Qafiḥ, Jerusalem: Mosad ha-Rav Kook.
– 1980. *Daniel and the Scroll of Antiochus with the Translation and Commentary of Saadia Gaon* (Hebrew), Ed. Joseph Qafiḥ, Jerusalem: Association for Publishing the Books of Saadiah Gaon.
Samuel, H. 2011. "ΙΣΤΡΑΕΛ – Anmerkungen zu einem altbekannten Phänomen und einem neuentdeckten Amulett aus Halbturn," *Zeitschrift des Deutschen Palästina-Vereins* 127: 185–196.
Sappir, I. 2007. "Linguistic Phenomena from Tel Kasila Inscriptions" (Hebrew), *Lĕšonénu* 69: 263–270.
Sarfatti, G. 1977. "*Erev Pesahim*" (Hebrew), *Lĕšonénu* 41: 21–28, 158 (Reprinted in Bar-Asher, (ed.) 1980: 327–334 (Translated in *Scripta Hierosolymitana* 37: 323–335).
– 1980. "On the Definiteness of Bound Construct Phrases in Mishnaic Hebrew" (Hebrew), in Sarfatti 1980 (ed.): 140–154.
– (ed.). 1980. *Studies in Hebrew and Semitic Languages, Dedicated to the Memory of Prof. Yehezkel Kutscher* (Hebrew), Ramat-Gan: Bar-Ilan University Press.
– 1983. "The Tradition of Mishnaic Hebrew – a Tradition of a 'Living Literary Language'" (Hebrew), in Bar-Asher et al. 1983 (eds.): 451–458.
– 1989. "Definiteness in Noun-Adjective Phrases in Rabbinic Hebrew", in *Studies in the Hebrew Language and Talmudic Literature Dedicated to the Memory of Dr. Menahem Moreshet* (Hebrew), M. Z. Kaddari and S. Sharvit (eds.), Ramat Gan: Bar Ilan University Press, pp. 153–158.
Schechter, S. 1910. *Documents of Jewish Sectaries: Volume 1: Fragments of a Zadokite Work.* Cambridge: Cambridge University Press.
Schiffman, L. 1997. "301. 4QMysteries[c]", in *Qumran Cave 4: XV: Sapiential Texts: Part 1.* Ed. T. Elgvin et al., Discoveries in the Judaean Desert XX Oxford: Clarendon Press, pp. 113–123.
Segal, M. H. 1908. "Mišnaic Hebrew and its Relation to Biblical Hebrew and Aramaic", *Jewish Quarterly Review* (Original Series) 20: 647–737.
– 1926. "The Language of the Mishnah: Its Origin and History" (Hebrew), *Studies in Jewish Studies* 1: 30–44.
– 1927. *A Grammar of Mishnaic Hebrew*, Oxford: Clarendon Press.
– 1936. A *Grammar of the Language of the Mishnah* (Hebrew), Tel-Aviv: Devir.
– 1939–1940. "*ḥălōm – ḥălōmōt – ḥ^{ă}lōmōt*", *Lĕšonénu* 10: 154–156.
– 1958. *The Complete Book of Ben Sira* (Hebrew), Jerusalem: Bialik Institute.

Seri, S. and Kesar, I. 2005. *Halikhot Qedem be-Mishkenot Teman*, Tel-Aviv: E'eleh be-Tamar.
Shabazi, Shalom. 1966. *Ḥafets Ḥayyim: Shirei Rabbeny Shalem Shabazi* (Hebrew), Jerusalem: ha-Aḥim Y. ve-S. Mekiton.
– 1976. *Shirim Ḥadashim le-Rabbi Shalem Shabazi: A Photocopied Edition of Two Manuscripts by the Poet* (Hebrew), Jerusalem: Ben-Tsevi Institute.
Sharon, M. 1996. "*Va-yifga' ba-maqom va-yalen sham*: Towards the Meaning of the Word *maqom* in the Bible", in *Studies in Bible and Education Presented to Prof. Moshe Arend* (Hebrew), Edited by Dov Rappel. Jerusalem: Touro College Press: 188–200.
Sharvit, S. 1976. "Versions and Language of Massekhet Avot, and Preparations for a Critical Edition" (Hebrew), Ph.D. diss., Bar-Ilan University.
– 1980. "The Tense System of Mishnaic Hebrew" (Hebrew), in Sarfatti 1980 (ed.): 110–125.
– 1981. "The Consolidation of the Study of Mishnaic Hebrew" (Hebrew), *Bar-Ilan* 18–19: 221–232.
– 1983. "Haplology in Mishnaic Hebrew" (Hebrew), in Bar-Asher et al. (ed.) 1983: 557–568 (= Sharvit 2008: 60–7).
– 1987. "The Syntax of Verbs that Require a Single Infinitive Complement in Mishnaic Hebrew" (Hebrew), *Language Studies* 2–3: 279–296.
– 1988. "Two Phonological Phenomena in Mishnaic Hebrew" (Hebrew), Te'udah 6: 43–61.
– 1990. "Nouns with Two Plural Forms in Mishnaic Hebrew" (Hebrew), *Language Studies* 4: 335–373.
– 1993. "Modal Infinitive Sentences in Mishnaic Hebrew" (Hebrew), in Bar-Asher (ed.) 1993: 413–437.
– 2004. *Leshonah ve-Signonah shel Massekhet Avot le-Doroteha* (Hebrew), Beer-Sheba: Ben-Gurion University of the Negev Press.
– 2005. "The Growth and Crystallization of the Verbal Nouns in Ancient Hebrew" (Hebrew), in M. Bar-Asher and M. Florentin (eds.), *Studies in Samaritanism, Hebrew, and Aramaic Presented to Avraham Tal* (Hebrew), Jerusalem: Bialik Institute: 177–188.
– 2008. *Pirqe Mehqar bi-Lshon Hakhamim* (Hebrew), Jerusalem: Bialik Institute.
Shivtiel, Y. 1971. "The Yemenite Tradition in the Grammar of the Sages" (Hebrew), in Bar-Asher (ed.) 1971: 207–251.
Sinaceur, Z. I. 1994–1996. *Le Dictionnaire Colin d'arabe dialectal marocain*, 8 Vols, Rabat: Al-Manahil, Ministère des Affaires Culturelles.
Smith, M. 1991. "4Q462 (Narrative), Frg. 1: A Preliminary Edition", *RevQ* 15: 55–77.
– 1995. "462. 4QNarrative C (Pl. XXVI)", in Broshi et al 1995 (eds.): 195–209.
Sokoloff, M. 1971. "The Hebrew of Bereshit Rabbah, According to MS Vatican 30" (Hebrew), in Bar-Asher (ed.) 1971: 257–301 (originally published in *Lĕšonénu* 33: 25–42, 135–149, 280–279).
– 1974. *The Targum to Job from Qumran cave XI*, Ramat-Gan: Bar-Ilan University.
– 2002. *A Dictionary of Jewish Babylonian Aramaic*, Ramat-Gan: Bar-Ilan University.
– and Yahalom J. 1999. *Jerusalem Palestinian Aramaic Poetry from Late Antiquity* (Hebrew), Jerusalem: Israel Academy of Sciences and Humanities Press.
Sperber, A. 1939. "Hebrew Based upon Biblical Passages in Parallel Transmissions", *Hebrew Union College Annual* 14: 153–249.
– (ed.). 1959–1968. *The Bible in Aramaic*, 5 vols., Leiden: Brill.
Stadel, C. 2008. "Hebraismen in den aramäischen Texten vom Toten Meer", M. A. thesis, Heidelberg University.
Stegemann H. and Schuller, E. 2009. *Qumran Cave 1: III: QHodayot^{a}*. Discoveries in the Judaean Desert XL, Oxford: Clarendon Press.

Steiner, R. C. 1979. “From Proto-Hebrew to Mishnaic: The History of ךְ- and הָּ-”, *Hebrew Annual Review* 3: 157–174.
– 1992. “A Colloquialism in Jer. 5:13 from the Ancestor of Mishnaic Hebrew”, *Journal of Semitic Studies* 37: 11–26.
Strugnell, J. 1999. “4QInstruction[d] (Pls. XII–XXVII)”, in *Qumran Cave 4: XXIV: Sapiential Texts Part 2*. Ed. J. Strugnell et al. Discoveries in the Judaean Desert XXXIV. Oxford: Clarendon Press: 211–474.
Sturtevant, E. H. 1968. *The Pronunciation of Greek and Latin*, 2nd edirion, Gröningen: Bouma’s Boekhuis.
Sukenik, E. L. 1954. *Otzar Ha-Megillot Ha-Genuzot she-b-idei ha-Universita ha-‘Ivrit*, Jerusalem: Bialik Institute.
Sussman, Y. 1974. “A Halakhic Inscription from the Beth Shean Valley: A Preliminary Discussion” (Hebrew), *Tarbiẓ* 43: 88–158.
Sznejder, M. B. 1930. “The Relationship of the Mishnaic Grammar to Biblical Grammar” (Hebrew), *Lĕšonénu* 3: 15–28.
– 1936. “Literary Hebrew Language” (Hebrew), *Lĕšonénu* 6 (1934–5): 301–326 (part 1), *Lĕšonénu* 7: 52–73 (part 2).

Tal, A. 1994. *Samaritan Pentateuch* (Hebrew), Tel-Aviv: Tel-Aviv University.
– 2000. *A Dictionary of Samaritan Aramaic*, 2 vols., Leiden: Brill.
Talmon, S. 1956. “Double Readings: A Fundamental Phenomenon in the Transmission History of the Biblical Text” (Hebrew), Ph.D. diss., Hebrew University.
– 1960. “Double Reading in the Massoretic Text”, *Textus* 1: 144–184.
– 1961. “Synonymous Readings in the Textual Traditions of the Old Testament”, in *Studies in the Bible*. Ed. C. Rabin, *Scripta Hierosolymitana* VIII, Jerusalem: Magnes: 335–385.
Talshir, D. 1987. “The Status of Late Biblical Hebrew, Between Biblical Hebrew and Mishnaic Hebrew” (Hebrew), *Language Studies* 2–3: 161–172.
– 1992. “Mishnaic Hebrew Through the Lens of Personal Names” (Hebrew), *Language Studies* 5–6: 225–244.
– 1993. “Second Temple Hebrew: Its Place of Origin and History” (Hebrew), *Mehqere Talmud 2:* 285–301 (Translated as “The Habitat and History of Hebrew During the Second Temple Period” in Ed. I. Young *Biblical Hebrew; Studies in Chronology and Typology*, London: T & T Clark International, 2005: 251–275).
– 2004. “Is the Jehoash Inscription Genuine? A Philological Analysis” (Hebrew), *Lĕšonénu La‘am* 54: 3–10.
Theodor, J. and C. Albeck 1965. *Midrash Bereshit Rabba*, 2nd edition 3 Vols., Jerusalem: Warhmann books.
Thorion, Y. 1984. *Studien zur klassischen hebräischen Syntax*, Berlin: Reimer.
Tobi, J. and Seri, S. 1988. *Diwān umlal Shir: A Selection of the Poems of Yemen* (Hebrew) Israel: E’eleh be-Tamar.
Tov, E. 2007. “On the Writing and the Language of the Dead Sea Scrolls: A New Finding” (Hebrew), in Bar-Asher et al. (ed.) 2007: 333–351.

VanderKam, J. and Milik, J. T. 1994. “4QpseudoJubilees[b]”, in *Qumran Cave 4: VIII: Parabiblical Texts,* Part 1. Edited by H. Attridge, et al. Discoveries in the Judaean Desert XIII. Oxford: Clarendon Press: 141–156.

Wartski, I. 1970. *Leshon ha-Midrashim*, Jerusalem: Mosad ha-Rav Kook.
Weinfeld, M. and Seely, D., “4QBarkhi Nafshi[a] (Pls. XVII–XIX)”, in *Qumran Cave 4 XX*, Ed. E. Chazon et al., Discoveries in the Judaean Desert XXIX: 270–278.

Weinreich, U. 1968. *Modern English–Yiddish, Yiddish–English Dictionary,* New York: Yivo.
Weiss, I. H. 1867. *Mishpat Leshon ha-Mishnah*, Wein.
Wernberg-Möller, P. 1957. *The Manual of Discipline*, Leiden: Brill.

Yadin, Y. 1957. *The Scroll of the War of the Sons of Light Against the Sons of Darkness* (Hebrew), Jerusalem: Bialik Institute.
– 1983. *The Temple Scroll*, 3 Vols. (Hebrew), Jerusalem: Israel Exploration Society.
Yahalom, J. 1985. "The Passive in Piyyut, Poetic Language, Prosaic Language, and Verbal *binyanim*" (Hebrew), *Lĕšonénu* 45 (1981): 17–31.
– *Śefat ha-Shir shel ha-Piyyut ha-Eretz Yisraeli ha-Qadum*, Jerusalem: Magnes.
Yalon, H. 1963. *Quntresim le-'Inyenei ha-Lashon ha-'Ivrit ve-'Inyenei Lashon* (reprint edition), Jerusalem: Wahrmann Books.
– 1964. *Introduction to the Vocalization of the Mishnah* (Hebrew), Jerusalem: Bialik Institute.
– 1967. *Megillot Midbar Yehudah: Matters of Language* (Hebrew), Jerusalem: Shrine of the Book Fund and Qieyat Sefer.
– 1971. *Pirqe Lashon*, Jerusalem: Bialik Institute.
Yalqut Shim'oni, 1944, New York: 1944.
Yardeni A. 2000. *Textbook of Aramaic, Hebrew, and Nabataean Documents from the Judean Desert, and Related Materials* (Hebrew), 2 vols., Jerusalem: Dinur Center of the Hebrew University.
– 2008. "A New Dead Sea Scroll in Stone", *Biblical Archeology Review* 34.1: 60–61.
– and Elizur B. 2007. "A Prophetic Text from the First Century B.C.E: Initial Report" (Hebrew), *Cathedra* 123: 155–166.
Yeivin, I. 1983. "The Meaning of the *Dagesh* in the 'Expanded' Tiberian Vocalization System" (Hebrew), in Bar-Asher et al. (eds.) 1983: 293–307.
– 1985. *The Hebrew Language Tradition as Reflected in the Babylonian Vocalization* (Hebrew), 2 Vols., Jerusalem: Academy of Hebrew Language.
Yellin, D. 1972. *The Writings of David Yellin*, Vol. 6: *Biblical Studies*, Jerusalem: Center for Publishing the Writings of David Yellin.
Yuditsky, A. E. 2005. "Reduced Vowels in the Transcriptions in the Second Column of Origen's Hexapla" (Hebrew), *Lĕšonénu* 67: 121–141.

Zakovitch, Y. 1987. "The Many Faces of Inner-Biblical Interpretation" (Hebrew), *Tarbiẓ* 56: 136–143.
– 1992. *An Introduction to Inner-Biblical Interpretation,* Even-Yehudah: Rekhes Press.
Zaks, N. 1972, 1975 (ed.). *Mishnah Zera'im 'im Shinuyei Nusha'ot mi-Kitvei Yad shel ha-Mishnah* (Hebrew). 2 Vols, Jerusalem: Mekhon ha-Talmud ha-Yisraeli ha-Shalem.
Zer-Kavod, M. 1980. *'Ezra-Neḥemiah 'im Perush Da'at Miqra* (Hebrew), Jerusalem: Mosad ha-Rav Kook.
Zuckermandel, M. S. (ed.). 1970. *Tosefta*, New Edition, Jerusalem: Wahrmann Books.
Zurawel, T. 1984. "The Abandonment of the *Qal* in Samaritan Hebrew" (Hebrew), *Massorot* 1: 135–151.
– 1987. "Comparison of the Tradition of Maimonides' Autograph of the Mishnah" (Hebrew), *Language Studies* 2–3: 217–223.
– 2004. "*Linguistic Tradition of Maimonides, According to the Autograph Copy of his Commentary of the Mishnah* (Hebrew), Eda ve-Lashon XXV, Jerusalem: Magnes Press.

Indexes

Index of texts cited

Hebrew Bible

Gen. 1:26 204 n. 45
Gen. 1:31 129–130
Gen. 4:15 120
Gen. 4:22 236
Gen. 5:3 204 n. 45
Gen. 5:29 30–31, n. 42
Gen. 6:3 402
Gen. 8:19 140, 146
Gen. 8:22 92 n. 33
Gen. 9:9 105 n. 8
Gen. 10:5 140, 331
Gen. 10:6 75
Gen. 10:13 75
Gen. 10:15 75
Gen. 10:32 331
Gen. 11:9 192
Gen. 12:7–22:9 124 n. 37
Gen. 12:10 124
Gen. 12:17 58, 59 n. 36
Gen. 12:18 58
Gen. 12:19 58
Gen. 13:14 247
Gen. 14:14 47 n. 1
Gen. 14:15 120
Gen. 14:24 57 n. 33
Gen. 17:26 340
Gen. 18:16 132
Gen. 19:20 124 n. 37
Gen. 21:12 58, 59
Gen. 21:14 59 n. 36
Gen. 21:15 59 n. 36
Gen. 21:16 59 n. 36
Gen. 21:17–20 59
Gen. 21:20 47 n. 1, 58–59
Gen. 22:1 220 n. 63, 221
Gen. 22:2 33
Gen. 22:9 124
Gen. 23:20 252
Gen. 24:10 132
Gen. 24:11 269
Gen. 24:14 58–59
Gen. 24:15 58
Gen. 24:16 59
Gen. 24:28 58–59
Gen. 24:43 58–59
Gen. 24:44 58
Gen. 24:55 59
Gen. 24:61 57 n. 33
Gen. 25:27 57 n. 33
Gen. 26:3 182
Gen. 26:4 182
Gen. 26:34 75 n. 1
Gen. 27:11 44
Gen. 27:23 44
Gen. 27:43 52
Gen. 28:2 52
Gen. 28:5–6 52
Gen. 28:10 133 n. 71
Gen. 28:13 134
Gen. 28:17 98
Gen. 30:38 47 n. 1, 56
Gen. 31:18 52
Gen. 31:21 132
Gen. 31:30 340 n. 89
Gen. 31:42 120
Gen. 31:46–47 53
Gen. 31:47 249 n. 70
Gen. 32:12 18
Gen. 32:25–32 124
Gen. 32:29 124
Gen. 34:19 98
Gen. 34:22 340
Gen. 36:40 146
Gen. 37:11 51
Gen. 37:31 377
Gen. 38:14 234 n. 19
Gen. 38:29 98
Gen. 41:1 134
Gen. 41:51 342 n. 100
Gen. 45:6 92 n. 33
Gen. 47:32 113 n. 11
Gen. 48:7 52 n. 16

Gen. 49:3 43 n. 19
Gen. 49:5 142, 270
Gen. 49:7 48
Gen. 49:11 48
Gen. 49:23 59 n. 37
Gen. 49:27 56

Exod. 1:7 137 n. 86
Exod. 1:13–14 136
Exod. 1:13 175–176
Exod. 2:1 79 n. 11
Exod. 2:3 403
Exod. 2:5 57 n. 33
Exod. 2:23–25 136
Exod. 2:23 136–137
Exod. 3:1 49 n. 6
Exod. 3:15 49
Exod. 3:21 119–120
Exod. 4:4 251
Exod. 4:15 84
Exod. 6:29 50 n. 7
Exod. 7:14 97
Exod. 8:28 96
Exod. 9:7 97
Exod. 9:9 269
Exod. 9:10 269
Exod. 10:3 384
Exod. 11:3 120
Exod. 12:3 269
Exod. 12:7 230 n. 6
Exod. 12:15 130
Exod. 12:22 230 n. 6, 389
Exod. 12:23 230 n. 7, 239 n. 32
Exod. 14:18 98
Exod. 15:1 217
Exod. 15:7 135
Exod. 15:8 98–99 n. 19
Exod. 15:10 347 n. 147
Exod. 15:15 189 n. 42
Exod. 17:11 117
Exod. 17:14 49
Exod. 19:5 29 n. 39
Exod. 20:4 269
Exod. 20:7 51 n. 14, 52
Exod. 20:8 51
Exod. 20:13 53
Exod. 20:14 51
Exod. 21:6 234
Exod. 21:7 234
Exod. 22:4 61 n. 41
Exod. 22:12 52
Exod. 22:22 384 n. 5
Exod. 23:5 61 n. 41
Exod. 23:17 379
Exod. 25:5 306 n. 80
Exod. 25:40 306 n. 81
Exod. 28:16 235 n. 23
Exod. 28:32 111–112
Exod. 28:39 377 n. 7
Exod. 29:13 251
Exod. 29:22 220
Exod. 29:33 331 n. 12
Exod. 30:10 331 n. 12
Exod. 34:6 387
Exod. 34:13 146
Exod. 34:21 91, 92 n. 33
Exod. 35:3 91
Exod. 36:34 146
Exod. 39:9 235 n. 23
Exod. 39:23 111–112

Lev. 4:7 222
Lev. 4:18 222
Lev. 4:25 222
Lev. 6:2 54–55, 100
Lev. 6:3 56
Lev. 6:15–16 55
Lev. 7:2 55 n. 24
Lev. 7:8 55 n. 24
Lev. 7:9 369 n. 74
Lev. 7:17 118
Lev. 7:18 13 n. 27
Lev. 8:22 220
Lev. 11:35 332 n. 19
Lev. 11:38 332 n. 19
Lev. 12:2 13–15
Lev. 12:5 13
Lev. 13:56 111
Lev. 14:4 377
Lev. 14:21 85
Lev. 15:13 14
Lev. 15:19 13–14
Lev. 15:20 13–14
Lev. 15:24 13–14
Lev. 15:25 13, 13 n. 23
Lev. 15:26 13

Lev. 15:33 13
Lev. 16:16 146 n. 35
Lev. 17:7 13 n. 27
Lev. 18:19 13
Lev. 19:12 52
Lev. 19:21 388
Lev. 19:24 217, 220
Lev. 19:28 376
Lev. 20:21 11, 13
Lev. 21:1 101, 341 n. 92
Lev. 21:10 410
Lev. 21:14 85
Lev. 22:27 238
Lev. 23:40 252
Lev. 24:10 77
Lev. 24:11 76

Num. 1:5 391
Num. 1:16 43 n. 128
Num. 5:2 100
Num. 7:13, 50
Num. 11:15 250
Num. 12:1–2 132 n. 69
Num. 14:6 112
Num. 14:14 359, 360 n. 13
Num. 15:38–39 60 n. 40
Num. 15:38 101
Num. 16:2 43
Num. 16:30 215
Num. 19:9 10 n. 6
Num. 19:13 10 n. 6
Num. 19:20 10 n. 6
Num. 19:21 10 n. 6
Num. 20:13 190
Num. 20:17 347 n. 147
Num. 24:21 16
Num. 26:9 43
Num. 27:7 140
Num. 28:5 192
Num. 30:3 258 n. 114
Num. 30:4 314 n. 127
Num. 30:6 258 n. 114, 314 n. 127
Num. 31:23 10 n. 6

Deut. 2:8 258
Deut. 4:37 34 n. 59
Deut. 5:12 51
Deut. 5:18 51–52
Deut. 5:19 51 n. 14
Deut. 6:4–9 234
Deut. 6:4 103
Deut. 6:5 120
Deut. 7:6 29 n. 39, 129
Deut. 7:7 116 n. 18
Deut. 7:26 13 n. 27
Deut. 8:2 221
Deut. 8:6 144 n. 20
Deut. 10:16 184
Deut. 11:13–21 234
Deut. 11:30 168
Deut. 13:14–18 387
Deut. 13:18 83–84, 387
Deut. 14:2 29 n. 39, 116 n. 18, 129
Deut. 17:15 190 n. 50
Deut. 17:17 153 n. 3
Deut. 18:4 18–19, 86
Deut. 19:15 53
Deut. 20:2 98–99 n. 19
Deut. 20:13 379
Deut. 21:6 247
Deut. 21:8 84, 331
Deut. 21:12 258 n. 111, n. 113, 314
Deut. 21:15–17 43
Deut. 22:15 43
Deut. 22:19 57 n. 33
Deut. 25:4 234 n. 19
Deut. 25:6 49
Deut. 25:19 49
Deut. 26:18 29 n. 39, 116 n. 18, 129
Deut. 28:66 367 n. 68
Deut. 28:40 319
Deut. 31:26 243
Deut. 32:7 192
Deut. 32:47 119 n. 3
Deut. 33:12 24, 26–28, 35–36

Josh. 1:1–8 99
Josh. 1:9 99, 100
Josh. 2:3 163
Josh. 2:9 89 n. 42
Josh. 2:18 163 n. 59
Josh. 3:28 100
Josh. 8:31 18
Josh. 10:24 360 n. 12
Josh. 11:9 101
Josh. 15:34 234 n. 19

Judg. 3:11 116
Judg. 3:16 68, 378, 391
Judg. 3:30 116
Judg. 5:3 396 n. 5
Judg. 5:7 267, 402
Judg. 5:31 116
Judg. 6:14 100
Judg. 6:17 401 n. 33, 402
Judg. 6:37–39 18
Judg. 8:28 116
Judg. 9:10 105 n. 8
Judg. 9:18 135
Judg. 10:4 60–61 n. 40
Judg. 11:3 119 n. 3
Judg. 12:13 236
Judg. 13:15 236
Judg. 14:14 217
Judg. 18:3 79 n. 11
Judg. 20:4 79 n. 11
Judg. 20:18 132
Judg. 20:26 163

1 Sam. 1:6 191 n. 52
1 Sam. 2:3 212, 216
1 Sam. 2:29 175
1 Sam. 3:14 331 n. 12
1 Sam. 4:4 377, 389
1 Sam. 4:21 65–66
1 Sam. 7:9 55 n. 26, 56
1 Sam. 8:12 92 n. 33
1 Sam. 9:9 53
1 Sam. 13:14 132
1 Sam. 16:12 57 n. 32
1 Sam. 17:12 163
1 Sam. 17:55 57, 59
1 Sam. 17:56 56–59
1 Sam. 17:58 57, 59
1 Sam. 18:23 359
1 Sam. 20:22 57
1 Sam. 21:3 348
1 Sam. 21:10 21
1 Sam. 21:11 132
1 Sam. 24:11 83 n. 13
1 Sam. 25:4 19
1 Sam. 25:7 19
1 Sam. 27:1 351 n. 180

2 Sam. 3:25 173 n. 46
2 Sam. 6:6 96
2 Sam. 6:29 98
2 Sam. 7:16 340
2 Sam. 12:24 37, 54
2 Sam. 12:25 37, 54
2 Sam. 13:5 77
2 Sam. 13:6 77
2 Sam. 13:32 16, 21
2 Sam. 19:33 217 n. 49
2 Sam. 20:2 75
2 Sam. 20:21 306 n. 81
2 Sam. 20:22 57
2 Sam. 21:12 367 n. 68
2 Sam. 22:37 259
2 Sam. 22:46 141
2 Sam. 23:10 132

1 Kings 7:3 26 n. 18
1 Kings 7:7 26 n. 18
1 Kings 7:33 140
1 Kings 11:9 359
1 Kings 11:31 111
1 Kings 11:33 233
1 Kings 13:5 111
1 Kings 13:28 236 n. 25
1 Kings 14:16 176
1 Kings 15:7 18
1 Kings 15:30 176
1 Kings 21:19 236 n. 25

2 Kings 4:8 12 n. 20
2 Kings 6:19 125 n. 38
2 Kings 10:8 233
2 Kings 10:33 75
2 Kings 12:24 30
2 Kings 12:25 30
2 Kings 14:22 258
2 Kings 17:25 78 n. 9
2 Kings 18:26 75 n. 1
2 Kings 18:28 75 n. 1
2 Kings 19:29 92 n. 33
2 Kings 22:25 306 n. 81
2 Kings 23:22 369 n. 74
2 Kings 23:23 369 n. 74
2 Kings 23:25 120

Isa. 1:13 13 n. 27
Isa. 1:17 71

Isa. 3:9 183
Isa. 3:18–23 86
Isa. 3:21 86, 388
Isa. 5:1 25–28, 37
Isa. 9:3 123
Isa. 11:8 209
Isa. 13:1–4 204 n. 45
Isa. 13:4 131 n. 63
Isa. 14:2 163
Isa. 16:2 19
Isa. 17:9 17
Isa. 17:10 17
Isa. 17:11 16–18
Isa. 19:4 188
Isa. 19:5 188
Isa. 19:7 188
Isa. 19:8 188
Isa. 19:11–16 188
Isa. 19:11–22 191
Isa. 19:16–17 189
Isa. 19:16 192
Isa. 19:17 188–192
Isa. 19:20 53
Isa. 19:22 188
Isa. 20:6 383
Isa. 25:10 383
Isa. 26:2–3 218
Isa. 26:8 49, 56
Isa. 29:9 132
Isa. 30:2 207 n. 6
Isa. 33:23 47 n. 1, 56
Isa. 34:15 214
Isa. 35:2 216
Isa. 36:22 111
Isa. 37:11 182
Isa, 37:18 182
Isa. 37:30 92 n. 33
Isa. 40:3 160
Isa. 40:20 207 n. 6
Isa. 40:22 190
Isa. 40:23 72 n. 38
Isa. 41:2 207 n. 6
Isa. 41:8 26, 34–25
Isa. 41:27 119 n. 4
Isa. 42:17 340
Isa. 43:1 221
Isa. 43:17 220
Isa. 43:23 175–176
Isa. 43:24 175
Isa. 44:13 190
Isa. 50:4 223
Isa. 51:20 50
Isa. 52:3 120
Isa. 52:5 348
Isa. 52:11 158
Isa. 52:12 158
Isa. 52:13 158
Isa. 52:15 158
Isa. 53:7 384
Isa. 53:11 143 n. 14
Isa. 54:6 12 n. 20
Isa. 54:11 175 n. 55
Isa. 54:13 223
Isa. 56:3 78 n. 8, 359
Isa. 58:1 159 n. 41
Isa. 58:2 159 n. 41
Isa. 58:3 159 n. 41
Isa. 58:4 158, 159 n. 41
Isa. 59:5 158, 209
Isa. 59:7 147–148
Isa. 59:8 147–148
Isa. 60:6 123
Isa. 62:9 345, 347
Isa. 65:18 216
Isa. 66:4 147
Isa. 66:5 11

Jer. 2:23 341 n. 92
Jer. 2:24 223 n. 73
Jer. 3:7 71, 232
Jer. 3:9 21 n. 51
Jer. 3:10 71, 232
Jer. 3:19 182–183
Jer. 4:20, 306 n. 80
Jer. 5:13 68
Jer. 6:7 71
Jer. 6:27 232
Jer. 6:29 232
Jer. 7:29 217
Jer. 10:11 249 n. 70
Jer. 11:15 24–29, 32, 36
Jer. 12:7 35 n. 61
Jer. 12:13 92 n. 33
Jer. 16:4 145 n. 29
Jer. 17:4 175
Jer. 17:1 258

Jer. 17:22 91
Jer. 19:13 145
Jer. 21:12 71
Jer. 22:3 71, 232
Jer. 22:14 26 n. 18, 221 n. 67
Jer. 23:17 345 n. 137
Jer. 23:20 216
Jer. 25:16 348
Jer. 26:6 125
Jer. 27:8 71, 232
Jer. 27:9 232
Jer. 29:9 71
Jer. 31:17 331 n. 11
Jer. 32:29 145
Jer. 33:8 143 n. 14
Jer. 36:14 75 n. 1
Jer. 37:16 293, 314
Jer. 38:14 168
Jer. 40:4 131 n. 63
Jer. 40:11 75
Jer. 46:7 348
Jer. 51:34 391
Jer. 51:56 403
Jer. 51:58 193

Ezek. 1:4–5 204 n. 45
Ezek. 1:11 140 n. 3
Ezek. 1:18 140
Ezek. 1:23 140 n. 3
Ezek. 7:19–20 14
Ezek. 7:19 13 n. 24
Ezek. 7:20 13 n. 24
Ezek. 8:3 60 n. 40
Ezek. 8:5 167 n. 10, 216
Ezek. 8:16 88
Ezek. 9:2 306 n. 81
Ezek. 9:7 129
Ezek. 11:21 140
Ezek. 13:6 133
Ezek. 16:4 316
Ezek. 16:7 340
Ezek. 16:49 116
Ezek. 18:6 12–15
Ezek. 20:6 182
Ezek. 20:15 182
Ezek. 20:30 341 n. 92
Ezek. 22:10 13 n. 24, 14–15
Ezek. 23:3 174
Ezek. 23:4 140 n. 3
Ezek. 23:8 174
Ezek. 23:21 174 n. 51
Ezek. 23:48 331
Ezek. 24:26 183
Ezek. 26:10 168–169
Ezek. 26:17 360 n. 11
Ezek. 27:3 168–169
Ezek. 27:32 214 n. 39
Ezek. 29:18 176
Ezek. 33:31 168
Ezek. 36:17 13 n. 24, 14–16
Ezek. 43:10 143 n. 14
Ezek. 46:22 354

Hos. 5:5 384
Hos. 7:10 384
Hos. 8:7 92 n. 33
Hos. 9:7 220
Hos. 9:8 72 n. 38
Hos. 9:17 19
Hos. 10:3 92 n. 33
Hos. 10:13 92 n. 33
Hos. 11:7 367 n. 68
Hos. 12:13 52
Hos. 13:3 348

Joel 2:17 88

Amos 5:26–27 154 n. 10, 198
Amos 5:26 200–201
Amos 5:27 161
Amos 6:3 11
Amos 7:1 18–19
Amos 9:11 154 n. 11, 198 n. 9
Amos 9:13 92 n. 33

Jon. 1:11 117 n. 21

Mic. 1:4 218
Mic. 4:3 140
Mic. 6:15 92 n. 33

Nah. 2:4 306 n. 80
Nah. 3:7 306 n. 80
Nah. 3:8–10 115
Nah. 3:9 116, 129

Hag. 1:4 26 n. 18, 221 n. 67

Zech. 2:17 340
Zech. 7:14 182
Zech. 13:1 10 n. 6, 11 n. 13, 11 n. 15, 11 n. 17

Mal. 1:2 33
Mal. 1:11 168
Mal. 2:17 175

Ps. 1:1 105
Ps. 2:3 143 n. 14
Ps. 15:4 359
Ps. 17:7 135–136
Ps. 18:34 105
Ps. 18:35 104
Ps. 18:37 259
Ps. 18:46 141
Ps. 24:8 220 n. 61
Ps. 25:3 120
Ps. 29:2 104
Ps. 29:3 191
Ps. 30:11 104
Ps. 31:23 104
Ps. 32:9 105
Ps. 36:8 98
Ps. 38:8 359
Ps. 41:5 105 n. 8
Ps. 45:1 25 n. 13, 27–28, 35 nn. 61–68, 36
Ps. 49:4 105
Ps. 50:15 105
Ps. 51:6 50 n. 7
Ps. 51:21 55 n. 26, 56
Ps. 55:20 215
Ps. 59:2 136
Ps. 60:7 24–28, 37
Ps. 62:4 345 n. 138
Ps. 63:12 50 n. 7
Ps. 66:3 98
Ps. 68:25 215
Ps. 69:37 36
Ps. 71:4 71
Ps. 72:6 18–19
Ps. 74:10 345 n. 137
Ps. 84:2 25–29, 35–37
Ps. 89:28 105
Ps. 89:40 105
Ps. 89:48 105
Ps. 89:51 105
Ps. 91:3 72 n. 38
Ps. 91:14 29
Ps. 104:19 168
Ps. 101:5 348
Ps. 106:24 182
Ps. 106:35 315
Ps. 107:1 142
Ps. 107:6 142
Ps. 107:13 142
Ps. 107:14 142
Ps. 107:17 142–143
Ps. 107:19 142
Ps. 107:20 143
Ps. 107:23 191
Ps. 107:26–27 188–189
Ps. 107:26 189
Ps. 107:27 189–191
Ps. 107:28 142
Ps. 107:30 142
Ps. 108:7 24–28, 37
Ps. 109:13 49
Ps. 116:10 384
Ps. 119:28 133
Ps. 119:99 217
Ps. 119:106 133–134
Ps. 119:107 384
Ps. 119:161 120
Ps. 120:2–3 217
Ps. 126:1 217
Ps. 126:5 92 n. 33
Ps. 127:2 25–28, 37
Ps. 130:4 215
Ps. 132:12 125 n. 38
Ps. 133:2 324
Ps. 133:3 324
Ps. 139:15 174 n. 53
Ps. 139:21 136

Prov. 1:6 147
Prov. 2:16 12 n. 20
Prov. 3:32 340
Prov. 8:24 98 n. 16
Prov. 8:30 72 n. 38
Prov. 9:1 25 n. 13, 187 n. 34
Prov. 10:7, 49
Prov. 11:3 306 n. 80

Prov. 11:22 12 n. 20
Prov. 12:25 161
Prov. 14:10 315
Prov. 14:14 21
Prov. 14:28 72
Prov. 22:8 92 n. 33
Prov. 23:2 69
Prov. 25:19 21
Prov. 25:26 306 n. 81
Prov. 27:8 19
Prov. 27:9 111
Prov. 27:17 384 n. 4
Prov. 27:25 403
Prov. 29:19 331 n. 11

Job 4:8 92 n. 33
Job 6:9 122
Job 9:15 348
Job 9:20 21 n. 50
Job 12:11 233
Job 12:20 50 n. 13
Job 20:26 345
Job 20:27 135
Job 22:9 122
Job 22:14 190
Job 22:30, 65
Job 26:3 98
Job 26:9 127–128
Job 26:10 190
Job 27:7 135
Job 27:21 348
Job 31:20 18

Ruth 1:21 120
Ruth 2:8 100 n. 24
Ruth 4:5 133

Shir ha-Shirim 1:4 105 n. 8
Shir ha-Shirim 4:3 49
Shir ha-Shirim 5:2 277 n. 118, 312
Shir ha-Shirim 5:3 377
Shir ha-Shirim 7:3 21

Eikhah 1:8 11, 13, 15 n. 29
Eikhah 1:17 12 n. 21, 13–16
Eikhah 2:12 145 n. 29
Eikhah 3:12 188 n. 38
Eikhah 3:62 135
Eikhah 4:10 51 n. 13 114, 317
Eikhah 4:16 73
Eikhah 4:20 143 n. 15
Eikhah 4:21 251–252

Qohelet 1:13 369 n. 74
Qohelet 1:14 369 n. 74
Qohelet 1:17 25 n. 13, 187 n. 34
Qohelet 2:12 25 n. 13
Qohelet 2:17 369 n. 74
Qohelet 2:20 351
Qohelet 2:22 316
Qohelet 3:18 316
Qohelet 4:3 369 n. 74
Qohelet 5:7 143 n. 14
Qohelet 6:10 402
Qohelet 8:9 369 n. 74
Qohelet 8:11 360 n. 13, 369 n. 74
Qohelet 8:14 369 n. 74
Qohelet 8:16 369 n. 74
Qohelet 8:17 369 n. 74
Qohelet 9:2 369 n. 74
Qohelet 9:6 369 n. 74
Qohelet 9:12 324
Qohelet 10:3 402
Qohelet 10:5 324

Esth. 1:1 190
Esth. 1:17 101
Esth. 1:18 68
Esth. 2:5 75–76
Esth. 2:8 383
Esth. 3:15 340
Esth. 3:38 76
Esth. 8:17 76
Esth. 9:27 78
Esth. 9:31 134

Dan. 2:5 69
Dan. 2:8 31 n. 46, 128
Dan. 2:35 128
Dan. 2:39 123
Dan. 2:47 31 n. 46 128
Dan. 3:29 69
Dan. 4:9 353
Dan. 4:15 184 n. 11, 187 n. 32
Dan. 5:12 187 n. 32
Dan. 6:3 123

Dan. 8:1 359–360
Dan. 9:9 215
Dan. 9:24 235 n. 23
Dan. 10:10 182
Dan. 10:16 204 n. 45
Dan. 10:19 182
Dan. 11:11 331
Dan. 12:2 163 n. 59

Ezra 2:63–64 128
Ezra 4:21 353 n. 200
Ezra 5:7 123
Ezra 5:8 76
Ezra 6:11 69
Ezra 7:9 222 n. 69
Ezra 7:16 183–184 n. 11, 187 n. 32
Ezra 9:1 113 n. 11
Ezra 9:2 315
Ezra 9:11 13–14

Neh. 5:18 369 n. 74
Neh. 7:3 251
Neh. 9:3 132
Neh. 9:4 132
Neh. 11:25 140
Neh. 13:24 75 n. 1

1 Chron. 3:5 337 n. 63
1 Chron. 5:16 142
1 Chron. 20:8 337 n. 63
1 Chron. 22:9 116

2 Chron. 17:12 126 n. 45
2 Chron. 20:7 34
2 Chron. 20:19 133
2 Chron. 23:13 168
2 Chron. 23:20 129
2 Chron. 29:5 13–14
2 Chron. 30:27 132
2 Chron. 34:33 180 n. 78

APOCRYPHA

Ben Sira 3:26–27 97
Ben Sira 4:17 221
Ben Sira 5:5 215
Ben Sira 6:35 216
Ben Sira 7:9 146
Ben Sira 8:8 147
Ben Sira 8:15 96 n. 7
Ben Sira 9:4 147
Ben Sira 9:15 146
Ben Sira 12:2 398
Ben Sira 13:30 96 n. 7
Ben Sira 14:6 398
Ben Sira 16:3 147
Ben Sira 16:16 215
Ben Sira 35:9 136 n. 85
Ben Sira 36:1 220
Ben Sira 37:25 147 n. 40
Ben Sira 40:29 221
Ben Sira 41:22 135, 136 n.86
Ben Sira 42:19
Ben Sira 43:10 146
Ben Sira 44:1 146
Ben Sira 44:4 146
Ben Sira 44:20 220
Ben Sira 44:23–25 32 n. 53
Ben Sira 45:11 220 n. 60
Ben Sira 45:13 146
Ben Sira 45:18 220
Ben Sira 47:17 217
Ben Sira 48:5 146
Ben Sira 49:10 146
Ben Sira 51:24 125 n. 41

Versions

Targum Onqelos

Gen. 21:20 58
Gen. 28:17 98 n. 13
Gen. 32:12 18

Exod. 1:13 176
Exod. 19:5 29 n. 39
Exod. 20:7 52
Exod. 20:13 53
Exod. 29:13 251

Lev. 7:17 118
Lev. 12: 2 13
Lev. 12:5 13

Lev. 15:19 13
Lev. 15:20 13
Lev. 15:24 13
Lev. 15:25 13, 13 n. 23
Lev. 15:26 13
Lev. 15:33 13
Lev. 18:19 13
Lev. 20:21 13
Lev. 23:40 252

Deut. 4:37 34 n. 59
Deut. 7:6 29 n. 39, 129
Deut. 14:2 29 n. 39, 129
Deut. 18:4 19
Deut. 26:18 29 n. 39, 129
Deut. 33:12 24

Targum Pseudo-Jonathan

Deut. 4:37 34 n. 58
Deut. 7:7 116 n. 18
Deut. 14:2 116 n. 18
Deut. 26:18 116 n. 18

Targum Jonathan

Judg. 3:11 116
Judg. 3:30 116
Judg. 5:3 396
Judg. 5:31 116
Judg. 8:28 116
Judg. 9:27 217–218

1 Kings 7:3 26 n. 18
1 Kings 7:7 26 n. 18

Isa. 5:1 25
Isa. 17:11 17
Isa. 41:8 26

Jer. 11:15 24
Jer. 22:14 26 n. 18, 221 n. 67

Ezek. 7:19 13 n. 24
Ezek. 7:20 13 n. 24
Ezek. 16:49 116
Ezek. 18:6 13 n. 24
Ezek. 22:10 13 n. 24
Ezek. 24:26 183 n. 6
Ezek. 29:18 176
Ezek. 36:17 13 n. 24
Amos 5:27 161
Amos 7:1 19

Nah. 3:9 116

Hag. 1:4 26 n. 18, 221 n. 67

Zech. 13:1 10 n. 6

Targum Neofiti

Deut. 4:37 34 n. 59
Deut. 7:7 116 n. 18
Deut. 14:2 116 n. 18
Deut. 26:18 116 n. 18
Deut. 33:12 24

Other Targumim

Frag. Tg. Deut. 7:7 116 n. 18
Frag. Tg. Deut. 14:2 116 n. 18
Frag. Tg. Deut. 26:18 116 n. 18

Tg. Psalms 60:7 24–25
Tg. Psalms 72:6 19
Tg. Psalms 84:2 25
Tg. Psalms 108:7 24–25
Tg. Psalms 139:15 174 n. 53

Tg. Job 6:9 122
Tg. Job 22:9 122
Tg. Job 26:9 127–128

Tg. Eikhah 1:8 15 n. 29
Tg. Eikhah 1:17 13, 15 n. 29

Tg. Qohelet 2:17 369 n. 74
Tg. Qohelet 8:11 369 n. 74
Tg. Qohelet 9:6 369 n. 74

Tg. Rishon to Esther 8:17 77
Tg. Sheni to Esther 8:17 77

Peshitta

Gen. 8:19 146
Gen. 9:9 105 n. 8
Gen. 10:5 331
Gen. 10:32 331
Gen. 12:7–22:9 124 n. 37
Gen. 12:10 124
Gen. 13:14 247
Gen. 19:20 124 n. 37
Gen. 22:9 124
Gen. 36:40 146

Exod. 7:14 97
Exod. 8:28 96
Exod. 9:7 97
Exod. 20:13 53
Exod. 22:12 53
Exod. 28:32 112
Exod. 34:13 146
Exod. 36:34 146
Exod. 39:23 112

Lev. 12:5 13
Lev. 15:13 14
Lev. 16:16 146 n. 35
Lev. 20:21 13

Num. 14:6 112

Deut. 2:8 258
Deut. 33:12 26

Isa. 5:1 26
Isa. 17:11 17
Isa. 19:20 53

Jer. 11:15 26

Ezek. 18:6 14
Ezek. 7:19–20 14
Ezek. 22:10 14
Ezek. 36:17 14

Amos 5:27 161

Zech. 13:1 10 n. 6

Ps. 60:7 26
Ps. 84:2 26, 27 n. 26
Ps. 127:2 26

Eikhah 1:8 13
Eikhah 1:17 13

Qohelet 2:17 369 n. 74
Qohelet 8:11 369 n. 74
Qohelet 9:6 369 n. 74

Ezra 9:11 13–14

2 Chron. 29:5 13–14

Septuagint

Lev. 12:2 14
Lev. 15:19 14
Lev. 15:20 14
Lev. 15:24 14

Deut. 33:12 26

2 Sam. 3:25 173 n. 46
2 Sam. 12:24–25 37

Isa. 5:1 26–27
Isa. 17:11 17

Jer. 11:15 27
Jer. 26:6 125 n. 40

Ezek. 22:10 15
Ezek. 36:17 14

Amos 5:27 161

Ps. 60:7 27
Ps. 84:2 27
Ps. 108:7 27
Ps. 127:2 27

Eikhah 1:8 15 n. 29
Eikhah 1:17 15

Ben Sira 41:22 136 n. 85

Vulgate

Gen. 21:20 58

Lev. 12:2 15

Deut. 33:12 26–27

Josh. 8:31 18

1 Kings 15:7 18

Isa. 5:1 27
Isa. 17:11 17–18

Jer. 11:15 27

Ezek. 18:6 15
Ezek. 22:10 15
Ezek. 36:17 15

Ps. 45:1 27
Ps. 60:7 27
Ps. 84:2 27
Ps. 108:7 27
Ps. 127:2 27

Eikhah 1:17 16

Qumran

Community Rule (1QS)
1QS 2:14–15 213
1QS 3:1 219
1QS 3:15 212 n. 35
1QS 4:3 213
1QS 4:9 214
1QS 5:3 220
1QS 6:2 208
1QS 6:7 212
1QS 7:17 222
1QS 9:8 214
1QS 10:3–4 184
1QS 10:3 171–172
1QS 10:4–5 173
1QS 10:10 172
1QS 10:25 218
1QS 11:21 205
4QpapS^c (4Q257) III 4 214
4QS^h (4Q262) 1 3 213

Copper Scroll
3Q 2 12 213 n. 37
3Q 3 13 213 n. 37

Damascus Document
CD A 161
CD A 1:6 202 n. 31
CD A 1:8–9 156
CD A 1:9 202 n. 31
CD A 2:4–5 213
CD A 2:13 156 n. 26
CD A 3:9 202 n. 31
CD A 4:20 202 n. 31
CD A 4:21 212
CD A 5:1–4 153
CD A 5:15 202 n. 31
CD A 5:17 213
CD A 7:1–2 202 n. 29
CD A 7:5 219
CD A 7:8 219
CD A 7:13–14 157
CD A 7:14–18 154, 198
CD A 8:15 202 n. 29
CD A 9:14–15 156
CD A 11:22 219

CD B 19:10 157
CD B 19:17 202 n. 29
CD B 20:4 223

4QD^a 156
4QD^a (4Q266) 2 III 201
4QD^a (4Q266) 2 3:18 155
4QD^a (4Q266) 11:18 219
4QD^f (4Q275) 5 I 15 219

Halakhic Letter
MMT 2:15 184

Isaiah Scrolls
1QIsa[a] 123, 147, 158–159, 163
1QIsa[a] 11:14 131 n. 63
1QIsa[a] 23:7 184
1QIsa[a] 35:7 119 n. 4

1QIsa[b], 158–159

Pesher Habakkuk (1QpHab)
1QpHab 7.2 208
1QpHab 8.6 214

Pesher on Psalms 148

Sabbath Sacrifice
4QShirShab[c] [4Q402] 1:1 171 n. 29
4QShirShab[f] [4Q405] 23 I 8 172 n. 35
4QShirShab[f] [4Q405] 23 I 9 171
4QShirShab[f] [4Q405] ii 20–23 13 213
10:26 209
4QShirShab[f] [4Q405] 14 15:4 172
11QShirShab (11Q17) 4:4 171 n. 29

Temple Scroll
29:9 212
52:21 222
60:4 219
11QT 37:14 124
11QT 45:6–7 124
11QT[b] (11Q20) 14:2 129 n. 57
11QT[b] (11Q20) I 20 219

Thanksgiving Scroll
1QH[a] (4Q427) 4:14–19 147
4QH[a] (4Q427) 8 ii 212 n. 35
4QH[a] (4Q427) 8 ii 11 171 n. 32
1QH[a] (4Q427) 6:27–28 171–172
1QH[a] (4Q427) 12:4 171–172
4QH[b] (4Q428) 10:7 222–223
4QH[c] (4Q429) 4 ii 9 214 n. 40
9[7]:19–20 20
10 [2] 18 214
12 [2] 39 223 n. 74
14 [6] 12 213
15 [7] 13 222–223
19 [9] 4 214
19 [11] 22a 214
20 [12]:10–11 222
22, 34 202 n. 35
25 [7] 22–32 212 n. 35

War Scroll
1QM 1:12 147
1QM 2:8 209
1QM 2:14 147
1QM 3:11 213
1QM 4:64 6 219
1QM 5:13 207–208
1QM 6.13 220
1QM 7:3 147
1QM 9:8 213
1QM 14:13 171 n. 29
1QM 16:12 212
1QM 17:8–9 208
1QM 26:10–11 219
4QM[a] (4Q491) 1–3 12 212
4QM[a] (4Q491) 11 ii 1 212

Numbered Scrolls
3Q14 3 2 214 n. 40

4Q158 (RP[a]) 124

4Q169 (pNah) 3 III 1 147
4Q169 (pNah) 3 III 3 208

4Q176 (Tanḥ) 21:3 147

4Q185 1–2 ii 1 208

4Q216 (Jub[a]) V 9 212

4Q223–224 (Jub[h]) 2 I 50 212

4Q225 1:7 129 n. 57, 212
4Q225 2 ii 7 208

4Q251 1–2 4 213

4Q252 1:9–10 129

4Q253 2 3 212

4Q300 (4QMyst^{b}) 1 ii 1 214
4Q300 (4QMyst^{b}) 8 6 213

4Q324 167 n. 10
4Q324 1 7 213
4Q324a ii 2 213

4Q334 4 4 213

4Q374 131 n. 63
4Q374 2 i 4 131 n. 63
4Q374 2 ii 181–195
4Q374 2 ii 5 131 n. 63
4Q374 2 ii 6–9 187 ff.

4Q375 1 i 9 213

4Q379 12:5 167 n. 10

4Q385 6 ii 11 115

4Q386 ii 7 116

4Q387a 2 113

4Q389 8 113

4Q418 (Instruction^{d}) 123 n. 27
4Q418 (Instruction^{d}) 55 7 116
4Q418 (Instruction^{d}) 96:4 123
4Q418 (Instruction^{d}) 127 6 220

4Q422 iii 7 208

4Q424 1 3 214 n. 40

4Q433a 1 4 214

4Q434 1 4 184, 223 n. 72

4Q440 3 I 21 178 n. 70

4Q451 3 219

4Q461 (Narrative B) 1 10 214

4Q462 (Narrative C^{a}) frg. 1 119
4Q462 (Narrative C^{a}) 116 n. 18, 137
4Q462 (Narrative C^{a}) 1:5 119
4Q462 (Narrative C^{a}) 1:8 127
4Q462 (Narrative C^{a}) 1:11 129, 131
4Q462 (Narrative C^{a}) 1:12 131, 133, 137
4Q462 (Narrative C^{a}) 1:13 131

4Q464 3 i 7 208

4Q470 1 I 4 177–178

4Q487, 3 112
4Q487 frg. 24:4 97 n. 12

4Q504 1–2 iv 7 219
4Q504 1:17–18 219

11Q5 (11QPs^{a}) 18:5–6. 172
11Q5 (Ps^{a}) XVIII 12 214

11Q13 ii 6 (11QMelch) 147

Midrash

Midrash Rabbah

Gen. Rabbah 29 240
Gen. Rabbah 53:15 58
Gen. Rabbah 69:3 134
Gen. Rabbah 87:5 135 n. 83

Exod. Rabbah 1:35 335 n. 44

Lev. Rabbah 7:8 251
Lev. Rabbah 11:7 251
Shir ha-Shirim Rabbah 1:9 254

Mekhilta' de-R. Ishmael

BaḤodeš 7 51
Bešallaḥ 5 23 n. 1
Va-yassa' 1, 411–412
Va-yassa' 3 337
Shira 4:4 (15:3) 124
Shira 9 144

Mekhilta' de-RŠBY

14:27 271
15:14 144

Sifra'

96:1 100
ṣav Millu'im 322
ṣav Millu'im 1 216
Nega'im 8:1 288 n. 178
Qedošim 11:1 14 n. 28
Emor 3:1 410
Behar 5:2 144

Sifre

Numbers 1 100
Numbers 6 353
Numbers 19 334
Numbers 22 242
Numbers 23 275
Numbers 32 352 n. 188
Numbers 42 322 n. 168
Numbers 83 144, 271
Numbers 84 283 n. 147
Numbers 110 288
Numbers 153 350

Deuteronomy 32 221
Deuteronomy 42 144–145
Deuteronomy 47 338
Deuteronomy 128 337
Deuteronomy 352 31, 33, 39 n. 91
Deuteronomy 452 30

Other Midrashim

Sifra' Zuṭa Naśo' 5:2 88 n. 25

Midr. Eikhah 1:36 15 n. 29
Midr. Eikhah 1:60 15 n. 29

Pesiqta 33 177 n. 65
Pesiqta Ten Commandments 113:2 123
Pesiqta de-Rav Kahana 5 240

Yalqut Šim'oni 2:955 30 n. 40
Yalqut Šim'oni 2:950 161 n. 49

Mishnah

Berakhot 1:2 269
Berakhot 1:5 269
Berakhot 2:3 269
Berakhot 2:8 345 n. 128
Berakhot 7:1 343
Berakhot 7:3 377, 389
Pe'ah 1:1 185 n. 21
Pe'ah 2:7 252
Pe'ah 3:7 251
Pe'ah 5:1 333
Pe'ah 6:8 233
Pe'ah 7:2 243
Pe'ah 7:5 85

Demai 3:4 231 n. 11

Kil'ayim 1:7 348
Kil'ayim 2:7 364–365
Kil'ayim 3:1 378
Kil'ayim 3:2 378
Kil'ayim 3:3 364
Kil'ayim 3:5 402 n. 34
Kil'ayim 5:1 84, 364
Kil'ayim 5:3 364
Kil'ayim 5:7 349
Kil'ayim 6:3 373
Kil'ayim 6:4 374
Kil'ayim 9:3 254
Kil'ayim 9:6 242

Ševi'it 2:2 250, 343
Ševi'it 3:4 343
Ševi'it 4:2 350
Ševi'it 4:4 85
Ševi'it 6:4 331
Ševi'it 8:4 243
Ševi'it 8:6 413

Ševi'it 9:1 130
Ševi'it 9:3 414
Ševi'it 10:3 216, 236

Terumot 2:5 391
Terumot 3:4 72
Terumot 3:5 368 n. 72
Terumot 3:8 364–365
Terumot 3:9 144
Terumot 4:11 319
Terumot 8:10 269
Terumot 8:12 238
Terumot 11:1 170

Ma'aśerot 1:5 343
Ma'aśerot 1:7 343, 402 n. 34
Ma'aśerot 1:8 331

Ma'aśer Šeni 3:4 365 n. 41
Ma'aśer Šeni 3:6 364
Ma'aśer Šeni 3:8 145 n. 30
Ma'aśer Šeni 3:10 364–365
Ma'aśer Šeni 5:2 258

Ḥallah 1:2 305
Ḥallah 1:8 343
Ḥallah 2:2 320–321 n. 155, 339
Ḥallah 2:3 413–414
Ḥallah 2:8 336
Ḥallah 4:3 244

Bikkurim 1:3 69
Bikkurim 1:6 241
Bikkurim 3 229
Bikkurim 3:5 336
Bikkurim 3:6 244
Bikkurim 3:8 336

Šabbat 1:3 242
Šabbat 1:11 378
Šabbat 3:4 331
Šabbat 3:5 340
Šabbat 6:5 12
Šabbat 7:2 89–90
Šabbat 9:7 241
Šabbat 10:1 391
Šabbat 10:6 311 n. 107, n. 109
Šabbat 12:4–5 337–338
Šabbat 16:1 169 n. 20
Šabbat 16:5 121
Šabbat 17:3 336
Šabbat 19:3 343
Šabbat 24:3 64 n. 4, 354
Šabbat 24:5 53 n. 19

'Eruvin 1:1 169 n. 20, 170 n. 28, 180
'Eruvin 1:2 169 n. 20
'Eruvin 4:1 72
'Eruvin 5:2 169 n. 21
'Eruvin 6:8 169 n. 21
'Eruvin 7:5 244
'Eruvin 7:7 250, 353
'Eruvin 9:3 169 n. 21
'Eruvin 10:3 252
'Eruvin 10:15 88 n. 23

Pesaḥim 2:7 373
Pesaḥim 3:4 162 n. 53
Pesaḥim 4:4 170
Pesaḥim 4:6 242
Pesaḥim 5:6 122, 185 n. 22
Pesaḥim 5:8 185 n. 22
Pesaḥim 5:9 67
Pesaḥim 6:1 185 n. 22, 215 n. 42
Pesaḥim 6:2 277 n. 118
Pesaḥim 7:1 376
Pesaḥim 7:9 333
Pesaḥim 9:5 230 n. 6, 239 n. 32, 389
Pesaḥim 9:8 321
Pesaḥim 10:2 252
Pesaḥim 10:4 238
Pesaḥim 10:5 254, 330

Šeqalim 3:2 104
Šeqalim 4:3 275
Šeqalim 4:5 303 n. 61
Šeqalim 5:3 85
Šeqalim 7:3 247, 333
Šeqalim 8:3 69

Yoma 1:2 305
Yoma 1:7 309 n. 96
Yoma 3:8 88 n. 23
Yoma 4:1 193
Yoma 5:4 122
Yoma 6:4 343

Yoma 7:3 361 n. 22, 365–366, 368
Yoma 7:5 391
Yoma 8:1 216

Sukkah 3:1 129
Sukkah 3:4 252
Sukkah 3:9 193
Sukkah 4:5 343

Beṣah 1:8 340
Beṣah 3:2 39
Beṣah 4:4 235 n. 23
Beṣah 5:1 319
Beṣah 5:6 49 n. 6

Roš Haššanah 1:2 339
Roš Haššanah 1:3 403
Roš Haššanah 1:7 305
Roš Haššanah 1:9 305
Roš Haššanah 1:9 83
Roš Haššanah 2:4 319
Roš Haššanah 2:6 247
Roš Haššanah 2:9 144
Roš Haššanah 3:5 373
Roš Haššanah 3:8 340

Ta'anit 2:2 122
Ta'anit 2:3 143
Ta'anit 3:1 239

Megillah 3:3 186 n. 26
Megillah 4:4 260

Mo'ed Qaṭan 1:7 402
Mo'ed Qaṭan 3:4 234
Mo'ed Qaṭan 3:9 214 n. 39, 330

Ḥagigah 2:10 122
Ḥagigah 3:3 320–321 n. 155

Yevamot 2:10 241, 319
Yevamot 3:7 304
Yevamot 6:1 167–168 n. 10
Yevamot 6:3 241, 319
Yevamot 6:4 304
Yevamot 8:3 143
Yevamot 9:4 305
Yevamot 11:3 13
Yevamot 11:4 162 n. 53
Yevamot 12:6 352 n. 189
Yevamot 13:4 241, 319
Yevamot 15:1[2] 168 n. 14
Yevamot 16:3 387

Ketubbot 2:1 241, 319
Ketubbot 4:2 241, 305, 319
Ketubbot 4:4 214 n. 39
Ketubbot 5:1 246 n. 54, 319
Ketubbot 5:8 44 n. 134
Ketubbot 6:1 241
Ketubbot 6:7 44 n. 134
Ketubbot 10:7 414
Ketubbot 8:1 72
Ketubbot 8:4 334 n. 39
Ketubbot 10:2 238
Ketubbot 11:1 339–340
Ketubbot 11:4 246 n. 54

Nedarim 1:3 415
Nedarim 1:4 415
Nedarim 3:11[9] 364–365
Nedarim 4:3 144
Nedarim 5:3 373
Nedarim 5:4–5 303 n. 61
Nedarim 9:2 365, 368
Nedarim 9:8 391
Nedarim 9:9 277 n. 118
Nedarim 9:10 69, 303 n. 61
Nedarim 10:1 269
Nedarim 10:2 121, 350
Nedarim 11:6 410
Nedarim 11:9 241
Nedarim 11:10 241, 319

Nazir 1:5 402 n. 34
Nazir 7:3 408–409
Nazir 7:4 167 n. 10

Soṭah 3:8 364–366, 372, 374
Soṭah 7:2 247
Soṭah 9:1 247
Soṭah 9:6 84, 269
Soṭah 9:7 248
Soṭah 9:12 260

Giṭṭin 1:5 331
Giṭṭin 2:6 345
Giṭṭin 3:1 144 n. 21
Giṭṭin 3:3 319
Giṭṭin 3:5 335 n. 42
Giṭṭin 3:6 43
Giṭṭin 5:2 339
Giṭṭin 8:8 319
Giṭṭin 9:3 251
Giṭṭin 9:8 177

Qiddušin 1:2 364–365
Qiddušin 1:3 364–365
Qiddušin 1:6 365, 365 n. 41

Bava Qamma 1:1 402
Bava Qamma 2:10 122
Bava Qamma 3:13 340
Bava Qamma 8:1 311
Bava Qamma 9:10 67 n. 17, 361 n. 22
Bava Qamma 10:2 349–350

Bava Meṣi'a 1:4 20
Bava Meṣi'a 4:8 361 n. 22

Bava Batra 2:3 239
Bava Batra 4:4 414
Bava Batra 5:3 64 n. 5
Bava Batra 9:4 185 n. 21
Bava Batra 9:6 251

Sanhedrin 1:3 248
Sanhedrin 2:1 361 n. 22, 364–365
Sanhedrin 4:7 379
Sanhedrin 6:2 372
Sanhedrin 6:4 361 n. 22, 364–366, 379
Sanhedrin 6:6[12] 344
Sanhedrin 8:1–4 361 n. 22
Sanhedrin 8:1 365
Sanhedrin 8:2 365
Sanhedrin 8:3 365
Sanhedrin 8:4 365
Sanhedrin 10:5 387
Sanhedrin 10:6 387
Sanhedrin 10:10 83

Makkot 1:1 241, 319
Makkot 1:7 343
Makkot 2:2 383 n. 3, 384
Makkot 3:5 245
Makkot 3:6 376
Makkot 3:21 388

Ševu'ot 1:2 365
Ševu'ot 1:3 361 n. 22, 365
Ševu'ot 1:6 361 n. 22, 365
Ševu'ot 1:7 365
Ševu'ot 2:1 216
Ševu'ot 4:12 387

'Eduyot 1:14 402
'Eduyot 3:5 309 n. 96
'Eduyot 5:6 129
'Eduyot 6:3 277, 334
'Eduyot 8:3 334

'Avodah Zarah 1:9 324
'Avodah Zarah 2:1 186 n. 25, 324
'Avodah Zarah 3:3 361 n. 22, 365
'Avodah Zarah 3:4 378
'Avodah Zarah 3:7 221 n. 68
'Avodah Zarah 3:9 322, 332
'Avodah Zarah 3:10 243
'Avodah Zarah 4:4 361 n. 22
'Avodah Zarah 4:8 365

Avot 1:2 185 n. 21
Avot 1:6 46
Avot 1:7 350
Avot 1:8 244
Avot 2:2 270
Avot 2:4 233, 244
Avot 2:5 260
Avot 2:10 244
Avot 3:1 319
Avot 3:4 337
Avot 4:3 337
Avot 4:22 337
Avot 5:2 387
Avot 5:9 186 n. 25
Avot 6:1 361 n. 22
Avot 6:2 365 n. 50, 366, 372

Zevaḥim 1:4[6] 185 n. 22, 274
Zevaḥim 1:5 274
Zevaḥim 3:5 274

Zevaḥim 5:1 274
Zevaḥim 5:2 274
Zevaḥim 5:4 274, 333
Zevaḥim 6:6 253
Zevaḥim 11:3 221
Zevaḥim 12:1 185 n. 22
Zevaḥim 12:2 55 n. 24

Menaḥot 2:3 335
Menaḥot 2:4 335
Menaḥot 10:4 361 n. 22, 364
Menaḥot 11:1 361 n. 22, 364–366
Menaḥot 11:9[11] 361 n. 22, 364–366, 372
Menaḥot 12:6 244
Menaḥot 13:9 321

Ḥullin 1:2 311 n. 109
Ḥullin 1:6 248
Ḥullin 2:2 128
Ḥullin 2:5 307, 320–321 n. 155
Ḥullin 3:1 391
Ḥullin 3:6 309 n. 96
Ḥullin 4:1 333
Ḥullin 4:6 336
Ḥullin 8:10 320–321 n. 155
Ḥullin 10:4 244
Ḥullin 11:1 86
Ḥullin 12:1 214 n. 39

Bekhorot 3:4 361 n. 22
Bekhorot 6:2 409
Bekhorot 6:7 309 n. 96
Bekhorot 7:5[6] 361 n. 22, 364, 365 n. 49
Bekhorot 7:6 259
Bekhorot 8:6 416

'Arakhin 2:2 361 n. 22
'Arakhin 8:1 361 n. 22, 364–365

Temurah 3:1 143
Temurah 6:3 143
Temurah 6:5 143

Karetot 3:9[11] 361 n. 22, 365 n. 44
Karetot 4:2 215–216

Me'ilah 1:2–4 185 n. 22
Me'ilah 2:1 331
Me'ilah 5:1 361 n. 22, 365
Me'ilah 5:2 361 n. 22
Me'ilah 6:2 361 n. 22, 364, 365 n. 45, 366 n. 52

Tamid 1:1 58
Tamid 2:1 345
Tamid 2:2–3 243
Tamid 2:2 83
Tamid 2:3 83
Tamid 2:5 345 n. 128
Tamid 3:4 335
Tamid 3:7 335
Tamid 4:1 343
Tamid 4:2 235 n. 23, 391
Tamid 4:3 251
Tamid 5:5 344
Tamid 5:6 88 n. 23
Tamid 6:1 83
Tamid 6:3 46, 83 n. 12

Middot 3:6 88
Middot 4:2 335
Middot 5:1 88 n. 23

Kelim 1:5 308
Kelim 1:6–9 86–87
Kelim 1:9 88 n. 23
Kelim 2:2 143, 307
Kelim 3:1 308
Kelim 3:4 330
Kelim 3:7 308
Kelim 4:1 308
Kelim 4:2 330
Kelim 4:4 288
Kelim 5:1 288
Kelim 5:2 288
Kelim 5:4 307
Kelim 5:5 376
Kelim 5:9 307
Kelim 5:10 308
Kelim 6:3 308
Kelim 8:2 308
Kelim 8:3 308
Kelim 8:7 241
Kelim 8:9 242, 276
Kelim 8:10 308, 320–321 n. 155
Kelim 9:1 308

Kelim 9:3 308
Kelim 9:6 307
Kelim 10:2 339
Kelim 10:3 309 n. 96
Kelim 10:4 376
Kelim 10:6 308
Kelim 11:3 380
Kelim 11:8 86, 388
Kelim 12:1 307
Kelim 12:4 72, 305
Kelim 12:6 308
Kelim 12:8 203, 308–309
Kelim 13:2 255
Kelim 13:3 308
Kelim 13:5 308
Kelim 14:1 308
Kelim 15:2 347
Kelim 16:4 308
Kelim 17:5 307
Kelim 17:9 307, 309 n. 96
Kelim 17:11 308
Kelim 17:12 307
Kelim 18:5 308
Kelim 18:9 247
Kelim 19:1 308
Kelim 19:8 308
Kelim 20:1 308
Kelim 20:7 287–288
Kelim 22:9 305
Kelim 23:2 190
Kelim 24:7 253
Kelim 24:8 305
Kelim 24:11 308
Kelim 24:17 308
Kelim 25:8 308
Kelim 26:1 307
Kelim 26:5 132
Kelim 26:8[9] 310, 349
Kelim 27:6[8] 367
Kelim 28:10 308
Kelim 29:1 68, 378, 392
Kelim 29:3 245

Ohalot 1:6 307, 331
Ohalot 1:8 259, 308, 309 n. 96
Ohalot 1:9 245
Ohalot 2:1 308
Ohalot 2:2 308
Ohalot 2:3 308
Ohalot 3:3 311
Ohalot 3:5 336
Ohalot 3:7 53 n. 19, 383 n. 3
Ohalot 6:2 307
Ohalot 6:6 307
Ohalot 7:2 309 n. 96
Ohalot 9:3 335
Ohalot 9:10 230 n. 6, 390
Ohalot 9:16 308
Ohalot 10:1 347
Ohalot 10:7 230 n. 6, 308, 390
Ohalot 11:7 230 n. 6
Ohalot 11:8 308
Ohalot 12:8[10] 230 n. 6
Ohalot 16:3 305
Ohalot 18:1 361 n. 22, 362–363, 365
Ohalot 18:7 383 n. 3, 184

Nega'im 2:3 310
Nega'im 2:4 361 n. 22, 362–365
Nega'im 4:3 267 n. 35
Nega'im 4:5 333
Nega'im 4:10 337
Nega'im 5:1 168–169 n. 14, 408
Nega'im 6:8 312, 312 n. 106
Nega'im 7:4 267 n. 35
Nega'im 8:3 168–169 n. 14
Nega'im 11:4 361 n. 22, 362, 366, 372
Nega'im 11:10[11] 310
Nega'im 11:11[12] 308, 310
Nega'im 12:3 308
Nega'im 12:4 230 n. 6
Nega'im 14:7 85
Nega'im 14:9 377

Parah 1:4 238
Parah 2:5[7] 242, 307, 361 n. 22, 362, 365, 372
Parah 3:3 308
Parah 3:11 299 n. 39
Parah 4:4 376
Parah 5:5 308
Parah 7:8 367
Parah 9:6 122
Parah 10:5 122
Parah 11:1 340
Parah 11:6 122, 308

Parah 11:7 64 n. 6
Parah 11:9 64 n. 6
Parah 12:2 253
Parah 12:5 308
Parah 12:10 308

Təharot 1:2–3 312, 311 n. 109
Təharot 2:1 320–321 n. 155
Təharot 2:7 307
Təharot 3:5 20, 215 n. 41
Təharot 3:8 300 n. 42, 308
Təharot 4:12 215 n. 41
Təharot 5:7 215 n. 41
Təharot 5:9 339
Təharot 6:3 299 n. 39
Təharot 7:3 307
Təharot 7:8[9] 310
Təharot 7:9[11] 310
Təharot 8:3 307
Təharot 9:9 215 n. 41

Miqwa'ot 3:1 376
Miqwa'ot 5:6 308
Miqwa'ot 6:2 347
Miqwa'ot 6:5 305
Miqwa'ot 7:1 334 n. 39
Miqwa'ot 7:2 334 n. 9
Miqwa'ot 7:5[7] 361 n. 22, 362, 365, 372
Miqwa'ot 9:2 308, 312
Miqwa'ot 9:4[5] 312, 311 n. 107
Miqwa'ot 10:3 308
Miqwa'ot 10:8 361 n. 22, 362–363

Niddah 3:5 305, 308, 347
Niddah 4:2 144, 270
Niddah 4:4 235
Niddah 5:4 367
Niddah 6:2 312, 312 n. 114
Niddah 7:1 169 n. 15
Niddah 7:2 169 n. 20, 170
Niddah 8:1 308
Niddah 10:1 16
Niddah 10:2 12 n. 18
Niddah 10:6 414
Niddah 10:7 414
Niddah 10:8 310

Makhširin 1:1 332 n. 19
Makhširin 2:1 254, 348 n. 154
Makhširin 2:3 186 n. 26
Makhširin 2:7 308
Makhširin 2:9 307
Makhširin 3:3 269
Makhširin 3:5 231, 308
Makhširin 4:1 308
Makhširin 5:1 367
Makhširin 5:2 337 n. 57
Makhširin 5:7 170 n. 23
Makhširin 6:3 258

Zavim 1:4 254
Zavim 1:5 305
Zavim 2:1 308
Zavim 2:2 122
Zavim 2:4[5] 361 n. 22, 362–363, 364 n.40, 365–366, 372, 374
Zavim 5:2 336

ṭevul Yom 2:2 320–321 n. 155
ṭevul Yom 2:3 190, 320–321 n. 155
ṭevul Yom 4:1 320–321 n. 155
ṭevul Yom 4:7 186 n. 25

Yadaim 3:1[2] 168, 169 nn. 14–15

'Uqṣin 1:1 121
'Uqṣin 1:2 308
'Uqṣin 1:3 121, 342
'Uqṣin 1:5 121, 342
'Uqṣin 1:6 308
'Uqṣin 2:8 342

Tosefta

Berakhot 6:3 23 n. 1
Berakhot 6:13 33 n. 57
Berakhot 9:2 90

Pe'ah 1:1 185 n. 21
Pe'ah 3:5 160 n. 48
Pe'ah 4:6 185 n. 23

Demai 2:7 185 n. 22

Terumot 1:3 112
Terumot 1:6 144

Šabbat 12:14 221 n. 66

'Eruvin 6:1 353

Pesaḥim 1:5 337
Pesaḥim 2/3:8 162 n. 53
Pesaḥim 8:4 176
Pesaḥim 8:5 176–177, 367
Pesaḥim 9:2 321 n. 157

Roš Haššanah 1:18 144

Ta'anit 2:10 222

Nedarim 10:2 350

Soṭah 4:7 335
Soṭah 6:4 144, 270
Soṭah 7:5 353

Giṭṭin 7:6 112

Bava Qamma 3:7 121

Bava Meṣi'a 11:9 93 n. 34

Sanhedrin 1:1 185 n. 23
Sanhedrin 2:11 367 n. 62
Sanhedrin 4:1 231

Šavu'ot 3:4 185 n. 23

Menaḥot 1:8 112

Ḥullin 3:19 132

Bekhorot 4:2 410

Kelim BQ 6:4 322 n. 168
Kelim BQ 6:17 276
Kelim BM 5:1–2 288 n. 178

Parah 12:10 321 n. 157

Yerushalmi

Berakhot 3:5 [6d] 241
Berakhot 4:5 [14d] 239
Berakhot 5:1 [8d] 233
Berakhot 9:1 134 n. 81
Berakhot 9 [14a] 23 n. 1
Berakhot 9:2 90

Šeqalim 5:1 91

Šabbat 5:2 [5b] 254
Šabbat 11:2 [13a] 231

Yevamot 11:4 [12a] 162 n. 53

Ketubbot 4:11 [29b] 144 n. 28

Nedarim 9:6 [39d] 177

Qiddušin 51c 167 n. 10

Sanhedrin 1:2 [18d] 177
Sanhedrin 1:3 [19a] 185 n. 24

'Avodah Zarah 2 [42a] 243

Bavli

Berakhot 2a 167–168 n. 10
Berakhot 3a 254
Berakhot 17a 194
Berakhot 18a 68
Berakhot 32b 123
Berakhot 58a 90
Berakhot 59b 345

Šabbat 18a 221
Šabbat 73b 89–90
Šabbat 137b 23 n. 1, 32–33, 39
Šabbat 144b 155 n. 28

'Eruvin 53a 239

Pesaḥim 12a 241
Pesaḥim 112a 239
Pesaḥim 117a 30 n. 40

Yoma 39b 71
Yoma 75a 161

Beṣah 20b 123 n. 31

Ta'anit 26b 185 n. 23

Megillah 12b 75 n. 2
Megillah 13a 76 n. 4

Ḥagigah 24b 320–321 n. 155

Yevamot 24b 78
Yevamot 45b 190

Soṭah 8b 68
Soṭah 10b 353 n. 199
Soṭah 42b 161 n. 49

Qiddušin 53a 71

Bava Qamma 82b 400 n. 24
Bava Qamma 100a 185 n. 21
Bava Batra 9a 177
Bava Batra 25b 239
Bava Batra 53b 221

Sanhedrin 99b 177
Sanhedrin 100b 161 n. 49

Avodah Zarah 75b 10

Zevaḥim 27b 55 n. 24

Menaḥot 11a 235 n. 23
Menaḥot 53a 39
Menaḥot 53a–b 23 n. 1, 32, 40
Menaḥot 53b 25
Menaḥot 64b 400 n. 24

Ḥullin 33b 321 n. 156

'Arakhin 10b 345

Epigraphic texts

Bar Koseba 1 270
Bar Koseba 2 241
Bar Koseba 7 270
Bar Koseba 8 270, 279 n. 126
Bar Koseba 8:3–4 257
Bar Koseba 8:3 252
P. Yadin (from the Cave of Letters) 44 line 7 323

Kefar Devora 402

Mesha Stele 125 n. 38

Murabba'at 24, 2.13 323
Murabba'at 24, 5.8 323

Nahal ṣe'elim 13:9–10 400

Rehov Inscription 130

Index of Hebrew and Aramaic Words

Hebrew

-אַ ("in", for -בְּ) 257, 278
אב 141–147, 270–271
אָבַס 64
אב"ק
– מְאָבְקִין/מְאַבְּקִין 250, 343–347, 355
אֵבֶר
– אֵבָרִים/אֲבָרִים 247, 284, 392
אג"ד 279 n. 126
אגרוף 159, 307–308
אוֹגְנִין 283 n. 151
אַגָּס 63
אדיר 189 n.39, 347 n. 147
אדמה 163 n. 59
אדם
– מְאָדָּם/מְאָדָּמִים 306 n. 80
אֲדוֹן/אֲדוֹנָי 107

אה"ב 25, 29–38, 46 n. 143, 60
אוי 324
או"י (או"ה), 10, 51–52
אויל 44
אומן 307
אונאה 351 n. 179
או"ת
– נֵיאוֹתִין 340
אותו 269
אותה 303
אזן (אָזְנוֹ) 308
אִזְמֵל 253
אָח (הָאָח) 310
אחות 246, 312–315
אֶחָד 107
– מאחד 127–128
אָחַז 251
– מְאָחֵז 128
אח"ר
– מואחר < מאוחר 321
אִי/אֵי 65–67, 317 n. 139
אי אפשר 65–66
אי הכרח 67
אילן 19 n. 43, 83 nn. 11–12
אילת (אֱיָלֶת/אַיֶּלֶת) 258–259
אין (spelling) 399
אישים 156
אכילה 210 n.26, 216
אכ"ל
– אכלין 270
– ניתאָכלו 344–345
– אֱכָל 324 n. 171
– נתאכל 347–348
אכ"ל “burn”, 345 n. 128
אַל 98–99
אלא 304 n. 64
אלו אלה 125–126, 240
אוּלָם 172
אלמ"ן
– נתאלמנה 241–242, 278, 319–320
אם (הָאֵם) 416
אֵם, אמותן 144–145, 270
אָמוֹן 72 n. 38
אמ"ן
– תַּאֲמֵן 244
אמנם 121
אמצע/אמצַע 309
אמ"ר 101
אמור(ה) 310
אֵינָב see עינב
אָנוּ 208, 238–239
אנחנו 238–239
אנ"ח
– מתאנח 345, 356
אסטגיות 276, 278
אס"ף
– מאספיו 345–347
אסקופה 252
אִסָּר/אֱסָר 258 n. 114, 315 n. 127
אסור 279 n. 126
אַף (anger) 48, 84
אַף (nose) 86, 387–389
אפ"ה
– נאפה 361, 364–366, 372–374
אפ"ך
– יוֹפַךְ 208
אָפֵל (with the definite article) 310, 316 n. 134
אַפָּר 272 n. 68
אצבע 309
אָרִיג (with the definite article) 310, 313, 316 n. 134
ארישתובול 398–400
אורך 307–308
ארמ"ל
– נתארמלה 241–242, 278, 281, 319
ארנון 117
ארוסין 218, 356 n. 208
אר"ס
– אֵרֵס 249, 343
– מארס 305
– מאורסה 269
ארצה 120
אשה 12 n. 20
אשמורה 146–147
אשפה 64
אש"ש
– נתאשש 73
אֶת, תיכול (< אֶת הכול) 398–399
אַתָּה 250, 267
אתר 319
אתרוג 252, 307

ב- 257, 278
– בית < בבית 401
בֵּאֵר 342–343

בָּגוֹד 71
בָּגוֹדָה 70–71, 232
בָּד/בַּד 309
בְּדִיל 44
בְּדִילָה 304 n. 63
בו"א 167–174
– בָּאָה/בָּאָת 408–409
– בא spelled -בָּ 416
בו"ך
– נָבוֹכָה 340

בּוּרְיָה 308
בַּיְשָׁן/בּוֹישָׁן 260, 271
בז"י
– נִבְזֶה 359
בִּזָּה 16, 20
בזיון 64, 68, 231
בָּחוֹן 70–72, 232
בְּתִיר 182
בִּיאָה (entryway) 213, 216
בֵּין (syntax of) 89
בִּינָה 146–147, 213, 216, 346
בֵּיצֵי: ביצים 159
בירה/בירניות 126–127 n. 45
בירן 126–127 n. 45
בית 234 n. 19, 399
– בית עמר 401
– בתי כנסיות 159
– בתי מדרשות 159
בְּכוֹר 105
בטלן 311
בל"ל
– נָבָל, בָּלַל 20, 192
בְּנִיָּה 214 n. 40
בסיס 254
בַּעַל 403
בְּעֵר 61 n. 41
בָּצָל 391
בַּקָּר 380
בק"ש
– מְבַקְשִׁים 346 n. 146
בר"א 175
בְּרִיאָה/בְּרִיָּה 212, 214–215
בר"ח 52
בְּרִיחַ 44
ברית 105
בֹּר/בָּרוּר/בריר 21 n. 50, 22
מן ברור 128 n. 50

גא"ל
– נוגאלו 337
גְּבוּל 378
גְּבוּל 208, 218, 221, 224
גִּבְצָל 64 and n. 6
גְּבִיר 39 n. 91, 44, 45 n. 140
גג 144–145
גדי 40
גֵּדֶל 224
גּוֹדְלָן 307
גְּדוּלִים 218
גֹּדֶל 207–208, 223
גד"ף 113–114, 317
גִּדּוּפִים 210 n. 26
גומא 243, 402
גו"ר
– מתגיירים 77–78
– נתגייר 244
גִּזָּה 18–21
ראשית הגז 86
גזלן 113, 233, 311
גז"ר
– גָּזְרוּ 304 n. 64
– גֵּזֶר 343, 347
גל"ה
– גָּלַת 384
– נִגְלָה/נִגְלֶה 361, 364–365, 372–374
גִּילָה 213, 216
גליד 44
גל"ח
– גולח (= גִּילַּח), 334
גֻּלָּה 188 n. 38
גָּלְיוֹת/גָּלוּת 299
גַּלְעֵד 53
גּוּמֶד/גֹּמֶד 68, 378–379, 391
גמילות חסדים 184 n. 11, 185–186
גּוּמָּה 308
גַּיִס 22
גמר (noun) 208
גִּנָּה 20
גס"ס 22
גע"ש
– וְהִתְגָּעֲשׁוּ 348
גֶּפֶן 48
גַּרְגְּרָן 113, 311

גְּרֶדֶת 380–381
(גָּרְנוֹ) גֹּרֶן 308
גָּרוֹסוֹת 72
גַּרַע 305
גרורת/גרורות 380
גירש 304–305
גרושין 218, 251 n. 81, 356 n. 208

דא"ג
– דאגין 270
דִּבָּה 10
דֶּבִין 306
דב"ק
– מודבקת 308
דב"ר 236, 282–283
דָּבָר (noun) 68–69, 274
דִּבּוּר 274
דַּבְּרָן/דַּבְּרָנִית 73
דוגמא 318
דוֹד 25 n. 16, 29
דוה 14
דו"ך
– נידוֹכין 340
דח"א
– דחָאו/דחיו 318
די"ן
– נידון/נדון 274, 339–340, 363–364, 370
– נודן 337
דַּיִשׁ
– דִּישׁוֹ 234 n. 19
דַּל 84–85
דל"ה
– מדלה 373
(דלתותיהם) דלת 142
דמות 204 n. 45
דק"ק
– דיקא 22
דָּרוֹכוֹת 72
דר"ם
– ידרים 239
דרשה/דרישה 184 n.19
דרשן 113

-ה 129–130, 287, 352 n. 188, 405 n. 47
-ָה 119–121, 124, 127, 234 n. 19
הא 416
האם 416
הג"י
– נהגה 337–338
הוראה/הוריה 318
הי"י 107 n. 17
– היות 411–412
– יהי 244
הימנו 256–257, 278, 281, 301, 319, 322–325
הכי 41
(הלוא) הלא 100 n. 24
הלאה 85 n. 17, 161, 238
הילוך 274 n. 101
הליכה 212, 215
הל"ך
– ללכת/לילך 144,
הִלֵּל/הֶלֵּל 236–237, 259, 266–267, 283, 304 n. 64
הוללוֹת 25 n. 13, 187 n. 34
(הכרות) הכרה 183–184, 186
הלולים 217, 219–220
הלקט 354
הנ"י
– נהנה 337–338, 361, 364–366, 372–374
הִנָּם 119 n. 4
הערבות שמש 184, 186
(אפ"ך >) הפ"ך 208
– יופך 208, 223
הקטר 357
הקצע 354
הקפדה 304 n. 64
השמעות 183, 186
השתחוה 244, 275, 331

זאת (see also זו) 125, 235
זַגָּג 242
זה 235, 405 n. 47
זות זו 83 n. 11, 125, 235
זוּגִין 307
זו"ן
– זונים 273
– ניזונת 339
זכ"ר
– זָכַר 51
– הוזכרו 307, 331
זְכָר 105
זֵכֶר 49
זְכוּר/זָכוּר 379–380
זל"ף
– מזלפין 343

זִמָּה 20
זמ"מ
– מזמם/מזוממים 343, 346
זמיר 41
זנ"ה
– זונה 12 n. 20
זנות 202 n. 29
זע"ק 131–133 136–137
זְעָקָה 356
זערת 235 n. 23
זק"ן
– נזדקן 73
זקנים 51 n. 13
זק"ק
– זוקקה 333
זרת 235 n. 23
זוֹרֵעַ 89–92
זְרוֹעַ 105
זְרִיקוּת 185

חב"ב 24–36, 116 n. 18
עם החביב 129–131
– See also חב"ב in Aramaic section
חבוקים 210 n. 26
חב"ר
– התְחָבֵר 348 n. 155
חָבֵר 23, 38 nn. 88–89, 39, 46 n. 141
חג"ג 187–195
חדות 320
חידה 147, 214, 217
חדרים 277 n. 119
חוט 163 n. 59
חולדה 307
חוליה 307–308
חומר 309
חז"ק
– נתחזק 133, 353 n. 202
חזרת 63
חט"א
– חטאתם 146 n. 35
– חטא/החטיא 176–178
חט"ף
– מחטפין 343
חַיָּטִין 242
חֹתֶם 86, 387–388
חט"ף
חי/חיה 31, 267, 274, 363–364, 370

חייב
– נתחייב 244
חיל (rampart) 87
חכמוּת 25 n. 13, 187 n. 34
חלזון 410
חל"ט
– הוחלטה 308
חל"ל
– הֵחֵל/התחיל 77, 83, 243, 308
חלחל
– מחֲלחלת 335
חָלוּם 70–72, 232
חליפה 212, 215
חל"ק
– נוחלק 337
חמ"ד 51–52
חמדה/חמדוּת 182–187, 195
חמ"ם
– הוחמו 331
חמ"ס 71 n. 37
חמסנים 311
חמוץ 70–72
חמ"ץ 71–72
חמצן 71–72
חנות 267, 283, 299–300, 32
חנם 120–121
חָפְנָיו 308
חֵץ 20
חָצֵר 390
חֹק/חֻקָּה 21, 188 n. 38, 307
חרדל 63
חוֹרֵשׁ 89–93
חָרָשׁ 377
חָרָשׁ/חֹרֵשׁ 236
חֶשְׁבָּן 398
חת"ך 235 n. 23
– חוּתך 333
חֲתִיכָה 215
חֲתִיכָּה 281

טב"ל
– הוּטבלו 308
טבעת 86, 388
טבור 324
טו"ח
– נֵטח/ניטוח 337
טָחוֹן 231

טמ"א
– טוּמֵא 318 n. 141, 334
– נטמא 133, 319
– ניטמא 339–341, 355
טומטום 308
מטפחת 304 n. 64
טר"ף
– מטורף 342
– ניטרפה 192–193

יא"ש
– נתיואש 349–352
יג"ע
– יָגַע and הוֹגִיעַ 175–178
יד"י
– התודה 331
– מודה 396, 398
ידיד 23–46, 54, 60
ידיעה 212, 215–217
יד"ע
– יודעתי 348
– להודעותני 184 n. 11
– נודע 340 n. 84
יה"ב
– יוהב 397 n. 11
יה"ד
– מתיהדים 76–78
יהודי 75–79
יום 235 n. 20
ייִנין 263 n. 1, 275
יכח
– נִתּוֹכַח 353
– נוכח 126 n. 44
יל"ד
– יֻלָּד 323 n. 171
– נולד 126
– נוּלדה 337
יֶלֶד 59 n. 36
ולד, וולדותיהן 143
ימין 75–76, 347 n. 147
יס"ד
– נוּסדו 337 n. 64
יסוד 222
יסורים 219, 221
יס"ף
– נִתוסף 250, 352–353
יס"ר
– נִוַּסְּרוּ 73, 331
יפ"י
– יֻפִּי 334
יצ"א
– מִתּוֹצֵאת 353
יצאה/יציאה 284 n. 19
יָצַר 175
– נוֹצר 126
– נוּצר 337
יק"ד
– מִתּוֹקֶדֶת 250, 353
יקוש 72 n. 39
יר"א
– נורא 98, 126
ירד
– לֵרֵד/לרדת 207 n. 6
ישיבה 217 n. 49
ישב
– מיושבת 193 n. 59

יש"ן
– לישן 239
יהושוע 153–154
יש"ר
– נוּשרו 337 n. 65
ישתראל (= ישראל) 106
ית"ר
– נִתּוֹתַּר 353

כב"ד 96–101
כִּבּוּס 219, 221
כַּד 309
כוס 243, 251–252
כוחל 388
כך 84, 269
כוּך 308
כו"ן
– להכין 207 n. 6
– נכון 340
– מיתכוין 345
כיור 219, 221
כל, תיכול (< את הכול) 398–399
כלוב 377, 390
כְּלִי 302 n. 52
כַּלָּה 10
כְּלָל 208
כָּל 398
כליל 55 n. 26
מכמר 50

כֵּן, כיני 154– 164, 197–205
כנ"ן 136
כנ"ס 383–384
כנ"ע
– נוכנעים 209, 338
כנען 75
כס"ה
– נכסה 361, 365, 372–373
כסיל 44, 45 n. 140
כס"ף
– נכספת 340 n. 89
כַּעַס 387
כֶּפֶל/כָּפֵל 283
כפורים 210, n.26
כְּפִיר 39 n. 91
כפ"ף
– ניכפה 364–366, 372–373
כפ"ר
– נתכפר 319
– נִכַּפֵּר 73, 331
– כִּיפֵּר 343–344, 347
כַּפְּרָן 311
כרוב 377, 389
כָּרוֹז 71–72
כָּרֵשׂ/כָּרֵס 391
כר"ת
– כֹּרֶת 307
כרתן 280
כָּשַׁל and נִכְשַׁל 98, 133, 384
כש"ר
– הוכשר 331
– הוכשרו 307–308
כת"ב
– כּוֹתֵב/כָּתוּב 335
– כתוב 18, 21, 22 n. 52
כְּתָב 105 n. 9, 397–398, 404
כתובה 127 n. 45
כְּתוֹבֶת 376–377, 388–389
כּוֹתֶל, כותלי כותלין 309, 378, 392
כתֹּנֶת 377, 380, 391

לַ- for לָהּ 413–415
ל for לֹא 415–416
לא 415–416
לאין 319
לאלתר 319–320
לאן 319
לבלר 253
לוּגְמִיּוֹת לֹגֶם 309
לה 413–415
להלן 238
לוּגִין 307–308
לו"ז
– נָלוֹז 340
לו"ט
– לוּטָה 21
לוי 79 n. 11
לו"י
– נִלְוָה 359–360
– נִלוים 77, 78
לו"ש
– נִילוֹשָׁה 339
לח"ם
– נִלְחֵם 331
ליזביז 276, 278
ליל, לילה 120, 234–235
למ"ד
– לֻמַּד 307
לִמּוּד 220 n. 61, 222–223
לקח
– לָקַח 83, 243–244
– נלקח/ניקח 276, 278
– לֻקָּח 324 n. 171
– יקח 51 n. 13
לָקוֹחוֹת 72
לק"ט
– לוּקַט 333
– הַלְקֵט see הלקט
לק"ק
– לקקו 236 n. 25
לש"ן
– מלושני 348
לשון הקודש 208

מִ- 106
-ָם 119–121
מאבקין see אב"ק
מאד 119–120, 123, 127
מאחד see אחד
מבוי/מבוא 168–174
מְגוּרָה 147–148
מגלות (= מגילות) 303 n. 62
מִדְבָּר 49–50
מדיכה 190, 324
מִדְיָן (spelled מדים) 123
מדינה 190

מַה 98
מו"ל
– נְמוֹל 043
– מולים 273–274
מושב 142, 147
מזבח 146
מזוזה 234
מזון 144–145
מזרק 50
מחיגה 187–195
מי written -מ 416
מחוז 142 n. 13
מח"ל
– מְחֹל 31
מְטוֹתָם, מְטָּה 146–147
מַטָּרָא 188 n. 38
מיגמר/מוגמר, 318
מל"א
– נתמלא/מתמלא 319
מלאך 82
מלואים 219 –220
מל"ט 157
מל"ך
– מְלֹכִי 105 n. 8
מלך, מלככם 157 n. 34, 162
מלכות 299–300, 318, 324
מילים/מילין 233
ממון 208, 216, 224, 278
מן, ממנו 128 –129, 256–257, 301, 319, 322–
325
מסילה 147–148
מס"ר
– מוֹסָרוֹת 142, 143 n. 14
מְסָרָה 184, 186
מע"ט
– מָעַט 133
– נתמעט 133, 244
– מועט/ממועט 313, 318, 322 n. 171, 324,
374
מעיל 44
מעין 242, 278
מצ"א
– מצאנו/מצינו 169 n. 16
– נִמְצָא 366, 369
מציאה 20, 214–215
מְצוּקוֹת 142, 143 n. 14
מצרי 75
מק"ק
– נִימוֹקִים 340
מקרא 22 n. 52
מרחץ 318
מְרִיא 39 n. 91
מריבה 190
מַרְכּוֹף 304 n. 64
מרפק 304 n. 64
משהו 241
משוגע 194
מָשׁוֹחַ 72
מְשׁוֹפְטִי 348
משיחה 213, 215–217
מש"ך
– משכני 105 n. 8
משיכה 213, 215–217
משימה 190
משמר 142, 146–147
משקוף 230 n. 6, 239 n. 32, 389–390
מֵת 20

נא"ם 50–51 n. 13
נאמן 50–51 n. 13
נא"ץ
– נִאֵץ 343
– מנאֵץ 344, 347
– מְנֹאָץ 348
נִבְזֶה see בז"י
נביא 43, 54, 60
נָבָל (נב"ל) 20, 192
נג"ב
– הנגיב 239
נגבה 120
נג"ד
– הוגד 307
נגחן 311
נְגִילָה 233
נד"ב
– התנדב 244, 275
נֵד 16–18
נִדָּה 9–22
נדה (מי) 9–11
נד"ף
– נִדַף 207 n. 6
– נודף 207 n. 6, 209
נה"ג
– נוהגין 338
נוגאלו see גא"ל

נו"ד 11 n. 16, 15 n. 29, 20
נו"ח
– הונח 308
נְוָלִי/נְוָלוּ 69
נו"ע
– ינועו 190, 192
נז"ק
– נְזָק 364, 370
– נְזוֹק 364, 370
– נִיזּוֹקִים 340
נז"ר 10 n. 7, 300
נח"ש ("spell") 410
נחושת, נחושתו 308
נח"ם
– נִחֵם 342–344, 347
נחתומין 308
נט"ל 83, 243–244
– נוּטל 260, 336–338
נט"ר 10 n. 7
נֵיאוֹתִין see או"ת
נִידָה see נו"ד
נכ"ה
– מוכה 373
נמ"י
– נִמֵּיתִי 334
נֵס 117
נסוי 219 –220
נס"ס 221
נס"ק (< סל"ק)
– הוסק 308
נעים (< מעין) 242, 278
נַעַר 47 n. 1, 57–60
נפ"ל
– נופלין 304 n. 64
נפקנית 73 n. 42
נִצָּב 134
נציב 44
נצ"ל
– ניצל/נוצל 336
– ניצולת 340
– להנצל 383
נִצָּן (< נֵץ) 127 n. 45
נְקִיק 39 n. 91
נש"א 169 n. 16
– נוּשָׂא 336–338
– נשא שם 52
נשואין 251, 356
נשיאות 185
נַשְׁכָנִית 311
נש"ל 319–320
נתאלמנה see אלמ"ן
נת"ז
– הותָּזו 307, 331
– נותזין 337 n. 57
נת"ן
– כי יותן 332 n. 19
– נותנו 336–338
נת"ר
– הותר 331

סא"ב
– מוסאבות/מסואבות 308, 313, 318, 321, 322 nn. 161–162, 324–325, 342, 344
סב"ב
– יָסֹבּוּ 191 n. 52
– מסובב 194
– סוֹבֵב 346
– מְסַבִּין < מְסֻבִּין 351
סִבָּה 10, 16, 20
סְגֻלָּה 29 n. 39, 116 n. 18, 129–131
סג"ר
– הסגירו/היסגירו 302 n. 52
– מוסגר 308
סו"ג
– סוּגָה 21
– נָסֹגוּ 340
סו"ר
מֵסִיר 51 n. 13
סֻכָּה 21
סוּכַּת/סֻכּוֹת 154 n. 10, 162, 201–202
סי"ע
– סייעתו 349, n. 160
סכ"ן
– מְסֻכָּן 335 n. 42
סָכִין 44, 69
– see also שכ"ן
סַכָּר 380
סלח 31
סליחה, סליחות 127 n. 45, 213, 215
סם, סממנים 126–127 n. 45
סְמִיכוּת 185–186
סעד (בסעדך) 115–116, 129
סע"ר
– נִסְעַר < סָעַר 133
– יסֹער 348
– סוערתו/סיערתו 349, 351 n. 182

ספ"ג 253–254
– נסתפג 345–348
סיפגן/סופגן 318
סָפִּיוֹת (שָׂפָה <) ספה 276, 278
ספון 26 n. 18
ספסל 253
סקיי/סקאי 380
סרבן/סורבן 113, 233, 311
סר"ג
– סירגן 305
סר"ס
– מסורס 306, 313, 347
סָרוֹק 231 n. 10
סר"ק
– סִרְקָן 347

עב"ד 131, 136–137
– העביד 175–178, 180 n. 78
עבדן/עובדן 113, 310–311
עב"ר
– תעבר/תעובר 333
עֶבְרָה 48
עֶגְלָה 247–248, 287, 303
עַגְמוּת 186–187
עַד 56
עדוד 21 n. 50
עוֹלָה 54–55
עו"ר
– נֵעוֹרָה, נֵעור 337, 339–340
עז"ב 61 n. 41
עִזּוּז 219–220
עַז 19, 48, 309
עֹז 21, 53 n. 19
עזרה, בעזרתך 115–116, 129
עי"ן 234 n. 19
עינב/עֵנב 399, 409–411
עֲיָרוֹת 61 n. 40, 144–145
עכ"ב
– מעוכב 335
עכשו 208, 216, 223–224, 267 n. 35, 402
על"י
– מעלין/מועלין 334 n. 39
עֶלֶם 56–60
עמ"ד 134–135
עַם החביב 129–131
עני 84–85
ענ"י
– נענה 384

עס"ק
– העסיק 175
עסקני/עוסקני 73 n. 42, 311
עץ 83 n. 11
עצמות 408–409
עצרת 69
עקיבה/עקיבא 318
עק"ד
– מעקדין 343
צֹקֶץ, עוקצה/עוקצו 308
ער"ב
– מעורב בדעת 194
– עֵרֵב 249, 285, 312, 315, 347
– ניתערב 305, 315
– מצֹרבת 347
ער"י
– לְעָרוֹת 249
ערלוּת 184, 186
ערער 193
ער"ר
– עורר/נתעורר 330
עשב, עִשְׂבוֹת 403
עָשׁוֹק 70 –72, 232
עש"י
– עשת/עשתה 384
– תעשו 84
– נעשה 247, 361–374
– מעשׂה 20–21
– העשה 174–178
עושי זכוכית 242
צֹשֶׁף, עושפו 308
עש"ק
– הִתְעַשֵּׁק 135
עש"ר
– לַעשר 174 n. 51

פִּגּוּל 13 n. 27
פג"ל
– מפֻגל 335
פג"ם
– נִתפגמה 345
פד"י
– נִפדה 361, 364–366, 372–374
– נפדת 384
פַּדָּן 52
פולחן 176
פולמוס 253
פורנה 276

פורענות 299–300, 318, 403–404
פט"ר
– פטור 380–382
– פוטר 398–399, 403 n. 43
פי"ס
– פייסת 343 n. 108
פלונית 285
פל"ל
– התפלל 275, 331
פנקס 253, 318
פנ"י
– פִּנָּה 10
– מָפנה 307 n. 81
– מפונה/מופנה 322
פנאי 318
פסול/פיסול 376, 380
פסוק 22 n. 52
פק"ד
– הפקיד 339 n. 80
– הַמְּפקדים 306 n. 81
פָּקיד 39 n. 91
פר"ד
– נִפְרדו 331
פֵּירוּשׁ/פֵּרוּשׁ 219, 221–222, 306
(פורקדן) פרקדן 113
פר"ש
– פֵּרֵשׁ 342
– מפורש/מופרש 322
– פורשנו 334–335
פתאם 121 n. 7
פת"ח
– פּוֹתֵחַ טֶפַח 53 n. 19
– נפתח 153
פתילה 304 n. 63
פַּת 202

צִבּוּר 233
צד 309–310
צו"ד
– נוצד 337, 339
צו"ה 95–96, 99–100
צידוני 232 n. 13
ציצית 60 n. 40
צלמים 154–164, 197–205
צפון 239, 247
צפורן 246, 258, 312–315
צר 147
צָרכו/צָרכה 309
צר"ף
– מצטרפין 249
צָרוֹף 70–72, 232
צְרִיף 44
צר"ר
– צָרוּר 22

קִבּוּל 274
קב"ל
– נתקבלה 246 n. 54
– התקבלתי 246 n. 54
– התקבלת 404
– קִבֵּל 263 n. 1
– קובלתי 318
– התקבל 331
– קובלנו 334–335
קַבְּלָן 311
קבר 19 n. 43
קדמותה 184, 186
קדקד 307
קד"ש
– קידש 32–35, 40, 330
– נקדש 133
– מקַדש 335
– מקֻדש 335
– נתקדש 330
קדושין 218, 251 n. 81, 356
קולמוס 308
קו"ם 15 n. 29, 21, 31, 52, 133–137, 339 n. 80, 346, 399, 403 n. 43, 404
– אקומה 232
– התקומם 135–136
– התקיים 131–135
– יקום 233
– קם 131–134
קומקומוס/קומקום 307–308
קו"ץ
– נתקווצה 350, 355
קִטְרֵג 254
קי"ן
– מקוננות 330
קינה 214, 217
קֵיפָּה 343, 348
קלגס 351
קל"ה
– נקלֶה 359
קלוסטר 308

קל"ל
– נָקֹל 340 n. 84
– קל 19, 21, 309
– קל וחומר 53 n. 19
קל"ס
– קֶלֶס 254
קולר 307
קומץ 307
קנ"א
– קניה/קנאה 318
קנ"י
– ניקנה 364–366, 372–373
קעקע 376–377
קפדן/קופדן 310
קפ"ח
– מקפיח 344, 347
קוּפָּא/קוּפָּה 308, 402 n. 34
קצ"ה 413–414
קצ"ע 354
קצ"ץ 380
קצ"ר 89–93
קציר 17
קר"א
– נקרא 366, 369
– הקרא/הוקרא 334 n. 39, 352 n. 188
– וקראני 105 n. 8
– קרוא 43
– קריא 16, 43
קר"ב
– לקֱרבה 307
קְרָב 105 n. 9
קרדום 245, 308, 318, 324, 351
קרסול 245, 318
קר"ע 111–112
קרקע 309
קרקר 143, 307–308
קרסול 259, 308, 324
קָשָׁה 48
– נקשה/נוקשה 338 n. 69
קֶשֶׁת 47 n. 1, 148
קשתותם 148, 403
קתדרה 253

רא"י
– רואה 54, 60
– נראה 274, 359–366, 372–374
– מָראה 306 n. 81
רֹאשׁ 173, 305
ראשית הגז 86
רב"ב 59 n. 37
– רַב/רָבֶה 267, 274, 363–364, 370
– מרבה/מרובה 334, 374
– רבה/נתרבה 133
רֹבַע 408–409
רבצן 311
רג"ז
– מרוגזין 344
רד"ף
– נֶרדפנו 338 n. 70
רוֹבֶה 47 n. 1, 58–59
רוח 144–147, 271
רו"ם 77 n. 5, 330
רו"ע 77 n. 5, 239
רזון 70–72
רֹחַב 309
רחמן 113–114, 311
רחמניות 51 n. 13, 73, 317
רחיצה 213, 215–217
רח"ק
– הרחיק 18 n. 41
– מרוחק 342
רֵיקָם 119–127
רֵקָן 343, 347–352, 355
רְמִיה 214, 217
רֵעַ 23, 39
רצ"ח
– תְּרָצְּחוּ 345 n. 138
רַצְעָן 311
רע"ם
– הרעים 191 n. 52
רע"ע
– רֹעָה/רעועה 21–22
– נתרעעה 330
– הֵרע/הורע 334 n. 39
רע"ש
– נרעש 133
רפ"א
– רפאה 105 n. 8
רְצִין 45 n. 140
רק"ק
– רַק/רָקַק 303
רשוּת 398–399
רשעים 105

-ש, שֶׁל 63, 241–242, 246, 267, 277–278, 285, 305–306, 318, 324–325, 401–402

שא"ר
– מְשׁוֹאר 342
שְׂאֵת 53 n. 19
שבוקין 218, 251
שְׁבִיב 39 n. 91
שבט 379 n. 15
שבע
– נשבע בשם 52
שב"ק 348 n. 155
שב"ר
– שָׁבַר/שְׁבֶר 236 n. 25
שב"ש
– שיבש/משובש 357
שג"ג 10 n. 11
שג"י 10 n. 11
שֶׁגֶם 309
שד"ד
– שדוד 22
– שׂדדה 307 n. 80
שָׂדֶה 52, 251–252
שֶׁדֶף 116–117
שדרה/שזרה 318
שיבה 15 n. 29, 214, 217
שׂי"ם
– שׂוּמָה, שִׂימָה 16, 21
שורקה 48 n. 3
שחיטה 210 n. 25
שח"ל
– משילין < משחילין 319–320, 380
שִׁחְרֵר 330, 354
שח"ת
– מָשחת 306 n. 81
שחית 142–143
שִׂיחָה 214, 217
שי"ר
– אשירה 232
שיר ידידות 35–36
שירה 28, 32, 214, 217, 343
שָׁכֵב מְרַע 251
שׂכין 69
– see also סכין
של"ח
– שׁוֹלח 332 n. 23
שְׁלוּתִים 218
שָׁלִיחַ 16, 43, 45, 82
של"ך
– מֻשְׁלָךְ 306 n. 81, 308
שָׁלָל 56
שְׁלוֹם 220
של"ק
– מְשָׁלֵק 343–344, 347, 356
שליש 44
שָׁם 124, 127
– שָׁמָּה 120, 124
שֵׁם 49, 156 n. 26
– מִשּׁוּם 318
– שמותן 144–145
שמאי 318
שמירה 356
שמ"ע 103–104
– הִשָּׁמַע 383
שמעון 398
שמ"ר
– שָׁמוֹר 51
– שָׁמוּר
שנ"א 263 n. 1
– משנאיך 283 n. 147
– שנוא 43
– שניא 43
– שניאה 16
שָׁעָה 255
שועל 398
שע"ן
– נשען 374
שע"ר
– וישׂערהו 348
– משתער 342
שָׂעִיר 43–44
שפוד 376
שפ"ה
– נשתפה 345, 355
– שֵׁיפה 347
שפיות 276, 278
משפחה 142, 143 n. 14, 146
שפיכות דמים 186
שְׁפִיר 44
שפ"ה
– שָׂפַת 64 n. 5
שק 309
שָׁקֵד 390
שקוף 230 n. 6, 389–390
שקט 116
שֹׁקֶת המים 56
שרביט 379 n. 15
שָׂרִיד 39 n. 91

שר"י
– תִּשְׁרֵי/תִּשְׁרָה 373
שר"ץ 105 n. 8
שֹׁרֶשׁ 309
שת"ק 117 n. 21
– יִשְׁתְּקוּ 142

ת- (feminine marker) 125
תבונות 105
תועבה 13 n. 27, 113 n. 11, 147
תוצאה, תוצאותם 142
תורבד/תורווד 308
תורגמן 260, 311
תורמל 308
תורפה 308
תתִינה תתִינות 142
תכון 220
תל"י
– נתלה 361, 363–366, 372–374
תל"ש
– מתלשין 343, 347
תְּנוּךְ 377
תקוה 162 n. 59
תק"ן
– מותקן 308, 321
תַּקָּנָה 356
תרגם
– נִתַּרְגֵּם 330
תר"ם 77 n. 5
תרנגול 300
תשלמה 398 n. 14

Aramaic

אחד 127–128, 251
ארעא 123

בוסרן 13 n. 24
ביה (בית >) 397, 400, 404
ברא 123

ד- 324–325
דא דה 125 n. 38, 235
דחילו 98 n. 14

האמנו see מן האמנו
הנון 25 n. 14

זל"ל
– זִילָא 22

חב"ב
– חביב 24–26
חדא, כחדה 128
חקל 252
חֲשבן 397

יגר 53
יה"ב 397 n. 11

כלא 123, 127
כס 252
כסלו 398, 403
כפ"ף
– כֵּיף 22
כְּתָבָא 397

לוות 397, 399

מטא 17
מן האמנו (Samaritan) 128 n.51

נד"ב
– התנדבוּת 184, 187 n. 32
ניר 17
נכ"ס 398

סה"ד see שה"ד.
סל"ק 55
סעלב 398, 400

עב"ד 174 n. 53
– שעבד 354
עלא 123, 127
על"ל
– עֵיל 22

קב"ל 397–398, 404
קל"ל
– קיל 22
קשט 31 n. 46, 128
רה"ט 56
רח"ם 24–26, 332 n. 23

רח"ק
- מרחקא 13, 17 n. 37
- ריחוק 13

שא 401
שאיוהב 398

שהדותא 53
שׁוּמַיִן 106 n. 16
של"ם 397

תרי עשר 397 n. 12

Index of *binyanim* and grammatical categories

Binyanim, Other Verbal Forms and Noun Patterns

I-guttural 368
I-w 273
I-y 126, 239, 250, 335–339 *passim*
I-n 308, 335ff, 355

II-weak 16, 20, 335 ff.
II-w 239, 273, 339–341, 355

III-’ 167ff, 366–372
III-y 10, 217, 247, 338 n. 66, 359–374, 384

’af‘ēl 187 n. 32

’ef‘ōl 240

’eppĕ‘ēl 341 n. 94
’etpĕ‘ēl 341 n. 94
’ettaf‘al 353

haf‘ālāh 357
haf‘ēl 187 n. 32, 354
hef‘ēl 37
hetpa“al 397 n.
hif‘il 136, 273, 279 n. 126, 302 n. 52, 329, 354, 357
hitpa“al 234, 329–330, 397 n. 9
hitpa“ēl 77, 234, 244, 266, 273, 275, 331
hitpā‘al 331
hitpā‘ēl 315
hitpōlel 135–136
hittaf‘al 251
hof‘al 308

huf‘al 307–308, 322, 329, 331–332, 338, 357
- false *huf‘al* 334 n. 39

māfôl 170 n. 23

*m*ᵉ*fa‘al* 335, 356
*m*ᵉ*fa“ēl* 335, 356
*m*ᵉ*‘ēlāh* 190 n. 45
*m*ᵉ*fo‘āl* 356
*m*ᵉ*fûlāh* 190 n. 45
*m*ᵉ*fu“āl* 335, 341 ff.
mif‘āl (*miqṭāl*) 50, 168 n. 11
mitpa“ēl 233, 274, 281, 319
mitpā‘ēl 356
muf‘āl 338–339

naf‘al 340

nif‘al 126, 234, 247, 260, 266, 279 n. 126, 331, 335–341 *passim*, 351, 355–356, 368, 372, 383
- passive participle 10 n. 11
nif‘eh 359–374 *passim*
nif‘ōl 240, 329
nippa‘al 112
nippĕ‘al 273, 329, 339–341, 355

nitpalpal 330
nitpa“al 73 n. 44, 81, 112, 234, 241, 245, 248, 266, 279 n. 126, 329–331, 341, 350, 355–357, 397 n. 9
nitpā‘al 272–273, 329–331, 341 ff.
nitpa“ēl 73, 233, 244, 246 n. 54, 248, 273–274, 281, 319

nitpayyel 136
nitpawwel 136

nitpi'al 354
nitpōlal 330
nitpōlel 343 n. 112
nitpō'al 329–330, 349–352
nitpo'ēl 348
nittaf'al 250, 273, 329, 331, 352, 355
nuf'al 207 n. 6, 209, 273, 279 n. 126, 329, 335–341, 355

pa'' (*qaṭṭ*) 203, 309, 387
pa''āh (*qaṭṭāh*) 10 n. 5, n. 8
pa''āl 380
pa''ālāh 356
pā'ēl 272–274, 279 n. 126, 329, 341 ff., 391
pā'îl (*qāṭîl*) 16, 20–21, 26, 39 n. 91, 41, 43, 45 n. 140
pa'lān 51 n. 13, 72–73, 113, 233, 311, 313–314, 317
pā'lōn 231 n. 11
pā'ôl 70–73, 231
pā'ûl (*qaṭûl*) 21, 378–379, 389

pē' (*qēṭ*) 16, 20–21

pᵉ'ăl 105 n. 9
pᵉ'ālāh 184 n. 19, 211 n. 27, 303, 356
pᵉ'ālîm 56 n. 30

pē'ēl 250, 329–330, 341 ff.

pᵉ'i' (*qeṭiṭ*) 22
pᵉ'îl (*qĕṭîl*) 22, 26, 39 n. 91, 41, 44
pᵉ'îlāh 184 n. 19, 186, 207–225, 356
pᵉ'illāh 212 n. 33
pᵉ'îlût 185

pᵉ'î 302 n. 52

pᵉ'ōl 159 n. 45
pᵉ'ōlet 376–380, 388
pᵉ'ûl 222 n. 69, 377–379

pi'' (*qiṭṭ*) 16, 20–21
pī'' (*qīṭṭ*) 21

pi''ēl 250, 282, 318 n. 141, 329–330, 333–338 *passim*, 355–356
– Yemenite vocalization, 40 n. 95
pī'ēl 331 n. 10
pi''āh (*qiṭṭāh*) 10–21 *passim*
pi'lāh 303
pîl (*qîl*, middle weak) 16, 20–22
pilpēl 330
pi''ûl 207–225, 251, 356
piwwel 136
piyyel 136

pō' (*qōṭ*) 21
po'al 341ff
pō'el 391–392
pō'ēl 274, 308, 329–330, 348–349
pōl 308
po'lān 113, 233, 260, 311, 313, 317
pōlel 135–136, 330, 343 n. 112

pu'' (*quṭṭ*) 21
pu''āh 188 n. 38
pu''al 81, 112 n. 1, 322, 329, 332–335, 338, 355
– false *pu''al* 334
pûl (*qûl*) 21
pu'l 159 n. 45
pu'lān 260
pu'' 308

qal 273, 281, 329, 331–332, 356
– active participle and 72, 279 n. 126
– geminates and 16, 21
– internal *qal* passive 332 n. 19
– passive 279 n. 126, 324 n. 171

šif'el 354
yāf'ûl 232–233

Subject Index

adverbial suffix 119–121, 124, 127

assimilated *lamed* 276

compensatory lengthening 305

diachronicity 54, 82, 165 ff., 233–234
diphthong 234 n. 19, 318
directional *he* 120
– geminate roots 9–10, 16, 20–22
– geminate verbs 239

hollow roots 15 n. 29
intervocalic *he* 383

metathesis 242
metonymy 16 n. 31, 234
monphthongization 398

nomen rectum 209
nomen regens 209

numbers
– ordinal numbers 129

paragogic *nun* 84
parallelism 31, 47–52
participles 53 n. 19
passive participles 43
plural 139–148

quadriliteral roots 330, 354

synonymy 49, 56

Yemenite vocalization 40 n. 951

www.ingramcontent.com/pod-product-compliance
Lightning Source LLC
Chambersburg PA
CBHW050847160426
43194CB00011B/2058
* 9 7 8 3 1 1 0 4 8 5 9 3 6 *